THE LAW OF OBLIGATIONS

The Law of Obligations

Essays in Celebration of John Fleming

Edited by

PETER CANE and JANE STAPLETON

Law Program
Research School of Social Sciences
Australian National University

CLARENDON PRESS • OXFORD
1998

This book has been printed digitally and produced in a standard specification in order to ensure its continuing availability

OXFORD
UNIVERSITY PRESS

Great Clarendon Street, Oxford OX2 6DP

Oxford University Press is a department of the University of Oxford. It furthers the University's objective of excellence in research, scholarship, and education by publishing worldwide in

Oxford New York

Auckland Bangkok Buenos Aires Cape Town Chennai Dar es Salaam Delhi Hong Kong Istanbul Karachi Kolkata Kuala Lumpur Madrid Melbourne Mexico City Mumbai Nairobi São Paulo Shanghai Singapore Taipei Tokyo Toronto

with an associated company in Berlin

Oxford is a registered trade mark of Oxford University Press in the UK and in certain other countries

Published in the United States by Oxford University Press Inc., New York

Reprinted 2002

ISBN 0-19-826484-4

Photograph: John Fleming at Berkeley Law School, July 1996, by Jim Block

Contents

Preface

John Fleming was one of the most influential writers on the law of torts and comparative law in the English-speaking world this century. His towering contribution to scholarship is evidenced not only by the great prestige his work attracts in academic circles, but also by the frequency and high respect with which his work is cited by judges in appellate courts of many jurisdictions. The authors of this collection of essays on the law of obligations intend it as a tribute to his achievements.

In his great work, *The Law of Torts*, John was able to synthesize vast areas of precedent, uncovering and distilling broad principles of law applicable throughout the common-law world while also noting the local variations in legal doctrine which are the lifeblood of an area of law so patently sensitive to social mores. The sweep of John's coverage allowed him not merely to record legal rules but also to analyse areas of instability in the law of one jurisdiction in the light of the variety of approaches taken to the problem in other places. This approach revealed much of the common law as necessitating policy choices and also demonstrated to the common lawyer a practical benefit of engaging in comparative law studies. It is an approach which academics continue to find richly rewarding and students find a revelation.

Most of the contributors also knew John as a kind friend whose personal and intellectual generosity was legendary. Each of us could cite many instances when John freely gave much-valued support, encouragement, and wise counsel. We hope that this work will be a token of our gratitude to him and a reflection of the warmth in which his memory is held.

This book was commenced before John fell ill and we had intended it as a surprise for him. However, when John was visiting Oxford in the early summer of 1996 he lightly told us over lunch that he was not well. We decided to reveal to him the planned book (then already under way) and the number and range of people keen to contribute essays in his honour. As editors we wish to thank all the contributors warmly for their commitment to this project, the news of which gave John great pleasure.

We had hoped to have contributions from both judges and academics across many jurisdictions. The exigencies of judicial and professorial life have, in the result, prevented the contributions planned from Canada, a gap we regret given the great influence John's work has in that jurisdiction.

Peter Cane and Jane Stapleton
Canberra
March, 1998

Notes on Contributors

Lord Bingham of Cornhill is Lord Chief Justice of England.

Peter Cane is Professor of Law, Research School of Social Sciences, Australian National University.

Lord Cooke of Thorndon was formerly President of the Court of Appeal of New Zealand and is a Lord of Appeal.

James Gordley is Shannon Cecil Turner Professor of Law, University of California at Berkeley.

Dr Nils Jansen is Academic Assistant to the Chair of Private Law, Roman Law and Comparative Legal History, University of Regensburg.

Hein Kötz is a Director of the Max-Planck-Institut Für Ausländisches und Internationales Privatrecht, Hamburg.

Werner Lorenz is Professor Emeritus and former Director of the Institute of International Law, Ludwig-Maximilians-Universität, Munich.

Harold Luntz is George Paton Professor of Law, University of Melbourne.

Basil Markesinis is Clifford Chance Professor of Law and Director of the Centre for the Advanced Study of European and Comparative Law, University of Oxford.

Sir Anthony Mason was formerly Chief Justice of the High Court of Australia and is a National Fellow, Australian National University.

Gary T. Schwartz is William D. Warren Professor of Law, University of California, Los Angeles.

Jane Stapleton is Professor of Law, Research School of Social Sciences, Australian National University.

Stephen D. Sugarman is Agnes Roddy Robb Professor of Law, University of California at Berkeley.

André Tunc is Professeur émérite, University of Paris I, Panthéon-Sorbonne.

Tony Weir is a Fellow of Trinity College, Cambridge and Reader in Law in the University of Cambridge.

Reinhard Zimmerman is Professor of Law, University of Regensburg.

Table of Cases

Table of Statutes

UK STATUTES

OTHER NATIONAL STATUTES

AUSTRALIA

AUSTRIA

CANADA

FRANCE

GERMANY

ITALY

NEW ZEALAND

SWITZERLAND

THE NETHERLANDS

US

Table of International Instruments

An Appreciation of John G. Fleming

Stephen D. Sugarman

The international legal community lost one of its most distinguished members when John Gunther Fleming, the Cecil Shannon Turner Professor of Law Emeritus at the University of California, Berkeley (Boalt Hall) died on 22 September 1997.

'He was a giant in the law of torts.' That was the first thing that Judge Guido Calabresi said when I informed him of Fleming's death. In that comment, Yale Law School's former Dean was speaking for all of us who work in Fleming's field of the law. And Lord Cooke captured Fleming well in a recent judgment, calling him 'the doyen of tort writers'.

Fleming was best known for his path-breaking treatise *The Law of Torts*. Ever since its first appearance in 1957, generations of law students, professors, and judges throughout the Anglo-American legal system have depended upon Fleming's work as a guide to the traditions, subtleties, and modernization of the law of personal injury. Mr Justice Gerald LaForest, perhaps Canada's greatest torts judge, attested to this reliance in his tribute to Fleming: 'whenever I was stymied by a torts problem that seemed to have no answer, I turned to Fleming, who was the person who offered *the* insights needed to solve the problem.'

Just weeks prior to his death, Fleming completed the book's ninth edition. Unlike any other volume on the subject, Fleming's *The Law of Torts* weaves together the analysis of legal developments in Australia, Britain, Canada, New Zealand, and the United States. This comparative law approach reflects Fleming's long and celebrated academic career on three continents.

Although our public memory of Fleming will be as a scholar, many of my fondest memories are about his personal life. For example, there was a truly memorable party at the Flemings' home in Berkeley for what must have been his 55th birthday. The wine flowed. Lots of charming people were surrounding him. As I recall it, Valerie, his wife served salmon—not just any salmon, but several whole salmons that were each, in my memory, at least three or four feet long. Had they been caught in England, surely they would have been claimed by the Queen. Suddenly, and I never found out whose idea this was, a genuine belly-dancer arrived and began to perform her art right in front of the birthday boy. If it had been me, I would probably have fainted. But Fleming, eyes twinkling, behaved as though he had been a Middle Eastern pasha-in-training for twenty years. It was wonderful.

Fleming's ability to have great fun in what might be called an off-beat way was re-enforced at the time of what I call the Veedercrest wine caper. Before most of us knew the difference between a cabernet and a chardonnay, Fleming knew a lot about wine. He also knew about special wine opportunities. For example, he once sent me to a half-hidden, backyard garage in Berkeley to buy from some dentist a cache of vintage port with the labels almost washed off. This time it turned out that Veedercrest, a good Napa Valley vineyard, was liquidating its stock at incredible prices. Faculty at Berkeley and visitors to the campus may recall that the Women's Faculty Club for some years thereafter featured Veedercrest on its wine list; Fleming, who was then on the Club's Board, was the reason. But the zaniest thing about the Veedercrest adventure was that we could buy it, not only bottled by the case, but also in the barrel. So, at Fleming's urging, several of us suddenly found ourselves in a wine warehouse—rinsing out recycled bottles, running the bottling machine, jamming in the corks in a totally disorganized way that, a colleague noted at the time, would have made the Volvo assembly plant proud. I still have two or three bottles of that 1980 red, which, when I finally drink them, will bring back wonderful memories of Fleming's instigation of that caper.

Now, Fleming's eldest son has planted grapes at the family's weekend home in California's Sonoma County—as pretty a location, I should say, as anywhere in Provence. In a few years we will have a living reminder of Fleming's love for wine in what I suppose will be called something like Fleming Zin.

Born in Berlin in 1919, Fleming was sent from Germany by his anti-Nazi and Anglophile father to be educated in England. As a result, Fleming obtained his secondary-school training at the Brentwood School in Essex. From there he went on to receive a BA in Jurisprudence from Brasenose College, Oxford in 1941. During the Second World War, Fleming performed distinguished military service in the British Royal Tank Corps in North Africa and Italy from 1941 until 1945. Moving to London after the War, he married, was called to the Bar at Lincoln's Inn, and began his academic career as a law lecturer at King's College, University of London. In 1948 he received his Doctor of Philosophy from Oxford; later, in 1959, Oxford awarded him the DCL. In 1949, Fleming responded to an advertisement for a teaching post in Australia, a land of especially great opportunity after the War. Once selected, he promptly emigrated with his young family to take up a position at Canberra University College. He flourished in this, his third home country, and in 1956 he became the founding father and Dean of the Law School at the newly established Australian National University. There he published the first edition of *The Law of Torts*, which promptly won him international acclaim. For example, Justice Allen M. Linden, of the Federal Court of Canada and a former student of Fleming's, has said that Fleming's book 'has been a bible for Canadian law students and judges for more than forty years'. In 1985 Fleming received an honorary doctorate in law from Canada's York University.

After living about ten years in Australia, Fleming was wooed away to America. Following a period as a visiting professor at the University of California at Berkeley, a permanent position was extended that Fleming tried to accept. But diplomatic snafus got in the way, forcing him to return to Australia for two years before he was eventually able to resettle in California.

According to news accounts at the time, the US State Department initially denied Fleming the necessary visa on the ground that American raiding of top Australian educators might damage US–Australian relations. Although Fleming had, so to speak, been previously raided from England, University of California President Robert Sproul protested in vain. Other assistance was then proffered. Fleming had published a review of a then recent book by Melvin Belli, a Berkeley law graduate and famed personal injury lawyer, terming Belli (or his legendary trial techniques) 'dangerous'. Apparently on the theory that any publicity helps sales, Belli, on hearing about Fleming's visa problems, sent then Berkeley Dean William Prosser a hilarious telegram: 'Offer my services for free to help prevent Australian tort professor Fleming's deportation', signing it 'dangerous doctor Belli, Alias the King of Torts'. So much for Belli's legal help; the Fleming family shipped out. Berkeley did not give up, however, and by 1960 the brouhaha subsided, allowing Fleming to join the Boalt Hall law faculty where he remained until his death.

During his years at Berkeley, Fleming was several times recognized with honours by the country where be obtained his legal education. Brasenose College made him an honorary fellow in 1980, in 1987–8 he served as the Goodhart Professor of Law at Cambridge University, and in 1996 he was made a Corresponding Fellow of the British Academy. Soon after Fleming's death, Peter Birks, the Regius Professor of Civil Law at Oxford, wrote to me: 'Here in Oxford we regarded John Fleming as the pre-eminent torts lawyer of the age. We are proud that the University played a part in the development of his interest in that field. We deeply valued his continuing association with this University. [He was] an analyst of unrivaled learning and vision. His influence will long continue to be felt through his immensely important books, and posterity will regard him, without doubt, as one of the formative figures of twentieth-century jurisprudence.'

Between 1972 and 1987, Fleming was editor-in-chief of *The American Journal of Comparative Law,* and his leadership solidified that journal's reputation as the leading publication in the field. He served as president of the International Association of Legal Science and the American Association of Comparative Law, and as a member of the International Academy of Comparative Law, the Society of Public Teachers of Law (UK), the American Law Institute, and the American Academy of Foreign Law.

Although his scholarly base remained at Berkeley until the end of his life, Fleming's international reputation led to visiting professorships at the National University of Singapore, the University of Michigan, and the University of Witwatersrand in South Africa, as well as countless lectureships and public consultantships throughout the world.

Besides the major opus, Fleming published two other books—*The American Tort Process* (1988) and *Introduction to the Law of Torts* (1967)—as well as more than a hundred articles, reviews, and the like in academic journals around the world.

Fleming's persistent attention to the ways that other nations solve their legal problems has left a lasting mark on today's academics and lawyers in the United States, in the European Union, and in the Commonwealth, where we now see a broad willingness to look outward to find new legal arrangements to fit today's global economy.

We should also not forget Fleming's commitment to teaching. For one thing, during my first, say, twenty years at Berkeley, Fleming always taught a large section of Torts (90–120 students). He knew he was effective in that forum. In addition, I used to accuse him of wanting to protect as many students as possible from the rest of us who also teach in the field. Some years after he formally retired, however, Fleming decided one fall term to teach a small section instead (30 students). Not surprisingly, he was very popular in that setting as well. During that term, alas, what he called a 'medical episode' landed him in the hospital. The others who were teaching Torts that term pitched in to cover some classes, and just as two of us were figuring out how we would share teaching his students for the remaining weeks, there was Fleming ready to reclaim the lectern—against doctor's orders, I'm sure. Although the students kindly tolerated us, the substitutes, I am also sure they were very happy to have Fleming back.

Although is most respects a model of the academic man, Fleming sometimes ventured into the political aspects of his field. For example, one year many colleagues were surprised to see his name appear on the California ballot pamphlet in support of a voter initiative intended to curb legal fees in personal injury cases.

Fleming was 78 when he died—from amyotrophic lateral sclerosis (commonly called 'Lou Gehrig's disease' in the United States, after the famous baseball player whose affliction gave widespread visibility to the disease). In addition to Valerie, his wife of fifty-one years, he is survived by his four children, Anthony, Barbara, Colin, and Stephen, and his five grandchildren, Olivia, Tori, Peter, Alex, and Kristin.

The last time I saw him, rather shortly before he died, Fleming was reading the novel *Changing Places* by David Lodge. As many academics know, this is a very amusing book about two professors who exchange jobs and go off to teach in new countries. It then struck me that Fleming alone changed places—that is, changed his home country—more times than the two of them together. And he found great admirers in every one of those places. We miss him.

9 February 1998

HUMAN RIGHTS

1

Tort and Human Rights

Lord Bingham of Cornhill

For most English lawyers of (or above) a certain age, Human Rights formed no named or identifiable part of the legal landscape in which they grew up. They had heard of the Declaration of the Rights of Man and the Citizen approved by the National Constituent Assembly at Versailles in August 1789 and knew of the rights protected by the first ten amendments to the United States Constitution, but these were no more than historical titbits, of little or no practical significance to the practice of the law in England. They had heard or came to hear of the Universal Declaration on Human Rights adopted by the United Nations in 1948, of the European Convention for the Protection of Human Rights and Fundamental Freedoms ratified by the United Kingdom in 1951, and of the International Covenant on Civil and Political Rights which the United Kingdom signed in 1968 and ratified in 1976; but these again were matters of mere general knowledge, interesting but (from a professional point of view) useless. Even the most rudimentary legal education did, of course, involve some exposure to legal provisions giving protection against (for example) unlawful detention, wrongful arrest, the issue of general search warrants, the imposition of cruel and unusual punishments, and the right to a fair trial according to law, but in the absence of an entrenched written constitution or any statutory code of human rights with any claim to be comprehensive, these provisions were not generally seen as part of a coherent attempt to protect rights identified as being of particular importance to the citizen as a human being and a member of society.

In the international instruments already mentioned, and in the charters and bills of rights adopted by an ever-increasing number of countries, it has been the practice to define (subject to appropriate qualifications) a series of different rights identified as deserving special protection. This is no doubt necessary and desirable for drafting purposes, to avoid undue generality and complexity. But it would seem that most if not all of the primary rights usually singled out for special protection are related directly or indirectly to the belief that the individual citizen should enjoy as much personal autonomy as is consistent with the reasonable interests of other citizens and the community as a whole. In other words, the individual citizen should be left to do his or her own thing to the maximum extent possible without impinging on the rights of others; where restraints on personal autonomy are called for they should be the minimum needed to serve their purpose; where penalties for anti-social conduct are called for, they should be for proved breaches of known rules, imposed by a fair and impartial body. The right to life; to freedom from inhuman and degrading treatment and slavery; to liberty of the person; to a fair trial before an independent and impartial tribunal within a reasonable time; to privacy; to freedom of thought, conscience, and religion; to freedom of expression; to freedom of association; to freedom to marry and found a family; to own property: all fit into this pattern. In referring to Fundamental Freedoms, as its full name does, the European Convention makes an important point: freedom from unwarranted interference with an individual citizen's right to do his or her own thing lies at the heart of what is now recognized as a discrete field of legal study known as Human Rights.

The absence in the United Kingdom of an entrenched written constitution or any comprehensive statutory code of human rights has not, of course, meant that such rights have been unprotected. But it has inevitably meant that protection, where it exists, has been piecemeal and ad hoc. Various fields of law have made their contribution to this protection: statute, constitutional law, criminal law, equity, rules of practice and procedure. But it would seem clear that it is the law of tort, to which the late Professor Fleming made such a notable and enduring contribution, which has borne the heat and burden of the battle.

To define or accurately to describe what is meant by tort law is one of the oldest and most intriguing of legal conundrums. For present purposes, however, one may perhaps borrow the definition to be found in *Street on Torts*, where the aim of the law of torts is said to be

> to define the obligations on one member of society to his or her fellows, and to adjust, once it is decided that some adjustment is to be made, those losses which must inevitably result from the ever-increasing activities of those who live in a common society. The adjustment is made by providing compensation for the harm suffered by those whose interests have been invaded owing to the conduct of others.[1]

[1] M. Brazier, *Street on Torts*, (9th ed., 1993), 1.

The interests protected by the law of tort, it is suggested in *Street*, include:

(1) intentional invasion of personal and proprietary interests;
(2) interests in economic relations, business and trading;
(3) interests in intellectual property;
(4) negligent interference with personal proprietary and economic interests;
(5) further protection of personal and proprietary interests;
(6) reputation;
(7) due process; and
(8) miscellaneous interests.[2]

If this definition and this breakdown are accepted, the aptness of tort law as a vehicle for protecting human rights can be readily recognized, for both acknowledge that the personal autonomy of A, his freedom to do his own thing, must be circumscribed at the point where his activity becomes harmful to B to the extent that the law gives B a right to complain. So, at any rate *faute de mieux*, the law of tort is a suitable vehicle for protecting human rights. But whereas an entrenched written constitution or a statutory code of rights will set out and identify the rights to be protected, with any appropriate qualifications, the law of tort operates in a quite different and negative way, by proscribing and providing remedies for certain acts and omissions judged to be unacceptable. To the extent that the law of tort proscribes all acts and omissions which undermine or encroach on the rights which a constitution or a statutory code would protect, it may give the citizen the same rights, the same personal autonomy, the same freedom from unwarranted interference, as a constitution or a code. If, as seems likely at the time of writing, the United Kingdom is at last set to incorporate the European Convention into its municipal law, it is timely and perhaps interesting to consider how effective the law, and in particular the law of tort, has been in practice in safeguarding the basic human rights and fundamental freedoms of the British citizen.

It is probably safe to assume that most citizens would in the last resort, however unheroically, value their own physical security above all else. This is recognized in the international instruments already mentioned. It is also recognized by the law of tort. If A threatens B with unwelcome physical contact, he commits the tort of assault. If he deliberately makes

[2] *Ibid*. 5–7. And see the valuable contribution by Robert S. French, 'Statutory Modelling of Torts', to Nicholas J. Mullany (ed.), *Torts in the Nineties* (1997), a fascinating survey of the law of tort in several jurisdictions from which I have derived much benefit.

unwelcome physical contact with B, he commits the tort of battery. If, without lawful authority, he confines B and restricts the freedom of B to go where B wishes, he commits the tort of false imprisonment. If, owing a duty to take reasonable care not to cause physical injury to B, A fails to take such care and so causes or allows such injury to be caused to B, A is liable to B for the tort of negligence. Generally speaking, the law of tort protects the individual's right to physical autonomy.

The old adage that an Englishman's home is his castle reflects another aspect of personal autonomy, the right of the individual who is causing no harm to anyone to live peaceably in his habitation and refuse entry to all unwelcome intruders. Over the years an increasing number of public officials have won the right, in defined circumstances, to enter the castle against the wishes of the occupier, but the basic right, subject to these exceptions, survives. And that is, of course, because the law of tort proscribes unauthorized entry on to land owned or occupied by another.

True to form, neither the law of tort nor any other branch of English law provides any guarantee of the individual's right to publish (by speech or writing) what he wishes. Such a right, if it may be called such, exists only by default, by the absence of any legal objection to such publication. Various branches of the law proscribe different forms of publication: that which is libellous or slanderous; that which breaches confidence; that which discloses official secrets or is subversive or incites public disorder or racial hatred; that which is blasphemous; that which is prohibited by statute; that which breaches orders made by the court; and so on. But despite the multiplicity of grounds upon which publication may be proscribed, the citizen's freedom to publish what he wishes is in practice much more than interstitial. It conveys a truer impression to state that the British citizen may publish what he wishes with impunity in the absence of legal objection than to state that in the absence of legal objection the British citizen may publish what he wishes with impunity.

So far this is all plain sailing through smooth water safely protected by the harbour wall. But beyond the harbour wall the condition of the sea is more taxing. There are breakers and cross-currents and sunken wrecks and uncharted waters. No survey of the efficacy of tort law in protecting human rights can respectably shirk the challenge of the open sea.

The torts of assault and battery afford adequate protection against the more crude and obvious threats or acts of physical violence. And the courts have avoided undue literalism in their approach to these torts. It was long ago held to be a battery to throw water over a person or spit in his face,[3] or to overturn a chair on which he is sitting[4] or a ladder on

[3] *R v Cotesworth* (1704) 6 Mod. 172.
[4] *Hopper v Reeve* (1817) 7 Taunt. 698.

which he is standing.[5] It is now clear that a criminal defendant may commit an assault over the telephone,[6] and there would seem to be no good reason why a defendant sued in tort would not be similarly liable as has been held in Australia.[7] In *R v Chief Constable of Devon and Cornwall, ex parte CEGB*[8] Lord Denning MR relied on old authority in holding that 'an unwanted kiss may be a battery' and most lawyers would surely regard this as an acceptable conclusion. But the requirement that to be actionable contact must be non-consensual may, and in the past has, led to strange (and to modern eyes) unacceptable results. In *Latter v Braddell*,[9] for example, a female servant was examined by a doctor on the instructions of the employer who thought (wrongly) that the servant was pregnant. The servant submitted to the examination believing that she was obliged to do so but protested and sobbed throughout. It was held, by a majority, that the servant's reluctant obedience did not amount to a lack of consent, so her claim failed. One can only hope that the result would be different today. One could not, however, be sanguine about a plaintiff's chances of success if she invoked the tortious law of assault to complain of a friendly but unsolicited invitation to indulge in sexual relations. This might be deeply offensive to the plaintiff, but if accompanied by no threat of force and if not persisted in, and if made in the belief that the invitation would be welcome, would not at all obviously amount to an assault.[10] Even if the English law of tort embodied the rule in section 46 of the American Law Institute's *Restatement (Second) of Torts* (1965) that 'One who by extreme and outrageous conduct intentionally or recklessly causes severe emotional distress to another is subject to liability for such emotional distress', it must be doubtful whether a case such as this would be covered; and it must further be doubted whether *Wilkinson v Downton*[11] or any later English authority could or would be extended so far.[12]

In its continuing tolerance of corporal punishment inflicted on children (provided it is not 'excessive', whatever that may mean), the English law of tort would be held by international and progressive opinion to have failed to acknowledge what would now be widely recognized as the rights of the child. But this is an area in which, even now, there is perhaps no consensus of domestic opinion. More significant, certainly in practical terms, are the difficulties which face plaintiffs seeking to

[5] *Collins v Renison* (1754) Sayer 138. [6] *R v Ireland* [1997] 3 WLR 534.

[7] *Barton v Armstrong* [1969] 2 NSWR 451. J. Conaghan & W. Mansell, *The Wrongs of Tort* (1993), 133. [8] [1982] QB 458.

[9] (1881) 44 LT 369. [10] Conaghan & Mansell, n. 7 above, 137.

[11] [1897] 2 QB 57.

[12] Account should, however, be taken of P. B. Birks' erudite and sustained argument to the contrary in 'Harassment and Hubris: The Right to an Equality of Respect', John Maurice Kelly Memorial Lecture of 1995, (Univ. Coll. Dublin, 1995).

complain as adults of sexual abuse suffered as children. There can be no doubt that such abuse, if inflicted without consent and if the subject of timeous action, can found a successful complaint of battery. But save, it seems, in Canada, there appear to have been few actions,[13] and the explanation can scarcely be the absence of grounds for complaint. In England the House of Lords in *Stubbings v Webb*[14] applied the limitation rules in a way which posed real difficulties for plaintiffs, but the European Court of Human Rights was content to accept that decision.[15] The Canadian cases, however, show that difficulty arises from the requirement that conduct must, to be a battery, be non-consensual.[16] Even where an initial act of abuse was non-consensual, courts have been willing to hold that later acts in a sustained course of abuse took place with the consent of the child. The problem may perhaps have been resolved, or at least clarified, by the decision of the Supreme Court of Canada in *Norberg v Wynrib*,[17] holding that the traditional assumption of individual autonomy and free will could not safely be made, even between adults, in the case of 'power dependent relationships' such as those of parent–child, psychotherapist–patient, physician–patient, priest–penitent, professor–student, attorney–client and employer–employee. Unless, in a similar case, the English courts were to adopt a similar approach, the protection given by tort law to a human right of obvious importance would seem clearly defective.

The essential mischief of false imprisonment, where A without lawful authority detains B, is clear enough. But even this tort becomes a little fuzzy at the edges.[18] A surprising number of questions arise. Where an act of detention is established, must the plaintiff show that the detention was wrongful or the defendant show that it was not? English law, it would seem, gives the first answer,[19] Australian law the second.[20] Is the tort established if the detention complained of is not intentional but reckless or negligent? To this question English law gives a negative,[21] Australian law an affirmative,[22] answer. So if A turns off the power to a lift on Friday evening, carelessly failing to check whether any passenger is in the lift, with the result that B spends the weekend in a stationary lift between floors with no means of escape, his claim for damages for false

[13] See P. B. Feldthusen, 'The Canadian Experiment with the Civil Action for Sexual Battery' in Mullany, n. 2 above, 274.

[14] [1993] AC 498.

[15] (1997) 23 EHRR 213.

[16] *Madelena v Kunn* (1989) 38 BCLR (2d) 273; (1989) 61 DLR (4th) 392; *Lyth v Dagg* (1988) 46 CCLT 25.

[17] [1992] 2 SCR 226.

[18] See F. A. Trindade, 'The Modern Tort of False Imprisonment' in Mullany, n. 2 above, 229, to whose analysis I am much indebted.

[19] *Fowler v Lanning* [1959] 1 QB 426.

[20] *McHale v Watson* (1964) 111 CLR 384; *Tsouvalla v Bini* [1966] SASR 157; *Carnegie v State of Victoria*, (Supr. C. Victoria, Sept. 1989).

[21] *Letang v Cooper* [1965] 1 QB 232.

[22] *Williams v Milotin* (1957) 97 CLR 465; Trindade, n. 18 above at 252.

imprisonment would (it seems) fail in England but succeed in Australia. What if the restraint on B's freedom of movement is brought about indirectly, as by an indication that harm will follow to B, or to another close to B, if B moves from where he is? It appears that Australian courts would give a remedy in such circumstances.[23] If A, claiming to be an eyewitness of a serious crime, dishonestly and maliciously identifies B to a police officer as the perpetrator, with the result that the officer, reasonably believing the information to be reliable, arrests B, is A liable in tort for the ensuing detention of B? Until recently, English law would again have given a negative answer, unless A asked the officer to take B into custody.[24] But the recent decision of the House of Lords (relating to malicious prosecution) in *Martin v Watson*[25] may throw doubt on earlier authority. It seems likely that the Australian courts would regard A's conduct as causative of the detention. If B is lawfully ordered to serve a term of imprisonment, has he any right of complaint against the prison authorities if his residual liberty as a prisoner is infringed or if the conditions of his confinement fall clearly below the minimum acceptable level? After some hesitation,[26] English law appears for the present to give a clearly negative answer.[27] Whether this negative answer can survive incorporation of the European Convention may be doubtful; there is perhaps less room for doubt whether it should. Must a detention, to be tortious, be total, or does A avoid liability if he leaves B with some means of escape? The answer here must surely turn on the acceptability, in fact, of the means of escape. A can scarcely be liable if he locks B in a room which B is free and able to leave by an open French window. But it would be otherwise if A drove off in his car with B an unwilling passenger, able to leave only by throwing himself out of the moving car. What if B, having voluntarily agreed to some restraint on his freedom of movement, seeks to revoke his agreement in breach of contract? Earlier this century it was held that B could not complain of false imprisonment if detained in accordance with the conditions of the original contract.[28] There is, however, authority in England,[29] Canada,[30]

[23] Trindade, n. 18 above at 232; *R v Garrett* (1988) 50 SASR 392; and see *Chaytor v London, New York and Paris Association of Fashion Ltd* (1962) 30 DLR (2d) 527.

[24] *Grinham v Willey* (1858) 4 H & N 496; *Pike v Waldrum and Peninsular & Oriental Steam Navigation Co.* [1952] 1 Lloyd's Rep. 431; *Davidson v Chief Constable of North Wales* [1994] 2 All ER 597.

[25] [1996] AC 74.

[26] *Middleweek v Chief Constable of Merseyside (Note)* [1992] 1 AC 179 at 186; *Weldon v Home Office* [1992] 1 AC 58 at 139.

[27] *R v Deputy Governor of Parkhurst Prison, ex p Hague* [1992] 1 AC 58; *Weldon v Home Office*, ibid.

[28] *Robinson v The Balmain New Ferry Co. Ltd* [1910] AC 295; *Herd v Weardale Steel, Coal and Coke Co. Ltd* [1915] AC 67.

[29] *Sunbolf v Alford* (1838) 3 M & W 248.

[30] *Bahner v Marwest Hotel Co. Ltd* (1969) 6 DLR (3d) 322.

and Australia[31] that A is not entitled to detain B for non-payment of a contractual debt, and it would seem clear in principle that B should not be personally detained as security for his contractual performance. Is it necessary to establish the tort that B should know at the time that he is being detained? Both in England[32] and the United States[33] it was held or thought that it was. But doubts were expressed.[34] In the United States the rule was changed.[35] In England knowledge of the detention was authoritatively held not to be a necessary ingredient of a successful claim.[36] This view has found favour in Australia.[37] Need A, to be liable, know that he is wrongfully detaining B? Not in Australia: in *Cowell v Corrective Services Commission of New South Wales*[38] the prison authorities were held liable in false imprisonment for detaining the plaintiff beyond the period permitted by law as a result of miscalculating the remission to which he was entitled. There can be little doubt that the same result would follow in England.

It not infrequently happens, often following the end of an acquaintance or the breakdown of a relationship, that the rejected party finds it impossible to accept the finality of the rupture and reacts by bombarding the other party with oral and written communications, messages, presents, and telephone calls, or by loitering at or near the other party's home or workplace or places where they spend their leisure time. The same behaviour may of course have quite other motivations (it is an affliction to which many well-known public figures are subject) but the harmful effect on the victim may be the same, and is often serious. This is conduct which plainly infringes the personal autonomy of the victim, representing as it does an unwarrantable violation of the victim's right to be left alone. Yet the courts in England have been curiously slow to treat such conduct as tortious. In *Patel v Patel*[39] it was roundly stated that no tort of harassment existed. This view was soon rejected by the Court of Appeal in *Khorasandjian v Bush*[40] and *Burris v Azadani.*[41] But the majority decision in the earlier of those cases, holding that a daughter living as a licensee in her mother's house could complain of unwanted telephone calls in private nuisance, has since been disapproved by the House of Lords.[42] The House did not, however, go on to hold that there existed no tort of harassment. The criminal law witnessed a similar development: in *R v Burstow,*[43] a case in which conduct of the kind described had caused

[31] *Gold v Healco Services (Vic) Pty Ltd,* (Supr. C. Victoria, 15 Apr. 1988).
[32] *Herring v Boyle* (1834) 1 CM & R 377. [33] *Restatement of Torts* (1934), para 42.
[34] *Meering v Grahame-White Aviation Co. Ltd* (1919) 122 LT 44; Trindade, n. 18 above at 247. [35] *Restatement of Torts, Second* (1965) para 35.
[36] *Murray v Ministry of Defence* [1988] 1 WLR 692.
[37] *Myer Stores Ltd v Soo* [1991] 2 VR 597. [38] (1988) 13 NSWLR 714.
[39] [1988] 2 FLR 179. [40] [1993] QB 727. [41] [1995] 1 WLR 1372.
[42] *Hunter v Canary Wharf Ltd* [1997] 2 WLR 684. [43] [1997] 3 WLR 534.

the victim to suffer psychiatric damage, the defendant was convicted of inflicting grievous bodily harm. In the light of these developments it must be doubted whether there was a lacuna in the law which the Protection from Harassment Act 1997 was needed to fill.[44]

The most notable breach in the walls of the Englishman's castle came to light with the decision, in *Malone v Metropolitan Police Commissioner*,[45] that the civil law of England offered no protection against the official interception of telephone communications or, by necessary analogy, postal communications. It required resort to Strasbourg, and an Act of Parliament,[46] to remedy the deficiency. The remedy was only partial, however, for although the Security Service was subjected by statute[47] to strict controls and scrutiny in entering private premises to plant electronic listening devices, the police were subject to no such control or scrutiny, and when this obviously lawless conduct by the police came to light the initial response of the government of the day, supported by the Opposition, was not to outlaw such behaviour but to give it statutory sanction. Happily, in the end, more principled counsels prevailed,[48] largely as a result of judicial criticism. Such entry by the police was, of course, tortious, but since it was covert the victim never became aware of it and so was unable to sue; and even if he suspected such entry he would be likely to face insuperable problems of proof. That the law of tort in this instance afforded inadequate protection of the citizen's basic rights seems clear; that a constitutional guarantee would afford more effective protection in practice is perhaps less clear.

Reviewing the law of defamation from a New South Wales perspective, the Hon Mr Justice Dennis Mahoney has written,

> The law of public defamation is seen publicly to be a failure: it does not do what it should do and what it does it does not do in an efficient, effective and timeous way.[49]

Most commentators familiar with the English law of defamation would tend to take a similar view, regarding this as a field in which the law of tort most obviously failed to protect the rights of the citizen in the way and to the extent the citizen could reasonably expect.

While most would agree in expressing dissatisfaction, however, the grounds of dissatisfaction would be quite different. The media, and particularly the Press, criticize the English law of defamation (and perhaps, to a lesser extent, contempt) as so onerous and restrictive as to inhibit valuable investigative journalism and confine within too narrow

[44] This statute was enacted to criminalize what is popularly known as 'stalking'. Where such conduct caused physical or psychiatric injury it was already criminal. It was also, even in the absence of injury, restrainable by civil injunction.

[45] [1979] Ch 344.

[46] Interception of Communications Act 1985.

[47] Security Service Act 1989.

[48] The Police Act 1997, Pt III.

[49] 'Defamation Law—A Time to Rethink', in Mullany, n. 2 above, 261.

a compass the basic right of free expression. Particular objection is taken to the rule which requires a defendant to prove the truth of a defamatory statement rather than the plaintiff its untruth, to the absence of a rule such as that laid down in *New York Times v Sullivan*[50] giving special protection to publishers of statements made about public figures, to the inadequate protection accorded to journalists' sources, to the willingness of the courts to impose restraints prior to publication, and to the disproportionate awards of damages not infrequently made by juries to successful plaintiffs.

Others, notably including those exposed to adverse or unwanted publicity in the Press, voice a different complaint: that the cost and risk of suing any major organ of the Press are such as can be contemplated, in the absence of Legal Aid, only by those who are very wealthy or very foolhardy or (preferably) both, so that in practice the law affords little or no protection to the ordinary citizen; and that the law does too little to protect the privacy of the citizen against the intrusions of a vulgar and often irresponsible Press.

Many objective observers would probably see force in both sides of this argument. It is perhaps contrary to general principle and surprising that a plaintiff who comes to court to complain of a false and defamatory statement should not have to show that the statement is false as well as defamatory, although it may be questionable how much practical difference a change in the rule would make. On the merits of the rule in *New York Times v Sullivan* there is much to be said both for and against, as evidenced by the rejection of the rule in England[51] and Canada[52] and its acceptance in Australia.[53] But the courts have resolved a long-running issue as to whether local authorities enjoyed a reputation protected by the law of defamation in favour of free speech.[54] It has long been the rule that an interlocutory injunction restraining publication should not be granted where a defendant plausibly undertakes to justify.[55] And the level of jury awards, already the subject of adverse decision in Strasbourg,[56] has in recent years become the subject of more effective control and review.[57]

The problems facing a defamation plaintiff are indeed formidable, and

[50] 376 US 254 (1964).

[51] *Derbyshire County Council v Times Newspapers Ltd* [1993] AC 534.

[52] *Hill v Church of Scientology of Toronto* [1995] 2 SCR 1130.

[53] *Theophanous v The Herald & Weekly Times Ltd* (1994) 182 CLR 104.

[54] *Derbyshire County Council v Times Newspapers Ltd*, above, resolving a difference between *Manchester Corporation v Williams* [1891] 1 QB 94 and *National Union of General and Municipal Workers v Gillian* [1946] KB 81 and *Bognor Regis Urban District Council v Campion* [1972] 2 QB 169.

[55] *Bonnard v Perryman* [1891] 2 Ch 269.

[56] *Tolstoy Miloslavsky v United Kingdom* (1995) 20 EHRR 442.

[57] *John & MGN Ltd* [1997] QB 586.

it remains to be seen how effective a judicially–inspired statutory reform which has recently been enacted proves in practice.[58] But in the view of many the most glaring failure of English tort law in this area has been in declining to recognize the invasion of personal privacy as an independent tort. As has been pointed out before,[59] much has been done, in particular by extending and adapting equitable rules on breach of confidence, to protect the privacy of the citizen. But the Court of Appeal did hold, in the notorious case of *Kaye v Robertson*,[60] that English law recognized no right to privacy, and felt unable to grant the substantial relief it would have wished. This decision has provoked much criticism and disagreement,[61] and it seems clear that in (for instance) the United States, France, Germany, Switzerland, and Canada the plaintiff would have fared better.[62] In his thought-provoking contribution to *Torts in the Nineties*, Professor Todd has valuably drawn attention to several cases which give pause for thought.

As long ago as 1931, a Californian court held that giving publicity eight years after the event to the facts that the plaintiff had worked as a prostitute and had been tried and acquitted of murder was an actionable violation of her right to privacy.[63] In *Tucker v News Media Ownership Ltd* a New Zealand plaintiff, seeking by means of a publicity campaign to raise funds for a major operation abroad, learned that the media proposed to publish details of his previous convictions of sex offences and applied for interim injunctive relief. This he was successful in obtaining at first instance and on appeal.[64] Before trial, disclosure was made by other sources, and the injunctions were discharged, but McGechan J tentatively supported the view taken by the earlier courts.[65] In *Bradley v Wingnut Films Ltd*[66] the defendants made a horror film part of which was shot in a public cemetery and the plaintiff complained (among other things) that the inclusion of his family tombstone in the film was an unlawful invasion of his privacy. The claim failed on the facts, but Gallen J was willing to hold that the law of New Zealand recognized in principle the cause of action sued upon.

It would be very strongly arguable, to say the least, that under the English common law all three of these claims would be struck out as

[58] Defamation Act 1996.

[59] Notably by D. J. Serpp in his important article 'English Judicial Recognition of a Right to Privacy', (1983) 3 OJLS 325; also by myself, 'Should there be a Law to Protect Rights of Personal Privacy?', (1996) 5 EHRLR 450.

[60] [1991] FSR 62.

[61] See, e.g., Peter Prescott QC '*Kaye v Robertson*—A Reply', (1991) 54 MLR 451, Birks, n. 12 above; Stephen Todd, 'Protection of Privacy' in Mullany, n. 2 above, 174 at 210.

[62] See Basil Markesinis, 'Our Patchy Law of Privacy—Time to do Something about it', (1990) 53 MLR 802.

[63] *Melvin v Reid* 297 P.91 (1931)

[64] High C., Wellington, 20 Oct. 1986, Jefferies J; CA, 23 Oct. 1986.

[65] [1986] 2 NZLR 716.

[66] [1993] 1 NZLR 41.

disclosing no course of action. The result would then necessarily be to deprive the plaintiff of relief (unless some other cause of action could be ingeniously adapted to cover the facts). Are these cases in which the plaintiff ought to be protected? That is a much more difficult question, and one to which reasonable people could give different answers. The value of free speech has been described so frequently and so eloquently as to leave no room for doubt of its importance. The international instruments mentioned at the outset also recognize a right to privacy, as would most ordinary citizens. It is, however, difficult and sensitive to determine where free speech ends, or should end, and privacy begins. Wherever the line is drawn, there will be cases clearly falling on one side of it or the other. But there will be other cases (touching, for example, on private activities of political figures unrelated to performance of their public duties, or the private lives of collateral members of the Royal Family with no realistic prospect of succession to the throne) which would be much more problematical. These are problems which, until now, the English courts have scarcely had to confront. If, as expected, the European Convention is incorporated into English law (protecting privacy in article 8 and free speech in article 10) the nettle of reconciling the two will have, it would seem, to be grasped. It must be hoped that on a case by case basis, and guided by authority and academic commentary here and elsewhere, a pattern and thence a discernible dividing line, will emerge—unless, of course, Parliament takes the initiative and lays down statutory rules to define the bounds of privacy. But it seems perhaps unlikely that statutory rules could be devised which were so clear, so comprehensive, and so easy of application that a body of case law would not build up, putting the flesh of real-life experience on the bones of the statutory skeleton.

It seems clear that the law of tort has the fertility and flexibility to protect nearly all of the most basic of human rights. But remedies may only be developed in the cases which happen to come before the courts. In the absence of any principled frame of reference judicial responses are inevitably partial and to some extent inconsistent. So perhaps the end-of-term report on the performance of the English courts in this field, on the eve of incorporation, should be: 'Has done some good work, and tried hard, and set a good example. But there are areas of weakness which call for attention. The next few terms will call for energy, imagination, an open mind, and, above all, a willingness to learn.'

2

Human Rights and the Law of Torts

Sir Anthony Mason

Introduction

The object of this essay is to discuss the impact of human rights on the law of torts. This is no easy task as the protection of human rights was at most a speck on the horizon when the law of torts took shape—though some would deny that it has ever taken shape. The law of torts protects and has protected a range of rights and interests long recognized by the common law. Some of the rights and interests so recognized fall within the much wider catalogue of human rights; others do not.

The fact that there is some degree of commonality between interests protected by the law of torts and human rights poses the question whether the law of torts can be moulded and, if so, to what extent, to provide a remedy in those cases in which human rights have been violated. A related question is to what extent the principles of the law of torts will be influenced by human rights jurisprudence. Answers to these questions turn on a complex of considerations. They include (a) the nature of the law of torts, (b) the relationship between the interests which it protects and human rights, and (c) the adequacy of alternative available remedies for human rights violations.

The Nature of the Law of Torts

The purpose of the law of torts is to adjust 'losses and afford compensation for injuries sustained by one person as a result of the conduct of another'.[1] Our inability to base the law of torts on a single unifying principle led Sir John Salmond to the conclusion that the law of torts consists of a series of unconnected wrongs. That view has been contested by many commentators, including such celebrated jurists as Pollock,

[1] C. A. Wright, 'Introduction to the Law of Torts', (1942) 8 Camb. L.J. 238.

Winfield, Harper, and Wigmore. The law of torts remains in essence however, the offspring of its history, a body of principles developed around particular causes of action, imposing liability in a variety of situations for wrongful conduct which occasions loss or damage to another. For the most part that liability gives rise to an award of damages but it can result in an injunction or a specific order for the return of goods, as in detinue. Generally speaking, the emphasis is on the wrongful conduct of the defendant, rather than on the violation of the plaintiff's right, though in some cases, as in trespass, the emphasis is on the infringement of the plaintiff's right. On the other hand, with human rights, the emphasis and the basis of relief are concerned with the infringement of the plaintiff's human right or fundamental freedom.

The character of the law of torts as a body of principles centred on particular causes of action does not mean that the category of actionable torts is closed. Far from it. Fleming makes the point that new and innominate torts have emerged over the years.[2] This capacity to generate new causes of action suggests that the law of torts may be capable of being moulded in such a way as to provide remedies for human rights violations. As illustrations of Fleming's point, it is enough to refer to such instances as the doctrine in *Rylands v Fletcher*,[3] the tort of intimidation,[4] interference with contractual relations,[5] and conduct intended or calculated to inflict mental harm.[6] To these instances we can add the new advances in the tort of negligence culminating in liability for negligent mis-statement and purely economic loss.[7] We can also mention the tort of intentionally causing unlawful harm recognized in *Beaudesert Shire Council v Smith*,[8] but, after extensive criticism, ultimately rejected in *Northern Territory v Mengel*.[9]

The United States provides additional illustrations of new torts. They include strict products liability,[10] invasion of privacy, and wrongful discharge from employment. Of particular importance for present purposes is the creation of the tort of invasion of privacy. If the common law in the United Kingdom and Australia were to recognize such a tort, then it could play a valuable role in providing a remedy for conduct amounting

[2] *The Law of Torts* (9th ed., 1998), 7–8.

[3] (1868) LR 3 HL 330; but see now *General Jones Pty Ltd v Burnie Port Authority* (1994) 179 CLR 520.

[4] *Rookes v Barnard* [1964] AC 1129.

[5] *Bowen v Hall* (1881) 6 QBD 333.

[6] See *Wilkinson v Downton* [1897] 2 QB 57 (the precise effect of this decision is a matter of debate).

[7] *Hedley Byrne & Co. Ltd v Heller & Partners Ltd* [1964] AC 465.

[8] 120 CLR 145.

[9] (1995) 185 CLR 307.

[10] *Restatement (Second) of Torts* § 402A. At its annual meeting in Washington, DC in May 1997 the American Law Institute voted to adopt the *Restatement (Third) of Torts: Products Liability* (*Proposed Final Draft*, April 1, 1997), subject to amendments approved at that meeting.

to a violation of the human right of privacy. Whether such a tort might be recognized is a matter to be discussed later in this essay.

The list of new torts thus created is fairly short. Even in the United States, the judicial approach to the creation of new torts is extremely conservative.[11] There, as in England, Australia, Canada, and New Zealand, judges are anxious to present a new tort as if it is an inevitable consequence of principles long accepted, thereby downplaying its novelty.[12]

Interests Protected by the Law of Torts

The common law has historically provided remedies for intentional wrongful interference with the physical integrity of the person through the tort of trespass to the person, that is, battery, and assault. Likewise, the action for false imprisonment provides a remedy for interference with the liberty of the individual. The tort of negligence also enables a plaintiff to recover damages not only for physical injury, but also for emotional distress and nervous shock.[13] It would seem to follow inevitably that intentionally inflicted purely mental distress would be actionable. Actions for trespass to land, trespass to goods, detinue, and conversion do not call for discussion. Nor do actions in deceit, for injurious falsehood, passing-off, intimidation, or conspiracy. Interference with contractual relations and the action for interference with trade or business by unlawful means stand in a different position simply because they are regarded as economic torts designed to provide a remedy for intentional conduct which results in economic loss or damage. Malicious prosecution and abuse of process also stand in a different position but for a different reason, in that they provide remedies against use of curial process for an improper purpose.

It would be a mistake to place too much emphasis on interests hitherto protected by the law of torts. We should keep in mind the entire array of interests protected by the common law, an array which is continuing to expand, as the later discussion of privacy will demonstrate. This expansion may be facilitated by the greater judicial willingness to take account of, if not to evaluate, policy issues which underlie the principles of the law of torts, a willingness which is readily discernible in such recent decisions as *Stovin v Wise*.[14] In this respect, the formulation of tort law

[11] A Bernstein, 'How to Make a New Tort: Three Paradoxes' (1997) 75 Texas L.R. 1539 at 1546.
[12] Ibid at 1545–1546.
[13] *McLoughlin v O'Brian* [1982] 2 All ER 298; *Jaensch v Coffey* (1984) 155 CLR 149.
[14] [1996] AC 923 (dealing with the liability of a highway authority for failure to remove an obstruction to visibility at a road junction).

principles ultimately rests on policy considerations, sometimes competing policy considerations, as does judicial enforcement of human rights. On the other hand, the failure of the plaintiffs to establish as against the public authority defendants in *X (minors) v Bedfordshire County Council*[15] the existence of a duty of care in relation to discretionary decisions concerning the welfare, including psychological and material welfare, and education of children, demonstrates that tort remedies have a limited role to play in challenging discretionary and policy-based decisions.

Special mention should be made of the action for defamation, not because it is capable of providing a remedy for violation of human rights but because the principles applicable to the action have been significantly influenced by the existence of a guarantee of freedom of expression and, for that matter, freedom of expression as an interest or value traditionally protected by the common law. I shall return to this topic which is important, as perhaps is the relatively new cause of action for negligent mis-statement, though as yet its potential for conflict with freedom of expression has not excited interest. A similar comment might be made about the potential for conflict between freedom of expression and interference with contractual relations.[16]

It should be noted that not all actionable wrongs are classified as torts. Some wrongs give rise to equitable relief attracting compensation. Compensation has even been awarded for loss sustained as a result of undue influence[17] and, in Canada, the fiduciary duty has been extended so that a doctor *vis-à-vis* his patient and a parent *vis-à-vis* his child can be liable for compensation for sexual acts in breach of that duty.[18] This extension of the fiduciary duty, particularly to embrace tort-like duties, finds no echo in Australia and the United Kingdom where the fiduciary duty is confined to the no conflict, no unauthorized profit rules.[19] Perhaps the law of torts will expand to fill the void.

Before concluding my comments on the nature of the law of torts, I should point out that its emphasis on the wrongful conduct of the defendant and the emphasis in human rights jurisprudence on the infringement of the plaintiff's rights, reflects a difference in the legal foundations of the two branches of law. The law of torts constitutes a system of legal rules regulating the conduct of members and institutions of society in the interests of the members of society and allocating

[15] [1995] 2 AC 633 at 736.

[16] As to the position in the US, see D. A. Anderson 'Torts, Speech, and Contracts' (1997) 75 Texas L.R. 1499.

[17] *Mahoney v Purnell* [1996] 3 All ER 82.

[18] *Norberg v Wynrib* (1992) 92 DLR (4th) 449; *McInerney v MacDonald* (1992) 93 DLR (4th) 415; *M(K) v M(H)* (1992) 96 DLR (4th) 289.

[19] *Breen v Williams* (1996) 186 CLR 71; *Bristol & West Building Society v Mothew* [1996] 4 All ER 698.

compensation for loss and damage sustained in breach of those rules. On the other hand, human rights protection is designed to affirm and safeguard the rights and dignity of the individual as an autonomous member of society. The nature of the rights so affirmed and protected have consequences, however, for the framework of government of the society. Hence the inclusion in guaranteed human rights and freedoms of the holding of free elections entails democratic government; so also the inclusion of the right to a fair trial, along with a requirement for an independent judiciary, spells out elements of the Rule of Law.

All this leads to another point, namely that the object of guaranteeing protection of human rights is to ensure that human rights are respected by government, using that term in a broad non-specific sense. The law of torts, on the other hand, is concerned with wrongful conduct on the part of anyone, whether individual, government, or government official, which causes loss or damage. Indeed, initially, because the Sovereign was immune from suit, the law of torts was primarily concerned with the conditions under which an individual was liable for tortious conduct. It is only in modern times that the elimination of the barriers to maintaining an action against the Crown in tort has effectively opened the way to making tort remedies available against the Crown.

The Catalogue of Human Rights

Just what that catalogue of human rights comprises is not altogether certain. The catalogue varies across the jurisdictions, depending upon such variables as the nature and extent of constitutional entrenchment, statutory protection, and the implementation and enforceability of international and regional conventions protecting human rights. For present purposes it will be sufficient if we assume that the catalogue contains those rights which are protected by both the European Convention on Human Rights and Fundamental Freedoms and the International Covenant on Civil and Political Rights (ICCPR). The rights common to the Convention (and its protocols) and the ICCPR include the following:

- the right to life, liberty and personal security
- freedom from torture, or inhuman, cruel or degrading treatment and punishment
- freedom from slavery
- the right to a fair trial and fair hearing by an independent court or tribunal
- freedom from retroactive criminal laws and penalties
- the right to privacy, correspondence, family and marriage rights

- freedom of thought, conscience and religion
- freedom of expression, assembly and association
- freedom from the death penalty
- freedom of movement and residence
- protection of aliens from expulsion
- the holding of free elections
- minority rights.

Human rights may be classified in various ways. The rights which are common to the European Convention and the ICCPR fall into the category of civil and political rights. Other human rights, such as social and economic rights, are not relevant to this essay. The classification 'civil and political rights', as the very description suggests, is one which can be subdivided into political rights connected with the individual's participation in the democratic process, and civil rights which stand outside that participation. Some rights, such as freedom of expression, however, have both characters, the freedom being critical both to participation in the democratic process and the individual's right to self-expression.

The Difference between Common-Law Interests and Human Rights

Even in those cases where there is a correspondence between an interest recognized by the common law and a specific human right, for example, liberty of the individual and freedom of expression, the correspondence is far from complete. The paramountcy of statute over the common law means that the interest protected by the common law is inevitably subject to statutory impairment or extension, whereas constitutionally entrenched human rights are not subject to statutory impairment. Statute-based human rights and internationally protected human rights, though subject to statutory alteration, are less likely to be altered by statute than common-law rights.

Of more importance for present purposes is the classification of the law of torts as private law and the classification of human rights jurisprudence as public law. The difference in classification reflects not only the historical development of the law of torts but also the different purposes served by the law of torts and human rights jurisprudence, the former being principally directed to the regulation of private rights and obligations, the latter being directed to the protection of individual rights from excessive exercise of public power. The difference in classification is not easy to maintain by reason of the absence of a bright-line distinction between public and private law. Yet the difference is important. In England, the divide has procedural consequences for the availability of relief by way of judicial review and damages. More significantly, tort law provides a remedy by way of damages, injunction, and specific orders, whereas human rights protection has been primarily directed to the provision of remedies invalidating the exercise of government powers.

For the future, too much should not be made of the difference. Just as the law of torts expanded to make relief available against government, so human rights jurisprudence is expanding to protect individuals against human rights violations by those exercising non-governmental powers. Statutes rather than the common law now impose human rights obligations on employers outside government, such as the obligation not to discriminate in various ways.

The Nature of Human Rights

Regimes for the protection of human rights take various forms. In most jurisdictions they are constitutionally entrenched, as they are in the Constitution of the United States and the Canadian Charter of Rights and Freedoms.[20] Human rights may be statute-based, rather than constitutionally entrenched, as they are in the New Zealand Bill of Rights Act 1990. Statute-based human rights are, of course, subject to statutory repeal and modification,[21] though repeal and modification *may* require compliance with certain procedures.

The national protection of human rights by international and regional conventions depends partly on whether the relevant provisions form part of domestic law, even if they have been ratified by the executive government. Implementation by statute is necessary in the United Kingdom, Canada, and Australia,[22] though it is not necessary in the United States. Ratification may, however, result in the exercise of jurisdiction by a supra-national tribunal, established by a convention, with respect to a complaint of human rights violations by a ratifying State: hence the exercise of jurisdiction by the European Court of Human Rights in relation to violation by the United Kingdom of its obligations under the Convention. Likewise the Human Rights Committee, established by the ICCPR, has exercised jurisdiction with respect to a violation by

[20] Constitution Act 1982, Sch. B, s. 33.

[21] S 6 of the New Zealand Bill of Rights Act 1990 provides that wherever an enactment can be given a meaning that is consistent with the rights and freedoms declared, that meaning is to be preferred.

[22] *Attorney-General for Canada v Attorney-General for Ontario* [1937] AC 326 at 347; *R v Secretary of State for Home Department, ex p Brind* [1991] 1 AC 696; *Minister for Immigration and Ethnic Affairs v Teoh* (1995) 183 CLR 273.

Australia of the ICCPR,[23] Australia having ratified but not implemented the ICCPR and the First Protocol.

Human rights are amenable, in appropriate circumstances, to the protection afforded by the private-law forms of action which constitute the law of torts. That is only to be expected, as the object of guaranteeing human rights is to protect the autonomy and the dignity of the individual. Just how far human rights are amenable to private-law forms of action depends in part upon the juristic nature of human rights, that is, whether they operate merely as a negative restriction on the exercise of power or whether they give rise to civil liability and, if so, in an action *sui generis* or in an action in tort.

The Influence of Human Rights in Jurisdictions where International Conventions have not been Implemented in Domestic Law

The rule that an international convention, unless implemented by legislation, does not form part of the law of the land has impeded the potential of human rights jurisprudence to influence the common law. That rule has led to a reluctance on the part of English judges to formulate the common law by reference to the European Convention on Human Rights. So, in *Malone v Metropolitan Police Commissioner*,[24] Megarry VC refused to expand the common law by reference to article. 8 of the Convention protecting the right of privacy, so as to make phone-tapping without authority a breach of such a right, despite the consequence that English law would not conform with Convention requirements.[25]

In later cases, however, it would seem that the Convention has had an indirect influence, especially in cases concerning freedom of expression,[26] leading to judicial assertions that the common law is consistent with Convention requirements.[27] There is, in principle, no reason why judges should not draw on the provisions of the Convention or for that matter, an international convention, for the purpose of resolving problems in the common law and, where necessary, if thought appropriate, to develop the common law.[28]

[23] *Toonen v Australia*, Comm. No. 488/1992, UN Doc CCPR/C/50/D/488/1992, 4 Apr. 1994.

[24] [1979] Ch 344.

[25] See *Klass v Germany* (1978) 2 EHRR 214.

[26] See *Sunday Times v United Kingdom* (1979) 2 EHRR 245 and *Attorney-General v British Broadcasting Corporation* [1981] AC 303 at 354 per Lord Scarman.

[27] *Attorney-General v Guardian Newspapers (Spycatcher) (No. 2)* [1990] 1 AC 109 at 283–4 per Lord Goff of Chieveley; *Derbyshire County Council v Times Newspapers* [1993] AC 534 at 550 per Lord Keith of Kinkel.

[28] *Minister for Immigration and Ethnic Affairs v Teoh* (1995) 183 CLR 273.

The Juristic Nature of Human Rights and the Enforcement of Human Rights Obligations

The traditional view in the common-law world was that an entrenched right operated as a negative restriction on legislative and executive power. There is no inherent reason why an entrenched right or freedom should not also be cast as a restriction on judicial power,[29] though in Canada[30] and Australia[31] that step has not been taken. If a human right is no more than a negative restriction on the exercise of power, two consequences may follow. One is that it operates as a restriction on state or government power only and it is not enforceable against individuals. The other, and more debatable, consequence is that the right may not be enforceable by an action for damages.[32] Framing constitutionally entrenched human rights guarantees as mere negative restrictions on power is no longer fashionable. The Canadian Charter authorizes a court of competent jurisdiction to award such remedy as the court considers 'appropriate and just in the circumstances' when a person's guaranteed rights or freedoms have been infringed or denied.[33] The European Convention enables the Court, in certain circumstances, to afford 'just satisfaction to the injured party' where a State is in breach of its obligations under that Convention.[34]

The New Zealand Court of Appeal has decided that, although the New Zealand Bill of Rights Act contains no remedies clause, let alone a provision authorizing the award of damages, an action for damages for violation of a guaranteed right may be maintained. In *Simpson v Attorney-General (Baigent's Case)*,[35] the plaintiff sought damages *inter alia* for breach of the Bill of Rights Act in making an unreasonable search contrary to section 21 of that Act. The section provides:

> Everyone has the right to be secure against unreasonable search or seizure, whether of the person, property, or correspondence or otherwise.

Police officers made a search of premises under a warrant in circumstances where there was reason for thinking that the search was not

[29] S 3 of the New Zealand Bill of Rights Act 1990 applies the Bill of Rights to legislative, executive, and judicial acts.

[30] S 32 of the Charter applies the Charter to legislative and executive acts only.

[31] *Lange v Australian Broadcasting Commission* (1997) 145 ALR 96.

[32] Thus, in Australia, it has been held that there is no action for damages under the Constitution for government failure to observe the restrictions on power which the Constitution imposes. That is because the Australian Constitution concerns itself with the powers and functions of government and reveals no intention to confer a private right of action for damages in addition to those conferred by the common law: *James v Commonwealth* (1939) 62 CLR 339 at 362; *Kruger v Commonwealth* (1997) 146 ALR 126 at 142, 203–5.

[33] S 24(1).

[34] Art. 50.

[35] [1994] 3 NZLR 667.

authorized by the warrant. A majority of the Court concluded that the Bill of Rights Act implied that effective remedies should be available for its breach. The main remedy granted for breach of section 21 was exclusion of unlawfully obtained evidence. In *Baigent's Case*, the persons subjected to unreasonable searches were innocent of wrongdoing and were not facing any criminal charge. So the main remedy was inappropriate. Damages were appropriate as being the only effective remedy.

The principle that an effective remedy is authorized for violation of a guaranteed human right has powerful support in both international law and national legal systems. The principle is expressed in article 8 of the Universal Declaration of Human Rights and article 2(3) of the ICCPR and has been acted upon by the United Nations Human Rights Committee.[36] Moreover, the European Court of Human Rights has awarded damages from time to time, where it is authorised so to do by article 50 of the European Convention.

The New Zealand Court of Appeal was able to point to the award of damages for violation of constitutionally entrenched fundamental rights by the Supreme Court of Ireland,[37] and the Supreme Court of India.[38] The Irish Constitution contains no provision for a remedy in the case of infringement. Reference was also made to the decision of the Supreme Court of the United States in *Bivens v Six Unknown Named Agents of the Federal Bureau of Narcotics*[39] where, despite the absence of a provision affording such a remedy, the plaintiff was held entitled to sue federal officers for damages for breach of a constitutional right. Brennan J remarked, '[W]here federally protected rights have been invaded, it has been the rule from the beginning that courts will be alert to adjust their remedies so as to grant the necessary relief.'[40] *Bivens* had attracted some unfavourable comment, a matter referred to by Gummow J in the Australian decision *Kruger v Commonwealth*,[41] where, in the light of Australian developments which differed from those which had been influential in the United States, it was not followed.

Particularly influential in *Baigent's Case* was *Maharaj v Attorney-General of Trinidad and Tobago (No. 2)*[42] where there was a provision in the Constitution of Trinidad and Tobago enabling a person alleging contravention of constitutional rights, including guaranteed fundamental rights, to apply to a court for redress. That provision was held by the Privy Council

[36] *Mbange v Zaire* (1983) (Comm. No. 16/1977) and *Acosta v Uruguay* (1983) (Comm. No. 110/1981), both reported in *Selected Decisions of the Human Rights Committee*, vol 2 (1990), 76 & 148, respectively. *Valenzuela v Peru* U.N. Doc. CCPR/C/48/D/309/1988, 10 Aug. 1993 (Comm. No. 30/1988).

[37] See *Kearney v Minister for Justice* [1986] IR 116; *Conway v Irish National Teachers Association* [1991] 2 IR 305.

[38] *Nilabati Bahera v State of Orissa* [1993] Cri L.J. 2899.

[39] (1971) 403 US 388.

[40] Ibid at 624.

[41] (1997) 146 CLR 126 at 222.

[42] [1979] AC 385.

to authorize a court to award damages for breach of a fundamental right. Lord Diplock, delivering the advice of the majority, said:

> The chapter is concerned with public law, not private law. One man's freedom is another man's restriction; and as regards infringement by one private individual of rights of another private individual, section 1 implicitly acknowledges that the existing law of torts provided a sufficient accommodation between their conflicting rights and freedoms to satisfy the requirements of the new Constitution as respects those rights and freedoms that are specifically referred to.[43]

In other words, the constitutional provision affording redress was seen as a provision of public law, offering a remedy against the State, the individual's rights against others being adequately safeguarded by private law remedies, notably remedies in tort. The difference in the nature of the remedies led Cooke P in *Baigent's Case* to describe the action against the State as one for 'compensation' not 'damages', the latter being the term appropriate to describe a private-law award of monetary compensation.[44]

Underlying the approach adopted in *Maharaj* and *Baigent* is the view that guaranteed human rights are restrictions on government power, not on the conduct of individuals. On that view, human rights jurisprudence does not provide a remedy at the suit of one individual against another; if a remedy is available for a 'human rights violation' by an individual, it is a remedy that arises under the general law, such as the law of torts. So far as government is concerned, a violation of human rights giving rise to 'compensation' may also be actionable as a tort, thereby attracting an award of 'damages'. One would expect the remedies to be concurrent.

If we assume that a human rights regime expressly or impliedly authorizes the award of damages or other relief for infringement, recourse to the law of torts will be subject to some limitations. In other words, tort remedies will be available only in situations in which direct enforcement is either unavailable, inadequate, or less favourable than a tort remedy. If human rights obligations are imposed on government only, then the law of torts will continue to regulate the conduct of individuals and non-government organizations in conformity with the approach adopted in *Maharaj* and *Baigent*.

In his contribution to this publication, 'Torts and Human Rights', Lord Bingham of Cornhill has reviewed comprehensively the ways in which, in various jurisdictions, the law of torts currently provides relief in relation to conduct which amounts to a violation of human rights. There is no point in my undertaking a similar exercise and exposing myself to the making of an unfavourable and invidious comparison. Instead, I shall confine my energies to a consideration of the capacity of the law

[43] Ibid at 396–7.

[44] *Baigent's Case* [1994] 3 NZLR at 677–8.

of torts to be moulded into a body of principles which reflect, to a significant degree, human rights jurisprudence and provide, in a range of appropriate situations, relief for human rights violations, concentrating on the areas of privacy and freedom of expression.

Privacy

So far, outside the United States, the law of torts provides no general remedy for invasion of privacy. The recognition of that remedy in the United States is an interesting story to which the existence of entrenched constitutional rights in the United States Constitution is a relevant consideration. The Supreme Court has affirmed the existence of a constitutional right to privacy, even though the Constitution makes no mention of such a right. The right has emerged by way of implication. Judicial development of the tort of invasion of privacy has been credited to a celebrated article by Warren and Brandeis.[45]

That there has been no corresponding development elsewhere may be due in part to difficulties associated with the cause of action which have arisen in the United States as a result of the conflicting interests which are at play. But it is also attributable to the controversy which surrounds political proposals to protect the right of privacy. Those proposals are strongly resisted by media interests and those who oppose judicial enforcement of human rights. In England, the Calcutt Commission on Privacy[46] and, in Australia, the Australian Law Reform Commission, recommended that a general right to privacy not be introduced, though the Australian Commission favoured the adoption of a tort remedy against commercial appropriation, publicity of private facts, and data misuses.[47]

There has been a wealth of academic discussion on the question of whether the law should protect a person's privacy and, if so, to what extent.[48] The effect of this discussion, along with desultory references in the cases to a 'right of privacy' might give some encouragement to bold judicial spirits to recognize a tort of invasion of privacy. The expression 'right of privacy' is to be found in the judgments in *Prince Albert v Strange*.[49] More recently, Lord Scarman referred to the 'fundamental right of privacy in one's home'.[50]

[45] 'Right to Privacy', (1890) 4 *Harvard* L.R. 193.

[46] Cmd 1102 (1990).

[47] Australian Law Reform Commission, Report No. 11 (1979) on *Unfair Publication: Defamation and Privacy*; Report No. 22 (1983) on *Privacy*.

[48] See, e.g. P. H. Winfield, 'Privacy', (1931) 47 LQR 23; R. Wacks, 'The Poverty of Privacy', (1980) 96 LQR 73; D. J. Seipp, 'English Judicial Recognition of a Right to Privacy', (1983) 3 OJLS 325.

[49] (1849) 2 De G and Sm 652; 64 ER 293.

[50] *Morris v Beardmore* [1981] AC 446 at 465.

On examination, however, these statements fall short of recognizing a general right of privacy and are confined to specific situations, such as to the contents of private correspondence and privacy in one's home. Thus, the so-called reference to privacy in one's home derives from the occupier's possession or right to possession which enables him to treat as wrongful acts undertaken by a trespasser on the occupier's premises. Hence the unauthorized installation of listening devices[51] and the taking of photographs on the premises by a trespasser is unlawful.[52] On the other hand, the taking of a photograph of a person when in a public place or of a person's property without that person's consent is not tortious conduct.[53] The difference between taking a photograph in a public or a private place is fairly well entrenched.[54]

Add to these restricted recognitions of privacy the strong judicial rejections of a general right of privacy. One only has to read the discussion of the old authorities in Sir Owen Dixon's judgment in *Victoria Park Racing and Recreation Grounds Co. Ltd v Naylor*[55] to appreciate that the common law did not value privacy highly. In that case it was held that an occupier of land was entitled to avail himself of any overview of neighbouring land and activities thereon which the occupier's land offered. The occupier by building a platform on land was able to view and broadcast races run on the neighbouring racecourse. Latham CJ rejected the argument that there was a general right of privacy.[56]

Even more daunting to bold spirits is *Kaye v Robertson*,[57] a decision of the Court of Appeal. In that case the plaintiff, a well-known actor, was taken to a private room in a hospital after suffering severe head injuries requiring brain surgery. Despite a notice on the door listing visitors authorized to enter the room, journalists from a tabloid newspaper entered the room without authority, interviewed the plaintiff and took photographs. Once discovered by hospital staff, the journalists were forced to leave. The plaintiff was not in a fit condition to consent to the interview and to be photographed or to be interviewed. The court granted an interlocutory injunction restraining the publication of material which could be reasonably understood as suggesting that the plaintiff voluntarily agreed to give the interview and the photographs. This

[51] *Coco v The Queen* (1994) 179 CLR 427.

[52] *Lincoln Hunt v Willesee* (1986) 4 NSWLR 457; *TV3 Network Services Ltd v Broadcasting Standards Authority* [1995] 2 NZLR 720.

[53] *Sports and General Press Agency Ltd v 'Our Dogs' Publishing Co. Ltd* [1916] 2 KB 880; affd. [1917] 2 KB 125; *Bathurst City Council v Saban* (1985) 2 NSWLR 704; *Bernstein v Skyviews & General Ltd* [1978] QB 479.

[54] *Bradley v Wingnut Films Ltd* [1993] 1 NZLR 415; but cf. *Burnett v The Queen* (1979) 94 DLR (3d) 281.

[55] (1937) 58 CLR 479 at 506–8.

[56] Ibid at 496.

[57] [1991] FSR 62.

relief was based on a cause of action for malicious falsehood; otherwise relief was refused.

Glidewell LJ said that in English law, '[T]here is no right to privacy and accordingly there is no right of action for breach of a person's privacy.'[58] Though lamenting the absence of an adequate remedy, their Lordships considered that the matter was one for the legislature.

On the other hand, as Professor Stephen Todd has noted, '[T]he boundaries of existing torts have been extended to give deserving plaintiffs a remedy.'[59] He points to disclosure of private facts, intrusions upon solitude and breach of confidence. Breach of confidence, though largely governed by the equitable obligation of confidence, does provide protection against the disclosure of private and personal information.[60]

In New Zealand, the courts have followed the United States development in recognizing in principle a cause of action for disclosing private facts about a plaintiff.[61] Disclosure of private facts is one instance or category of the American tort of invasion of privacy. The cause of action is made out if the plaintiff can establish a disclosure of private facts, the facts being such that disclosure would be highly offensive and objectionable to a reasonable person of ordinary sensibilities. In Canada[62] and Australia[63] also there are indications that the law may move in a similar direction, at least so far as photographs are concerned.

At its present stage of development some elements of the cause of action are rather fuzzy. The extent or reach of the disclosure raises the question whether disclosure to a third party as opposed to disclosure to the public is requisite; the former rather than the latter would accord more closely with privacy considerations. Likewise, there is a question as to what is meant by 'private facts'. The circumstance that they are known by a small circle of people closely associated with the plaintiff would not seem to take them outside the field of protection. The emphasis given in some cases to the highly objectionable and embarrassing nature of the disclosures, especially a photograph of someone in a seriously wounded condition, supports this view. But the emphasis also suggests that something more than mere invasion of privacy is required.

There is, of course, a very considerable tension between the protection of privacy and freedom of expression, which also includes freedom of

[58] Ibid at 66. A like view was expressed by Kirby P in *Australian Consolidated Press Ltd v Ettingshausen* (13 Oct. 1993, NSW Court of Appeal).

[59] 'Protection of Privacy' in N. J. Mullany (ed), *Torts in the Nineties* (1997), 174 at 176.

[60] *Duchess of Argyll v Duke of Argyll* [1967] Ch 302.

[61] *Bradley v Wingnut Films Ltd* [1993] 1 NZLR 415; see also *Tucker v News Media Ownership Ltd* [1986] 2 NZLR 716, discussed by S. Todd, n. 59 above at 179–180; *T v Attorney-General* (1988) 5 NZFLR 357.

[62] *Burnett v The Queen* (1979) 94 DLR (3d) 281.

[63] *Bathurst City Council v Saban* (1985) 2 NSWLR 704 at 708.

the media. It is that tension which underlies some of the uncertainties just discussed. Aggressive intrusion by the media into the private life of individuals has become one of the ugly features of modern society as media interests desperately seek drama and sensation in the quest for increased readership and larger audiences. Reading the judgments, one senses that they are influenced as much, if not more, by a sense of the need to curb the abuse of power by the media as by the desire to protect the privacy of the individual as such. Once the existence of the tension between privacy and freedom of expression is acknowledged, that influence is a material, if not a decisive, consideration.

Discussing in these terms the existence of a remedy in tort protecting privacy brings home the point that judicial articulation of the principles of the law of tort requires an assessment and balancing of competing and material policy considerations in much the same way as the judicial interpretation of a guaranteed right of privacy, such as that enshrined in article 8.1 of the European Convention on Human Rights. The right is subject to article 8.2, which prohibits interference by a public authority with the exercise of the right

> except such as is in accordance with the law and is necessary in a democratic society in the interests of national security, public safety or the economic well-being of the country, for the prevention of disorder or crime, for the protection of health or morale, or for the protection of the rights and freedoms of others.

The quartet of English prisoners' correspondence cases, *Golder v UK,*[64] *Silver v UK,*[65] *Raymond v Honey*[66] and *R v Secretary of State for the Home Department, ex p Leech (No. 2),*[67] though not concerned with a remedy in tort, demonstrate that interests protected by the common law have much in common with interests that are protected by the Convention. So, quite apart from privacy, the citizen's right or interest in access to the courts and access to legal advice as well as other rights or interests of the citizen, provide a foundation for the presumptive common-law rule that there shall be no interference with the exercise of such rights except by an unmistakable and unambiguous manifestation of statutory authority so to do.[68]

Although *Raymond v Honey* and *Leech (No. 2)* are administrative law decisions, they reveal that the courts can mould general principles in a way that will protect rights and interests which are commonly recognized by both the common law and the European Convention. If that

[64] (1975) 1 EHRR 524. [65] (1981) 3 EHRR 475. [66] [1983] AC 1.
[67] [1994] QB 198.
[68] *Coco v The Queen* (1994) 179 CLR 427; *Morris v Beardmore* [1981] AC 446 (where the House of Lords applied a similar presumption against the authorization of what would otherwise have been tortious conduct).

result can be achieved in the area of public law, simply as a matter of development of the common law, it may also be capable of achievement in terms of providing appropriate tort remedies, whether by providing a new remedy to protect a right recognized by the common law or, what is more likely, by extending an existing remedy.

In the context of privacy, what is happening in the area of disclosure of private facts suggests that too much can be made of judicial rejection of a general right of privacy. Future development of tort law on privacy is likely to take the form of granting relief in particular categories of case, disclosure of private facts being one such category. As Professor Todd observed,[69] Dean Prosser considered that in the United States invasion of privacy consisted of four separate torts, the sole unifying element being the right of the plaintiff to be left alone. The four torts Dean Prosser identified are:

(1) appropriating the plaintiff's identify for the defendant's benefit.
(2) placing the plaintiff in a false light in the public eye;
(3) publicly disclosing private facts about the plaintiff; and
(4) unreasonably intruding upon the seclusion of solitude of the plaintiff.[70]

It has been suggested that there is an arguable case for treating breach of confidence as a tort.[71] The suggestion derives little, if any, support from the decided cases where relief is based on contract or equity.[72] As a matter of principle and policy, however, there seems to be no reason why tort should not provide a remedy if confidential or secret information is an interest recognized and protected by law. The fact that it has been protected by equity does not, in a post-Judicature Act world, seem to be an insuperable reason for refusing to develop the common law in an appropriate way, all the more so if disclosure of private facts is accepted as a tort remedy. That said, there is obvious force in Meagher, Gummow, and Lehane's comment[73] that the views expressed by Mr North twenty-five years ago in his article 'Breach of Confidence: Is there a New Tort?'[74] have not borne fruit.

Physical interference with a person's privacy or solitude attracts, as already mentioned, tort remedies appropriate to interference with the

[69] See n. 59 above, 177. [70] W. L. Prosser, 'Privacy', (1960) 48 California L.Rev. 383.
[71] By Prof. Todd, see n. 59 above, 187 fn 62.
[72] See R. P. Meagher, W. M. Gummow & J. R. F. Lehane, *Equity: Doctrines and Remedies* (3rd edn 1992), 865. The authors point out that the reference to 'an established tort' in *McKaskell v Benseman* [1989] 3 NZLR 75 at 88 is supported by the citation of equity not tort cases. [73] Ibid.
[74] (1972) 12 JSPTL 149.

person and to unauthorized entry upon land. In addition, nuisance provides a remedy in the case of interference with the use and enjoyment of land, such as watching and besetting premises.[75] The English Court of Appeal was prepared to extend the remedy to enable a plaintiff who is an 'occupier' of land having no proprietary or possessory interest in it at all to obtain relief against aggressive, abusive, and threatening telephone calls amounting to persecution;[76] but the House of Lords has subsequently rejected this development.[77]

Of greater significance for present purposes than the extension of the law of nuisance is the recognition by the Court of Appeal, in *Burris v Azadani*,[78] of a tort of harassment, resulting in that case in the grant of an interlocutory injunction restraining the defendant from engaging in certain acts, including harassment. This step, one would think, was an inevitable development from the preceding nuisance cases in which relief against harassment was granted. To refuse to grant relief against harassment dissociated from use and enjoyment of land when relief is available against harassment affecting use and enjoyment of land would be to insist on an unacceptable distinction, a distinction that would suggest that judge-made law is trapped in a time-warp.

The step-by-step progression just recounted is typical of the way in which the law inches forward. That is not to say that judicial development of the law is incapable of advancing by way of overarching principle. The adoption of a Bill of Rights in the United Kingdom might conceivably generate such an advance in the area of tort law and privacy, though, having regard to the United States experience and the deep-seated nature of the problems, that outcome is unlikely. And, in any event, in the common law, formulation of overarching principle is more often designed to eliminate unnecessary or inconvenient distinctions. That said, it is possible to view the emergence of harassment as an independent ground of relief as the creation of an overarching principle.

Freedom of Expression

The conjunction of freedom of expression as a guaranteed human right or fundamental freedom and the law of torts has had a significant impact on the law of torts. Here the effect of human rights jurisprudence is not to be measured in terms of creating a new cause of action but in terms of re-shaping an old cause of action, namely defamation. In the United States, the influence of the First Amendment on defamation is

[75] *Hubbard v Pitt* [1976] QB 142. [76] *Khorasandjian v Bush* [1993] QB 727.
[77] *Hunter* v *Canary Wharf Ltd* [1996] 2 WLR 348. [78] [1995] 1 WLR 1372.

well-known. It culminated in the celebrated decision in *New York Times Co. v Sullivan*[79] where the Supreme Court of the United States, giving weight to the First Amendment's requirement of free speech and a free Press, held that a defamatory publication was not actionable by a plaintiff who is a 'public figure' unless the plaintiff could establish that the defendant published the defamatory statement knowing that it was false or recklessly not caring whether it was true or false. This decision radically altered the common-law defence of qualified privilege so as to give the publisher of defamatory material significantly more protection than he had formerly enjoyed. The decision rested on the paramount importance in a democratic society of maintaining freedom of expression and a free Press and the consequential necessity of ensuring that the 'chill factor' arising from liability to heavy damages for defamation did not operate to inhibit free discussion of matters of public importance.

In *Derbyshire County Council v Times Newspapers Ltd,*[80] the House of Lords rejected the argument that the *Sullivan* principle should be adopted in English law. Their Lordships, relying heavily on the importance of freedom of expression in a democratic society, held that a local authority could not sue for defamation in relation to defamatory material published of the authority on the ground that the bringing of such an action could stifle criticism of a public authority. Yet at the same time their Lordships acknowledged that individual councillors could sue in relation to defamatory imputations relating to them, those imputations arising from the material which reflected adversely on the authority itself. The decision is vulnerable to the comment that the protection given to a free press by one hand is taken away by the other hand. It seems that the House of Lords conducted a balancing exercise, holding that as between the reputation of a public authority and a free press the balance must come down in favour of the press but, as between individual reputation and a free press, the balance must favour individual reputation.

One aspect of *Derbyshire* which should be mentioned is that the House of Lords declined to apply article 10 of the European Convention, which guarantees freedom of expression, on the ground that the Convention had not been enacted as part of domestic legislation. Nevertheless, Lord Keith of Kinkel was at some pains to say that it was a matter of some satisfaction to note that the English common law was consistent with the requirements of article 10. It is difficult to resist the temptation of saying that their Lordships, in shaping the common law, are looking over their collective shoulder at the Convention. It is curious that they should arrive at a result consistent with the Convention by the indirect route

[79] (1964) 376 US 254. [80] [1993] AC 534.

of relying upon United States and Commonwealth authorities rather than upon article 10.

Whether their Lordships were correct in thinking that their reasoning was entirely consistent with the requirements of the Convention is another question. The decision of the European Court of Human Rights in *Lingens v Austria*,[81] indicates that a prominent politician has higher hurdles to surmount in a defamation action arising out of criticism of his activities in public office than would an ordinary citizen. The Court noted that freedom of expression as secured in article 10(1) constitutes one of the essential foundations of a democratic society and one of the basic conditions for its progress and for each individual's self-fulfilment. The Court considered the limits of acceptable criticism are wider in relation to a politician as such than in relation to a private individual. The politician, unlike the individual, lays himself open to close scrutiny by journalists and the public and must display a greater degree of tolerance. The protection of reputation under article 10(2) must be weighed in relation to the interests of open discussion of political issues.

As yet the English common law has not advanced as far as the Australian common law in protecting freedom of expression in actions of defamation. In Australia, the recent implication in the Constitution of freedom of communication as to government and political matters[82] has resulted in a re-formulation of the defence of qualified privilege so that it is consistent with the constitutionally mandated freedom. In *Lange v Australian Broadcasting Commission*,[83] the High Court held unanimously that a defendant who publishes defamatory material in the course of discussing federal matters of government or politics has a defence of qualified privilege if the publication is reasonable in the circumstances. The defence will be destroyed by the existence of malice or other improper motive; it will also be destroyed if the defendant knows the material is false or cares not whether it is true or false; the publication would not then be reasonable.

In Canada, in *Hill v Church of Scientology of Toronto*,[84] the Supreme Court of Canada rejected a defence of qualified privilege in a case in which a lawyer and his client made defamatory remarks about the plaintiff who was a Crown lawyer. The case for qualified privilege was that the plaintiff was a public official and that the statements were made about him in relation to his performance of his public duties. *Hill* is a not altogether satisfactory case. The balance was set in favour of individual reputation, the constitutional guarantee of freedom of

[81] (1986) 8 EHRR 407 (the case arose out of published criticism of Chancellor Kreisky).

[82] *Nationwide News Pty Ltd v Wills* (1992) 177 CLR 1; *Australian Capital Television Pty Ltd v Commonwealth* (1992) 177 CLR 106.

[83] (1997) 145 ALR 96.

[84] (1995) 126 DLR (4th) 129.

expression in article 2(b) of the Canadian Charter of Rights and Freedoms having no application to the exercise of judicial powers.[85]

The American, the Australian, and the European Convention experience with freedom of expression, even though in Australia the freedom is limited to federal government and political matters, indicates that the affirmation of the freedom as an entrenched or human right has a significant impact on the law of defamation. In the three jurisdictions, the courts have given more emphasis to the role of a free Press and to freedom of discussion in a democratic society than was formerly the case. It is possible that the common law of qualified privilege would have developed in this way in any event. But the reasoning in the judgments suggests that it was the focus on the entrenched or guaranteed freedom that was decisive in shifting the balance in favour of the public-interest factors flowing from the freedom over the individual interest in vindication of reputation.

Freedom of expression has also had an impact upon the law of defamation in relation to the assessment of damages. The courts had consistently held that the assessment of damages in defamation was at large and a matter for the jury, with great emphasis placed on the special role of the jury and on the difficulties involved in a challenge to its verdict, particularly its award of damages.[86] This meant that an appellate court could not substitute itself for a jury and set aside its award of damages unless it was so manifestly too large or so manifestly too small that no sensible jury properly directed could have made the award.

The magnitude of damages awards in defamation cases became a matter of increasing concern. One aspect of this concern was the lack of any rational relationship between awards in defamation cases and awards in personal injury cases, a situation brought about by the practice of refusing to recognize any relationship between awards in the two categories of case. The other aspect was the tendency of very large awards for defamation to deter media organizations and others from engaging in public discussion of important issues lest they should become liable for heavy damages.

In Australia, in *Carson v John Fairfax & Sons Ltd*,[87] the High Court by majority addressed the first aspect and held (1) that an appellate court, in reviewing the quantum of damages awarded in defamation, may consider verdicts in personal injury in personal injury cases for the purpose of comparison on the footing that a rational relationship should exist between the two categories; and (2) that trial judges may provide to

[85] Charter of Rights and Freedoms, s 32.

[86] *Broome v Cassell & Co.* [1972] AC 1027 at 1065; *Coyne v Citizen Finance Co. Ltd* (1991) 172 CLR 211.

[87] (1993) 178 CLR 44.

juries an indication of the ordinary level of general damages component of person injury awards for comparative purposes and counsel may do likewise. Subsequently, the English Court of Appeal, in *Rantzen v Mirror Group Newspapers*[88] considered an argument, presented by a newspaper appealing against a defamation award of £250,000 on the ground that it was excessive, that the award was so great as to be a restriction or penalty on the exercise of freedom of expression and was neither prescribed by law nor necessary in a democratic society as required by article 10.2 of the European Convention. Relying on statements in the House of Lords on the consistency of the common law and article 10,[89] the Court of Appeal subjected the award to closer scrutiny and allowed the appeal, holding that the practice of allowing juries to assess damages, without clear instructions, could limit freedom of expression and that such a limitation was not sufficiently certain to be 'prescribed by law'.

Rantzen was a precursor to the decision of the European Court of Human Rights in *Tolstoy Miloslavsky v United Kingdom*[90] where it held that the Court of Appeal's power to review defamation awards was so limited that there was no safeguard against disproportionately large awards which would put the guaranteed freedom at risk. The Court held that English law did not provide for a principled review of defamation awards. The award of £1.5 million in favour of Lord Aldington, the plaintiff in the English action, could not be supported as being necessary in a democratic society. A postscript to the *Tolstoy* case is the later Court of Appeal decision in *John v MGN Ltd*[91] where the Court held that defamation awards must be subjected to closer scrutiny on appeal and sanctioned the use of awards in personal injury cases for comparative purposes along lines similar to those adopted in *Carson*, though the Court avoided direct reliance on article 10 of the Convention.

Conclusion

The defamation cases illustrate the way in which human rights jurisprudence can influence the substantive principles of the law of torts, while the privacy cases indicate how the law of torts can extend its remedies to protect human rights. It would be unwise, however, to exaggerate the potential for judicially managed change. Curiously enough, some of the

[88] [1994] QB 670 (in which the newspaper defamed a well-known television personality and child welfare campaigner).

[89] *Attorney-General v Guardian Newspapers Ltd (Spycatcher No. 2)* [1990] 1 AC 109 at 283; *Derbyshire Council v Times Newspapers Ltd* [1993] AC 534 at 550.

[90] (1995) 20 EHRR 442. [91] [1996] 2 All ER 35.

most notable examples of judicial creativity have occurred in equity where the Supreme Court of Canada has expanded the fiduciary relationship to non-traditional relationships, such as doctor and patient[92] and parent and child[93] in order to grant tort-like remedies for sexual acts in breach of fiduciary duty. Yet it is the Supreme Court of Canada that has voiced the most recent warning against judicial creativity that goes beyond incremental change. In *Winnipeg Child and Family Services (Northwest Area) v G (DF)*,[94] the court was confronted with the question whether the law of tort would support a remedy in injunction or damages for the purpose of preventing harm to an unborn child arising from the pregnant mother's addiction to glue-sniffing. The question, by majority, was answered in the negative. Writing for the majority, McLachlin J stated[95] that, '[A]s a general rule, judicial change is confined to incremental change "based largely on the mechanism of extending an existing principle to new circumstances"; courts will not extend the common law "where the revision is major and its ramifications complex".'[96] This statement was supported by reference to the case-by-case mode of judicial decision-making and the courts' difficulties in fully appreciating relevant policy issues. Yet, in the application of the provisions of the Charter, the Supreme Court encounters and surmounts similar difficulties.

In the *Winnipeg* Case, McLachlin J also invoked, more significantly, 'the long-established principle that in a constitutional democracy it is the legislature, as the elected branch of government, which should assume the major responsibility for law reform'.[97] That sentiment has been strongly expressed by members of the House of Lords[98] and the High Court of Australia[99] in recent times. The reiteration of that sentiment across the jurisdictions indicates that the law of torts is more likely to pursue the even tenor of its way than engage in a dramatic leap forward.

[92] *Norberg v Wynrib* (1992) 92 DLR (4th) 449; *McInerney v MacDonald* (1992) 93 DLR (4th) 415.
[93] *M(K) v M(H)* (1992) 96 DLR (4th) 289.
[94] (1998) 152 DLR (4th) 193.
[95] Ibid at para 18.
[96] See *Watkins v Olafson* [1989] 2 SCR 750 at 760–1; approved in *R v Salituro* [1991] 3 SCR 654 at 668–9.
[97] See n. 94 above at para 18.
[98] *Woolwich Equitable Building Society v Commissioners of Inland Revenue* [1993] AC 70 at 173; *Airedale NHS Trust v Bland* [1993] AC 789 at 780.
[99] *Craig v South Australia* (1995) 184 CLR 163; *Breen v Williams* (1996) 186 CLR 71 at 99, 114–5.

ASPECTS OF NEGLIGENCE

3

The Right of Spring

Lord Cooke of Thorndon

Heuston, Glanville Williams, Fleming, Gower: in all-too-rapid succession the gods have stolen from the world of academic legal scholarship in English a select range of its acknowledged leaders, leaving sad gaps in the front rank. Two of them may be described without exaggeration as the most influential all-round writers in the field of torts. John Fleming survived just long enough to make accurate my description of him in the *Canary Wharf* case[1] as the doyen of living tort writers, though whether he saw that small tribute I do not know. It is good that his passing has not discouraged Peter Cane and Jane Stapleton from continuing with the project of a Festschrift for him. For a contribution I have chosen a subject of topical importance which falls squarely within the area of his expertise—evolution of legal principle to meet changing conceptions of social requirements: a clash between apparently solidly-settled black-letter precedents and new public policy.

A Question of Compatibility

Robert Heuston mentioned in a letter to me that he was 'very surprised' at the decision of the House of Lords in *Spring v Guardian Assurance plc*.[2] As is in outline well-known, in that case the House of Lords, by a majority of four (Lords Goff of Chieveley, Lowry, Slynn of Hadley and Woolf) to one (Lord Keith of Kinkel), reversed a decision of the Court of Appeal in England (Glidewell, Rose LJJ and Sir Christopher Slade), restored the first instance judgment (Judge Lever QC) and held that, notwithstanding that for over two centuries the common law of England had accorded qualified privilege to an employer giving a reference

[1] *Hunter v Canary Wharf Ltd* [1997] 2 All ER 426.
[2] [1995] 2 AC 296, revg [1993] 2 All ER 273.

concerning a former employee, the latter was owed a duty of care by the employer. Hence an action in negligence could be maintained by him or her against the employer, it being immaterial that an action for defamation would fail if the plaintiff could not prove malice. In *Spring*'s case the former employee had been found at first instance to have been working under a contract for services, not of service (in other words he was an independent contractor), but that distinction was not regarded by the House of Lords as significant. Nor was any significance attached, at least by most of their Lordships, to the fact that the reference was given (to a prospective employer who in the event did not employ the plaintiff) in the name of one subsidiary company in a group. There were four relevant associated companies in the group, and the plaintiff had a contract with one or perhaps two of the subsidiaries only. The officer in the parent company who actually prepared the reference was found to have been personally neither malicious nor negligent; but two of the officers of subsidiaries from whom she obtained information, although exonerated of malice, were found to have been negligent in the supply to her of information in such terms as to reflect on the plaintiff's honesty.

In reaching their decision the majority of the Appellate Committee distinguished the New Zealand Court of Appeal decisions in *Bell-Booth Group Ltd v Attorney-General*[3] and *South Pacific Manufacturing Co. Ltd v New Zealand Security Consultants and Investigations Ltd; Mortensen v Lang*,[4] and impliedly disagreed with some of the reasoning of that Court in *Balfour v Attorney-General*.[5] Of these cases *Balfour* was the closest on the facts to *Spring*. It was a case concerning a schoolteacher who claimed that his career had been damaged by a memorandum in his file at the Department of Education stating that he was a long practising and blatant homosexual. His action for damages for breach of statutory duty and negligence failed principally on the issue of causation, but in giving the judgment of the Court Hardie Boys J described the alleged negligence cause of action as coming perilously close to defamation, and said that any attempt to merge defamation and negligence is to be resisted. While Lord Keith emphatically regarded this as sound,[6] the majority of their Lordships treated defamation and negligence as discrete branches of tort law. So Maitland's famous aphorism can be amended. The forms of action are alive and well. The most forthright

[3] [1989] 3 NZLR 148. [4] [1992] 2 NZLR 482. [5] [1991] 1 NZLR 519.

[6] Lord Keith saw the New Zealand decisions as all the more important because they were from a jurisdiction 'well known to be tender in its approach to claims of negligence involving pure economic loss'. This delightful epithet is eloquent of unease at the philosophy guardedly favourable to imposing liability on those who, in pursuing their own activities, selfishly omit reasonable precautions for the interests of others whom they ought to have in contemplation.

comment in the majority speeches on *Balfour* was by Lord Slynn, who said,

> [T]he inspector who wrote the comment on the teacher 'Entirely unsuitable', giving detailed reasons, concluded 'check file to make absolutely sure I have the right person then ring Mrs Brocklesby and inform her'. It seems to me extraordinary that, if the remarks were untrue about the named individual and written without malice (so that no claim lay in defamation) but that the teacher lost a job as a result, there should be no possibility for the employee to claim in negligence.[7]

Lord Goff[8] said that the issue of assumption of responsibility did not appear to have been considered in that case, while Lords Lowry and Woolf made no separate express mention of the case.

If any of the comments or silences about *Balfour* in *Spring* are to be construed as strictures, they are unlikely to disturb my former brother Sir Michael Hardie Boys in the serenity of his office as Governor-General of New Zealand.[9] I did not sit in *Balfour* but must declare an interest in that I wrote the judgment of the court in *Bell-Booth* and also an unwontedly long individual judgment in *South Pacific*. May what follows acquit the writer of being prejudiced by that interest. Neither of the two cases last mentioned was a case of an employer–employee reference. But it has to be admitted that the judgments included dicta *capable* of being extended from the context in which they were uttered to the field of such references, and thus capable of supporting an argument against a duty of care in that field.

In *Bell-Booth* the plaintiff company had been marketing a product, consisting basically of seaweed powder diluted in water, represented to do wonders for pasture- and plant-growth. In a national television advertising campaign, farmers were advised to 'get your money out of the country' by spreading this product. Officers of the Ministry of Agriculture, believing the product to be useless, communicated their opinion to the makers of a consumer-complaints television programme. The result was a thirty–minute programme presenting perfectly fairly the differing views of the spokesmen for the company and the Ministry, but ending with a reference to 'at least giving you and your plants a little food, if only for thought'. Sales of the product having fallen, the

[7] [1995] 2 AC 296 at 335. [8] Ibid at 324.

[9] His Excellency has kindly provided the following note of his views and given me permission to reproduce it: 'I would have liked to find for Balfour, but had I done so it would have been seen as an example of a hard case making bad law, because I remain firmly of the view I expressed in the judgement. The law of defamation has well-established principles which I do not believe should be circumvented by resort to negligence. I am all in favour of the more liberal approach the Privy Council and the House of Lords are now taking to duty of care, but there must be limits.'

company sued the Ministry for defamation, misfeasance in public office, and negligence. The alleged negligence related to the results of certain field trials. The company claimed that the Ministry, was under a duty to disclose to it fully all the results before publishing them; to give it an opportunity of being satisfied about them; and to consult it as to their presentation. In effect the company was claiming more time for marketing the product without adverse publicity, followed at worst by a 'commercially sensitive' withdrawal from the market.

After a trial lasting slightly more than a year, during which a mass of expert evidence was called (mainly by the defence), Ellis J. found it proved, although the good faith of the company was not questioned, that when applied in the quantities directed by the plaintiff the product did not work: it produced no significant increase in growth or quality. Thus the defence of truth or justification was made out, so on that ground alone the defamation claim must fail. On appeal that result was not challenged. The judge also found that the Ministry's officers had not been actuated by malice: their dominant motive had been to stop the sale of a worthless product. That disposed, in his view, of the cause of action for misfeasance in public office; and following a fairly strong hint from the Court of Appeal, that cause of action likewise was ultimately not pursued on appeal. But the judge, while negating any contractual duty, did find a tort duty of care and breach, awarding some damages. It was on the negligence cause of action that the appeal hearing came to focus.

The Court of Appeal held that the cause of action in negligence could not succeed, essentially because to accept a tortious duty of care not to publish the truth would be to introduce a distorting element in the law as to injury to reputation and freedom of speech. It was also said that 'in our opinion justice does not require or warrant an importation of negligence law into this class of case. Where remedies are needed they are already available in the form of actions for defamation, injurious falsehood, breach of contract or breach of confidence.' In the course of the judgment we mentioned *Lawton v BOC Transhield Ltd*[10] where Tudor Evans J had accepted that a former employer owed to its former employee a duty of care in giving a reference but had found that the reference in question was honest, accurate, and not negligently written. We noted that it was a difficult case, as the judge had not discussed the law of defamation at all, and we cited academic criticisms of, or doubts about, the reasoning by Dr Andrew Demopoulos and Mr Philip Lewis. We developed the point that the law as to injury to reputation and freedom of speech is a field of its own. It was this passage of our

[10] [1987] 2 All ER 608.

judgment that understandably provided some ammunition for the argument against a duty of care in *Spring* and was treated by the Court of Appeal and Lord Keith as assisting their conclusions.

The fact remains that *Bell-Booth* was not concerned with careless *misstatements*, nor with the rights of an employee. I can vouch that the Court gave no consideration to whether the employment relationship is a special one entailing duties of care in the giving of adverse references, superadded to such duties as the law of defamation imposes. In contrast *Spring* was concerned solely with the employment relationship, and solely with untrue statements.

Of the majority speeches, those of Lord Slynn and Lord Woolf bring out those limitations most clearly. Lord Slynn emphasizes the need to attain a fair, just, and reasonable result in the master–servant situation;[11] speaks of the far greater duties imposed on the employer than in the past, whether by statute or judicial decision, to care for the physical, financial, and even psychological welfare of the employee;[12] and approves a definition of the right of the former employee as being to 'a careful and accurate assessment of his qualities',[13] while making it clear that no warranty of accuracy is propounded—the duty is simply one of reasonable care. Lord Woolf attaches weight to contemporary practices in the field of employment and unreservedly accepts that there can be no action of negligence if the statement is true.[14] He underlines that the views he expresses are confined to the class of case with which he is dealing; possible extensions by analogy are best considered when they arise. The limitations appear to be implicit also in the reasoning of Lord Goff and Lord Lowry. In accordance with his approach in 'pure' economic loss cases,[15] Lord Goff uses the technique of imputing to the employer an assumption of responsibility of care to the employee in ensuring the accuracy of adverse factual considerations,[16] thus bringing the case within *Hedley Byrne*.[17] Lord Lowry's reasoning is founded on proximity and a balancing of moral and practical arguments.[18] It too does not extend beyond the kind of situation exemplified by *Spring*. So *Bell-Booth* and *Spring* can stand together, as indeed the House of Lords considered.

The same can be said of *South Pacific*[19] (and *Mortensen*)[20] and *Spring*.

[11] [1995] 2 AC 296 at 334, 337. [12] Ibid at 335. [13] Ibid at 338.

[14] Ibid at 349. Lord Slynn and Lord Woolf both accepted that *Bell-Booth* was correctly decided on its facts. [15] Cf. *White v Jones* [1995] 2 AC 207.

[16] [1995] 2 AC 296 at 324.

[17] *Hedley Byrne & Co. Ltd v Heller & Partners Ltd* [1964] AC 465. Paradoxically Lord Goff refrained from expressing an opinion on whether the maker of the reference would also owe a duty of care to the recipient (see [1995] 2 AC 296 at 320), a question on which *Hedley Byrne* would seem much more closely in point. [18] Ibid at 326.

[19] [1992] 2 NZLR 482. [20] Ibid.

The two New Zealand cases, heard together, related to whether investigators reporting to an insurer on the cause of a loss (apparently suspicious fires in both cases) owe a duty of care to the insured. Proximity is an unhelpful test in negligence law, since it is only a shorthand for a combination of circumstances which leads the court to hold in favour of a duty of care. But in any ordinary sense there is very close proximity between an insured and the insurer's investigators. The policy obliges the insured to co-operate with the insurer's representatives and the likelihood is strong that the report will affect the insured's interests. Indeed the New Zealand legislature had recognized as much, in that such private investigators had to be licensed, and persons interested could complain of their negligence to the disciplinary authority, which right was conferred expressly without prejudice to any civil remedy. These statutory provisions are not confined to intrusions on privacy.

Nevertheless the Court of Appeal held against a duty of care at common law, for an accumulation of reasons. *Inter alia* it was said that the balance of public interest embodied in the detailed rules of law relating to defamation, malicious prosecution, witness immunity, and evidential privilege would be unjustifiably disturbed by superimposing the claimed duty of care.[21] Also it was stressed that the insured had a reasonable, even if not entirely comprehensive, remedy against the insurer. The case is in truth quite distant from *Spring*.

Some Reactions to *Spring*

There were a few American state decisions holding insurance investigators to owe a duty of care to the insured,[22] but in my own judgment I was able to express indebtedness to Professor John Fleming for a reference to a Californian appellate decision rejecting the notion that an adjuster hired by the insurer owed the insured a fiduciary duty.[23] If memory is correct, I had mentioned to John Fleming, after hearing him deliver a fine address to a university audience in Christchurch, New Zealand,[24] that our court was considering the *South Pacific* issue, and he subsequently sent me the reference.

This leads one to speculate whether Fleming was as surprised by *Spring* as was Heuston. It may be suspected that the answer is Yes, but that he accepted the decision. In the eighth edition of his *Law of Torts*,[25]

[21] Ibid at 304. [22] Collected in ibid at 292–3.

[23] Ibid. at 293, the case being *Thompson v Cannon* 224 Cal. App. 3d 1413 (1990).

[24] In case it is not mentioned elsewhere in the Festschrift, I should add that he was a skilled presenter of prepared lectures, with a clear and attractive multicultural voice and in content striking a good balance between generalities and detail. [25] (1992), 565 & 140.

after describing an employee's character reference from an employer as one of the most common instances of qualified privilege, he added, 'Nor is there a duty of care, sounding in negligence'. As regards extension of duties of care, he identified among 'the more general countervailing policies the concern of not impinging on other areas of civil liability. For example, settled rules of tort liability, conditioned on malice, like defamation on occasions of qualified privilege or malicious prosecution, would be undercut if a plaintiff could succeed on mere negligence.' In support he cited *Bell-Booth*,[26] *Balfour*,[27] and *South Pacific*,[28] merely noting that *Lawton*[29] was to the contrary. He hinted at no doubt and certainly did not forecast *Spring*. In the posthumous ninth edition, however, he has written,

> Yet the interface with a related but competing rule does not always categorically halt the path of negligence. An exceptional example was the decision to allow an ex-employee's claim for economic loss resulting from a negligent character reference by his former employer. The argument, that to allow a claim for negligence would undercut the required proof of malice in actions for defamation or injurious falsehood, had in this instance to yield to the felt necessity of providing a remedy for loss of employment, whatever might otherwise be appropriate for an overlap between protecting reputation and economic loss.[30]

For the second sentence he cites *Spring* as authority, while noting that it was not followed in *Sattin v Nationwide News*, a New South Wales case to which I will turn shortly. For 'whatever might otherwise be appropriate for an overlap . . . ', he instances *Bell-Booth*. Fleming's message would appear to be that he had come to see a carelessly inaccurate account of facts in an employee's reference as something of a special case.

The 1998 edition of *Gatley on Libel and Slander* rehearses the arguments against and for the view that the introduction of liability for negligence for incorrect employment references improperly subverts the policy of the law in respect of other torts.[31] The obvious point is made that most 'policy' arguments on the duty of care are not capable of accurate measurement. The argument that *Spring* will discourage candid references is put in that category: 'All one can say is that the majority of the House of Lords has found the argument unconvincing.' In a footnote the editors comment that their Lordships 'presumably do not write many

[26] *Bell-Booth Group Ltd v Attorney-General* [1989] 3 NZLR 148.

[27] *Balfour v Attorney-General* [1991] 1 NZLR 519.

[28] *South Pacific Manufacturing Co. Ltd v New Zealand Security Consultants and Investigations Ltd* [1992] 2 NZLR 482.

[29] *Lawton v BOC Transhield Ltd* [1987] 2 All ER 608.

[30] I am indebted to his new editor, Carolyn Sappideen of the Univ. of Western Sydney, for this extract from the book about to be published, at 156. See also a more general passage at 585.

[31] (9th ed.), para 21.4.

references'. Such does not entirely accord with my own experience and impression (though the 'many' renders the comment strictly accurate), but I believe that senior judges, like everyone else, prefer writing guarded references to writing critical ones. The considerations prompting the industry association rule applicable in *Spring*—'A member [asked by another member for a reference] shall make full and frank disclosure of all relevant matters which are believed to be true to the other member or his representative'—may have been rather played down by the majority in *Spring*.

A most important question is left unanswered in *Spring*. In *Lawton*, Tudor Evans J was definite that an employer giving a reference could protect itself from negligence liability to the employee by a *Hedley Byrne* disclaimer.[32] In the speeches in *Spring*, only Lord Slynn adverts to the issue, but he merely says that this may be so if the employer makes it clear to the subject of the reference that he will only give one if the latter accepts that there will be a disclaimer of liability both to him and to the recipient.[33] It is not difficult to forecast what employers often required to give references will be advised to do if they wish to avoid negligence liability. Whether such disclaimers would be acceptable industrial practice is another matter.

Before parting with *Gatley* one should note an observation in the ninth edition on *X (minors) v Bedfordshire County Council*,[34] where the House of Lords held that a social worker investigating, on behalf of a public authority with statutory functions, a case of suspected child abuse owed no duty of care to the child. It is pointed out that Lord Browne-Wilkinson, with whom the other members of the Appellate Committee simply agreed, did not even mention *Spring* in his speech, although it had been cited in argument. His Lordship had not sat in *Spring*. Conceivably, this suggests that at least some members of the House will favour restricting the potential ambit of the *Spring* reasoning. On the other hand a more likely explanation may be that the cases were seen as simply too far apart on the facts to warrant mention of *Spring*.

Some of the textbook reaction to *Spring* in the jurisdiction where *Bell-Booth, Balfour* and *South Pacific* were decided is interesting. In the title Defamation in *The Laws of New Zealand*, *Bell-Booth* is treated as supporting absence of liability in a *Spring*-type case, the same wide interpretation being placed on *Bell-Booth* as was adopted by Lord Keith in his dissenting speech in *Spring*.[35] The contributor of the title[36] goes on to say

[32] [1987] 2 All ER 608 at 617–8. [33] [1995] 2 AC 296 at 336.
[34] [1995] 2 AC 633. See *Gatley*, n. 30 above, para 21.5. [35] (1992), para 103, n.1.
[36] The Rt Hon. Ian McKay, who was a member of the CA when he contributed the title. McKay J did not sit in *Bell-Booth, Balfour* or *South Pacific*.

that whether the Privy Council in a New Zealand case would follow *Spring* or *Bell-Booth* is problematical.

The 1997 edition of *Todd on Torts* has the following passage in a chapter written by Professor Stephen Todd:

> The policy underlying the defence of qualified privilege in defamation is the removal of a disincentive to speak caused by a fear of legal liability and the promotion of frankness or candour, which policy would seem as relevant to an action for negligence as to an action for defamation. The argument in *Spring* that the ingredients of the tort of negligence are not the same as those of defamation and that the two torts cover different ground and may compensate for different damage does not answer this point. Denying a remedy in negligence to the subject of an incorrect reference may be seen as unjust, but this is as true of a claim in defamation. In the end a policy choice must be made as between specially protected speech on the one hand and individual accountability for negligence on the other. The Court of Appeal has favoured the first and the House of Lords the second. The implications of the latter view are significant. Lord Keith, the dissentient in *Spring*, thought that on the majority view the negligence principle logically should extend to cover all situations where the defence of qualified privilege would be available if the action were one for defamation. It may be that their Lordships will now need to overhaul this part of the law of defamation.[37]

All in all, it is fair to say that, like most pioneering judgments, *Spring* leaves many consequences to be worked out.

An Australian Approach

In a jurisdiction not bound by the House of Lords one available way of dealing with *Spring* is to decline to follow it. Such was the course apparently favoured by Levine J in the New South Wales Supreme Court in *Sattin v Nationwide News Pty Ltd*.[38] The plaintiff was suing on a newspaper publication of a photograph with the caption 'Newlyweds David Leslie and Janette Sattin enjoyed a celebratory drink at the Beach Bistro'. In truth she was not married to Leslie newly or at all: she was the separated wife of another man. The claim was originally for defamation only. Relying on *Spring*, the plaintiff's advisers sought leave to amend the statement of claim to introduce a cause of action in negligence. This the judge disallowed, pointing out that it was not a reference case but one of publication in the mass media. He noted that the trend in Australia is against the inhibition of freedom of speech in instruments of mass communication. Nevertheless he saw no possibility that a defence

[37] (2nd ed.), 165. [38] (1996) 39 NSWLR 32.

of qualified privilege could be established, nor was it a case where the plaintiff was complaining of publication of the truth.

These factors were enough to distinguish the actual decisions in both *Spring* and *Bell-Booth*, but the judge's observations went further. He preferred the approach in the New Zealand judgments, read in their wider sense, and Lord Keith's dissent in *Spring*, to the majority reasoning in that case. He thought that the majority had overlooked the significance of the public policy according qualified privilege to a communication made in performance of a legal or moral duty owed to the recipient. In that connection he referred, as had the House of Lords in *Spring*, to Lord Diplock's exposition of the public policy in *Horrocks v Lowe*.[39] Levine J said that public policy should logically transcend mere forms of action, it not being merely a matter of a defence being applicable to one cause of action but not to another: 'the view of Lord Goff fundamentally frustrates the policy behind the defence of qualified privilege and clearly so.'

Levine J's observations about public policy would seem incontestable. Indeed the majority in *Spring* did not, as I see it, deny that they were partly subverting the public policy underlying qualified privilege. Rather they treated it as overridden by the public policy applying as between employer and employee. And Lord Slynn said,

> If to recognise that such a duty of care exists means that there have to be such changes—either by excluding the defence of qualified privilege from the master–servant situation or by withdrawing the privilege where negligence as opposed to express malice is shown—then I would in the interests of recognising a fair, just and reasonable result in the master–servant situation accept such change.[40]

Two other aspects of *Sattin*'s case deserve mention. First, Levine J's judgment includes a useful collection of the legal periodical writings on *Spring*.[41] The judgment was reserved for eight months; perhaps the judge spent some of the time conscientiously trawling through this material. Secondly, an amendment pleading damages for personal injury (shock?) was allowed, Australian authorities tending to support the availability of such damages in defamation being also collected.[42] This is a reminder of the potential width of defamation damages. The majority in *Spring* do not hold that loss of employment chances are irrecoverable in defamation, and in principle such loss must be recoverable if causation can be proved.[43] Of course there must be defamation in the first place. Lord Slynn in *Spring* makes the point that a careless statement

39 [1975] AC 135 at 149.

40 [1995] 2 AC 296 at 337. See the passage from *Todd on Torts* reproduced above, text at n. 36.

41 (1996) 39 NSWLR 32 at 42.

42 Ibid at 45.

43 Cf. *Longdon-Griffiths v Smith* [1952] 2 All ER 662 at 678.

may not be defamatory, instancing untrue statements that a labourer is lame or a secretary very arthritic.[44] But, if malice can be proved, such mis-statements are actionable as injurious falsehood.[45] The 'undermining' argument accordingly remains. It has to be remembered that, in so far as undermining other branches of the law was a major factor in the *Bell-Booth* and *South Pacific* equations, the law of defamation was by no means the only branch in jeopardy, as the judgments in both these cases make clear.

The Dynamics of Public Policy

The true explanation of *Spring* is a sea change in public policy. How vast the change has been is rather hidden by the shape of the speeches in the Lords. Only one of the old cases concerned with privileged references is there cited.[46] In fact the decisions holding or accepting that an employee's reference given by a former employer to a prospective employer is privileged in the absence of malice go back to at least the middle years of the eighteenth century.[47] There are literally scores, perhaps hundreds, of reported English cases to that effect. In the common-law world as a whole, thousands of cases must have been decided or settled on that basis. Late in the nineteenth century the established law was stated simply by Lord Esher MR:

> An occasion is privileged when the person who makes the communication has a moral duty to make it to the person to whom he does make it, and the person who receives it has an interest in hearing it. Both these conditions must exist in order that the occasion may be privileged. An ordinary instance of a privileged occasion is the giving of a character of a servant. It is not the legal duty of the master to give a character to the servant, but it is his moral duty to do so; and the person who receives the character has an interest in having it. Therefore the occasion is privileged, because the one person has a duty and the other has an interest. The privilege exists against the person libelled; it is not a question of privilege as between the person who makes and the person who receives the communication.[48]

When the House of Lords decided in *Hedley Byrne*[49] in 1963 that, in the absence of a disclaimer, a bank giving a reference as to the creditworthiness of a client owed a duty of care to the requesting party, there were

[44] [1995] 2 AC 296 at 334.
[45] As is pointed out in *Gatley*, n. 30 above, para 21.4, n. 26.
[46] *Whiteley v Adams* (1863) 15 CBNS 392.
[47] The earliest authority cited in *Gatley*, n. 30 above, para 14.17, n. 5, is *Edmonson v Stephenson* (1766) Buller's N.P. 8.
[48] *Pullman v Hill & Co.* [1891] QB 524 at 528.
[49] [1964] AC 465.

forecasts of possible liability to the *recipient* of an employer's reference;[50] but I have not come across any anticipation of a duty of care to the *subject* of a reference before *Lawton*[51] in 1986. The prospect of some development of the principle of contractual co-operation to add to the duties of employers was certainly recognized.[52] Still (while I stand to be corrected) no writer was prescient enough to foresee the application of the principle in favour of a former employee as in *Lawton*. Indeed the reasoning of Tudor Evans J in *Lawton* was itself based on the general principles of *Dorset Yacht*,[53] *Anns*,[54] and *Junior Books*[55] rather than on any particular development in the law of master and servant.

Yet the seeds of an outstanding particular development had been sown almost a decade before *Lawton* by decisions in England of the Employment Appeal Tribunal and the Court of Appeal under the employment protection legislation. While the details of such legislation differ from jurisdiction to jurisdiction, its general aim is to ameliorate the harshness of some of the old common-law rules regarding the rights of employers against employees. Rights not to be unfairly dismissed or subjected to other unfair industrial action are conferred on employees. Discretionary monetary and other remedies, even including reinstatement, are made available from specialist tribunals, typically with provision for appeal to the ordinary appellate courts on questions of law only. In one of the earlier English cases[56] Sir John Donaldson P, giving the judgment of the National Industrial Relations Court, described the common law rules and authorities on wrongful dismissal as irrelevant. That cause of action, he said, was quite unaffected by the 1971 Act which had created an entirely new cause of action, namely the 'unfair industrial practice' of unfair dismissal. Similarly, some years later in the House of Lords,[57] Lord Salmon described the 1971 Act as a remarkable piece of social legislation in that it had given birth [in England] to the concept of unfair dismissal.

Although such legislation may not purport to alter the common law—with the result, for instance, that a former employee may still be able to bring a common law action for damages for wrongful dismissal[58]—by its

[50] As by *Hepple and O'Higgins on Employment Law*, (2nd ed., 1976), para 512; note also *Technovision Ltd v Reed*, The Times, 14 Apr. 1964, cited by Tudor Evans J in *Lawton v BOC Transhield* [1987] 2 All ER 608 at 612.

[51] N. 49 above.

[52] See for instance M. R. Freedland, *The Contract of Employment* (1976), 37–9; 372–6.

[53] *Home Office v Dorset Yacht Co. Ltd* [1970] AC 1004.

[54] *Anns v Merton London Borough Council* [1978] AC 728.

[55] *Junior Books Ltd v Veitchi Co. Ltd* [1983] 1 AC 520.

[56] *Norton Tool Co. Ltd v Tewson* [1973] 1 All ER 183 at 186

[57] *Nothman v London Borough of Barnet* [1979] 1 All ER 142 at 144. The New Zealand legislation antedated the UK legislation; legislation elsewhere in the Commonwealth may also have done so.

[58] In *Ogilvy & Mather (New Zealand) Ltd v Turner* [1994] 1 NZLR 641, it was held that under the New Zealand legislation a dismissed employee could choose to invoke either

emphasis on fairness it has indirectly influenced the development of the common law. This is an interesting illustration of cross-fertilization in public policy between the legislature and the courts. Thus, in a New Zealand case,[59] where the Court of Appeal held that a local authority's statutory power of dismissal of a general manager had to be exercised by a fair procedure and with reasonable cause, it was said that the position had probably been reached where there were few, if any, relationships of employment, public or private, to which the requirements of fairness had no application whatever.

And so, in both England and New Zealand, the courts and tribunals, founding on some of the statutory language, evolved the concept of constructive dismissal, whereby an employee forced to resign by culpable conduct on the part of the employer may be treated as dismissed.[60] In England this produced an issue that was controversial for a time. To bring the concept into play, did the employer's conduct have to be a significant breach going to the heart of the contract of employment? Or was it enough that the employer had conducted itself so unreasonably that the employee could not fairly be expected to put up with it any longer? That issue was resolved by the Court of Appeal in favour of the first alternative, Lord Denning MR saying[61] that the new test of 'unreasonable conduct' of the employer was 'too indefinite by far'.

But, scarcely was the ink dry on that limiting decision, when it was outflanked by a skilful extension of the principle of contractual co-operation. In a line of cases, including what is now seen as the *locus classicus* in *Woods v W. M. Car Services (Peterborough) Ltd*,[62] a decision of the Employment Appeal Tribunal delivered by Browne-Wilkinson J (as he then was), an implied contractual term was identified. The key passages in *Woods* read:[63]

> In our view it is clearly established that there is implied in a contract of employment a term that the employers will not, without reasonable and proper cause, conduct themselves in a manner calculated or likely to destroy or seriously damage the relationship of confidence and trust between employer and

the statutory personal grievance procedures or sue *in the specialist Employment Court* at common law. P, a dismissed chief executive, pursued a common-law claim, no doubt being advised that in the particular circumstances the award was likely to be higher, but in the event the amount was reduced on appeal, chiefly because the CA held that the evidence did not support the Employment Ct's finding that a period of 3 years' notice was required at common law: ibid.

59 *Marlborough Harbour Board v Goulden* [1985] 2 NZLR 378 at 383.

60 For the theoretical basis of the doctrine, see *Auckland Shop Employees Union v Woolworths (NZ) Ltd* [1985] 2 NZLR 372.

61 *Western Excavating (ECC) Ltd v Sharp* [1978] QB 761 at 770.

62 [1981] ICR 666. For other cases and some doubts see 16 *Halsbury's Laws of England* (4th ed.) para 444.

63 [1981] ICR 666 at 670–2.

employee: *Courtaulds Northern Textiles Ltd v Andrew.*[64] To constitute a breach of this implied term it is not necessary to show that the employer intended any repudiation of the contract: the tribunal's function is to look at the employer's conduct as a whole and determine whether it is such that its effect, judged reasonably and sensibly, is such that the employee cannot be expected to put up with it: see *British Aircraft Corporation Ltd v Austin*[65] and *Post Office v Roberts.*[66] The conduct of the parties has to be looked at as a whole and its cumulative impact assessed: *Post Office v Roberts.*

. . .

Experience in this appeal tribunal has shown that one of the consequences of the decision in the *Western Excavating*[67] case has been that employers who wish to get rid of an employee or alter the terms of his employment without becoming liable either to pay compensation for unfair dismissal or a redundancy payment have had to resort to methods of 'squeezing out' an employee. Stopping short of any major breach of the contract, such an employer attempts to make the employee's life so uncomfortable that he resigns or accepts the revised terms. Such an employer, having behaved in a totally unreasonable manner, then claims that he has not repudiated the contract and therefore that the employee has no statutory right to claim either a redundancy payment or compensation for unfair dismissal.

It is for this reason that we regard the implied term we have referred to as being of such importance. In our view, an employer who persistently attempts to vary an employee's conditions of service (whether contractual or not) with a view to getting rid of the employee or varying the employee's terms of service does act in a manner calculated or likely to destroy the relationship of confidence and trust between employer and employee.

Woods went to the Court of Appeal.[68] Although the Court took a rather different view of the facts from that of the Appeal Tribunal, they agreed with the Appeal Tribunal that the first instance Industrial Tribunal, who had expressly referred to the implied term as to the preservation of trust and confidence, had fallen into no error of law. Ironically, on this occasion Lord Denning MR, while referring to that formulation of the implied term, said[69] that he preferred 'to look at it in this way: the employer must be good and considerate to his servants. Just as a servant must be good and faithful, so an employer must be good and considerate.' When we had to consider the matter in the New Zealand Court of Appeal in the *Woolworths* case,[70] we indicated a respectful preference for the formulation adopted by Browne-Wilkinson J. as being 'somewhat less nebulous than Lord Denning's later wording'. Speaking judicially I

[64] [1979] IRLR 84. [65] [1978] IRLR 332. [66] [1980] IRLR 347.
[67] [1978] QB 761. [68] *Woods v W. M. Car Services (Peterborough) Ltd* [1982] ICR 693.
[69] Ibid at 698.
[70] *Auckland Shop Employees Union v Woolworths (NZ) Ltd* [1985] 2 NZLR 372 at 376.

was inhibited as an essayist is not, so I refrained from echoing 'too indefinite by far'.

In another respect as well, an attempt at deference or tact was made in the *Woolworths* judgment. We added that we did not have the benefit of the view of the Arbitration Court (as the present Employment Court was then called) on how best to define an implied term so as to serve the needs of industrial relations in New Zealand. So we refrained from stating a final opinion on that general question. Sadly this attempt at cross-fertilization miscarried. The Chief Judge of the Employment Court said[71] that in *Woolworths* the Court of Appeal had expressly left open the precise extent of the obligations of a private-sector employer to be a good employer. 'No one knows,' he continued. As far as I know neither he nor his fellow judges have ever expressly responded to our invitation.[72] Yet there are a multitude of cases in their jurisdiction in which the implied term relating to trust and confidence has been applied, so *sub silentio* it has apparently been accepted as alive and well in New Zealand—at any rate, in the specialist Employment Court.

In the ordinary courts of New Zealand, led by the Court of Appeal, the future potency of the implied term may be more doubtful. The existence of the term has been accepted, but its use by the Employment Court to make some quite modest awards of compensation for redundancy, where unfair procedures had been followed and a reasonable employer with the resources to do so would have made some payment, was upheld by three–two majority decisions only.[73] The composition of the Court of Appeal has changed since. The minority view brought to the application of the employment protection legislation a philosophy closer in some degree to that promulgated by the New Zealand Business Roundtable, a pressure group wholeheartedly enamoured of market forces and given to attacking inimical judicial decisions by techniques less than Arthurian.

Australian Caution

Whereas in New Zealand the implied term as to the employer's duty not to violate trust and confidence has been seen as a natural corollary of the

[71] *New Zealand Public Service Association (Inc.) and the State Insurance Office and the State Services Commission* [1990] 1 NZILR 655 at 685.

[72] The compilers of the standard loose-leaf work, *Mazengarb's Employment Law*, vol. 2, B/59 (Nov. 1997), are equally unappreciative of the invitation extended to the Employment Ct, but they go on to give sundry instances of the working of the implied term in practice.

[73] *G. N. Hale & Son Ltd v Wellington Caretakers Union* [1991] 1 NZLR 151; *Brighouse Ltd v Bilderbeck* [1995] 1 N.Z.L.R. 158; *Jones Schindler Lifts Ltd v Johnston* [1995] 1 NZLR 190.

employee's duty of fidelity,[74] Australian law is apparently not yet committed to the implied term. In the title Employment in *Halsbury's Laws of Australia*[75] one finds the cautious statement, with reference to the English authorities, 'It has been suggested that there is an implied duty on employers to be good and considerate to their employees, and not to do anything likely to destroy the relationship of confidence between them. As a corollary to the employee's duty to disclose relevant information about himself or herself, it has been suggested that there is an implied duty on employers to disclose to employees terms of the contract incorporated by reference to agreements negotiated between the employer and a body representing employees generally'.[76]

Such caution is warranted because of the tenor of the judgments in the leading Australian case of *Byrne v Australian Airlines Ltd*.[77] Baggage-handlers had been dismissed for alleged pilfering from passengers' luggage. Their claims against the employer centred on a provision in their industrial award that 'termination by an employer shall not be harsh, unjust or unreasonable'. The trial Judge, Hill J, dismissed the claims, finding *inter alia* that there were reasonable grounds for the employer to conclude that each claimant had been participating in criminal acts. On appeal a majority of a Full Court of the Federal Court, without expressing an opinion on that question, held that there were shortcomings in the employer's investigation of the allegations, which made the dismissal at least procedurally unreasonable. Damages they held to be not recoverable, but they remitted the case to the court of first instance for consideration of the question of penalty for breach of the award. On further appeal the High Court agreed unanimously that damages were not available for breach of the award but that it had been wrong to isolate the procedural aspect of the dismissal from the substantive grounds. The case was remitted to the Full Court to consider whether the trial judge was correct in concluding that there was sufficient evidence to establish that the appellants were involved in the misconduct. A minority joint judgment in the High Court (McHugh and Gummow JJ) stated specifically[78] that, if Hill J's findings were upheld, it would be very difficult to see how the dismissal could be regarded as harsh, unjust, or unreasonable. The majority joint judgment (Brennan CJ, Dawson and Toohey JJ) did not go so far in terms.

[74] *Schilling v Kidd Garrett Ltd* [1997] 1 NZLR 253. Cf. *Secretary of State for Employment v ASLEF (No. 2)* [1972] 2 QB 455.

[75] Vol. 10, para. 165–470 (1995). There is a cross-reference to para. 165–765, where by contrast the English view appears to be accepted. The contributor of the title is Prof. Adrian Brooks.

[76] This 'suggestion' is the description given to the cited unanimous decision of the House of Lords in *Scally v Southern Health and Social Services Board* [1992] 1 AC 294.

[77] (1995) 131 ALR 422 (HCA), varying 120 ALR 274 (FCA).

[78] 131 ALR 422 at 464.

It chances that I have long held and sometimes expressed the view that, in administrative law generally and in employment law, fairness is an ultimate question requiring an overall assessment of the merits of a case, a question in which procedure and substance should not be divorced. Thus in a case of gross and palpable misconduct the procedural restraints on an employer are clearly less than in one where the issue is more evenly balanced. To that extent I now venture to express respectful agreement with the High Court of Australia. There may be more room, however, for reservation about the High Court's ruling that the provisions of governing industrial awards, as they stand from time to time, are not to be treated as incorporated into individual contracts of service. And, more to the point for present purposes, at first sight it does seem rather odd that the *Woods* line of cases in England are not even mentioned in the High Court judgments in *Byrne* (nor, for that matter, the *Woolworths* line of cases in New Zealand), although in the Full Court of the Federal Court some indirect allusions are to be found in the judgments of Black CJ[79] and Gray J.[80]

One can only hazard a guess that, mindful of the existence of *some* evidence against their clients (particularly certain video evidence), the claimants' advisers thought it impolitic to dwell on duties of trust and confidence. Whatever the explanation, their arguments were evidently focused on the clause in the award and whether it was imported into the contracts of service or could found a statutory cause of action. No contention that a *Woods* implied term exists in employment contracts generally seems to have seen the light of day in any of the courts in *Byrne*. The tone of most of the judgments, especially the minority High Court judgment, may be unpromising, but it would seem that the issue could hardly be taken as concluded for Australia by *Byrne*.

A Major Development in the House of Lords

If doubts remain in Australia, or if past decisions are questioned in New Zealand, a decision of high persuasive authority in both jurisdictions must henceforth call for close attention. This is *Malik v Bank of Credit and Commerce International SA (in liquidation)*.[81] It may be seen as part of an escape from *Murphy*.[82] As for decisions of the House of Lords itself, some

[79] 120 ALR 274 at 285–6.

[80] Ibid at 333–9. Gray J's judgment was a dissenting one favouring 'prising employment law in Australia from the grip of 19th century judges' and favouring the recognition of international standards.

[81] [1997] 3 All ER 1.

[82] *Murphy v Brentwood District Council* [1991] 1 AC 908, where the House held that no duty of care was owed by a local authority, in approving designs, to subsequent owners

would date the tendency from *Scally v Southern Health and Social Services Board*,[83] where any relevant duty of care on the part of the employer was negated but their Lordships, for reasons given by Lord Bridge of Harwich, held that the employer nevertheless owed an implied contractual duty to inform employees of a superannuation option, negotiated at a general level, of which they might reasonably not otherwise be aware. It was said that if the issue was analysed in contract rather than tort the starting-point was quite different. 'Proximity' is a notorious linguistic trap. I do not wish to start that hare in the present context. What is clear, since *Scally* and now *Malik*, is that when a contractual claim can plausibly be mounted there will be decidedly fewer judicial inhibitions against allowing just remedies for economic loss.

Malik came before an Appellate Committee consisting of Lord Goff of Chieveley, Lord Mackay of Clashfern, Lord Mustill, Lord Nicholls of Birkenhead and Lord Steyn. They were unanimous, their reasons being given in speeches by Lord Nicholls and Lord Steyn. They reversed the courts below. The case is well summarized in the headnote in the All England Reports, from which (by permission) I extract the following.

> The two appellants were long-serving employees of a bank which collapsed as the result of a massive and notorious fraud perpetrated by those controlling the bank. The appellants were unaware of and had no part in the fraud. After the bank went into liquidation the appellants were made redundant by the liquidators and thereafter they found difficulty in obtaining employment in the banking field because of their association with the bank. The appellants lodged a claim in the liquidation for 'stigma compensation' arising out of the fact that they had been put at a disadvantage in the employment market. The appellants appealed to the court against the liquidators' rejection of their claim, contending that it was an implied term of their contracts of employment that an employer would not conduct his business in a manner calculated or likely to destroy or seriously damage the relationship of confidence and trust between the employer and employee. The judge held on the trial of a preliminary issue that a claim for stigma compensation did not disclose a reasonable cause of action or a sustainable claim for damages because the term contended for could not be implied in a contract of employment as it was not part of that contract that the employer should prepare an employee for employment with future employers or that he should ensure that employees were not put at a disadvantage in the employment market in the event of their employment being terminated. On appeal, the Court of Appeal held that although the employees had an arguable case that there had been a breach of the implied mutual obligation of trust and confidence the employees had no remedy as damages were not recoverable in contract for

of the house. If the house collapsed or had to be reconstructed because of danger to the occupants, the damage was to be classified as purely economic and irrecoverable in tort.

[83] [1992] 1 AC 294.

damage to or loss of an existing reputation except in certain limited situations which did not apply. The Court of Appeal accordingly dismissed the appeal. The appellants appealed to the House of Lords. The liquidators contended that injury to reputation was protected by the law of defamation, that the implied obligation of trust and confidence was not breached if the employer's dishonest behaviour was directed at defrauding third parties, not the employees, and that the employee had to have been aware of such conduct while he was an employee.

Held—The appeal would be allowed for the following reasons—

(1) In appropriate cases damages could in principle be awarded for loss of reputation caused by breach of contract. Furthermore, provided a relevant breach of contract was established and the requirements of causation, remoteness and mitigation were satisfied, financial loss in respect of damage to reputation caused by a breach of contract could be recovered for breach of a contract of employment.
(2) An employer was under an implied obligation that he would not, without reasonable and proper cause, conduct his business in a manner likely to destroy or seriously damage the relationship of confidence and trust between employer and employee, and an employer who breached the trust and confidence term would be liable if he thereby caused continuing financial loss of a nature that was reasonably foreseeable. Thus, if it was reasonably foreseeable that conduct in breach of the trust and confidence term would prejudicially affect employees' future employment prospects and loss of that type was sustained in consequence of a breach, then in principle damages in respect of the loss would be recoverable. The trust-destroying conduct need not be directed at the employee, either individually or as part of a group, in order to attract liability, nor was it necessary that the employee must have been aware of the employer's trust-destroying conduct while he was an employee.
(3) Since the bank had promised, in an implied term, not to conduct a dishonest or corrupt business the promised benefit being employment by an honest employer which benefit did not materialise the appellants were entitled to damages if they proved that they were handicapped in the labour market in consequence of the bank's corruption.

Technically the case might be suggested not to have decided the implied term issue, because it was argued on the agreed footing that the contracts contained an implied term that the bank would not, without reasonable and proper cause, conduct itself in a manner likely to destroy or seriously damage the relationship of trust and confidence between employer and employee. But the speeches leave no doubt that their Lordships endorsed the existence of such a term in contracts of employment generally. Lord Nicholls spoke[84] of it as a 'portmanteau, general obligation'. Lord Steyn spoke[85] of 'the change in legal culture

[84] [1997] 3 All ER 1 at 5. [85] Ibid at 15.

which made possible the evolution of the implied term of trust and confidence'. *Woods*[86] was approved; *Norton*[87] used as an analogy; *Addis v Gramophone Co. Ltd*[88] virtually discarded as outdated, as has occurred elsewhere.[89]

Spring in Perspective

Malik helps us, I think, to put *Spring* in its most convincing perspective. Although Lord Nicholls did not expressly refer to *Spring* in his speech, Lord Steyn did so—first as part of the history of the development of employment law in this century,[90] secondly as containing dicta showing that there is no rule preventing the recovery of damages for injury to reputation where that injury is caused by breach of contract.[91] Three of the majority Law Lords in *Spring* did accept that the situation there could be seen as one of concurrent duties in tort and contract.[92] Another and possibly more realistic way of putting it is that the employer has a duty of reasonable care originating in both tort and contract: only one duty, but with two sources. Their Lordships there defined the duty in terms of the giving of a reference. *Malik* enables us to classify this more broadly as a specific illustration of the portmanteau duty to take reasonable care to act consistently with the trust and confidence which should exist between employer and employee, a duty which survives for a reasonable time the period of the employment.[93] In a *Spring* type of case, where several companies in a group collaborate in the reference-compilation process but not all of them are in contractual relationship with the employee, the relationship will be so close that the same duty is owed by each in tort and perhaps equity, even if not in contract.[94] The key feature is the relationship of trust and confidence.

Such a relationship may exist between employer and employee whether the contract is of service or for services.[95] Other sufficient relationships may emerge from common sense and case law. They are best left to be considered where they arise, as Lord Woolf says in *Spring*.[96] If trust and confidence continue to provide the touchstone,

[86] *Woods v W. M. Car Services (Peterborough) Ltd* [1982] ICR 693.

[87] *Norton Tool Co. Ltd Tewson* [1973] 1 All ER 183. [88] [1909] AC 488.

[89] See *Ogilvy & Mather (New Zealand) Ltd v Turner* [1996] 1 NZLR 641 at 653–4.

[90] [1997] 3 All ER 1 at 15. [91] Ibid 21.

[92] Lord Goff in [1995] 2 AC 296 at 320; Lord Slynn at 340; Lord Woolf at 354.

[93] See Lord Goff in *Spring*, ibid at 320, and Lord Woolf at 354.

[94] In *Spring* Lord Goff intimates a doubt on this point, ibid at 322, but it was not shared by the three other majority Law Lords.

[95] See Lord Goff in *Spring*, ibid at 322, Lord Slynn at 337, and Lord Woolf at 341.

[96] Ibid at 354.

there should be no major undermining of defamation law or other departments of law.[97] As a general rule, however, injury to reputation should remain the exclusive province of the branch of the law that has been built up specifically to deal with it. In offering these opinions I believe that I am in tune with Professor John Fleming's thinking after *Spring v Guardian Assurance*; and in welcoming, on balance, the right of Spring as defined by the House of Lords, I am certainly fulfilling a prophecy made by Dr Yvonne Cripps.[98] Stravinsky's famous work caused a furore when it first appeared, but no longer shocks. This decision of the House of Lords may have more than one thing in common with it.

[97] In *Bell-Booth* [1989] 3 NZLR at 157, the action for breach of confidence was mentioned as one of the remedies whose existence made the importation of negligence law neither required nor warranted in the *Bell-Booth* class of case. Once *Spring* is classified as applying between parties bound by special mutual obligations to maintain confidence, the 2 cases may be seen as complementary. I do not claim, of course, that the employer–employee relationship was specifically in mind when the general reference to breach of confidence was made in *Bell-Booth*.

[98] *The Legal Implications of Disclosure in the Public Interest* (2nd ed., 1994), 237.

4

Duty of Care Factors: a Selection from the Judicial Menus

Jane Stapleton

One of the many great qualities of John Fleming's masterpiece, *The Law of Torts*,[1] is its ability to unmask the apparently formulaic reasoning of judges and reveal the real concerns motivating judgment in this notoriously open-textured field, once aptly described as law's most patent experiment in 'applied morality'.[2] Following his inspiring lead, I will try in this essay to unmask and draw together some of the recent achievements of British (and some Commonwealth) appellate judges in coming to terms with the complex moral and policy concerns underlying their resolution of novel claims for a duty of care in the tort of negligence. Through this continuing project[3] to unmask the variety of the concerns which such claims throw up to courts it will be made clear why no 'test' for the recognition of a duty of care is possible and how courts in future might best proceed.

Donoghue v Stevenson: Four Advances but no 'Test' for Duty

There is a core dilemma for judges seeking to rationalize their determination of disputes in the tort of negligence. It is that a much wider range of conduct, and conduct includes omissions, (a) might be implicated in the occasioning of (actionable classes of) injury and (b) might plausibly be described as 'careless', than any judge, however radical, would accept

[1] (8th ed., 1992).

[2] S. Stoljar, 'Concerning Strict Liability' in P. Finn (ed.), *Essays on Torts*, (1989), 267.

[3] Some factors drawn together here have been discussed in greater detail in earlier work: J. Stapleton, 'Duty of Care: A Wider Agenda', (1991) 107 LQR 249; J. Stapleton, 'In Restraint of Tort', in P. Birks (ed.), *Frontiers of Liability* (1994); J. Stapleton, 'Tort, Insurance and Ideology', (1995) 58 MLR 820; J. Stapleton, 'Duty of Care: Peripheral Parties and Alternative Opportunities for Deterrence', (1995) 111 LQR 301.

as properly giving rise to liability. Early on it was appreciated, even if only indirectly, that quite apart from the flexibility provided by the analytical devices represented by the requirements of a breach of standard of care, causation and damage not being too 'remote', more general 'systemic'[4] control of this tort's ambit was necessary. Such control emerged under the label of duty of care: only those to whom a duty of care was owed by the defendant would be able to sue for the injury which the carelessness of the defendant had caused to them. So far so good. But merely providing an analytical label for systemic control was widely regarded as insufficient: a search developed among both judges and academic commentators for a core 'test' to be used to determine whether a duty of care would be owed. Much of the confusion in the field of negligence law has been generated by this misguided enterprise and the false belief that such a 'test' was feasible.

There *is* no 'test' for the duty of care. There *can* be no 'duty test' given what it is that judges do under the cloak of this analytical label. Indeed, the underlying nature of judicial reasoning here is distorted when any case is seen as laying down a 'test' for duty. This distortion occurred most famously with the later academic and judicial treatment of the judgment of Lord Atkin[5] in *Donoghue v Stevenson*.[6] Contrary to the shorthand commonly used to describe the importance of the case, *Donoghue*'s case did not lay down any 'test' of duty. In the context of the duty of care analysis[7] the real importance of *Donoghue*'s case lay elsewhere, namely in four clear and sound principles:

1. The idea that a plaintiff had to bring himself within or incrementally close to a pre-existing 'pocket' of recognized factual situations giving rise to a duty was denounced as wrong and rightly abandoned.
2. The argument that a plaintiff could not base his claim in negligence on conduct of the defendant where that conduct was related to the performance of the defendant's contractual obligations to a third person, was exploded as false. This argument has became known as the 'privity fallacy'.[8]
3. It was made clear that foreseeability of some description was a necessary requirement before a duty of care would be recognized.
4. By the use of the restricted notion of 'neighbour', Lord Atkin

[4] On the utility of the duty concept to signal systemic concerns of the law see Stapleton, 'Peripheral Parties' n. 3 above at 303–5.

[5] That well-known Brisbane boy-made-good: G. Lewis, *Lord Atkin*, (1983) 1.

[6] [1932] AC 562.

[7] As opposed to the specific issue of manufacturer's liability.

[8] In other words, after *Donoghue*'s case no defendant could argue that his contractual obligations to a third party were necessarily exhaustive of his civil obligations.

seemed to emphasize that while foreseeability was a necessary factor for a duty to be recognized, it may not always be a sufficient factor.

The first two principles operate to open up the field of negligence liability by removing two irrational barriers to its coherent development. At first it was these two principles and their intellectually liberating effect on how that tort was seen and deployed by courts which captured the attention of commentators and judges alike. They served well the mid-century moods for rejecting unintelligible historical relics and for increasing social obligation. In contrast, the last two principles emphasized that even with these two barriers removed still other barriers should and must remain. The first barrier, the requirement of foreseeability is straightforward enough: one cannot even be careless with regard to a risk which one could not foresee; *a fortiori* there can be no duty to avoid it.

But what of the fourth 'principle', the neighbour concept? It is here that the confusion has centred. Many commentators and judges in the past have appeared to believe that the term 'neighbour', and its modern cousin, 'the relationship of proximity', can do more than merely warn of the fact that besides foreseeability there are complex concerns that judges may legitimately weigh in the duty analysis. Thus, for example, there are many judgments[9] which suggest that the 'relationship of proximity' is an element common to duty situations; the basis, general conceptual explanation and *determinant*, unifying theme, rationale, and integral constituent of the duty concept which allows an understanding and *identification* of duty situations. But these are all dangerously misleading statements because they might suggest that merely by intoning this phrase over a particular fact situation a coherent working criterion for the determination of the duty question is provided for the particular case. It clearly is not. The bald phrase 'relationship of proximity' has no content.

Its banal role can be usefully compared to that of the phrase 'breach of the standard of care'. A 'relationship of proximity' is only a determinant of duty and therefore of liability in the same banal sense that the phrase 'breach of the standard of care' is a determinant of negligence-in-fact

[9] Particularly from the High Ct of Australia when Deane J was on that court. All the descriptions of the 'relationship of proximity' cited in the text are from such cases (though parallel descriptions are also found in British, Canadian, and New Zealand cases): *Gala v Preston* (1990–1) 172 CLR 243 at 252–3; *Stevens v Brodribb Sawmilling Co. Pty Ltd* (1986) 160 CLR 16 at 52; *Burnie Port Authority v General Jones Pty Ltd* (1992–4) 179 CLR 520 at 543–4; *Sutherland Shire Council v Heyman* (1985) 157 CLR 424 at 497; *San Sebastian Pty Ltd v The Minister* (1986) 162 CLR 341 at 355.

and therefore of liability. Both phrases merely flag the existence of a particular gate through which the plaintiff must pass. Neither bald phrase reveals what precise substantive issues will, in the relevant circumstances of a particular case, be regarded as relevant to whether the plaintiff is, respectively, owed a duty or can establish negligence-in-fact.

Moreover, as we will see, sometimes a duty factor, such as the concern not to encourage abortion, weighs in favour of a duty, sometimes it weighs against a duty, and sometimes it is simply not raised by the facts of the case at all. So, just as the diversity of fact situations means that in the determination of breach a particular feature may be judged relevant in one circumstance but of little or no weight in another, so among the concerns weighing with judges in duty cases there is no one concern which is always relevant on the facts. In other words, the phrase 'relationship of proximity' cannot even be interpreted as code for some constant common denominator in all duty situations. Even a minimal prior relationship between the parties, as misleadingly suggested by the phrase itself, is not always judged necessary for a duty: for example, I owe a duty not carelessly to knock down a total stranger. In short, the bald phrase a 'relationship of proximity' can no more deliver 'underlying unity or consistency'[10] to the duty field than can the bald phrase 'breach of the standard of care' to that of negligence-in-fact.

What is needed is the unmasking of whatever specific factors in each individual case weighed with judges in their determination of duty. It is not acceptable merely for a judge baldly to assert that the plaintiff was proximate; or that a duty was justified because the parties were in a 'special relationship', or because the plaintiff had 'reasonably relied' on the defendant, or merely because it was 'fair, just and reasonable'. Without more, these are just labels. Judgment should focus explicitly on why this plaintiff is proximate, why the relationship was special, why reliance was reasonable, and so on.

Over the past twenty years many British and Commonwealth appellate judges have adopted a franker style of analysis, packaged less in the formulaic labels common in earlier case law but more in clearly enunciated considerations for and against recognition of a duty. Of course, there are still many instances where judges mask their reasoning behind empty labels of no content such as 'a relationship of proximity' but these instances should not overshadow the achievement of other judges in openly analysing factors which have weighed in their determination. The judgments in *Stovin v Wise*,[11] *X (minors) v Bedfordshire County*

[10] *Burnie Port Authority v General Jones Pty Ltd* (1992–4) 179 CLR 520 at 543.
[11] [1996] 3 All ER 801.

Council,[12] *Elguzouli-Daf v Commissioner of Police*[13] and *Winnipeg Child and Family Services v G (DF)*[14] are all admirable examples of the latter phenomenon. On investigation some of these unmasked factors are less than convincing, but many are convincing. In any case, the trend towards greater transparency in judgments allows direct evaluation of the soundness of factors which concerned individual judges and represents a healthy and necessary stage in the maturing of this, the most potentially explosive of all torts.

The chapter ends with a summary of the factors discussed: full-size numerals in the text refer to these lists. A final caveat: the following discussion has had to be highly selective. There are many more duty factors surfacing in the case law than space allows me to deal with here. But I have tried to give some flavour of how diverse the judicially cited factors are and how they range from simple, easily spotted notions such as the concern not to discourage rescue to much more complex but commercially important factors such as the concern not to encourage parties to be dependent and 'free-ride' on tort where they could have helped themselves.[15]

Unconvincing Factors

In Favour of Recognition of Duty

Some factors which appear in appellate judgments concerning novel duties of care are unconvincing. It is as important to tease out some of these and to explain in what way they are incoherent as it is to identify convincing factors.

A common weakness in the reasoning of judges in this field is the temptation to elevate the effect of a determination into a reason for it. Thus, while it is true that a finding of a duty of care is owed will promote compensation (of the plaintiff) (1), perhaps deterrence (of the defendant) (2) and loss-spreading (given that virtually all defendants against whom cases are actually taken are insured) (3), none of these factors can be a convincing reason for the determination. They are simply corollaries of it.[16]

[12] [1995] 3 All ER 353, where it is particularly refreshing to see a judge concede that the specific duty issue at hand was 'a difficult question on which my views have changed from time to time' (per Lord Browne-Wilkinson at 391).

[13] [1995] 1 All ER 833.

[14] (1998) 152 DLR (4th) 193.

[15] In an appropriate manner, namely protect themselves from the risk occurring or obtain contractual protection in relation to the threatened loss in a way which directly or indirectly deters the careless party: see below.

[16] There is a more general point here. It is as banal and misleading to say that the

The reason these factors are unconvincing in cases recognizing duties is that they are present and would also weigh in favour of a duty in all cases, including the plethora of recent cases in which a duty has been denied. The real issue is *why* the compensation/deterrence/loss-spreading results are to be allowed in the former class of case but not the latter. Judicial observations that these results will flow in the former cases and are not 'justified' in the latter do not explain, let alone justify, the distinctions courts draw between the two groups.

Of course, sometimes in cases such as these judges may not intend their references to the compensation of the plaintiff, deterrence of the defendant, and so on, to be taken as part of the reasons for the finding of a duty. But unless this is made clear, such comments are very dangerous: for they can appear to support the misleading claims of some commentators that compensation and deterrence (even loss-spreading) are acceptable and potent reasons for recognizing a duty of care.

A parallel trap for judges who have determined that a novel duty of care should be owed in a particular case is to refer to the financial impact such a finding may have on the defendant. Thus, comments that a defendant or a class of defendants is likely to be insured[17] (4) and/or have a deep pocket[18] (5) are again liable to mislead some observers into the mistaken belief that the resources of a defendant class is a generally valid factor in the resolution of duty issues. As a general proposition this is demonstrably false as a matter of description[19] (even though in a specific context, such as the defendant being a public authority or landowner, resources may form *part* of a rationale specific to that defendant class[20]) and is bewildering from a normative point of view given that the basis of the normative framework of tort law is personal responsibility.

Also unconvincing are the currently fashionable attempts in some cases to refer to 'voluntary assumption of responsibility' (6) as a factor which justifies the finding of a duty of care. So far none of these attempts has been convincing because, just as with other 'labels' such as 'proximity', this phrase has not been given precise content. Of course if a person, X, not only undertakes a particular task but explicitly undertakes the legal risk of liability for any injury thereby caused, this would be a convincing factor in favour of a duty on that person being recognized.

'function' of tort is compensation as it is to say that the 'function' of a petrol station is to dispense petrol: the question of interest is who is entitled to have the benefit dispensed and why.

[17] See cases cited in J. Stapleton, 'Tort, Insurance and Ideology', n. 3 above at 823ff.

[18] The defendant's 'shoulders are broad enough to bear the loss': *Dutton v Bognor Regis Urban District Council* [1972] 1 QB 373 at 398 (per Lord Denning MR).

[19] See J. Stapleton, 'Tort, Insurance and Ideology' n. 3 above at 823ff.

[20] See, e.g., the later discussion of the concern not to distort public budgets and/or activities.

But as is the case with the defence of 'voluntary assumption of risk', the mere undertaking of a task does not justify a conclusion of an undertaking of *legal* risk and responsibility. Moreover, in practice the facts of a case rarely provide evidence of such an undertaking. A mere judicial assertion that this was the case is not convincing.[21] The law is thrown back on the normative question: *should* the defendant be under a duty, should he be *taken in law* to have undertaken the legal responsibility? A mere judicial assertion that this should be the case is also not convincing.[22]

COUNTERVAILING TO THE RECOGNITION OF DUTY

More varied are the unconvincing reasons sometimes given by judges for the *denial* of a duty of care. Again there are judicial observations based on insurance[23] (1) and wealth (2) which are the mirror-images of those in cases recognizing novel duties. In cases denying a duty, observations that the plaintiff is or could be insured or that the plaintiff has a deep pocket are both unconvincing and demonstrably not applied as a general principle (as they would need to be if they were to be convincing): in the vast majority of cases where a duty is recognized the plaintiff could have insured. As with all the above factors, these observations mask whatever real factors are influencing courts to cite these factors *selectively*.

But there is also a range of other unconvincing factors, typically found in case law of the time when the confidence of the *Anns*[24] period was giving way to the wariness of cases such as *D&F Estates*[25] and *Murphy*.[26] Here the determination of the Law Lords to confine liability (particularly for economic loss) led them to enunciate a series of factors which at best were dangerously misleading observations and at worst bad 'reasons' for denial of duties of care.

Concern that, in a particular context, imposition of a duty of care might expose defendants to a large volume of claims (3) (as opposed to an indeterminate number of claims—see below) are unconvincing given that the law is content elsewhere to impose liability where the

[21] For an example see the mere assertion of Lord Goff in *Henderson v Merrett Syndicates Ltd* [1994] 3 All ER 506 at 534–5 that such assumption was present in that case but not in *Simaan General Contracting Co. v Pilkington Glass Ltd* [1988] 1 All ER 791.

[22] See, e.g., the mere assertion of Lord Goff in *White v Jones* [1995] 1 All ER 691 at 710 that the defendant in that case 'should be held in law' to have assumed responsibility to the plaintiff.

[23] See J. Stapleton, 'Tort, Insurance and Ideology' n. 3 above at 823ff and cases cited therein.

[24] *Anns v Merton London Borough Council* [1978] AC 728.

[25] *D&F Estates Ltd v Church Commissioners for England* [1988] 2 All ER 992.

[26] *Murphy v Brentwood District Council* [1990] 3 WLR 414.

potential plaintiff class is large.[27] Indeed, it would be very odd if a defendant could argue in his own favour that he should not owe a duty became he had many victims!

Clearly observations[28] that the law had never recognized a duty here before (4) are analytically unhelpful in explaining why a duty should be rejected now that it is being argued for.[29] What is more, some of the greatest landmarks of the common law, including *Donoghue v Stevenson*, are cases in which it is recognized that what had never been done before should now be done.

Similarly, in some cases judges refer to the fact that in a particular context the recognition of a duty would have a substantial socio-economic and/or redistributional effect (5), or would create a large new area of liability (6).[30] Now, while there may be sound reasons for extra care in analysis in such cases,[31] this is not the same thing as providing a specific justification for rejecting a duty. Again, as *Donoghue v Stevenson* and *Hedley Byrne & Co. Ltd v Heller & Partners*[32] demonstrate, some cases which have had all these dramatic effects are some of the most widely approved 'landmark' cases of the common law.

The *bald* assertion, often made, that restraint must be exercised because the claim is for a duty in relation to pure economic loss (7) is also unconvincing. With hindsight it was ironic that the first recognition of a duty of care in negligence in relation to pure economic loss (save for two obscure earlier cases[33]), *Hedley Byrne*, concerned negligent words in a context where indeterminate liability threatened. As we will see, it is a sound and well-settled reason against a duty that it would expose defendants to indeterminate liability (the 'floodgates' concern). For many years after *Hedley Byrne* there seemed to be a widespread assumption in judgments and commentaries that *any* claim in relation to a duty

[27] E.g., an individual's single moment of carelessness gave rise to liability in negligence (*inter alia*) towards 182 plaintiffs in *AB v South West Water Services* [1993] 1 All ER 609.

[28] E.g., see *Murphy v Brentwood District Council* [1990] 3 WLR 414 at 432 (per Lord Keith), 448 (per Lord Oliver); *Leigh & Sillivan Ltd v Aliakmon Shipping Co. Ltd (The Aliakmon)* [1986] AC 785 at 815 (per Lord Brandon); *Junior Books Ltd v Veitchi Co. Ltd* [1983] 1 AC 520 at 551–2 (per Lord Brandon); *D&F Estates Ltd v Church Commissioners for England* [1989] 1 AC 177 at 211 (per Lord Oliver). See Stapleton, 'Agenda' n. 3 above at 253.

[29] A point well made by the majority of the Australian High Ct in *Northern Territory of Australia v Mengel* (1996) 185 CLR 307 at 339.

[30] See e.g. *Murphy v Brentwood District Council* [1990] 3 WLR 414 at 419 (per Lord McKay), 430, 432 (per Lord Keith), 451 (per Lord Oliver), 457 (per Lord Jauncey). See Stapleton, 'Agenda', n. 3 above at 253 and 268.

[31] See, e.g. *Winnipeg Child and Family Services v G (DF)* (n. 14 above) where the majority gave specific reasons why in this particular case the legislature was the proper forum for resolution of 'the serious policy concerns' (para 45) raised by the claim.

[32] [1964] AC 465.

[33] *Morrison Steamship Co. Ltd v Greystoke Castle (Cargo Owners)* [1947] AC 265; *Wilkinson v Coverdale* (1793) 1 Esp. 75, 170 ER 284.

to avoid pure economic loss would involve this indeterminacy problem and that therefore (a) all economic loss claims formed a class and (b) that they must be treated with especial caution: that is, the mere *fact* that a claim concerned pure economic loss was seen to provoke the concern of indeterminacy which weighed heavily against recognition of a duty.

As we will see, there may be a deeply rooted moral view of the common law that physical security is an interest worthy of more protection than economic. If accepted and made explicit this might constitute a sound restraining factor in all claims for pure economic loss, but the oft-cited fear of indeterminacy does not justify restraint across the entire class of such claims. As demonstrated by later cases such as the acquisition of property cases,[34] *White v Jones*[35] and so on, this indeterminacy problem is not endemic to all economic loss cases. It is not even endemic to all cases where negligent words cause economic loss. There is a whole range of economic loss situations where both the class of plaintiffs and the quantum of loss is foreseeable and determinate. But echoes of and references back to earlier case law sometimes still allows this crude reasoning to infect judgments.

Conversely, the fact that *Hedley Byrne* involved words led some judges, concerned with restraining liability, to attempt to confine economic loss liability on the artificial basis of the form of defendant conduct involved. The consequent unconvincing assertion was that the precedent of *Hedley Byrne* was confined to negligent words causing the economic loss. The idea conveyed was that words are, in some significant but often unstated way, different from acts; and that while the law might recognize a duty in a specific case involving words, the mere fact that in the present parallel case the conduct was an act took it outside the 'pocket' of liability recognized by *Hedley Byrne* (8).[36] Where an attempt is made to state what this crucial difference is the explanation is, at bottom, merely the concern with floodgates: an observation that sometimes, perhaps even often, the context in which economic loss is caused by careless words triggers this concern. This is not a convincing reason why *all* cases of negligent words causing economic loss form a coherent class because not every case of negligent words triggers the indeterminacy concern. The concern should be declared for what it is, indeterminacy, and the fallacious distinction between acts and words *per se* should be abandoned.

[34] i.e., cases where the plaintiff suffers economic loss because he has acquired property of a certain quality as in *Bryan v Maloney* (1994–5) 182 CLR 609 and *Smith v Bush (Eric S.)* [1989] 2 All ER 514.

[35] [1995] 1 All ER 691.

[36] For a detailed criticism of the lack of policy justification for a 'pocket' of liability devoted to negligent words see Stapleton, 'Agenda', n. 3 above at 259ff.

The most dramatic illustration of this fallacy is the still unresolved problem of claims for economic loss suffered by the acquisition of defective property.[37] Here, despite the absence of any floodgate threat,[38] the House of Lords has rejected the claim that a negligent builder owes a duty of care to the acquiring owner while nevertheless recognizing that a duty is owed to the owner by a professional adviser when the owner acquired the property in reliance on the latter's negligent advice. Thus, if X carelessly surveyed land and carelessly advised that it required foundations of no more than three feet deep, X may well owe a duty of care to an owner of the subsequent building when its foundations are discovered to be inadequate; or if X carelessly advised a prospective purchaser that a property has adequate foundations when it did not, X may well owe a duty of care to that purchaser; but if X is actually a careless builder who creates a building with inadequate foundations he owes no duty in the tort of negligence to the subsequent owner!

There have been cases in which the denial of a duty was accompanied by the assertion that a particular piece of legislation impliedly 'covers the field' (9).[39] But in *Donoghue v Stevenson* the House of Lords clearly did not consider that the warranties of quality recognized by sale of goods legislation impliedly covered the field of the safety of commercially supplied ginger beer. The mere assertion that legislation covers the field begs the underlying substantive question of when, if ever, and why a piece of legislation which is itself silent on the matter[40] should be taken to have pre-empted the common law developing obligations in the area.[41]

A close but equally weak argument against a duty is the bald unqualified assertion that an area is more appropriately to be seen as the province of Parliament (10) and that to recognize a duty here would be to engage in illegitimate 'judicial legislation'.[42] Thus in the *D&F*

[37] On which see ibid at 277–83. For a bizarre illustration see *Lanchashire and Cheshire Association of Baptist Churches Inc. v Howard & Seddon Partnership* [1993] 3 All ER 467. For a way forward in acquisition cases which does not distinguish between words and acts see Stapleton, 'Peripheral Parties', n. 3 above at 335–7.

[38] Because the plaintiff class is determinate (indeed it is usually only 1 or 2 people who acquire ownership) and the relevant quantum of loss is also determinate.

[39] See, e.g., the discussion of the Defective Premises Act 1972 in *Murphy v Brentwood District Council* [1990] 2 All ER 908. On this point see Stapleton, 'Agenda', n. 3 above at 268–9. Compare the discussion in *White v Jones* [1995] 1 All ER 691 at 707 by Lord Goff of the Carriage of Goods by Sea Act 1992 which 'solved, as a matter of urgency' the type of difficulty revealed by the plaintiff's claim in *The Aliakmon* [1986] AC 785.

[40] Contrast the Occupiers' Liability Acts (1957 & 1984) enacting rules 'in place of the rules of the common law', s 1(1) in both Acts.

[41] Contrast *X (minors) v Bedfordshire County Council* [1995] 3 All ER 353, 'I can see no legal or commonsense principle which requires one to deny a common law duty of care which would otherwise exist just because there is a statutory scheme which addresses the same problem' (per Lord Browne-Wilkinson at 395).

[42] See Stapleton, 'Agenda', n. 3 above at 268–9.

Estates case[43] and *Murphy*'s case[44] we are told that consumer protection in the field of economic loss resulting from the acquisition of property is more properly the province of Parliament, and specifically that the recognition of a duty of care in *Anns'* case was 'judicial legislation'. Again such assertions beg the question of why the particular field is regarded as more properly the province of the legislature when so many other fields are accepted as areas in which the common law can recognize obligations.[45] The poverty of these particular bald assertions is exposed most dramatically when note is taken that, between the two above cases, the Lords decided the case of *Smith v Bush (Eric S.)*[46] citing as a reason *for* the recognition of a duty the need to protect consumers such as Mrs Smith who had suffered economic loss through the acquisition of property.

Yet another bald assertion which has surfaced in appellate case law is that an area was more properly seen as the province of contract (11).[47] This idea was deployed in the early days of judicial concern with recovery for pure economic loss. Its incoherence again lies in the failure to give a substantive explanation of why it should operate in the particular context in which it was used, namely claims for economic loss against manufacturers or builders of property by acquirers of that property, who were therefore relegated to such protection as might be available by private ordering through contract. This is particularly troublesome when in other contexts the point is ignored and plaintiffs given tort protection, even including some instances of economic loss occurring through acquisition of defective property.[48]

Though, as we will see later, courts may now be teasing out more fine-tuned and coherent factors for and against recognizing a duty in cases of economic loss occurring by acquisition of defective property, in the early days of such claims appellate courts enunciated a number of other unconvincing factors allegedly countervailing to liability. Of all these perhaps the most superficially alluring was that set out by Lord Brandon in his influential dissent in *Junior Books Ltd v Veitchi Co. Ltd*:[49] that to

[43] *D&F Estates Ltd v Church Commissioners for England* [1989] 1 AC 177 at 208 (per Lord Bridge).

[44] *Murphy v Brentwood District Council* [1990] 3 WLR 414 at 433 (per Lord Keith), 451 (per Lord Oliver) & 457 (per Lord Jauncey).

[45] Contrast the explicit analysis on this point in *Winnipeg Child and Family Services v G (DF)* (n. 14 above).

[46] [1989] 2 All ER 514.

[47] See J. Stapleton, 'Agenda', n. 3 above at 253.

[48] e.g., as in *Smith* v. *Bush (Eric S.)* [1989] 2 All ER 514.

[49] [1983] 1 AC 520 at 551–552. See also, *Murphy v Brentwood District Council* [1990] 3 WLR 414 at 433 (per Lord Keith), 441 (per Lord Bridge), 451 (per Lord Oliver) & 457 (per Lord Jauncey); *D&F Estates Ltd v Church Commissioners for England* [1989] 1 AC 177 at 207–8 (per Lord Bridge); *White v Jones* [1995] 1 All ER 691 at 694 (per Lord Keith) and the

recognize a duty here would be tantamount to giving the plaintiff the benefit of a contract to which he or she was not a party (12). This idea I call the 'evasion of privity fallacy'. There are two ways of seeing why this factor must be rejected. First, if we focus on the defendant: since *Donoghue*'s case, it is no bar to recognition of an entitlement in the tort of negligence and the parallel obligation on the defendant that the defendant owed a similar or identical obligation to a third party with whom he was in contractual privity. Thus Mrs Donoghue was protected by a duty even though the defendant was in contract with a third party who thereby had the benefit of contractual obligations resting on the defendant with regard to the quality and safety of the ginger beer. Secondly, if we focus on the plaintiff: by definition, whenever any tort entitlement is recognized it benefits the plaintiff regardless of whether he or she bargained and paid for it in a contract; indeed this is a corollary of a tort entitlement as currently understood: it is available despite not having been paid for. Mrs Donoghue was given the protection of a duty even though she did not buy the ginger beer and in that way pay for protection. Inasmuch as Lord Brandon's objection is to the plaintiff's failure to have a contractual entitlement against the defendant, most if not all tort entitlements would thereby be rendered objectionable.

This last criticism can also be made of the argument sometimes made that recognition of a duty would in effect make the defendant the insurer of the plaintiff (13). The very term 'insurer' here is confused because defendants, unlike insurers, only have to pay when and because they have breached an obligation. Moreover, even if we decide to use the term 'insurer' for this situation, it is still true that wherever any tort entitlement is recognized this in effect makes defendants insurers in that sense. Were this type of 'insurance' objectionable, it would render all tort obligations objectionable.

As Lord Brandon's failed attempt to draw a line excluding certain cases concerning the acquisition of property from the reach of negligence liability illustrates, the relation of tort to contract has been seen as particularly troublesome in the period since *Hedley Byrne* recognized that pure economic loss was an actionable form of loss (that is, it could form the 'gist damage' in a claim in negligence). Judicial concern in this area occasionally manifested itself in observations, cruder than, but similar to, Lord Brandon's reasoning, about the defendant's expectations.[50]

discussion in Stapleton, 'Agenda', n. 3 above at 253, 268–70. Later cases recognizing duties, such as that to the plaintiff in *White v Jones* and to the indirect Names in *Henderson*'s case, clearly ignore Lord Brandon's concern.

[50] E.g., see *Candlewood Navigation Corporation Ltd v Mitsui OSK Lines Ltd (the Mineral Transporter)* [1986] 1 AC 1 at 15 (PC); *The Aliakmon* [1986] AC 785 at 816–17 (per Lord Brandon).

Where these reflect a concern not to upset such expectations (14) and this concern is elevated into a reason for denying a duty of care we are presented with no more than the privity fallacy which was so comprehensively demolished in *Donoghue*'s case.[51] If a defendant's expectations are not to be unsettled, no expansion of common-law obligations would be acceptable: it is only by unsettling expectations that novel obligations can be recognized.

To show the variety of unconvincing countervailing arguments which recent case law have thrown up, let me give one final example. In *Spring*[52] the Court of Appeal denied the victim of a careless reference the protection of a duty of care on the basis that he already had another cause of action against the defendant arising from the same facts, namely defamation, in relation to which the law recognized that the defendant had a defence (qualified privilege) (15). Given that separate torts protect separate interests, it is likely that any set of facts may, *prima facie*, trigger claims in more than one tort. To reject the possibility of concurrent liability here[53] is to disturb this rich pattern of common law response and would set us the impossible task of ranking all causes of action and justifying the ranking. Thus, in *Spring*'s case the court would need to explain why it implicitly ranked the policy concern reflected in the defence of qualified privilege in the tort of defamation above the pro-liability concerns operating in the tort of negligence. Why not vice versa: if a reference was careful (thereby providing an answer to the claim in negligence), why would that not be sufficient to deny an entitlement in defamation? It is true that qualified privilege reflects an important concern of the law which reason demands should not be overlooked when a different cause of action is argued for. But mechanically and across the board to reject a duty of care (or any other cause of action) *merely* on the basis that it would undermine or outflank this policy concern pre-empts the real possibility that on the facts a court might judge this factor to be outweighed by strong factors in favour of liability where a careless untrue statement causes physical or economic loss to the plaintiff.

[51] That someone else has a 'suitable' claim against the defendant is also a version of this fallacy: Stapleton, 'Peripheral Parties', n. 3 above at 324. Sometimes there are ways of reading a judgment to avoid such an embarrassing construction: J. Stapleton, 'Tort, Insurance and Ideology' n. 3 above at 827, n. 21.

[52] *Spring v Guardian Assurance plc* [1993] 2 All ER 273; rev'd by HL, [1994] 3 All ER 129. Compare *Bell-Booth Group Ltd v Attorney-General* [1989] 3 NZLR 148.

[53] As elsewhere: see *Northern Territory of Australia v Mengel* (1996) 185 CLR 307 at 368 where Deane J resorted to the same unconvincing argument to assert that the Beaudesert proposition 'impermissibly' intruded on the domain of the tort of negligence and other torts. See also 359 (per Brennan CJ).

Convincing Factors

In Favour of Recognition of Duty

Judgments are remarkably thin on explicit convincing pro-liability factors. The most powerful of all such factors is one which can, in effect, merely be deduced from a remarkably consistent pattern of outcomes in the relevant sphere: namely, a defendant who, by his own positive act, has carelessly caused physical damage to the plaintiff or his property is *always* held to owe a duty of care to the victim. This is so even if the plaintiff and defendant are complete strangers; plaintiff and defendant are physically distant; the plaintiff is rich and insured; the defendant is a public authority; and so on. In other words, apart from Crown privilege no factor countervailing to the recognition of a duty has yet been identified which has the force to outweigh this pro-liability factor. Thus, if I carelessly trip a stranger into a swimming-pool where he drowns it will be held that he is my 'neighbour', that we are 'proximate' and that it would be fair, just, and reasonable to impose a duty on me.

But although this 'trump' factor[54] should clearly be placed on the top of our menu of convincing pro-liability factors, its formulation can be little more than a recital of the relevant fact pattern: proper vindication of the law's concern with the physical security of persons and property is currently regarded as justifying a duty being imposed on a party by whose own careless act the plaintiff's person or property has been physically damaged (1). Of course, this does not mean that whenever I cause you physical damage by my act I will always be *liable*. Courts still have a range of analytical devices which they can use to exculpate me: my act was not a *breach* of duty; the damage was too *remote*; you had voluntarily assumed the risk or were acting in a way which the court is willing to recognize justifies raising the defence of illegality against you; and so on. But the fact that a duty is *always* recognized in such cases confirms that judges want to give a very forceful 'systemic' message about the importance the common law[55] places

[54] Trump factors such as this and the trump countervailing factor discussed later might be described as 'principles' constituting assertions of rights which stand to be justified, if at all, in moral terms. Other factors might be described as 'policies' which, because they are generated and justified by consequentialist (though not only economic) concerns, may be subject to being outweighed in any particular case by countervailing policies.

[55] Statutes commonly go further to reflect the detail of social values and to elevate particular sorts of physical security: thus personal injuries are treated preferentially in many statutory regimes of liability (see e.g. the Occupiers' Liability Act 1984, s 1(8), (9)) as is damage to buildings which are dwelling houses (e.g. Defective Premises Act 1972, s 1). Is it possible that the common law might develop such fine tuning in relation to physical loss?

on physical security from careless acts. Moreover, so well-recognized and accepted is this concern that courts rarely attempt to justify or explain its eminence within the common law. Their silence on such a key factor is, of course, understandable given that the task of justification here would require the handling of delicate issues of moral philosophy.

More specific concerns which weigh convincingly in favour of liability have been raised explicitly by appellate judges. For example, courts routinely justify holding that those who create situations of peril owe a duty to those who intervene in order to rescue others on the basis that to deny a duty would tend to discourage rescue (2). Since the common law should not discourage that which the community consensus wants encouraged, a duty is convincingly justified.

The unwanted baby cases throw up another specific sound pro-liability concern. When the first such case came before the courts it was brought by the child.[56] Analytically the only damage of which the child could complain, the only formulation of damage which could be said to form the gist of the action, was life itself. As we will see, courts are generally concerned with the symbolic messages the law sends out. Here this led to the court denying the claim of a duty of care owed to the child: for, given the limits of the law's conceptual apparatus, recognition of a duty would require the law to acknowledge that healthy life could be 'damage' to the individual baby, a proposition wholly at odds with community morality. Cleverly the next unwanted baby case was presented in a way which avoided this sound countervailing concern: here it was the parents who sued for their own loss, the economic loss in bringing up the child. Here not only was the previous countervailing concern absent but a separate pro-liability argument was convincingly cited by the court in justifying its recognition that the careless medical defendant owed the parents a duty of care: a denial of duty would tend to encourage abortion (3),[57] again a result which would have flown in the face of a community consensus that this is a phenomenon which should not be positively encouraged.

Countervailing to the Recognition of Duty

Just as at the top of the list of convincing pro-liability factors there is a factor which can be defined so precisely that it trumps all others when present on the facts, so too we can spell out from case law a sound countervailing factor so powerful in a narrow formulation that it trumps all others. The common law recognizes the core libertarian impulse that I

[56] *McKay v Essex Health Authority* [1982] QB 1166.
[57] *Emeh v Kensington Area Health Authority* [1985] QB 1012 at 1021.

am not my brother's keeper where he is a stranger! The concern here is to maximize a person's freedom of choice of action and at present the very heavy weight given to this concern has produced a clear bright-line of outcomes: no duty of affirmative action is recognized towards a stranger. In other words, the concern with freedom of action is currently given such weight that it is seen to justify denial of all duties of affirmative action towards strangers (1). Thus the law accepts that were I to walk past a baby stranger drowning in a paddling-pool I would be under no legal duty to assist. In the eyes of the law at present, he or she is not my 'neighbour', we are not 'proximate', and it would not be 'fair, just and reasonable' to impose on me a duty to roll the baby out of the pool, so powerful is this concern with freedom of action.

Of course, the fact situations which trigger the pro-liability trump factor (that the plaintiff was physically injured by the affirmative act of the defendant) and the fact situations which trigger the trump countervailing factor (that the defendant failed to act in relation to a stranger) are mutually exclusive. But the law also allocates weight (albeit rebuttably) to weaker versions of both. Thus, in cases of *physical injury* courts seem keener to protect plaintiffs by recognition of a duty of care than in cases of pure economic loss, even where the act causing physical injury was committed not by the defendant but by someone over whom the defendant merely had some form of control. On the other hand, in cases where the complaint is of an *omission* by the defendant, courts are more reluctant to recognize a duty than in cases where the complaint is about a positive act of the defendant even where the case is between non-strangers: because it is possible for the court to regard the passive defendant, relative to the active source of injury, as a merely peripheral party (2).[58]

Clearly some fact situations can raise both of these weaker versions of our two trump factors. This is seen most clearly in cases where the omission of the defendant to control the behaviour of a third party has resulted in physical injury to the plaintiff: cases such as *Topp*[59] and *Smith*

[58] A view often bolstered by the fact that the party of central causal importance is being sued or has already been successfully sued by the plaintiff: *Investors in Industry Commercial Properties Ltd v South Bedfordshire District Council* [1986] 1 QB 1034; *Curran v Northern Ireland Co-ownership Housing Association* [1987] AC 718; *Richardson v West Lindsay District Council* [1990] 1 WLR 522; *Ancell v McDermott* [1993] 4 All ER 355; *Clough v Bussan (West Yorkshire Police Authority)* [1990] 1 All ER 431; *Governors of the Peabody Donation Fund v Sir Lindsay Parkinson & Co. Ltd* [1985] 1 AC 210; *Wood v Law Society* (1993) 143 NLJ 1475 (QBD); *Stovin v Wise* [1996] 3 All ER 801 (for the point see [1994] 3 All ER 467 at 469); *Banque Financière de la Cité SA v Westgate Insurance Co. Ltd* [1991] AC 249. See Stapleton, 'Peripheral Parties', n. 3 above at 316. Contrast the recognition of a duty in *Pyrenees Shire Council v Day* [1998] HCA 3 (23 Jan. 1998), para 8 where the principle wrongdoer had been successfully sued.

[59] *Topp v London Country Bus (South West) Ltd* [1993] 1 WLR 976.

v Littlewoods.[60] Such cases[61] pose some of the most difficult cases for judges to handle since the two concerns in tension with one another reflect powerful but ultimately incommensurate moral impulses. In such cases, even where judges agree on the relevant factors to be weighed, it is inevitable that sometimes different judges will give the competing factors different weight, yet each will be unable to explain his particular determination in a way which convincingly justifies it in preference to the different determination of his fellow judges.

Sometimes in these 'failure to control third party cases' additional sound countervailing factors can be discerned in judgments denying a duty of care. Thus not only are there a large number of cases in which there are judicial references to the fact that the defendant is of peripheral causal importance and another party the principal actor,[62] but there are many cases where it is emphasized that the victim himself had adequate means of avoiding the risk eventuating and causing loss (3).[63]

Of course, even in the set of cases of failure to control a third party where the plaintiff did *not* have adequate means of avoiding the risk eventuating, a duty may be denied on the basis of the perceived strength of the libertarian concern and the associated view that, relative to the

60 *Smith v Littlewoods Organisation Ltd* [1987] 1 AC 241.

61 Discussed in Stapleton, 'Peripheral Parties', n. 3 above at 314–17. Such cases are even more troublesome when overlaid with the concerns which may be triggered when the defendant is a public authority, see e.g. *Stovin v Wise* [1996] 3 All ER 801; *Home Office v Dorset Yacht Co. Ltd* [1970] AC 1004; *Pyrenees Shire Council v Day* [1998] HCA 3 (23 Jan. 1998); J. Stapleton, 'Peripheral Parties', n. 3 above at 313–14.

62 See e.g. *Yuen Kun-Yeu v Attorney-General of Hong Kong* [1988] AC 175 at 195; *Richardson v West Lindsay District Council* [1990] 1 WLR 522 at 546; *Ancell v McDermott* [1993] 4 All ER 355 at 363; *Clough v Bussan (West Yorkshire Police Authority)* [1990] 1 All ER 431 at 434; *Murphy v Brentwood District Council* [1991] AC 398 at 487. On the general point see Stapleton, 'Peripheral Parties', n. 3 above at 310–17. That the primary wrongdoing is that of the third party seems an important theme in the judgment on the abuse claims in *X (minors) v Bedfordshire County Council* [1995] 3 All ER 353: 'the courts should proceed with great care before holding liable in negligence those who have been charged by Parliament with the task of protecting society from the wrongdoing of others' (per Lord Browne-Wilkinson at 382).

63 See e.g. *Barrett v Ministry of Defence* [1995] 3 All ER 87 at 95; *Banque Financière de la Cité SA v Westgate Insurance Co. Ltd* [1991] AC 249 at 271; *James McNaughton Paper Group Ltd v Hicks Anderson & Co.* [1991] 2 QB 113 at 128; *Pacific Associates Inc. v Baxter* [1990] 1 QB 993 at 1031; *Minories Finance Ltd v Arthur Young* [1989] 2 All ER 105 at 110; *Investors in Industry Commercial Properties Ltd v South Bedfordshire District Council* [1986] 1 QB 1034 at 1062; *Governors of the Peabody Donation Fund v Sir Lindsay Parkinson & Co. Ltd* [1985] 1 AC 210 at 241; *Yuen Kun-Yeu v Attorney-General of Hong Kong* [1988] AC 175 at 195; *Richardson v West Lindsay District Council* [1990] 1 WLR 522, 539; *Van Oppen v Trustees of the Bedford Charity* [1990] 1 WLR 235. These cases are discussed on the general point in Stapleton, 'Peripheral Parties', n. 3 above at 305–10. For an Australian example, see *San Sebastian Pty Ltd v The Minister* (1986) 162 CLR 341 at 360 (that the plaintiff could have used private advisers). It applies even in cases where the defendant's conduct was a careless act and the loss was physical, e.g. *Philcox v Civil Aviation Authority*, The Times, 8 June 1995 (no duty on supervisory public authority re negligent airworthiness certificate.)

active injurer, the defendant was a mere peripheral party. This is what happened in both *Topp* and *Smith v Littlewoods*, particularly noteworthy examples as they both involved denial of duty in relation to physical loss and in both the principal wrongdoer was not good for judgment. But in a subset of these cases, namely the subset where the defendant is a public authority, we find the denial of a duty being explicitly bolstered by other sound countervailing factors relevant to the conduct of such bodies.[64] One of these is that the imposition of a duty might produce a *specified* unattractive socio-economic impact, namely the *disproportionate* distortion of the budgets of public bodies and/or the diversion of their efforts to the detriment of a specified public interest (4).[65] Interestingly, this factor has been recognized in cases involving physical loss as well as cases involving pure economic loss.[66]

Among other sound countervailing factors are some we have already touched on, for example the indeterminacy concern (5). Even though different commentators elaborate the concept of the rule of law differently, it seems agreed that at least one requirement of that touchstone of legal legitimacy is that a person should be able to know what the law demands of him. The confluence of this constitutional idea and a specific notion of fairness produces the common-law restraining requirement that liability rules allow defendants to know the *extent* of their obligations in advance. Efficiency concerns also demand this: for how else can a person decide whether it is worth engaging in an activity if he cannot know what its costs will be. This means that a powerful countervailing factor is present wherever a duty would expose the defendant to the risk of liability for an indeterminate time or to an indeterminate class or for an indeterminate[67] extent of loss. This is known loosely as the 'floodgates' concern.

Another well-known factor is generated by another constitutional principle, namely the separation of powers. This is the so-called policy/operational distinction (6) which arises in disputes concerning the liability of public bodies. Though this distinction is, at the margins, much easier to state than to apply,[68] it is a restraining factor which has

[64] Whether acts or omissions.

[65] See e.g. *Elguzouli-Daf v Commissioner of Police* [1995] 1 All ER 833 at 842; *Welton v North Cornwall District Council* [1997] 1 WLR 570 at 581, 585; and cases discussed and cited in Stapleton, 'Peripheral Parties', n. 3 above at 313–14.

[66] See *Stovin v Wise* [1996] 3 All ER 801 at 813, 832; the abuse claims in *X (minors) v Bedfordshire County Council* [1995] 3 All ER 353 at 381. See also the police cases such as *Hill v Chief Constable of West Yorkshire* [1988] 2 All ER 238 and *W v Commissioner of Police of the Metropolis*, The Times, 21 July 1997.

[67] Not merely *extensive*, see above. On the general point see *Ultramares Corp. v Touche* (1931) 174 NE 441; Stapleton, 'Agenda', n. 3 above at 253ff.

[68] On the current position in the UK see *X (minors) v Bedfordshire County Council* [1995]

wide support in principle and operates powerfully over a wide range to suppress duties in negligence.

The earlier discussion of the unwanted baby cases also touched on another sound countervailing factor: that to assist this plaintiff would bring the law into disrepute or otherwise injure its dignity (7), in that case by signalling the socially unacceptable view that healthy life could constitute actionable damage in the eyes of the law. This concern with the dignity of the law[69] not only underlies other cases where a duty is in effect denied[70], but also underlies many other controls of the common law of obligations such as the rules of assessment of damages,[71] the defence of illegality[72], sometimes the defence of *volenti*, and sometimes even causation.[73]

In passing let me also note that the concern with the dignity of the law should also be an important factor courts consider when faced with the problem of the civil law being used to evade the demands of criminal law procedure or in effect challenge the outcome of the criminal process.[74] The most notorious recent example of the sort of challenge that

3 All ER 353 at 368–71, 380: if the decision complained of falls within the ambit of a statutory discretion it cannot be actionable at common law; if the decision is so unreasonable that it falls outside that ambit it *may* give rise to common-law liability; but if the factors relevant to the exercise of the discretion include matters of policy (here meaning matters judged unjusticiable such as the 'allocation of resources or the determination of general policy', 380) the court cannot reach the conclusion that the decision was outside that ambit.

[69] Sometimes the law falls between two stools: e.g., in an attempt to avoid the floodgates potential of liability for nervous shock courts formulated artificial duty requirements (spatial, temporal, and relational) widely regarded as themselves bringing the law into disrepute, see Stapleton, 'In Restraint', n. 3 above at 84, 94–5.

[70] Such as the recent decision of the CA that a Health Authority owed no duty to a schizophrenic to provide after-release care (and thereby prevent his killing a stranger): *Clunis v Camden & Islington Health Authority*, The Times, 10 Dec. 1997. For *ex turpi causa* ideas operating at the duty stage see also Cory J (221–222) in *Hall v Hebert* (1993) 2 SCR 159, 101 DLR (4th) 129, 142ff.

[71] See, e.g. *Burns v Edman* [1970] 2 QB 541 (dependency claim related to proceeds of crime).

[72] Albeit in an impressionistic manner which 'cannot be expressed in a way that is self-executing': *Gala v Preston* (1990–1) 172 CLR 243 at 273 (per Brennan CJ). None the less, the better view is that the law recognizes illegality as a defence or a factor countervailing to the recognition of a duty of care in cases where 'for the law to lend its support to the recovery of damages by a plaintiff who suffers injury while participating with the defendant in the commission of a serious criminal act' (Toohey J, at 292) would be repugnant to prevailing community standards and therefore would bring the law into disrepute.

[73] E.g., the better view of *Baker v Willoughby* [1970] AC 467 where the plaintiff was the victim of 2 sufficient tortious causes, was that the law is justified in abandoning the but-for threshold test for factual causation where to apply it would leave the victim of 2 torts worse off than the victim of one. (Note here dignity of the law acts as a *pro-liability* factor.) The same is true in cases of multiple *possible* sufficient causes such as *Cook v Lewis* [1951] SCR 830 and *Summers v Tice* 199 P 2d 1 (Cal. 1948). On the general point of dignity of the law see Stapleton, 'In Restraint', n. 3 above at 94–6 and cases cited therein.

[74] On which see Stapleton, 'Peripheral Parties', n. 3 above at 326–7, and cases cited therein. Compare the comment of Brennan CJ (in a different context) that the law should

can be thrown out to the common law of obligations in this way is the trial and subsequent civil case brought against O. J. Simpson in the United States. A variety of such challenges are feasible (and some are also surfacing in the United Kingdom and elsewhere) not merely in the intentional torts such as assault, but also sometimes in the context of the duty of care: where a person acquitted of murder seeks to establish that his legal team owed him a duty of care to advise him about the potential for a claim for false imprisonment; or a victim or a victim's family sue their legal representatives for failing to advise carefully on the potential of a civil claim against an acquitted person.

An associated countervailing factor is that recognition of a duty of care here might threaten to involve substantial and systemic evidentiary difficulties (which may even bring the law into disrepute) (8). Perhaps the haphazard[75] reluctance of the courts to recognize duties of care in relation to pure loss of a chance is motivated by this concern. Certainly a thread in the judicial concern in nervous shock cases seems to be related to the evidential difficulties, if not impossibility, of drawing a convincing distinction between this syndrome of symptoms and that associated with non-actionable 'mere grief'.

Similar to these last factors is a concern with the judicial system in general. Where a duty might threaten the orderly pursuit and administration of justice (9) courts recognize a powerful countervailing factor.[76]

Clearly that imposition of a duty might threaten the control of public order, the conduct of military operations or national security (10) would also constitute a sound countervailing factor to the recognition of that duty.[77]

We saw earlier that the fact that the plaintiff had means to avoid the risk eventuating and causing loss has often been cited as a factor bolstering a finding that the defendant was a mere peripheral party who should not be burdened with a duty of care. But even where the defendant's carelessness is regarded as causally important and where, therefore, one might expect the law, *prima facie*, to be interested in deterring such conduct, there may be in particular cases more powerful reasons against

'limit the admission of a civil duty of care in order not to trespass upon the operation of the criminal law': *Gala v Preston* (1990–1) 172 CLR 243 at 272.

[75] The curious dichotomy by which loss of a chance arguments are treated differently according to whether the loss is economic or physical began to emerge more than a decade ago: J. Stapleton, 'The Gist of Negligence: Part 1', (1988) 104 LQR 213 at 235.

[76] See, e.g. *Saif Ali v Sydney Mitchell & Co.* [1980] AC 198, Al-*Kandari v J. R. Brown & Co*, [1988] 1 All ER 833 at 836; *Kelley v Corston*, The Times, 20 Aug. 1997, NLJ 5 Sept 1997, 1276 (civil justice); *Elguzouli-Daf v Commissioner of Police* [1995] 1 All ER 833 at 842; *Hill v Chief Constable of West Yorkshire* [1988] 2 All ER 238 (criminal justice).

[77] See, e.g. *Hughes v National Union of Mineworkers* [1991] 4 All ER 278 at 288 and *Mulcahy v Ministry of Defence* [1996] 2 All ER 758 at 772.

the imposition of a duty consistent with an interest in deterring such potent carelessness. For example, in a solid series of cases such as *Simaan* British appellate courts have refused the protection of a duty of care to plaintiffs who, despite not being in contractual privity with the defendant, were linked by a chain of contracts through a middle party to the defendant (these are the so-called 'contractual matrix' cases).[78] A similar phenomenon exists in cases such as *The Esso Bernicia*, where though the plaintiff may have had no dealings with the defendant, the plaintiff had had dealings with the owner of property the injury to which by the careless defendant had caused economic loss to the plaintiff (the damage to property of third party cases).[79] It is noteworthy that all these cases involved pure economic loss and all involved commercial plaintiffs.

In each case the commercial plaintiff was seeking to use tort to provide it with an entitlement against a distant defendant. In each case this was an entitlement which the plaintiff could have obtained in contract against the middle-party in contractual matrix situations or the property owner in the damage to property of third-party cases. Had such protection been secured it would thereby have introduced, in the contractual matrix cases, an incentive on that middle party to extract similar protection from the defendant (and thereby effect deterrence of the defendant without the intervention of tort). In the damage to property of third-party cases the securing of such contractual protection from the owner would have given the plaintiff a claim against the owner who could then have recovered the relevant amount as part of his loss in his negligence claim against the defendant for injury to his own property, again a situation which allows deterrence of the defendant without the intervention of tort.

In these circumstances recognition of a duty would in the future positively encourage advertent parties in the position of the plaintiff to be dependent, to refrain from available self-help conduct (namely, contractual protection from the middle party or owner) which would have secured protection from economic loss for them (while also achieving deterrence of the defendant). Courts seem almost uniformly unwilling

[78] See, e.g. *Simaan General Contracting Co. v Pilkington Glass Ltd* [1988] QB 758 (approved by Lord Goff in *Henderson v Merrett Syndicates Ltd* [1994] 3 All ER 506 at 534–535); *Muirhead v Industrial Tank Specialities Ltd* [1986] QB 507; *Pacific Associates Inc. v Baxter* [1990] 1 QB 993. See also the New Zealand cases discussed below.

[79] See, e.g. from the House of Lords *Esso Petroleum Co. v Hall Russell & Co. (The Esso Bernicia)* [1989] AC 643 at 663, 665, 676; *The Aliakmon* [1986] AC 785 at 819. See also the dissent of La Forest in *Norsk Pacific Steamship Co. Ltd v Canadian National Railway Co.* (1992) 91 DLR (4th) 289 at 349: 'it is hard to imagine a more sophisticated group of plaintiffs than the users of railway bridges. These parties have access to the full range of protective option . . . (including) contracts with the bridge owner.' For a detailed discussion of both types of case see Stapleton, 'Peripheral Parties', n. 3 above at 327ff.

positively to encourage such dependency and 'free-riding' on the tort of negligence, at least in relation to economic loss, whether it be in a contractual matrix case (which we might call 'the *Simaan* principle') or a case concerning damage to property of a third party (which we might call 'the *Esso Bernicia* principle') (11).

The force of this countervailing concern not to assist those who have adequate means of deterring the defendant and protecting themselves is underscored by the fact that the only major case out of line with this approach in the U.K. is the contractual matrix case of *Junior Books* (where the plaintiff not only had adequate alternative protection in place, via its contract with the middle party,[80] to protect itself and deterring the defendant but had that contractual entitlement *and* had exploited it to recover damages from the middle party[81]). Significantly, although *Junior Books* was a decision of the House of Lords, it has not been applied by an appellate court in England[82] and even judges elsewhere known for their sensitivity to pro-liability factors have strongly hinted that the case is one which should not be followed.[83]

That the plaintiff in contractual matrix cases had an adequate opportunity to use his contract with the middle party to protect himself and achieve (albeit indirectly) the deterrence of the defendant is not only a sound rationale for the denial of a duty in such cases, but it also provides a convincing distinction to be drawn between these cases (some of which, like *Simaan*, involved economic loss resulting from the acquisition of property from the middle party) and *Smith v Bush Eric S.*[84] In the latter case a duty to avoid economic loss was recognized in the context of the acquisition of property in favour of a non-commercial plaintiff who, despite being in a contractual chain that led to the defendant, was prevented by standard terms within that chain (and their presence in all alternative transactions in that market sector) from obtaining contractual protection from the middle party for the risk involved. In an exceptionally important analogue, the High Court of Australia similarly allowed a subsequent non-commercial owner of a dwelling to sue a contractually distant builder in circumstances where the relevant market conditions (*caveat emptor* in the sale of used dwelling houses) prevented

[80] The subtle implication of this factual feature is discussed below.

[81] See, e.g. *Pacific Associates Inc. v Baxter* [1990] 1 QB 993; *Banque Financière de la Cité SA v Westgate Insurance Co. Ltd* [1991] AC 249; *Marc Rich & Co. AG v Bishop Rock Marine Co. Ltd* [1994] 1 Lloyd's Rep. 492. See Stapleton, 'Peripheral Parties', n. 3 above at 330.

[82] Contrast the position in Scotland: J. M. Thomson, 'A Prophet Not Rejected in His Own Land', (1994) 110 LQR 361.

[83] See later discussion of Cooke P's comments in *Invercargill City Council v Hamlin.*

[84] [1990] 1 AC 831. On this general point see Stapleton, 'Peripheral Parties', n. 3 above at 335–7.

the plaintiff from obtaining the relevant protection from the middle party with whom she was in privity.[85]

Note that courts are not necessarily adopting some unexplained differential between commercial and non-commercial plaintiffs here. The concern not positively to encourage dependency and free-riding is only triggered where the plaintiff has sufficient muscle in the relevant contractual context to be able to negotiate for protection with the middle party were a duty to be denied. This simply tends to be more likely in cases involving commercial plaintiffs and less likely where the plaintiff is a consumer.

Further subtlety in the courts' approach here is revealed when we consider contractual matrix cases where the plaintiff already has protection from economic loss by his contract with the middle party.[86] Importantly, even here we see that powerful commercial plaintiffs such as *Simaan* are denied the protection of a tort duty. In contrast, those plaintiffs perceived as prone consumers, such as the indirect Names were perceived to be in *Henderson*,[87] are allowed such protection. The countervailing concern about dependency and free-riding provides a sound rationale for this otherwise baffling distinction: that whereas the recognition of a duty to protect the former type of plaintiffs might positively encourage them to use their negotiating power to 'cash in' on their tort entitlement in their dealings with the middle party, protection of the prone consumer will not result in such exploitation.[88]

Now that judgments have begun to reveal judicial sensitivity to the possibility that plaintiffs could secure both protection from and deterrence (albeit indirect) of the defendant using contract, the reason for certain stress points in the law becomes clearer. We have already seen how this broad concern about not encouraging dependency on and exploitation of tort explains the widespread rejection of the decision in *Junior Books*. But the concern also allows us to formulate the anxiety

[85] Though it must be conceded that the principle under discussion was not directly expounded: *Bryan v Maloney* (1994–5) 182 CLR 609. Note Toohey J's sensible concern that 'confining liability to the first purchaser might encourage sham first sales as a means of insulating builders from liability' (at 663).

[86] Significantly, this was also the case in a number of other cases from which the principle under discussion is drawn: e.g. *Simaan General Contracting Co. v Pilkington Glass Ltd* [1988] QB 758; *Muirhead v Industrial Tank Specialities Ltd* [1986] QB 507; *Pacific Associates Inc. v Baxter* [1990] 1 QB 993; *Banque Financière de la Cité SA v Westgate Insurance Co. Ltd* [1991] AC 249; *Marc Rich & Co. AG v Bishop Rock Marine Co. Ltd* [1994] 1 Lloyd's Rep. 492.

[87] *Henderson v Merrett Syndicates Ltd* [1994] 3 WLR 761.

[88] This suggests however that consumers and buyers of goods should be able to sue distant manufacturers for pure economic loss (e.g. where the item, say a TV, simply does not work): a matter which has yet to receive authoritative determination by an appellate court in the UK (presumably because the warranty remedy for consumers against retailers is so effective).

which surrounds apparently more established precedents. Take two examples. First, *D&F Estates*: in this case might it not be argued that the *Simaan* countervailing concern was absent on the ground that the plaintiffs could not realistically have obtained contractual protection from the middle party against the defendant's negligence, nor were they part of a class likely positively to become dependent on and to exploit any tort entitlement granted them? Secondly, *Hedley Byrne*: if the plaintiffs in *Simaan* and so on are required to seek protection (and thereby secure indirectly the deterrence of the defendant) via contractual arrangements with the middle party, why is not a commercial plaintiff who had *direct* dealings with the defendant, whether amounting to a contract or not, told that it had an adequate avenue of self-protection (and route to deter the defendant), namely by contract with that party for that protection; and that, just because it had failed to help itself, tort was not willing to step in and bail such a party out of its economically unwise gamble in relying on the defendant's advice without contractual or other protection?[89]

The law is concerned to prevent itself being the instrument by which parties may exploit others in breach of (even minimal) good faith principles. Thus it has been held, for example, that a duty would be denied where its imposition would allow the plaintiff to circumvent a positive arrangement or understanding (to which *both* the plaintiff and defendant were clearly parties) as to where the relevant risk would fall and/or the avenues of legal complaint the plaintiff would use (12).[90]

Another feasible countervailing factor is that, for some *specified* and sound reason, the area is one more appropriate for Parliamentary action (13).[91] Of course, the force of such reasoning rests on how convincing those reasons are.

A final example of a convincing countervailing factor can be deduced from the reasoning of the House of Lords in *Spring v Guardian Assurance plc*.[92] In that case the view was taken that there would be no liability in

[89] See, e.g. the attitude of the court in *Pacific Associates Inc. v Baxter* [1990] 1 QB 993 at 1037, 1020. See also *South Pacific Manufacturing Co. Ltd v NZ Security Consultants and Investigations Ltd* [1992] 2 NZLR 282 at 308. See Stapleton, 'Peripheral Parties', n. 3 above at 321–4.

[90] *Pacific Associates Inc. v Baxter* [1990] 1 QB 993 at 1032, 1010–11, 1020–3; *Norwich City Council v Harvey* [1989] 1 WLR 828 at 837 (a physical loss case); *The Pioneer Container* [1994] 3 WLR 1 at 10. But caution is required here to avoid the privity fallacy: see Stapleton, 'Peripheral Parties', n. 3 above at 328–31 and cf. *British Telecommunications plc v James Thomson & Sons (Engineers) Ltd*, The Times, 28 Jan. 1997. Cf. also *Morris v Ford Motor Company Ltd* [1973] QB 792 (a case on subrogation not duty) where there was a judicial concern not to allow the party claiming subrogation to disturb such a joint understanding (which was crucial to harmonious industrial relations).

[91] See, e.g. *Winnipeg Child and Family Services v G (DF)*, n. 14 above, discussed below.

[92] [1994] 3 All ER 129.

the tort of negligence where carelessly made true statements cause injury. Although the Law Lords did not spell out which analytical label was most appropriate to carry this message, the 'no-duty' packaging is clearly the most convenient. What needs to be signalled is the *generality* of the concern here: that liability would be inconsistent with free (true) speech (14). That would not be conveyed as forcefully if, for example, the no-liability result was packaged as a case of there being a duty of care *even with regard to the truth* but liability ultimately never attaching because the damage is always caused by the underlying truth and not by the carelessness of the statement.[93]

A Few Examples from New Zealand, Australia and Canada

Just as many appellate judges in the United Kingdom have become more open about the substantive factors they have considered in resolving claims for novel duties of care, so too have many judges in New Zealand, Australia, and Canada. Space here precludes the rigorous discussion which these many factors deserve. But for three reasons it is worth mentioning a few examples. First, there will always be factors in the jurisprudence of other countries which, by mere happenstance, have not yet been thrown up by the fact situations litigated in one's own system but which could well weigh with local appellate judges if a suitable case came before them: indeed, in my view this is the most fruitful harvest of comparative legal study. Secondly, a few Commonwealth examples help confirm the variety of factors to which the common law is sensitive and help bolster the associated argument I have been making that this phenomenon prevents any formulation of a common denominator 'test' of duty in the same way no common denominator 'test' of 'breach of a standard of care' can be formulated. Thirdly, this variety ranges from factors, such as the indeterminacy concern, whose weight is uniformly recognized, to factors such as a concern with preserving local customs of rural hospitality (see below) whose recognition and weighting obviously varies across jurisdictions: the source of that divergence in the common law world is to be welcomed not feared.

Judgments of the New Zealand Court of Appeal contain some of the clearest statements of the earlier important principle that the law should not positively encourage dependency and free-riding on tort, where the

[93] See also the explicit rejection of a duty 'not to injure the plaintiff's reputation by true statements' in *Bell-Booth Group Ltd v Attorney-General* [1989] 3 NZLR 148 at 156 (per Cooke P.). Cf. *Lonrho plc v Fayed (No. 5)* [1994] 1 All ER 188 at 195 (CA) where a similar refusal to allow the telling of the truth to be actionable is made by the CA in the context of the tort of conspiracy to injure by lawful means.

plaintiff could have protected himself in contract either directly with the defendant or with a middle party. So, for example, in *Invercargill City Council v Hamlin*[94] President Cooke strongly hinted that were a case parallel to *Junior Books* to come before that court, a duty would be denied on the basis that 'the network of contractual relationships normally provides sufficient avenues of redress to make the imposition of supervening tort duties not demanded'. Indeed in *South Pacific Manufacturing Co. Ltd v NZ Security Consultants and Investigations Ltd*[95] Richardson explicitly recognised that this countervailing concern could arise between commercial parties who had had *direct* dealings, stating, 'I cannot see any justification for allowing [the plaintiffs] a greater recovery through tort than they were prepared to pay for in contract'.[96]

That courts are able to draw clear and convincing restraining force from a specific statute is well-illustrated by the judgments of the New Zealand Court of Appeal in *Kavanagh v Continental Shelf Company (No. 46)*.[97] Here the judges rejected the claim that the agent of a council owed a duty in the circumstances on the basis that to recognize such a duty would undermine the clear policy of a statute (sound countervailing factor 15). The relevant statute was designed to protect public bodies from liability in contract for unauthorized contracts purportedly made on their behalf. Were the 'carelessness' of the agent in making such an unauthorized contract to lead to his liability in the tort of negligence, the council might well have been vulnerable, via the doctrine of vicarious liability, to the very sort of liability from which the statute sought to protect it.

Another potent countervailing factor was cited by the High Court of Australia in the *San Sebastian* case.[98] Here the claim that a public body owed a duty of care to a property developer was rejected on the grounds, *inter alia,* that recognition of a duty to an individual might clash with, inhibit, or frustrate a specifiable 'public interest' with which the defendant has been charged (sound countervailing factor 16). In other words, even where a court may characterize the defendant's conduct as 'operational', a duty might be denied to an individual on the basis of such a clash of interests. Of course, such a factor, also often deployed by British appellate judges,[99] can only have weight if the

[94] [1994] 3 NZLR 513 at 520. [95] [1992] 2 NZLR 282. [96] Ibid at 308.

[97] [1993] 2 NZLR 648. A parallel concern seems to underlie the rejection of a duty on the individual social workers and the psychiatrist in *X (minors) v Bedfordshire County Council* [1995] 3 All ER 353 at 384.

[98] *San Sebastian Pty Ltd v The Minister* (1986) 162 CLR 341 at 374.

[99] See, e.g. *X (minors) v Bedfordshire County Council* [1995] 3 All ER 353 at 371 (per Lord Browne-Wilkinson), a common-law duty should be denied if it would be 'inconsistent with, or have a tendency to discourage, the due performance by the local authority of its statutory duties'; *Davis v Radcliffe* [1990] 1 WLR 821 at 827 (per Lord Goff), typically 'the

specific clash of private and public interests can be convincingly established. That this *is* feasible is shown by some of the police cases. That it is even feasible in the case of regulatory bodies with only one field of operation is shown by cases where a public body is authorized solely to monitor the soundness of companies or banks. Such a body might decide not to warn individual investors and depositors of evidence of maladministration of the company or bank, or not to warn them of its financial plight in the hope that the company or bank can put its house in order or trade out of its difficulties rather than risk damage to public confidence in the company or banking system.

The *San Sebastian* judgments contain another explicit sound countervailing factor (17): that 'to impose a legal duty of care on the unsolicited and voluntary giving of any information and advice on serious or business matters would chill communications which are a valuable source of wisdom and expertise for a person contemplating a course of conduct'.[100] This is yet another concern which might be thought to throw doubt on the correctness of the decision in *Hedley Byrne*.

The Australian High Court has also recently concerned itself with a factor, known as the doctrine of 'general reliance',[101] from whose problematic form it is possible to tease out a sound pro-liability factor. It was noted earlier that where the complaint against a defendant is merely that it did not control the principal author of the plaintiff's injury there is, for statable reasons, a greater reluctance to impose a duty than in cases of the defendant's overt act causing harm. Since many complaints against public bodies relate to their regulatory functions this countervailing factor often arises in cases involving public authority defendants. (It was in an attempt to define cases where, nonetheless, public bodies would owe duties that it was thought that a concept of the public's general 'reliance or dependence'[102] might assist.)

very nature of the task, with its emphasis on the broader public interest' militates against a duty to an individual; *W v Home Office*, The Times, 14 Mar. 1997 (CA); *Welton v North Cornwall District Council* [1997] 1 WLR 570 at 581, 585 'the interests of the individual may have to be sacrificed for the greater common good' (per Ward LJ). On the general point see Stapleton, 'Peripheral Parties', n. 3 above at 313–14 and case law cited therein. This factor is closely associated with that couched in terms of the distortion of public budgets and/or activities (see above).

100 *San Sebastian Pty Ltd v The Minister* (1986) 162 CLR 341 at 372.

101 Formulated by Mason CJ in *Sutherland Shire Council v Heyman* (1985) 157 CLR 424 at 463–4, 470.

102 Mason was happy to formulate the idea in both terms: ibid at 470. Unhappily it came to be known by its weaker limb: general reliance. Mason appreciated that simply because the public is vulnerable to a risk and subliminally 'relies' on a government agency would not be sufficient (after all, citizens 'rely' on police to catch criminals but no duty is owed here) but attempts to define the idea more narrowly were couched in terms of general *reliance* and were perceived as unconvincing: see *Pyrenees Shire Council v Day* [1998] HCA 3 (23

In rare cases, however, the regulatory activity of a public body does not consist of the surveillance of risky behaviour of third parties: rather, the public body has *alone* been allocated the role of the organization of behaviour of others and is the sole creator of the risk. Air traffic control is a good example, where the public body charged to allocate air space carelessly orders two aircraft on to a collision course and they obey and collide. In such cases, the public body is clearly the principal causal player and the public is not only completely prone to the relevant risk but is dependant solely on the public body discharging its role carefully. The dependence is not only complete but it is a dependence which is exclusively focused on the public body by the nature of how the risk came about. This can be contrasted with similar public regulatory roles such as checking on the safety of aircraft where the aircraft's operator and manufacturer might be regarded as being the principal parties in relation to how the risk came about and the regulator occupying a merely peripheral role.[103] Were the doctrine to be couched only in terms of 'general dependence' or better still, *'exclusive dependence'*, and narrowly defined to catch only cases where it is the public body *alone* which has control over the relevant risk, it would undoubtedly constitute a sound if rarely triggered pro-liability factor (sound pro-liability factor 4).

On the other hand, the fact that the plaintiff was exclusively dependent on the conduct of the defendant may, nevertheless, be outweighed by the strength of countervailing concerns. This is well-illustrated by the recent judgment of the majority of the Canadian Supreme Court in the extraordinary case of *Winnipeg Child and Family Services v G. (D.F.)*[104] where, *inter alia*, the question arose whether a pregnant woman owed a duty of care to her unborn child in relation to 'lifestyle choices'. Such a child is, of course, exclusively dependant on its mother in relation to risks arising from such choices. Among the range of countervailing factors cited by McLachlin J writing for the majority were the following: a duty here might encourage abortion (sound countervailing factor 18);[105] recognition of a

Jan. 1998); *Stovin v Wise* [1996] 3 All ER 801. Even where the regulator has entered into some course of action to control the third party then (carelessly) omits some possible 'follow-through', this may not necessarily be judged sufficient to warrant imposition of a duty. For example it is not uncommon for police to decide to caution rather than charge a person who goes on to re-offend: would it be in the public interest for all such incidents potentially to give rise to legal challenge on the basis that care required some type of post-caution surveillance of the person?

[103] The role may even be judged peripheral relative to that of another party where the damage suffered was physical and the regulator's conduct was: an act, for example see *Philcox v Civil Aviation Authority*, The Times, 8 June 1995 (CA) (contrast the recognition of a duty in *Perrett v Collins*, The Times, 23 June 1998 (CA); or a failure to continue to act, for example see *Stovin v Wise* [1996] 3 All ER 801 on which contrast *Pyrenees Shire Council v Day* [1998] HCA 3 (23 Jan. 1998).

[104] See n. 14 above.

[105] Ibid, para 44.

duty might overall have deleterious effects on those in the position of the plaintiff (19);[106] recognition of a duty here would render actionable defendant conduct (such as drug abuse) which was not a free choice and so would not be effective in deterring it (20);[107] the content of the duty could not be defined adequately narrowly with bright lines (21);[108] avoidance of breach of such a duty would be particularly onerous on disadvantaged groups (22);[109] the duty would effect a major departure from traditional legal categorization of a fundamental relationship and such change is best left to the legislature (23);[110] and since a duty here would constitute a potentially extensive invasion of a 'fundamental' aspect of liberty, women's autonomy over their own bodies, this justified 'great caution' and supported the view that it was an area best left to the legislature (24).[111]

Concluding Remarks

Let me make a few remarks before I summarize the above selections from the 'judicial menus' of duty factors. A first and obvious point is that these lists are by no means complete or closed. The changing nature and diversity of social circumstances will continue to reveal factors which might convincingly weigh with courts in determining the appropriate limits of the obligation in negligence. Moreover, just as the lists will change over time, so too may the judicial weight given each factor. In both these phenomena lies the richness and flexibility of the common-law method.

Secondly, concerns which have sound weight in this field must, by modern common-sense juridical logic, run throughout the law: the law should not speak with a forked tongue.[112] The parallel point also holds: factors which sensibly concern judges elsewhere in the law might well have a valid resonance here. An example which also illustrates the cultural specificity which relevant factors may have can be drawn from Australian jurisprudence dealing with the issue of landowners' liability for the escape of fire. Since 1914 the Australian High Court

[106] Ibid, paras 42–4. Because, e.g., an addicted mother might choose not to seek pre-natal health care for fear of legal action against her.

[107] Ibid, para 41.

[108] Ibid, para 39. The legislature was in a better position to craft a 'solution that is principled and minimally intrusive to pregnant women' (para 56).

[109] Ibid, para 40.

[110] Ibid, para 29. 'The pregnant woman and her unborn child are one' (para 55).

[111] Ibid, paras 34, 37, 45, 50, & 55.

[112] We have seen, e.g., that the concern not to bring the law into disrepute underlies other analytical compartments of this tort itself such as the defence of illegality and even causation. Similarly many sound concerns of the law have earlier surfaced under the 'packaging' of remoteness of damage and these might also be considered relevant to the duty question.

has rejected the special *ignis suus* rule (which makes the landowner vicariously liable for such escapes caused by the negligence of mere licensees) on the explicit basis that 'contemporary conditions in this country have no real similarity to urban conditions in medieval England'[113] and that such a liability rule would have been an intolerable restriction on 'the tradition of hospitality in the bush and would have been a disincentive to pastoralists to allow Aboriginal communities to camp on their holdings'.[114] Presumably equivalent concerns not to discourage socially beneficial forms of hospitality (sound countervailing factor 25) would have weight in duty-of-care cases where the facts raise the issue. Similarly, given the law is keen elsewhere to frustrate dishonesty, bad faith, duress, and so on, we might confidently predict that such factors would not be ignored in the duty analysis where the facts raise the issue.

Thirdly, while the listing of these judicial menus of sound factors relevant to the duty issue help unmask the substantive determinations being made by judges in this field, they cannot operate as some sort of mechanical guide as to how a novel case will be decided in the future. This is because, at the end of the day, even if judges agree on the relevant factors to be weighed in the individual case, different judges may well place different weight on competing factors and do so quite reasonably. As we have seen, this is often the case. It is, after all, the source of the embarrassment for the law in claims asserting that the defendant should be under a duty of affirmative action.

Fourthly, there are areas in which, even were judges to agree on the relevant duty factors *and* their weight, the common law does not possess the tools necessary to draw coherent non-arbitrary lines around an obligation. A classic example of this sort of conceptual helplessness is liability for nervous shock. To the evident and understandable frustration of appellate judges, this is an area where it seems that all that can be done with common-law techniques to restrain the tort within acceptable limits is to adopt the sort of artificial and incoherent boundary rules which currently exist, and which are a sore humiliation to the law.

Fifthly, drawing together these judicial policy menus allows us to pinpoint areas of inconsistency and tension in the current law. Thus it allows us to see why, in the area of economic loss resulting from the acquisition of property, claims against a local authority should, contrary to past judicial treatment in the United Kingdom, be treated separately

[113] '[W]here the escape of domestic fire rivalled plague and war as a cause of general catastrophe': *Burnie Port Authority v General Jones Pty Ltd* (1992–4) 179 CLR 520 at 534 (per the majority).

[114] Ibid at 566 (per Brennan CJ). See also *Whinfield v Lands Purchase and Management Board* (1914) 18 CLR 606 at 616 (per Griffiths CJ).

from claims against builders. This is because in the former cases a powerful countervailing factor is present which is absent in the latter cases: namely, that imposition of a duty on such a public body might produce a particular unattractive socio-economic impact, namely the disproportionate distortion of public budgets and activity.

Sixthly, it is noteworthy that among factors explicitly cited by judges recently in the analysis of duty, there seem to be significantly more factors countervailing to recognition of a duty than factors weighing in favour. This phenomenon, probably[115] caused by the unwise adoption of sequential two- and three-step duty 'tests' which separate the 'proximity' determination from, and therefore tend to emphasize, countervailing factors, might superficially mislead observers into thinking that the project of recording such judicial menus of recognized duty factors is somehow motivated by a crude concern to rein in liability. This would be misguided as well as short-sighted because only by carefully pinpointing and determining the limits of countervailing factors can we guard against the emphasis on restraint being misapplied. Thus, for example, even this short study allows us to see that though there may be powerful reasons for the denial of duty in *Murphy*'s case, the denial in *D&F Estates* is much less convincing.

Seventhly, in constructing these menus I have simply examined appellate judgments and evaluated the coherence of the reasons actually stated by the judges. There is a separate project to be pursued which looks at which factors *should* be considered relevant to duty even though they do not yet surface in judgments.

Eighthly, these judicial menus underscore why there can be no 'test' for duty. The fact situations are so various and raise such a variety of different factors for courts to weigh in their determination that no directive formula is feasible. Cases such as *White v Jones* and *Henderson*, for example, are characterized by the *dissimilarity* of relevant factors not their similarity.

Finally, we might ask what will the most powerful judgments in the field of novel duties of care look like?

1. They will be judgments which explicitly eschew any purported reliance on a directive 'test for the duty of care', explicitly eschew the incantation of formulaic labels as devices for *determining* the specific duty issue at hand and which instead spell out in detail from the facts the substantive factors weighing with the judge, both those for and those weighing against recognition of a duty. Under

[115] Conversely it might be the result of a period of concern with the rapid growth of liability in the field.

this approach where all factors for and against are balanced together and not evaluated separately and in sequence, the analysis does not contain the sort of potential for pro-plaintiff (or pro-defendant) bias which bedevilled the sequential application of the well-known two- and three-stage 'tests' for duty.[116]

2. Earlier case law would not be pre-classified into 'pockets'[117] based on crude factual similarity but examined to see where such substantive factors had arisen before and how courts had dealt with them. Thus a case involving, say negligent words, would not be pre-assigned to a pocket of precedent relating to 'liability for negligent statements' which is an association of cases with no coherent policy basis. Instead it would be considered in the light of any case law there might be[118] relating to whatever individual *substantive* factors the fact situation threw up, even where the overall factual contexts of such precedents look quite different to the case in hand: for example, the facts of the case in hand may throw up the indeterminacy concern; or a concern to safeguard public budgets from disproportionate distortion; or a concern not to encourage dependency and free-riding on tort; or all of these factors.
3. The caution of incrementalism would be transformed into a caution in relation to departing too radically from past judicial weightings of substantive policy factors. Thus if, in the past, the libertarian concern has consistently prevented a duty of affirmative action being owed to strangers, caution in overturning this strong position would be both understandable and acceptable in the light of the law's interest in certainty.
4. If it is thought helpful, this entire process could be couched in terms which, though previously troublesome because of their vague and/

[116] Even the otherwise admirable judgment of Kirby J in *Day*'s case [1998] HCA 3 (23 Jan. 1998) finally falls into this sort of trap by separating out the establishment of 'proximity' from 'a third question' where issues of legal policy might justify rejection of a duty even to a party who had established proximity. The separation of stage 2 'proximity factors' from stage 3 'legal policy factors' is productive of confusing and unnecessary line-drawing: is the sort of concern underlying the denial of a duty in *Simaan* one of the former or the latter? Why should lower courts be sent on the fruitless errand of allocating relevant factors between stage 2 and stage 3? Might it threaten an unintended bias against claims, given that a whole step (i.e. step 3) is devoted entirely to countervailing concerns? Conversely, might this rigidly sequential analysis of factors generate a pro-plaintiff dynamic in much the way the *Anns* approach allegedly did?

[117] For a detailed criticism of 'pockets' and 'incrementalism' when defined in relation to analogous fact situations rather than in terms of substantive policy factors, see Stapleton, 'In Restraint', n. 3 above.

[118] Of course some cases will present concerns which have not yet been presented to appellate courts. As *Donoghue*'s case established, this lack of a relevant 'pocket' of analogous cases should not be fatal to the claim.

or shifting meaning, could now be used with sharpened and therefore more effective definition:

- First, the judge would state that the plaintiff must establish that the relevant risk was ***foreseeable***.
- Secondly, the judge would state that the plaintiff must establish why the law should conclude he was owed a ***duty*** by the defendant and the judge would state that to do this the plaintiff must show that, taken together and on balance, the pro-liability concerns raised by the facts outweigh factors countervailing to liability.
- Next, the judge would identify with sufficient precision to give later guidance to practitioners and judges alike which pro-liability and countervailing concerns are raised by the particular fact situation.
- The judge would consider previous case law, if any, in which these concerns were raised and the weight given them by previous courts (being cautious about departing more than ***incrementally*** from such earlier weightings).
- The judge would determine what weight, *in this judge's own view*, it would be ***fair, just and reasonable*** to give to the relevant factors and therefore, on balancing them together, whether a duty of care should be recognized.
- After such an open analysis, but only then, it would be acceptable for the judge to deliver his conclusion in the form of the familiar 'packaging' of: the defendant owed a ***duty*** of care; the plaintiff was ***proximate*** to the defendant; and the plaintiff was a ***neighbour*** of the defendant whom the latter ought reasonably have taken care not to injure.

Summary of Selected Duty Factors

Unconvincing Factors

In Favour of Recognition of Duty

(1) Recognition of a duty will promote compensation (of the plaintiff).
(2) Recognition of a duty will promote deterrence (of the defendant).
(3) Recognition of a duty will promote loss-spreading (e.g. via the insurance of the defendant).
(4) The defendant is (and the defendant class is likely to be) insured.
(5) The defendant has (and the defendant class is likely to have) a deep pocket.
(6) A mere assertion that the defendant voluntarily assumed responsibility or a mere assertion that in law the defendant should be taken to have voluntarily assumed responsibility.

Countervailing to the Recognition of Duty

(1) The plaintiff is (and the plaintiff class is likely to be) insured.
(2) The plaintiff has (and the plaintiff class is likely to have) a deep pocket.
(3) A duty would expose the defendant to a large volume of claims.
(4) The law has never recognized a duty here before.
(5) Imposition of liability would have a substantial socio-economic and/or re-distributive effect.
(6) Imposition of liability would create a large new area of liability.
(7) The bald assertion that the loss here was pure economic loss (on the erroneous assumption that all such claims threatened indeterminate liability).
(8) A bald unqualified assertion that words are different to acts and that while the law may recognize a duty in a parallel case involving words, the mere fact that in the present case the conduct was an act takes it outside that 'pocket' of liability.
(9) A bald unqualified assertion that a particular piece of legislation impliedly 'covers the field'.
(10) A bald unqualified assertion that this is an area more properly to be seen as the province of Parliament.
(11) A bald unqualified assertion that this is an area more properly to be seen as the province of contract.
(12) To recognize a duty here would be tantamount to giving the

plaintiff the benefit of a contract to which he or she was not a party (I call this 'the evasion of privity fallacy').

(13) That the duty would in practice make the defendant the insurer of the plaintiff.

(14) That recognition of a duty would upset the defendant's expectations (and other forms of the 'privity fallacy').

(15) The plaintiff had another cause of action against this defendant and/or that the defendant had a defence to a different cause of action which the plaintiff had against him.

Convincing Factors

In Favour of Recognition of Duty

(1) That the proper vindication of the law's concern with the physical security of persons and property justifies a duty being imposed on a party by whose careless act the plaintiff's person or property has been physically damaged.

(2) Denial of a duty would tend to discourage rescue.

(3) Denial of a duty would tend to encourage abortion.

(4) That the relevant risk was in the exclusive control of the defendant on whom the plaintiff was, therefore, 'exclusively dependent'.

Countervailing to the Recognition of Duty

(1) That the proper vindication of the law's concern with the liberty of the individual justifies a refusal to recognise any duty of affirmative action towards a stranger.

(2) The defendant is causally only a peripheral party.

(3) The plaintiff himself had adequate means of avoiding the risk eventuating and causing loss.

(4) The imposition of a duty might produce a *specified* unattractive socio-economic impact such as the disproportionate distortion of the budgets and/or activities of public bodies to the detriment of a specified public interest.

(5) A duty here would expose the defendant to the risk of liability for an indeterminate time or to an indeterminate class or for an indeterminate (not merely extensive) extent of damage (the 'floodgates' or 'indeterminacy' concern).

(6) The concern to separate executive and judicial powers requires

the denial of a duty in relation to the broad policy decisions of public bodies as opposed to operational conduct.

(7) Recognition of a duty here might bring the law into disrepute or otherwise injure its dignity.

(8) Imposition of a duty here might threaten to involve substantial and systemic evidentiary difficulties which may even bring the law into disrepute.

(9) Imposition of a duty here might threaten the orderly administration of justice.

(10) Imposition of a duty might threaten the control of public order, the conduct of military operations or national security.

(11) Recognition of a duty would in the future positively encourage advertent parties in the position of the plaintiff to be dependent on tort, to refrain from available self-help avenues, namely contract with the middle-party (in contractual matrix cases), the third party owner (in the damage to property of a third party cases) or directly with the defendant, which self-help would have secured protection from economic loss while also achieving deterrence of the defendant. This is the concern about encouraging 'dependency' or 'free-riding' on tort.

(12) Recognition of a duty might encourage exploitation of others in breach of good faith principles, for example recognition of a duty here would allow the plaintiff to circumvent a positive arrangement/understanding (to which both the plaintiff and defendant were parties) as to where the relevant risk would fall and/or the avenue(s) of complaint the plaintiff would use.

(13) For some explicit and sound reason(s) the area is one more appropriate to Parliamentary action.

(14) Imposition of a duty would be inconsistent with free (true) speech.

(15) Imposition of a duty here would undermine the clear policy of a piece of legislation.

(16) Recognition of a duty to this individual, even in relation to what is judged 'operational' conduct of the defendant, might clash with, inhibit or frustrate this public authority defendant's pursuit of the public interest with which it has been charged.

(17) To impose a legal duty of care on the unsolicited and voluntary giving of any information and advice on serious or business matters would chill communications which are a valuable source of wisdom and expertise for a person contemplating a course of conduct.

(18) Recognition of a duty would tend to encourage abortion.

(19) Recognition of a duty might overall have deleterious effects on those in the position of the plaintiff.
(20) Recognition of a duty would render actionable defendant conduct which was not a free choice and so would not be effective in deterring it.
(21) The content of the duty could not be defined adequately narrowly with bright lines.
(22) Avoidance of breach of such a duty would be particularly onerous on disadvantaged groups.
(23) The duty would effect a major departure from traditional legal categorisation of a fundamental relationship and such change is best left to the legislature.
(24) The duty would constitute a major invasion of a 'fundamental' aspect of liberty (such as autonomy over one's own body) and such change is best left to the legislature.
(25) Recognition of a duty would discourage socially beneficial forms of hospitality.

5

The Staggering March of Negligence

Tony Weir

Although the twentieth century has been in many respects what Shakespeare called 'The expense of spirit in a waste of shame'[1]—as it maunders to its end, we see the leaders of Western Europe adamant to create an insanely bureaucratic and multilingual ideological empire such as the nations of Eastern Europe have just broken loose from, and England, in an anachronistic preference for geography over history, abandoning the law it gave to the English-speaking world and turning its back on those to whom it was given—yet for the time being the common lawyers of England can take comfort in the success of the tort of negligence: announced in hieratic terms in 1932, its principle of liability has become so dominant that sixty years later Lord Goff could state that 'the law of tort is the general law, out of which the parties can, if they wish, contract'.[2] The contrast with the position in 1900 could hardly be more marked.

This royal progress has not been uniformly welcomed.[3] Lord Templeman has been scathing. In a case where an attempt was made to extend the rights of sureties he said: '...the tort of negligence has not yet subsumed all torts and does not supplant the principles of equity or contradict contractual promises or complement the remedy of judicial review or supplement statutory rights'.[4] In a later case where debtors' rights had been extended he added,

> The House of Lords has warned against the danger of extending the ambit of negligence so as to supplant or supplement other torts, contractual obligations,

[1] Sonnet 129.

[2] *Henderson v Merrett Syndicates* [1994] 3 All ER 506, 532 (HL). Lord Goff does not add that the extent to which parties can contract out of the law of tort is now greatly curtailed by the Unfair Contract Terms Act 1977.

[3] See, e.g. J. C. Smith & P. Burns, 'Donoghue v Stevenson—The Not so Golden Anniversary', (1983) 46 MLR 147.

[4] *China and South Sea Bank v Tan* [1989] 3 All ER 839 at 841 (PC).

statutory duties or equitable rules in relation to every kind of damage including economic loss. . . . If the defined equitable duties attaching to mortgagees and to receivers are replaced or supplemented by a liability in negligence the result will be confusion and injustice.[5]

The indication is that a general principle may imperil solutions inconsistent with it but better adapted to particular situations, in other words that the intellectual appeal of the abstract may prove pragmatically unhelpful.

The purpose of this unhappily posthumous tribute to the half-century's foremost academic contributor to the anglophone law of tort is to investigate the extent to which ideas associated with the tort of negligence have indeed affected the operation of other established heads of liability at common law, such as trespass, nuisance, defamation, *Rylands v Fletcher*, breach of statutory duty, and breach of contract, with a glance at its effect on rules of equity and of public law.

The basic principle of negligence as a tort is that one is liable for the foreseeable consequences of one's unreasonable behaviour: the test as to conduct is its *reasonableness*, the test as to its effect is its *foreseeability*. The concept of *duty* need not detain us long.

The Duty Concept

The 'duty' concept, as John Fleming made clear in his invariably luminous prose, is a control device[6]—a way of keeping the negligence principle within practical bounds; this is necessary since the negligence principle, 'You must pay for the foreseeable harm you were at fault in causing,' is a very powerful one, rather like the principle of having to disgorge an unjust enrichment. Of the latter John Dawson said; 'a general principle prohibiting enrichment through another's loss appears first as a convenient explanation of specific results; it is an instrument for quite practical and intelligible purposes. Yet once the idea has been formulated as a generalization, it has the peculiar faculty of inducing quite sober citizens to jump right off the dock.'[7] Sober tort lawyers can keep their feet on the ground by deploying the notion of 'duty' so as to

[5] *Downsview Nominees v First City Corporation* [1993] 3 All ER 637 (PC).

[6] 'The mechanisms associated with liability for negligence, such as the duty and causation concepts, are nothing more or less than the control devices fashioned by the courts to achieve that purpose [sc. limitation of liability].' J. G. Fleming, 'Remoteness and Duty: Control Devices in Liability for Negligence', (1953) 31 Can. Bar Rev 471 at 474.

[7] J. P. Dawson, *Unjust Enrichment: A Comparative Analysis* (1951), 8.

deny liability in cases where the principle would impose it with results which would not be 'fair, just and reasonable'.[8]

It may be said that it is better as a control than as a device, for its formulation is unfortunate. It is not, after all, the imposition of a duty which may be unfair or unjust or unreasonable, but the imposition of liability: the question is not really whether a defendant should have behaved better, but whether he should be made to pay for not having done so. The distinction is clear in public law, where a body may be ordered by a court to do something, but not to pay for not having done it; in such a case one cannot say that the body was not under a duty—it certainly was—but it is not under any liability in damages for having failed in its duty. In the *Dorset Yacht* case, for example, the preliminary question of law was 'regrettably'[9] phrased as 'whether on the facts pleaded . . . the Home Office, their servants or agents owed any duty of care to the [plaintiffs] capable of giving rise to a liability in damages with respect to the detention of persons undergoing sentences of Borstal training, or with respect to the manner in which such persons were treated, employed, disciplined, controlled or supervised whilst undergoing such sentences'.[10] The allegations were that the warders went to sleep instead of preventing the bad boys from scarpering and trashing the plaintiff's yacht in the moonlight. Of course the warders were under a duty to do their job—to say otherwise gives quite the wrong signal—but it is quite another question whether the Home Office should have to pay, and the answer given was surely wrong.[11]

Secondly, the appeal of the duty device is so great that it is sometimes applied where it is inappropriate or harmful. For example, while it is generally admitted that the contributory negligence of a plaintiff who

[8] First used in a case of actual property damage in *The Nicholas H* [1995] 3 All ER 307 (HL) so as to produce a decision manifestly right; had it gone the other way the surveyor would have been ultimately liable for $4.5m with no claim for contribution from the shipowner, whose liability for the loss of the cargo owing to known unseaworthiness of the vessel in which he had contracted to carry it was limited to only one-ninth as much.

[9] *Home Office v Dorset Yacht Co.* [1970] 2 All ER 294 at 323 (HL) per Lord Diplock.

[10] The decision, long taken as an instance of liability for pure omission, is now read as one where the Home Office positively created the danger by bringing the boys to the island in the first place. See Lord Hoffmann in *Stovin v Wise* [1996] 3 All ER 801 at 823, and *Skinner v Secretary of State* [1995] TLR 3: the Home Office 'created a danger and then negligently let it loose'. There is certainly a principle that if you create a danger, even without negligence, you come under a duty to try to defuse it, unlike a person who merely had the ability to defuse a danger created by someone else. The best instance is where a driver, without negligence, runs into a drunk on the highway: though free from fault in causing the injury, he must take steps to protect the injured drunk from further injury by third parties.

[11] The *only* bodies to benefit from the decision are the insurers of property damaged by escaping criminals: those who suffer attack will recover (from the Home Office) under the Criminal Injuries Compensation Scheme, and those who suffer property damage (*unless* it is insured) recover under the Home Office's own *ex gratia* scheme. See C. Harlow, *Compensation and Government Torts* (1982), 154f.

fails to take care of his own safety does not rest on breach of any duty by him, estoppel by careless conduct is said to do so. In consequence, a company which had carelessly omitted to register the fact that one of its vehicles was subject to a hire-purchase agreement was able to claim its value from a tradesman who would never have bought it had the charge been registered.[12] It was in this case that Lord Edmund-Davies observed that 'In most situations it is better to be careful than careless, but it is quite another thing to elevate all carelessness into a tort. Liability has to be based on a legal duty not to be careless, and I can find none in this case.'[13] But of course the question was not whether there was a tort, or liability, but whether there was preclusion, disability; conduct which falls short of what is required to make one pay may nevertheless bar one from claiming: after all, there are certain promises in breach of which one may not sue but for breach of which one cannot be sued.[14]

The notion of 'duty' also intrudes unhelpfully in the law of damages. While it is clearly sensible that a plaintiff should not recover compensation for an item of harm or expenditure he could and should reasonably have avoided suffering or incurring, it is perverse and misleading to describe him as being under a 'duty to mitigate damage', when only preclusion being in issue and not liability.[15]

The duty device has also been embraced by the parliamentary draftsman. This is needless. Parliament can impose liability directly subject to whatever pre-conditions seem appropriate, as is done, for example, in the Consumer Protection Act 1987 and the Animals Act 1971. It is not a question of whether the liability so imposed is strict or not, as under those statutes. 'Breach of statutory duty' may well be strict, but the liability really has nothing to do with duty. Indeed, it is with some surprise that we read that the liability of our Government for trying to restrict to nationals the quota of fish which Brussels had accorded to us as a nation is a liability for breach of statutory duty rather than an instance of misfeasance in office.[16]

Given that 'The law of negligence has been deliberately limited in its range by the courts' insistence that there can be no actionable negligence

[12] *Moorgate Mercantile v Twitchings* [1976] 2 All ER 641 (HL). [13] Ibid at 659.

[14] *Central London Property Trust v High Trees House* [1947] KB 130 for the former, *Snelling v John G. Snelling* [1973] QB 87 for the latter.

[15] The only suggestion known to me that there may be *liability* for failure to mitigate damage is Schlechtriem, *Uniform Sales Law* (1986) 99 n. 408, on art. 77 CISG.

[16] *R v Secretary of State, ex p Factortame (No. 5)* [1997] TLR 482 (Div. Ct.): 'Their Lordships can find no similarity between a claim of tortious misfeasance by a government servant and the claims made by the applicants for the United Kingdom's breach of its obligations' (at 484); otherwise punitive damages would have been payable! On the general problem, see C. Harlow, 'Francovich and the Problem of the Disobedient State' 2 (1996) Eur. L.J. 199 at 216ff .

in vacuo without the existence of some duty to the plaintiff',[17] we may ask if the 'duty' device is specific to negligence as a tort. One would not have expected an authoritative answer to so jurisprudential a question, but the House of Lords has provided one. The very issue in *Stubbings v Webb*[18] was whether a claim for damages in respect of personal injury deliberately and directly caused fell within the statutory words 'action for damages for negligence, nuisance or breach of duty'.[19] It was held that a claim in trespass did not, and that the phrase 'carries with it the implication of a breach of duty of care not to cause personal injury, rather than an obligation not to infringe any legal right of another person'.[20] On this one might compare *Westwood v Post Office* where it was held that it was not contributory negligence to trespass in breach of the rights of others, only to fail to take care of one's own safety.[21]

The position as regards deceit is much the same. We do not speak of a duty to be honest: you are liable for lying. But where there is dishonest silence rather than speech, or a dishonest failure to correct honest speech, then perhaps we do need to invoke the duty concept in order to limit the situations in which we want to tolerate an inquiry into why the defendant maintained silence.

The Hallmarks of Negligence as a Tort

With these words we can leave aside the duty question, and consider the two basic aspects of negligence liability, namely unreasonableness of conduct and foreseeability of harm.

To be noted at the outset is the fact that these requirements are double-edged. Where negligence is the dominant tort, there will be no liability where the conduct is reasonable, and none for harm which is not foreseeable: the corollary of liability for unreasonable conduct is no liability where the conduct is not unreasonable, and the corollary of liability for foreseeable harm is no liability for harm which is not foreseeable. Thus the plaintiff, who had won in the Australian courts, lost his claim when the Privy Council in *The Wagon Mound (No. 1)*[22] laid down in terms more dogmatic than convincing that the harm must be foreseeable, and the same thing nearly happened in *The Wagon Mound (No. 2)*[23] when they

[17] *Hedley Byrne & Co. Ltd v Heller & Partners* [1963] 2 All ER 575, 613 (HL) per Lord Pearce.

[18] [1993] 1 All ER 322 (HL).

[19] Limitation Act 1980, s 11.

[20] *Stubbings v Webb* [1993] 1 All ER 322 (HL).

[21] [1973] 1 All ER 184 (HL).

[22] *Overseas Tankship (UK) Ltd v Morts Dock and Eng. Co. (The Wagon Mound (No. 1))* [1961] AC 388.

[23] *Overseas Tankship (UK) Ltd v Miller Steamship Co. (The Wagon Mound (No. 2))* [1967] 1 AC 617.

held that the negligence rule applied in nuisance claims as well. The pattern is also observable in the *Cambridge Water Co.*[24] case where the House of Lords allowed the defendant's appeal on the sole ground that the harm resulting from the escape of the chemical from his land could not reasonably have been foreseen. Accordingly, when we find a modification of the rules of liability so as to impose liability when, and only when, the conduct is unreasonable or the harm foreseeable, we may take it that the tort of negligence is having an influence.

Negligence and Nuisance

Although Lord Atkin famously took 'neighbours' as the paradigm of a relationship giving rise to a duty of care in negligence, the common-law regime for the relationship between actual neighbours had previously been quite distinct from that of negligence. It is true that the rules of nuisance did not positively require that the parties be neighbours—provided that the plaintiff was complaining of a non-trespassory effect on his land,[25] he could sue his neighbour's predecessor, contractor, or even a person outside on the highway—but actual suits in nuisance were overwhelmingly suits between neighbours-in-fact.

It was just eight years after *Donoghue v Stevenson* that Lord Atkin had an opportunity in *Sedleigh-Denfield v O'Callaghan* to apply his negligence doctrine to the relations between actual neighbours.[26] The plaintiff's land was flooded after a cloudburst because a culvert in a boundary ditch was blocked. The culvert had been placed there by trespassers on the defendants' land, and it got blocked because they put the grating in the wrong place. The defendants had done nothing whatever. Both lower courts held them not liable, the Court of Appeal expressly discounting the relevance of negligence. The House of Lords reversed the decision. The defendants were held liable, on the factitious ground that the unprotected culvert was a nuisance and they had 'continued' and 'adopted' it. They had 'continued' it because they should have seen that it was dangerous and done something about it. The decision was not overtly based on negligence, and *Donoghue*, not mentioned in argument, was not cited in the speeches. Furthermore, Lord Wright said 'Negligence here is not an independent cause of action, but is ancillary to the actual cause of action, which is nuisance.'[27] But that

[24] *Cambridge Water Co. v Eastern Counties Leather* [1994] 1 All ER 53 (HL).

[25] There is rather a dubious decision to the effect that a person who repairs a house undermined by tree roots and then buys it can sue for the damage: *Masters v Brent London orough Council* [1978] 2 All ER 664 (CA).

[26] [1940] 3 All ER 349 (HL), reversing [1939] 1 All ER 725 (CA).

[27] Ibid at 365.

the defendant's liability in nuisance had been affected by considerations relevant in the tort of negligence seems beyond doubt.

This became explicit in the next case, one of fire rather than flood, where the decision of the Privy Council was explicitly based on *Sedleigh-Denfield*.[28] Lord Wilberforce said: 'The present case is one where liability, if it exists, rests on negligence and nothing else; whether it falls within or overlaps the boundaries of nuisance is a question of classification which need not here be resolved' and reached the 'conclusion that the respondents' claim for damages, on the basis of negligence, was fully made out'.[29] Previous cases which had held a defendant not liable for doing nothing about a knowable or known danger on his land not resulting from any activity of his were now said to turn on the conclusion that his inactivity was not unreasonable, that is, no nuisance because no negligence; this involves rather creative rereading of the relevant decisions. This was made clear in the High Court of Australia when Windeyer J (citing *Hedley Byrne*!) observed that 'new situations are being subsumed under rules and principles that are proving extensive rather than restricted. This is largely the result of the expansive scope of the tort of negligence today.'[30] Certainly one may say that it is one thing to put out a fire in a tree which has been felled, quite another to prevent rocks from falling; but whether the Court of Appeal was right to hold that preventing a hill from crumbling was more like the former than the latter is another matter.[31]

Like penalizing silence, to make a person liable for inactivity almost inevitably involves speaking of a 'duty' to act: conditions, such as having to pay for resulting harm, may be attached to activities, but hardly to inactivity. But once the duty to take steps to remove existing dangers is admitted, it is easy to extend it to include a duty to take steps to prevent persons coming on to the land and creating dangers. This has led to a rather unfruitful discussion of whether or not there is a general duty on occupiers to take such steps, as in negligence.[32]

The intrusion of negligence into nuisance law now appears nearly complete. In the recent re-analysis of nuisance as a tort characterized by undue interference with the enjoyment of rights in land,[33] Lord Goff appeared sympathetic to the view that not only claims for personal injury but also claims in respect of actual damage to the land should henceforth be treated as claims in negligence rather than in private nuisance,[34] the

[28] *Goldman v Hargrave* [1966] 2 All ER 989 (PC). [29] [1966] 2 All ER 989 at 996.
[30] *Hargrave v Goldman* [1964] ALR 377 at 385 (1963).
[31] *Leakey v National Trust* [1980] 1 All ER 17 (CA).
[32] *Smith v Littlewoods Organisation* [1987] 1 All ER 710 (HL).
[33] *Hunter v Canary Wharf* [1997] 2 All ER 426 (HL).
[34] This is in line with the argument of C. Gearty, 'The Place of Private Nuisance in a

latter being reserved for claims in respect of disamenity due to noises, smells, and so on,[35] a kind of damage not traditionally redressable in a negligence suit.[36]

Does it make any difference if claims for actual damage to land are reclassified as sounding in negligence, bearing in mind our twin reference points of unreasonableness of conduct and foreseeability of harm? As to the latter, we have the holding of the Privy Council in *The Wagon Mound (No. 2)*[37]—a case of actual property damage caused by negligent conduct—that harm has to be foreseeable in order to be actionable in a nuisance claim.[38] In the *Cambridge Water Co.* case[39]—a case of damage to water rights due to conduct not negligence—this was endorsed and extended to claims under *Rylands v Fletcher*, where actual damage has always been required. There is no point in objecting to this, especially as it will apply only in cases where damages are sought for past encroachments: where the activity is continuing and an injunction is sought, the foreseeability for future harm will have been established. Thus if the defendants in the *Cambridge Water Co.* case had been continuing to allow their chemicals to escape, an injunction would unquestionably have issued.[40]

Modern Law of Torts', [1989] Camb. L.J. 214, and also of Fleming: '[T]he problem of overlap sows confusion and, if only for the sake of protecting nuisance against infection from negligence in the core area of non-physical harm, it might be better now to exclude all physical harm from the province of nuisance.' *The Law of Tort* (8th ed., 1992), 409.

[35] The disamenity is proprietary rather than personal, so to speak, in the sense that a claim in respect of it cannot be brought by the discommoded individuals on the land but only by its owner or possessor, doubtless often corporate with neither ears nor nose. Lord Hoffmann said that 'nuisances productive of sensible personal discomfort do not constitute a separate tort of causing discomfort to people but are merely part of a single tort of causing injury to land.' *Hunter v Canary Wharf* [1997] 2 All ER 426 at 452 (HL).

[36] Other recent cases which suggest an extension of the kinds of harm redressible in a negligence suit are *Hague v Deputy Governor of Parkhurst Prison* [1991] 3 All ER 733 at 746f. (HL) (discomfort falling short of injury or disease, Lord Goff doubting Lord Bridge on this point) and *X (minors) v Bedfordshire County Council* [1995] 3 All ER 353 at 400 (educational disadvantage—actually held compensable in *Phelps v Hillingdon London Borough Council*, The Times, 10 Oct. 1997). It is gratifying that in *Hotson v East Berkshire Area Health Authority* [1987] 2 All ER 909 the House of Lords repelled the notion that exposure to risk of personal injury or loss of the chance of not suffering it constituted acceptable damage. In *Barrett v Enfield London Borough Council* [1997] 3 All ER 171 at 180 Evans LJ raised, but did not answer, the question whether 'a personality disorder not amounting to personal injury or mental illness' was actionable.

[37] [1967] 1 AC 617.

[38] Whether the restriction, if that is what it is, is being properly applied may be a question. In *Lewis v Sadiq* [1996] TLR 660 D's building works, improper because unannounced, damaged P's house, and P was allowed to recover the loss suffered as a result of delay in selling the house as well as the increased cost of building the house abroad to which he planned to move.

[39] [1994] 1 All ER 53 (HL).

[40] Compare *British Road Services v Slater* [1964] 1 All ER 816, where an occupier whose tree overhung the highway, but at a height such as to make a collision most unlikely, was held not to be liable when such a collision occurred, though of course he could have been required to lop the overhanging limb.

Much more problematical, however, is the question of whether a landowner who has suffered foreseeable harm as a result of a past short-term activity on his neighbour's land should have to prove that the neighbour's conduct was unreasonable. As to personal injury, such a rule is quite acceptable—it would be wrong and undemocratic to give better protection to A's body than to B's when both are injured on A's premises[41]—but as to damage to the land, the matter is very debatable.

There is ample authority that liability in nuisance is strict, that is, it is not dependent on fault, but it comes from decisions relating to damage resulting from activities or constructions on the neighbour's land, not mere passivity or natural phenomena. The extension of liability to cases where there had been a failure to correct a situation procured by a stranger or by natural forces was itself an outgrowth of negligence law, and such failure must certainly be culpable for such inactivity to be actionable. Where, however, the damage results from an activity of the defendant's, there are good arguments for allowing the damaged neighbour to recover without having to prove any fault. It hardly conduces to neighbourly relations if I have to prove that it was my neighbour's fault that a projectile from his garden broke my window. Lord Hoffmann's reference to the mutuality between neighbours is apt where the harm results to one from the activities of the other.[42] Take the leading case on liability, or rather non-liability, for damage done by independent contractors. In *Salsbury v Woodland* an occupier of land had a man cut down a tree of moderate size and he did it so clumsily that the tree fell against some wires and caused them to curl up on the highway. A spectator who had been watching from the neighbour's garden went on to the highway to clear up the mess and was injured by a motorist. The occupier was held not liable to the young man.[43] Consider, however, the position if the tree had fallen on the neighbour's greenhouse, as it might well have done. Would no action lie? Surely it would. In a subsequent case the plaintiff's house was flooded when rain percolated through the junction between the roof of his terraced house and the roof which his neighbour had had a builder replace. The defendant neighbour was held liable, though on very tortured grounds.[44] It would surely be better to admit that the relationship between neighbours is such that each pays for the actual damage done to the other's land by his activities, however reasonable. Mrs Stone may not be able to recover for

[41] That is why Animals Act 1971, s 4(1)(a) restricts claims in cattle trespass to damage to property, overruling *Wormald v Cole* [1954] 1 QB 614.

[42] *Stovin v Wise* [1996] 3 All ER 801 at 819 (HL).

[43] [1970] 1 QB 324.

[44] *Alcock v Wraith* [1991] TLR 600 (CA).

her broken head when she is standing on the highway outside her house, but she should surely recover for a broken window.[45]

This strict liability for physical damage to land and buildings would be justified by the situation of mutual exposure in which neighbours find themselves as a result of their prolonged proximity. Trees provide the best example.[46] Prior to the invasion by negligence and after it had been reasserted that the remedy of lopping was insufficient,[47] the rule used to be that if my tree roots subverted your house, I paid, no questions asked; likewise if it were your roots and my house. As was said in the Privy Council in a case involving four pohutukawa trees, 'it has long been established as a general proposition that . . . if an owner of land grows or permits the growth on his land . . . of trees whose roots penetrate into adjoining property and thereby cause or continue to cause damage to buildings upon that property, he is liable.'[48] However, in 1981 this old rule was somewhat surreptitiously changed.[49] Under the influence of the cases which had held that an occupier was under a duty to take reasonable steps to defuse natural dangers on his land, the rule as to tree roots was changed, and it now appears to be the law that the occupier must be shown to have been at fault, and certainly that the damage has to be foreseeable—though one would have supposed that everyone knows that tree roots go hunting for water and that the withdrawal of water may cause the collapse of superjacent buildings.[50] This example of the

[45] *Bolton v Stone* [1951] AC 850.

[46] Not all the hazards to which neighbours expose each other are reciprocal: fire may go in any direction but water will go only downwards. It appears to be established law that whereas the liability for fire is rather strict (*Balfour v Barty-King* [1957] 1 QB 496), liability for flooding is less so (*Hawkins v Dhawan* (1987) 19 HLR 232 (CA)). Of course it is only academics who will be offended by differences they have problems in explaining: the practising lawyer has no problem provided the facts to which the different rules apply are easily ascertained and delimited. Distinguishing between fire and explosion may be difficult (*Hughes v Lord Advocate* [1963] 1 All ER 705 (HL)), but not between fire and flood. Likewise between digging and draining (a distinction criticized by John Fleming in 'Negligence and Property Rights' 104 LQR 183 (1988)), though an unexpected problem did arise when D, wishing to extract salt from under his land, sent down steam which provoked brine, the removal of which caused P's property to subside. (*Brace v South Eastern Regional Health Authority* [1984] C.A.T. 20.)

[47] *Smith v Giddy* [1904] 2 KB 448. Tree roots are, of course, relevantly different from tree limbs in that their progress is imperceptible.

[48] *Morgan v Khyatt* [1964] 1 WLR 475, 477; *Davey v Harrow Corporation* [1958] 1 QB 60.

[49] In *Solloway v Hampshire County Council* (1981) 79 LGR 449. This was taken to result from *Leakey v National Trust* [1980] 1 All ER 17 (CA) (itself an improper extension of *Goldman v Hargrave* [1966] 2 All ER 989 (PC)) which has now been extended from the duty to prevent your hill falling on D's house to a duty to prevent your land slipping in such a way as to cause P's land to slip: *Holbeck Hall Hotel v Scarborough Borough Council* (The Times, 15 Oct. 1997) (Official Referee) which sounds rather like a King Canute case.

[50] Liability seems to depend on knowledge or possible knowledge of the geological strata: in *Solloway* D was excused since he had no means of knowing that there was a pocket of clay under P's building. It is true that householders' insurance policies now

purely doctrinaire influence of negligence concepts on nuisance law has not been to the benefit of the legal system as a whole.

Negligence and *Rylands v Fletcher*

The emphatic holding that nuisance is a tort which exists to protect property, taken in conjunction with the close association effected in the *Cambridge Water Co.*[51] case between nuisance and *Rylands v Fletcher*,[52] now makes it virtually impossible to argue that liability under the latter head can be asserted by the victim of personal injuries. This is a useful clarification. It may be worth emphasizing that the recent decision in the *Cambridge Water Co.* case does not reduce liability under *Rylands v Fletcher* to that of negligence. Certainly the requirement of foreseeability of damage has been introduced, but the requirement that the conduct be unreasonable has not: it remains a tort of strict liability for the foreseeable consequences of an escape of materials brought on to the defendant's land. Indeed, its scope has been greatly extended by the narrowing of the defence of 'natural user': it now appears that any industrial material which escapes will entail liability for the foreseeable damage which ensues. Needless to say, the cases where the damage is unforeseeable will be rather rare.

This is very different from the position adopted by a majority of the High Court of Australia in *Burnie Port Authority v General Jones Pty*,[53] where the plaintiff licensee's stock was burnt by a fire started on premises retained by the defendant and caused by negligent welding on the part of his independent contractor.[54] As John Fleming observed, the majority 'did not shrink from absorbing *Rylands v Fletcher* itself into negligence'[55]

regularly cover damage by subsidence, though subject to a considerable deductible or excess, but this does not justify the extra work given to courts by the change introduced in 1981. For the liability of the highway authority in respect of tree roots encroaching on private land from the highway, see *Hurst v Hampshire County Council* [1997] TLR 339, where Stuart-Smith LJ appears to think that a suit for personal injury might be brought in nuisance by a highway-user or riparian owner: Highways Act 1980, s 96(6) makes the authority strictly liable for planted trees which become a nuisance, and the common law makes the authority liable as owner for all trees (and other vegetation) rooted in the soil under the adopted highway, even if planted before adoption. What is not clear is whether, foreseeability of damage being required, unreasonableness of conduct is also required. The cases are far from emphasizing this dubious requirement. In *Hurst* the tree was an oak over 170 years old.

[51] [1994] 1 All ER 53 (HL).

[52] (1866) LR 1 Exch 265; aff'd (1868) 3 HL 330.

[53] (1994) 179 CLR 520.

[54] There would have been liability in England without reference to *Rylands* because it is well established that an occupier is liable for damage done to neighbouring premises by a fire carelessly started by anyone on his premises not a stranger—*Balfour v Barty-King* [1957] 1 QB 496.

[55] J. Fleming, 'The Fall of a Crippled Giant', [1995] Tort L. Rev 56 at 58.

and indeed the headnote itself states that 'the rule in *Rylands v Fletcher* has been absorbed by the principles of negligence'. But Fleming is not happy with the result in either country. In England he notes that the 'only remaining attribute of strict liability is that the escape itself need not be negligent' (surely an important attribute?), and in Australia he sides with the minority, though he would rather that the original rule of *Rylands* had not been etiolated by subsequent decisions inimical to strict liability, such as 'non-natural user', escape from land, and so on.[56] All in all, he concludes, 'it would be an historical misinterpretation to suggest that negligence had at last overtaken a rule redolent of archaism',[57] but his point is less that negligence has not played a role than that the original rule has modern validity, as its development in the United States shows.

Negligence and Trespass

The most obvious take-over of one tort by another took place in 1959 when Diplock, L. J. decided at first instance that it no longer stated a cause of action to plead 'You shot me'—a classic allegation of trespass to the person—but that in order to get into court one must add 'intentionally or negligently'.[58] There had been straws in the wind.[59] This point has been adequately discussed elsewhere. Nevertheless, it is clear from the decision of the House of Lords in *Stubbings v Webb*[60] that trespass still exists as an independent tort and has not been entirely suppressed.

That the tort of trespass protects person as well as tangible property is unquestionable, but what it protects is the *right* of physical integrity rather than actual safety: no damage to limb or thing need be shown. Indeed the requirements of trespass in its classic form and the tort of negligence are completely at odds. As to the defendant's conduct, negligence requires that it be unreasonable and accepts that it may be an omission, whereas trespass, insistent that the conduct be positive, is indifferent to its reasonableness. In negligence the damage, which is

[56] 'Escape' is not simply a dotty English requirement. In Germany escape from D's land is required for strict liability for damage done by specified substances previously contained in a production plant or conduit: *Haftpflichtgesetz* of 4 Jan. 1978, best found in B. S. Markesinis, *The German Law of Obligations* vol. 2 (Torts), (3rd ed., 1997) 859ff. In France, of course, any damage done by any thing is compensable—art. 1384(1) Civil Code.

[57] J. G. Fleming, n. 55 above at 61.

[58] *Fowler v Lanning* [1959] 1 QB 426.

[59] In *National Coal Board v J. E. Evans* [1951] 2 KB 861 D, excavating on council land, grubbed up a cable clandestinely laid there by P or his predecessor. In unreserved judgments the CA reversed the holding below that D was liable for trespass to goods, Singleton LJ observing that 'where the plaintiffs are at fault and the defendants are free from fault . . . there is in fact no trespass' (at 875).

[60] [1993] 1 All ER 322 (HL).

requisite, ideally physical, must be foreseeable, for *The Wagon Mound (No. 1)*[61] laid down that directness was not enough; in trespass, on the other hand, the invasion, whether or not it causes damage, must be direct: it is a trespass to pump oil on to someone else's land, not a trespass to pump it into the sea even though it inevitably proceeds thence to the land.[62]

Now the foreign observer might be forgiven for thinking that the common law is schizophrenic in having two torts with fundamentally opposite ingredients, and it is indeed a question how they can properly co-exist. The case of *Wilson v Pringle* may be illuminating in this context.[63] Both parties were schoolboys. After a mathematics class they were walking down the corridor, the plaintiff in front, when the defendant, as a merry prank, pounced on him and pulled at the bag slung over his shoulder. The plaintiff fell awkwardly and injured his hip. The second-instance judge held on the pleadings that it was no defence to the claim in trespass to assert that this was just normal horseplay between schoolmates, and ordered that the case proceed to the assessment of damages. On the defendant's appeal the Court of Appeal ordered a trial on the merits, not because the harm was unintended—it was enough that the invasion be intended—but because it was not established that the pouncing was 'hostile', a quality said to be required in order for it to be trespassory. Now it is perfectly clear that this is nonsense, quite apart from its being in conflict with the views of Lord Goff, already expressed and subsequently reasserted. That the pouncing was trespassory, though amicable, is perfectly clear when one considers (a) that unconsented osculation, though amatory, is clearly a wrong, and (b) that the pouncee, had he turned round in time, was certainly entitled to protect himself by battering the pouncer. So what actuated the Court to say what it did?

Surely the reason is that here the plaintiff was complaining, so to speak, of a broken leg. Broken limbs come before the courts every day, normally resulting from industrial or traffic accidents. The courts know what law applies: the plaintiff has to establish that the fracture was the foreseeable result of culpable behaviour on the part of the defendant. In this case, unless the decision below was reversed, the plaintiff was going to get damages for a broken leg when it was neither alleged nor established that the harm was foreseeable as a result of what the defendant did nor that what he did was unreasonable ('normal horseplay').

What this suggests is that where the plaintiff is seeking compensation for harm, the rules of negligence seem so appropriate nowadays as to be

[61] [1961] AC 38.
[62] *Esso Petroleum v Southport Corporation* [1956] AC 218. Likewise the operators of the *Wagon Mound* did not trespass to P's riparian installations.
[63] *Wilson v Pringle* [1986] 2 All ER 440 (CA).

almost mandatory, whereas they have, or ought to have, no place where the plaintiff is seeking, not compensation for harm, but rather vindication of the rights by whose infringement he is aggrieved. It is not a great step to move from the proposition that no harm need be established in a trespass claim to the position that if harm is alleged, the rules of negligence apply.

This distinction is quite justifiable. If the plaintiff's rights have been invaded it cannot be relevant that he is none the worse for the experience, nor that it was the defendant's fault that he invaded them. If negligence intrudes here, the results are problematic, and it is certainly the tendency of the courts to think that if the defendant behaved reasonably, he cannot be liable in tort.

Of course trespassory behaviour can often be justified. While it is no justification for the defendant simply to show that what he did was reasonable in all the circumstances, he may well be able to rely on a mistake, provided that it is reasonable: the police may arrest an innocent person if they reasonably believe him to have committed an arrestable offence. Not all reasonable mistakes will serve, however: the police may not arrest a person for a non-arrestable offence just because they believe it to be an arrestable one. Or at least they ought not to be able to do so.

Recent decisions bring this into question, however, in rather an alarming manner. In *Percy v Hall*[64] the Court of Appeal held that persons arrested (150 times!) for breach of a bye-law apparently making it an offence to enter a certain (barely identifiable) area could not sue for wrongful arrest even if the by-law were void for uncertainty. 'As it seems to me, the position can be no different whether byelaws are eventually condemned for substantive invalidity or for procedural invalidity: either way, I repeat, the actions of the constables concerned . . . would be beyond criticism.'[65] It is clear beyond a peradventure that the Lord Justice was much moved by the consideration that the policemen were not to blame for what they did. That is an immaterial consideration when the plaintiffs' liberty is in issue: the fact that a person liable to be arrested may complain if arrested in an unreasonable manner[66] does not entail that a person not liable to be arrested cannot complain if the person effecting the arrest was behaving reasonably.[67]

To much the same effect is a decision of a bare majority in the House of

[64] [1996] 4 All ER 523 (CA). [65] Ibid, per Simon Brown LJ at 541.

[66] *Christie v Leachinsky* [1947] AC 573.

[67] In *R v Wicks* [1997] 2 All ER 801 (HL) doubt was cast on the proposition that a person could be convicted of an offence under a bylaw later held to be invalid, though criminal sanctions for breach of other acts done under statutory authority could not be avoided by offering to demonstrate bad faith or irrationality, though these would ensure their invalidation in proceedings for judicial review.

Lords in 1982.[68] There the question was whether a policeman with statutory power to arrest a person who committed a stipulated offence within his sight was acting in the exercise of his duty in arresting a person whom he erroneously but reasonably supposed to be committing such an offence. Lord Bridge, with the unreasoned assent of Lords Wilberforce and Russell, was ready to extend the power, unswayed by the two powerfully argued dissents in favour of the liberty of the citizen.

The worst case, however, from our point of view, involved no statutory power. In *Chic Fashions (West Wales) v Jones*[69] constables lawfully on premises removed goods which they reasonably believed to be stolen, though they neither were nor were believed to be the goods described in their search warrant. The county court judge correctly held that there was no power at common law to seize goods suspected stolen, but the Court of Appeal reversed. Diplock, L. J., admittedly making new law, observed,

> The plaintiffs' cause of action for interference to their property in goods lies in trespass—a cause of action which historically did not necessarily involve blameworthiness on the part of the defendant. The development of the common law in the last thirty years, however, has tended towards equating civil liability with conduct which right-minded men in contemporary society would regard as blameworthy and towards protecting those who act reasonably in intended performance of what right-minded men would deem a duty to their fellow men.[70]

The five cases he cited as authority are all cases of claims for actual damage, three of them cases where it was the reasonableness of the *plaintiff's* conduct which was in question. The tone of the judgment is given by Lord Denning: 'In these present times, with the ever-increasing wickedness there is about, honest citizens must help the police and not hinder them in their efforts to track down criminals.'[71] The consequences of this disgraceful[72] decision may be seen in *Ghani v Jones*,[73] where the police sought to retain the plaintiffs' passports and papers as of 'evidential value' concerning a suspected murder, although there was no evidence of the plaintiffs' implication in the crime, if actually committed. The trial judge peremptorily ordered the police to return the documents,

[68] *Wills v Bowley* [1982] 2 All ER 654 (HL).

[69] *Chic Fashions (West Wales) v Jones* [1968] 1 All ER 229 (CA).

[70] Ibid at 238.

[71] Ibid at 236.

[72] All the more disgraceful because (a) unnecessary, since the Theft Bill, already published, contained the power desiderated by the Court, but limited, unlike the judicial invention, to stolen goods, and (b) mean-minded, since the award to P below was only £5,500 (the then limit of the county court's jurisdiction) and the CA made P pay the costs below and in front of them, whereas D's damages and costs would have come from public funds.

[73] [1969] 3 All ER 720 (CA).

and Lord Denning, while upholding the order, repeated the observation quoted above, adding that to decide otherwise than in favour of the plaintiffs 'would be to accord to the police powers to take charge of property which they believe might be of evidential value irrespective of any connection the owners might have with the crime',[74] as indeed followed from his decision in *Chic Fashions*.

There are, of course, other explanations for the clear tendency of the courts to expand police powers at the expense of the liberty of the citizen, but there is no doubt that the climate of juridical opinion created by the dominance of negligence in the field of tort, where normally these debates are situated, has contributed by suggesting that a person can have no complaint in respect of conduct which appears reasonable at the time and to the court.

How can the law of trespass, with its vital vindicatory function, be kept free from such infection? Perhaps, as in nuisance law, one should distinguish between the functions of the law in the area. Is the plaintiff seeking compensation for actual harm or is he seeking redress for a grievance? Just as undue noise is really, in layman's speech, a nuisance in a way in which a broken greenhouse or a flooded warehouse is not, so the person wrongfully arrested is not really seeking compensation for harm. And if he is beaten up, a claim in negligence will be quite adequate, since in almost all such cases the unreasonableness of the defendant's conduct will be manifest. That is why it is appropriate that prisoners, whose rights are restricted, should be able to sue the authorities in negligence but not in trespass.[75]

One further interface of negligence and trespass law occurred in the sad case of F, an adult woman mentally, though not sexually, backward. Given that she was incapable of consenting or dissenting, could the doctors sterilize her so as to protect her from the adverse consequences of pregnancy and parturition? As Lord Bridge said:

> It would be intolerable for members of the medical, nursing and other professions devoted to the care of the sick that, in acting for those lacking the capacity to consent to treatment, they should be put in the dilemma that, if they administer the treatment which they believe to be in the patient's best interests, acting with due skill and care, they run the risk of being held guilty in trespass to the person, but, if they withhold that treatment, they may be in breach of a duty of care owed to the patient. . . . If . . . the professionals . . . have acted with due skill and care . . . they should be immune from liability in trespass, just as they are immune from liability in negligence.[76]

[74] Ibid at 723.
[75] *Hague v Deputy Governor of Parkhurst Prison* [1991] 3 All ER 733 (HL).
[76] *In Re F, F v West Berkshire Health Authority* [1989] 2 All ER 545 at 548–9 (HL).

Such categorical considerations in so human a case may seem wholly irrelevant, and they are surely not determinative, but cases must be decided in terms of the legal concepts.

Where trespass to goods is in question, it is clear that the duty to care for them will be more relaxed and the privilege of interfering with them more extensive. Sometimes, out of deference to inherited views, the courts eschew mention of 'reasonableness' as such, but lay down specific rules, in rather a legislative manner, which have the same effect. So it was in *Arthur v Anker*,[77] where it was held that an occupier of premises was not liable for trespassing to a trespassing car by affixing a clamp provided that (1) there was a clearly visible notice forbidding unauthorized parking, and (2) release was undertaken against a reasonable fee and within a reasonably short time. Likewise in *Ghani v Jones*[78] Lord Denning laid down a complete set of do's and don'ts to enable the police to confiscate passports and seize chattels without incurring liability.

Negligence and Conversion

That a person in unauthorized possession of someone else's goods must be bound to return them is clear. Likewise if he has sold them he must hand over the price obtained. This liability is naturally strict: it is futile to say 'It's not my fault I have your goods or their price.' Other systems procure this result by using the law of property or its obligational counterpart, the law of unjust enrichment, but the common law could not do so, since the property remedy was lacking and the latter head of liability was imperfectly recognized. The law of tort was used for this purpose. The tort nature of the remedy affected both title to sue and the requisite conduct of the defendant. As to the former, title to sue was not accorded to the owner as such (who was rather difficult to identify, since in the absence of a *vindicatio* there was no reason to do so) but to anyone who had an immediate right to possession (and not to the owner if he did not); and—typically for tort—the law looked not to the defendant's possession or enrichment but to his conduct. Liability remained strict, however, or the purpose of the enterprise would have been frustrated. The result was that a person who bought or sold goods without the authority of the person entitled to their immediate possession was strictly liable to that person, even though he acted without negligence and retained neither the property nor the price. The prime case is that of the careful auctioneer, deluded by a thief into selling the goods and accounting to him for the price so obtained.

[77] [1996] 3 All ER 783 (CA). [78] [1969] 3 All ER 720 (CA).

This is so odd as a matter of tort law that the question arises whether it has been affected by thinking more characteristic of tort. In the case of cheques it clearly has been so affected. When the courts decided to extend to cheques the rules applicable to chattels, thereby escaping the need to speak in terms of unjust enrichment (or the quasi-contract of 'money had and received to [the plaintiff's] use'[79]) they produced a situation intolerable to banks which process cheques in huge numbers, effectively buying and selling them: to make banks strictly liable would be like making the Royal Mail strictly liable for the loss of posted items. Accordingly statutory protection has been given to them provided they act with reasonable care.[80] Then the question of the plaintiff's contributory negligence arose. Donaldson J. held that this reduced the plaintiff's claim.[81] Then the silly Torts (Interference with Goods) Act 1977 laid down that contributory negligence was no defence to a claim in conversion. Further legislation was required to reinstate the position as decided by Donaldson J.[82]

If we turn to chattels, we are faced with the position of the bona fide purchaser. In principle, the purchaser of stolen goods is liable to the person from whom they were stolen, and it is immaterial that he effected his purchase in good faith and without negligence. Certain exceptions are made in the Sale of Goods Act 1979, and the purchaser can avail himself of them if he buys them 'in good faith and without notice'. The Act itself provides that 'A thing is deemed to be done in good faith . . . when it is in fact done honestly, whether it is done negligently or not.'[83] There has fortunately been very little attempt to introduce 'constructive notice' into such cases in order to deprive the careless but honest purchaser of his statutory defence: a person without actual notice will be deprived of his defence only if he has wilfully closed his eyes to suspicious circumstances inviting successful investigation.[84] This insistence on dishonesty or extreme fecklessness is quite right, given that the owner may sue though it was through his fault that the goods got into commerce. What is not right is that the owner through whose carelessness the goods get into circulation should be able to make their purchaser strictly liable for what is, after all, merely economic loss.[85]

[79] As in *Down v Halling* (1825) 107 Eng. Rep. 1082.

[80] Crossed Cheques Act 1876; Bills of Exchange Act 1882, s 82; Cheques Act 1957, s 4.

[81] *Lumsden & Co. v London Trustee Savings Bank* [1971] 1 Lloyd's Rep. 114.

[82] Banking Act 1979, s 47.

[83] Sale of Goods Act 1979, s 61(3).

[84] See A. G. Guest (ed.), *Benjamin's, Sale of Goods*, (4th ed., 1992) para. 7-048, and *Forsythe International v Silver Shipping* [1994] 1 WLR 1334, 1349f.

[85] This is the result of Torts (Interference with Goods) Act 1977, s 11(1) (what a daft enactment that is!), and the decision in *Moorgate Mercantile v Twitchings* (n. 12 above) that the owner is not estopped by his negligence unless his conduct was in breach of a duty owed to the defendant.

Negligence and Defamation

If there is one tort which would have benefited from the introduction of the rules of negligence, it is defamation. Not only is it actionable in this country to say something disobliging about someone else although you reasonably believe it to be true and it causes no provable harm, but in certain circumstances it is not actionable to defame another even if it does cause harm and your belief in the truth of what you said was not reasonable at all.[86] The existence of these circumstances of qualified privilege are also independent of the reasonableness of your belief in their existence: you must actually be under a duty to speak—it is not enough that you believe yourself to be so—and the person you speak to must be the right person, not the person you quite reasonably believe to be the appropriate addressee of your message. At common law reasonableness had no part at all to play in this tort.[87]

Indeed, not so long ago, the Court of Appeal amazingly held that the rules of defamation actually ousted the rules of negligence altogether, that if what you said was defamatory and the circumstances of qualified privilege were present there *could* not be a duty to take reasonable care that what you said was true. The defendant, effectively the plaintiff's ex-employer, was found by the trial judge to have believed, though unreasonably, in the truth of the unnecessarily damning reference on the plaintiff he sent to a potential employer—that is, no malice, but negligence. The Court of Appeal reversed judgment for the plaintiff, holding that the rules of negligence were quite inapplicable.[88] Happily, the House of Lords reversed and held that a suit might lie if it was in breach of a duty of care to the plaintiff that a person gave information about him to a third party which was inaccurate and damaging, whether or not it was defamatory.[89]

On the question of liability for writing disagreeable things about politicians, there have been good developments in Australia, where it is now held that defendants may escape liability if they show that they took reasonable care to check the veracity of what they wrote.[90] The

[86] *Horrocks v Lowe* [1974] 1 All ER 662 (HL).

[87] The Defamation Act 1996 now provides a defence for persons other than the author, editor, or publisher of the defamatory statement if they 'took reasonable care in relation to its publication' and 'did not know, and had no reason to believe' that they were causing or contributing to the publication of a statement which was defamatory.

[88] [1993] 2 All ER 273 (CA). [89] [1994] 3 All ER 129 (HL).

[90] *Lange v Australian Broadcasting Corporation* (1997) 145 ALR 96, subject to this, that 'Reasonableness of conduct is an element for the judge to consider only when a publication concerning a government or political matter is made in circumstances that, under the English common law, would have failed to attract a defence of qualified privilege' (at 107). The publisher (not necessarily the media, but intending wide dissemination) must

position in England, to judge by the deplorable conduct of the House of Commons in the face of the Defamation Bill, is unlikely to improve.[91] It is true that the introduction of a defence of reasonable belief makes it impossible to use the courts as a forum for ascertaining the truth of an allegation or imputation, but in fact the courts in defamation cases never ascertain the truth: even if the plaintiff wins huge damages, all he can say is that the defendant was unable to prove the truth of what he said—a very different thing.

If reasonableness of conduct is irrelevant in defamation suits, the Court of Appeal has nevertheless introduced the other principle of negligence law. It used to be the law that a defendant was not liable for the harm due to repetition of what he had uttered unless he had authorized it or it were a necessary consequence of his utterance.[92] This was a very useful constraint on the extent of a liability which can be incurred very easily indeed, as the bona fide repeaters themselves would find if sued. However, when the BBC broadcast a film making mock of the plaintiff, a sort of Inspector Clouseau, it was held potentially liable for the damage done by newspaper reports the next morning, simply because newspaper comment was foreseeable. Bingham LJ said, 'There cannot, I think, for this purpose be a difference in principle between negligence and other tortious conduct.'[93] With respect, the difference is clear enough. It is a general principle that when liability is very easily incurred, its extent should be the more readily restricted. This is clear not only in trespass and in claims for breach of contract,[94]

have had an honest and reasonable belief in the truth of the imputation, taken proper steps to check its veracity and, if practicable, sought a response from the present plaintiff. This goes less far than the US, which in *New York Times v Sullivan* 376 US 254 (1964) required P to prove absence of belief or reckless indifference to the truth. Canada has rejected both positions: *Manning and Church of Scientology v Hill* (1995) 126 DLR (4th) 129. See Kentridge, 'Freedom of Speech—A Primary Right?' 45 Int. Comp. L.Q. 253 (1996).

[91] Tartuffe MP and his friends in the House of Commons rejected a sensible clause (13) to the effect that a plaintiff could not sue for damage to a reputation which the defendant could show was undeserved, and substituted the present s 13 of the Defamation Act 1996, which allows a Member of Parliament to sue in respect of what has been said regarding his conduct in Parliament, thereby qualifying the important constitutional principle that the courts may not take cognisance of what happens in that august body.

[92] So held in *Speight v Gosnay* (1891) 60 LJQB 231: 'the original utterer is not responsible in damages for the subsequent repetition of the slander by persons who have no authority from him to repeat what he had said'. The treatment of this authority in *Slipper*, n. 93 below, is perplexing. It would be nice to know whether this decision was the trigger for the Slander of Women Act 1891, but Hansard is silent on the point.

[93] *Slipper v BBC* [1991] 1 All ER 165 at 178 (CA). Admittedly this was a striking-out action, but it is the sort of action which should be struck out.

[94] This is surely the explanation of the distinction drawn in *The Heron II* [1967] 3 All ER 686 (HL).

but also *e contrario* from the rule in deceit[95] and the rule that intended consequences are never too remote. The different torts are different, and if foreseeability is the appropriate test of remoteness in negligence, *non constat* that it is appropriate in defamation. Indeed it is not. You may be liable in defamation although your conduct is perfectly reasonable and you are liable for publications to third parties even if they cause no harm to the plaintiff. One might as well say that the policeman who makes a wrongful arrest should be liable for the detention when the magistrate remands the person arrested in custody.

It might be supposed that this decision was not very important, since in suits for libel no damage need be proved, and that given the present level of illiteracy, the difference between the number watching television and those extra persons reading the next day's tabloids would be immaterial. However, one must see the decision in the light of Community law as regards jurisdiction. In *Shevill v Presse Alliance*,[96] the Court in Luxembourg held that state courts could hear suits only as regards publications in their jurisdiction; the extension of liability to repetitions, even if unauthorized, will clearly increase the number of cases which can be heard in England, with all the associated advantages which that brings to the socially parasitic libel bar.

Negligence and the Torts requiring Malice

It will soon enough be a question whether malicious falsehood is to fall victim to negligence thinking. At present the *mere* fact that one is talking about a person raises no duty to take care that what one says is true, provided it is not defamatory, but *Spring v Guardian Assurance*[97] is good authority that an anterior relationship with that person may well contain such a duty, whether or not the statement is defamatory. It is entirely possible that our courts may hold that such a relationship exists between persons in competition, that competitors owe each other a duty to take care and/or to act reasonably in what they say about each other.[98]

Other torts requiring malice or something worse than mere negligence are malicious prosecution and misfeasance in a public office. 'In the case of the former, a plaintiff has to establish the absence of reasonable and

[95] *Smith New Court Securities v Scrimgeour Vickers (Asset Management) Ltd* [1996] 4 All ER 769 (HL).

[96] Case C-68/93, [1995] All ER EC 289n (ECJ).

[97] [1995] 2 AC 296, rev'g [1993] 2 All ER 273.

[98] Thus by statute, claims that a competitor has infringed one's intellectual property rights may well generate liability in damages: see Cornish, *Cases and Materials on Intellectual Property* (2nd ed., 1996), 670ff. At common law malice is still required: *Granby Marketing Services v Interlego* [1984] RPC 209, cited ibid.

probable cause and malice. In the case of the latter, knowledge of the want of power is an essential element.'[99] In a case where the plaintiff was suing the Crown Prosecution Service for negligent delay in discontinuing a prosecution as soon as it was evidently doomed to failure, Morritt L. J. proceeded to say, 'If the plaintiffs are right, want of reasonable care will suffice'. In holding them wrong, he prevented the intrusion of negligence into the tort of malicious prosecution. As in *Spring*, however, it was accepted that the prosecution service might in an unusual case assume responsibility for taking steps favourable to the suspect and be liable for negligent failure to comply with the duty of care so arising.[100]

Likewise Clarke J, in his very extensive review of the tort of misfeasance in office, said, 'I accept . . . that the tort of misfeasance is to be sharply distinguished from the tort of negligence.'[101] However, where the infraction of Community rights is concerned the validity of the requirement of knowledge of want of power has been questioned by the Court in Luxembourg,[102] which seems determined to make liability turn on the gravity of the breach rather than the attitude of the relevant legislative or executive body, a posture certainly consistent with concern to protect the rights of the citizen rather than restrain improper conduct by those in authority. A pity, perhaps, that the rights are principally economic.

Negligence and Contract

Introduction

Before we advert to the question of whether negligence thinking has had an effect on the liability of contractors, a few preliminary remarks on the relationship of contract and tort are called for.

The great majority of claims against contractors have absolutely no connection with the law of tort. It is not a tort not to pay your debts, and most contract claims are claims of debt, claims to enforce *in specie* the defendant's promise to pay for what he asked for and got.[103] It is quite

[99] *Elguzouli-Daf v Commissioner of Police* [1995] 1 All ER 833, per Morritt LJ.

[100] *Welsh v Chief Constable of the Merseyside Police* [1993] 1 All ER 692 (QB), where D failed to inform the court that certain offences committed by P had already been taken into account.

[101] *Three Rivers DC v Bank of England (No. 3)* [1996] 3 All ER 558 at 582, where the requirements are set out.

[102] See *Brasserie du Pêcheur v Germany//R v Secretary of State ex p Factortame (No. 4)* Cases C-46/48–93, [1996] QB 404 at 502.

[103] There is no liability at all for non-payment of damages: *President of India v Lips Maritime Corporation* [1987] 3 All ER 110 (HL). Indeed, it is only recently that contractual damages may be claimed for non-payment of a debt, and then only in narrow circumstances: *Wadsworth v Lydall* [1981] 2 All ER 401 (CA). There is still no entitlement to interest, unless stipulated for or sued for before payment: *President of India v La Pintada Cia* [1984] 2 All ER 773 (HL).

different where the claim is for damages for breach of a non-monetary promise, for when we are concerned with compensation (as opposed to enforcement) questions of fault, harm, causation, remoteness, and mitigation are as relevant as they are in a negligence claim. On such contractual claims negligence thinking could well have an effect.

Since the same function is performed by damages claims whether they are based on a contract or not, it is easy for a legal system to shift from one source of liability to the other when this seems desirable. Thus at a time in France when there was no liability in delict in the absence of fault, the courts turned to contract in order to protect the injured passenger (and his dependants, if he was killed) and held that the carrier contractually guaranteed his safety.[104] The German courts, unable to impose liability for purely economic harm in the absence of a contract, developed the idea of pre-contractual liability and expanded its scope to protect third-party victims of non-performance of the implicit duty of care.[105] In England if a customer was physically injured by a breach of contract and could not sue his contractor because of an exemption clause, he was allowed to sue the peccant employee in tort and the employee was not allowed to invoke the exemption clause even if it purported to cover him[106]—a device, unsatisfactory in both respects, now rendered superfluous by legislation invalidating exemption clauses in respect of personal injury or death caused by negligence.[107] The most dramatic development took place in 1964, when Lord Devlin, deciding 'to settle the law so that the presence or absence of consideration makes no difference', held that 'wherever there is a relationship equivalent to contract, there is a duty of care' even though the harm resulting from breach was of a purely financial order.[108] The relationship, not only of those negotiating a contract,[109] but also of those who had contracted,[110] came to be regarded, inevitably, as 'equivalent to contract', and relevant conduct has been extended from mis-statements to misperformance[111] and now even to non-performance.[112] The position arrived at now is that it is a tort negligently to fall short of a duty one has assumed by contract, and the practical consequence is that most damages claims against

[104] Civ., 21 Nov 1911, D. 1913.1.249, Note Sarrut.

[105] See B. S. Markesinis, *The German Law of Obligations*, vol 1, (3rd ed., 1997) 688f.

[106] *Adler v Dickson* [1955] 1 QB 158.

[107] Unfair Contract Terms Act 1977, s 2(1). As to property damage, the courts have managed (only just) to extricate themselves from the mess they unnecessarily created: see *The Makhutai* [1996] 3 All ER 502 at 506 ff. (PC) per Lord Goff.

[108] *Hedley Byrne v Heller* [1963] 2 All ER 575 at 611, 612 (HL).

[109] *Esso Petroleum v Mardon* [1976] 2 All ER 5 (CA).

[110] *Midland Bank Trust Co. v Hett Stubbs & Kemp* [1978] 3 All ER 571.

[111] *Henderson v Merrett Syndicates* [1994] 3 All ER 506 (HL).

[112] *White v Jones* [1995] 1 All ER 691 (HL).

professionals brought in the courts today allege both breach of contract and tortious negligence.[113]

Not every legal system agrees that liability in tort can concur with liability for breach of contract. In France a contractor's liability for breach of contract is, as against his contractor, exclusively contractual. This is not so in Germany where, however, the range of concurrence is limited by the fact that there is no liability in tort for merely economic harm. England has gone much further than either neighbour, as a consequence of accepting liability in tort for mere financial loss and confirming the principle of concurrence of claims in the strongest terms, despite murmurs below.[114]

But it is one thing to say that the contractor who is in breach of contract may be sued in tort; another to say that he can be sued in tort although a claim for breach of contract would fail on the merits. Can the general tort duty be used to increase the obligations of a contractor? The answer is that it cannot. The critical case involved the relationship of banker and customer.[115] Previous decisions in such disputes, necessarily contractual prior to *Hedley Byrne*,[116] had held that the customer's only duty as regards cheques was to take care to draw them in such a way as to minimize the risk of fraud and to notify the bank once the customer was aware that cheques were being fraudulently drawn. Now the bank sought to argue that in running his business so carelessly that he did not realize that cheques were being fraudulently drawn the customer was in breach of his duty of care to the bank. Lord Scarman repelled the argument with vigour, taking a strong position against 'searching for a liability in tort where the parties are in a contractual relationship.'[117] The view that '[i]t should be no part of the law of tort to fill in contractual gaps'[118] was strikingly applied in a case where 'the tortfeasor had contracted to be liable for failure to use reasonable skill and care in the design of the . . . operation and in the selection of materials and goods . . . but the contract was significantly silent as to liability for the manner in which the work was executed', with the result that he

[113] The practical result of *Hedley Byrne* (a case in which an advertising agent lost its claim for damages) has been to extend by very many years the period of the exposure of architects to successful claims. This is surely an odd way for the law to develop.

[114] 'That precisely the same breach of precisely the same [obligation] should be capable of generating causes of action which arise at different times is in my judgment an anomaly which our law could well do without.' *Bell v Peter Browne & Co.* [1990] 3 All ER 124 at 134 per Mustill LJ.

[115] *Tai Hing Cotton Mill v Liu Chong Hing Bank* [1985] 2 All ER 947 (PC).

[116] The banker could be liable in defamation for denying that there were funds to meet the customer's cheque; and also liable in conversion, subject to legislative protection.

[117] [1985] 2 All ER 947 at 957.

[118] *Banque Financière v Westgate Insurance* [1989] 2 All ER 952 at 1011, per Slade LJ.

was not liable for the pure economic loss resulting from his careless performance.[119]

Breach of Contract

Is negligence relevant to the question of whether or not a contractor is in breach of his contract? Standard teaching is that 'in general, liability for breach of contract is absolute and is not, like liability in tort, dependent on wrongful intent or negligence.'[120] The assumption that liability is strict has become an axiom.[121] Axioms ought to be questioned. True it is that fault is often irrelevant. The unpaid creditor need not show that his debtor was at fault in failing to pay as and when promised. Promises to supply other commodities are likewise strict, and sellers are strictly liable for defects in the goods delivered. Accordingly, when we add to promises to pay (the commonest of all promises), undertakings to deliver generic goods, and warranties of quality, we can safely go so far as to say that strict liability is *characteristic* of contract.

Even so, fault is often relevant. '[I]n the ordinary employment of a professional man, whether it is a medical man, a lawyer, or an accountant, an architect or an engineer, his duty is to use reasonable care and skill in the course of his employment.'[122] It is for the client to show that the professional was at fault. The position of the bailee—the garage, the laundry,[123] the hirer—who fails to return the goods is slightly different: he is not liable if it is not his fault or that of his delegates that he cannot return the goods, but it is for him to prove it. This sensible rule should have been generalized by the court in *Taylor v Caldwell*,[124] where the proprietor of a concert-hall was unable to provide it as promised by reason of an accidental fire, but it was unwisely held instead that the fire terminated the whole contract, with the consequence that now the proprietor who carelessly lets his hall burn down will be liable, not because his duty is only to take care of it (like the bailee's), but because the frustrating event, being 'self-induced', does not terminate the contract and he remains absolutely liable. [!] This unnecessarily complex solution has led to the absurd position that it is for the disappointed creditor to

[119] *Greater Nottingham Co-op v Cementation Ltd* 971 at 984 per Purchas LJ.

[120] Salmond and Williams, *Principles of the Law of Contract* (2nd ed, 1945), 510.

[121] 'It is axiomatic that, in relation to claims for damages for breach of contract, it is, in general, immaterial why the defendant failed to fulfil his obligation, and certainly no defence to plead that he had done his best.' Per Lord Edmund Davies in *Raineri v Miles* [1980] 2 All ER 145 at 158 (HL).

[122] *Greaves v Baynham Meikle* [1975] 3 All ER 99 at 104–5 (CA).

[123] There is a marvellous relevant passage, too long to quote, in *Alderslade v Hendon Laundry* [1945] KB 189 at 192, *per* Lord Greene MR.

[124] (1863) 112 Eng. Rep. 826.

prove the fault of the debtor of a supposedly absolute obligation once the latter invokes a frustrating event.[125]

Accordingly, fault *is* frequently relevant to the question of contractual liability. Is it becoming more relevant? Lord Devlin has observed that 'in every branch of the law we are getting away from the idea that absolute liability is the ideal'.[126] An instance of this is provided by the Occupier's Liability Act 1957, section 5. Prior to that enactment if one paid to enter premises to watch an event, the safety of one's seat was guaranteed and the occupier was strictly liable;[127] now the occupier's duty is reduced to the common duty of care unless the contract specifies otherwise. Equally Mr Silverman, who was bitten by fleas during his overnight stay in the defendant's hotel, would now have to show that their presence was due to negligence, not simply that they were present in unreasonable numbers, contrary to the implied warranty.[128] The carrier of goods by sea used to be held to a guarantee of the seaworthiness of his vessel. Now, 'There shall not be implied . . . any absolute undertaking by the carrier of the goods to provide a seaworthy ship.'[129] Furthermore, the duty of the carrier to 'load, handle, stow, carry, keep, care for and discharge the goods' is one to do those things 'properly and carefully' in the light of the knowledge of the nature of the cargo he did or should have had.[130] Again, when it was suggested that the employer warranted the safety of the equipment he provided for his employees to use, the suggestion was repelled with vigour.[131] There is some truth, then, in Lord Devlin's observation. It will be a question of the construction of a specific term whether it entails an obligation to procure a result or simply to try to do so, and the courts now tend to avoid the guarantee.[132] The matter may be quite complex. Thus in relation to the charterer's obligation to nominate a safe port for the vessel to proceed to, the House of Lords has reversed lower court decisions to the effect that the nomination constituted a continuing guarantee of the safety of the port, while accepting that the nomination was a guarantee that the port was safe

[125] *Joseph Constantine v Imperial Smelting* [1942] AC 154; see, too, *Lauritzen v Wijsmuller (The Super Servant Two)* [1989] 1 Lloyd's Rep. 148, and [1990] 1 Lloyd's Rep. 1 (CA), where it is said that fault in the sense of tortious negligence or breach of contract is not necessary if the allegedly frustrating event is one within the control of the party alleging it. It is also said (perhaps in view of the terms of the contract, but otherwise surprisingly) that a contractor who requires an item for future performance of his contract owes the other party no duty in contract or tort to look after it carefully in the meanwhile.

[126] Devlin, 'The Treatment of Breach of Contract', [1966] Camb. L.J. 192 at 202.

[127] *Francis v Cockrell* (1870) LR 5 QB 501.

[128] *Silverman v Imperial London Hotels* (1927) 43 TLR 260, (1927) 137 LT 57.

[129] Carriage of Goods by Sea Act 1971, s 3.

[130] *Albacora v Westcott and Laurance Line* [1966] 2 Lloyd's Rep. 53.

[131] *Davie v New Merton Board Mills* [1959] AC 604.

[132] *Thake v Maurice* [1986] 1 All ER 497.

at the time.[133] Consistent with this is the view that where 'the question is one of implication . . . the court will imply the least onerous obligation necessary to give the contract business efficacy'.[134]

Unreasonable Exercise of Rights

Even if a duty of a tortious nature cannot impose liabilities on a contractor over and above those he has assumed, it could possibly restrict the exercise of the rights he has given himself. The question arose in *Johnstone v Bloomsbury Health Authority*[135] where the contract of employment expressly empowered the hospital to require the employee to work up to forty-eight hours per week on average, over and above the forty hours laid down as his basic stint. The employee, seeking a declaration, asserted that the exercise of this power would endanger his health and breach the employer's duty to take care for the health of his employees. Stuart-Smith LJ was ready to hold that since the duty of care was implied by law it could not be cut down even by an express term (as indeed a statutory duty could not be so cut down). His colleagues disagreed with this, but Sir Nicholas Browne-Wilkinson VC agreed with his conclusion on the ground that the employer's right to require the contractual overtime was not absolute but rather a discretion to be exercised 'subject to its ordinary duty not to injure the plaintiff'.[136]

A term can clearly be implied that a contract right will be exercised reasonably, but in the absence of such a term is there such a duty? For a time it seemed not. Lord Reid famously said 'It might be, but it never has been, the law that a person is only entitled to enforce his contractual rights in a reasonable way and that a court will not support an attempt to enforce them in an unreasonable way.[137] Hot on its heels followed an astonishing statement in the Court of Appeal that 'A person who has a right under a contract or other instrument is entitled to exercise it and can effectively exercise it for a good reason or a bad reason or no reason at all.'[138] And this was said very shortly after that Court had had to backtrack in disarray from a suggestion that a finance company might be unable to claim damage for loss of bargain if its termination of the hire-purchase contract for non-payment was unreasonable.[139]

133 *Kodros Shipping v Empresa Cubana de Fletes (The Evia)* [1982] 3 All ER 350 (HL).
134 *Pagnan v Tradax* [1987] 3 All ER 565 at 572 (HL).
135 [1991] 2 All ER 293 (CA). 136 Ibid at 305.
137 *White & Carter (Councils) v McGregor* [1961] 3 All ER 1178 at 1182 (HL).
138 *Chapman v Honig* [1963] 2 All ER 513 at 522, per Pearson LJ.
139 See *Brady v St Margaret's Trust* [1963] 2 All ER 275, noting the correction of *Overstone v Shipway* [1962] 1 All ER 52 in *Financings v Baldock* [1963] 1 All ER 443 (CA). As a result of the last-mentioned case, the financier's loss is held irrecoverable not on grounds of his fault

But Lord Reid's statement was part of his swing speech in a decision much criticized and now being taken as authority for the very opposite of what it held;[140] in *Chapman v Honig* Lord Denning dissented powerfully, and the outcome in the hire-purchase cases has been maintained by a quick shift from fault to causation. All in all there is no doubt that developments in contract law over the past decades have been towards the imposition of a duty on contractors to exercise their rights with some circumspection and consideration for the other party, though the discussion is taking place in terms of good faith and fairness rather than reasonableness. Even so, recent statutory amendments to the Sale of Goods Act prevent a businessman from rejecting goods for disconformity when it would be unreasonable to do so,[141] and under the Unfair Contract Terms Act 1977 a party who unreasonably relies on a non-contractual notice of exemption from liability will rely in vain.[142] Clauses which allow one party unilaterally to alter the terms of a contract are naturally suspect. Building contracts may contain a clause which permits the employer to determine how much is due from the contractor; such a clause has been held valid, but the employer must have acted 'fairly, honestly and reasonably' even if the contract does not say so.[143]

Remoteness of Damage

The rules of remoteness of damage in contract and negligence are so intertwined that it is almost impossible to say which has been affected by the other. One would expect the rules to differ depending, not so much on the source of liability, but rather on whether the defendant was at fault (bad people pay more!) and on the nature of the harm: not only is mere economic loss more tolerable (and publicly tolerated) than physical

but of causation. It is otherwise where payment of each instalment is expressly made of the essence: *Lombard North Central v Butterworth* [1987] QB 527. See Opeskin, 'Damages for Breach of Contract Terminated under Express Terms', (1990) 106 LQR 293.

140 See, e.g. *Stocznia Gdanska v Latvian Shipping* [1996] 2 Lloyd's Rep. 132 (CA), where Staughton LJ says: 'To be a legitimate interest, the innocent party must have reasonable grounds for keeping the contract open, bearing in mind also the interests of the wrongdoer' (at 139). 'Absence of legitimate interest' was one of the tests used by French lawyers to ascertain the presence of an actionable *abus de droit;* this degenerated into the question whether the exercise of the right in question was *reasonable* or *fautif*. The trend echoed by Staughton LJ is all the more remarkable in that we are not supposed to have any doctrine of abuse of rights (but it is only the doctrine which is lacking).

141 Sale and Supply of Goods Act 1994, s 4 (quality and quantity), modifying Sale of Goods Act 1979, ss 13, 14, 15 & 30. Furthermore, the test of disconformity refers to the reasonable able buyer (s 1, modifying Sale of Goods Act 1979, s 14).

142 Unfair Contract Terms Act 1977, s 11.

143 *Balfour Beatty v Docklands Light Railway* [1996] 78 BLR 49 (CA).

harm but the failure to get something is manifestly not so serious as losing something you had. Although the typical contract claim for damages is based on the defendant's failure to act resulting, even without any negligence on the defendant's part, in the plaintiff's failure to acquire, whereas the typical tort consists in the defendant's unreasonable conduct causing harm to an existing asset or resource, there are instances of both kinds of case in both types of liability, and now that concurrence is so rampant it would be perplexing to relate the rules to the sources of liability.

What of the authorities? In *Hadley v Baxendale* in 1854[144] it was effectively held that a carrier who loses the goods is liable to the consignor for their value but not for any consequential loss unless he at least had notice of its likely occurrence;[145] the word 'foreseeable' does not occur in the judgments. In *Re Polemis* (whose very title indicates that it was a contract case) the charterer was held liable to the shipowner when the ship was destroyed as the direct but unforeseeable result of the negligence of a servant of an independent contractor retained by the charterer; the loss of the ship, though unforeseeable, was within the limits of *Hadley v Baxendale*—no consequential loss was claimed, only the value of the vessel under charter.[146] So far so good. In *The Wagon Mound (No. 1)*, however, where the parties were total strangers, the Privy Council, relying on a supposed rule in *Hadley v Baxendale* which they were surprised to find had not been cited in *Re Polemis*, held that a negligent defendant was not liable for consequent physical harm unless it was foreseeable as a result.[147] A few years later the House of Lords had another suit against a carrier for delay in delivery—*The Heron II*[148]—and held that the test in contract cases was more restrictive than in tort cases such as *The Wagon Mound*. To this confusion Lord Denning has added the view, not shared by his colleagues, that the more restrictive rule in contract cases does not apply when the harm is physical rather than merely economic.

There is not much point in discussing the matter. The principles enunciated are at too high a level of abstraction to be meaningful or even applicable. As Brian Simpson said in this connection, 'As law becomes more abstract and more generously endowed with doctrinal axioms and categories, the doctrines themselves seem to become

[144] (1854) 156 Eng. Rep. 145.

[145] Florian Furst in 'Hadley v Baxendale; an Understandable Miscarriage of Justice', (1994) 15 J. Leg. Hist. 41 at 48 states and shows that 'most surprisingly . . . this classic case as to the measure of contract damages, is not a contract case.' It was a claim based on the common custom of the realm, against an unincorporated common carrier.

[146] *Re Polemis and Furness Withy & Co.* [1921] 3 KB 560.

[147] [1961] AC 388.

[148] *Koufos v C. Czarnikow Ltd* [1969] 1 AC 350.

emptied of real significance; they become compatible with more or less any conclusion in concrete cases.'[149] The attempt to equate causation in the physical and economic fields (whether liability is in contract or in tort) is doomed to failure; so is the attempt to find a rule applicable to contracts of all types; and the pretence of ignoring fault in contract cases does not help.

Indeed the supposed connection may be a fantasy. Suppose that in the contract between Hadley and Baxendale's firm there had been an express clause limiting the carrier's liability to a certain figure.[150] No one supposes that its application would have anything to do with causation or remoteness of damage. Is the rule in *Hadley v Baxendale* not simply an *implied* limitation-of-liability clause, limiting liability to the value of the goods bailed? And would liability have been so limited if, shortly after the mill-shaft set out on its trip to Greenwich, one of Hadley's competitors had bribed Baxendale to delay its re-delivery? That the contract rules may have to do with quantum rather than the recoverability of particular items of loss is also indicated by the fact that where one would have made an unexpectedly profitable use of a chattel which the defendant has failed in breach of contract to supply, one may recover what one would have made from normal use, even though one would never have used it normally.[151]

As to our main theme, impossible to develop in this murky area, one may simply quote Treitel, who says, 'developments in England suggest that the tort analogy may have been pushed too far, but there is no doubt of its influence in the development of the foreseeability test in contract'.[152]

Negligence and Equity

Damages, the hallmark of tort, were not awarded as such by the courts of equity.[153] It might therefore be supposed that the links between

[149] A. W. B. Simpson, 'Innovation in Nineteenth Century Contract Law', (1975) 91 LQR 247 at 278, repr. in his *Legal Theory and Legal History* (1987), 171 at 202.

[150] It is worth noting what Martin B, who participated in *Hadley v Baxendale*, said (as he was to do later in *Horn v Midland Railway* (1873) 42 LJQB 42 at 59 in *Wilson v Newport Dock Co.* (1866) LR 1 Ex 177 at 184: dissenting, he emphasised that it was a case of carriage, and that the only effect of the decision was to bar a claim for consequential loss in such a case. Those from whom he dissented used *Hadley* to restrict the liability of the dock-owner who wrongfully refused entry to a vessel which thereupon came to (physical) grief outside it.

[151] *Cory v Thames Ironworks* (1868) LR 3 QB 181; *Victoria Laundry v Newman Indus.* [1949] 2 KB 528.

[152] G. H. Treitel, *Remedies for Breach of Contract—A Comparative Account* (1988), 152–3.

[153] The courts were very keen to keep distinct the damages payable by a fraudulent party for the loss suffered by the defrauded party through reliance on the lie and the indemnity which equity was prepared to require of the innocent misrepresentor when

negligence and equity must be slight. The equity courts did, however, issue decrees that the defendant pay money by reason of his breach of an equitable duty, so it is a question whether negligence thinking has affected the range of circumstances under which such a decree might issue, whether by modifying a strict liability imposed by equity or by inducing equity to afford its remedies where there was mere carelessness as opposed to wickedness. Secondly, whereas equity's money decrees were often directed to the replacement of money improperly dealt with by the defendant or to the disgorgement of profits improperly made or received by him, and damages in negligence are directed to compensating the plaintiff for appropriate damage or loss, the second question nevertheless arises of whether the restrictions which the rules of negligence place on recoverable harm have had any effect on the remedies of equity.

Scope of Duties in Equity and at Law.

It is first necessary to revert to the 'duty' question, for equity acknowledged duties unknown to common lawyers. As Lord Dunedin observed, '[W]henever we come to the idea of breach of duty we see how nearly the domains of law and equity approach, or perhaps, more strictly speaking, overlap.'[154] After a long period when there seems to have been little cross-fertilization or infection, the notion of 'fiduciary duty' has exploded, especially in Canada, where it has been deployed to deal, *inter alia*, with the conduct of a doctor who in return for sexual favours from a patient prescribed drugs she wanted but did not need, misbehaviour rather remote from that which traditionally attracted the critical attentions of the Lord Chancellor. This is but an extreme example of the way the notion of 'fiduciary duty' has been used to expand liability.[155]

If there were any doubt about the interaction of equity and negligence, one need only instance the role which *Nocton v Lord Ashburton* has played in the development of liability for negligently causing economic loss. In that case the defendant solicitor had written a misleading letter advising the plaintiff to release a security, the effect of which was to

the contract induced was rescinded. The best, though narrow, formula was that of Bowen LJ: 'Complete rescission would not be effected unless the misrepresenting party not only hands back the benefits which he has himself received but also re-assumes the burthens which under the contract the injured person has taken upon himself.' *Newbigging v Adam* (1886) 43 Ch. D. 582, 593. The matter has now been resolved (?) by the Misrepresentation Act 1967, which so far as damages is concerned appears to treat as a fraudulent misrepresentor the person who cannot prove that his mis-statement was not negligent.

[154] *Nocton v Lord Ashburton* [1914] AC 932 at 964.

[155] *Clark Boyce v Mouat* [1993] 4 All ER 268 (PC).

benefit the solicitor himself.[156] Actual fraud was negatived, and the common-law claim for contractual negligence was not open on the pleadings, but the House held that the defendant was in breach of his fiduciary duty to his client and that he was liable 'to restore to the mortgage security what he had procured to be taken out of it'.[157] This decision in equity was used in *Hedley Byrne & Co. Ltd v Heller & Partners*[158] as the catalyst to release a common-law liability in damages for economic loss carelessly caused outside the parameters of both contract and fiduciary duty. Indeed Lord Browne-Wilkinson VC regards *Nocton* as the 'genesis' of the conception of 'assumption of responsibility' in negligence,[159] and went so far as to say that 'The paradigm of the circumstances in which equity will find a fiduciary relationship is where one party, A, has assumed to act in relation to the property or affairs of another, B.' Even if it is true that in all cases where equity would find a fiduciary duty the party obliged has had dealings with the property or affairs of the creditor, his 'paradigm' is sadly insufficient as a statement of the further conditions which equity would demand before imposing a duty which can reasonably be called fiduciary,[160] even if he stated it to be adequate to found a duty of care at common law.

In a slightly earlier case his Lordship had deplored as 'misconceived' the plaintiffs' allegation, alternative to that of tortious negligence at common law, of a breach of fiduciary duty on the part of their agents, on the ground that (contrary to what was actually held in *Nocton v Lord Ashburton*) a fiduciary is under no special liability as such for negligent conduct of the affairs he has undertaken to conduct. This accords with a commentator's observation that 'While a solicitor is a status-based fiduciary, his negligence in carrying out his duties does not amount to a breach of fiduciary duty.[161]

One would be tempted to conclude that the common-law duty has absorbed that of equity, especially when one reads that '[I]t is likely that the equitable duty will eventually be folded into the common law to

[156] In an earlier case a solicitor's misrepresentation procured him an estate at the expense of his client, and he was treated as a constructive trustee: *Bulkley v Wilford* (1834) 6 Eng. Rep.1094.

[157] *Nocton v Lord Ashburton* [1914] AC 932 at 958 *per* Viscount Haldane. In fact the order in the CA for an inquiry into damages was upheld by the House since D had not objected to it.

[158] [1964] AC 465.

[159] *White v Jones* [1995] 1 All ER 691 at 712 (HL).

[160] Thus his Lordship arrives at the extremely extensive view that whenever a person does or agrees to do anything which he should realize would benefit another if properly done, he is liable in damages if owing to his failure to do it properly that benefit is not achieved, a proposition which Lord Mustill convincingly depotentiates in his marvellous dissenting judgment in that unhappy decision.

[161] So held in *Bristol and West of England Building Society v Mothew* [1996] 4 All ER 698 in a luminous judgment by Millett LJ.

produce a single standard of care and a single measure of recovery for breach of it'.[162] However, 'It is one thing to mould the tort of negligence by analogy with an equitable rule. . . . It is another to contend that once the tort of negligence has been moulded into its new form . . . the equitable rule thereby becomes somehow annihilated.'[163] In fact it appears that while the care required of a fiduciary is now identical with that of non-fiduciaries who are managing the plaintiff's affairs, he is subject to other duties whch remain wholly equitable and with which common-law negligence has nothing to do. As Lord Mustill observed, 'The essence of a fiduciary relationship is that it creates obligations of a different character from those deriving under the contract itself.'[164] Indeed in such cases negligence is sometimes not enough and sometimes not required.[165]

The principal thrust of the fiduciary duty is one of loyalty rather than care, and while care is always required, loyalty is in issue only when disloyalty is possible, where there is a conflict of interest. In order to ensure loyalty in such cases the courts of equity imposed the strictest of standards, not always involving fault in the particular case. As has been said, 'The reasonable man labours at law not in equity which sets higher standards for fiduciaries.'[166] This hortatory or deterrent concern is rather absent from negligence law, which has little to do with the proper area of fiduciary duty, namely the misuse of power conferred in the private sphere, a power over property in which another has an interest, or which one has only for a particular purpose, or a power to bind the other or commit him to dispositions and engagements. While it is true that agreement between the parties may profoundly modify the duty, equity has been much more discriminating in determining the duties of fiduciaries in various situations than has the common law of negligence, which treats the question of breach as one of mere fact, the legal standard of 'reasonable care' being virtually constant.[167]

[162] R. P. Austin, 'Moulding the Content of Fiduciary Duties', in A. J. Oakley (ed.), *Trends in Contemporary Trust Law* (1996), 153 at 174.

[163] Hayton in (1995) 111 LQR 1 at 3.

[164] *Re Goldcorp Exchange* [1994] 2 All ER 806 at 821 (PC).

[165] Where the fiduciary has been transacting with the principal 'even inadvertent failure to disclose will entitle the principal to rescind the transaction', whereas in other cases, 'Mere incompetence is not enough. A servant who loyally does his incompetent best for his master is not unfaithful and is not guilty of a breach of fiduciary duty.' *Bristol and West Building Society v Mothew* [1996] 4 All ER 698 at 712 per Millett LJ.

[166] R. P. Meagher, W. M. C. Gummow & J. R. F. Lehane, *Equity Doctrines and Remedies* (3rd ed., 1992), para 229.

[167] In his critical note on Lord Browne-Wilkinson's speech in *Henderson v Merrett Syndicates* Hayton notes differences between the duties of the various parties in whom equity is interested, independently of the effect of legislation applying to some and not others, and the specifics of the constituent instrument under which they take their powers: (1995) 111 LQR 1 at 6–7.

If the fiduciary makes a profit his liability is strict (like that of the donee of someone else's property), though the law may allow him something for his pains if he is deserving.[168] In the absence of such profit, where there is only loss—the cases where tortious negligence would be relevant—statute has sometimes intervened to protect those who have acted reasonably and excusably, in particular trustees and company directors. But there are other cases of equitable liability where the question of the intensity of the obligation is a matter of debate. In general terms, whereas equity, looking to the conscience of the defendant, is much interested in whether he acted with knowledge or in ignorance, there is the question whether, though he did not know, he should have known, whether he had 'constructive knowledge', that is, was at fault in not knowing. The extension from actual to constructive knowledge entails an intrusion of negligence thinking, and a diminution of the conditions of liability.

Thus in *Re Horsley & Weight Ltd*,[169] where the question was whether directors were liable for granting a pension which the company could not afford, it was suggested by Templeman LJ that negligence on their part in failing to realize the company's financial position might be enough, whereas generally misfeasance or serious fault or bad faith is required.[170]

But it was not only on fiduciaries that equity imposed monetary liability: a non-fiduciary who, without receiving trust funds, assisted in a breach of trust might be found liable for the 'equitable tort' of *Barnes v Addy*.[171] The question was what conduct rendered such a person liable: 'Whether . . . negligence will suffice is an issue on which there has been a well-known difference of opinion.'[172] The suggestion that negligence was sufficient unsurprisingly arose in 1968,[173] but it has now been definitively held that dishonesty is required: negligence is not enough. In the absence of dishonesty the disappointed beneficiary will have no claim unless the negligent defendant owed him a duty of care; this will not often occur—for in general there is no duty to check that trustees are behaving honestly—and if they are behaving honestly, the trustees will have an action for the benefit of the trust, for they will certainly be owed a duty by the person they retain to assist them in its management.[174]

The duties of the mortgagee have caused confrontations between the

[168] *Boardman v Phipps* [1966] 3 All ER 721 (HL).

[169] [1982] 3 All ER 1045 (CA).

[170] Cooke J expanded this liability for negligence in *Nicholson v Permakraft (NZ) Ltd* (1985) 3 ACLC 453 at 459–60, cited in J. D. Heydon, 'Directors' Duties and the Company's Interests', in P. D. Finn (ed.), *Equity and Commercial Relationships* (1987), 120 at 128.

[171] (1874) LR Ch App 244.

[172] *Royal Brunei Airlines v Tan* [1995] 3 All ER 97 at 104 per Lord Nicholls (PC).

[173] *Selangor United Rubber Estates v Cradock* [1968] 2 All ER 1073.

[174] See *Royal Brunei Airlines v Tan* [1995] 3 All ER 97 at 107–8.

rules of negligence and the dictates of equity. In *Cuckmere Brick Co. v Mutual Finance*[175] a Court of Appeal not including Lord Denning held that though a mortgagee was free to sell when he chose, he owed a duty in tort towards a mortgagor to take reasonable care to obtain the best price when he did sell.[176] This duty of care was extended by Lord Denning in a later case[177] to cover the surety as well as the mortgagor, but when it came to the question whether a like duty was owed to a beneficiary, the later Court was distinctly cool, and asserted that the duty was equitable only, and not one in the law of tort.[178]

The case which started the rot has been referred to in frosty terms in the Privy Council. *Downsview Nominees v First City Corporation*[179] concerned the liability of a receiver and mortgagor company towards a second debenture holder, and the Court of Appeal of New Zealand had held that 'if there were any duties on the part of the [defendants] . . . they would have to be based in negligence.'[180] The Privy Council reinstated the judgment of Gault J on a quite different ground, namely bad faith. Lord Templeman said, 'The general duty of care said to be owed by a mortgagee to subsequent incumbrancers and the mortgagor is inconsistent with the right of the mortgagee and the duties which the courts applying equitable principles have imposed on the mortgagee.'[181] The receiver and the mortgagee are given the powers they have for a purpose, and are liable only if they act in bad faith for other purposes. Just as the general duty of reasonable care is not to be invoked in order to increase the duties undertaken by a contractor,[182] so it must not be introduced where it would have the effect of modifying the precise powers and duties held by equity courts to be vested or incumbent on mortgagees and receivers. Likewise it is wrong to invoke the principles of equity in order to increase the duties of a solicitor beyond those assumed by him under his contract or imposed by the common law.[183]

Quantum of Recovery

Though it is true, as we have seen, that '[I]n recent cases the standard of care is increasingly being treated as merely an application of the

175 [1971] 2 All ER 633 (CA).

176 For this they much relied on a case where the mortgagor had actually caused physical damage to the property to be auctioned, by driving the mortgaged horses too hard to the sale: *McHugh v Union Bank* [1913] AC 299.

177 *Standard Chartered Bank v Walker* [1982] 3 All ER 938 (CA).

178 *Parker-Tweedale v Dunlop Bank* [1990] 2 All ER 577 (CA).

179 [1993] 3 All ER 626 (PC).

180 Ibid at 633. It can be said that for the New Zealand judges liability in negligence is not just a principle but an obsession.

181 Ibid at 637.

182 *Tai Hing Cotton Mill v Liu Chong Hing Bank* [1985] 2 All ER 947 (PC).

183 *Clarke Boyce v Mouat* [1993] 4 All ER 268 (PC).

common law of negligence with no special equitable measure of damages',[184] it remains the case that the measure of recovery where the duty breached is purely equitable is often different from that where the duty is one now arising at common law. This can be seen in a recent case where a building society obtained a money judgment against a solicitor found at first instance to be liable for breach of fiduciary duty and trust as well as for tortious misrepresentation in breach of contract: on appeal it was held that since there was no equitable liability the judgment must be vacated and the matter remanded so that the plaintiff could prove, if possible, what loss had resulted from the defendant's common law negligence.[185] We therefore turn to the second question, whether the rules of negligence about causation, remoteness, and mitigation have had effect on the remedies granted by equity in comparable cases.

In *Re Bell's Indenture*[186] a solicitor was liable as constructive trustee for the improper sale of a farm. Had the farm been retained in the trust, estate duty would have been payable and the benefit to the beneficiaries thereby reduced. The defendant was not allowed to reduce his liability in this respect, but such a reduction would certainly have been permitted in a negligence action.

By contrast in *Target Holdings v Redferns*[187] Lord Browne-Wilkinson regarded it as a 'novel point' whether a trustee is 'liable to compensate the beneficiary not only for losses caused by the breach but also for losses which the beneficiary would, in any event, have suffered even if there had been no such breach'. He held that a 'bare trustee' need not, as the Court of Appeal had held, replace the funds mishandled unless the mishandling had contributed to the loss. 'Equitable compensation for breach of trust', he observed, 'is designed to achieve exactly what the word compensation suggests: to make good a loss in fact suffered by the beneficiaries and which, using hindsight and common sense, can be seen to have been caused by the breach,'[188] and that while 'The detailed rules of equity as to causation and the quantification of loss differ, at least ostensibly, from those applicable at common law . . . the principles underlying both systems are the same'.[189] The 'at least ostensibly' is rather suspicious, but the actual holding undoubtedly goes in the direction of importing common-law notions of causation, at least, into equitable proceedings.

Commentators have suggested that the liability in question was not

[184] R. P. Austin, 'Moulding the Content of Fiduciary Duties', in A. J. Oakley (ed), *Trends in Contemporary Trust Law* (1996) 153 at 169.
[185] *Bristol and West Building Society v Mothew* [1996] 4 All ER 698.
[186] [1980] 3 All ER 425. [187] [1995] 3 All ER 785 (HL). [188] Ibid at 798.
[189] Ibid at 792.

really that for breach of trust, but for breach of fiduciary duty regarding the funds in question. One of them has said that

> once a truly compensatory approach is adopted and that approach is applied to breaches of non-traditional trusts (and other forms of equitable obligations), issues of causation, remoteness and foreseeability come to the fore. Tort law, with its greater learning on these matters, is a tempting model. . . . The consequence is that then one starts to ask questions about the linkages between tort duties and equitable duties.[190]

Those questions may have to touch on matters of contributory negligence and mitigation of damage as well as causation, remoteness, and foreseeability, but it is not unpredictable what the outcome will be.

Negligence and Public Law

Judicial Review

One does not have to read very far into the material on judicial review of the decisions of public bodies to come across the word 'unreasonable' as an indicator of probable judicial sanction. However, it is commonly preceded by the word 'Wednesbury'.[191] Woden, after whom that Staffordshire town, like the day of the week, is named, was doubtless unreasonable as gods tend to be, but the citizens may not appreciate the fact that for lawyers their local brand of unreasonableness means *very irrational indeed*, and indicates that a decision not vulnerable on grounds of bias or irrelevance or procedural irregularity may yet be annulled if quite unreasonable. As Lord Reid observed, 'the word has come to acquire a rather artificial meaning'[192] but even so Lord Diplock pitches it perhaps a little high when he says, 'It applies to a decision so outrageous in its defiance of logic or of accepted moral standards that no sensible person who had applied his mind to the question to be decided could have arrived at it.[193] Close though this comes to the 'gross negligence' which the courts have, perhaps unwisely, rejected as a criterion in tort cases,[194] one author questions whether this test actually adds

[190] C. E. F. Rickett, Note in (1996) 112 LQR 27 at 32, referring to Heydon, Note in (1994) 110 LQR 328.

[191] See J. Jowell & A. Lester, 'Beyond *Wednesbury*' [1987] PL 368; G. L. Pieris, '*Wednesbury* Unreasonableness—The Expanding Canvas', [1987] Camb. L.J. 53; Lord Irvine, 'Judges and Decision-Makers: The Theory and Practice of *Wednesbury* Review', [1996] PL 59f.

[192] *Westminster Bank v Beverley Borough Council* [1971] AC 508 at 530.

[193] *CCSU v Minister for the Civil Service* [1984] 3 All ER 935 at 951 (HL).

[194] In admiralty law the idea of *crassa neglegentia* still exists in connection with the unjustified arrest of a vessel: see *The Kommunar (No. 3)* [1997] 1 Lloyd's Rep. 22 (Colman J).

anything to the other tests specific to the area.[195] Certainly it is not enough that the reviewing court believes that a different decision would have been more reasonable, since to substitute its own view for that of the public body with power to decide would be to confuse adjudication with administration; but it is also true that in normal negligence cases it is not generally enough to persuade the court that the defendant could have acted more reasonably: the court has to conclude that no reasonable man would have behaved as the defendant did.[196]

Nevertheless, it is clear that, at any rate in its original formulation by Lord Greene in the 1948 case about the local authority's decision to ban the showing of a film to those under 16, a decision not (otherwise) *ultra vires* has to be very unreasonable before it can be struck down. The tort lawyer of course would ask what harm resulted from the decision, and might find that being prevented from watching a film did not rate very high, but it is significant that administrative lawyers pay rather little overt attention to the nature of the harm occasioned by the decision impugned.

Has there been an increase in the application of the criterion of unreasonableness in this area? Although Lord Templeman has said that 'It is not the function of the court to determine whether a decision is reasonable or not',[197] others have observed that 'The criterion moves closer to asking whether the courts believe that the exercise of discretion was reasonable',[198] and that 'the courts have used the *Wednesbury* sense of unreasonableness to invalidate exercises of discretionary power which could not realistically be regarded as absurd, or manifestly irrational'.[199] It has also been suggested that 'the courts in deciding cases tend to lower the threshold of unreasonableness to fit their more exacting ideas of administrative good behaviour'.[200] The answer is probably that although judicial intervention has undeniably increased over the past twenty or thirty years it is attributable to factors other than a cross-over from negligence law.

DAMAGES

Yet the impact of negligence law on local authorities has been profound and troubling. As warrant for this we need simply note that the

[195] P. P. Craig, *Administrative Law* (3rd ed., 1994), 410.

[196] As H. W. R. Wade & C. F. Forsyth make clear, This is not . . . the standard of the '"man on the Clapham omnibus".' (*Administrative Law* (7th ed., 1994), 400). Yet the analogy of negligence law has been invoked in an odd way: '[E]veryone by now knows Lord Greene MR's summation of the *Wednesbury* principles by heart and, as has happened to *Donoghue v Stevenson*, no one now ever opens the report of the *Wednesbury* case' (per Hodgson J in *R v Secretary of State, ex p Benwell* [1985] QB 554 at 568).

[197] *Re Westminster City Council* [1986] AC 668 at 701. [198] Craig, n. 187 above, 411.

[199] Ibid at 441. [200] Wade and Forsyth, n. 188 above, 401.

revolution effected by *Anns*[201] and the counter-revolution in *Murphy,*[202] which have set the legal world by the ears and divided the Commonwealth,[203] both turned on the application of the law of tortious negligence to local authorities exercising public powers. And if one were to list the five most important cases in the years since *Murphy,* one could omit neither *X (minors) v Bedfordshire County Council*[204] nor *Stovin v Wise,*[205] which also considered at length the question of the liability in damages of governmental bodies for doing or not doing what they decided to do or did. The underlying idea is that unreasonable governmental *decisions* should not involve liability for consequent loss, if within the accorded area of discretion, but that unreasonable *action* should or may do so if not in proper implementation of a permitted decision, but it is extremely difficult to formulate an applicable criterion. We have toyed with 'discretionary' and 'operational', but as Steyn LJ observed, 'The criteria upon which one determines whether a decision is one of policy or of operation has not been worked out in the courts. It is as yet a most obscure corner of the law'[206]—for all that it is of vital importance.

Given the appropriate reluctance of the courts to hold that breach of statutory duty by a public body gives rise to liability in damages,[207] it is not surprising that they are unready to impose liability in negligence at common law when the exercise of statutory powers is questionable and proves harmful. If the statutory power simply replicates a liberty enjoyed by private citizens, such as driving a motor vehicle or providing medical treatment, there is no problem, but when the powers are special to governmental bodies, such as the power to interfere with the custody of children, the courts tend to hold that it would be 'unfair unjust or unreasonable' to impose a common-law duty regarding their exercise with consequent liability for failure to exercise them properly.[208] On

[201] *Anns v Merton London Borough Council* [1977] 2 All ER 492 (HL).

[202] 194) *Murphy v Brentwood District Council* [1990] 2 All ER 908 (HL).

[203] See *Invercargill City Council v Hamlin* [1996] 1 All ER 756 (PC).

[204] [1995] 3 All ER 353. [205] [1996] 3 All ER 801.

[206] *Lavis v Kent County Council* (1992) 90 LGR 416 at 420, where the question was whether the highway authority was liable for failure to signal a bend in the road which proved dangerous to the plaintiff motor-cyclist; the case was remitted to the trial court which held the decision one of policy.

[207] The overruling of *Thornton v Kirklees Metropolitan Borough Council* [1979] 2 All ER 349 (CA) in *O'Rourke v Camden London Bourough Council* [1997] 3 All ER 23 (HL) removed a significant exception (duty to provide a facility). But perhaps the justifiable reluctance as regards public bodies is causing the courts to be unduly reluctant where D is a private person: *Richardson v Pitt-Stanley* [1995] 1 All ER 460 (CA—company director guilty of offence of conniving at company's failure to have the mandatory insurance against liability to employees, not liable to injured employee uncompensated because of such failure).

[208] This may be the explanation for the otherwise curious holding in *X v Bedfordshire County Council* [1995] 3 All ER 353 (HL) that a local authority is not liable at common law for unreasonable exercise or failure to exercise powers relating to the prevention

political grounds, the tendency of the tort of negligence to expand its scope must be restrained when it unduly threatens the exercise of governmental powers. Indeed, it is to this threat that we must attribute the introduction of the much criticized division between public law and private law in *O'Reilly v Mackman*:[209] it says much for the power of negligence doctrine that the courts felt forced to describe its use as an 'abuse of the process of the court' in cases where a governmental decision was being impugned.

Yet if negligence liability cannot use the front door of the local authority, it can try to use the employees' entrance at the back, and this is happening under our very eyes. We have already seen the ambiguity in the nature of the liability of the Home Office in the *Dorset Yacht* case:[210] was it primarily liable for breach of its own duty through the warders, or vicariously liable for the warders' breach of their own duties? In several cases recently a local authority has been held liable for the misconduct of its employee in the exercise of powers as to which the authority itself would have been held to be under no common-law duty to the party affected. It was so in *Welton v North Cornwall District Council*,[211] where a restaurateur was put to unnecessary expense when an employee of the local authority, in purported pursuance of its health powers, required the unnecessary work. The Court of Appeal used standard negligence law to hold that the employee would be liable to the restaurateur, and that consequently his employer was liable; it is unimaginable that the authority could have been held directly liable for giving such an instruction, yet it is only through employees that local authorities can have any effect on the outside world. Something is going to have to be done about this development unless the law is be unacceptably self-contradictory.[212]

of child abuse but may be liable as regards its powers relating to education of the disadvantaged.

[209] [1982] 3 All ER 1124 (HL). [210] Above, text at n. 9. [211] [1996] 1 WLR 570.

[212] The question arose also in *Barrett v Enfield London Borough Council* [1997] 3 All ER 171 (CA), concerning the liability of a local authority to a child in care who ended up with severe personality problems as a result of mismanagement by D's social services and social workers. Evans LJ accepted that the authority might be vicariously liable when not primarily liable: 'The distinction rests . . . on the different relationships with the child or patient in the two cases' (at 181). This is not enough to justify the distinction, and the reason he proceeds to give (physical harm to the child) does not justify it either.

It is not only in the area of governmental liability that the problem presents itself. Suppose a misrepresentation appears in a company document addressed to P: is the liability of the company primary, or vicarious? Is the draftsman or human originator of the misrepresentation personally liable or not? Can it make any sense to hold the secretary liable for a typing error? Or the managing director? See *Williams v Natural Life Health Foods* [1996] 1 BCLC 288. Now that *Hedley Byrne* has been extended from statements to services, and from positive action to omission, we have here a battering ram to pierce the corporate veil, if we may mix metaphors as readily as the law mixes policies.

Conclusion

As was to be expected, the influence of negligence thinking in the various areas of obligations law is very varied, but far from negligible. As Lord Templeman accurately and acidly observed, '[A] fashionable plaintiff alleges negligence. The pleading assumes that we are all neighbours now, Pharisees and Samaritans alike, that foreseeability is a reflection of hindsight and that for every mischance in an accident-prone world someone solvent must be liable in damages.'[213] Although, as we have seen, the rules of negligence exclude liability without fault as well as liability for unforeseeable harm, the thrust of the tort has certainly been to render persons liable who previously would not have had to pay, and this effect has been in line with the public belief that a society is progressive in proportion as it answers complaints, the complainants in our context being plaintiffs. In more recent years there has perhaps been some retrenchment, best instantiated by the dramatic overruling of *Anns* in *Murphy*,[214] and the equity lawyers seem to be quite good at maintaining their territory, though not without a struggle. The pull of the negligence principle—pay for the foreseeable harm you are at fault in causing—is immensely strong. This can be seen in France. There the principle is enshrined in a text. Desperate remedies have been employed to prevent a deluge—including, in the hope of preserving the law of contract, a refusal to allow a concurrent claim in tort,[215]—but in vain. Likewise, we have had to hold that negligence suits against public bodies may constitute an abuse of the system, and have adopted a discretionary escape-hatch in the form of 'not fair, just and reasonable'. The German draftsmen were wise, having seen what article 1382 of the French Civil Cote could do, to refrain from adopting such a general clause, and though Italy and Switzerland do have a clause like the French one, they have in fact largely followed the German model.

The pull of the principle is not purely emotional, encouraging us to be

[213] *CBS Songs v Amstrad plc* [1988] 2 All ER 484, 497 (HL). This paper has not considered the (happily unsuccessful) attempts to render liable those who, with arguable carelessness, merely facilitated an invasion of P's intangible property rights by a third party: *Paterson Zochonis & Co. v Merfarken Packaging* [1986] 3 All ER 522 (CA).

[214] It is to be noted, however, that the objections to *Anns* were quite as much doctrinal as political.

[215] Unfortunately the result has been to pervert the law of contract by making it largely a law of damages rather than enforcement, which is its proper aim. '[O]n donne indûment à la 'responsabilité contractuelle' une fonction de réparation de dommages corporels empruntée à la responsabilité délictuelle, en incluant artificiellement dans le contrat une obligation de sécurité.' P. Rémy, 'Nouveaux Développements de la responsabilité civile', (1995) rev. gén. ass. terr. 529. See also P. Rémy, 'La 'responsabilité contractuelle': histoire d'un faux concept' (1997) rev. trim. dr. civ 323, and D. Tallon, 'L'inexécution du contrat: pour une autre présentation', (1994) rev. trim. dr. civ 223.

generous with other people's money; it is also aesthetic—in this rather like the idea of a single Europe. Despite its double appeal, it would be right to be mindful of the characteristically sound observation of John Fleming that 'An undifferentiated approach may satisfy the quest for uniformity but it is unlikely to produce desirable decisions'.[216]

[216] J. Fleming, 'Remoteness and Duty: Control Devices in Liability for Negligence', (1953) 31 Can. Bar Rev 471 at 481.

THEORETICAL PERSPECTIVES

6

Retribution, Proportionality, and Moral Luck in Tort Law

*Peter Cane**

Introduction

According to traditional wisdom, tort law is about compensation, not punishment. Even as applied to the assessment of damages, this pithy shibboleth misses an important part of the truth, if only because tort law recognizes disgorgement damages and punitive damages as well as compensatory damages. But applied more generally, the dictum is positively misleading. Tort law compensates people for harm, but only if some other person can be said to be responsible for that harm in one of the senses of 'responsible' recognized by tort law in its heads of liability. Every cause of action in tort is a two-sided affair concerned with the interests of the plaintiff on the one side and with the conduct of the defendant on the other. Tort law is as much a set of ethical rules and principles of personal responsibility as a mechanism for compensating victims of harm.[1] Indeed, it could be said that responsibility for conduct underpins all of the plaintiff-oriented functions of tort law, including compensation. There can be no tort liability without a judgment that the defendant was responsible in some relevant sense. The fact that punitive remedies play only a minor role in tort law should not divert our attention from the fact that being held liable in tort is a sanction.

Viewed as a set of rules and principles of personal responsibility, tort law has some puzzling features. For instance, under the objective test of negligence, a person may be held liable for failing to act 'reasonably' even if the person could not have met the standard of reasonable

*Thanks to John Braithwaite, Richard Holton, Tony Honoré, Jane Stapleton and Lucia Zedner for valuable comments and advice.

[1] See generally P. Cane, *The Anatomy of Tort Law* (1997), esp ch 1.

conduct in the circumstances of the case. Under rules of strict liability a person may be held liable for outcomes which could not have been avoided by the exercise of reasonable care by that person or anyone else. Under the rules of assessment of damages, a negligent driver who happens to injure a low-earner will, other things being equal, pay less compensation for loss of income than one who happens to injure a high-earner, even if the former's tort was no less culpable than the latter. The puzzle in each of these examples is that a person is held responsible for conduct or events or outcomes which were, to a greater or lesser extent, outside their control. How can we justify imposing legal responsibility on a person for something which they could not have prevented?

In this essay I seek to cast light on these puzzles by drawing on two sources: ideas in criminal law about retributive justice, and the philosophical concept of 'moral luck'. In order to avoid misunderstanding, it should be stressed at this point, as will be clear from what has already been said, that the concept of retributive justice used in this essay is not tied to punishment but refers more generally to the link between responsibility for conduct and legal liability. As applied to tort law, retributive justice embodies two ideas: first, that a person should not be held liable unless they were, in a relevant sense, responsible for that which they are being held liable for; and secondly, that any sanction imposed by the law should be proportional, in some sense, to the ground of the liability. The main conclusions about the application of ideas of retributive justice to tort law will be, first, that while fault-based tort liability can be understood in retributive terms, strict liability cannot be so understood; and secondly, that the rules governing tort remedies for 'faulty' conduct can be said broadly to take account of the demands of proportionality.

The philosophical notion of 'moral luck' refers to the fact that many aspects of a person's conduct and the circumstances in which that conduct occurs and takes effect are, to a greater or lesser extent, outside their control. This raises the fundamental question of how we can justify holding a person responsible for conduct or events over which they had only partial or no control. This question is fundamental to the moral legitimacy of legal rules, such as the rules of tort law, criminal law, and contract law, which are predicated upon judgments of personal responsibility for conduct. I will argue that the phenomenon of moral luck does not, by itself, undermine attributions of responsibility because taking responsibility for conduct and outcomes, even those outside our control, is essential to having a sense of ourselves as moral agents rather than mere victims of fate.

The issues addressed in this essay are not ones to which tort lawyers or the mainstream literature on tort law have given much attention. They are, however, crucial to understanding tort law and to assessing its legitimacy. They are large and difficult issues, and I cannot hope to do more here than introduce them. If this essay stimulates tort lawyers to think more deeply about the foundations of their subject, it will have fulfilled its main objective.

Three Basic Ideas

According to a widely-held view, one of the fundamental principles of sentencing in the criminal law is that the punishment should, in some sense, 'fit the crime'; or, in other words, that the sanction imposed on a convicted criminal should, in some sense, be proportional to the seriousness of the offence and the culpability of the criminal.[2] On this view, such proportionality is a pre-condition of a criminal sanction being (retributively) just. This quantitative aspect of retributive justice has two elements. First, the punishment for any particular crime should not be too severe: we should not, for instance, imprison someone merely for parking on a double yellow line. This is called 'cardinal proportionality'. Secondly, punishments for different crimes should be proportional *inter se*; that is, they should reflect the relative seriousness of various offences and the relative culpability of those committing them. This is called 'ordinal proportionality'. Besides this dual quantitative aspect, retributive justice also has (what might be called) a qualitative aspect which is concerned not with the appropriateness of particular punishments but with whether a person ought to be punished at all; that is, with whether the person was, in some relevant sense, responsible for what they did or failed to do.

Underlying both the quantitative and the qualitative aspects of retributive justice are notions of moral desert. Judgments of moral desert are based on ideas about the responsibility of persons for their conduct and for consequences of their conduct. Central to ideas of personal responsibility is the concept of control.[3] We are often loath to hold people responsible for events outside their physical or mental control. Extreme determinists would entirely reject the idea of personal responsibility on the basis that everything we do is, to a greater or lesser extent, the result of causal processes beyond our control. But even if we reject extreme determinism (as most people do), we might still have qualms about the idea of personal responsibility which are based on what philosophers

[2] A. Ashworth, *Sentencing and Criminal Justice* (2nd ed., London, 1995), 69–72 & ch 4.

[3] Control may be a matter of degree; and it may have an evaluative element in the sense that we may treat as being beyond a person's control something which was not literally so but which it would not be reasonable to expect the person to control.

call 'moral luck'.[4] 'Moral luck' refers to the phenomenon of subjecting a person's conduct to moral judgment[5] even though some aspect of their conduct or its consequences was beyond their control. Thus, we might judge someone negatively for some bad conduct or some outcome even though the conduct or the outcome was, in some respect, outside their control. Conversely, we may confer moral approval on a person for some conduct or outcome even though things turned out well for that person for some reason beyond that person's control. In short, people can have good moral luck and bad moral luck. Luck is an inevitable and pervasive feature of the human condition because our conduct and its consequences 'nearly always depend on factors beyond our control'.[6] There are two types of luck, which I shall call 'dispositional'[7] and 'circumstantial'.[8] Dispositional luck is a function of 'the kind of person you are';[9] of your personality, temperament, emotions, desires, and capacities. Of course, not all of our internal characteristics are beyond our control, but there are practical limits to the extent that the typical person can consciously regulate their behaviour. Our ethical sense makes some allowance for such limits, but the allowance is not infinite. Circumstantial luck is a function of the circumstances in which you find yourself.[10] Once again, human beings have great capacity to control their surroundings, but in the total order of things, that capacity is nevertheless very limited, especially when the surroundings include other human beings.

In this essay I will examine the relevance to tort law of these three related ideas of retributive justice, proportionality, and moral luck. The basis of my approach is that tort law is a set of ethical rules and principles of personal responsibility. The relationship between legal ethics and extra-legal ethics (which I shall call 'morality') is complex: law reflects morality in certain respects, but in others diverges from it. Important to understanding the relationship is the fact that tort law is ultimately underwritten by the power of the State. The ethical rules and principles it embodies must, therefore, possess qualities of clarity, internal consistency, and widespread social acceptability which extra-legal

[4] This term was coined by Bernard Williams in 'Moral Luck' (1976) *Procs Aristotelian Soc.*, Supp. vol L, 115. For a useful collection of essays on the subject see D. Statman (ed.), *Moral Luck* (1993). See also M. Moore, *Placing Blame* (1997), ch 5.

[5] I use this term to cover both judgments that a person is responsible for conduct and consequences, and attributions of praise or blame in respect of conduct and consequences. However, as we will see later, there is an important distinction between the two.

[6] T. Nagel, *Mortal Questions* (1979), 25. Most basically, our coming into existence is a matter of luck.

[7] Also called 'internal' or 'constitutive'.

[8] Also called 'external'.

[9] Nagel, n. 6 above, 28.

[10] I use this phrase in a broad sense to cover both 'resultant luck' (luck in the way our behaviour turns out) and 'situational luck' (luck in the situations we face or do not face). Philosophers tend to use the term 'circumstantial luck' only to cover the latter, but for present purposes, nothing turns on the distinction between the two.

ethical principles may not possess.[11] If politics is the art of compromise, law is one of the most important products of such compromise. Extra-legal morality may tolerate disagreement and conflict to an extent that law cannot, because morality is not enforceable in the way law is.

Retributive Justice and Moral Luck in Tort Law

It is a corollary of viewing tort law as a set of ethical rules and principles of personal responsibility that retributive justice is a possible criterion for evaluating the fairness of the rules and principles of tort law and of their application in individual cases. As noted above, retributive justice has both a qualitative and a quantitative aspect. The first demands that tort liability should only be imposed on a defendant (D) if D was personally responsible (in some sense) for the conduct and outcomes of which the plaintiff (P) complains; and the second demands that D's liability should be proportional (in some sense) to that conduct and to those outcomes. Both aspects of retributive justice turn on the seriousness of the conduct and the outcomes complained of, and on the culpability of the alleged tortfeasor. The phenomenon of dispositional luck is relevant to making judgments of culpability, and the phenomenon of circumstantial luck is relevant to making judgments about the seriousness of conduct and outcomes, that is about the nature and circumstances of the allegedly tortious conduct and about events and states of affairs consequential on that conduct.

How important is it that the rules and principles of tort law and individual applications of them should be retributively just? It might help in answering this question to consider the criminal law first. The relevance of retributive justice to questions of guilt and sentencing in criminal law is easy to understand because the prime focus of criminal law is on the offender, on *actus reus*, and on *mens rea*. Victims play only a minor role in the process of determining guilt and sentence;[12] and although victim-oriented sanctions play a part in the criminal justice system, they are arguably subsidiary to offender-oriented punishment.[13] Some people would argue that criminal law and the criminal justice system should be much more concerned with ameliorating the plight of victims, but retributive ideas are currently central to both.

In tort law, by contrast, the victim plays a more important role. Tort claims, unlike the vast majority of criminal prosecutions, are initiated by

[11] See also J. L. Austin, 'A Plea for Excuses' in his *Philosophical Papers* (1961), 134–7.
[12] Concerning sentencing, see Ashworth, n. 2 above, 309–13.
[13] L. Zedner, 'Reparation and Retribution: Are They Reconcilable?' (1994) 57 MLR 228.

victims. As a group, tort remedies are at least as much concerned with protecting the interests of plaintiffs as with sanctioning the conduct of defendants. This helps to explain why attempting to commit a tort is not a tort, whereas attempting to commit a crime is itself a crime. Tort law is a bilateral affair in a way and to an extent that the criminal law is not. It is concerned as much with what we might call 'reparative justice' as with retributive justice. Conflict between these two forms of justice is not inevitable. For instance, requiring a criminal or tortfeasor to compensate a victim for harm suffered as a result of the crime or tort may satisfy the demands of retributive justice in the circumstances of the case. But they may conflict, as when, for instance, minimally culpable conduct produces great harm. When such conflicts arise, a choice needs to be made to prefer the demands of one form of justice to those of the other. The basic point is that only if retributive justice were the sole criterion for evaluating tort law would departures from it in the law provide, *per se*, grounds for condemning the law as unjust. Reparation and retribution are potentially competing moral and social goals, and one of the functions of tort law (but, as we will see, not its only function) is to embody a socially (and ethically) acceptable compromise between them.

The Qualitative Aspect of Retributive Justice

This section lays the groundwork for the later discussion by giving a very brief account of the grounds of tort liability viewed as a set of rules and principles of responsibility for conduct. In other words, this section examines what tort law means by the term 'responsible'. The distinction in tort law between matters of liability and matters of remedy roughly corresponds to the distinction between the qualitative and the quantitative aspects of retributive justice. Tort liability rules are concerned both with the 'seriousness' of the alleged tort and the culpability of the alleged tortfeasor. The seriousness of the alleged tort is a function, first, of the aspects of the allegedly tortious conduct which are external to the tortfeasor and, secondly, of the states of affairs and the events which result from that conduct. The culpability of the alleged tortfeasor is a function of an evaluation of the moral quality of the allegedly tortious conduct.

The Seriousness of the Alleged Tort

Causes of action in tort have at least two elements: on the plaintiff's side, a protected interest; and on the defendant's side, sanctioned conduct.[14]

[14] See generally Cane, n. 1 above.

At a very general level, the external aspects of sanctioned conduct can be described as interference with an interest protected by tort law. Such interests include an interest in bodily and mental health and safety, dignitary interests (such as reputation and privacy), civil and political interests (such as liberty and freedom of movement), interests in tangible and intangible property, rights under contracts, an interest in making contracts, and an interest in the preservation of wealth. Some interests are more valued by tort law (and, hence, better protected by tort liability rules) than others. For instance, property rights have traditionally been highly valued, whereas privacy has not been. Again, bodily health and safety is more highly valued than financial 'health' (that is, wealth as such). Other things being equal, the more highly tort law values an interest, the more seriously it treats interference with it.

Interferences with protected interests take different forms. For instance, tangible property may be misappropriated, exploited, or physically damaged; and the use and enjoyment of it may be disturbed. Intangible property, such as goodwill, may be exploited or damaged; as may reputation. Individuals may be physically injured or mentally disturbed or financially damaged. The various types of interference produce different states of affairs and events which bear upon the seriousness of the alleged tort. For instance, because tort law performs the vindicatory function of protecting title to property, misappropriation is treated by tort law as a more serious interference with tangible property (and, hence, more apt to attract tort liability) than damaging it (liability for the former being strict, while for the latter it is typically fault-based). Again, damaging someone only in their pocket is normally thought to be less serious (and, therefore, less properly the subject of tort liability) than injuring someone's body.

I am not suggesting that tort law recognizes a clear hierarchy of interests from the least to the most valued, or one of interferences with interests from the least to the most serious. My only claim is that embedded in tort law is an idea that interests are not all of equal value and equally deserving of the protection of the law, and that forms of interference with protected interests are not equally serious and equally deserving of being sanctioned by law.

The other element of the notion of seriousness concerns the impact on the victim of sanctioned interference with a protected interest. Tort liability may attach to interference with an interest regardless of its consequences. Liability for trespass to land is an example. Trespass to land is 'actionable *per se*'. By contrast, interference with some interests is only actionable in tort if the victim suffers some recognized harm or injury as a result. This is true of interference with an interest in personal health and safety, or in the use and enjoyment of land. 'Damage' is the 'gist' of liability for such interference. Where damage is the gist of liability, there must, of course, be a legally recognized causal link between the allegedly tortious conduct and the damage in order for the alleged tortfeasor to be held liable.

Actionability *per se* indicates that tort law puts high value on the interest in question. It is most commmonly used to protect title to (in the sense of possession and the right to possession of) property (the vindicatory role of tort law). It is not a feature of liability for nuisance, which does not threaten title. It is, however, a feature of liability for defamation in that the plaintiff need not prove injury to reputation resulting from the making of the defamatory statement, and in the sense that material injury is not the gist of liability. To some, at least, the high value thus placed on reputation seems increasingly unjustifiable.

The Culpability of the Alleged Tortfeasor

In tort law, there is an important distinction between fault-based liability and strict liability. As I will argue in more detail later in this essay, the former is based on ideas of culpability, while the latter is based on a principle that disturbances of settled distributions of resources and risks in society ought to be reversed.

Fault-Based Liability

In tort law, fault is defined in terms of two concepts: failure to reach specified standards of behaviour, and behaviour accompanied by certain states of mind.[15] In relation to neither concept does tort law impose liability on persons who lack a certain minimum capacity to control their minds or bodies. Such lack of capacity may be particular or general. If A overpowered B and used B as a weapon to injure C, B would not be liable in tort for C's injuries. If a car being driven by B knocked C over after B unexpectedly suffered a stroke which rendered B totally unconscious, B would not be liable in tort for C's injuries. In these examples, B suffered from a lack of capacity for controlling his or her conduct in the *particular* circumstances of the case (which might be called 'particular lack of capacity'). By contrast, a concept which might be called 'general lack of capacity' underpins the rule that a very young child cannot be

[15] In drawing this distinction I do not mean to enter the debate about the relationship between physical conduct and mental states (see R. A. Duff, *Intention, Agency and Criminal Liability* (1990), ch 6), but only to point out that certain forms of tort liability pay no regard to the mental state associated with the conduct to which liability attaches. The issue in that debate, it seems to me, concerns the relationship *between* 2 phenomena (however they may best be described) rather than about whether there *are* 2 phenomena.

liable in tort. The notion of general lack of capacity has a normative element lacking in the concept of particular lack of capacity. Children below a certain age are immune from tort liability not only on the basis that very young children typically lack certain capacities, but also on the basis that such children should not be expected to have or exercise such capacities. Conduct (that is, acts or omissions) of a person who falls below the minimum level of capacity is 'involuntary'.[16] However, the minimum level of capacity in tort law is low, and those who meet it cannot, as a general rule, avoid tort liability by pleading lack of capacity, even if the lack is genetic and incorrigible. This is what is meant by saying, for instance, that standards of care and the concept of negligence in tort law are objective: people with the minimum level of general capacity cannot escape liability for failing to meet the required standard by proving that they could not have reached the standard.

Sometimes tort liability will attach to conduct only if it was accompanied by a particular state of mind. The states of mind found in tort law are deliberation, intention, and recklessness. Acting deliberately is contrasted with acting automatically or inadvertently or inattentively. Deliberation is a condition, for instance, of secondary liability in tort for assisting, inducing, or authorizing the commission of a tort by another. Whereas deliberation refers to conduct, intention and recklessness refer to the consequences of conduct.[17] To act intentionally is to act with the aim of producing a certain consequence thereby; and to act recklessly is to act with the awareness that a certain consequence may follow from the action, but not caring whether it does or not. Intention to injure is a condition, for instance, of liability for interference with trade. Both intention and recklessness involve deliberation: it would make no sense to say that a person intended or foresaw the actual consequences of some inadvertent conduct. The converse is not true: a person may not intend or foresee the natural consequences of some deliberate conduct. Acting deliberately, intentionally, or recklessly is (other things being equal) more culpable than acting inadvertently.

Being in a particular state of mind may not only be a condition of liability but may also affect the quantum of liability. For instance, liability for making a fraudulent mis-statement is more extensive than liability for making a negligent mis-statement because fraud is considered more culpable than negligence.

[16] Another sense of 'involuntary' is '(morally or legally) obligatory'.

[17] The distinction drawn here between deliberation and intention is rarely drawn (explicitly, at least) in discussions of tort law. The term 'intention' is used indiscriminately to mean either deliberation or intention in my sense. Failure to draw the distinction is a rich source of confusion: see Cane, n. 1 above, 32–3.

Strict Liability

Strict tort liability does not depend on whether the sanctioned conduct fell below any particular standard[18] (unless it was involuntary) nor on whether it was done in any particular state of mind. Strict tort liability falls into three categories. In the first, the sanctioned conduct is defined simply in terms of interference with an interest of the plaintiff, such as unauthorized exploitation of another's property or the publication of a defamatory statement. The second category is exemplified by vicarious liability, which is based on the existence of a particular relationship between the tort and the tortfeasor on the one hand and a relevant activity of the defendant on the other. The third category might be referred to as 'outcome-based' strict liability. The elements of such liability are the conduct of a defined activity, the occurrence of a defined outcome, and a causal connection between the activity and the outcome. This form of strict liability is rare in the common law of tort, but is not uncommon under statute: for instance, the liability of a keeper of an animal which belongs to a dangerous species under section 2(1) of the Animals Act 1971; and liability for causing pollution under section 85(1) of the Water Resources Act 1991.[19]

All these forms of strict liability are based on a judgment that as between the two parties, the defendant ought to bear the risk that their conduct will interfere with a protected interest of the plaintiff regardless of whether the conduct was faulty.

Moral Luck and the Qualitative Aspect of Retributive Justice

The issue addressed in this section is how we can justify imposing tort liability on a person in accordance with the principles of responsibility discussed in the previous section when the allegedly tortious conduct or its consequences was, to a greater or lesser extent, outside the defendant's control.

Circumstantial Luck

Circumstantial luck is luck in respect of the circumstances in which a person's conduct occurs and takes effect. The mere fact that a person's conduct occurs or has effects in circumstances which were, to a greater or

[18] This is a controversial statement (see K. M. Stanton, *The Modern Law of Tort* (1994), 38–41. Detailed elaboration of the point must await another occasion.

[19] Concerning the latter, see *Empress Car Company (Abertillery) Ltd v National Rivers Authority* [1998] 1 All ER 481.

lesser extent, beyond the person's control, is not a basis for claiming immunity from responsibility for the conduct or its effects either within tort law or outside it. Indeed, the very concept of human agency pictures human beings as acting against and bringing about changes in a background which is, in some sense and to a greater or lesser extent, 'given'. So, for instance, a negligent driver who[20] knocks down and injures a non-negligent pedestrian cannot escape tort liability on the basis that the pedestrian's presence on the road at the crucial time and place was beyond the driver's control, and that if the pedestrian had not been there, the driver's negligence would not have attracted tort liability. So far as concerns responsibility for adverse effects of our conduct on others, the starting-point of judgments both within and outside tort law is that human agents must take the world around them as they find it if things turn out badly, and may take it as found if things turn out well.[21]

Some writers have attempted to explain this starting-point by seeing life as a lottery or as a series of gambles—'you win some, you lose some'.[22] However, this approach does not explain why we start from the position that agents rather than victims[23] should accept the burden of events and outcomes beyond their control.[24] In the example given in the previous paragraph, why should the pedestrian not accept the bad luck of being in the wrong place at the wrong time? A much better explanation is that our starting-point of agent-responsibility rests on basic ideas about relationships between individuals and between human beings and the world around us.[25] Taking responsibility for our conduct

[20] Neither intentionally nor recklessly.

[21] This formulation assumes that the issue of causation can be separated from that of luck. It cannot be, and in this way, the formulation is circular: the judgment that the driver caused the pedestrian's injury implies and involves that the pedestrian is not required to bear the consequences of bad luck in being in the wrong place at the wrong time. In other words, identifying who is the agent of harm, and who the victim, may involve allocating the risk of relevant bad luck. This point becomes clearer if we consider defences: if liability is denied or damages are reduced because of some conduct of the sufferer of the harm, this is partly because the sufferer was, in some sense, the cause of their own harm. A sufferer may be treated as an agent of their own harm even though the harm was partly the result of factors beyond their control (i.e. bad luck: the negligent pedestrian would not have been injured if the road had been clear of cars). The concept of causation is, therefore, pivotal in allocating the burden of luck. This point explains why the pedestrian in the example in the text is 'non-negligent'—this stipulation rules out any attribution of legal causation to the pedestrian. It also requires us to distinguish between sufferers and victims of harm. A sufferer of harm may be an agent of that harm. I use the term 'victim' to refer to a sufferer of harm who is not an agent of it.

[22] T. Honoré, 'Responsibility and Luck' (1988) 104 LQR 530; J. Waldron, 'Moments of Carelessness and Massive Loss' in D. G. Owen (ed.), *Philosophical Foundations of Tort Law* (1995), 387.

[23] See n. 21 above for the meaning of this term.

[24] I owe this point to a personal communication from Wilfred Beckerman.

[25] Of course, such ideas may vary from culture to culture and according to whether the

and its effects is important to having a secure sense of ourselves and others as moral agents whose conduct an have effects in the world. We are prepared to make and accept judgments of our own behaviour which ignore luck because refusal to do so would threaten our sense of selfhood and our ability to act purposively. Similarly, ignoring luck in our judgments of the behaviour of others is an important part of respecting their personhood and practical projects. To the extent that we view human conduct or its effects as matters of luck, we see humans as victims (or passive beneficiaries) of fate. The ultimate conclusion of viewing humanity in this way would be the destruction of the distinction between sentient human beings and the non-sentient world. Furthermore, I agree with Margaret Walker[26] that a world in which moral evaluations of people's conduct were fully sensitive to circumstantial luck would be morally repellent. Human beings who live in societies are interdependent, and it is a moral virtue to accept responsibility and show concern for the adverse consequences of our actions on others[27] despite the role of luck in producing those consequences. Such ideas are more attractive than any lottery analogy. It is preferable to see responsibility as the price of having a sense of ourselves as agents and not victims, rather than as the outcome of a lottery forced on us by the nature of the world.

Nevertheless, neither within tort law nor outside it are people held responsible for all the effects of their conduct. Sometimes we can disclaim responsibility on the basis that some circumstance surrounding our conduct was beyond our control. A morality which entirely ignored circumstantial luck would be as damaging to our sense of our own and others' responsibility for conduct as one which was entirely sensitive to it. If people could be held responsible for all aspects and effects of their conduct, they would lose any sense of being able to act purposively and to influence events. Thus, the crucial ethical distinction is not between factors within and outside our control but between factors outside our control which should be ignored in making moral judgments and those of which account should be taken. In allocating moral and legal responsibility for conduct and outcomes, some judgment must be made about

luck in question is circumstantial or dispositional. The ideas I espouse in this essay are based on a vision of human beings as agents rather than patients, actors rather than victims, masters rather than slaves, active rather than passive. It is some such vision which, I believe, underpins modern tort law. I do not deny that other visions are possible or legitimate, and in such visions responsibility may be much more sensitive to circumstantial luck than in mine.

[26] M. U. Walker, 'Moral Luck and the Virtues of Impure Agency' in Statman n. 4 above, 236–50.

[27] And to accept responsibility for the adverse consequences to ourselves of our own actions rather than seeking to place responsibility on others.

when pleas of 'lack of control' should and should not succeed. In tort law, an important distinction at work here is that between the ordinary and the extraordinary. This distinction finds expression in a number of principles of tort law. One is that in judging whether a person acted negligently or not, it is relevant to ask whether the person was faced with an 'emergency': that is, extraordinarily demanding circumstances. This rule is an application of a second, more general, principle in tort law, namely that a person should not be held liable for the unforeseeable. As a quantitative criterion concerned with the extent of tort liability for harm suffered, foreseeability (as we will see later) is widely, but not universally, applied throughout tort law. As a qualitative criterion concerned with the imposition of tort liability, foreseeability is a very common pre-condition of liability for harm. Indeed, it is probably true to say that in the common law of tort there can be no tort liability for harm unless *some* of the harm (or, at least the type of harm) alleged to flow from the conduct of the alleged tortfeasor was foreseeable.

A second concept of tort law used to define the acceptable scope of appeals to moral luck is that of causation. For the sake of simplicity, I shall confine the discussion to the central case of causation in tort law, namely the doing of harm by one's actions. I shall ignore cases of what we might call 'secondary causation' which may attract tort liability, such as failing to prevent harm occurring (omission), authorizing, inducing, or assisting tortious behaviour, or providing the opportunity for tortious behaviour. In the central case, the traditional legal distinction between the *causa causans* (or 'effective cause') of an event and the conditions *sine qua non* (or 'necessary conditions')[28] of that event reflects the distinction between agents and the background against which their conduct occurs and takes effect. In the central case, a human agent's lack of control of the causal background will only lead us to deny the status of effective cause to an agent whose tortious conduct was a necessary condition of harm if there was something abnormal or extraordinary in the background. This is the idea underlying the concept of an 'act of God'.

Thirdly, in relation to many heads of tort liability, the basic rule of remoteness is that a defendant will not be liable for harm caused by a tort if the harm was of an unforeseeable type; and this rule gives effect to the distinction between the ordinary and the extraordinary so far as the consequences of conduct are concerned. However, when examined in more detail, rules of remoteness present a complex picture in this regard because they often allow recovery for unforeseeable (and, hence, uncontrollable) losses.

[28] Or, more accurately, conditions which can be called a necessary element of a set of conditions sufficient to produce the harm.

For the purposes of attributing personal responsibility for harm in tort law, the distinction between 'normal' and 'abnormal' causal factors is often an evaluative or normative one. This point is obvious if one considers, for instance, the liability of a negligent driver for ulterior harm resulting from negligent medical treatment consequent upon the harm suffered by the victim in the road accident. Negligent medical treatment is clearly not 'normal' in any everyday or statistical sense of that term; and yet the judgment of the law is that a tortfeasor ought to take the risk of merely negligent medical treatment when the treatment was necessitated by the tort.

Perhaps the most explicit reference to circumstantial luck in tort law is contained in the principle that the tortfeasor must 'take the victim as found'. In the context of remoteness, the principle is used to extend liability for personal injury (and, possibly, property damage; but not purely economic loss) to the results of interaction between the tortious conduct and pre-existing susceptibilities of the plaintiff which may not have been foreseeable. In the context of assessment of damages, the principle dictates that the defendant must compensate the plaintiff for all the harm P suffers as a result of the tort, however much or little it may be (the 'shabby millionaire'[29] illustrates this point). The principle makes it crystal clear that in tort law, at least, luck may be no answer to a judgment of personal responsibility.[30] Taking the victim as found is one aspect of the *prima facie* principle that agents must take the world as found. On the other hand, in the context of deciding, in the tort of negligence, whether the defendant measured up to the required standard of care, the rule is that D will be held liable for failure to take precautions to protect an abnormally sensitive person from injury only if those precautions would have been necessary to protect a normal person from injury. In this context, the tortfeasor is not required to take the risk of abnormality. By combining the two principles, the law (as it were) distributes the luck between the tortfeasor and the victim.

My basic argument is that circumstantial luck is an ineradicable and pervasive feature of the human condition which does not stand in the way of attributing responsibility to individuals either inside or outside the law. To allow that any element of luck in a bad outcome resulting from a person's conduct would justify relieving that person of responsibility for the outcome would be to destroy human beings as moral agents. The really difficult ethical job, therefore, is to develop principles

[29] *The Arpad* [1934] P 189 at 202.

[30] But taking the victim as found may work to a tortfeasor's advantage; e.g., where the same damage results from 2 independent sufficient tortious causes which are separated in time. In such a case, responsibility is allocated to the prior tortfeasor because (luckily for the later tortfeasor) the victim was already damaged at the time of the second tort.

to determine when the slings and arrows of a person's fortune are so outrageous that the person should be relieved of responsibility for their effects. Tort law contains certain principles which clarify and give concrete content to relatively vague and usually unexpressed moral intuitions about how to do this job.

Dispositional Luck

Whereas circumstantial luck is luck pertaining to the circumstances in which conduct occurs and takes effect, dispositional luck is luck pertaining to conduct. Tort law is a set of rules and principles of personal responsibility for conduct and its effects. This is true of strict liability as well as of fault-based liability. The difference between these two forms of liability lies in the fact that the principle underlying the latter is that the tortfeasor did what ought not to have been done or failed to do what ought to have been done, whereas the basis of the former is simply that the tortfeasor did a particular act[31] or engaged in a particular activity, without any implication that it was wrong so to do.[32]

As we have seen, there are three different bases on which conduct may give rise to tort liability: that it was accompanied by a particular state of mind (deliberation, intention, or recklessness); that it fell short of a specified standard (that is, it was 'negligent'); and that it occurred (strict liability). The role of dispositional luck is most obvious in relation to liability for negligence[33] by virtue of the fact that the standard of careful conduct which the law establishes is explicitly stated to be 'objective' rather than subjective. This means that whatever the law's standard may be, it is no answer for the defendant to say that he or she could not have met it because of personal mental, physical, or financial characteristics. It is important to distinguish the objectivity principle from the question of the extent to which, in setting its standard, the law takes account of the personal characteristics of the defendant. The law's starting-point is to establish a relevant universal standard of conduct by constructing a sort of average ('reasonable') person and asking what that person would have done in the circumstances in which the defendant was placed. The word 'relevant' refers to the fact that there are different categories

[31] In tort law there is no strict liability for omissions.

[32] The only problem for this analysis arises out of vicarious liability. Vicarious liability is often said to be based on ideas of efficient loss distribution rather than on any notion of personal responsibility. On the other hand, it has been argued that vicarious liability is properly based on an ethical principle along the lines that a person who enagages in an activity for profit ought to bear the cost of injuries generated by that activity: J. Stapleton, *Product Liability* (1994), ch 8.

[33] The following analysis is also relevant, *mutatis mutandis*, to the defence of contributory negligence.

of average person for different types of case. For instance, in a road-accident case, the average person is the average driver; in a medical negligence case against a surgeon, the average person is the average surgeon; and so on. In a few cases, however, the law takes account of the individual physical or financial characteristics of the defendant. Such personalization ensures that the average person of the relevant type looks like the defendant in some particular respect; but it does not 'subjectivize' the standard of care. The question is still whether the defendant measured up to the standard which the average person who shared the particular characteristic with the defendant would have reached.

One of the reasons why the law of negligence does not allow a defendant to argue that he or she could not have met the required standard of care on the relevant occasion may be the difficulty of proving such a proposition in the typical case; and another reason may be that to allow such an argument would remove the defendant's incentive to attempt to do better next time. However, even if the proposition could be proved, or even if the defendant would never be capable of doing better, there would still be a strong ethical justification for applying an objective standard of care. Dispositional luck is luck pertaining to 'the (sort of) person you are'. A person's capacities and characteristics define the person as a moral being. To relieve a person of responsibility for their failure to reach a required standard of conduct because it was an inevitable consequence of their capacities and characteristics would be to deprive them of the status of a moral agent.[34] A chief distinguishing feature of human beings is their capacity for purposive action. To the extent that we see ourselves as victims of our genes, we undermine that capacity. Moreover, as Judith André argues,[35] one aspect of moral virtue is the ability to know what is the right thing to do and the desire to do it even if it is beyond our capacity. The morally virtuous person regrets their bad conduct and its adverse consequences even if they could not have acted otherwise. The only basis on which we are prepared to suspend moral judgment of a person's conduct is that the person, either on the occasion in question or generally, was incapable of operating as a moral agent. We do this only in the most extreme cases because of the dire implications of categorizing someone as a moral non-being.

I would argue, therefore, that the objectivity of the legal test of negligence is not a ground of ethical criticism of the law, for two reasons. One

[34] Nicholas Rescher goes further and argues that one's disposition is not a matter of luck but rather the very essence of oneself. Disposition is part of the concept of a person which is logically prior to moral judgment of conduct: 'Luck and Desert' in Statman n. 4 above, 156–7.

[35] J. André, 'Nagle, Williams and Moral Luck' in Statman n. 4 above, 123–9.

is that moral judgment outside the law is also objective in the sense that typically it does not allow dispositional bad luck as an excuse. The other is that objectivity of moral and legal judgments of personal responsibility is a necessary condition of our having and retaining a sense of ourselves as autonomous moral agents rather than as slaves to our genes. It does not follow, of course, that the standards of care which the law establishes may not be open to criticism. If the law set it standards so high that most people would be incapable of meeting them most of the time, it could well be considered unfair as a system of personal responsibility. The unfairness would not reside in the objectivity of the standard but in the sorts of conduct which would, under the standard, attract judgments of personal responsibility. In theory, the law avoids this criticism by adopting the standard of the average person. In practice, it is often alleged that the law attributes to the average person characteristics which most people simply do not have. My view is that such allegations are generally unjustified.

Dispositional luck is relevant not only to negligent conduct. Although we might be sceptical of a plea that a person could not but have formed a particular state of mind and translated it into conduct, we perhaps cannot logically deny the possibility that such a plea might be well-founded. However, to allow people, as a matter of course, to plead that a mental state of deliberation, intention, or recklessness[36] was beyond their control would be even more destructive of their personhood than generally allowing people to plead inability to meet particular standards of conduct. A person's conscious mental states are basic to their individuality and moral identity. Moreover, a world in which 'morally capable' people who were conscious and unintoxicated could, as a matter of course, disown responsibility for their mental states, would be a nightmare. By a 'morally capable person' I mean a person of sufficient mental capacity to be fairly an object of judgments of personal responsibility for their conduct.

What are we to say of strict liability?[37] Honoré treats liability for breach of an objective standard of care and strict liability as ethically equivalent.[38] However, as noted earlier, there is an important difference between strict liability and fault liability which resides in the fact that the latter is, but the former is not, based on a judgment that the person held liable should have behaved otherwise than they did. Another way of putting this point is to say that a person may be held responsible for

[36] This analysis is also relevant, *mutatis mutandis*, to the defences of consent and *volenti non fit injuria*, both of which differ from contributory negligence in being based on a particular state of mind, not on failure to reach a standard of conduct.

[37] The defence of illegality has structural features in common with strict liability.

[38] T. Honoré, n. 22 above.

conduct without being blamed for it; and a person may be prepared to accept responsibility for some consequence of their conduct and even acknowledge an obligation to compensate another for some adverse effect of their conduct without being prepared to accept blame, let alone punishment, for the conduct.[39] Blaming someone for their conduct (and their being to blame) implies (at least) that the person *should* have behaved otherwise. If a morally capable person causes harm deliberately, intentionally, or recklessly, they will almost certainly be blamed. If a morally capable person fails to meet an objective standard of care, they will typically be blamed for it. Even if they *could* not have done otherwise because of some incorrigible personal characteristic, they may be blamed for engaging in the relevant activity in the first place. And even if they were unaware of their incapacity, they might still not avoid blame if the average person would have been aware of it. Conduct to which strict tort liability may attach may also attract blame if it was done deliberately, intentionally, recklessly, or negligently. But the whole point of strict legal liability is that it does not involve any judgment that the defendant should have behaved differently. In other words, it involves responsibility without blame. Therefore, the question of whether the defendant could have behaved differently is simply irrelevant to strict liability.

Thomas Nagel says that strict liability may have its legal uses, but it is irrational as a moral position.[40] He explains this statement by saying that it is morally irrational to 'hold people responsible for the contributions of fate as well as their own'. For reasons which I have already given, I believe that it not only makes moral sense to hold people responsible for *at least some* of the contributions of fate, but also that it would be ultimately destructive of our humanity not to do so. Anyway, it is a feature not only of strict legal liability but of fault-based legal liability as well that it may hold people responsible for contributions of fate. It is a mistake to equate strict legal liability alone with responsibility for 'contributions of fate'. The ethical difference between strict liability and liability for fault does not reside in their relationship to luck. Under either head a person may be held liable for consequences beyond their control or conduct which could not have been otherwise. The difference is that fault liability rests on a judgment that the defendant *should* have behaved differently, whereas strict liability rests on no such judgment.

However, even if this argument is accepted, it might still be said that strict legal liability is morally unfair exactly because it does not entail that the defendant should have acted otherwise. But this is not the only

[39] J. André, n. 35 above, 127–8.
[40] T. Nagel, n. 6 above, 31; cited by Honoré, n. 22 above, 537.

basis on which it can be fair to hold a person responsible for their conduct and its consequences. It may also be fair to do so in order to protect some especially valuable institution, such as private property; or in order to correct disturbances of a settled distribution of risks throughout society, regardless of fault or blame. Strict liability in tort law is imposed either as a mechanism for protecting highly valued interests, especially property rights (the vindicatory function of tort law); or as a sort of taxation mechanism for internalizing risks to particular activities which, it has been decided, ought to bear them (as in the case of vicarious liability).

To summarize: dispositional luck is as inevitable and pervasive a feature of the human condition as circumstantial luck. Neither inside nor outside the law is it normally an answer to a judgment of responsibility for conduct to say that one could not have behaved otherwise. In tort law, this is true both of fault-based liability and strict liability. The distinction between the two forms of liability is that fault-based liability rests on a judgment that the defendant should have behaved differently, whereas strict liability does not. It does not follow, however, that in a moral sense, strict legal liability is necessarily either irrational or unfair.

Fault-Based Liability, Strict Liability, and Retributive Justice

From the foregoing discussion, I conclude that neither circumstantial nor dispositional luck prevents fault-based liability complying with the requirements of the qualitative aspect of retributive justice. This is because judgments of responsibility and blame are not dependent on the absence of luck. However, I also conclude that because the basis of strict liability is not a judgment that the defendant should have behaved otherwise, such liability does not rest on ideas of retributive justice, because this form of justice is concerned with moral desert. Whereas fault-based liability in tort law rests on a judgment that a person deserves to be sanctioned for their conduct, strict liability is not so grounded. If strict tort liability is to be justified, it must be on some basis other than retribution. In my view, strict tort liability rests on a principle that disturbances of settled distributions of resources and risks within society should be reversed. Strict tort liability performs two main functions: it protects the institution of private property, which is concerned with the allocation of certain resources amongst members of society; and it allocates certain risks of harm amongst members of society regardless of questions of fault or blame. In performing the first of these functions, tort law accepts as given the distribution of property resources dictated by the rules of property law. In relation to the second function, the rules establishing the distribution of risks, disturbances of which tort law reverses, are also part of tort law. In other words, in the former case tort law provides remedies to protect rights established by a different department of the law; whereas in the latter case, tort law both defines the right and provides the remedy to protect it. This taxonomic difference is of no great significance. But reflection on the role of the property torts does alert us to the very important point that the principle that disturbances of settled distributions of resources and risks within society should be reversed which, in my view, underpins strict tort liability, operates independently of the fairness of those settled distributions. A person might accept that strict tort liability has a proper role to play in the legal system without accepting the fairness of the distributions of risks and resources in society which are settled by the law. Moreover, a person who thought that the settled distributions of resources or risks in society were unfair would consider rules of strict tort liability which reversed disturbances of those distributions to be unfair even if they also thought that strict tort liability had a proper place in the legal system. The only claim I am currently making is that strict tort liability is best understood as a mechanism for reversing disturbances of settled distributions of risks and resources regardless of culpability. I make no claim about the fairness or otherwise of the distributions of risks and resources currently settled by the law, disturbances of which strict tort liability reverses.

My argument, then, is that strict tort liability does not rest on ideas of retributive justice but on some idea of 're-allocative justice' (as we might call it).[41] Retributive justice is only one of the forms of justice relevant to evaluating legal rules. The fact that particular legal rules are not retributively just does not mean that they are unjust *tout court*. The importance of this conclusion will become clearer in the next section of this essay.

The Quantitative Aspect of Retributive Justice

Having examined the relationship between tort liability and the qualitative aspect of retributive justice, this section looks at the place given in tort law to the idea that legal sanctions ought to be proportional to the ground of legal liability. In this context, the quantitative aspect of retributive justice would require that the sanction (or remedy) should be

[41] I would have preferred to use the term 'corrective justice' but decided not to because Ernest Weinrib (*The Idea of Private Law* (1995)) uses this term to describe the structure of tort law in which, in his view, strict liability has no proper place. Another useful term would be 'restorative justice', but this has a very particular meaning (irrelevant to the present discussion) in modern theorizing about the criminal justice system.

proportional to the tort in some sense. Cardinal proportionality would require that the sanction for each tort should be proportional to that tort; and ordinal proportionality would require that more 'serious' torts should attract greater sanctions, and that less serious torts should attract lesser sanctions. The remedies of tort law fall into two main categories: non-monetary and monetary.

Non-Monetary Remedies

The most important non-monetary remedy is the injunction. By its nature, this remedy is only available in relation to tortious conduct likely to occur after the date of the award of the injunction. In respect of such conduct, damages may sometimes be awarded as a substitute for (in lieu of) an injunction. In this type of situation, one would expect an injunction to be viewed as a greater sanction than damages because an injunction forbids the conduct in question. This expected ranking is borne out by the facts: (1) that in some contexts, damages will be awarded in lieu of an injunction only if the award of an injunction would be unfair to the defendant, whereas in other contexts an injunction will be awarded only if an award of damages would be unfair to the plaintiff; and (2) the former contexts are those in which the interest to be protected is a highly valued property interest. In other words, injunctions are reserved for cases in which the interest to be protected is particularly highly valued or the impact of the tort on the plaintiff would be so great as to make an award of damages inadequate (typically because any injury suffered would be serious and irreparable). Thus, the rules regulating the relationship between monetary and non-monetary remedies in tort law are sensitive, in a general way, to the requirement of ordinal proportionality. It might also be argued that the award of an injunction in cases where it seems likely that a defendant will in the future engage in tortious conduct which would interfere with a particularly highly valued interest of the plaintiff or inflict serious or irreparable injury on the plaintiff could satisfy the requirement of cardinal proportionality: prevention is better than cure unless effecting the cure will be a simple matter and the cure will be complete. If this argument is acceptable, the real puzzle is why injunctions are never available in negligence actions to restrain anticipated (deliberate) future conduct in breach of the required standard of care. The probable basis for this rule is the mistaken notion that negligent conduct is, by definition, inadvertent (that is, not deliberate). This mistake is a result of treating negligence as a state of mind rather than what it is, namely failure to meet a standard of conduct.

Monetary Remedies

Injunctions are exceptional remedies in tort law. The typical remedy is a monetary award to compensate for injury, loss, damage, or harm suffered before the date of the award and likely to be suffered after the date of the award as a result of tortious conduct which occurred before the date of the award.[42] As we shall see, monetary awards may perform other functions besides compensation, but these are subsidiary to compensation. The primacy of compensation in tort law is a function of viewing tort law in terms of 'reparative' justice (as I shall call it), that is, the justice of making good harms caused to others. However, compensation is payable in tort law only if harm is caused in certain ways defined as 'tortious'. Tort law strikes a balance between the interest of the plaintiff in protection from harm and the interest of the defendant in freedom of action by compensating victims of harm, but only if the harm was caused in certain ways. There is, potentially at least, a resulting tension in tort law between the demands of reparative justice and the principles of justice which support the classification of certain sorts of conduct as tortious.

It was argued above that fault-based tort liability can be evaluated in terms of the qualitative aspect of retributive justice, and that strict tort liability can be evaluated in terms of the notion of re-allocative justice. It might be thought to follow that the quantitative aspect of retributive justice would be relevant to evaluating the rules about monetary remedies as they apply to fault-based tort liability, but not as they apply to strict tort liability. This hypothesis will be tested in the following sections, each of which deals with a different category of tort damages.

Nominal and Contemptuous Damages

These two types of damages are monetary in form but non-monetary in substance. Both are designed to mark the fact that a legal right of the plaintiff has been interfered with by tortious conduct but that no substantial injury has resulted. They are, therefore, only available in the case of torts actionable *per se*. Because they merely declare that a tort has been committed, principles of qualitative rather than quantitative justice are relevant to the evaluation of their incidence.

Compensatory Damages

Compensation is the primary function of damages in tort law. For present purposes, three sets of rules are of the greatest importance in

[42] Concerning the difficult case of defamation see Cane, n. 1 above, 47–8.

evaluating the quantitative justice of compensatory tort damages. They are the rules which give effect to the 'full compensation principle', the rules governing burden of proof of causation, and the rules governing the assessment of damages for losses under the multiplier system.

The Full Compensation Principle

This principle has two limbs: the 100-per-cent principle and the standard-of-living principle. The former requires that tort victims be compensated for all their financial losses flowing from the tort and that they receive a 'fair' measure of compensation for non-financial losses resulting from the tort. The latter specifies that damages for financial loss should be related to the plaintiff's pre-tort financial position so as to enable P to maintain his or her pre-tort standard of living. The quantum of compensatory damages is calculated exclusively by reference to a comparison of the pre-tort and post-tort positions of the plaintiff. In this respect, the tortfeasor must take the victim as found. In other words, the tortfeasor bears the risk (in cases of physical harm, anyway) that the adverse pecuniary or non-pecuniary effects of the tort on the victim might, for reasons beyond the tortfeasor's control, be unusually severe. Consistently with my earlier conclusions, I would argue that the mere fact that the full compensation principle ignores circumstantial luck in this way does not make it inconsistent with retributive justice.

Under the full compensation principle no attempt is made to achieve any degree of proportionality between the quantum of compensatory damages and the nature or quality of the tortfeasor's conduct. In this respect, *so far as fault-based liability is concerned*, the full compensation principle might seem to be inconsistent with the requirements of the quantitative aspect of retributive justice. We must be careful not to overstate the inconsistency. In criminal law, ideas of retribution currently play a much more dominant role than they do in tort law because criminal law sanctions focus on the criminal and largely ignore the needs or plight of the victim. In criminal law, proportionality between punishment and crime is an important criterion of quantitative justice. Tort law, however, is bilateral: the interests of the victim are just as important as the conduct of the tortfeasor. Tort law involves a trade-off between reparative and retributive justice. Moreover, we have already concluded that fault-based tort liability is not inconsistent with the qualitative aspect of retributive justice. On this basis, it might be said in relation to fault-based tort liability that taking the two aspects of retributive justice together, the full compensation principle strikes a compromise between the demands of reparative and retributive justice because it only comes into operation once the defendant has been held liable for the commission of a fault-based tort. In other words, the rule of tort law that as between a person who has committed a fault-based tort and an innocent victim[43] the former should bear the burden of all the losses suffered by the latter regardless of how culpable the tortfeasor's conduct was,[44] may be viewed as a reconciliation of the tension between the demands of retributive and reparative justice.

The full compensation principle has also been attacked for taking no account of the financial means of the tortfeasor.[45] In criminal law, the principle of equality before the law may be interpreted to require that monetary fines should be adjusted to take account of the means of the offender (the principle of equal impact).[46] In relation to tort law, the force of the attack is blunted in practice by the fact that tort actions are rarely mounted against defendants who do not carry adequate liability insurance or who lack sufficient personal means to meet any damages payable. But the fact that a tortfeasor is insured against liability would not remove any underlying injustice there might be in imposing monetary liability which could only be met (if at all) at the cost of financial ruin. How can it be fair to hold a poor defendant who lives on the financial brink liable to pay enormous damages to a rich plaintiff who could manage perfectly well without them? Framing the attack in this way supplies the traditional answer: the pre-tort wealth of the two parties to a tort action is a matter of distributive justice. Fault-based tort liability, by contrast, is a system of retributive and reparative justice. According to the traditional argument, the fact that satisfying the demands of retributive and reparative justice may create or aggravate a distributional injustice does not detract from the fairness of the move as a matter of retributive and reparative justice. On the other hand, the fact that the tort system is apt to generate distributional injustices may create an obligation to redress such distributional injustices. In this light, liability insurance may be seen not only as a necessary pre-condition of the achievement of tort law's reparative function, but also as required in practice, in some cases at least, to redress distributional injustices generated by tort law. At all events, it must be accepted that the demands of various dimensions of justice may conflict in such a way that satisfying one involves failing to satisfy another. The way to deal with such con-

[43] The proposition applies even to a victim found guilty of contributory negligence because the damages payable to such a victim, although rateably reduced to take account of the fault and 'causal contribution' of the plaintiff's conduct, are calculated according to the full compensation principle.

[44] Joel Feinberg, *Doing and Deserving* (1970), 212–21 describes this principle in terms of 'weak retributivism'.

[45] P. Cane, *Atiyah's Accidents, Compensation and the Law* (5th ed. 1993), 150–2.

[46] Ashworth, n. 2 above, 194–5; but this principle was rejected in the abolition of unit fines by the Criminal Justice Act 1993.

flicts is not to deny the demands of the one dimension of justice but to seek to redress the derogation from the other in some other way.

What are we to say of *strict tort liability* in this context? Tony Honoré argues that strict liability can only satisfy the requirements of the quantitative aspect of retributive justice if it is 'not unduly burdensome'. In his view, this condition may be met if liability insurance is compulsory (or, at least, freely available), or if the defendant is in a position to distribute the cost of the liability amongst those who benefit from the activity to which the strict liability attaches.[47] However, my view is that strict tort liability should be seen as resting on the notions of re-allocative justice, not retributive justice. So far as strict liability for harm (as opposed to liability for interference with property rights) is concerned, paying tort damages is not a matter of repairing a wrong but of re-allocating the costs of certain risks from those on whom they initially fall to those on whom they should fall according to the rules which establish the distribution of such risks within society. Strict liability for harm is a mechanism for reversing disturbances of settled distributions of certain risks within society. If such a disturbance has occurred, the re-allocative principle underlying strict liability requires that the full cost generated by the disturbance should be shifted from P to D. In this context, retributive justice is simply irrelevant to the analysis of tort law.

It does not follow, of course, that ability to bear the burden of particular risks ought not to to be taken into account in deciding how those risks should be distributed throughout society. On the contrary, the issue of liability to pay might be thought particularly relevant to the resolution of such distributional questions. However, once the answer to the distributional question has been settled, the principle of re-allocative justice operates independently of the question of ability to pay even though, of course, ability to pay on the part of any strictly liable tortfeasor is a precondition of the achievement of re-allocative justice.

My conclusion, then, is that in relation to fault-based tort liability, the full compensation principle can be viewed as a compromise between the demands of reparative and retributive justice. Strict tort liability, by contrast, is a matter of re-allocative justice to which considerations of retributive justice are irrelevant.

Burden of Proof of Causation

In tort law, the plaintiff must prove, on the balance of probabilities, that the defendant's tort caused the harm in question in the sense that the former was a necessary condition of (or a necessary element of a set of conditions sufficient for) the latter. This rule operates in an all-or-nothing

[47] T. Honoré, 'The Morality of Tort Law', in D. G. Owen, n. 22 above, 88–90.

way: if P satisfies the burden of proof, P recovers full compensation; but if P fails to satisfy it, P recovers nothing. In other words, tort liability for harm is not proportional to risk. Does this make the burden-of-proof rule retributively unjust (so far as fault-based tort liability is concerned) or re-allocatively unjust (so far as strict tort liability is concerned)?

Note, first, that whether or not P is able to satisfy the burden of proof may well be, to some extent, a matter of circumstantial luck; but this, as I have argued, does not make the burden unjust. Observe, next, that the burden of proof (of causation) in tort law is lower than that in criminal law: 'on the balance of probabilities' as opposed to 'beyond reasonable doubt'. *So far as fault-based tort liability is concerned*, the lower burden of proof might be explained either as a compromise between the demands of reparative and retributive justice or as a reflection of the fact that the social stigma which attaches to being held liable in tort is less than that which attaches to being held guilty of a crime (although whether this is always true in cases where the punishment imposed for the crime is monetary, is perhaps open to argument). On the other hand, it might be argued that while it may seem fair that the strict test of causation in criminal law should operate in an all-or-nothing way (on the basis that typically, 'beyond reasonable doubt' is the closest we can practically get to incontrovertible proof), it seems less fair that the less strict test of causation in tort law should operate in an all-or-nothing way. Why should a defendant have to pay full compensation even though there may be a very substantial chance that the tort was not the cause of the harm? Even if we accept that having a lower burden of proof in tort is not unfair, we might still think it unfair that a burden of proof test as low as a bare balance of probabilities should operate in an all-or-nothing way. The only answer to this objection that I can imagine is this: while in theory a person might be held liable in tort on a bare balance of probabilities, in practice the test operates in an imprecise way and actually depends on the court being *satisfied* that the tort more probably than not caused the harm. An adjudicator is unlikely to feel such satisfaction unless the probability that the tort caused the harm is not just greater than even, but considerably greater than even.

In fact, pressure to abandon the all-or-nothing balance-of-probabilities test has arisen not because it is thought unduly generous to plaintiffs but because it is thought too difficult for plaintiffs to satisfy. Courts have been asked to lower the test to 'substantial contribution to risk', even if that contribution is 50 per cent or less, while at the same time retaining the full compensation principle. Such a development would aggravate any perceived unfairness in the causal test, and has rightly been rejected by English courts. Alternatively, courts have been asked to introduce a rule of liability proportional to risk such that if, for example, the plaintiff could prove that the tort increased the risk of the harm by 25 per cent, the plaintiff would recover 25 per cent of the damages which would have been recoverable if the plaintiff could have proved that the tort more probably than not caused the harm. English courts have refused the request partly out of fear of encouraging speculative claims: but also, I think, because the all-or-nothing balance-of-probabilities test is seen as a fair compromise between the interests of tortfeasors and victims. There certainly must come a point, short of incontrovertible proof, at which it is fair to the tortfeasor to award full compensation to the victim; but fairness to the victim requires that this point should not be too high. Opinions might differ about what the right point is. However, opinions might also differ about whether a system under which damages proportional to risk could be awarded if the all-or-nothing point was not reached, provided the increase in risk was substantial, would not be even fairer than the simple all-or-nothing, balance-of-probabilities test.

There is another rule of causation which bears on this discussion. All causal questions in tort law involve a hypothetical or counterfactual inquiry: what would have happened if the tort had not been committed? If, in answering this question, it is necessary to speculate about whether, if the tort had not been committed, someone other than the victim would have behaved in such a way that the victim would not have suffered harm or whether, on the contrary, the victim would have suffered the harm in question even if the tort had not been committed, the applicable test is not how the third party would have behaved on the balance of probabilities. Rather, the chance that the third party would have behaved in such a way as to obviate the harm is estimated and the plaintiff's damages are assessed according to that chance. The basis for this rule is by no means clear.

Assessment of Damages under the Multiplier System

At all events, the fairness or otherwise of the basic all-or-nothing balance-of-probabilities rule of causation cannot be judged independently of the rules about assessment of damages under the multiplier method. This method is used in fatal accident cases for the assessment of damages for continuing losses occurring after the date of death, and in all other cases for the assessment of damages for continuing financial losses occurring after the date of assessment. The rule most relevant to the present discussion is that the multiplier must be discounted for future contingencies or 'vicissitudes'. In other words, the amount awarded must (admittedly in a rough-and-ready way) take account of the chance that the harm would have occurred even if the tort had not occurred. This rule not only moderates the all-or-nothing balance-of-probabilities approach to causation; it can also affect the operation of the take-victim-as-found rule. For instance, suppose an industrial worker receives a burn at work as a result of the negligence of the employer, and that the burn triggers off a dormant cancer. The employer will be liable not only for loss caused by the burn but also for loss caused by the cancer. However, in assessing damages under the multiplier method in such a case, account will be taken of the chance that even if the worker had not received the burn, the cancer might still have developed. Taken together, therefore, the rules of causation and the rules of assessment of damages strike a complex compromise between the demands of reparative and retributive justice. While it is true that tort damages are not proportional to fault, they are, to an extent at least, proportional to causality.

So far as *strict tort liability* for harm is concerned, since it is based on the idea that the costs of certain risks of harm imposed on P by D's conduct should be shifted back to D, the quantum of strict liability should accurately reflect that risk. In other words, in order to satisfy re-allocative justice, damages to compensate for harms for which liability is strict should be proportional to the relevant risk of harm imposed by D on P. There is no question in this context of striking a compromise between conflicting principles of justice; the only issue is a technical one of whether the rules of causation and assessment of damages generate the correct quantum of liability. Is the all-or-nothing balance-of-probabilities rule of causation coupled with the rule of risk-related assessment of damages sufficiently accurate or would a full-blown rule of risk-related causation satisfy the demands of re-allocative justice to a significantly greater extent? In this context, the lack of any liability for risks of 50 per cent or less may seem a much more serious problem than in respect of liability for fault.

Disgorgement Damages

Damages representing gains made by a tortfeasor as a result of tortious conduct which do not correspond to loss suffered by the victim are recoverable on only two bases in tort law. The first is exploitation of another's property without their consent, and the second is deliberate gain-seeking. The latter is sanctioned through the medium of awards of punitive damages, which may contain a disgorgement element. There are two measures of disgorgement damages: expense saved and profits made. The former measure is embodied in awards of so-called 'mesne profits' (rental value) in the case of land, hire value in the case of chattels, and licence fees in the case of intellectual property. The remedy used to secure disgorgement of profits is the account of profits. In tort law, this is only available in respect of exploitation of intellectual property. In that context, therefore, the court has a choice between the two measures of disgorgement. Expense saved tends to be chosen when any profits made are significantly attributable to value added to use of the property by the exploiter's own exertions, at least in cases where the infringement of the plaintiff's rights by the defendant was innocent.

Because disgorgement damages do not represent any harm suffered by the plaintiff, they cannot be justified in terms of reparative justice. In the property context, they may best be seen as resting on ideas of re-allocative justice. A retributive analysis is unsatisfactory in this context because liability to pay such damages is often not fault-based. By contrast, a retributive analysis seems right in relation to awards triggered by deliberate gain-seeking. The requirement of deliberation satisfies the demands of the qualitative aspect of retributive justice. The quantitative aspect is satisfied by the requirement that there be a suitable causal connection between the tort and the gain which must be disgorged.

An objection which may be made to the award of disgorgement damages is that since they represent no loss to the plaintiff, they constitute an undeserved windfall. However, this objection simply assumes that tort law's only function is to repair harms. It ignores the re-allocative function of strict tort liability. In fulfilment of this function, tort law may order a person who has, by using another's property without their consent, disturbed the distribution of property rights settled by property law, to account to the property owner for the benefit of that use which, according to the rules of property law, belongs to the property owner. When tort law performs its vindicatory function of protecting property rights, its concern is not with reparation or even with retribution, but with reversing disturbances of the settled distribution of resources in society.

So far as deliberate gain-seeking is concerned, the principle of retributive justice has nothing to say about the proper destination of the damages. Perhaps this should be decided simply on pragmatic grounds: where would the damages do most good?

Punitive Damages

Leaving aside elements of disgorgement in awards of punitive damages, such awards are, as their name implies, designed to punish. They are unarguably retributive in the sense that they rest on a judgment that the defendant should have acted differently. In England, they are available if statute so provides, and to punish deliberate gain-seeking (whether successful or not) or 'oppressive, arbitrary, or unconstitutional action' by persons exercising governmental (or 'public') powers. Under the third head, such awards are most commonly made in actions for wrongful detention or prosecution by the police. Under the second head, one suspects that there is an element of punishment in many of the larger awards of damages by juries in defamation actions. The requirement of deliberation under the second head arguably satisfies the qualitative aspect of retributive justice. Deliberation (either in the form of intention to injure or knowing illegality) is probably also required under the third head. In addition, it might be argued that deliberate abuse of public power is more serious in some sense than abuse of private power.

So far as the quantitative aspect of retributive justice is concerned, the only guidance which the law gives concerning the quantum of punitive damages is that such damages should be 'moderate'. The amount awarded is in the discretion of the court, which is thus free to give effect to notions of proportionality.

It is often argued that punitive damages are out of place in tort law, the aim of which is to compensate. However, I believe that one of the functions of damages awards in tort is to express disapproval of and to discourage certain kinds of tortious conduct. Viewed in this way, even compensatory damages may have a punitive aspect.[48] There is, therefore, no *a priori* reason why tort law should not have punishment as one of its aims. The only question is whether we think that punitive damages express a degree of disapproval and discouragement out of proportion to the seriousness and culpability of any conduct which we call tortious. Ultimately, it seems to me that a judgment that they are disproportionate to tortious conduct is the only basis on which we could pronounce punitive damages, or disgorgement damages based on deliberate gain-seeking, not properly part of tort law.

Conclusions

My conclusions will address the three elements of the title of this essay, namely moral luck, retribution, and proportionality.

Moral Luck

Luck, both in the sort of person one is (dispositional) and in the way things turn out (circumstantial) is an ineradicable and pervasive feature of human experience. The mere fact that our conduct or its effects are (partly) a function of luck does not immunize us from attributions of responsibility or blame. In extreme cases, luck may immunize us from being judged responsible or blameworthy. But such cases must be excep-

[48] See Zedner, n. 13 above.

tional if we are not to undermine our sense of ourselves and others as autonomous agents. This sense is a precondition of human interaction and of ethical meaning in our lives. To make widespread allowance for luck in forming ethical judgments would be self-defeating. Luck need not, therefore, threaten the legitimacy of the judgments of personal responsibility and blame which underlie tort law.

Retribution

This conclusion about moral luck removes a major obstacle in the way of viewing fault-based tort liability in terms of retributive justice, whether it is based on a state of mind or on failure to meet an objective standard of conduct. On the other hand, strict tort liability should not be assessed in terms of retributive justice but in terms of re-allocative justice. The function of strict tort liability is to reverse departures from settled distributions of resources or risks in society.

So far as the extent and quantum of tort liability are concerned, once again the relevant question in relation to strict tort liability is whether the rules governing these matters are re-allocatively fair. In relation to fault-based tort liability, the full compensation principle, the all-or-nothing balance-of-probabilities test of causation and the rules about assessment of damages may, together, be seen as a complex compromise between the demands of reparative and retributive justice. Furthermore, unless one believes that no faulty tortious conduct could be culpable enough to deserve to be sanctioned by awards of non-compensatory damages, there is no need to conclude that the availability of disgorgement damages and punitive damages in respect of certain sorts of deliberate tortious behaviour is inconsistent with the demands of retributive justice.

Proportionality

These conclusions about moral luck and retributive justice make it possible to conclude that in a general sense, the law of tort remedies, so far as it relates to fault-based tort liability, is sensitive to the demands of both cardinal and ordinal proportionality on the basis that (1) the rules regulating the relationship between monetary and non-monetary remedies reserve the former for more 'serious' cases; (2) the rules governing compensatory damages strike a compromise between the demands of reparation and retribution; and (3) non-compensatory damages are only available in response to particularly serious tortious conduct.

Finally, we can also conclude that since strict tort liability does not rest on ideas of retributive justice, the notion of proportionality inherent in the quantitative aspect of retributive justice is irrelevant to the legitimacy of such liability; but also that the principle of re-allocative justice which underlies strict tort liability requires that the remedy should accurately reflect the value of the resource or the nature of the risk which is the subject of the liability.

Some will find these conclusions and, indeed, the whole project pursued in this essay, deeply uncongenial because they rest on forging a link between personal responsibility and retributive ideas. Retribution, it would be said, is a primitive instinct which should be suppressed. Moreover, the idea of cardinal proportionality is highly problematic because there is no convincing way of establishing that any particular sanction is proportional to the conduct of any particular tortfeasor. Even if this problem did not exist, ordinal scales of sanctions and of tortious conduct would be difficult to establish and justify, at least in detail. Much better, it might be said, to explain and evaluate tort law in terms of desirable consequences such as compensating the injured, reducing the number of injury-causing incidents, or maximizing social wealth.

A fundamental analytical problem with most consequentialist interpretations of tort law is that they cannot successfully explain the correlativity of tort law.[49] For instance, the law's pursuit of the compensation goal is constrained by its search for a responsible tortfeasor; and its pursuit of the accident-reduction goal is constrained by its focus on victims. A serious practical problem is that such empirical evidence as we have suggests that tort law is very inefficient at furthering the major social goals commonly attributed to it.[50] It is only by viewing tort law as a system of rules and principles of personal responsibility that we can make analytical sense of it or have any hope of justifying its existence in the face of its consequentialist inefficiency.

Even if this is accepted, however, it does not follow that tort law must be interpreted in terms of the principles of retributive justice outlined in this essay. Holding people responsible for their conduct might itself be viewed in terms of its consequences. On this basis, having a secure sense of ourselves as moral agents would be a desirable consequence of principles of personal responsibility of the sort embodied in tort law (assuming a traceable causal connection between such principles and people's self-image) rather than an expression of basic ideas about what it means to be human. Proportionality would be viewed not as a value in its own right but instrumentally in terms of reinforcing people's sense of their identity and worth.

At this level of abstraction, it may be that the choice between a 'deontological' approach (such as I have adopted in this paper) and a

[49] E. Weinrib, n. 41 above, esp. 46–9.

[50] See generally Cane, n. 45 above.

consequentialist or instrumentalist approach is really one of intellectual and moral temperament rather than of logic. I can make more sense of tort law by viewing it as an expression of our sense of what it means to be human rather than as being in some sense 'good for us'. To interpret tort law as giving content to, rather than as deriving from, our sense of what it means to be human puts the trailer before the lorry. It does not follow from this conclusion (for me at least) that tort law deserves our support or approval. In fact, at least in relation to personal injuries, I think that it is indefensible and ought to be abolished exactly because its character as a set of rules and principles of personal responsibility militates against the efficient performance of precisely those social goals which we want it to realize. There is no point in looking to tort law to do jobs which, by its nature, it is ill-fitted to perform, when other more efficient techniques are available to achieve desired ends. My aim in this essay has been to understand tort law in its own terms ('immanently', as the jargon goes), not to analyse its shortcomings or to suggest what the future of tort law should be.

7

Responsibility in Crime, Tort, and Contract for the Unforeseeable Consequences of an Intentional Wrong: A Once and Future Rule?

*James Gordley**

Responsibility in Crime and Tort

The Modern Problem

Suppose A accidently shot B when aiming at C. It has seemed to many people that A should be held criminally and civilly responsible for shooting B. Yet modern jurists have trouble explaining why. They recognize two types of responsibility based on fault. A person is responsible for causing harm intentionally or negligently. In the example just given, the defendant's objective was not to cause the harm he did. So it seems odd to say he caused it intentionally. Moreover, he may not have been negligent. He may have used due care to avoid shooting a bystander.

In Anglo-American criminal law, A is held responsible by invoking a doctrine known as 'transferred intent' or 'transferred malice'. A's intention to kill C is said to 'transfer' to the death of B.[1] In Italy, article 82 of the Criminal Code provides that one who mistakenly harms a different person than he intended will be held responsible as though his intention had not miscarried.[2]

*I would like to thank Stefano Mechelli for helping with my research. I am especially grateful to John Fleming for encouraging me to take an historical and comparative approach to modern problems.

[1] As the Model Penal Code puts it, the requirement that the defendant have acted 'purposefully' is satisfied even if the actual result is different only in that a different person or property is affected. Model Penal Code § 2.03(2)(a).

[2] Italian Criminal Code (*Codice penale*) art. 82.

Neither the Italians[3] nor the English[4] have a similar doctrine in tort although in two old English cases the defendant was held liable in situations like the one just described.[5] But American lawyers say that the intent to commit a tort can be transferred from one victim to another and from one tort to another so that if A shoots at C or at C's dog he will be liable if he hits B.[6]

Italian critics have claimed that their rule violates the principle, enshrined in their Constitution,[7] that a person is criminally responsible only for his 'personal' fault.[8] English and Americans have called their doctrine 'a curious survival of the antique law',[9] an 'archaic survival',[10]

[3] Nevertheless, the defendant might be civilly liable under art. 185 para. 2 of the Italian Criminal Code which says that 'every crime that has caused a harm . . . obligates the guilty party to make compensation'.

[4] Some say that liability even for an intentional wrong is limited to the foreseeable consequences; e.g., R. F. V. Heuston & R. A. Buckley, *The Law of Torts* (20th ed., 1922). Others think an English court might follow the Canadian case of *Allan v New Mt. Sinai Hospital*, [1980] 125 DLR (3d) 276, in which the court said that there would be liability for the unforeseeable consequences as well. See John Fleming, *The Law of Torts* (8th ed., 1992), 25 (approving the rule); K. M. Stanton, *The Modern Law of Tort* (1994), 101 (asking if it is part of English law). But *Allan* was not like the American transferred intent cases. The defendant, who had committed a battery by giving the plaintiff an injection despite his protests, was held liable for consequences to which he was abnormally and unforeseeably susceptible.

[5] *Scott v Shepard*, [1773] 2 Wm. Bl. 892, 96 Eng. Rep. 525 (D liable when he had thrown a fire cracker toward one person who threw it toward another who threw it towards P); *James v Campbell*, [1832] 5 Car. & P. 372, 172 Eng. Rep. 1015 (D liable when he tried to hit one person in a fist-fight at a parish dinner and accidentally struck P).

[6] e.g., *Alteiri v Colasso*, 362 A 2d 798 (Conn. 1975) (D liable when he hit P with a rock thrown in order to frighten someone else); *Singer v Marx*, 301 P 2d 440 (Cal. App. 1956) (same, except the rock was thrown to hit someone else). In other cases sometimes cited as authority for the doctrine of transferred intent courts have reached similar results but have spoken of the 'unlawfulness' of the defendant's action: e.g., *Talmage v Smith*, 59 NW 656 (Mich. 1894) (a man threw a stick at two boys who were trespassing on his property but struck a third boy who, he claimed, was out of sight); *Lopez v Surchia*, 246 P 2d 111 (Cal. App. 1952) (D shot when he had not been attacked with deadly force, and therefore he is liable when a bystander is accidentally hit); *Morrow v Flores*, 225 SW 2d 621 (Tex. App. 1949) (same); *Carnes v Thompson*, 48 SW 2d 903 (Mo. 1932) (if D struck at P's husband, he is liable if he accidentally hit P).

In Anglo-American criminal law, the doctrine of transferred intent permits the 'intention' to be transferred from one person to another or one physical object to another but not from one crime to another. According to the Italian Criminal Code, art. 83, except as provided by art. 82 (described in the text), a person who causes an 'event' other than the one he intended is liable for the event he caused 'for negligence' (*a titolo di culpa*). Commentators disagree whether this provision means he is punished as though he caused this event negligently or whether he is liable only if he caused it by his negligence. See Giovanni Fiandaca & Enzo Musco, *Diritto penale Parte generale* (3rd ed., 1995), 581 (taking the former position); Ferrando Mantovani, *Diritto penale Parte generale* (3rd ed., 1992), 386 (supporting the latter position on the grounds that in cases of doubt one must follow the principle that punishment is due only in cases of personal fault); Francesco Antolisei & Luigi Conti, *Manuale di diritto penale Parte generale* (13th ed., 1994), 392–3 (same).

[7] Italian Constitution art. 27, para. 1. [8] Fiandaca and Musco, n. 6 above, 576–81.

[9] William L. Prosser, 'Transferred Intent', (1967) 45 Texas L. Rev. 650.

[10] Cardozo in *Sinram v Penn*. R.R. Co, 61 F 2d 767, 770 (2d Cir. 1932).

'an historical aberration',[11] 'an arbitrary exception to normal principles'.[12] No one believes that A's intention to kill C really transmutes to an intention to kill B.[13] To say so merely expresses the conclusion that A should be held responsible.[14] It has proven hard to explain why he should be.

One reason, suggested by both Italian and Anglo-American writers, is that A's intention is as culpable as if he had wanted to kill B.[15] But, as critics have pointed out, his intention would have been as culpable if he had missed them both, and yet he would be punished less severely.[16]

Other reasons, discussed only to be dismissed by Italian writers, are that holding him responsible adds to deterrence and simplifies problems of proving what his intentions were.[17] But the deterrent effect is small when the harm is unforeseeable; and the problem of proof is minimal when the defendant had no motive for shooting the person he did.

Michael Moore has suggested that, instead of speaking of transferred intent, we define intentional homicide to require merely the intent to kill a human being rather than to kill a specific individual.[18] As Douglas Husak has pointed out, that approach has the paradoxical consequence that a person is held responsible for killing intentionally when there is no one whom he intentionally killed.[19]

Husak has suggested that although A is not guilty of intentional homicide he should be punished as severely as if he were. He argues that the severity of the punishment should depend on the degree of fault and the harm done. Here, A's intention was as culpable and the harm done as serious as if he had shot C.[20] But if A is not guilty of intentional homicide, for what crime is he to be held responsible? If the crime is killing B, then what crime could that be, since B was killed neither

[11] Don Stuart, *Canadian Criminal Law* (1982), 196–7.

[12] Glanville Williams, *Criminal Law: The General Part* (2nd ed., 1961), 134. Similarly, Martin R. Gardner, 'The Mens Rea Enigma: Observations on the Role of Motive in the Criminal Law Past and Present', (1993), Utah L. Rev. 635 at 734 ('an unnecessary exception').

[13] Douglas Husak, 'Transferred Intent', (1966) 10 Notre Dame J.L. Ethics & Pub. Pol. 65 at 83.

[14] Husak, 'Transferred Intent', n. 13 above at 67; Paul H. Robinson, 'Imputed Criminal Liability', (1984) 93 Yale L.J. 609 at 619.

[15] Antolisei & Conti, n. 6 above, 390; Robinson, n. 14 above at 619; Douglas Husak & Craig A. Collender, 'Wilful Ignorance, Knowledge, and the 'Equal Culpability' Thesis: A Study of the Deeper Significance of the Principle of Legality', (1994) Wisconsin L. R. 29 at 58 n. 102.

[16] Husak, n. 13 above at 89–90; Kimberly Kessler, 'The Role of Luck in the Criminal Law', (1994) 142 U. Pa L. Rev. 2183 at 2211.

[17] Fiandaca and Musco, n. 6 above, 574–6.

[18] Joshua Dressler, *Understanding Criminal Law* (2nd ed., N.Y., 1995), 109; Michael Moore, 'Intentions and *Mens Rea*' in R. Gavison, *Issues in Contemporary Legal Philosophy* (1987), 267–8; Kenneth W. Simmons, 'Criminal Law: Mistake and Impossiblity, Law and Fact and Culpability: A Speculative Essay', (1990) 81 JCL 447 at 506.

[19] Husak, n. 13 above at 74.

[20] Ibid at 92.

intentionally or negligently? If it is the attempted murder of C, then why should an attempt be punished as severely as a completed crime if, by sheer accident, it happens to have produced a corpse? As Martin Gardner has said, although there is a *mens rea* and an *actus reus* in a case of transferred intent, the two 'do not concur in the same crime'.[21]

The same objection has been made to the doctrine in tort law. According to Ernest Weinrib, the doctrine is anomalous because '[t]he duty breached by the defendant must be with respect to the embodiment of the right whose infringement is the ground of the plaintiff's cause of action'.[22]

In tort law, an additional difficulty is that the defendant must intend to commit one tort before this intention can be transferred to another. Whether he is liable for the harm he actually caused therefore turns on whether he would have committed a common-law tort had he committed the wrong that he intended. Consequently, the distinctions among common-law torts, which normally determine whether the defendant is liable for interfering with the plaintiff, are used to answer the quite different question of whether he is liable for the unforeseen consequences of trying to interfere with someone else. The logical consequences are anomalous, and it is not clear courts would actually live with them. If A shot B intending to hit C or to put C in imminent apprehension of harm, he would be liable because he had the intent necessary to commit battery or assault. But A would not be liable if he did not have the intent requisite to any common-law tort: for example, if, intending to scare C, he shot when C's back was turned and immediately threw down his gun, or he mailed C a bomb which he thought would be intercepted before arrival.[23]

[21] Gardner, n. 12 above at 708.

[22] Ernest Weinrib 'The Gains and Losses of Corrective Justice', (1994) 44 Duke L J 277 at 295, 295 n. 42.

[23] Indeed, on the basis of some doubtful historical speculation, Prosser claimed that intent can be transferred only among torts that were once redressed by an action of trespass *vi et armis*. Such an action was once brought against a person who trespassed on P's land (trespass *quare clausum fregit*) or against someone who intentionally struck P (trespass in assault and battery). Therefore, a person who entered land without permission is liable if he accidentally struck P. Prosser thought that this limitation was a good one because it kept the doctrine of transferred intent within reasonable bounds (Prosser, n. 9 above at 655–6). But if we take it seriously, if a child was physically injured because D locked up the child's parent, D would be liable merely because of the historical accident that false imprisonment was also redressed by an action of trespass *vi et armis*. If P's goods suffer harm because D beat a servant who was looking after them, P would recover because this injury was also redressed by such an action. But he could not recover if the goods were harmed because D enticed away his servant, or if a mob mistook them for the goods of someone D had falsely accused of being a child molester, because these injuries were once redressed by actions of trespass on the case. It seems irrational to allow recovery to turn on considerations like these.

Some Italian and Anglo-American jurists have concluded that the doctrine should be abolished. If A shoots at C and kills B he should be criminally responsible for negligent homicide.[24] Some Americans believe that if he was not negligent, he should not be liable in tort except possibly to C for assault.[25]

The trouble is, illogical as the doctrine appears to be, it enables courts to reach results that seem to be more in accord with our sense of justice than those they would reach otherwise.[26] If A aims at C and shoots B, few people would want to treat him the same way as if he missed.[27] Those who disagree, Husak suggests, should ask themselves how they would react if A shot first at B and then at C meaning to kill them both, and due to some freak event (chance ricochets or gusts of wind) the bullet meant for B hit C and vice versa.[28] Is A really guilty, at the most, of attempted murder?

Prosser said that while 'it would be easy to dismiss all this as one more illustration of the survival of absolute rules . . . nevertheless . . . as between the innocent plaintiff struck by the bullet and the guilty defendant who fired it with intent to kill another man, it put the loss on the one upon whom it ought in obvious justice to fall'.[29] And so we have a curious state of affairs. A thoroughly illogical doctrine is needed to reach an 'obviously' just result.

Moreover, if we abandoned the doctrine our law would not be logically consistent unless we tolerated further conflicts with our sense of justice. Suppose that A and B are rival track stars and that A shot at B's legs to cripple him but instead hit his hand. Surely, A would be held criminally and civilly responsible. The English would hold him liable in tort on the grounds that, to commit a battery, the defendant need only

[24] Mantovani, n. 6 above, 384; Fiandaca & Musco,n. 6 above, 576; Gardner, n. 12 above at 710; Gail Hollister, 'Using Comparative Fault to Replace the All-or-Nothing Lottery Imposed in Intentional Torts Suits in Which Both Plaintiff and Defendant are at Fault', (1993) 46 Vanderbilt L. Rev. 121 at 155 ('defendant was at most negligent as to plaintiff' and the fact that he intended to harm another should be irrelevant); David Karp, Note, 'Causation in the Model Penal Code', (1978) 78 Columbia L. Rev. 1249, 1267–72 (there should be a rebuttable presumption of recklessness). This approach is described by Husak, n. 13 above at 70.

[25] That seems to be Prosser's view of what we would conclude if we applied tort principles logically. Prosser, n. 9 above at 660, 652.

[26] Husak, n. 13 above at 70. See Robinson, n. 14 above at 619 (speaking of a 'community consensus').

[27] As in other respects, the sense of justice in Dodge City on the American frontier was different. In 1878, Jim Kennedy shot at Mayor Dog Kelley and killed Dora Hand by mistake. He was tracked down and arrested by a blue ribbon posse composed of Wyatt Earp, Bat Masterson, Charlie Bassett, and Bill Tilghman, only to be acquitted. The reason, apparently, was that 'Kelley had not even been hit so there was no reason for him to squawk, and Miss Hand had not been shot on purpose, so it was ridiculous to talk about assaulting with intent to kill'. John Myers, *Doc Holliday* (1973), 91.

[28] Husak, n. 13 above at 70.

[29] Prosser, n. 9 above at 662.

intend the act that causes contact but need not intend the harm inflicted.[30] Yet logically, the same problem arises. Why should the defendant be liable for harm he neither intended nor, perhaps, was negligent in causing?

Or suppose that A trespassed on B's land and, without negligence, started a fire that destroyed the plaintiff's house. American courts have held such a person liable in tort.[31] Though Prosser regarded these cases as kindred to transferred intent,[32] there is no need to say the defendant's intent is transferred from one crime or tort to another or from one victim to another. Yet, as in cases of transferred intent, the same question arises as to why A is held responsible for a harm to B that he did not intentionally or negligently inflict. Yet many people feel that he should be.

The difficulty of achieving logical consistency even if we abandon the doctrine of transferred intent is illustrated by the experience of legal systems that have no such doctrine. Germany is a good illustration. In German criminal law, if A shoots at C and kills B, he is guilty of attempting to murder C and, at most, of negligently killing B.[33] The result is said to be the same in tort.[34]

In criminal law, this result may seem logical if not intuitively correct. In tort, however, German courts have held the defendant liable when he inflicted a different kind of harm than he intended on the same person. That result seems intuitively correct but is reached at the cost of logical consistency.

In such cases, German courts have applied a general rule that once the defendant has violated a right of the plaintiff enumerated in section 823

[30] Margaret Brazier, *The Law of Torts* (8th ed., 1988), 21; R. F. V. Heuston & R. A. Buckley, *Salmond and Heuston on Torts* (20th ed., 1992), 127.

[31] E.g., *Farm Bureau Mutual Ins. Co. of Arkansas v Henley*, 628 SW 2d 301 (Ark. 1982) (2 6-year-olds who started a fire that spread to D's gift shop by tossing a lighted match in D's trash bin are liable if they committed trespass); *Brown v Dellinger*, 355 SW 2d 742 (Tex. Civ. App. 1962) (2 children ages 7 and 8 are liable who had entered a man's property without his permission and started a fire in the charcoal burner in his garage); *Cleveland Park Club v Perry*, 165 A 2d 485 (DC 1960) (child liable for damage to swimming-pool when he put a rubber ball under a drain cover because the act was a trespass); *Wyant v Crause*, 86 NW 527 (Mich. 1901) (adult who trespasses and starts fire in forge liable for its spread).

[32] Prosser, n. 9 above at 658.

[33] Adolf Schönke & H. Schröder, *Strafgesetzbuch Kommentar* (24th ed., 1991) no. 57 to § 15; *Bundesgerichtshof*, 4th Strafsenat., 10 Apr. 1986, Entscheidungen des Bundesgerichtshofes in Strafsachen 34, 53 (D who tried to run down one person in his car and accidentally struck another is liable for attempted murder as to the first and for the negligent infliction of bodily harm as to the second).

[34] In OGH, Schleswig, 10 Aug. 1976, (1977) NJW 718, the court held that if D hit P with an object thrown at another, he would be liable to P for negligence, not for an intentional wrong. The court, however, was not deciding a case in which D argued he was not negligent as to P. P's injury was covered by an insurance policy if harm was inflicted negligently but not intentionally.

of the Civil Code, he is liable even for unforeseen consequences.[35] Section 823 says that the defendant is liable for intentional or negligent injury to a plaintiff's life, body, health, freedom of movement, or 'similar' right. Economic harm does not count as the invasion of a 'similar' right. The defendant is liable for causing economic harm only if he does so intentionally, and then only if the harm he inflicts is the harm he intended. But if he negligently or intentionally injures the plaintiff's life, body, health, or freedom, he is liable for unforeseen consequences.[36]

One result is that in Germany, as in the United States, the defendant must 'take the plaintiff as he finds him'. If he causes him a physical injury, he will be liable if the injury is more severe because the plaintiff had some unforeseeable physical condition.[37] But another result is that the defendant who violated one of the plaintiff's protected rights is liable for the unforeseen consequences to some quite different interest. For example, in one case, the plaintiff's property was destroyed in an allied bombing raid in the Second World War. He claimed he could have saved it, had he not been arrested by the German authorities on information given them by the defendant. He was allowed to recover if he could prove the giving of the information was unlawful.[38]

Such a result raises the same problems as the doctrine of transferred intent. The defendant is held liable for harm he neither intended nor negligently caused. Why should it matter that this harm was the accidental consequence of a harm that he did intend? If he should be liable

[35] German writers distinguish 2 causal relations: that between D's act and a violation of one of the rights enumerated in s 823 (*haftungsbegründende Kausalität*) and that between the violation and any further harm of whatever type that P suffers (*haftungsausfüllende Kausalität*). Karl Larenz & Claus-Wilhelm Canaris, *Lehrbuch des Schuldrechts*, vol 2 pt 2 (13th ed., 1994), § 27 III b 1. The first of these causal relations also embraces unforeseen consequences. Nevertheless, a limit is imposed by the requirement that P must cause these consequences negligently or intentionally. Wolfgang Grunsky in Kurt Rebmann & Franz Juergen Säcker, *Münchener Kommentar zum Bürgerlichen Gesetzbuch* (ed., 1985) vor § 249 no. 38 There is no analogous requirement that P must intentionally or negligently bring about the consequences of the initial violation of a right.

[36] According to some German jurists. Defendant is liable provided that his violation of P's rights was the 'adequate cause' of the harm done, meaning that the harm 'would not appear wholly improbable from the standpoint of an experienced observer'. Larenz & Canaris, n. 35 above, §27 III b 1. Others say that the defendant is liable only if the harm suffered falls within the 'protective purpose of the norm' that was violated. Ibid § 27 III 3; Grunsky, n. 34 above vor § 249 no. 43. All agree, however, that D may be liable even for harm that he could not foresee.

[37] e.g., *Bundesgerichtshof*, 3rd Zivilsen., 17 Oct. 1955, Entscheidungen des Bundesgerichtshofes in Zivilsachen 18, 286, 289 (D liable for P's adverse reaction to an injection even if it was due to abnormal susceptibility); *Reichsgericht*, 6th Zivilsen., 26 Apr. 1937, Entscheidungen des Reichsgerichts in Zivilsachen 155, 38, 41 (D liable for consequences of accident that were due to P's nervous condition).

[38] *Bundesgerichtshof*, 3rd Zivilsen., 8 Mar. 1951, (1951) NJW 596 (holding the loss of freedom was the 'adequate cause' of the loss of property).

for this sort of accident, why shouldn't he be if, by accident, the victim was a third party?

Moreover, why should it matter that the harm the defendant did intend happened to constitute the violation of a right enumerated in section 823? When the draftsmen listed these rights, they were not considering how to limit liability for the unforeseen consequences of one's acts. They were trying to limit liability, particularly in negligence, so that one would not be responsible for any foreseeable adverse consequence to another person. One can make the same criticism as in the case of transferred intent: the question of liability for unforeseeable harm is answered by distinctions drawn for a quite different purpose. Moreover, as in the case of transferred intent, the answer can depend on some fine distinctions. For example, in German law, the plaintiff's property right to a ship is violated if the ship cannot leave a channel the defendant has obstructed but not if it cannot enter the channel to unload.[39] By analogy, and as in Anglo-American law, the plaintiff's right to freedom of movement would be violated if he is prevented from leaving a confined space but not if he is prevented from entering.[40] Such distinctions may be appropriate for determining when a foreseeable harm is actionable. But if the defendant locked the plaintiff in or out of his hotel room, and the plaintiff suffered serious consequences because he had a heart attack and could not reach a telephone, it would be odd if liability turned on whether he had been locked in or locked out.

In German law, it is easier to see these anomalies because the German jurists are precise about the grounds for giving relief. Nevertheless, the same difficulty is implicit in the tort law of other continental legal systems. Typically, their codes contain a general provision that the defendant is liable for harm he causes negligently or intentionally.[41] Logically, these provisions seem to leave only two alternatives: to deny relief for harm that was neither foreseeable nor intended, or to

[39] *Bundesgerichtshof*, 2nd Zivilsen., 21 Dec. 1970, *Entscheidungen des Bundesgerichtshofes in Zivilsachen* 55, 153.

[40] Gottfried Schiemann in Walter Erman, *Handkommentar zum Bürgerlichen Gesetzbuch* (9th ed., 1993), to § 823 no. 31.

[41] e.g., French Civil Code (*Code civil*) arts. 1382–3; Italian Civil Code art. 2043. The new Dutch Civil Code (*Burgerlijk Wetboek*) art. 6.162 is an exception. It provides that a person is responsible if his action was 'due to fault or another ground which, according to statute or the opinion of society, should make him accountable'. But the provision is not meant to impose liability for the unforeseen consequences of unlawful acts. It was meant to deal with cases in which a person is held liable even though he is not personally to blame for the way he acted. It was thought, e.g. that a novice driver or newly-trained physician should be liable if he fails to act like a more experienced person although he is not at fault. It was thought more honest to acknowledge that liability is imposed without fault than to say, as other legal systems do, that D was 'negligent' as judged by an 'objective standard'. See The Netherlands Ministry of Justice, *The Netherlands Civil Code Book 6 The Law of Obligations Draft Text and Commentary* The Netherlands Ministry of Justice, (1977), 384–5.

give relief and claim that somehow the harm was caused negligently or intentionally.

In France, a hunter came on the plaintiff's land in violation of a French statute and in defiance of posted 'no trespassing' signs. The plaintiff angrily grabbed the man's firearm, knocked it against a cement block, and was injured when it fired. The highest court, the *Cour de Cassation*, allowed him to recover.[42] It did not say whether it regarded the consequences of the defendant's intentional wrong as, in some mysterious way, intended as well, or whether it thought that a prudent hunter would remove his cartridges when entering another's land for fear that the owner would grab his gun and injure himself by knocking it against a cement block.

American law might not be more consistent even if, like continental legal systems, it rejected the doctrine of transferred intent. Yet the doctrine of transferred intent seems to be illogical. What is to be done?

An Older Solution

Before the nineteenth century, English jurists did not speak of transferred intent. They said that if A unintentionally harmed B, he was responsible if he was either negligent or engaged in an unlawful activity. He would be liable if he shot B when aiming at C or trespassing on B's land because these were unlawful activities. One can find that doctrine in Blackstone[43] and Hale[44] who took it from Coke[45] who took it from Bracton.[46] As Shulz has shown,[47] Bracton took it from the famous thirteenth-century canon lawyer Raymond of Penafort.[48] Raymond had simply been stating the opinion generally accepted among the canon lawyers of the day. Italian scholars say that this medieval doctrine also inspired article 82 of their Criminal Code.[49]

Although, in the nineteenth century, English jurists thought it more sensible to speak of transferred intent, we will argue that this older

[42] Cass. 2c civ., 14 Dec. 1987, arret no. 1.307 [taken from Lexis and, so far as the writer knows, not pub. elsewhere].

[43] William Blackstone, *Commentaries on the Laws of England* 4 (W. C. Jones, ed., 1916), *182–3.

[44] Matthew Hale, *Historia Placitorum Coronae* 1 (S. Emlyn & G. Wilson, eds, London, 1800), *471–7. See also ibid *429–30, *431, *466.

[45] Edward Coke, *The Third Part of the Institutes of the Laws of England* (1817), *56–7.

[46] Bracton, *De legibus et consuetudinibus Angliae* 2 (G. E. Woodbine & S. E. Thorne, eds, 1968), *f 120b-121, p 341.

[47] F. Schulz, 'Bracton and Raymond de Penafort', (1945) 61 LQR 286 at 289–90.

[48] Raimundus de Penafort, *Summa de poenitentia* (Xaverio Ochoa & Aloisio Diez, eds, 1976), II.i.3.

[49] Fiandaca & Musco, n. 6 above, 574; Antolisei & Conti, n. 6 above, 361.

solution, which can still be glimpsed in the language of some judicial opinions,[50] was actually the best one. It is, of course, viable only if one can explain (1) what should count as an unlawful activity, (2) what the causal relation must be between that activity and the harm it unforeseeably causes, and (3) why one who engages in such an activity should be responsible for that harm. These are difficult questions. As we will see, the doctrine died out in continental Europe in the sixteenth and seventeenth centuries because jurists could not find answers to them. Before considering them, however, we will examine the doctrine itself and the advantages it might have over modern approaches.

The Doctrine

The canon lawyers accepted this doctrine, not because it was found in the texts they regarded as authoritative, but because it seemed to give the right result in a number of hypothetical cases.

The earlier canonists rested the doctrine on three texts in the *Decretum*, a collection of authorities made by Gratian about 1140. One was a vague statement by St Augustine that no one can be blamed for doing what is 'good and lawful'.[51] Another was a ruling by the Council of Worms in 868 that a person who cuts down a tree which crushes a passer-by 'while carrying out some necessary work' need only do penance if acted 'by will or by negligence'.[52] The third was a decision by Pope Urban I that a priest who killed a boy by throwing a stone should do penance as a homicide but would not be suspended from his functions as those guilty of homicide usually were. The text said nothing about why the priest threw the stone.[53]

Just because their authorities said so little, the canonists found themselves improvising. The earliest canon lawyers to consider the problem said that the priest would not be guilty if he threw the stone for a 'reason' (*causa*)[54] or 'good reason' (*iusta causa*)[55] and did so with 'diligence' in a place where people were not walking. Later canonists explained that the priest had a 'reason' to throw the stone if he was engaged in a 'lawful' activity rather than an 'unlawful' one.[56] The priest

[50] See n. 6 above.

[51] *Decretum Gratiani, Corpus iuris canonici* 1 (E. Friedberg, ed., Leipzig, 1876) C. 23, q. 5, c. 8. Hereafter, the *Decretum* is cited by standard abbreviation which merely gives the *causa* (C.), *questio* (q.), and *capitulum* (c.), as here, or the *distinctio* (D.) and *capitulum* (c.), as in n. 52.

[52] D. 50, c. 50. [53] D. 50, c. 37.

[54] Paucapalea, *Summa über das Decretum Gratiani* (J. F. Schulte, ed, 1891; repr. 1965), to D. 50 c. 37.

[55] Stephanus Tornacensis, *Die Summa über das Decretum Gratiani* (J. F. Shulte, ed., 1891; repr. 1965), to D. 50 c. 37.

[56] Huguccio, *Summa*, Admont, Stiftsbibliothek, MS 7, to D. 50, c. 37, f. 71ra.

would not have been guilty if he threw the stone to chase a wild boar or a pig out of a field of grain unless he had been careless.[57] He would be guilty if he engaged in an unlawful activity or failed to use the diligence he should.[58]

After the doctrine became generally accepted, Popes referred to it in their own decisions which were in turn regarded as authoritative. Raymond of Penafort included two such decisions in his authoritative collection known as the *Decretals* of Pope Gregory IX. In one, the Pope exonerated a chaplain who had gone riding to restore his appetite after an illness and killed someone when the reins broke.[59] In the other, he exonerated a priest who was building a church and killed a co-worker by dropping a load of wood on him. In both decisions, the Pope noted that the activity was a lawful one.[60] As a sixteenth-century critic pointed out, these texts supported the doctrine only by negative inference: because a priest engaged in a lawful activity was exonerated, one was asked to infer that the priest engaged in an unlawful one would be held responsible.[61] Nevertheless, the canon lawyers read these texts as authority for their doctrine, and, indeed, they read the doctrine into other Papal decisions that had never mentioned it.[62]

The canon lawyers, then, did not accept this doctrine on authority. Neither did they do so for any theoretical reason. Instead, they seem to have liked it because it produced results that seemed intuitively correct. They gave some instances in their commentaries. One was the hypothetical case just mentioned of a priest who kills a boy when he throws a stone to chase a boar or pig from a grain-field. He was not to be held responsible, but, presumably, he would be if he had thrown the stone at another boy. Raymond of Penafort said that a person would not be

[57] *Glossa Palatina*, Vatican City, Biblioteca Apostolica Vaticana, Cod. palatini latini MS. 658, to D. 50, c. 37, f. 13va; Huguccio, n. 56 above to D. 50, c. 37, f. 71ra; Iohannes Teutonicus, *Glossa ordinaria*, Vatican City, Biblioteca Apostolica Vaticana, Cod. palatini latini MS 624, to D. 50, c. 37 to *Clerico*, f. 40rb.

[58] e.g., *Glossa Palatina*, n. 57 above, to D. 50, c. 37, f. 13rb; Huguccio, n. 56 above, to D. 50, c. 37, f. 71ra; to D. 50, c. 44, f. 72va; to D. 50, c. 50, f. 73 ra; Iohannes Teutonicus, n. 57 above, to D. 50, c. 37 to *Clerico*, f. 40rb; Guido de Baisio (Archidiacanus), *Archidiaconus super Decretum* (Lyon, 1549), to D. 50, c. 37; to D. 50, c. 44 to *casu*. For other references, see Stephan Kuttner, *Kanonistische Schuldlehre von Gratian bis auf die Dekretalen Gregors IX* (1935), 201 n. 1, 202 n. 1.

[59] *Decretales Gregorii IX, Corpus iuris canonici* 2 (E. Friedberg, ed., Leipzig, 1876) 5.12.13. Hereafter, the *Decretals* are cited by the standard abbreviation 'X' which stands for *Liber extra* or 'extra book', which is how they were known in the Middle Ages.

[60] X 5.12.25.

[61] Domenicus Soto, *De iustitia et iure libri decem* (Salamanca, 1553), lib. 5, q. 1, a. 9.

[62] e.g., *Glossa ordinaria* to X 5.12.14 (Venice, 1595); Raimundus de Penafort, n. 48 above, II.i.3; Hostiensis, *Summa aurea* (Venice, 1574), rubr. *Qua poena feriatur* sub *De homicidio volunatrai, vel casuali*, f. 359; Bernardus de Montemirato (Abbas Antiquus), *Commentaria ad libros Decretalium* (Venice, 1588), to X 5.12.13.

responsible for homicide if he threw a stone at his own animal and killed someone. He would be responsible if he threw the stone at another person's horse or cow in order to steal it.[63] A person who cut down his own tree with due care would not be responsible if it fell on someone. He would be responsible if he had been unlawfully cutting down another person's tree.[64] Sinibaldus Fliscus, later Pope Innocent IV, put the case of a man who advised someone else, not to kill anyone, but to perform an act which might cause someone to die: for example, to fire a ballista or to capture a castle or to attack a person who might defend himself. He rejected the opinion of some jurists that the man would be innocent of homicide only if 'if it were plausible that the act could be done without a person's death'. The better opinion, he said, was that he would be innocent only if the action that he had advised were lawful: for example, to attack a malefactor lawfully in order to apprehend him.[65]

In one respect, the canonists were in the same position as modern jurists. Results such as these intuitively appealed to them but they could not explain why.

Advantages of the Older Doctrine

In other respects, their position was more defensible than that of modern of jurists. According to them, causing harm while engaged in an unlawful activity is a distinct basis for responsibility alongside causing harm intentionally and causing it negligently. Consequently, they did not have to pretend that somehow the harm had been caused intentionally or negligently. They did not have to say that a person's intention transfers to an unintended harm. They did not have to redefine intentional homicide so that a person can intentionally kill someone he did not intend to kill.

Applied to criminal law, their approach would be less arbitrary than one based on transferred intent. Under the doctrine of transferred intent, A is held responsible for killing B only if he was trying to kill C. Under

[63] Raimundus de Penafort, n. 48 above II.i.3. [64] Ibid.

[65] Sinibaldus Fliscus (Innocent IV), *Commentaria in Apparatus in V Libros Decretalium* (Frankfurt, 1570), to X 5.12.12. Another and less fortunate example was based on a remark by Gratian that a blind man would be guilty if he injured someone while hunting with a javelin. Huguccio, n. 56 above, to C. 15, q. 1, dicta Gratiani post c. 2, f. 264rb; Iohannes Teutonicus, n. 57 above *ordinaria* to C. 15 q. 1 dicta Gratiai post c. 2 to *penitus*, f. 162 rb. The example was not a good one because the blind man should not go hunting precisely because it was too risky. As a critic pointed out, one did not need their doctrine to explain why someone was responsible in such cases. Leonardus Lessius, *De iustitia et iure, ceterisque virtutibus cardinalis libri quatuor* (Paris, 1628), lib. 5, cap. 9, dub. 15 no. 106.

this earlier doctrine, he could be held responsible if he killed B while engaging in any unlawful activity. He could be held responsible if he did not kill B but harmed him in some other way. If we were to adopt such an approach, we could allow the seriousness of the offence to depend on the wrongfulness of this activity as well as its consequences. If he were trying to kill C, it might well be, as Husak suggested, that the offence should be deemed as serious as if he succeeded. If he were engaged in some less wrongful activity, it could be deemed less serious. In any event, we would avoid the arbitrariness of convicting A of intentional homicide if he killed B while trying to kill C and exonerating him if he was engaged in some other unlawful activity or caused some other type of harm.

Indeed, we could avoid the idiosyncracies, not only of the doctrine of transferred intent, but also of the felony–murder and misdemeanour–manslaughter rules. These rules, like the doctrine of transferred intent, hold a person responsible for the unintended and sometimes unforeseen consequences of a wrongful act. As has often been pointed out, their operation can be arbitrary. The perpetrator of a felony that results in death is treated as though he had killed intentionally regardless of which felony he committed, whether it be armed robbery, theft, or drag-racing. But he is only held responsible if the unintended consequence is death. If he burns down a house while burglarizing it, he is not held guilty of arson under a felony–arson rule. It seems less arbitrary to hold people responsible for all the consequences of their unlawful acts, and then to let the seriousness of the offence depend upon the seriousness of the act.

In tort, this approach would avoid the arbitrariness of holding the defendant liable for the unintended consequences of his act only if he had the intention necessary to commit a common-law tort or only if he happened to violate one of the rights enumerated in section 823 of the German Civil Code. He would be liable if his act were unlawful. We will soon address the question of what sorts of unlawful acts should matter. The advantage of this older approach, however, is precisely that it allows this question to be asked. It does not sidestep the question and allow liability to depend on other rules that were framed to answer the quite different question of when a person should be civilly liable for consequences that he does intend.

As already mentioned, however, this approach was discredited in the sixteenth century when jurists asked, and were unable to answer, some fundamental questions about it. We will turn to those difficulties and how they might be resolved.

Some Difficulties and a Reappraisal

The Difficulties

Had the doctrine just described not been challenged in the sixteenth century, it might well have been passed into secular law. Other canon law doctrines did, such as the doctrine that one person may use another's property under conditions of necessity[66] and the doctrine that a party is not bound to his contract under changed circumstances.[67] Nevertheless, the civil lawyers did not adopt this older doctrine during the Middle Ages.[68] Then, in the sixteenth and seventeeth centuries, it was reconsidered and finally abandoned.

The jurists who reconsidered it belonged to a group known to historians as the Late Scholastics or the Spanish Natural Law School. Leading figures were Cajetan (1468–1534), Domingo de Soto (1494–1560), Luis de Molina (1535–1600), and Leonard Lessius (1554–1623). These jurists were self-consciously attempting to explain Roman and canon law with principles taken from their intellectual heroes, Aristotle and Thomas Aquinas. Paradoxically, many of their conclusions were borrowed by the seventeeth-century founders of the northern Natural Law School, Hugo Grotius (1583–1645) and Samuel Pufendorf (1632–94), and disseminated throughout Europe during the very centuries when the influence of Aristotle waned.[69] If the Late Scholastics had accepted the older doctrine, the northern Natural Lawyers might have done so as well.

[66] Johannes Teutonicus, n. 57 above to D. 47, c. 8 to *commune*, f 35vb.

[67] Ibid, to C. 22, q. 2, c. 14 to *furens*, f 188rb.

[68] Roman law recognized liability for causing harm to another by *culpa* or fault. The medieval Roman lawyers distinguished between *culpa* in the sense of intending harm and *culpa* in the sense of acting negligently. Azo Portius, *Summa super Codicem* to C. 3.35; Accursius, *Glossa ordinaria* (Venice, 1581), to Dig. 9.2.9.4 to *tenebitur*; Baldus degli Ubaldis, *Commentaria Corpus Iuris Civilis* (Venice, 1577), to Dig. 9.2.5 no. 1. They also observed that sometimes the fault precedes the harm, as when a person digs a pit in a public place; sometimes it concurs with the harm, as when a doctor operates unskillfully; and sometimes it occurs after harm has been done, as when a doctor operates correctly but then neglects to care for his patient. Azo to C. 3.35; Accursius to Dig. 9.2.8 to *reus*; Baldus to Dig. 9.2.8. But that is about as far as they delved into the principles underlying liability. Their chief accomplishment was to emancipate the *lex Aquilia* from archaic features that the Romans themselves had not discarded. See Reinhard Zimmermann, *The Law of Obligations: Roman Foundations of the Civilian Tradition* (1990), 1017–30.

[69] See James Gordley, *The Philosophical Origins of Modern Contract Doctrine* (1991), 69–133; Italo Birocchi, *Saggi sulla formazione storica della categoria generale del contratto* (1988), 25; Malte Diesselhorst, *Die Lehre des Hugo Grotius vom Versprechen* (1959), 6; Hans Thieme, 'Qu'est-ce que nous, les juristes, devons à la seconde scolastique espagnole?' in P. Grossi, ed., *La seconda scolastica nella formazione del diritto privato moderno* (1973), 20; Hans Thieme, 'Natürliches Privatrecht und Spätscholastik', (1953) 70 *Zeitschrift der Savigny-Stiftung für Rechtsgeschichte Romanistische Abteilung* 230.

Instead, Molina and Lessius rejected it. Grotius and Pufendorf ignored it.[70]

The doctrine fell into disrepute because of the difficulties just mentioned. Even Late Scholastics who approved of it could not satisfactorily explain which unlawful acts gave rise to liability nor the causal relationship necessary between such an act and the harm that ensued. Others rejected it because they could not see why the perpetrator of an unlawful act should be held responsible for its chance consequences. To do so seemed to them to violate some basic principles of Aristotelian and Thomistic moral philosophy. That was a curious conclusion because Thomas Aquinas himself had said that a person is responsible for the unintended consequences of an unlawful act.

Cajetan and Soto supported the doctrine but recognized that it would be absurd to hold a person liable for the consequences of any unlawful act. A priest should not be liable if he killed a co-worker while repairing a church on a religious holiday when he was forbidden to work.[71] If he was forbidden for religious reasons to ride a horse[72] or to hunt[73] he should not be responsible if he killed someone when his horse bolted or his arrow missed its mark. Soto argued that even though adultery is unlawful, if an adulterer unintentionally killed a husband while defending himself with permissible force, the adulterer should not be held responsible for his death.[74]

Cajetan and Soto recognized, then, that a person was responsible for the consequences of some unlawful acts but not others. But they never satisfactorily explained the difference. In trying to do so, they became entangled in the second difficulty mentioned earlier: explaining the causal relationship necessary between that act and the unforeseen result. Suppose one person struck and killed a person whom he wished to strike but not to kill. Cajetan thought he would be responsible for homicide because 'the blow is a path (*via*) to death'. In contrast, riding a horse or hunting is not 'generically (*de genere suo*) a path to death'.[75] Soto agreed.

[70] Hugo Grotius, *De iure belli ac pacis libri tres* (B. J. A. de Kanter-van Ketting Tromp, ed, 1939), II.xvii.1; Samuel Pufendorf, *De iure naturae et gentium libri octo* (Amsterdam, 1688), III.i.6.

[71] Soto, n. 61 above, V.i.9.

[72] Cajetan (Tomasso di Vio), *Commentaria* to Thomas Aquinas, *Summa theologica* (Padua, 1698), to II-II, Q. 64, a. 8; Soto, n. 61 above, V.i.9.

[73] Cajetan, n. 72 above to II-II, Q. 64, a. 8.

[74] Ibid.

[75] Cajetan, n. 72 above, to II–II, Q. 64, a. 8. Lessius, who thought one was only responsible for harm caused intentionally and negligently, sometimes spoke of harm that arises 'from the nature of an action' (*ex natura actionis*). He seems to have meant harm that arises 'frequently' (*ut plurimum*) rather than 'rarely' (*raro*) and so that undertaking the action would be negligent. Lessius, n. 65 above lib. 2, cap. 9, dub. 16, no. 111. He seems to have thought that Cajetan was referring to harm that naturally arose from an action in this sense. Ibid. lib. 2, cap. 2, dub. 15, no. 106. But in that event, Cajetan would have agreed with Lessius that there were only 2 bases for liability. Instead, Cajetan and Soto were to

As he put it, the unlawful activity must be a cause of death 'generically' (*de genere suo*), 'by its nature' (*ex natura sua*), or '*per se*'.[76]

These expressions may have been suggested to them by a remark of Thomas Aquinas. He agreed with the canon lawyers of his time that a person is responsible if, without intent or negligence, he kills someone while engaged in an unlawful activity.[77] His example, taken from the Bible,[78] was a person who strikes a woman and happens to kill her unborn child. According to Thomas Aquinas, 'he will not be excused from homicide, especially seeing that death is the natural result of such a blow.'[79]

It is not clear what Thomas Aquinas meant by 'the natural result'. It is not at all clear, even in the Scholastic terminology of the time, what it meant by saying an act was 'generically' or 'by its nature' or '*per se*' a cause of death.

Molina and Lessius decided that, in the absence of negligence, no one is responsible for the unintended consequences of an unlawful act. They may have been influenced by the difficulties that Cajetan and Soto encountered. Their chief difficulty, however, was that they could not see why someone should be liable for chance consequences. As Lessius put it, these consequences 'were willed neither themselves nor as to their cause'.[80] They were simply a matter of 'chance'.[81] The old doctrine was wrong.

For them, to hold someone responsible for 'chance' consequences that he did not 'will' would violate some of the basic principles of Aristotelian and Thomistic moral philosophy. For Aristotle and Thomas Aquinas, man is a rational animal. He acts by reason and will. When he fails to do so, for example, because he is ignorant of what he is doing or because his body is moved by force, he acts involuntarily.[82] Because such actions do not proceed from his reason and will, they are not caused by him *qua* human being.[83] They are the result of chance.[84] Aristotle said that a person could not be praised or blamed for such actions.[85] Thomas Aquinas concluded that he need not pay compensation when harm resulted from them.

Moreover, for Aristotle and Thomas Aquinas, the reason that someone should be held responsible for harming another is that he violated

preserve something of the old rule even at the cost of muddy expressions and apparent inconsistency.

[76] Soto, n. 61 above, V.i.9.

[77] *Summa theologiae* (Leonine text, 3rd ed., 1963), II–II, Q. 64, a. 8.

[78] Exodus 21: 22.

[79] *Summa theologiae*, n. 77 above, II-II, Q. 64, a. 8, ad 1.

[80] *De iustitia et iure*, n. 65 above, lib. 2, cap. 8, dub. 18, no. 103.

[81] Ibid, no. 102.

[82] Aristotle, *Nicomachean Ethics* III.i; Aquinas, n. 77 above, I–II, Q. 6, aa. 1, 5, 8.

[83] Aquinas, n. 77 above, I–II, Q. 6, a. 1.

[84] Ibid, II–II, Q. 64, a. 8.

[85] *Ethics*, n. 82 above, III.i.

commutative justice. Commutative justice is violated by harming or appropriating what belongs to another in order to gain through the victim's loss.[86] Aristotle himself was not clear about the sense in which a person who harmed another will 'gain'. He merely observed that 'when the suffering has been estimated, the one is called loss and the other gain'.[87] A first step toward an explanation was taken by the teacher of Thomas Aquinas, Albert the Great. He said that 'the one who acts has more of what he wants, and the one who suffers has less . . . and this is appropriately designated by the name gain and loss'.[88] Thomas Aquinas clarified: a 'person striking or killing has more of what is evaluated as good, insofar, that is, as he fulfills his will, and so is seen to receive a sort of gain'.[89] 'To gain', then, means to fulfill one's will. Therefore, it would seem, to gain through another's expense, one had to harm another's resources voluntarily.

For Thomas and for the Late Scholastics, one harmed another voluntarily not only when one intended the harm but also when one acted negligently. Negligence or lack of diligence meant a failure to act with prudence. Prudence was right reason about things to be done.[90] A prudent person weighs the good and evil consequences of his actions.[91] He accepts 'a small evil in order not to obstruct a great good',[92] taking into account 'what happens in the greater number of cases'.[93] Thus, a person who imprudently endangers another may have chosen to expose him to a more probable or more important evil for the sake of his own less probable and less important good.[94] Of course, he might be so lacking in prudence as not to realize that he was exposing another to a grave risk of harm. But in that case, he would still have acted voluntarily if he failed to have done what he could to develop prudence over the

[86] Ibid, V.ii 1130^b–1131^a; V.i–iv 1131^b–1132^b. Quotations are from *The Basic Works of Aristotle* (R. McKeon, ed., 1941).

[87] *Ethics*, n. 82 above, V.iv 1132^a.

[88] Albertus Magnus, *Ethicorum libri decem* in *Opera omnia* 7 (Bugnet, ed., 1891), lib. V, tract. ii, cap. 6, no. 25.

[89] *In decem libros ethicorum Aristotelis ad Nicomachum expositio* (A. Pirotta, ed., 1934), lib. V, lectio vi, no. 952.

[90] More technically, negligence (*negligentia*) was a lack of solicitude (*sollicitudo*) or diligence (*diligentia*). Solicitude or diligence was the virtue that enables the alert, adroit performance of the 'chief act' of prudence, *praecipere*, which could be translated as 'to command' or 'to execute'. Prudence required three 'acts': to take counsel or to consider what should be done (*consiliari*); to judge or decide what should be done (*iudicare*); and to execute this decision (*praecipere*). See *Summa theologiae*, n. 77 above, II–II, Q. 47, aa. 8–9; Q. 54, aa. 1–2; Q. 64, a. 8.

[91] *Summa theologiae*, n. 77 above, II–II, Q. 47, a. 4, obj. 1; Q. 49, a. 8; Q. 51, a. 8, ad. 1.

[92] Thomas Aquinas, *De veritate* Q. 5, a. 4, ad 4, in *Opera omnia* 9 (ed. P. Fiaccadori, 1859).

[93] *Summa theologiae*, n. 77 above, II–II, Q. 49, a. 1; a. 8 ad 3.

[94] See James Gordley, 'Tort Law in the Aristotelian Tradition', in D. Owen (ed), *Philosophical Foundations of Tort Law: A Collection of Essays* (1995), 131 at 140–51.

years by continual attention to the consequences his actions might have for others. If at no point could he have chosen to act otherwise, he was not responsible. He was the victim of chance.

In contrast, it would seem that the person held liable for the unforeseeable consequences of an unlawful act neither intended these consequences nor acted imprudently. Thomas Aquinas had said he was responsible nevertheless. To Molina and Lessius, that conclusion seemed irreconcilable with Thomas Aquinas' own principles.

William James, not intending to be complimentary, once described Scholasticism as 'common sense made pedantic'. While we have taken pains to see this difficulty in its intellectual context, it is the sort of objection that a person might make on the basis of common sense today. The harm that occurred had only a chance relationship to the unlawful act. Why then should the perpetrator be responsible? Stephan Kuttner and Martin Gardner have criticized the earlier doctrine for purporting to rest on fault but actually establishing a form of strict liability.[95] Giovanni Fiandaca, Enzo Musco and others have made the same criticism of article 82 of the Italian Criminal Code.[96]

As soon as the medieval doctrine was subject to careful scrutiny, then, it collapsed. The difficulties we have described seemed insurmountable.

A Reappraisal

But two features of this story should make us wonder if the older doctrine was rightly rejected. First, Molina and Lessius themselves seem to have had qualms about their own conclusions. There are indications that they, like ourselves, found it hard to reach intuitively correct results if a person is only held responsible for harm caused intentionally or negligently.

Molina denied that a person who, without negligence, cut down another person's tree should be held responsible if it fell on a servant or a cow.[97] He denied that a thief should be liable if, without negligence, he set fire to the house from which he was stealing.[98] Suppose, however, the thief had entered the house at night and stepped on something valuable and broke it. Or suppose a person who struck another harmed him in a different way than he intended. At this point even Molina refused to exonerate him. In these cases, he said, the unlawful act was the sort that might lead to the harm that actually occurred (*res illicita . . . est apta, ut damnum sequatur*). Consequently, 'it is easy for fault to be

[95] Kuttner, n. 58 above, 207; Gardner, n. 12 above at 734.
[96] Fiandaca & Musco, n. 6 above, 576–81.
[97] Ludovicus Molina, *De iustitia et iure tractatus* (Venice, 1614), disp. 728 no. 2 (reading *bovem* for *ovem*).
[98] Ibid.

present' and 'much easier' for it 'to be presumed' present by the court.[99] It sounds as if he is reassuring us that the court will always presume the thief or the assailant was negligent and so hold him responsible.

Lessius left himself no such line of retreat. Nevertheless, he did not discuss Molina's cases of theft and physical attack or the cases put by the medieval canon lawyers. He illustrated his thesis with Cajetan's examples of the priest who is forbidden to hunt and the adulterer who defends himself without excessive force.[100] He added several examples of his own. Suppose someone kills Peter, and malicious accusers and witnesses later see to it that Paul is punished for the crime.[101] Suppose someone robs Peter's treasure and Peter subsequently dies of grief.[102] Suppose someone sells arms to a knight knowing that the knight might put them to a bad use.[103] According to Lessius, in none of these cases should a person be held responsible for the death he did not intend.

The examples make one suspicious. They seem carefully chosen to make the conclusion sound plausible. In most of them, someone other than the perpetrator behaved in a strange or unlawful way: the homicidal husband, the malicious witness, the inconsolable robbery victim, the knight who misuses weapons that he is entitled to carry. Arguably, in these cases, the causal chain is broken. Just because it might be broken, it seems less unjust to exonerate the perpetrator than in the cases put by Lessius' predecessors.

There is a second reason for suspicion. The Late Scholastics thought that Thomas Aquinas had violated his own principles by accepting the doctrine. If so, one wonders why he didn't see the difficulty himself.

The easiest answer is that Thomas Aquinas did not think there was a difficulty. He may well have thought that the perpetrator of an unlawful act did act voluntarily in the sense required by his principles. As we have seen, Thomas Aquinas had two reasons to believe that a person must act voluntarily to be held responsible. First, a person must act voluntarily if the action is to be attributed to him *qua* human being rather than attributed to chance. Second, to violate commutative justice, a person must be seeking a gain for himself at the expense of another. When he culpably harms the other person, he 'gains' in the sense that he fulfills his own will at that person's expense.

Certainly, the unlawful act itself was voluntary and can be attributed to the perpetrator. It was voluntary even though he did not foresee the harm it would cause. Moreover, supposing that the unlawful act was a

[99] Ibid. no. 3.

[100] Lessius, n. 65 above, lib. 2, cap. 9, dub. 15, nos. 104–5. He added a similar case in which the priest who is an expert surgeon but prohibited by his religious station from practising his art operates on someone skillfully but happens to kill him. Ibid. no. 104.

[101] Ibid. lib. cap. 9, dub. 16, nos. 109–11. [102] Ibid. no. 113. [103] Ibid.

violation of commutative justice, then the perpetrator did choose to seek his own ends by causing another person harm. In this sense, he sought to 'gain' through another's loss. Perhaps Thomas thought it did not matter that he inflicted a different loss from the one through which he hoped to gain.

Earlier we saw that the Late Scholastic criticism can be restated in modern terms without losing its force. Whether or not Thomas Aquinas would have given the answer just described, it, too, can be restated rather simply, and in a way that does not depend on a specifically Thomistic or Aristotelian theory of human action and commutative justice. The defendant by mere chance did inflict a different loss from the one he intended. But it does not follow, as Molina, Lessius, Kuttner, Gardner, and Fiandaca and Musco thought, that holding him responsible is strict rather than fault-based responsibility, responsibility for chance rather than for choice. There are two senses in which one can say that the defendant inflicted the harm by chance: he could not foresee the harm, and he did not wish it to occur. But why should either of these make a difference?

Whether the defendant could have foreseen the harm matters in a negligence case precisely because the defendant is held liable for imposing an undue risk on someone else. When, however, the defendant is held liable for harm inflicted intentionally, it does not matter whether his action created a large or a small risk of harm. It does not matter whether he himself thought it probable that he would succeed in inflicting it. At the end of Faulkner's *Snopes Trilogy*, a man seeking revenge shoots Flem Snopes with a pistol so old and rusty that it was extremely unlikely to fire. Yet there is no doubt he is legally and morally responsible. That would still be so even if the pistol were so defective that he would not have been negligent if he fired it at someone as a joke. A person who succeeds in blowing up a building with a home-made bomb will be held responsible even if a dozen engineering experts agree that the bomb was so unlikely to explode that they would not have minded using it for a paper weight. Of course, the defendant's actions must have created some risk that harm would occur or else he could not be said to have caused the harm. But he is not held responsible because he created a risk. He is held responsible simply because he wanted the harm that he caused to occur.

Should it matter, then, that he caused, not the harm that he wanted, but a different harm? Certainly, it matters from his own perspective. His intention to bring about the very harm he wished was thwarted. His own ends, which would have been advanced, in his view, by causing this very harm, were not realized. But a defendant's failure to achieve his ends hardly exonerates him in criminal or tort law. The greedy nephew who shoots his uncle is not exonerated if the uncle turns out to have been poor rather than rich or to have left all his money to the University of California. Though the characteristic about which the nephew was mistaken—rich or poor, nephew's benefactor or not—mattered very much to him, it only matters from his own perspective. Similarly, if he missed the uncle and killed a bystander, it also matters from his perspective that the man he killed is not one from whose death he expected to profit. But it is hard to see why it should matter to anyone else that the harm he inflicted was not the one he wished.

This solution depends on defining a violation of commutative justice—or, if one prefers, on defining responsibility for culpably harming another—in much the same way that Michael Moore defined intentional homicide. As we have seen, according to Moore, intentional homicide requires that the defendant intended to kill someone and that he did so. But the person killed need not have been the one intended. Similarly, by the approach just described, the person held responsible must have wished to harm another, and he must have done so. But the harm he inflicted need not have been the one he intended. Moore's approach, however, entails the paradox that a person is held responsible for intentional killing when there is no one whom he has intentionally killed. The approach just described avoids that difficulty. It does not hold the perpetrator responsible for killing intentionally. It holds him responsible for culpably causing harm.

Moreover, the approach just described holds him responsible for a reason that answers to our sense of justice. Imagine a person's reaction if someone he loved were killed by a bullet aimed at someone else. If he were asked to regard the killing as merely an unfortunate accident, he might feel a sense of outrage. To explain that feeling, he might well say that the perpetrator should not have been trying to kill anyone at all. If he hadn't, the victim would still be alive.

If this approach is correct, then the other difficulties with the older doctrine can be resolved quite straightforwardly. A person should not be liable for the unforeseen consequences of all unlawful acts. He should be responsible for the unforeseen consequences of acts that are unlawful because they are unjust to others, because they harm or appropriate what belongs to them. As we have seen, Cajetan and Soto put cases in which it seems absurd to hold the defendant liable for the consequences of his unlawful act. But in those cases, the act in question was not unjust. The perpetrator hunted or worked on Sunday or in violation of the rules of his religious order.

Moreover, for the perpetrator to be held responsible, his action must have made the harm more likely to occur. But he himself need not have known that his act made this harm more likely.

This requirement does not mean that the risk must be greater because of the features of the act that made it unlawful. In the American cases described earlier, the defendant who trespassed on the plaintiff's land and built a fire was held liable when the fire spread and burned down his house. The risk may have been no greater than if the plaintiff had started the fire himself. But the fact remains that he did not, and that the defendant's unlawful act exposed him to the risk that did destroy his house. That is a sufficient reason for holding him liable. Moreover, any other rule would lead to strange results. If a would-be murderer shoots a bystander, it would be odd to ask whether he fired the shot in a hunting preserve or some other place where shots could lawfully be fired.

Nevertheless, this requirement is not the same as 'but-for' causation. If John Dillinger ran down a child who leaped in front of his car while he was driving to rob a bank, but for the unlawful act, the child would have lived. If Dick Turpin detained a traveller for ten minutes to rob him, and later the traveller was killed by a falling tree, then but for the unlawful act, the tree would have fallen before it could injure the traveller. But the fact that Dillinger is *en route* to a bank or that the traveller is delayed does not make it any more likely that someone will be harmed. The victim cannot complain that the unlawful act exposed him to an added risk.

A Postscript on Negligence

This discussion of intentional wrongs can throw light on whether the defendant should be responsible for the unforeseeable consequences of his own negligence. Jurists have disagreed. In German law, the prevailing view is that a person who is negligent should be liable even for unforeseeable consequences.[104] French and Italian jurists have said that he should only be liable for those that could be expected as a matter of ordinary experience.[105] In England and the United States, the question was addressed in some famous cases. In the English case of *In re Polemis & Furness, Withy & Co.*,[106] the plaintiff recovered when a board negligently dropped by a longshoreman in the hold of a ship unforeseeably struck a spark which ignited gasoline vapour. That decision was disapproved in *Overseas Tankship (UK) Ltd v Morts Dock & Engineering Co., Ltd*:[107] the defendant was not liable for a fire caused when his ship negligently spilled oil because he could not have foreseen that this

[104] See nn. 35 & 36 above.

[105] Philippe Malaurie & Laurnet Aynès, *Cours de droit civil Les obligations* (1985), no. 47; Boris Starck, Henri Roland & Laurent Boyer, *Obligations 1. Responsabilité délictuelle* (4th ed., 1991), no. 1219; Alberto Trabucchi, *Istituzioni di diritto civile* (32nd ed., 1991), no. 88.

[106] [1921] KB 560. [107] [1961] AC 388 (PC Aust).

type of oil was flammable. In the United States, in *Palsgraf v Long Island Railroad*,[108] a railroad employee negligently caused a passenger to fall who happened to be carrying fireworks which exploded, causing some scales at the other end of the platform to fall on the plaintiff. Cardozo, speaking for the court, said that the employee was not negligent as to the plaintiff since she was not in the zone of danger. Andrews dissented: 'when injuries do result from our unlawful act we are liable for the consequences [whether] unusual, unexpected, foreseen or unforeseeable'.

If our earlier conclusion is correct, a person who harms or appropriates what belongs to another to advance his own ends should be responsible for the unforeseeable consequences. It should not matter that the harm he inflicted was not the very one he intended. It would seem, then, that a person who acts negligently should be liable for the unforeseeable consequences if he made a similar decision: if he chose to inflict an undue risk of harm on another in order to advance his own ends.

If we consider the meaning of negligence, we can see why a person who acts negligently might or might not have made such a decision. American jurists have found it helpful to explain negligence with a formula once used by Learned Hand.[109] The defendant is negligent if he fails to take a precaution that would cost him less than the harm he should anticipate to others, taking into account both the severity of that harm and the likelihood it will occur if the precaution is not taken. While the formula is fashionable among those who do economic analysis of law, even those who do not should regard it as a piece of common sense. Precautions should be taken if they are worth it, given the risk and the severity of what might happen otherwise.

Using the formula in this common-sense fashion, we can see two different reasons why a person might act negligently. He might understand that a precaution is worth taking and still not take it because he himself must incur the cost of the precaution whereas the risk of harm falls on others. Or he may be so lacking in skill or judgment that he cannot take the precaution or cannot see that he should do so.

In the first case, he would have taken the precaution if his own person or property were endangered. Instead, he endangered others to save himself time, trouble, or expense or to benefit from some excessively dangerous activity. His decision to do so is like that of a person who intentionally inflicts harm on another to gain his own ends. If that person cannot object that the harm he caused is not the one he chose,

[108] 162 NE 99 (NY 1928).
[109] *United States v Carroll Towing Co.*, 159 F 2d 169 (2nd Cir. 1947).

then this person should not be able to object that he wished to endanger others in a different way.

If he omitted the precaution because of a lack of skill or judgment, he might not have made such a choice. Admittedly, his shortcomings may be due to choices he did make for which he is to blame: for example, to practise less than he should, to pay insufficient attention to the consequences of his actions, or to engage in a risky activity knowing his own limitations. Because of these choices, he saved himself time and trouble and others faced an undue risk, which is a sufficient reason for holding him liable. But he need not have chosen as he did because he knew that the risk would fall on others and cared less about their person or property than his own. Quite possibly he would have made the same choices if the risks to himself were as great as or greater than those to others. His choices were imprudent but not unjust. He should be liable only for the consequences of the risk that he imprudently created.

Usually, of course, a court cannot tell what choices the defendant made in the past or why he made them. Nevertheless, the court can conclude that the consequences to others were less important to him than his own concerns when, by a simple and obvious precaution, he could have avoided a great risk of severe harm. Such cases fit comfortably within the traditional definition of gross negligence: negligence that creates risks so great and so easy to avert as to manifest a wilful indifference to the consequences to others. And so once again we have reached an ancient conclusion: *culpa lata dolo aequiparatur*, gross negligence amounts to an intentional wrong.

Liability for Breach of Contract

If the defendant should be responsible in crime and tort for the unforeseen consequences of intentional wrongs, then it would seem that he should sometimes be liable for them when he breaches a contract. He should be liable, as before, when his breach is unjust because he seeks to appropriate or to harm what belongs to another.

Some might think that every intentional breach is wrongful or unjust. By definition, it is a violation of contractual duty. Others, particularly partisans of the efficient breach theory, might think that there is nothing wrong with breaching a contract provided one compensates the other party for the loss he suffers.

Every breach is a violation of contractual duty in the sense that the other party fails to receive something owed him and is entitled to a remedy. But not every breach is culpable, let alone wrongful or unjust. A party who finds it impossible to perform may sometimes be liable even though he failed through no fault of his own. That is so, not only in Anglo-American law, where liability is supposed to be strict, but in continental legal systems that supposedly require that the breaching party be at fault.[110]

Moreover, for a party to breach a contract intentionally may not be unjust or wrongful or even culpable. Any party who could perform but refuses to do so breaches his contract intentionally. But even Daniel Friedmann, in his critique of the efficient breach theory, does not claim a party should never refuse to perform. For example, according to Friedmann, he should breach if he finds that he can only perform at unexpectedly high cost to himself, and that someone else can make the same performance at a lower cost.[111] It would be wasteful for him to perform himself rather than to compensate the other party for any additional expense incurred by the other party in obtaining the performance from another. The breaching party may or may not have been at fault for putting himself in such a position. But having found himself in it, his decision not to perform is not culpable.

Under other circumstances, as Friedmann points out, the party who breaches, in effect, appropriates an asset that belongs to the other party even if he does pay compensation for the loss he causes. Suppose A agrees to sell B a Rubens. A then learned that C will pay a huge price for it—much more than it is worth to B. B does not know that C will pay so much and will not find out unless A tells him. Friedmann argues that it may not even be efficient to allow A to breach, compensate B for any loss he suffers, and sell the painting to C himself.[112] If he is not allowed to do so, he will tell B about C, charging for the information, and B will sell C the painting. The transaction costs of negotiating with B over the price for the information would be offset, if A breaches, by those of negotiating and possibly litigating over the value of the painting to B.

But even if it were efficient, Friedmann argues, A's breach would still be unjust.[113] A has sold the right to the painting to B. Therefore B should get the profits from the resale. A should no more be entitled to breach than to sneak into B's house after delivery, steal the painting, and sell it to C. Nor do modern legal systems allow him to breach and keep the painting. An Anglo-American judge would grant B specific performance because the Rubens is unique and therefore the damage remedy is deemed to be inadequate. A French judge would impose an *astreinte* or money fine unless the Rubens were delivered, a fine large enough to

[110] James Gordley, 'Contract in Pre-Commercial Societies and in Western History' ch 2, vol VII (*Contracts in General*), *International Encyclopedia of Comparative Law* (1997), §§ 89, 93.

[111] Daniel Friedmann, 'The Efficient Breach Fallacy', (1989) 18 JLS 1 at 10–11.

[112] Ibid. 6–7.

[113] Ibid. 1–2.

induce A to deliver it. A German judge would order performance because, under German law, that is the normal remedy.[114]

In the case just discussed, the breach is unjust because it amounts to an appropriation of the other party's assets. A breach would also be unjust if a party breaches because he hopes to evade paying compensation or when he knows that he cannot compensate the other party fully. In those circumstances, even adherents of the efficient breach theory would not claim the breach is efficient.

The situations in which a breach is unjust or wrongful thus correspond to those described earlier in which an unlawful act is unjust: the perpetrator knows he will be appropriating or harming what belongs to the other party. He should then be liable for the unforeseen consequences for the same reason as before. It should not matter that he intended one sort of harm and inflicted another.

As before, moreover, one can think of cases in which it seems intuitively right that he should be liable for unforeseen harm. Suppose that after A sells the Rubens to B but before he delivers it, B agrees to resell it to a private collector who will pay vastly more for it than anyone including A had imagined. If a thief steals the Rubens before A delivers it, it might be unfair to make A compensate B for the unexpected profit he would have made on resale. But it certainly seems fair to hold A liable for that amount if he helped the thief to steal the painting.

Suppose that the plaintiff owned a Rubens and stored it in the defendant's warehouse without telling him, and that the defendant would never have expected such a valuable object to be stored there. Suppose a fire broke out. It might be unfair to make the warehouse owner pay for the painting if it was destroyed because he negligently delayed calling the fire department. It seems perfectly fair to hold him liable if he did not call because he wanted to collect insurance on the warehouse when it burned.

Suppose someone sold penicillin that was diluted with a seemingly harmless chemical compound to a children's hospital. Or suppose he sold a rancher a horse that was infected with a disease that could be expected to infect other horses but not cows. If the seller was merely careless in not learning that the penicillin was diluted or the horse infected, it might be unfair to hold him liable if, unforeseeably, some children died of a severe allergic reaction or the rancher's cows were infected. It seems fair to hold him liable if, like Harry Lime in Orson Welles' film *The Third Man*, he deliberately diluted the penicillin to cut his costs, foreseeing that some children would die of disease but not of an allergic reaction. It seems fair

[114] James Gordley, 'Common Law und civil law: eine überholte Unterscheidung', (1993) 3 Zeitschrift für Europäisches Privatrecht 498 at 502.

to hold him liable for the death of the rancher's cows if he sold the horse knowing it would infect the rancher's horses.

Again, an Older Solution

As before, a doctrine was once developed to fit cases like these in which relief seems intuitively right. It was developed in France in the eighteenth century by Robert Pothier. He said that a breaching party should be liable only for harm that he could have foreseen at the time he contracted unless his breach constituted an intentional wrong (*dol*). If it did, he should be liable for unforeseeable harm as well. While this rule looks like an application to contract law of the canon law doctrine described earlier, Pothier developed it independently, long after the canon law doctrine had fallen into disfavour, to explain some notoriously intractable Roman texts.

One text said that if the seller fails to deliver, the buyer will get only damages that 'concern the thing itself' (*circa rem*). If the seller failed to deliver wine, the buyer would not get the profit he could have made reselling it; if he failed to deliver grain, the buyer could not recover the loss he suffered if his slaves starved.[115] Another text said that if the seller sold diseased cattle or unsound timber in ignorance of its condition, the buyer would only be compensated for the extra amount he paid because the parties did not know the truth. If the seller had known, however, the buyer could also recover damages if his other cattle died of contagion or the building he constructed with the timber collapsed.[116]

Pothier explained these cases by using a principle formulated in the sixteenth century by the French jurist Molinaeus: a party should be liable only for harm he could foresee when he entered into a contract. Molinaeus had used this principle to explain another Roman rule that put an upper limit to the damages recoverable for breach of contract. Pothier said that normally, a party should be deemed to foresee only those damages that occur as to the thing purchased itself (*par rapport à la chose même*) and not harm that occurs to other goods because of the lack of that thing (*propter rem ipsam non habitam*). If the seller failed to deliver a horse and the buyer had to pay a higher price for one, he can recover the difference in price but not the rents he was unable to collect from tenants because he did not have a horse. If a lessor leases property he did not own and his lessee is evicted, the lessee can recover for any increase in the rent he must pay elsewhere but not for the business he lost by changing locations or any furniture that is broken in moving.[117] These

[115] Dig. 19.1.21.3. [116] Dig. 19.1.13.pr.
[117] Robert Pothier, *Traité des obligations* no. 161, in *Oeuvres de Pothier* 2 (2nd ed., 1861).

'extrinsic damages' could be recovered only if they were foreseen at the time of contracting.[118] Nevertheless, unforeseeable damages could be recovered without limit if the breach constituted an intentional wrong (*dol*). As authority, Pothier cited the Roman text in which a person who knowingly sold defective cattle is liable when the buyer's other cattle are infected.[119] Similarly, he said, one who knowingly sold defective wood must pay for the damages suffered when the house that was built with the wood collapses.[120]

Modern Law

One way to test the merits of a rule is to see what happens when a legal system either adopts it or fails to do so. Pothier's rule was adopted in France and Italy and rejected in Germany, England, and the United States. We will examine the consequences.

French and Italian Law

The draftsmen of the French Civil Code adopted Pothier's rule[121] whence it passed to the Italian Civil Code.[122] The defendant is liable only for damages foreseeable when the contract was made unless, as Pothier said, he acted with *dol*, or the Italian equivalent, *dolo*. The French and Italians have experienced some difficulties with the rule but we can see from what has already been said how to resolve them.

One difficulty has been defining *dol* or *dolo*. French and Italian courts have swung between different and inadequate formulas: that the breaching party must want to injure the other party;[123] that he must act in bad faith and knowing he will injure him;[124] that he must breach intentionally.[125] Even when they use the last, they seem to mean the breach must

[118] Ibid, no. 162. [119] Ibid, no. 166. [120] Ibid, nos. 160, 166–7.

[121] French Civil Code (*Code civil*), art. 1150.

[122] Italian Civil Code (*Codice civile*), art. 1225.

[123] This position was taken in France before 1969. Christian Larroumet, *Droit civil*, vol 3, *Les Obligations Le Contrat* (3rd ed., 1996), no. 623; Geneviève Viney, *Traité de droit civil Les obligations La responsibilité: effets* (1988), no. 327.

[124] This seems to have been the position of Italian courts before 1984. See Cass., 16 Jan. 1954, no. 85, Giurisprudenza italiana 1954.I.1.513.

[125] This seems to be the current view of the Italian and French courts. Italy: Cass., 30 Oct. 1984, no. 5566, Giurisprudenza italiana 1986.I.1.276 (defendant refused to leave premises he rented even after a court had declared he had no right to remain); France: Cass., lère civ., 4 Feb. 1969, Dalloz 1969.601, Juris Classeur Périodique 1969.II.16030 (artist breaches by changing employers); Cass. lère civ., 22 Oct. 1975, Dalloz 1976.151 (same). In these cases, however, D appropriated an asset that belonged to the other: an apartment in the Italian case, and artistic services in the French ones. Moreover, the courts used more circumlocution than one would expect if they merely meant that he must breach intentionally. French jurists recognize that even after these decisions, a breach only constitutes *dol* if it is

be in some way wrongful as well as intentional.[126] Yet it has proven difficult to explain in what way it should be wrongful. It was in large part because of that difficulty that those drafting the Unidroit Principles rejected a provision, contained in the preliminary draft,[127] that the defendant would be liable for damages he could not have foreseen if his breach was 'intentional'. It was pointed out that not all intentional breaches are blameworthy or even undesirable. Nevertheless, we have already seen how this difficulty should be resolved. An intentional breach is wrongful when, for his own ends, the perpetrator appropriates or harms what belongs to the other party.

Some jurists have also objected that the rules governing liability for unforeseeable damages should be the same in contract as in tort. They have pointed out that the French and Italian Codes do not draw a distinction in tort analogous to this one.[128] If our analysis was correct, however, the problem is with the rules of tort which should be similar to those in the Codes dealing with breach of contract.

German Law

In Germany, in the nineteenth century, jurists claimed that Pothier's rule was wrong in principle. It was an age of conceptualism. They thought liability should be based on two simple concepts. First, a party should be liable only if he was at fault.[129] Second, the party who was at fault should pay the amount necessary to put the other party where he would have been had the contract not been breached.[130] If both parties were at fault, the damages awarded were to be reduced. These principles were adopted by the draftsmen of the German Civil Code of 1900.[131]

Nevertheless, German law has accepted these principles without

wrongful although they are not clear when that might be; e.g., Note by Jean Mazeaud to Cass., lère civ., 22 Oct. 1975, Dalloz 1976.151 at 152; Alain Sériaux, *Droit civil Droit des obligations* (1992), 236; Larroumet, n. 124 above, no. 623. On the dispute among Italian jurists, see Giovanna Visintini, *Trattato breve della responsibilità civile* (1996), 575.

126 See n. 125 above.

127 Art. 6.4.5, which was replaced by art. 7.44 of the final version. I argued against the change. *Comments by Professor James Gordley on Articles 7.44 and 7.4.13*, Unidroit, Study L–(WG) WP.2 (1993).

128 Malaurie & Aynès, n. 105 above, no. 489.

129 Karl Arndts, *Lehrbuch der Pandekten* (14th ed., 1889), § 86 n. 3; Georg F. Puchta, *Pandekten* (2nd ed., 1844), § 266; id, *Vorlesungen über das heutige römische Recht* 2 (2nd ed., 1849), §§ 264–67; Bernhard Windscheid, *Lehrbuch des Pandektenrechts* 1 (7th ed., 1891), § 101; Karl Vangerow, *Leitfaden für Pandekten-Vorlesungen* 1 (1847) § 107. For a dissenting view, see Aloys Brinz, *Lehrbuch der Pandekten* (2nd ed., 1879). See Gordley, n. 110 above, §§ 90–92.

130 Puchta, *Vorlesungen* 2, n. 129 above, § 224; Windscheid, n. 129 above, § 257. For a dissenting view, see Karl Vangerow, *Lehrbuch der Pandekten* 3 (7th ed., 1863) § 571 Anm. 3. See Zimmermann, n. 68 above, 833–4.

131 German Civil Code (*Bürgerlichesgesetzbuch*) §§ 249, 254, 275–7.

accepting what would seem to be their obvious consequences. According to section 254 paragraph 2 of the Civil Code, the damages awarded are to be reduced 'even if the fault of the injured party consisted in an omission to call the attention of the obligated party to the danger of an unusually serious injury of which the obligated party neither knew nor ought to have known'. Section 254 paragraph 1 provides that when the injured party was also at fault, the damages should be reduced by an amount that depends 'upon the circumstances and especially upon how far the injury has been caused by one party or the other'. Generally, courts make this determination by asking how dangerous and how culpable the conduct of each party was.[132] Nevertheless, the prevailing opinion is that when the plaintiff's 'fault' was a failure to tell the defendant that damages might be unusually high, he can recover no damages at all.[133] Moreover, according to the prevailing opinion, when one party's culpable action was merely negligent and the other's was intentional, the party who acted intentionally must pay damages in full.[134] Consequently, section 254 functions much like Pothier's rule. If the defendant's breach was culpable and intentional, he is liable even for unforeseeable consequences. If it was unintentional, he is only liable for harm he should have foreseen, either on the basis of his own knowledge or because of what he was told. The principal difference—which does not concern us here—is that for Pothier, though not under the German Civil Code, the damages must have been foreseeable when the contract was made.

Different provisions apply if the defendant sells the plaintiff defective goods. Normally, the plaintiff can only ask for either rescission or a reduction in price.[135] He can recover consequential damages, however, when the seller 'fraudulently conceals a defect'.[136] Fraud in the normal sense has not been required. It is enough that the seller knew of the defect and intentionally failed to reveal it.[137] Courts have not only allowed recovery for harm that was unforeseeable but have gone further than they should if our previous discussion of causation was correct. In one case, the plaintiff negligently wrecked a car he had just bought from the defendant. The defendant had falsely stated that the car had never been in an accident. He was allowed to recover its value on the ground

[132] Larenz & Canaris, n. 35 above, § 31 I e; Grunsky, n. 35 above, to § 254 no. 7.

[133] Grunsky, n. 35 above, to § 254 no. 59; Helmut Heinrichs in *Palandt Bürgerliches Gesetzbuch* (55th ed., 1996), to § 254 no. 51; *OGH*, Bremen, 20 Nov. 1975, Versicherungs Recht 1976, 558 at 560.

[134] Larenz & Canaris, n. 35 above § 31 I e; Grunsky, n. 35 above, to § 254 no. 7; Heinrichs in *Palandt*, n. 134 above, to § 254 no. 51. See *OGH*, Munich, 23 Feb. 1990, NJW—Rechtsprechungs Report Zivilrecht 1990, 828 at 829 (all the damages on the injured party when the injurer was grossly negligent).

[135] German Civil Code, § 462.

[136] Ibid, § 463.

[137] Hans Gramm in *Palandt*, n. 134 above, to § 463 no. 11.

that he would not have bought it, and therefore would never had wrecked it, had the defendant told him the truth.[138] Not only was the crash unforeseeable, but the lie did not make it any more likely to occur. It seems more like the cases discussed earlier in which John Dillinger runs over someone on his way to rob a bank or Dick Turpin detains someone who for that reason is later crushed by a falling tree.

In any event, despite the general principles that are supposed to inform German law, the plaintiff does recover for unforeseeable harm in the cases that Pothier would have described as intentional breach of contract. Nevertheless, while the results are similar, Pothier's formulation is more honest and straightforward. If the plaintiff normally should not recover for the unforeseeable consequences of the defendant's breach one should simply say so. It is artificial to presume he was at fault for not telling the defendant about these consequences and then to claim this fault was the entire cause of the harm he suffered. If the plaintiff should recover for the unforeseeable consequences when the defendant's breach was intentional and wrongful, then, again, one should say so. One should not claim that in that case the defendant's fault was the entire cause of the plaintiff's harm. One should not resolve it by a seemingly anomalous exception to the rules governing sale of defective goods.

Anglo-American Law

Anglo-American courts adopted Pothier's approach in part. In 1854, in *Hadley v. Baxendale*,[139] an English court adopted a rule that English and American courts still profess to follow. A party is liable only for damages he could have foreseen at the time of contracting, either because they would follow in the normal course of events, or because he had been told they might occur. Historians are agreed that the court took this rule directly from Pothier.[140] But they did not borrow Pothier's exception for cases in which the defendant's breach constituted an intentional wrong. Perhaps they would have done so if, while Pothier's prestige in the Anglo-American world was still great, a case had arisen in which someone knowingly sold infected cattle or unsound timber. By happenstance, it did not.

Nevertheless, as we have seen, the defendant is liable in the United States for the unforeseen consequences of an intentional tort under the

[138] *Bundesgerichtshof*, 7th Zivilsen., 14 Oct. 1971, Entscheidungen des Bundesgerichthofes in Zivilsachen 57, 137 at 142. The court held that the lie was the 'adequate cause' of the car wreck and that the wreck was within the 'protective purpose' of the norm that prohibits fraud. Nevertheless, since P was also at fault, he did not recover all of his damages.

[139] 9 Exch. 341. [140] See Zimmermann, n. 68 above, 830.

doctrine of transferred intent.[141] In some jurisdictions, he is liable for the unforeseen consequences of negligent acts. As a result, whether a defendant is liable for the unforeseen consequences of a breach of contract depends on whether the breach also happens to constitute a tort.

The results can be arbitrary. For example, the defendant has committed an intentional tort as well as a breach of contractual duty if he is a physician who intentionally removes the wrong organ from a patient as part of an unauthorized medical experiment; if he is a lifeguard who intentionally holds a swimmer underwater as a prank; or if he is a caretaker who intentionally lights a fire in order to burn down his employer's house. Supposedly, he is liable for all the harm he does, foreseeable or not. In contrast, a physician, a lifeguard, or a caretaker has committed a breach of contract but not an intentional tort if he deliberately refrains from acting and so a patient dies, a swimmer drowns, or a fire lit by another burns his employer's house. In principle, he is liable only for damages he might have foreseen at the time the contract was made.

In the case described earlier, the defendant who knowingly sold penicillin diluted with a compound he believes to be harmless might well be liable for committing an intentional tort. He might be liable for battery because he caused an unauthorized 'contact' between the chemical compound and the body of the plaintiff. One American court allowed women undergoing pre-natal care to recover for battery when, without their knowledge, they were given a pill containing a drug, DES (Diethylstilbestrol), as part of an experiment to determine its value in preventing miscarriages.[142] In contrast, the defendant who sold cattle that he knows to be infected could not be held liable in trespass for the unforeseeable consequences because he did not enter the plaintiff's property. At least, that was John Fleming's opinion when I put this hypothetical case to him years ago. It is hard to see any rational ground for such a distinction.

English law does not recognize the doctrine of transferred intent in tort. Nevertheless, in England, in both of the cases just described, the defendant might be liable for committing the tort of deceit. If so, then, as Lord Denning held in *Doyle v Olby*, he would be liable for the unforeseeable consequences.[143] In contrast, some American courts have said the

[141] On whether one is liable for any of the unforeseeable consequences of an intentional tort in English law, see n, 4 above.

[142] *Mink v University of Chicago*, 460 FSupp 713 (ND Ill 1978). In this case, the advantage of the action in battery was not that it permitted recovery of unforeseeable damages but that it permitted recovery even though P's were unable to prove that they themselves had suffered physical harm from the drug. The harm had been suffered by their unborn children.

[143] *Doyle v Olby*, [1969] 2 All ER 119, 122 (CA). See Heuston & Buckley, n. 4 above, 387; Stanton, n. 4 above, 100–1.

harm must be caused 'proximately' by the defendant's misrepresentation, an expression that usually excludes the unforeseeable.[144] But perhaps these statements are overly broad. In such cases, however, the plaintiff often suffered, not unforeseeable consequential harm caused by the circumstances that had been misrepresented, but harm that had nothing to do with those circumstances. The bonds or stock he purchased would have become valueless even if the defendant's representations had been true.[145]

To be liable in deceit, however, the defendant must have misrepresented some fact. He would be liable in England if he lied about whether the penicillin was diluted or the horse was infected.[146] In some American jurisdictions, he would be liable if he knew of such a defect and remained silent. For example, the seller of a house is liable if he does not reveal that it is infested with termites.[147] He must, however, have deceived the other party as to a presently existing fact, such as the defective condition of the goods, to be held liable in deceit.

His present state of mind counts as such a fact. Consequently, he is liable in deceit if he intends to violate his contractual obligations at the moment he contracts. Simply by contracting, he misrepresented his intentions. But he is not liable in deceit if he made his promise in good faith and then violated it.[148]

The results again can be arbitrary. One who owns a warehouse and rents space in it for storage would be liable in deceit if he lied about whether the warehouse was fireproof or whether it was equipped with a fire alarm that would automatically notify the fire department. He would be liable if he promised to fireproof the warehouse or to install such an alarm or to call the fire department if a fire broke out, intending at the time of making it to break his promise. He could therefore be liable if the Rubens stored by a customer burned. But he might not be liable if he later broke his promise to fireproof the warehouse or to install the alarm or to notify the fire department once a fire had started, even if he

[144] e.g., *Boatmen's National Co. v M.W. Elkins & Co.* 63 F 2d 214 (8th Cir. 1933). Similarly, courts have sometimes said that the proper measure of damages is the difference between the value of the object as it is and its value had it been as represented. *Waddell v White* 46 Ariz. 420, 108 P 2d 565 (1940); *Morrell v Wiley*, 119 Conn. 578, 178 A 121 (1935).

[145] *Boatmen's National Co. v M.W. Elkins & Co.* 63 F 2d 214 (8th Cir. 1933); *Waddell v White* 46 Ariz. 420, 108 P 2d 565 (1940). In other cases, the problem was not whether the damages were foreseeable but whether they could be established with any certainty: e.g., *Morrell v Wiley* 119 Conn. 578, 178 A 121 (1935).

[146] Stanton, n. 4 above, 330; Heuston & Buckley, n. 4 above, 382.

[147] e.g., *Obde v Schlemeyer*, 56 Wash 2d 449, 353 P 2d 672 (1960) (action lies for failure of seller of house to disclose termite infestation).

[148] England: Stanton, n. 4 above, 330; Heuston & Buckley, n. 4 above, 384. US: W. P. Keeton, D. Dobbs, R. Keeton, D. Owen & W. Prosser, *The Law of Torts* (5th ed., 1984), 763–4.

did so because he wanted the warehouse to burn so he could collect the insurance.

To avoid such anomalies, one might change the law of deceit to treat a later and wrongful decision to breach in the same way as an original intention to do so. One would then have arrived by the back door at the rule that the defendant is liable for the unforeseeable consequences of a wrongful breach. The more straightforward approach would be to acknowledge that we need such a rule if we are to avoid such results.

Conclusion

One might describe law as William James described Scholasticism. It, too, is often common sense made pedantic, or, if one prefers, made logically consistent. Working from common-sense intuitions that were much like our own, thirteenth-century canon lawyers and later, the eighteenth-century jurist Pothier, concluded that a person should be responsible even for the unforeseeable consequences of a wrongful act. That conclusion explains our intuitions better than any we have found since. It may be the only logically consistent way to explain them.

8

Rylands v Fletcher, Negligence, and Strict Liability

Gary T. Schwartz

Introduction

For twenty-eight years John Fleming and I were colleagues within the University of California. He, however, was at the University's Berkeley campus, 500 miles north of the Los Angeles campus where I teach. Despite this distance, over the years the support I received from John was very important to me, and very gratifying. (John, about a generation ahead of me, was already a scholar of international renown when I began at UCLA.) John's death in September 1997 has impoverished the University, just as it has impoverished the academy of tort scholars worldwide.

In May 1994, I met John at a professional meeting in Washington, DC. He told me that *Rylands v Fletcher*[1] was now under attack, having been narrowed by the House of Lords in England and rejected altogether by Australia's High Court. For American legal scholars, the status of *Rylands* is a very important question: *Rylands* is quite often cited by American judges in tort cases; and the various opinions in *Rylands* are set forth in almost every American torts coursebook, at the beginning of their chapters on traditional strict liability.

In our conversation, I asked John for citations, and received from him a week later a personal note in his compact, precise handwriting. The House of Lords case identified by his note is of course *Cambridge Water Co. v Eastern Counties Leather*,[2] decided in December 1993. The Australian case is *Burnie Port Authority v General Jones Pty*,[3] decided in March 1994.

Having received John's note, I promptly read the two cases. In doing

[1] (1866) LR 1 Exch 265; aff'd (1868) 3 HL 330. [2] [1994] 2 AC 264.
[3] (1994) 179 CLR 520.

so, I was reminded all over again of the pre-eminent role the Fleming treatise[4] has played in Commonwealth tort law. The High Court majority, in a joint opinion, relied on the treatise for purposes of the treatise's characterization of those English opinions that have interpreted *Rylands* narrowly.[5] The House of Lords, delivering its judgment in an opinion by Lord Goff, itself relied on the treatise for the latter's authoritative exposition of the elements of the tort of nuisance.[6] In addition, while the House of Lords ended up not accepting the treatise's position as to the proper scope of *Rylands* strict liability, Lord Goff went out of his way to set forth that position, to treat it with real respect, and in essence to recommend it for consideration by Parliament.[7]

In this essay I salute John Fleming by myself focusing on the issues to which he drew my attention: *Rylands, Cambridge Water Co, Burnie Port Authority,* and the general choice between negligence and strict liability. In doing so, I appreciate that my views on these issues may differ considerably from his.[8] But it is axiomatic that the opportunity for lively exchanges of views is one of the many things that makes a career as a law professor so satisfying. This is a career in which John so admirably excelled.

To some extent, our different views as to the place of strict liability relate back to a more basic point. I am comfortable enough with the values and structure of a traditional tort regime[9] yet John Fleming more than a decade ago expressed his position that in personal injury cases the tort system is largely a failure, and faces a declining future.[10] As it happens, Patrick Atiyah, another prominent Commonwealth scholar and treatise-writer, has quite recently gone even further, and actually recommended the repeal of tort law in its application to personal injuries.[11] That each of these distinguished scholars at some point experienced a loss of belief in the regime of tort is itself a fascinating, indeed quite important, development; still, the implications of this are beyond the scope of this essay.

While more time will be spent below on the facts in *Rylands v Fletcher,* for starters it suffices to say that the defendants arranged for the construction of a reservoir and that because of a problem with the reser-

[4] John G. Fleming, *The Law of Torts* (8th ed. 1992). The first edition of this highly authoritative treatise came out in 1957.

[5] (1994) 179 CLR 520 at 545.

[6] [1994] 2 AC 264 at 301, citing Fleming, n. 4 above, at 443–4.

[7] [1994] 2 AC 264 at 304–5, citing Fleming, n. 4 above, at 327–8, 341.

[8] See John G. Fleming, Comment, (1995) 3 Tort Law Rev. 57.

[9] See Gary T. Schwartz, 'Mixed Theories of Tort Law: Affirming Both Deterrence and Corrective Justice', (1997) 75 Texas L. Rev 1801.

[10] John G. Fleming, 'Is There a Future for Tort?', (1994) 44 La. L. Rev 1193.

[11] See P. S. Atiyah, 'Personal Injury in the Twenty-First Century: Thinking the Unthinkable' in Peter Birks (ed.) *Wrongs and Remedies in the Twenty-First Century* (1996).

voir's base, an incident occurred in which water burst from the bottom of the reservoir and ended up in the coal-workings being operated nearby by the plaintiff. The plaintiff's claim against the defendants began in the Court of Exchequer. Having found the defendants not guilty of negligence, the Court faced the question whether strict-liability should be deemed the appropriate standard. But a divided Court ruled against the plaintiff's strict liability claim.[12] On appeal, the Court of Exchequer Chamber unanimously concluded that this was a proper case for strict liability. Mr Justice Blackburn's opinion announced the 'true rule of law[:] the person who for his own purposes brings on his land and collects and keeps there anything likely to do mischief if it escapes, must keep it at his peril'.[13]

At the outset one can note a certain awkwardness in this formulation, as it applies to the *Rylands* facts. Though the defendants had indeed constructed on their land a reservoir, obviously the reservoir itself had not 'escaped'. And while the water in the reservoir did of course escape, that water had not been brought on to the defendant's land by any act of the defendants. As Melish stated on behalf of the defendants before the Court of Exchequer, 'the defendants did not themselves bring the water to their land; the water [came] to their land naturally'.[14]

On further appeal to the House of Lords, Lord Cranworth announced his support for Mr Justice Blackburn's opinion.[15] Lord Chancellor Cairns, though indicating general support for the Blackburn formulation, went on to offer his own standard. According to Lord Cairns, if water had been collected through 'a natural use' of the land, the defendant would not be liable; but the defendant bears strict liability for harms caused by 'a non-natural use'.[16] When scholars have discussed *Rylands*, the formulation set forth by Mr Justice Blackburn has commonly loomed large. Yet much of the litigation in the 130 years since *Rylands* has essentially accepted the framework of Lord Cairns' 'non-natural use' doctrine and attempted to work out its ongoing meaning. In fact, the Blackburn standard does seem to differ considerably from the Cairns standard. Blackburn's opinion, for example, relied significantly on the rule of strict liability for trespassing cattle as a familiar precedent which solidly supported the general standard he was recommending;[17] and that precedent does indeed fit comfortably within his 'mischief if it

[12] *Fletcher v Rylands* [1865] 3 H. & C. 774.

[13] (1866) LR 1 Exch 265 at 279.

[14] [1865] 3 3 H. & C. 114 at 785.

[15] Interestingly, Lord Cranworth's opinion avoids the problem mentioned in my previous paragraph by proposing strict liability for the party who 'brings, *or* accumulates, on his land anything which, if it should escape, may cause damage to his neighbour'. (1868) 3 HL at 330 340 [emphasis added.]

[16] Ibid at 338, 339.

[17] (1866) LR 1 Exch 265 at 280.

escapes' standard. Yet even if the range of possible meanings of 'non-natural use' is acknowledged,[18] none of those meanings readily includes the problem of wandering cattle. Cattle are not 'made by humans'; nor is the ownership of cattle either 'uncommon' or 'inappropriate' in rural English communities.

Fast-forward now to 1993. In *Cambridge Water Co.*, the defendant, a leather manufacturer, had used chemical solvents as part of its tanning process. Over the years, small amounts of this solvent had seeped into the soil below the tannery, and had finally reached the plaintiff's property many miles away, contaminating the plaintiff's water. Lord Goff's opinion for the House of Lords indicated (in *dictum*) that the 'storage of chemicals in substantial quantities' is 'an almost classic case of non-natural use' for *Rylands* purposes.[19] To this extent, *Cambridge Water Co.* is good news for environmentalists, and for those who favour a broad interpretation of *Rylands*.[20]

However, in *Cambridge Water Co.* the House of Lords also ruled that the foreseeability of harm is an essential prerequisite for the *Rylands* doctrine. Because the facts showed that at the time of the seepage the defendant could not have foreseen that its chemical would result in harmful contamination, the House of Lords found that the defendant was free of liability. More generally, the House of Lords characterized *Rylands* as simply a branch of nuisance law—or, alternatively, a limited extension of nuisance law, so that the nuisance doctrine can reach problems of isolated rather than ongoing harm. In light of that characterization, Lord Goff's opinion for the House of Lords seems to conclude that the *Rylands* rule is basically limited to disputes between neighbouring land-occupiers.[21] Moreover, since the House of Lords (having consulted the Fleming treatise) perceived that the nuisance doctrine presupposes foreseeability, the House of Lords ruled that the related *Rylands* doctrine calls for foreseeability as well.

Burnie Port Authority concerned a fire that began on the defendant's premises.[22] The fire was caused by the negligent welding of an employee of the independent contractor hired by the defendant. The plaintiff's

[18] See the discussion in W. Page Keeton *et al.*, *Prosser and Keeton on the Law of Torts* (5th ed., 1984), 545–6.

[19] [1994] 2 AC 264 at 309.

[20] See Tony Weir, 'Rylands v Fletcher Reconsidered', (1994) 53 Camb. LJ 216 at 218.

[21] [1994] 2 AC 264 at 298 (favourably quoting an article by S. H. Newark, 'The Boundaries of Nuisance', (1949) 65 LQR 480 at 488, which states that it is 'rash' to 'jump' to the conclusion that *Rylands* can 'be extended beyond the case of neighbouring occupiers'). Newark here assumes a somewhat narrow version of nuisance law: while nuisance generally requires that P suffer a land-related harm, it does not always insist that D be a land occupier. See R. A. Buckley, *The Law of Nuisance* (2d ed., 1996), 4–5. Lord Goff's opinion leaves open the question whether *Rylands* can apply when P as a neighbouring property-owner has suffered a personal injury. [1994] 2 AC 264 at 299.

[22] (1994) 179 CLR 520.

nearby property was damaged by this fire; and the plaintiff sued the defendant under several liability principles, including *Rylands*.[23] In reviewing the English cases interpreting *Rylands*, the High Court majority found a 'quite unacceptable uncertainty' about the scope of the *Rylands* rule.[24] More specifically, the High Court perceived that the Blackburn formulation had been 'all but obliterated by subsequent judicial explanations and qualifications'.[25] The High Court also perceived that at the time of *Rylands* the negligence doctrine in English tort law was itself quite feeble and incoherent. Negligence liability was at that time limited to 'a miscellany of disparate categories' of cases:[26] not until *Heaven v Pender*[27] in 1883 and eventually *Donoghue v Stevenson*[28] in 1932 was a defendant subjected to the general prospect of liability for any negligence that might injure a foreseeable plaintiff. Given this modern development of a broad and coherent body of negligence law, and given as well the unsatisfactory character of the *Rylands* doctrine, the High Court ruled that 'the rule of *Rylands v Fletcher*, with all its . . . qualifications and exceptions' should be 'absorbed into' and qualified by the basic principles of ordinary negligence.[29] In light of its repudiation of a precedent as well-known as *Rylands*, *Burnie Port Authority* has itself been described as 'one of the most spectacular [decisions] ever delivered in the history of the High Court'.[30]

In *Burnie Port Authority* there had been negligence on the part of the defendant's contractor. According to the High Court majority, certain doctrines of non-delegable duties are part of the modern negligence regime. More specifically, the High Court ruled that cases previously covered by the *Rylands* doctrine should now be covered by a doctrine of the defendant's non-delegable duty for the negligence of a contractor it employs.[31] Hence the High Court, though abandoning *Rylands*, was still able to rule in favour of the plaintiff. The High Court seemed not to notice two oddities in its own analysis. First, given the High Court's belief that the scope of the *Rylands* doctrine is unacceptably uncertain, it is hard to see why the Court should choose that doctrine as the basis or framework for rules of non-delegable duties.[32] Secondly, though the

23 On the extent to which *Rylands* has been held to apply to spreading fires, see Fleming, n. 4, at 350–52.

24 (1994) 179 CLR 520 at 540.

25 Ibid at 536.

26 Ibid at 543.

27 (1883) 11 QBD 503.

28 [1932] AC 562 at 580.

29 [1994] 179 CLR 520 at 556.

30 Jane Swanton, 'Another Conquest in the Imperial Expansion of the Law of Negligence: *Burnie Port Authority v General Jones Pty Ltd*', (1994) 2 Torts L.J. 101 at 101.

31 [1994] 179 CLR 520 at 552.

32 To be sure, the High Court indicated that non-delegable duties might go slightly beyond *Rylands*, so as to cover all situations in which the defendant 'take[s] advantage of . . . control of premises . . . to introduce a dangerous substance or to undertake thereon a dangerous activity'. Ibid at 551. Also, the Court spoke favourably of the possibility that

High Court praised the breadth and coherence of the negligence principle, the Court seemed not to recognize that vicarious liability—because of the way in which it automatically imputes one person's act to a non-negligent defendant—is itself an important form of strict liability. The High Court's opinion spends a paragraph discussing the considerations of both 'fairness' and 'utility' that justify a finding of non-delegable duty. These considerations include providing plaintiffs with a secure source of compensation, and giving all defendants—however non-negligent their conduct in the individual case—an ongoing 'spur to effective care'.[33] Yet if these are indeed important considerations, they are considerations typically associated with strict liability.

Until now, this essay has devoted itself to describing *Rylands*, *Cambridge Water Co.*, and *Burnie Port Authority*. The time has now arrived to undertake evaluation. The pages that follow will discuss, first of all, whether *Cambridge Water Co.* interprets *Rylands* accurately in concluding that the *Rylands* rule of strict liability requires or presupposes foreseeability. Considered next is a more general question of principle: whether—quite apart from precedent—foreseeability ought to be a prerequisite for strict liability. A related question concerns how much weight should be placed on the defendant's 'causation' of harm in possibly assigning strict liability to the defendant. In reviewing this question, my essay is led into a close inquiry of the factual situation in *Rylands*. This inquiry identifies the ways in which the plaintiff's own conduct in *Rylands* played an important role in the 'causation' of the harm he incurred. Furthermore, that inquiry uncovers a landlord–tenant dimension in the *Rylands* facts that most of the commentary on *Rylands* has overlooked. My essay highlights the point that both the plaintiff and the defendants in *Rylands* were the tenants of the same landlord, and discusses the implications of this interesting point.

My essay next turns to *Burnie Port Authority* so as to review that case's suggestion that a broad negligence standard can serve as an adequate alternative to the *Rylands* realm of strict liability. It conducts this review by using *Rylands*-like reservoirs as a useful example. In cases involving bursting reservoirs, how likely is it that findings of negligence can be entered? Here my essay considers the range of likely causes of reservoir failures, the possible availability of the doctrine of *res ipsa loquitur*, vicarious liability rules that extend the significance of negligence find-

non-delegable duties, unlike *Rylands*, can serve to protect Ps who are on the premises of D. Ibid at 557.

[33] Ibid at 552, quoting Ezra R. Thayer, 'Liability Without Fault', (1916) 29 Harv L. Rev 800 at 809.

ings, and the very meaning of the negligence standard under English law.

Finally, my essay turns to strict liability as a supplement to negligence. In doing so, it considers the interpretation of *Rylands* that has been offered by Professor A. W. B. Simpson—that *Rylands* was formulated by the English judiciary as a specific response to the problem raised by recent incidents involving overflowing dams.[34] While my essay does not necessarily reject this interpretation, it finds that the evidence does not suffice to confirm the interpretation. The essay then reviews the American rule of strict liability for abnormally dangerous activities as a possible outgrowth of *Rylands*. (This is the rule that Lord Goff's opinion in *Cambridge Water Co.*, considered but declined to adopt.) Here the essay reports that the American rule is far more guarded and limited than Lord Goff may have realized. Indeed, despite their considerable differences in phraseology, English and American strict liability doctrines tend to converge—and they do so in ways that produce generally sensible results.

Foreseeability as a Prerequisite for Strict Liability

Even though a defendant's conduct is risky, under the conventional understanding, that conduct can be non-negligent for either of two reasons. First, the risky elements in that conduct might have been unknown and unforeseeable by the defendant. Secondly, even foreseeable risks might be those that the defendant is unable to eliminate by adopting appropriate precautions. Even as interpreted by *Cambridge Water Co.*, *Rylands* liability remains importantly strict in so far as the defendant's prevention burdens are deemed an irrelevant factor.[35] But *Cambridge Water Co.* denies that *Rylands* strict liability is appropriate in cases of unforeseeable risks.

Is this denial faithful to the original message of *Rylands*? In *Cambridge Water Co.*, Lord Goff consulted the language in the various *Rylands* opinions. Here he turned to one extended passage in Mr Justice Blackburn's opinion which refers to 'anything likely to do mischief if it escapes', to the defendant who collects things 'which he knows to be mischievous' if it escapes, and to the defendant's liability for the 'natural and anticipated consequences' of his conduct.[36] When the case reached the House of Lords, this passage from Mr Justice Blackburn's opinion

[34] A. W. B. Simpson, 'Legal Liability for Bursting Reservoirs: The Historical Context of *Rylands v Fletcher*', (1984) 23 J. Legal Stud. 209. This article is republished in a slightly different form in A. W. Brian Simpson, *Leading Cases in the Common Law* (1995), 195.

[35] [1994] 2 AC 264 at 300.

[36] (1866) LR 1 Exch 265 at 279, 280.

was quoted with approval by Lord Chancellor Cairns, and the Blackburn opinion was explicitly concurred in by Lord Cranworth.[37] The Blackburn passage, with all of its references to 'likely' and 'anticipated' consequences which the defendant 'knows' about, supports the idea that *Rylands* presupposes foreseeability.

Indeed, in considering further the Blackburn speech, one can find indications that his *Rylands* rule in fact requires not just foreseeability but the defendant's actual knowledge of risk.[38] In discussing livestock that kick or gore, Mr Justice Blackburn pointed out that the owner is ordinarily not liable, because it is 'not the general nature of horses to kick, or bulls to gore; but if the owner knows the beast has a vicious propensity to attack man, he will be answerable for that too'.[39] Here, then, the owner's actual knowledge of risk—'scienter'—is a prerequisite for automatic liability. Mr Justice Blackburn's opinion also relied on the liability of the livestock owner for livestock trespasses, and the liability of the operator of 'alkali works' for 'the fumes and noisome vapours'.[40] These are activities whose harm-causing nature is obviously known to the party conducting the activity. Consider also the example suggested by Mr Justice Blackburn during oral argument. 'Suppose a man leans against my cart, if I remove the cart suddenly, and without warning, not knowing he is there, I am not liable, but if I do so knowing that he is there, though he has no right to lean against my cart, yet I am liable if my act injures him'.[41]

The review so far supports Lord Goff's perception in *Cambridge Water Co.* that a requirement of at least foreseeability is implicit in *Rylands*. There is, however, one complication. In *Cambridge Water Co.*, Lord Goff relied on Mr Justice Blackburn's reference in *Rylands* to 'anything likely to do mischief if it escapes'. Yet this phrase suggests an ambiguity. Granted that an element such as water—once collected—will foreseeably cause significant harm if it escapes; still, how foreseeable is it that such an escape will occur? Only if such an escape is at least 'distinctly' foreseeable can one affirm in a meaningful way that the collection of

[37] (1868) 3 HL 330 at 339–40.

[38] Note here Lord Goff's somewhat guarded statement in *Cambridge Water Co.* that under *Rylands*, 'knowledge, or at least foreseeability of the risk, is a prerequisite for liability'. [1994] 2 AC 264 at 302.

[39] (1866) LR 1 Exch 265 at 286.

[40] Ibid at 280.

[41] Ibid at 274. Attention can also be given to the doctrine of strict liability associated with spreading fires (a doctrine that by the time of *Rylands* had been qualified by statute). As I understand this doctrine, it applied *only* to fires that D had deliberately set, and *not* to those fires which were accidentally initiated by D's conduct. (Thus, e.g., there is no mention of the strict-liability option in *Vaughn v Menlove*, which involved an accidental fire. (1837) Bing. N.C. 468 (CP)) The traditional rule relating to fire, then, is another example of strict liability that focuses on D's conduct that includes a kind of knowing risk-taking.

water in a reservoir is itself foreseeably risky.[42] On the other hand, if the risk of an escape is essentially zero, it would be hard to see why the activity of building a reservoir should be regarded as in any way problematic.

Observe in this regard that an ordinary nuisance produces continuing, ongoing harm in a way that eliminates this range of issues. For example, even if a defendant is unaware at first that his alkali works is producing noxious odours, within a few days his neighbours will be knocking on his door complaining (or going to court seeking an injunction) in a manner that will provide him with the relevant knowledge. Given this feature in nuisance law, when nuisance is extended to cover problems of isolated escapes (as it is by the *Cambridge Water Co.* characterization of *Rylands*), the foreseeability element in nuisance law becomes somewhat awkward as a precedent.

At this point in evaluating *Rylands*, however, the history uncovered by Professor Simpson becomes relevant. Simpson finds, first, that there were many dams in England in the nineteenth century, and that these dams—'constructed on the basis of common sense, hunch, and experience'—'not infrequently failed', for all kinds of reasons.[43] While most of these failures luckily did not inflict serious personal injuries, they almost certainly imposed harms on neighbouring properties. Moreover, in 1852 there was a 'sensational' dam disaster, and another such disaster in 1863, which together brought about over 300 deaths.[44] Discussed below are the lessons that Simpson himself draws from this pre-*Rylands* history. Whether or not one accepts these professed lessons, one can at least rely on Simpson's history for purposes of affirming that English judges at the time of *Rylands* would have perceived (and correctly so) that it is clearly foreseeable that a reservoir can experience a harm-causing incident.

Given all of this, the foreseeability of harm can be properly understood as playing a distinctive role in the positions taken by the *Rylands* judges. Furthermore, it can be noted that a foreseeability requirement is also affirmed by doctrines of strict liability that can be found in American law. As the *Cambridge Water Co.* opinion notes, the American rule of strict liability for abnormally dangerous activities bears some relationship to the *Rylands* rule. Lord Goff, having reviewed the treatment of that rule in the American *Restatement (Second) of Torts*, noted that the dangerous quality of the abnormally dangerous activities identified by the Restatement 'would be obvious to any reasonable person' undertaking such an activity.[45] In fact, the 'precedent' provided by the

[42] This problem has been discussed in Martin Davies, 'Strict Liability and Reasonable Foreseeability: *Cambridge Water Co. v Eastern Counties Leather Plc.*', (1994) 2 Torts L.J. 12 at 16–17.

[43] Simpson, n 34 above at 217.

[44] Ibid at 219, 219–31.

[45] [1994] 2 AC 264 at 304–5.

Restatement's rule is even stronger than the House of Lords realized. The First Restatement, released in the late 1930s, was explicit in posing a requirement that the actor be engaging in an activity which he 'should recognize as likely to' produce harm.[46] While this requirement was omitted in the Second Restatement's formulation, the internal documents of the American Law Institute clearly support an assessment that this omission was inadvertent.[47] Indeed, in every American case I have seen that has applied the strict liability doctrine that the two Restatements endorse, the dangerous quality of the defendant's activity was undeniably obvious. In the early 1990s, a committee of scholars organized by the American Law Institute considered expansions in the Restatement rule that might be advisable for purposes of protecting against a range of environmental harms. While that committee endorsed a number of reforms, the committee still perceived that unforeseeable risks should lie beyond the scope of strict liability.[48]

It can also be observed that at least two branches of the 'products' side of American strict liability support a foreseeability requirement. One branch concerns what are called manufacturing defects. When a product contains such a defect, the liability of the producer is meaningfully strict; but one rationale for this is that the prospect of manufacturing defects is something the producer can not only foresee, but can predict with some accuracy.[49] The second branch concerns the problem of what are called 'unknowable' risks. For many years American judges struggled with the question of whether manufacturers are liable for risks and side-effects of which the manufacturer was reasonably ignorant at the time of original product sale. But by the 1990s, a consensus had formed—now expressed in the new Restatement of Products Liability—that strict liability should not be applied in the case of unknowable risks.[50] It can be noted that products liability doctrine in Europe tends to reach the same result. As is well known, § 15(a) of the EEC Council Directive on Products Liability gives each Member State the option of rejecting liability for so-called 'development risks'—that is, risks that could not be identified by 'the state of scientific and technical knowledge at the time when [the manufacturer] put the product into circulation'; and the choice exercised by England, Germany, and almost all other Member States has been to exclude strict liability in cases of this sort.

[46] *Restatement of Torts* § 519 (1938).

[47] American Law Institute, *Restatement (Second) of Torts* (1964), 52.

[48] American Law Institute Reporters Study, *Enterprise Responsibility for Personal Injuries*, vol 2 (1991), 368.

[49] *Restatement of Products Liability* § 2 Comment a (Proposed Final Draft, 1 April 1997).

[50] Ibid at §§ 2(b), 2(c) (requiring that risks of harm be 'foreseeable').

Causation as a Possible Basis for Strict Liability

The precedent provided by various strict liability rules thus supports a foreseeability requirement for strict liability in tort. Some scholars, however, might seek to question such a requirement. Begin with the simple story that 'A's conduct is the cause of B's injury'. As a matter of moral theory, some would argue that liability is appropriate—that causation, unsupplemented by other elements, is a proper and satisfactory basis for strict liability. This, indeed, was the position taken by Professor Richard Epstein in a 1973 article;[51] and in his torts coursebook, Epstein sets forth *Rylands* as a prime example of strict liability in operation.[52] Moreover, even if the *Rylands* opinions are correctly interpreted by Lord Goff as requiring or presupposing foreseeability, it can still be noted that those opinions do contain passages which—standing on their own—seem to affirm the justice of liability based on mere 'but for' causation. Thus, according to Baron Bramwell in his Court of Exchequer dissent, 'this action is maintainable . . . on the plain ground that the defendants have caused water to flow into the plaintiff's mines, which but for their . . . act would not have gone there.'[53] According to Mr Justice Blackburn speaking for the Exchequer Chamber, 'but for [the defendants'] act . . . no mischief could have accrued.'[54] In the House of Lords, Lord Cranworth quoted this passage from Mr Justice Blackburn's opinion, and added the idea that 'when one person . . . causes, however innocently, damage to another, it is obviously only just that he shall be the party to suffer. . . . All that matters is that the defendant's acts have occasioned the plaintiff's injury.'[55]

These passages from the *Rylands* opinions are certainly interesting. Indeed, if you stop people on the street, tell them that 'A has caused B's injury', and ask them whether A should be held responsible, the answer that most people will intuitively give is in the affirmative. Even so, this response by people on the street depends on the situations they have in mind that may be covered by the question posed. To test out the public appeal of causation—standing alone—as the basis for (strict) liability, let me now offer the following hypothetical case. Somehow or other, A is about to come down with a significant illness. As of this morning, however, A has no idea of this; he is feeling fine. A leaves home, and in the course of the day encounters B. (Perhaps they stand next to each other in a check-out line in a supermarket). In this

[51] Richard A. Epstein, 'A Theory of Strict Liability', (1973) 2 J. Legal Stud. 151.

[52] Idem, *Cases and Materials on Torts* (6th ed., 1995), 120–32.

[53] (1865) 3 H. & C. 774 at 790.

[54] (1866) LR 1 Exch 265 at 280.

[55] (1868) 3 HL 330 at 341.

encounter, a germ carried by A is transmitted from A to B.[56] On account of this transmission, B soon afterwards begins suffering from A's illness.

Given these facts, it is undeniably true that 'A has been the cause of B's harm'. Even so, I find no appeal in the idea that A should be held legally liable (or for that matter found morally responsible) for that harm. And when (not having revealed to them my own views) I poll my own law students, they are essentially unanimous in rejecting the idea of A's strict liability.

From this homy example, I derive the conclusion that causation standing on its own is not a proper basis for liability. At a minimum, the defendant's conduct must be knowingly or at least foreseeably risky before imposing liability on the defendant begins to become morally attractive.

But let me now push somewhat further in assessing the relevance of 'causation' to the imposition of possibly strict liability. Assume that a defendant does engage in an activity whose risks *are* either known or foreseeable. Does the defendant's (foreseeable) causation of the plaintiff's injury provide an adequate rationale for strict liability? In his 1973 article, Professor Epstein, as noted, argued in the affirmative, and regarded as irrelevant any concern for the precautionary burdens a defendant might bear in seeking to avoid injuries.[57] I attempted to respond to Epstein in a 1981 article.[58] One point my article advanced is that a theory that assigns liability on the basis of causation is commonly indeterminate. This is because the typical accident occurs at the figurative (if not literal) intersection of a large number of activities. In *Bolton v Stone*,[59] for example, the injury suffered by the plaintiff may well have been caused by the defendant's activity in organizing a particular cricket match. But that injury was even more immediately caused by the activity of the batsman in striking the ball, and the activity of the plaintiff in walking next to the cricket-ground when a match was in progress. Also implicated, for causation purposes, is the conduct of the employer of the batsman, who both hired the batsman and brought his own team to the game. For that matter, lurking in a meaningful way in the causal background is the conduct of the local government, in building a highway next to the cricket-ground, and the activity of contractors, in building homes in the neighbourhood of a cricket-ground. It may well be that there is appeal in a strict liability result for a case such as *Bolton*, but that appeal cannot be rationalized in terms of a simple idea of strict liability based on but-for causation.

[56] 'Germ' is a word in public usage; the proper technical term is 'infectious agent'.
[57] Epstein, n. 51 above.
[58] Gary T. Schwartz, 'The Vitality of Negligence and the Ethics of Strict Liability', (1981) 15 Ga. L. Rev 963, 991–1005.
[59] [1951] AC 850.

In short, accidents typically result from a combination of causes in a way that makes it difficult to rely on causation, standing alone, as a criterion for liability. To be sure, in a certain number of cases causation does seem to be unitary rather than concurrent. And interestingly, in these cases the law's tendency—in England and in the United States—is indeed to impose strict liability. For example, if the defendant, blasting on its property, projects debris on to his neighbour's property that results in property damage, the defendant's blasting activity can easily be deemed the exclusive cause of the harm his neighbour suffers; and under American law, blasting has long been a prime example of strict liability. When a defendant landowner engages in an activity that generates odours on to adjacent properties that everybody would find noxious, it seems satisfactory to say that the defendant's activity is the only meaningful cause of the discomfort that the adjacent property owner experiences. And here nuisance law does impose what frequently amounts to strict liability.[60] A finding of exclusive causation also seems appropriate in the trespassing-cattle cases on which the Blackburn opinion in *Rylands* relies, and in the contamination of water (or land) cases dealt with by *Cambridge Water Co.*[61] These are situations in which English law does indeed affirm strict liability. Moreover, when a fire which the defendant deliberately sets on his own property spreads to the property of his neighbours, the resulting property damage seems exclusively due to the defendant's own activity. There is good sense, then, in the traditional notion of strict liability for fire, a notion implicated by the factual situation in *Burnie Port Authority.*[62] For that matter, if a dam or reservoir overflows and in doing so projects water on to the property of neighbours, a finding of exclusive defendant causation is sound. In such a case, *Rylands* would certainly call for strict liability. In all of these situations, the strict liability results that tort law reaches can be explained by the appeal in the idea of strict liability for harm caused solely by the defendant who deliberately engages in an activity which he knows to be risky. (This appeal, by the way, can find its justification both in perceptions of fairness and in a proper concern for deterrence.)[63]

Return now, however, to *Rylands*. From the perspective of the analysis

[60] The modern law of nuisance does not take account of the 'unreasonableness of the defendant's conduct'; but it does consider the 'unreasonableness of the result to the plaintiff'. B. S. Markesinis & S. F. Deakin, *Tort Law* (3rd ed., 1994), 419. It is the unreasonableness of defendant's conduct that is ordinarily seen as justifying a finding of negligence. The alkali works cases referred to by Blackburn J are described in Simpson, *Leading Cases*, n. 34 above at 176–9. These cases 'treated negligence as wholly irrelevant'. Letter to the author from Prof. Simpson (12 Nov. 1997).

[61] *Cambridge Water Co. v Eastern Countries Leather* [1994] 2 AC 264.

[62] *Burnie Port Authority v General Jones Pty* (1994) 179 CLR 520.

[63] See Schwartz, n. 9 above at 1820.

just developed, it proves quite possible to set forth a criticism of the strict-liability result reached by the *Rylands* court—given that case's actual facts. In the various strict-liability cases discussed above, the plaintiff is a property-owner who is essentially passive: the plaintiff merely receives whatever risks emanate from the defendant's activity. Indeed, in the 'nuisance' cases highlighted by *Cambridge Water Co.*, the plaintiff is (prototypically) a home-owner quietly trying to read a book in his own living-room.

However, such a characterization of plaintiff passivity turns out not to work at all in *Rylands* itself, the facts of which should now be more carefully considered. In *Rylands*, the plaintiff was not a property-owner; rather, he had entered into a lease with the actual owner, the Earl of Wilton. Moreover, the plaintiff, as a lessee, was not even a 'land occupier'. What he had leased were merely 'certain beds of coal lying under certain lands' owned by the Earl.[64] That is, the plaintiff had entered into what property lawyers call a 'mineral lease'; as far as the land itself is concerned, all one can say is that the plaintiff, given his mineral lease, had an implied easement to use the land for appropriate reasons. The special—and entrepreneurial—nature of the plaintiff's interest in the Earl's property is revealed by the method of payment set forth in the lease. The basic rent the plaintiff was required to pay the Earl was measured in terms of the actual amount of the 'coal gotten' by the plaintiff, though the plaintiff was also liable for a minimum yearly rent.[65]

As indicated above, strict liability has appeal when an overflowing dam sends water cascading on to the property of neighbours. But the reservoir in *Rylands* did not itself break in any way that brought about such a cascading overflow. Rather, water escaped from the bottom of the reservoir by breaking through certain shafts which led down into ancient coal-workings under the reservoir—coal-workings of which the defendants themselves were entirely unaware. In the ordinary course of events, this water would have remained in these old coal-workings—which were located under the reservoir and also under portions of the land owned by two immediate neighbours, John Whitehead and Walker Hutton. Because these old coal-workings were no longer in use, this flow of water ordinarily would have caused no appreciable harm. Yet in *Rylands*, the water, moving laterally, ended up filling the plaintiff's mine and hence causing the plaintiff's harm. It can be noted here that the plaintiff and the defendants were not even adjoining or adjacent;

[64] I draw here on the arbitrator's findings. *Fletcher v Rylands*, (1865) 3 H. & C. 774 at 774, 775. And for the time being, I somewhat simplify. See n. 92 below & accompanying text.
[65] [1865] 3 H. & C. 774 at 775.

rather, their relevant property interests were separated by the parcels of land owned by Whitehead and Hutton.[66]

How did it happen, then, that water coming from the bottom of the defendants' reservoir ended up in the plaintiff's mine? The answer to this question points to the causal role played by the plaintiff's own conduct. First of all, the plaintiff, having entered into his lease, in 1850 proceeded to 'sink a pit' (called the Red House Pit) under the Earl of Wilton's land, and to 'bor[e]' for coal in the beds in this pit.[67] Next, the plaintiff, as a somewhat ambitious coal operator, began looking at the coal lying under Whitehead's land. In 1851, the plaintiff, having secured Whitehead's permission, extended his boring from the Earl of Wilton's property to the property of Whitehead himself.[68] The plaintiff, that is, 'work[ed] through from the Red House Colliery into the coal lying under the said land of Mr. Whitehead'.[69] Then, having done this, the plaintiff, in 'gradually work[ing] through the seams of coal [came] into contact with the old and disused works underneath the close of the defendants'.[70] Only because of all of these activities undertaken by the plaintiff were the 'old coal workings' underneath the defendants' reservoir 'made to communicate' with the coal-mines the plaintiff had leased from the Earl.[71]

Given these circumstances, an argument for strict liability in *Rylands* that might be based on the equities of causation seems to be essentially unsuccessful. Even if 'but for' the defendant's action 'no mischief could have accrued',[72] the competing or complicating point is that 'but for' the plaintiff's own actions the plaintiff would have suffered no harm—would have been beyond the reach of the defendants' 'mischief'.[73] Accordingly, even if one concedes a narrow category of cases in which causation serves as an attractive basis for (strict) liability, on its own facts *Rylands* represents a larger category of cases in which accidents happen because of a combination of activities engaged in by several parties; and in such cases, causation turns out to be indeterminate as the criterion for assigning liability.

[66] The arbitrator's description is rather complicated: at the time the reservoir was being built, 'old coal workings under the site of the . . . reservoir communicated with old coal workings under the . . . land of Mr. Whitehead by means of other and intervening old coal workings under the . . . land of Mr. Walker Hutton'. Ibid at 778. Both Whitehead's parcel and Hutton's parcel were adjacent to the land of Lord Wilton under which the reservoir was being built.

[67] [1865] 3 H. & C. 774 at 775–76.

[68] While the plaintiff 'made arrangements' with Whitehead, ibid at 777, it is unclear whether these arrangements constituted a 'lease'. The arrangements were originally made without the knowledge of Lord Wilton—but at some point he learned of all of this, and did not object. Ibid.

[69] Ibid.

[70] (1866) LR 1 Exch 265 at 337–8.

[71] [1865] 3 H. & C. 774 at 779.

[72] (1866) LR 1 Exch 265 at 280.

[73] Simpson, n. 34, at 242, 245 & 248.

As noted, a previous article of mine[74] emphasized how concurring causes make causation an awkward basis for strict liability; and this article made its point by looking at *Bolton v Stone*.[75] Both Professor Jones and Professor Keating have criticized my analysis of that case, in so far as I identified as one possible accidental 'cause' the conduct of the plaintiff in walking near a cricket-ground as a game is in progress. What Jones and Keating claim is that the plaintiff has a moral 'entitlement'[76] to engage in such 'normal'[77] activities as walking on a city street. Therefore, they contend, no attention should be given to the plaintiff's conduct in thinking about the imposition of strict liability.

In this essay let me provisionally agree that when there is entirely normal conduct protected by a clear moral right, that conduct should be excluded from a strict-liability inquiry that focuses on causation.[78] When I discussed above (for example) the liability of the blaster, I took no account of the activity of the plaintiff in owning or buying property in a neighbourhood where blasting could at some future time conceivably occur. Yet even given my provisional agreement, it suffices here to say that the plaintiff's conduct in *Rylands*—entering into a mineral lease, digging a pit under the lessor's property, and extending that pit under the property of another—hardly comes within the category of altogether normal conduct to which there may be a basic moral entitlement. To be sure, the Bramwell opinion in *Rylands*, considering English precedent, indicates that a property-owner 'has the right to work his mines to their extent, leaving no boundary between himself and the next owner'.[79] Yet however accurate Baron Bramwell may here be in describing the results reached by prior English cases, the 'right' he identifies seems not to be not a natural right of property, but rather a conventional right—one which courts have chosen to recognize, at least in suitable contexts. If this evaluation is correct, then the point previously made about *Rylands* remains intact—the causal role played by the plaintiff's entrepreneurial activity in sinking and extending a mining pit makes it difficult to rely on the criterion of causation in imposing strict liability on the defendant.

[74] Schwartz, n. 58 above. [75] [1951] AC 850.

[76] See William K. Jones, 'Strict Liability for Hazardous Enterprise', (1992) 92 Colum. L. Rev. 1705 at 1757.

[77] Gregory Keating, 'The Idea of Fairness in Enterprise Liability', (1997) 95 Mich. L. Rev. 1303 at 1372 n. 246.

[78] In supporting, for causation-related reasons, the liability of D in *Bolton v Stone*, Jones and Keating do not consider the causal role played by the batsman and the batsman's employer. The conduct of these parties is hardly surrounded by any moral entitlement. Whether there *is* a clear moral right to walk on a city street during the limited period of time when a cricket match is in progress is a question I do not consider here. Note that in *Bolton v Stone* the cricket ground came first—it had evidently been constructed and was in use before the street and the plaintiff's residence were built.

[79] (1865) 3 H. & C. 774 at 788–89.

To be sure, in discussing the relevance of defendant causation to strict liability, I have indicated that the defendant's conduct must be foreseeably risky before it provides a possible basis for strict liability. Was there anything foreseeably risky about the activity of the plaintiff in *Rylands*, in boring through the beds of coal? The answer to this question is probably in the negative at the time the plaintiff began engaging in this activity in the early 1850s, and also when the plaintiff first 'worked through' into the old coal-minings.[80] Nevertheless, once the defendants initiated the construction of their reservoir, the plaintiff was in a good position to appreciate or foresee the risks entailed by the proximity of his mining and the defendants' activities. Indeed, the plaintiff was in a much *better* position than the defendants to anticipate those risks. In so far, then, as disparities or inequalities in the parties' ability to foresee risk are relevant to the assignment of liability, *Rylands* hardly seems an attractive case for strict liability. From this perspective, one can make sense of the reference by Melish for the defendants (in his argument in the Court of Exchequer) to the defendants' reservoir as having brought about a danger only 'by reason of the plaintiff's secret act'.[81] Melish could further argue, in the Exchequer Chamber, that it would be 'strange if those secret acts, not communicated to the defendants, should impose on them a liability'.[82]

The Common Landlord Problem in *Rylands*

Let me now proceed further with my somewhat revisionist account of *Rylands*[83] by calling attention to another element in the *Rylands* facts that is often ignored or downplayed. *Rylands* is often treated as a case involving nearby landowners, who are independent economic actors. As mentioned above, the plaintiff in *Rylands* was not a landowner, but

[80] However, Prof. Simpson's extensive review of the record in *Rylands* identifies one interesting possibility: that 'the critical connection between [the plaintiff's] mine and the disused passages under the reservoir' was effectuated by the plaintiff *after* the reservoir burst. Simpson, *Leading Cases*, 34 above, at 210. Simpson regards this sequence as unlikely, but at least possible. If this was the sequence, Simpson suggests, then the plaintiff was himself at fault 'for not following good practice'. Ibid. Even if the issue of fault is put to one side, this possible sequence highlights the significance of plaintiff causation in *Rylands*.

[81] [1865] 3 H. & C. 774 at 785.

[82] (1866) LR 1 Exch 265 at 272. Before the HL, Palmer replaced Melish as counsel for Ds. He argued that 'the fault, if any, is with the Plaintiff', [who] 'ought to have communicated his knowledge [of these passages] to the Defendants, who might then have provided against this mischief, but he did not'. (1868) 3 HL 330 at 334–5. For my purposes, it is not the plaintiff's possible fault, but rather the plaintiff's knowing contribution to the creation of risk, that makes a difference. Still, Palmer's indication of what the plaintiff's might have done illustrates how the plaintiff's knowledge in *Rylands* may have been causally relevant to the accident that finally happened.

[83] *Rylands v Fletcher* (1866) LR 1 Exch 265; aff'd (1868) 3 HL 330.

rather a lessee—and only a mineral lessee at that. A related observation is that the defendants were not owners, but rather lessees, as well.[84]

Consider, from this perspective, the *Cambridge Water Co.*[85] point that *Rylands* should be deemed an extension of nuisance law. Private nuisance cases are commonly brought by one property-owner against another. Still, it is obvious enough that a lessee who engages in a noxious activity can be a nuisance defendant; and it is equally obvious that the lessee who suffers a loss of enjoyment on his leased premises can be a nuisance plaintiff.

But the quite interesting point in *Rylands* is that if the defendants' lease came from the Earl of Wilton, the plaintiff's lease also came from the Earl. Both the plaintiff and the defendants, then, were lessees of the same lessor, tenants of the same landlord. And at this point the invocation of nuisance law does seem somewhat unusual. It is not ordinarily expected that one of a landlord's tenants will bring a nuisance claim against some other tenant. Rather, in so far as there may be problems concerning land uses among tenants that may be incompatible, these are problems that the landlord himself is in a good position to resolve. Indeed, one of the economic advantages in having nearby parcels of property owned by a single landlord is that this landlord is in an excellent position not only to resolve, but even to anticipate and hence minimize at the outset, possible conflicts among those who turn out to be property occupiers.[86]

Assume that an owner of a large parcel of land carves out a sub-parcel, and leases that to the plaintiff for residential purposes. Then, at some later point in time within the duration of the plaintiff's lease, the landlord on the remainder of the property begins operating 'alkali works' that generates 'fumes and noisome vapours'. In these circumstances, the plaintiff-tenant would evidently have an interesting claim against the landlord. In making this claim, the plaintiff would not need to rely on nuisance law. Rather, the plaintiff could allege that the landlord has violated the 'implied covenant of quiet enjoyment' that accompanies the lease;[87] and this allegation would probably turn out to be a winner. Moreover, if the landlord, having initially leased property to the plain-

[84] Indeed, it is even possible that the defendants were not lessees but instead mere licensees. See Simpson, n. 34 above, at 240. For purposes of my analysis here, the line between lessee and licensee does not make a difference.

[85] *Cambridge Water Co. v Eastern Countries Leather* [1994] 2 AC 264.

[86] See R. H. Coase, 'The Problem of Social Cost', (1960) 3 J. L. & Econ. 1 at 16; Henry Hansmann, 'Condominium and Cooperative Housing: Transactional Efficiency, Tax Subsidies, and Tenure Choice', (1991) 20 J. Legal Stud. 25.

[87] See Jesse Dukeminier & James E. Krier, *Property* (3d ed., 1993) 522–4. The recognition of this implied covenant is not at all a new development in the law. Still, it is hard to assess what the status was of the implied covenant in the 1860s. By then, however, the law had established that a tenant could sue a landlord in nuisance. See *Alston v Grant* (1854) 3 E. & B. 128.

tiff, later leases a sub-parcel to another party with the understanding that this party will construct and operate an alkali works, the plaintiff would again have a claim against the landlord, whose subsequent lease—which is responsible for the alkali works—would count as a violation of the covenant of quiet enjoyment.

But change now the terms of the hypothesis. Assume that at the time when the owner leases a sub-parcel of his land to the plaintiff for use as a residence, elsewhere on his property the owner is already operating an alkali works, with all its fumes and vapours. The plaintiff, having toured the property, is fully aware of these fumes and vapours as she makes up her mind about entering the lease; and all signs are that the owner–landlord expects to continue his alkali-works project. Though the fumes and vapours will obviously limit the tenant's enjoyment of her property, it seems clear enough that the tenant would have no claim against the landlord. Even given the implied covenant as a default rule for landlord–tenant law, the tenant's clear knowledge of the landlord's alkali works at the time she signed the lease would almost certainly count as a waiver of the covenant and hence would prevent her from complaining about the alkali works.[88] Similarly, if at the time the plaintiff's lease is entered into, the alkali works are being operated not by the landlord himself but rather by a previous tenant whose lease with the landlord specifically authorized the alkali works, the new tenant would plainly have no claim against the previous tenant. The landlord, having approved of those alkali works, obviously could not himself complain about them; and whatever rights the later tenant acquires are derived from the rights the landlord already possesses.

The facts in *Rylands* can now be compared to those in the above examples. In *Rylands*, the plaintiff entered into mineral leases in 1849 that were to last until 1871.[89] The defendants' lease was not created until about 1858.

With this sequence in mind, we can better understand the arguments made by the plaintiff in *Rylands* before the Exchequer Chamber. The plaintiff's first argument before this Court explicitly 'omitted' the lease arrangements, and assumed *arguendo* that the plaintiff and the defendant were 'mere strangers'—that is, parties not tied together by any sort of prior arrangements.[90] But the plaintiff, moving beyond this factually incorrect assumption, then accepted the sequence of actual events in

[88] See Lord Campbell's dictum on the lessee who submits to certain harmful conditions in *Alston v Grant* (1854) 3 E. & B. 128 at 133.

[89] In fact, 2 leases were signed on the same day in 1849. One lease, relating to location A, was due to run from 1849 to 1855. The second lease, relating to locations A and B, was to begin in 1855 and continue until 1871. [1865] 3 H. & C. 774 at 775. For a further complication, see n. 92 below.

[90] (1866) LR 1 Exch 265 at 269.

setting forth his second argument: according to the plaintiff, Lord Wilton's original lease with the plaintiff imposed on him a certain 'obligation'—and the defendants 'could only [lease the] land subject to the obligation which was imposed upon the landlord' by this original lease.[91] Obviously, what the plaintiff was claiming was that Lord Wilton's approval of the construction of a reservoir, with all the foreseeable risks this involved, violated an obligation he had impliedly assumed in his original lease with the plaintiff, and that this obligation should be deemed included in Lord Wilton's later lease with the defendants.

When, then, the plaintiff in *Rylands* actually focused on the case's facts, the plaintiff seemingly acknowledged that his claim depended on the implied obligations that could be found in the defendants' lease with the landlord, understood in the context of the landlord's previous lease with the plaintiff. So long as the defendants' reservoir is assumed to have posed a clearly foreseeable threat to neighbouring property interests (including those of the plaintiff), the argument advanced by the plaintiff seems essentially on the right track.[92] Indeed, in one important way the plaintiff's argument that builds on the combination of leases is stronger than the plaintiff's pure tort argument. As noted above, the latter argument is rendered somewhat problematic by the plaintiff's own activity in sinking the Red House Pit and working the coal-beds within that pit. But nothing in these facts poses any problem for the plaintiff's lease-related argument, since the plaintiff's lease with Lord Wilton specifically authorized him to engage in these activities.[93]

The neglect by the *Rylands* judiciary of the plaintiff's landlord–tenant argument, and the judiciary's consideration of the case based on the inaccurate factual assumption that the plaintiff and the defendants were 'mere strangers', therefore seems far from ideal. In fact, as later English cases have considered *Rylands* in cases of escaping water, they

[91] Ibid at 272.

[92] As it happens, the facts in *Rylands* contain a further wrinkle, which my previous account has left out. When the plaintiff began working the beds of coal covered by the original 1849 lease, the plaintiff found that these beds were not productive. The plaintiff and the Earl of Wilton then promptly agreed to substitute for these beds other beds owned by the Earl, north of the lands covered by the original lease. It was at this substitute location that the plaintiff actually sank the Red House Pit, in 1851. [1865] 3 H. & C. 774 at 775. The legal implications of this oral modification of the original lease are not entirely clear. Prof. Simpson suggests that given the failure to commit the modification to writing, the plaintiff was merely a tenant from year-to-year at the Red House Pit. Simpson, n. 34 above, at 241. Yet Simpson acknowledges another possibility—that the modification should be deemed incorporated into the 1849 lease, which was due to last until 1871. Ibid. This seems to me to best express the substance of the parties' transaction.

[93] To be sure, the problem remains intact of the significance of the plaintiff's activities under the land owned by Mr Whitehead. These activities were neither authorized nor anticipated by the plaintiff's original lease with the Earl of Wilton.

have concluded that *Rylands* does not apply in a variety of landlord–tenant situations. In *Ross v Fedden*,[94] *Rylands* was rejected in a suit by a ground-floor tenant against first-floor tenants when water escaped from the defendant's water closet. In *Kittle v City Business Properties, Ltd*,[95] the plaintiff rented a shop from the defendants, located in a building owned and mainly occupied by the defendants. Water which escaped from the defendants' premises entered into the shop of the plaintiff. The court denied strict liability, finding that the plaintiff, by renting from the defendants, accepted whatever risks were involved in the defendants' ongoing operations. The non-relevance of *Rylands* liability in cases of this sort seems confirmed by *A. Prosser & Son Ltd v Levi*.[96] Dealing with tenants' possible claims for intrusions of water, this case assumes that principles of landlord–tenant law are what governs, and further reasons that a tenant in renting space consents to the usual risks created by the landlord and other tenants, and consents as well to unusual risks if the plaintiff has knowledge of them.[97]

To be sure, this reasoning may end up supporting the claim of the *Rylands* plaintiff, since a reservoir is 'unusual' rather than 'usual' and since the *Rylands* plaintiff did not have knowledge of this unusual risk at the time he entered his lease. Yet if the plaintiff's claim is hence supportable, the support it receives comes from an analysis that operates within the framework of the landlord–tenant relationship. Admittedly, the cases discussed above involve situations among occupants of the same building.[98] But so long as the plaintiff and the defendant are tenants of the same landlord and are in close proximity to each other, the analysis set forth in the cases discussed above has considerable force. The obvious relevance of such a landlord–tenant analysis suggests an element of inadequacy in the *Rylands* opinions, insofar as they ignored the case's actual facts and considered instead an essentially hypothetical factual scenario.

The Adequacy of the Modern Negligence Doctrine

Let me turn now to the range of issues raised by *Burnie Port Authority* concerning the breadth and coherence of modern negligence law. My view that *Burnie Port Authority*[99] is quite wrong in denying a proper role to strict liability has been expressed above.[100] Yet if *Burnie Port Authority*

[94] (1862) 7 LR 661. [95] (1942) 1 KB 269. [96] [1955] 1 WLR 1224 (CA).
[97] Ibid at 1233.
[98] *Prosser* refers to parties all of whom are 'in a block of premises'. Ibid.
[99] *Burnie Port Authority v General Jones Pty* (1994) 179 CLR 520.
[100] See text at nn. 60–63 above.

is in error in denying this, it does not automatically follow that the court was wrong in claiming that the modern negligence doctrine has rendered rules of strict liability somewhat superfluous. It may well be—as one leading American law professor tells his students—that the entire issue of strict liability is simply No Big Deal.

Admittedly, the very effort to assess the significance of strict liability is rendered difficult by the wide range of situations in which rules of strict liability might be invoked.[101] Still, it should certainly be helpful to look at strict liability in the original *Rylands* context of bursting reservoirs. How likely is it that the victim of such a reservoir will be able to show any negligence on the part of the reservoir owner?

As Professor Simpson has indicated, the two dramatic dam failures that had preceded *Rylands* had both been caused by rather clear negligence by the dam managers.[102] Moreover, if one considers reservoir failures that might happen today, one can appreciate that intervening changes in both available information and safety technology make it even more likely that such failures can be avoided by the adoption of reasonable precautions. Improved information and more sophisticated engineering analysis enables reservoir managers more fully to understand whatever safety problems reservoirs entail; and improved safety technology commonly enables those managers to solve the problems they are now able to identify. The point made here about reservoirs can probably be generalized to many other forms of potentially dangerous activities: given both the information about risk facilitated by a modern analysis and the methods of protecting against risk provided by modern engineering, the vast majority of all incidents of harm can be avoided if all the precautions called for by negligence law are identified and implemented.[103]

Of course, as the saying goes, human error is human nature; and for that matter corporate error is probably corporate nature. Still, the negligence liability rule provides parties with an important incentive to avoid errors of this sort. True enough, despite this incentive a considerable level of negligent errors is doubtless predictable. But if such an error does bring about a harm-causing incident, the negligence liability

[101] *Rylands* itself has been applied to a considerable range of activities. Moreover, there are other rules of strict liability within tort law which seem quite independent of *Rylands*, and which no doubt call for separate review. American courts, e.g. have nurtured the doctrine of strict products liability (though this doctrine is interpreted by many as including major components of negligence law. See, e.g., Schwartz, n. 58 above, at 971–3.) The strict-liability dimension in the rule of vicarious liability has received increasing attention in recent years. See Corporate Tort Liability Symposium, (1996) 69 S. Cal. L. Rev 1679.

[102] Simpson, n. 34 above, at 222, 227.

[103] For a somewhat similar analysis, see Mark F. Grady, 'Res Ipsa Loquitur and Compliance Error', (1994) 142 U. Pa. L. Rev 887.

doctrine obviously affords the victim a sufficient basis for tort compensation.

Furthermore, if the likelihood of negligence when reservoirs fail is high enough, then the plaintiff—even if (for whatever reason) ignorant of or uncertain about the circumstances of the individual case—can prove negligence by relying on the doctrine of *res ipsa loquitur.* Having acknowledged this, one can point to the curious proximity in time between *Rylands v Fletcher,* decided by the Exchequer Chamber in 1865, and *Byrne v Boadle,* decided by the same court two years previously;[104] similarly, one can compare the Court of Exchequer's 1866 decision in *Rylands* with its decision the year before in *Scott v London & St. Katherine Docks Company.*[105]

The phrase '*res ipsa loquitur*' expressed by chief Baron Pollock in *Byrne v Boadle* has now become, in England and certainly in the United States, a formal and elaborate legal doctrine, one which (when it applies) enables the plaintiff to make a *prima facie* showing of negligence (and hence liability) merely by establishing the kind of accident that has brought about his injury. Given the modern version of the *res ipsa loquitur* doctrine, does it apply to water escaping dams and reservoirs? The answer to this question is quite possibly yes. Indicative of the many American cases that have considered the application of *res ipsa* to problems of escaping water are *Brizendine v Nampa Meridian Irrigation District*[106] and *Dye v Burdick.*[107] In *Brizendine,* the bank of an irrigation canal broke, resulting in a flooding of the properties of the land of adjacent property owners. In *Dye,* the dam owned by the defendant broke, resulting in the flooding of the plaintiff's home. Both the Idaho and the Arkansas Supreme Courts ruled in favour of the plaintiffs' *res ipsa* claims. The Idaho Court concluded that the jury, 'reasoning from . . . common experience' as supplemented by the 'expert testimony' in the record, could find that *res ipsa loquitur* was appropriate, and that the breaking of the canal had been probably caused by the defendant's negligence.[108] The Arkansas Court reasoned that 'in the ordinary course of things, the dam would not have broken if those in control had used ordinary care'.[109] The Courts' *res ipsa* holdings are not quite as broad as they might be, since in each case there was some evidence suggesting particular forms of negligence which the defendants might have committed. Still, those *res ipsa* holdings deprived the strict-liability issue of immediate significance. In *Brizendine,* the Court, having ruled in favour of *res ipsa,* was able to bypass the plaintiff's alternative claim that the

[104] (1863) 2 H. & C. 722.
[105] (1865) 3 H. & C. 595.
[106] 548 P 2d 80 (Idaho 1976).
[107] 553 SW 2d 833 (Ark. 1977).
[108] 548 P 2d 80 at 85.
[109] 553 SW 2d 833 at 839.

Rylands principle should be endorsed in a way that would justify strict liability.[110] And in *Dye*, the Court, in supporting *res ipsa*, explicitly rejected the plaintiff's *Rylands* strict-liability claim.[111] In doing so, the Court reasoned (in line with *Burnie Port Authority*) that strict liability was not appropriate in cases of this sort because the negligence standard was adequate—'the exercise of reasonable care would have eliminated the risk here'.[112] And the court then backed up its rhetoric with its holding, inasmuch as the court ruled in favour of the plaintiff's negligence-based *res ipsa* claim.

Of course, in *Rylands* itself, even if judges had accepted the *Byrne v Boadle* idea of *res ipsa loquitur*, the defendants would still have been able to challenge liability by rebutting with evidence of their non-negligence. *Res ipsa* is, of course, most decisive where neither party has effective access to the actual facts that explain why harm happened. In *Rylands*, those facts were readily available. The facts showed that the defendants were guilty of no negligence themselves, though negligence could be assigned to the defendants' contractor.

Who, then, was the contractor, and why did the plaintiff not bring a claim against that negligent party? This is a fascinating question the answer to which has eluded later scholars. In his careful study of the background for *Rylands*, Professor Simpson was unable to learn anything about the contractor.[113] In his new American torts coursebook, Dean Mark Grady suggests that the contractor may have gone out of business by the time of the plaintiff's lawsuit;[114] but he does not substantiate this suggestion. In their own coursebook, Professors Franklin and Rabin point to *Winterbottom v Wright*[115] as a case that might have erected a privity barrier to any suit by the plaintiff against the negligent contractor.[116] To confirm this suggestion, one would need to know how *Winterbottom*, decided in 1842, was understood in the 1860s—an inquiry that would be difficult to undertake. As an offset, however, to the Franklin–Rabin suggestion, it can be pointed out that the defendants in *Rylands* explicitly suggested that the contractor 'as wrong doer, is liable' to the plaintiff (and to the defendants as well) for the harm which the contractor's negligence had caused.[117] In any event, given the decline of the *Winterbottom* privity idea since the nineteenth century, it seems obvious that if the *Rylands* facts were re-enacted today, the plaintiff would be allowed to bring a negligence claim against the negligent contractor.

[110] 548 P 2d 80 at 87. [111] 553 SW 2d 833 at 839–40. [112] Ibid at 840.

[113] Simpson, n. 34 above, at 243 n. 131.

[114] Mark Grady, *Cases and Materials on Torts* (1994), 32. [115] (1842) 10 M. & W. 109.

[116] Marc A. Franklin & Robert L. Rabin, *Tort Law and Alternatives* (6th ed., 1996), 435.

[117] (1866) LR 1 Exch 265 at 276.

That contractor's negligence, moreover, raises another possibility. Can the defendants who hire such a contractor be held liable under some version of vicarious liability? In *Rylands*, the plaintiff in fact advanced such a claim, which turned out to produce divergent results. Without much discussion, Baron Bramwell thought that 'the defendants surely are as liable as their agents would be';[118] hence for Baron Bramwell, vicarious liability was apparently an easy result. For Chief Baron Pollock, factual uncertainties relating to the content of the engineer's negligence persuaded him to withhold any finding on the vicarious-liability issue.[119] In the Exchequer Chamber, Mr Justice Blackburn, having ruled in favour of strict liability, was able to reserve decision on the issue of vicarious liability.[120] The issue was not mentioned in the speeches in the House of Lords.

Overall, then, a property-owner's vicarious liability for the negligence of his contractor was very much an open question at the time of *Rylands*. How has modern tort law dealt with that question? At least in American law, the Restatement of Torts includes several rules that point in favour of the defendants' vicarious liability. One rule refers to work that creates 'a peculiar risk of physical harm . . . unless special precautions are taken';[121] another rule refers to 'work involving a special danger to others . . . inherent in or normal to the work'.[122] Most clearly pertinent, however, is the rule imposing vicarious liability on the 'possessor of land' who authorizes the 'construction' of a 'structure' on the land by an independent contractor and who 'retain[s] possession of the land during the progress of the work'.[123] Of course, as noted in my discussion of *Burnie Port Authority*,[124] vicarious liability, though originally requiring the negligence of some party, then imputes that negligence to the defendant in a manner that can properly be described in strict liability terms. Unfortunately, the discussion in the Restatement is quite thin as to what the policies or principles are that justify the Restatement's rules of strict vicarious liability.

Of course the facts in *Rylands* can be 'revised' so as to pose the strict-liability issue in an even starker, less ambiguous way. Specifically, one can assume that the 'defect' in the subsoil accompanying the reservoir was so 'latent' as to place it beyond the reach of all non-negligent inspections.[125] To be sure, in light of modern engineering knowledge, such an assumption becomes increasingly unreal. Even so, given the assumption, the defendant would be able to rebut any possible *res ipsa*

118 (1865) 3 H. & C. 774 at 791. 119 Ibid at 798.
120 (1866) LR 1 Exch 265 at 287. 121 See *Restatement (Second) of Torts* § 416 (1965).
122 Ibid at § 427. 123 Ibid at § 422. 124 See text at 214.
125 'Latent defect' is language used by Blackburn J. (1866) LR 1 Exch 265 at 278.

loquitur negligence claim; and there being no contractor negligence, no issue of defendant vicarious liability would arise.

To follow through on the inquiry invited by *Burnie Port Authority*, how would the modern law of negligence treat such a situation? Here one needs to know more about what the modern negligence doctrine entails. Two Canadian scholars, Stephen Perry and Ernest Weinrib, have each made a rather interesting claim about the negligence doctrine as worked out in England.[126] Relying in large part on Lord Reid's speech in *Bolton v Stone*,[127] both contend that a defendant is negligent under English law if the defendant's conduct creates a 'substantial risk'; a finding of negligence can be affirmed, they think, without regard to the magnitude of the burdens the defendant would need to bear in order to reduce or prevent that risk.

This is in a way a startling claim. Weinrib's book seemingly supports negligence liability and opposes strict liability.[128] Yet, as noted above, in many cases negligence liability is separate from strict liability insofar as the former—but not the latter—can be defeated by a showing of high prevention burdens. Weinrib hence supports a negligence-liability rule only by classifying as negligence what many American observers would understand to be strict liability.[129] Given Weinrib's characterization of the English negligence rule, *Rylands* can be re-interpreted as a negligence case. We know from *Cambridge Water Co.* that reservoirs pose 'foreseeable' risks; and so long as these risks are 'substantial' as well as foreseeable, Weinrib might classify the construction of a reservoir as a negligent act.

In any event, Weinrib's somewhat jarring understanding of the English negligence doctrine appears to be incorrect. The English cases are given careful consideration in a recent manuscript (as yet unpublished) by Professor Stephen Gilles.[130] Gilles finds that English law was vague as to the meaning of the negligence standard between 1860 and 1945; English courts often relied on unelaborated concepts such as 'ordinary

[126] Ernest Weinrib, *The Idea of Private Law*, (1995) 148–9; Stephen R. Perry, 'The Impossibility of General Strict Liability', (1988) 1 Can. J. Law & Juris. 147 at 169–71.

[127] [1941] AC 850.

[128] E. Weinrib, n. 126 above, at 145–203.

[129] Weinrib's view finds interesting support in Oliver Wendell Holmes' treatment of the negligence concept in his famous book, *The Common Law* (1881). Holmes regarded a defendant as free of negligence when D could not have reasonably foreseen the risks that his conduct turned out to involve. Yet as David Rosenberg has recently shown, much of the time Holmes assumed that if D could appreciate the element of risk in his conduct, then D's choice to engage in that conduct could properly be deemed negligent. David Rosenberg, *The Hidden Holmes* (1995). In his 1881 analysis, Holmes simply ignored precaution burdens as a factor that might bear on negligence determinations.

[130] Stephen G. Gilles, 'Cost-Benefit Analysis in Modern English Tort Law' (unpub. ms.). Gilles refers briefly to his English research in Stephen G. Gilles, 'The Invisible Hand Formula', (1994) 80 Va. L. Rev 1015 at 1026 n. 28.

care' and 'the reasonable man', and ducked the actual job of decision-making by recognizing the broad discretion of the civil jury. However, as the jury was replaced after 1946, English judges began reflecting self-consciously on the meaning of the negligence concept, and in doing so affirmed that the burden of precautions has a major bearing on findings of negligence or non-negligence. Some opinions suggest that judges should 'balance' the burden of precautions against the magnitude of the risk.[131] Yet other opinions talk about finding a defendant free of negligence only if the burdens of precautions are 'quite out of proportion' to risk magnitude.[132] Judicial language of this latter sort tilts the negligence doctrine in favour of liability. In so far as English doctrine indeed endorses such a tilt, one can better understand the position recently taken by Jules Coleman, that building the reservoir in *Rylands* was a negligent act. While Coleman does not accept the Weinrib idea that all 'substantial risks' are negligent, Coleman perceives that in England rainfall 'is adequate for all reasonable uses'; given this perception, he claims that maintaining a reservoir 'creates unnecessary, and therefore unreasonable risks'.[133]

To recap, Weinrib and Coleman would each extend the negligence doctrine—though each in his own way—so as to support the conclusion that the mere building and operation of a reservoir is a negligent act. Yet *if* it is correct to classify this as negligence, it seemingly follows that courts should be willing to enjoin the construction of a reservoir. (If conduct is accurately deemed faulty and wrongful, then courts—if given the opportunity to prevent that conduct—should be willing to do so.[134]) Almost certainly, however, at least in ordinary circumstances, a court would be unwilling to enjoin the construction of a reservoir. Instead, they would understand *Rylands* as regarding the reservoir itself as permissible, even though subjecting the reservoir-owner to liability if any harm should occur. If this assessment is right, then the effort by Weinrib and Coleman to re-interpret reservoir-building as negligent in and of itself ends up in failure. There really is no alternative but to appreciate *Rylands* as standing for strict liability.

[131] E.g., *Daborn v Baty Tramways Motor Ltd*, [1946] 2 All ER 333, 336 (CA).

[132] E.g., *Aiken v Port of London Authority*, [1962] 2 QB 30, 38.

[133] Jules L. Coleman, *Risks and Wrongs* (1992), 467–8.

[134] In fact, injunctions are rarely sought against negligent conduct. But the obvious reason for this is that in most cases the conduct cannot be anticipated in advance in a way that would make it possible as a practical matter to seek an injunction. Of course, equity intervenes only when the remedy at law is inadequate. Yet it is easy to argue that damages for injury after-the-fact is far less satisfactory than avoiding the injury in the first place.

Rylands and Strict Liability

A relevant question, then, concerns the nature and scope of the strict-liability rule *Rylands* properly supports. On this point, there has of course been an enormous debate over the years, both in the courts and in the scholarly literature. This essay has a limited a goal—to contribute to that debate by pursuing two specific lines of inquiry. One concerns the thesis about *Rylands* advanced by Professor Simpson. The other concerns the American rule of strict liability for abnormally dangerous activities, discussed by the House of Lords in *Cambridge Water Co.*[135]

Simpson's article, as noted above, identified two disasters involving overflowing dams that occurred in the years before the *Rylands* litigation, disasters that were responsible for massive harm to property and over 300 deaths. Simpson goes on to suggest that the English judges' concern about these recent disasters was the driving motive for the strict liability result reached in *Rylands* itself.[136] Given this explication of motive, *Rylands* can perhaps be understood as a strict-liability rule that could over time be extended to all the dramatically dangerous activities engaged in by modern enterprise.[137] In such an extension, strict liability would depart significantly from the norm I have previously discussed, a norm that would support strict liability mainly when the defendant's conduct has been the exclusive cause of the harm incurred by the plaintiff.

The Simpson thesis as to judicial motive, however, is poorly supported by the various texts in *Rylands*. Mr Justice Blackburn's opinion in the Court of Exchequer Chamber—later endorsed by both Lord Chancellor Cairns and Lord Cranworth—relied on various English strict liability precedents, such as the liability rules for trespassing cattle, overflowing privies, and alkali works that generate fumes and vapours. While these all are instances of conduct by defendants that may well bring about harm, the harms in question hardly rank as severe: for trespassing cattle, for example, all that happens is that the neighbour's 'grass or corn is eaten down'.[138]

If the precedents invoked by Mr Justice Blackburn do not support the Simpson thesis, neither does Mr Justice Blackburn's rhetoric. Strict liability applies to things brought on to one's land that are likely to cause 'mischief' if they escape. 'Mischief' is a mild term that hardly conveys the kind of terrible results that can be produced by collapsing dams and

[135] *Cambridge Water Co. v Eastern Countries Leather* [1994] 2 AC 264.

[136] See Simpson, n. 34 above, at 244–5.

[137] This is suggested in ibid at 264. (To be sure, elsewhere Simpson suggests that *Rylands* is really about dams and reservoirs, and nothing else. Ibid at 216.)

[138] (1866) LR 1 Exch 265 at 280.

other forms of modern technology; indeed, 'mischief' is what children commonly get into.

To be sure, at one point Mr Justice Blackburn departs from the rhetorical tendency here described. Towards the end of his opinion, he suggests there is 'no difference . . . between chlorine and water; both will, if they escape, do damage, the one by scorching, and the other by drowning, and he who brings them there must at his peril see that they do not escape and do that mischief'.[139] Simpson seems to treat this passage as though it were a kind of Freudian slip, revealing how deeply Mr Justice Blackburn had been affected by recent events.[140] Yet for all one knows, the passage should be taken at face value—simply as a casual reference, rather than as a revelation of a deep judicial motive. For that matter, it is not entirely clear that Mr Justice Blackburn's language was in fact alluding to these prior dam incidents. In presenting his case to the Exchequer Chamber, the plaintiff argued that the bursting reservoir had not only deprived the plaintiff of profits but had also induced a 'reasonable fear of being drowned in the [plaintiff's] mines, in those who were employed in the mines'.[141] It is at least possible that Mr Justice Blackburn, in referring to 'drowning', was remaining within the four corners of the immediate case, and was merely acknowledging the plaintiff's claim about that case's own facts.[142]

To be sure, later English opinions interpreting *Rylands* have expanded on Lord Chancellor Cairns' concept of 'non-natural use' as meaning a 'special risk bringing with it increased danger for others'.[143] This interpretation seems to refer less to the *severity* of the risk created by the defendant's activity, and more to its *distinctiveness*. Note, however, that when Oliver Wendell Holmes began reflecting on *Rylands* in the 1870s, he came up with the idea that a reservoir could be deemed an 'extra hazardous' activity that could properly be subjected to strict liability, even within a tort system generally committed to a negligence liability standard.[144] In America in the 1930s, the Restatement of Torts was published, and included a doctrine of strict liability for 'ultrahazardous activities'.[145] No doubt the Holmes characterization of *Rylands* played some role in the formulation of the Restatement rule. The rule in the First Restatement has now been supplanted by a rule in the Second

[139] Ibid at 286. [140] Simpson, n. 34 above, at 249–50.

[141] (1866) LR 1 Exch 265 at 266.

[142] Of course, the plaintiff, in making his claim about his workers' fear, may have been shrewdly seeking to remind the court of the recent events.

[143] *Rickards v Lothian*, [1913] AC 263 at 280.

[144] Oliver W. Holmes, 'The Theory of Torts', (1873) 7 Am. L. Rev 652 at 653.

[145] Restatement of Torts §§ 519–20 (1938).

Restatement, issued in 1977, imposing strict liability on 'abnormally dangerous' activities.[146]

In *Cambridge Water Co.*, Lord Goff rejected the idea that the precedent of *Rylands* should lead to an endorsement of this American strict-liability doctrine; according to Lord Goff, this doctrine is not without problems, and its consideration is more properly a function of Parliament.[147] This is a passage that has attracted the attention of commentators.[148] Here Lord Goff's apparent assumption, which the English legal community may well share, is that the American doctrine is itself broad and important. But from my American perspective, I can report that there is much less in this abnormally dangerous doctrine than meets the eye. Over the years, the doctrine has been applied to activities such as blasting, crop dusting, fumigation, and the contamination of land and water.[149] These, however, are activities involving adjacent property-owners that fit the 'nuisance' framework set forth in *Cambridge Water Co.* itself, as well as that case's own finding that the defendant's contaminated discharges justifies strict liability.[150] Meanwhile, the American doctrine has been found inapplicable to a huge number of other dangerous activities, including the handling of firearms and the transmission of electric power.[151] Overall, the doctrine plays a rather subsidiary role in modern American tort law, hardly standing for any general idea of strict liability for dangerous modern enterprise. American scholars who are devoted to the norm of enterprise strict liability generally make clear their disappointment with the American abnormally dangerous doctrine.[152] Indeed, this doctrine may in some circumstances be even more conservative than England's *Rylands* doctrine.[153] Yet overall, strict-liability doctrines in England and the United States agree far more often than they disagree.

[146] *Restatement (Second) of Torts* §§ 519–20 (1977). [147] [1994] 2 AC 264 at 305.

[148] See, e.g., W. V. H. Rogers, *Winfield and Jolowicz on Tort* (14th ed., 1994), 446–8.

[149] See Jones, n. 76 above at 1716, 1738–42.

[150] To be sure, the parties actually undertaking the blasting, crop dusting, and fumigation may not be property-owners themselves. But they are hired by property-owners in order to provide service to property. Strict liability was applied to the transportation of gasoline by truck in *Siegler v Kuhlman* 502 P 2d 1181 (Wash. 1972). The various opinions in *Siegler*, however, suggest that strict liability should not be applied if the mishap involving the truck is itself immediately caused by the negligence of P or a third party.

[151] See Jones, n. 76 above at 1745–7.

[152] See, e.g., Virginia E. Nolan & Edmund Ursin, 'The Revitalization of Hazardous Activity Strict Liability', (1987) 65 N.C.L. Rev. 257.

[153] It is not entirely clear that the American doctrine would even apply to the *Rylands* facts—to collections of water. The First Restatement included a caveat as to whether reservoirs are ultra-hazardous. *Restatement of Torts* § 520 Comment (a) Caveat (1938). In Mass., the Second Restatement's strict-liability rule has been applied to an overflowing canal. *Clark-Aiken Co. v Crowell-Wright Co.* 323 NE 2d 876 (Mass. 1975). But nationwide, the results are somewhat inconsistent as to whether strict liability applies to impounded water. The cases are collected in Jones, n. 76 above at 1733–7.

Conclusion

The positions taken in this essay can here be summarized. Strict liability in tort is proper when the defendant engages in deliberately (or at least foreseeably) risky conduct and when that conduct is the exclusive cause of the risk that injures an innocent bystander. Set forth in this manner, the theory favouring strict liability does not apply when the plaintiff has in some meaningful way contributed to the risk or assumed the risk. From the perspective of this theory, strict liability makes good sense when a reservoir operated by the defendant overflows and imposes harm on neighboring property-owners. Examined carefully, however, the factual situation in *Rylands* departs from this scenario in a way that makes *Rylands* an awkward model for strict liability. For one thing, the plaintiff's own business activities in *Rylands*—digging and extending a pit under property owned by others and boring underground for coal—substantially contributed to the risky situation; indeed, the plaintiff was in a better situation than the defendants to understand the particular problem that gave rise to the harm. For another thing, the plaintiff and the defendants were both tenants of the same landlord, and hence were involved in a network of leases. One needs to consult those leases in order to ascertain what risks the plaintiff had (and had not) assumed, and (likewise) to figure out what claims the plaintiff might bring under landlord–tenant law against his landlord and against the defendant as a subsequent tenant.

In any event, *Cambridge Water Co.* is right in requiring foreseeability as a pre-condition for strict liability. *Burnie Port Authority* is wrong in rejecting the doctrine of strict liability, but is on the right track in perceiving that the breadth of the modern negligence doctrine has reduced the significance of the strict-liability issue. Despite this reduction in significance, strict liability has a distinctive and interesting role to play in modern tort law. There are obvious differences in phraseology between the English and the American strict-liability doctrines. Nevertheless, those doctrines bear a considerable resemblance.

A EUROPEAN PERSPECTIVE

9

Towards a European Civil Code: The Duty of Good Faith

Hein Kötz

A few years ago the European Parliament in Strasbourg passed a resolution requesting the Commission to start work on a European Civil Code.[1] The European Commission does not yet seem to show much enthusiasm for this idea, and it is indeed far from clear whether a demonstrable practical need for such a Code exists at the present time, whether the Commission has the jurisdiction to undertake such a project, and what the political chances of success would be. What is clear, however, is that the project of a European Civil Code has proved to be a most challenging and stimulating idea to many legal academics.[2] There is no agreement on whether it is not too early to start work on a code that would not merely have the status of a Restatement but the binding force of a statute.[3] But there does seem to be agreement that a serious effort must be made to develop a common core of European legal principles and rules, to engage in the construction of a European legal *lingua franca*,

[1] Resolution of 26 May 1989 (OJ [1989] C158/400).

[2] See e.g. A. S. Hartkamp, M. W. Hesselink, E. H. Hondius, C. E. du Perron, & J. B. M. Vranken (eds.), *Towards a European Civil Code* (1994). A 2nd vol is to follow in 1997. See also the work of the Commission of European Contract Law: Lando & H. Beale (eds.), *The Principles of European Contract Law, Part I: Performance, Non-Performance and Remedies* (1995). Similar rules have been elaborated under the auspices of UNIDROIT, see International Institute for the Unification of Private Law (ed.), *Principles of International Commercial Contracts* (Rome 1994). The Principles of European Contract Law 'are intended to be applied as general rules of contract law in the European Communities' (art. 101.1 (1)) whereas the UNIDROIT Principles 'set forth general rules for international commercial contracts' (Preamble). Both texts provide that they shall be applied when the parties have agreed that their contract be governed by them, by 'general principles of law' or by the '*lex mercatoria*' or the like.

[3] See e.g. W. Tilmann, 'Eine EG-Kodifikation des wirtschaftsnahen Zivilrechts', (1991) Juristenzeitung 1023; G. Gandolfi, 'Pour un code européen des contrats', (1992) 91 Rev. int. dr. comp. 707; O. Lando, 'Is Codification needed in Europe?', (1993) Euro. Rev. Private Law 157, who are all in favour of starting work on a Draft Code immediately.

to develop a common European legal literature, and thus to lay the basis for what will be needed when the time is ripe to undertake the project of a European Civil Code.[4]

It is in this spirit that I would like to discuss the problem whether a general duty of good faith should be laid down in a future European Civil Code. To most Continental lawyers the answer will seem self-evident. All Continental civil codes have such provisions, and the new Dutch Civil Code (*Burgerlijke Wetboek*) (in particular Title 6 dealing with the 'General Part of the Law of Obligations' which came into force in 1992) is perhaps leading the field in this respect. Article 6.2 (1) provides that the parties must act in accordance with the requirements of reasonableness and equity. Subsection (2) provides that a rule, binding upon the parties by virtue of law, usage or a legal act, does not apply to the extent that, under the circumstances, this would lead to a result unacceptable according to the standards of reasonableness and equity.[5] § 242 of the German Civil Code simply says in quite general terms that everyone must perform his contract in the manner required by good faith giving consideration to common usage. Yet the courts have relied on this provision not only to solve the important economic and social problems which arose after the two world wars and the reunification of Germany, but also to qualify in many respects the rigorous individualism of the Code's original contract law and to adapt it to the changed social and moral attitudes of society. Not only have the German courts applied the good faith standard to the performance and enforcement of contracts, but they have also applied it to the negotiation phase by imposing constraints on the parties' pursuit of self-interest in negotiating a contractual agreement.

If the good faith standard is alive and well in all Continental civil codes why should it not be laid down in a European Civil Code as well? Even the Principles of European Contract Law provide that 'in exercising his rights and performing his duties each party must act in accordance

[4] See, e.g., H. Kötz, 'A Common Private Law for Europe', in de Witte & Forder (eds.), *The Common Law of Europe and the Future of Legal Education* (1992), 31; R. Zimmermann, 'Civil Code and Civil Law: The 'Europeanization' of Private Law within the European Community and the Re-Emergence of a European Legal Science', (1994/95) 1 Col. J. Eur. L. 63. *Contra*: P. Legrand, 'European Legal Systems are Not Converging', (1996) 45 Int. Comp. L.Q. 52; idem, 'Against a European Civil Code', (1997) 60 MLR 44.

[5] Cf. also arts. 6:248, 6:233, 6:258 *NBW* and A. S. Hartkamp, 'Judicial Discretion Under the New Civil Code of the Netherlands', (1992) 40 Am. J. Comp. L. 551. Art. 1134 French Civil Code provides that 'les conventions légalement formées doivent être exécutées de bonne foi'. While this provision has been of fairly little practical importance for a long time it has made considerable headway in French contract law over the past two decades. See, e.g., M. W. Hesselink, 'De opmars van de goede trouw in het Franse contractenrecht', (1994) Weekblad voor Privaatrecht 694 (with ample references to French cases and academic writers).

with good faith and fair dealing' (article. 1.106 [1]) and that each party 'owes to the other a duty to cooperate in order to give full effect to the contract' (article. 1.107). Why not use a similar formula in a European Civil Code?

The problem is that English law seems not to recognize and enforce a general principle of good faith. Its position is well summarized by Bingham LJ in *Interfoto Library Ltd v Stiletto Ltd*, where he said:

> In many civil law systems, and perhaps in most legal systems outside the common law world, the law of obligations recognises and enforces an overriding principle that in making and carrying out contracts parties should act in good faith. This does not simply mean that they should not deceive each other, a principle which any legal system must recognise; its effect is perhaps most aptly conveyed by such metaphorical colloquialisms as 'playing fair', 'coming clean' or 'putting one's cards face upwards on the table'. It is in essence a principle of fair and open dealing. . . . English law has, characteristically, committed itself to no such overriding principle but has developed piecemeal solutions in response to demonstrated problems of unfairness. Many examples could be given. Thus equity has intervened to strike down unconscionable bargains. Parliament has stepped in to regulate the imposition of exemption clauses and the form of certain hire-purchase agreements. The common law has also made its contribution, by holding that certain classes of contract require utmost good faith . . . and in many other ways.[6]

It can indeed be shown that there are a great many well-established rules of English contract law which reflect a concern for good faith, fair dealing, and the protection of reasonable expectations.[7] But these rules, although reflecting the general object of the law to do justice and ensure fairness, do not qualify as good faith rules. To distil from them a broad standard of good faith and to incorporate it in a code would, in the view of many English lawyers, amount to an invitation to judges to give vent to personal values, to refer everything back to supposed universals, and to give up the time-tested tradition of going cautiously from this case or that case to the next case.[8] There is also a concern that the adoption of a

[6] [1988] 2 WLR 615 at 620–1.

[7] See, e.g., Malcolm Clarke, 'The Common Law of Contract in 1993: Is There a General Doctrine of Good Faith', (1993) 23 Hong Kong L. J. 318; H. Collins, 'Good Faith in European Contract Law', (1994) 14 OJLS 229; Lord Steyn, 'The Role of Good Faith in Contract Law: A Hairshirt Philosophy?', (1991) Denning L. J. 131.

[8] See M. G. Bridge, 'Does Anglo-Canadian Contract Law Need a Doctrine of Good Faith?', (1984) 9 Can. Bus. L.J. 385, 413. Cf. also S. Waddams, 'Good Faith, Unconscionability and Reasonable Expectations', (1995) 9 J. Contract Law 55. On the other hand, Prof. Lücke has made a persuasive argument for his view that 'it would not be unreasonable to hope that good faith would ultimately make a significant and beneficial impact upon [Australian] law'. See H. K. Lücke, 'Good Faith and Contractual Performance', in P. D. Finn (ed.), *Essays on Contract* (1987), 155, 182. For the position of US law see E. A. Farnsworth,

broad concept of good faith would unsettle the commercial bargaining process and undermine the values of certainty and security. Professor Goode, a leading English commercial lawyer, said that,

> [T]he predictability of the legal outcome of a case is more important than absolute justice. It is necessary in a commercial setting that businessmen at least should know where they stand. . . . The last thing that we want to do is to drive business away by vague concepts of fairness which make judicial decisions unpredictable, and if that means that the outcome of disputes is sometimes hard on a party we regard that as an acceptable price to pay in the interest of the great majority of business litigants.[9]

A similar question was asked a few years ago by Lord Goff:

> Do we lack an overriding principle requiring good faith in the exercise of contractual rights? We know that there is such a principle in one of the most famous provisions of the German BGB. . . . Do we need such a principle as this in our commercial law? The vast majority of commercial judges and practitioners in this country would, I believe, instinctively answer that question in the negative.[10]

There is no doubt that Professor Goode's point is well-taken. I do not think, however, that it should carry the day, and what I propose to do is to set out a few arguments that might help to allay the fears expressed by our English friends. Before I do so I must turn to another objection likely to be raised by them. It is based on the deep-seated reluctance of English lawyers, perhaps not against codification as such, but against the adoption by a code or statute of broad and open-textured statements of principle. For example, English law has recently turned its back on the United Nations Commission on International Trade Law's Model Law of Arbitration and appears to be doing so in relation to the Vienna Convention on Contracts for the International Sale of Goods. One of the reasons given in each of these cases was the greater sophistication of English case law and the uncertainty that would result from the broadly formulated provisions of the Model Law and the Vienna Convention.[11] There is indeed a difference between the common law and the civil law in the style of statutory drafting and legislative technique, a difference which tends to be swept under the carpet by the *aficionados* of a European Civil Code.

'Good Faith in Contract Performance', in J. Beatson & D. Friedmann (eds.), *Good Faith and Fault in Contract Law* (1995), 153.

[9] Goode, 'The Concept of "Good Faith" in English Law' in Saggi, *Conferenze e Seminari, Centro di studi e ricerche di diritto comparato e straniero* (1992), 7.

[10] Lord Goff, 'Opening Address', (1992) 5 J. Contract Law 4.

[11] I owe this observation to J. Beatson & D. Friedmann, 'Introduction: From "Classical" to Modern Contract Law', in Beatson & Friedmann, at n. 8 above) 5. See also the sceptical observations by J. Hobhouse, 'International Conventions and Commercial Law: The Pursuit of Uniformity', (1990) 106 LQR 530.

The problem was canvassed thoroughly in the late seventies when the English and Scottish Law Commissions buried their original plans to codify the law of contract. Various members of the Commissions wrote epitaphs at the time, perhaps to rid themselves of a guilt complex, in which reasons were given for the demise of the projects.[12] What loomed large in the debate were arguments drawn from what were believed to be the main characteristics of codes in civil law countries. To the common lawyer, one of the characteristics of a code is its propensity for generalized statements of principle. Sir Michael Kerr described codification in the civil-law sense as involving the 'legislative formulation of a series of general rules in particular areas of the law which are then left to the courts to work out and apply in the infinitely varying situations which come before them'.[13]

As an example of this style of legislation the reader is normally referred to articles 1382–6 of the French Civil Code, which purport to cover virtually the whole of French tort law in a handful of majestic, if trivial, propositions. To adopt this style of legislation in England, so the argument continues, would be in clear conflict with what Sir Michael Kerr called 'a basic and apparently ineradicable feature of our constitutional philosophy' which requires all English legislation to be based on the premise 'that every statute must, so far as possible, seek to cover every foreseeable situation' and which is opposed to provisions expressed in general language that 'would leave unacceptably wide powers of interpretation and application to the judges'[14] and would therefore alter the traditional balance of power between Parliament and the judiciary.

I know that a lawyer from the Continent who ventures into English law is bound sooner or later to fall into error, but it does seem to me that the explanation given for the English style of legislative drafting has a somewhat hollow ring today. In his inaugural lecture at Oxford in 1978 Professor Atiyah suggested that England was already moving to an era when a great deal of strict and specific statute law is being replaced by discretions of one kind or another.[15] The proliferation of these discretions appeared to him to arise 'at least in part from the realisation that legislation . . . simply cannot anticipate and provide for the great variety of cases which are likely to arise, and that Parliament therefore prefers to proceed in partnership with the judiciary'.[16] Even for a civilian observer it is not difficult to point out a few examples of this type of legislation.

[12] M. Kerr, 'Law Reform in Changing Times', (1980) 96 LQR 515; A. E. Anton, 'Obstacles to Codification', (1982) Jur. Rev. 15; P. M. North, 'Problems of Codification in a Common Law System', (1982) 46 RabelsZ 490.

[13] Kerr, n. 12 above at 528.

[14] Ibid at 527–8.

[15] P. S. Atiyah, *From Principles to Pragmatism* (1978).

[16] Idem, 'Common Law and Statute Law', (1985) 48 MLR 1 at 5.

The example which comes first to mind is of course the Unfair Contract Terms Act 1977, which abounds with provisions under which the validity of an exemption clause depends on what has been called 'a reasonableness test'. This test, which has been said to stand 'at the centre of the strategy of the Act'[17] requires the judge to decide whether the clause in question 'shall have been a fair and reasonable one to be included having regard to the circumstances which were, or ought reasonably to have been, known to or in the contemplation of the parties when the contract was made'.[18] This is language at least as broad and vague as the texts used in the Continental statutes dealing with the control of unfair exemption clauses.

Nor does it seem plausible to me to link the traditional specificity of English legislation to a basic feature of English constitutional philosophy. If this were true the wide discretion exercised by English judges in fields governed by case law would seem highly objectionable on constitutional grounds. No one in England seems to find anything wrong with the judges using vague and indeterminate concepts and particularizing them as cases come up so long as these concepts are common-law concepts created not by the legislature but by the judges themselves. Both in England and on the Continent a defendant will be liable in negligence if he has failed to take reasonable care to avoid an unreasonable risk of causing physical injury to others. Both in England and on the Continent contracts may be void on grounds of public policy, assignees take subject to equities, and agreements can be terminated because of a fundamental breach. General propositions of this sort do not decide concrete cases, either in a civil-law system where such principles are codified, or in the common law where they are not. What they do achieve in both systems is that they help to organize legal thinking, to allow the formation of clusters of similar cases, to make the law manageable and findable, and to provide a language in which a meaningful discourse between lawyers can take place. It follows that if there is no major operational difference between the use to which general principles are put in code law and in case law, then it is difficult to see why the mere enactment of such principles would alter the balance of power between Parliament and the judges and thus violate basic tenets of British constitutional philosophy.

It seems to me that a better explanation of the specificity and elaborateness of English legislation can be found in the history of the common law. Until the nineteenth century the English regarded legislative activity as necessary only to counteract some specific social or economic

[17] *Cheshire and Fifoot's Law of Contract* (12th ed., 1991), 186.
[18] Unfair Contract Terms Act 1977, s 11(1).

mischief or to change an individual rule developed by the case law whose practical effects seemed to the monarch and his or her advisers, and subsequently to Parliament, to be inconvenient. For this reason English statutes used to be sporadic *ad hoc* enactments tightly drawn and designed to deal with specific issues only. The idea of codification which swept the Continent in the late eighteenth century was based on a different philosophy. Its aim was to replace the historically conditioned detail of the existing law by comprehensive legislation, consciously planned in a rational and transparent order covering whole fields of law by an exhaustive and complete regulation. This did not mean, of course, that every question that might possibly arise would get a precise answer in the code. The draftsmen of the French Civil Code, as indeed of all other Continental codes, knew very well that room had to be left for judicial decisions to make the law applicable to unforeseen individual cases. On the other hand, they wanted to remain faithful to the idea that a code was to provide a comprehensive and exhaustive treatment of the subject, and the compromise was to use in many places fairly broad and general clauses designed to be filled in due course by judicial decisions. To the English, the deliberate reliance of a code on judicial amplification, and indeed the whole idea of a conscious and planned partnership between the legislature and the judiciary, is a rather odd idea. Indeed, when an English statute emerges from the Parliamentary draftsman it is often couched in language so detailed, specific, complex and elaborate that its aim seems to curb the power of judges rather than to provide them with a framework for an intelligent and reasoned exercise of that power. The English do not seem to appreciate that the technique of going forward cautiously from this case or that case to the next case, as justice in each case requires, is equally possible where the judge has to work on the basis of a loosely-textured statutory formula, such as a good faith standard.

Some of them believe, indeed, that such a formula would be positively dangerous. In the view of Professor Bridge the articulation of a broad standard of good faith and fair dealing in formal terms would be

> [A]n imperfect translation of an ethical standard into legal ideology and legal rules. However much it might stimulate research or encourage inquiry into theories underlying contract law, its appropriate home is the university where it can perform these functions without wreaking practical mischief. . . . [G]ood faith is an invitation to judges to abandon the duty of legally reasoned decisions and to produce an unanalytical incantation of personal values [and is] more likely to produce idiosyncratic judgements.[19]

[19] Bridge, n. 8 above at 412–13.

I do not think that these dire predictions are borne out by the experience of the Continental legal systems. True, there are countless German cases relying in one form or another on § 242 of the Civil Code. But this does not mean that these cases form a 'wilderness of single instances'.[20] In some cases good faith is mentioned only as an afterthought and only to embellish a judgment based on other grounds. Most cases, however, can be assigned to one of a number of well-defined rules which have all been developed by the courts under the umbrella of § 242, but which now lead a separate and independent existence so that, figuratively speaking, the statutory foundation of § 242 could be withdrawn without any risk of having the judge-made edifice collapse. It would be a poor advocate who would simply cite § 242 to the judge and invite him to dispense justice to his client according to the principles of good faith and fair dealing. What would be expected of him would be a reference to the more specific doctrines of, say, laches, or frustration, or forfeiture, including the judgments applying these doctrines to individual cases.[21] There is hardly a case involving a problem of contractual interpretation or the implication of a term in which the court would not, for good measure, put in a reference to § 242. But this tells you more about the stylistic conventions to be followed in the proper drafting of a German judgment than about the substance of the rules employed to resolve omissions and incoherences of contractual expression. Differences there may be between the German and the English rules on the subject, and further research may well lead to the result that in some areas, like cases will not always be decided alike in Germany and in England. But if such differences exist the explanation must surely lie elsewhere than in the presence in German law and the absence in English law of a broad good faith standard. Indeed, instead of saying, as an English judge would, that implied terms should be read into a contract in accordance with the dictates of business efficacy, one could as easily say, as the German judge does, that a certain implied obligation should be imposed on a party because good faith requires it. Would it have made a difference if Lord Bowen in *The Moorcock*[22] or Lord Wright in *Luxor*'s case[23] had made a passing reference to the good faith principle? Is this not what Lord Bowen in fact did when he said in *Lamb v Evans* that '[T]he common law . . . treats the matter from the point of view of an implied contract, and assumes that there is a promise to do that which is part of the bargain, or which can fairly be implied as part of the good faith which

[20] Alfred, Lord Tennyson, *Aylmer's Field* (1894), 146.

[21] Cf. W. F. Ebke & B. M. Steinhauer, 'The Doctrine of Good Faith in German Contract Law', in Beatson & Friedmann, n. 8 above at 171.

[22] *The Moorcock* (1889) 14 PD 64.

[23] *Luxor (Eastbourne) Ltd v Cooper* [1941] AC 108.

is necessary to make the bargain effectual?'[24] Nor would it wreak havoc in the English law of contract if the judges were able to make use of a principle of good faith in their decisions on proprietary estoppel, mistake, acceptance by silence, or reliance on misrepresentation.

Let me illustrate this by the way German courts have treated standard-form contracts.[25] It had long been realized that most of the text on printed forms was not read and, if read, seldom understood by the signers, and that this made nonsense of the usual tests of mutual assent. In the mid-1950s the courts came to the conclusion that the traditional technique of construing ambiguous clauses *contra proferentem* was not sufficient. So they started to subject standard-form contracts to severe scrutiny, striking out terms found to be oppressive, unexpected, or one-sided. This was a very bold step indeed. But the proper limits of judicial activism need not concern us here. What is of interest here is that no provision in the Civil Code could serve in any way as a statutory basis for the newly created judicial power. Admittedly, the courts invoked § 242; and the fact that this was believed necessary shows that there is some truth in the statement that, in the civil law, judges generally do not feel safe until they have moored their ship to some statutory wharf. But this is often a largely ritual operation and so it was here, for § 242 only provides that contracts are to be performed in the manner required by good faith. On this basis, if basis it can be called, a considerable body of case law grew up, and guidelines for testing the fairness of such clauses were developed. Academic writers gave a helping hand, and while § 242 was gradually lapsing into benign neglect, they were busy lining up the cases in series, comparing and contrasting them, matching results against reasons given, and limiting the scope of decisions by imagining the effects of adding or subtracting particular facts. The techniques used were quite similar to those being used in England at the same time by the courts to create the doctrine (now defunct) under which an exemption clause was no defence to a claim based on what was called 'a fundamental breach'.[26] In other words, the view English lawyers seem to take by instinct, that a code provision on good faith would inevitably sound the death-knell of established techniques of developing the law by way of an orderly process of reasoning from case to case, is quite unproven.

[24] [1893] 1 Ch 218 at 229.

[25] I have made this point previously in H. Kötz, 'Taking Civil Codes Less Seriously', (1987) 50 MLR 1.

[26] See *Karsales (Harrow) Ltd v Wallis* [1956] 1 WLR 936; *Suisse Atlantique Société d'Armement Maritime SA v NV Rotterdamsche Kolen Centrale* [1967] 1 AC 361; *Harbutt's 'Plasticine' Ltd v Wayne Tank & Pump Co.* [1970] 1 QB 447. The doctrine of fundamental breach has been laid to rest in *Photo Production v Securicor Transport* [1980] AC 827.

Even if one accepts that there is no substantive reason why English law should *not* adopt a good faith obligation, there is still the question of whether this would be an improvement. Most German lawyers would answer this question in the affirmative: gathering together, under the roof of one overriding statutory principle, all the instances in which the law requires good faith in the exercise of contractual rights helps, he would argue, (a) to identify the common thread running through all the cases, (b) to prevent inconsistencies between the various practical applications of the principle, and (c) to make the law more orderly, accessible, and teachable. A civilian should say no more. Not only will he be told, as in the French proverb with a special meaning for comparative lawyers, 'A beau mentir qui vient de loin', he will also be told,

> that the failure to perceive or create in English law any decent order is more serious to the person looking at this system from outside than to the person working within it. The grimy and patched machine may operate very well, chaotic kitchens can produce good food, and if the index to a book is complete and accurate, it may not matter that the table of contents discloses profound disorder.[27]

But let me return to my main thesis: I think that the Continental experience does not support the view that the good faith principle would lead to an influx of vague requirements of contractual morality into the law, at least not when dealing with the rules on the performance of existing contracts. After all, an existing contract provides a framework of reference within which the court must move in ascertaining the intention of the parties and in protecting their reasonable expectations. Much more delicate ground would be entered if the good faith requirement were to be extended to the negotiation phase. This is the position taken by most Continental legal systems. Under German law, even in the absence of an express promise to negotiate in good faith, a relationship of trust and confidence comes into existence once the parties have entered into negotiations for a contract, and there is a liability for damages for *culpa in contrahendo* if a party fails to live up to the duties owed by a reasonable person in like circumstances to the other side. There is no doctrine of *culpa in contrahendo* in French law, but the courts reach similar results by other means. Reprehensible conduct during the negotiating phase may be a *faute* under article 1382 of the Civil Code, giving rise to an action for damages. The breach by one negotiating party of a pre-contractual duty of disclosure may constitute *dol par réticence* entitling the other party to avoid the agreement under article 1116 or to claim damages. All this is, or so it seems, anathema to English lawyers.

[27] Tony Weir, p. 2 of 'The Common Law System', in *International Encyclopaedia of Comparative Law* vol II, ch 2, (1974), 79.

But let us look at the matter a little more closely. In *Walford v Miles*[28] a draft agreement had been reached regarding the sale of a photographic processing business under which the prospective buyers, the brothers Walford, were to pay £2 million and the seller, Mr Miles, was to continue working in the business for twelve months after completion and to warrant that a certain net profit would be made by the buyers in the first year after completion. Furthermore, in consideration of a comfort letter provided by the Walfords from their bank, to the effect that they would be able to pay the price of £2 million, Mr Miles agreed on 17 March 1987 that he would not negotiate with anybody else or consider any alternative offers. Five days later he told the Walfords that to his regret he was unable to proceed with the sale, but was selling to a third party. This he did for £2 million, but under significantly different terms.

The Walfords brought an action for breach of contract. In their view the agreement of 17 March had laid upon Mr Miles a negative duty not to negotiate with a third party and a positive duty to bargain in good faith with them. In the view of the House of Lords the agreement was unenforceable for uncertainty in both aspects. The negative duty failed since no fixed time period had been agreed and it was not possible to imply a 'reasonable' time. The positive duty failed because under English law an agreement to negotiate is unenforceable for want of certainty. The reason for this rule was described by Lord Ackner as follows:

> [T]he concept of a duty to carry on negotiations in good faith is inherently repugnant to the adversarial position of the parties when involved in negotiations. . . . [H]ow is a vendor ever to know that he is entitled to withdraw from further negotiations? How is the court to police such an agreement? A duty to negotiate in good faith is as unworkable in practice as it is inherently inconsistent with the position of a negotiating party. It is here that the uncertainty lies. In my judgment, while negotiations are in existence either party is entitled to withdraw from these negotiations, at any time and for any reason. There can be thus no obligation to continue to negotiate until there is a 'proper reason' to withdraw. Accordingly, a bare agreement to negotiate has no legal content.[29]

This is a fairly sweeping and apodictic statement. To the Continental observer it is unacceptable, although he may find some consolation in the fact that most common-law commentators have criticized the decision as well.[30] This does not mean that the House of Lords reached the

[28] *Walford v Miles* [1992] 2 AC 128. [29] Ibid at 138.

[30] See, e.g., Jeff Cumberbatch, 'In Freedom's Course: The Contract to Negotiate', (1992) 12 OJLS 587; I. Brown, 'The Contract to Negotiate: A Thing Writ in Water', (1992) J. Bus. L. 353; Patrick Neil, 'A Key to Lock-Out Agreements', (1992) 108 LQR 405; R. P. Buckley, 'Walford v. Miles: False Certainty About Uncertainty, An Australian Perspective', (1993) 6 J. Contract Law 58; J. Shaw, 'Pre-contractual Negotiations in English Law: *Walford* v. *Miles* and its Aftermath', (1994) 2 Eur. Rev. Private Law 269; J. W. Carter & M. P.

wrong result. There are good reasons indeed to suppose that the Walfords would have lost their case had it been tried in a French, Dutch, or German court. Note that £700 had already been paid by Mr Miles to compensate the Walfords for the expenditure incurred on such matters as the preparation of the draft agreements. What the Walfords claimed were not just reliance damages. They claimed the performance interest. They said that Mr Miles's business was worth £3 million and that they were entitled to the sum of £1 million which they would have netted had the deal gone through. German and Dutch law do not rule out the possibility that fault in the pre-contractual phase may lead to a recovery of the performance interest.[31] But this would occur only in very rare cases, and *Walford v Miles* would not be one of them, if only because all agreements between the parties were explicitly made 'subject to contract'. Moreover, it is doubtful whether a Continental court would have found Mr Miles in breach of a duty to negotiate in good faith. There was no evidence that he had been stringing the Walfords along or that he had withdrawn from the negotiations simply to take advantage of a more attractive offer from a third party. His decision was based on the fear that, owing to his ailing health, he might not be able to continue working in the business for another year, that the staff might not get on with the Walfords, and that for these reasons the net profit he would have had to warrant might not be made by the Walfords in the first year after completion. There was therefore no basis for saying that the negotiations had been broken off by Mr Miles—in the words of the French *Cour de Cassation*—'sans raison légitime, brutalement et unilatéralement'.[32] English law and Continental law may therefore not be as far apart as one might conclude from taking Lord Ackner's speech at face value.

What about the extent to which a party is under a duty to disclose information during the pre-contractual stage? Here the situation seems to be similar. English cases are replete with general statements to the effect that a party may during the negotiations play his cards close to his chest and hold back information even if he is aware that a knowledge of the facts would deter the other side from entering into the contract. This

Furmston, 'Good Faith and Fairness in the Negotiation of Contracts', (1994) 8 J. Contract Law 1 and 93 at 112–15; H. Beale, Commentary on 'Good Faith and Fairness in Failed Contract Negotitations', (1994) 8 J. Contract Law 120 at 123–5; R. Brownsword, 'Two Concepts of Good Faith', (1994) 7 J. Contract Law 197; Nili Cohen, 'Pre-contractual Duties: Two Freedoms and the Contract to Negotiate', in Beatson & Friedmann, (n. 8 above) 25 at 34–7, 42–56. See also Sjef van Erp, 'The Formation of Contracts', in Hartkamp *et al.*, n. 2 above at 117 and various comparative case notes in (1994) 2 Eur. Rev. Private Law 274–327.

[31] See *Hoge Raad* 18 June 1982, Ned. Jur. 1983, 723 (*Plas v Valburg*) and more generally H. Kötz, *European Contract Law* (trans. Tony Weir) (1997) 37–41.

[32] Com. 20 Mar. 1972, JCP 1973.II.17543 annotated by Joanna Schmidt. See also Com. 17 Nov. 1993, JCP 1994.II.22283 annotated by H. Périnet-Marquet.

robust principle was stated in blunt language in *Smith v Hughes*[33] involving the sale of a specific quantity of oats. The buyer was a racehorse trainer who wanted old oats for his horses and believed that the oats on offer were indeed old. The seller, a farmer, knew full well that his oats were new, and he also knew that the buyer wrongly believed them to be old, but he did nothing to encourage the buyer's mistaken belief. Cockburn CJ said:

> The question is whether, under such circumstances, the passive acquiescence of the seller in the self-deception of the buyer will entitle the latter to avoid the contract. I am of opinion that it will not. . . . I take the true rule to be that where a specific article is offered for sale, without express warranty, or without circumstances from which the law will imply a warranty . . . and the buyer has full opportunity of inspecting and forming his own judgment, if he chooses to act on his own judgment, the rule caveat emptor applies. . . . The buyer persuaded himself they were old oats, when they were not so; but the seller neither said nor did anything to contribute to this deception. He has himself to blame. The case is not what a man of scrupulous morality or nice honour would do under such circumstances.[34]

True, there are now significant exceptions to, and mitigations of, the rule of non-disclosure. The law is more inclined than in the old days to imply a term and thus to hold the seller liable in damages not because he breached a *pre-contractual* duty to disclose that the product on offer is defective, but because he breached an implied *contractual* promise to deliver a product which is free from the defect.[35] There is a general duty of disclosure in contracts *uberrimae fidei* and in relationships of a fiduciary character. An increasing number of statutes now provide that information of various kinds should be disclosed, particularly in consumer contracts.[36]

On the other hand the Continental legal systems all recognize a broad 'obligation pré-contractuelle de renseignement'. Apparently French law goes particularly far in this respect,[37] but Dutch, German, and Swiss law do not seem to be far behind.[38] English lawyers are understandably reluctant to accept a broadly formulated duty to disclose information on the ground that this would impose on the negotiating parties a

[33] *Smith v Hughes* (1871) LR 6 QB 597.

[34] Ibid at 602 per Lord Cockburn CJ.

[35] See P. S. Atiyah, *An Introduction to the Law of Contract* (5th ed., 1995), 251f. with reasons 'why the courts have recently favoured the implied-term technique over the creation of duties of disclosure'.

[36] See B. Nicholas, 'The Pre-contractual Obligation to Disclose Information: English Report', in D. Harris & D. Tallon (eds.), *Contract Law Today, Anglo-French Comparisons* (1989), 166.

[37] J. Ghestin, 'The Pre-Contractual Obligation to Disclose Information: French Report', in Harris & Tallon, n. 36 above, 151 at 166.

[38] See art. 3.44(3) NBW and more generally Kötz, n. 31 above at 198–205.

general obligation to subordinate their own interests to those of the other side which is inconsistent with the adversarial interests of parties involved in negotiations. I am not sure that this fear is justified. Continental courts have not simply arrogated to themselves a licence to exercise an unfettered judicial discretion in this field. Instead the decisions turn on factors such as the materiality of the information, the cost and effort invested by the party in acquiring the information, the ease with which the other party may get the information himself, and the status of the parties as '*professionnel*' and '*consommateur*'.

Nevertheless, it has been argued that there is not only a difference in the conceptual structures of the English and Continental systems, but also a deep-rooted difference of values, attitudes, and policies: English law is said to tolerate 'a certain moral insensitivity in the interest of economic efficiency',[39] whereas French law is thought to rank solidarity higher than individualism.[40] Let me try to offer a more mundane explanation. Much of the doctrinal development of the contract law of a country depends on the types of contract litigated before the higher courts of that country. In comparing Australian and English contract law, Professor Ellinghaus has argued that

> [A] law of contract devised by a court most often confronted with one type of contract will differ from that devised by a court most often confronted with another type of contract. A court of ultimate appeal which draws on its own precedents in the development of a particular body of doctrine will naturally be influenced by the data most often placed before it.[41]

Professor Ellinghaus reported that about two-thirds of the contract cases decided by the Australian High Court concerned the sale of land, whereas the most litigated contracts before the House of Lords in the same period arose from charter parties, contracts for the carriage of goods, and contracts of insurance, particularly marine insurance. Lord Goff once said that

> [O]ne feature of our legal system which I find many of our continental friends are unable to understand or unwilling to accept is the worldwide importance of the English commercial court, of English commercial arbitration and of English commercial law. Yet, this is a fact of life. . . . I here refer not so much to London as a financial centre, but to London as the centre of the world's shipping, the centre of nearly all the world's commodity trades, and the centre of the world's insurance. One result of this is that more commercial arbitrations are held each year in London than in the rest of Europe put together . . . Yet another is, of

[39] Nicholas, n. 36 above, 187.

[40] P. Legrand, 'Pre-contractual Disclosure and Information: English and French Law Compared', (1986) 6 OJLS 322 at 349. See also van Erp, n. 30 above at 130–4.

[41] M. P. Ellinghaus, 'An Australian Contract Law?', (1989) 1 J. Contract Law 13 at 19–20.

course, the English Commercial Court itself . . . which must, I imagine, be by far the most important court in the world for the resolution of international commercial disputes. Certainly there is nothing like it anywhere else in Europe. You can judge its international character by the fact that, in one year during which I had the honour to preside over the court, in every single case tried in the court either one or both parties came from overseas.[42]

There is no commercial court in the English sense in Germany. But it can safely be said that the number of cases arising out of contracts for the sale of land or used automobiles or out of other personal non-commercial relationships or out of agreements between professionals and consumers is far greater in the Federal Court of Justice (the highest German court in civil matters) than in the English appellate courts. A study of the 415 decisions dealing with contractual disputes rendered by the Federal Court from 1986 to 1994[43] revealed that there were only six cases in which one or both parties were residing abroad. But there were no less than twenty-nine cases in which a consumers' association sought an injunction restraining the defendant firm from using allegedly unfair contract terms. The types of contracts litigated were spread fairly evenly over the whole spectrum but there were only eighteen cases involving contracts for the carriage of goods and insurance policies covering the attendant risks. In 212 cases (that is, slightly more than one half of the total sample) *both* parties were consumers in the sense that they had not entered into the agreements in the course of a business or in the exercise of a profession.

It would seem that there is more than a grain of truth in the observation that 'the English law of contract was designed for a nation of shopkeepers' while 'the French system was made for a race of peasants'.[44] If this assumption still holds in the present circumstances (except that 'shopkeepers' would have to be replaced these days by 'hard-nosed international business executives', and 'peasants' by 'consumers'), then it should come as no surprise that the English rules on disclosure, and indeed on good faith duties in the negotiation, performance, and execution of contracts, may differ in form and perhaps also in substance from those on the Continent.

The project of a European Civil Code is probably not a live issue yet. But it is perhaps not too early to speculate on the style of legislation we

[42] Lord Goff, n. 10 above, 2.

[43] Vols 95–127 of the official case reports (Entscheidungen des Bundesgerichtshofs in Zivilsachen).

[44] See O. Kahn-Freund, C. Lévy & B. Rudden, *A Source-book on French Law* (1979) 318: 'It certainly seems that the English law of contract was designed for a nation of shopkeepers. If that be so, the common lawyer might retort, then the French system was made for a race of peasants'.

must aim for when the time is ripe. In the light of my preceding remarks I would like to conclude by submitting three preliminary statements:

1. Obviously, the draftsman of a European Civil Code must find some passage or other between the Scylla of vague generalities and the Charybdis of mathematical precision. In the law of contract he will often have to opt for a legislative style guided by the determination to seek the general principle, to express it, and to follow up in an orderly and logical development with such detail as the circumstances require. An open texture calling for judicial amplification seems preferable because the whole project might fail unless European judges were left with an area of play larger perhaps than that acceptable in any national legal system. The reluctance of our English friends to accept this style of draftsmanship must not be overestimated. In particular, we must convince them of what is, to us, self-evident, namely that the adoption of a broad standard of good faith would not amount to a discretionary licence to judges to do whatever they think 'fair' and 'just' under the circumstances. It is neither a civilian plot to undermine the certainties to which they are accustomed, nor would it put an end to the incrementalist approach to which they are used. Any Continental judge worth his salt would, I believe, subscribe to the view that the technique of reasoning from case to case is not only permissible but indeed indispensable if sense is to be made of a broad statutory provision, and some judges will even agree that a lot can be learnt from the mature and tested techniques and methods developed in this regard by their English colleagues.
2. It has been said in England that a special characteristic of a code is that within its field it is the exclusive, authoritative, and comprehensive source of the law, and that the judges must accordingly wipe out their knowledge of prior law and concentrate on the statutory words. This is, to put it mildly, an overstatement. Recourse to pre-code cases is unobjectionable in principle. It has nowadays become very rare in Germany and even rarer in France but it is, I believe, quite common in Holland whose Civil Code is of recent origin. In order to allay any fears English lawyers might have in this regard it should be made clear that references by national judges to prior national cases would be admissible if that appears useful and appropriate in order to flesh out the details of an open-textured provision of a European Civil Code.
3. If a European Civil Code were enacted it would be most desirable to entrust to a European Court the power to control its uniform application. However, provision should be made to ensure that this

power is exercised sparingly, with judicial restraint and perhaps only (a) where a conflict between the positions taken by appellate courts of different Member States can be shown to exist and/or (b) where, in the view of the European Court, the result reached by the national court is clearly incompatible with the letter or the spirit of a European Civil Code. If such a Code is to be acceptable and practicable in the real world a good deal of play must be left in the machine.

10

Reading Through a Foreign Judgment

Basil Markesinis

Introductory Remarks

At the height of the so-called 'Beef Crisis' in 1996, Mr D. F. Williams, the Secretary-General of the European Commission and Britain's most senior Civil Servant in Brussels, warned against the Europhobic sentiments which were being whipped up by certain politicians and the Press.[1] He stressed the importance which the market of the European Union presented for Britain and the wider opportunities which 'Europe' offered to the British. While some English politicians bicker, as they try to shape a Europe *à la carte* which will allow them to profit from the European Union while also competing with it, or even undermining it, businessmen and law firms have long grasped the significance of the opinions contained in Mr Williams's speech.[2] The same cannot be said of academic lawyers who only grudgingly came to recognize the importance of Community law in the late seventies and, even more, in the eighties; and, arguably, still pay inadequate attention to the significance of the rulings of the Court in Strasbourg and even less to the Supreme Courts in the major continental systems.

The current 'rush' to complete legal studies through abridged courses also means that for the bulk of our law students there is simply no time for even trying to understand our major partners, their legal systems, and their way of thinking. Not surprisingly, therefore, in this country the level of research into and study of foreign law fell—with a few notable exceptions[3]—to a rather low point in the seventies and eighties. The

[1] At a speech given in York on 7 June 1996 to the Solicitors European Group Annual Conference.

[2] 'Britain exports more to Belgium and the Netherlands than to the United States; its exports to Germany equal those to the United States and Japan combined; it exports as much to France as to the whole of the Commonwealth'. Extract from Mr Williams's speech, kindly provided to the author.

[3] Such as at Oxford and King's College, London.

contrast with countries such as Germany could thus not be more striking. A recent prolonged stay in Munich, as the guest of their University's Institute of Comparative Law, frankly left me envious of the extent to which younger colleagues there were 'shadowing', each in their respective area, developments in the common law. Not even in an old and wealthy University such as mine can we rival them in their interest in and knowledge of foreign law, nor in their library equipment. Even a committed 'European' like myself cannot help but feel a pang of envy at this superiority of the best of Germany's institutions.

The scholar, to whom this volume is dedicated, is, however, one of those shining exceptions to whom I have alluded; and this country can lay some claim to his work because of his past association with King's College, London, and Brasenose College, Oxford. A piece on how one should try to approach and understand foreign judgments is thus a fitting if modest tribute to his work which has combined so forcefully Germanic scholarship with the eclecticism and willingness to speak one's mind which characterize the flourishing legal cultures of his two adopted countries: Australia and the United States of America. This piece is addressed mainly to teachers of law whose work might, one day, influence our judges, the senior partners of the law-making process in this country; but otherwise it forms part and parcel of my lifelong effort to give the study of foreign law the place it deserves in our law curriculum.[4]

The problems which this essay will look at arise in actions which, in the common-law world, have become known as actions for 'wrongful life' and 'wrongful birth'.[5] Since the way the teacher selects cases for discussion in the classroom can determine the breadth of his sweep, it is important to explain why this subject has been chosen. Five reasons at least can be given for this choice. They are the following.

First, similar relevant decisions can be found in almost all systems. Secondly, those decisions reveal clearly the areas where the systems are similar and where they are different. Thirdly, the decisions show how the wider legal background affects the style of reasoning as well as the final outcome of the case; and this, incidentally, also points to some of the dangers of legal transplants. Fourthly, the approach in some of these

[4] On which see the author's recent *Foreign Law and Comparative Methodology: A Subject and a Thesis* (1997).

[5] Since these terms have not been used consistently, especially in the American literature, it may be desirable to state that in this essay the first—*wrongful life*—is used in a way which refers to actions brought by the handicapped child and can include, among other things, claims for emotional harm and the cost of medical expenses. *Wrongful birth* actions are brought by the parents of the affected child and, likewise, can include claims for moral and pecuniary damages. *Wrongful conception* cases, including claims for the birth of a healthy but unwanted child, are not discussed in this essay though, as will be seen below, the distinction is not always clear in the French judgments.

cases does not depend on the inductive versus deductive way of reasoning which, we have been told time and again, differentiates the two ways of thinking: the English and the Continental. Finally, they show how relatively insignificant are the legal concepts used by jurists, at any rate for the purposes of comparing the results reached by the various systems. Let us look at these points in turn, focusing, because of lack of space but also out of deference to our honorand, on German and American law though, occasionally, also drawing attention to French law.[6]

Similar Litigation Found in Most Countries

At the outset the discussion requires two or three general qualifications.

The first is the obvious one, namely, that we are talking here of the countries which were once described as belonging to the 'Western World' but nowadays are best described as advanced or industrialized countries. For, clearly, the less 'developed' countries do not have the same level of litigation for these types of cases, partly for technological reasons and partly because their inhabitants are accustomed (perhaps with greater maturity) to treating many of these incidents as part of the normal vicissitudes of life which are best handled through family cooperation rather than through state help or litigation.

Secondly, even within this group of 'industrialized' countries with which we are concerned, indigenous factors may account for a lack of case law. For example, strong religious beliefs on the morality of abortion, coupled with criminal legislation on the subject which may vary in its breadth in significant details, affect the existence of case law on our subject.[7] Belgium is a good example of a country where no case law of any significance was found for the reasons given above; the Republic of Ireland is another, and that is one reason why they have been totally excluded from the purview of this essay.[8] Overall, however, one must

[6] Italian law offers interesting analogues—e.g. Cass Civ. 22 Nov. 1993, no. 11503, 1994 *La Nuoava Giurisprudenza Civile Commentata* 690, with note by Prof. Vincenzo Zeno Zencovich—and so do mixed jurisdictions such as Louisiana. For reasons of space, however, their consideration must be omitted from this essay.

[7] In *Trib. grande inst. Evreux*, 21 Dec. 1979, Dalloz. 1981. 185 the mother's first and unsuccessful abortion took place in France. By the time the mistake was discovered, the time-limit (10 weeks from the moment of conception) for having a legal abortion in France had passed; but it was still possible for her to have a legal abortion in England which she did. The (culpable) defendant was held liable for the extra costs of this second operation.

[8] This is also true of French law, though it does not figure in the opaque judgments. (Abortion was first legalized by the 'experimental' *loi Veil* of 17 Jan. 1975 and took its definitive form with the *loi Pelletier* of 31 Dec. 1979.) For Prof. Le Tourneau, note to *Cour d' Appel*, Riom of 6 July 1989, DS 1990, 284, 286, French law does not recognize a right to abortion but merely 'tolerates' it in certain circumstances.

note a degree of similarity in the social, economic, and political backgrounds of the countries which are looked at in this essay with the consequence that the transplantability of particular legal solutions can be considered with profit.

There is a third factor which may affect the levels of litigation. It is really a variant of the previous one: a county's constitution and its interpretation[9] can also have a bearing on these cases. An illustration of this can be found in the recent German case law. Thus, the re-affirmation by the German Constitutional Court that 'the child's existence cannot, in law, be classified as damage'[10] effectively continues to bar all direct claims by the child itself.

In America the 'constitutionalization' of private law can be seen by the effect which *Roe v Wade*[11] had on this branch of the law.[12] More ominously, one might wish to speculate on the fate of the wrongful life and wrongful birth actions if abortion rights are restricted as a result of the recent and politically orchestrated reactions of the 'pro-life' movement. Though one may take heart from the fact that the moods of the American public are often transient, it must be admitted that the current picture, from the claimants' point of view, is bleak if one is to judge from a series of statutes passed by many American states in the eighties which limit or totally eliminate such causes of action.[13] This trend (though not the reasoning) stands in marked contrast to the two most recent decisions of the *Cour de Cassation*[14] which may be heralding an expansion of plaintiffs' rights. We shall return to some of these ideas later on.

Similarities between the Systems

Let us first start with the most elementary observation. Many students (and some courts) have had difficulty in deciding what harm the doctor/defendant has caused in these cases. Both the landmark German and New Jersey cases in this field clarify this point at the outset; and do so using almost identical language. Thus, the German court states that 'the

[9] Which may remain consistent or alter over a period of time. Thus, in the US, changing attitudes about the constitutionality of abortion, have affected the availability and ambit of the tort actions of 'wrongful life' and 'wrongful birth'.

[10] BVerfGE 88, 203, s D.V.6. art. 2(2), which protects 'the right to life', is, of course, the one mainly considered in these cases.

[11] 410 US 113, 93 S Ct 705.

[12] See, for instance, the frank admissions which *Procanik v Cillo*, 97 NJ 339, 478 A 2d 755 (1984), contain on this matter.

[13] A summary can be found in B. S. Markesinis, *The German Law of Torts: A Comparative Introduction*, (3rd ed., 1994).

[14] La Semaine Juridique (JCP) 1996, 156. Contrast, *Conseil d'Etat*, 14 Feb. 1997, *La Semaine Juridique*, 1997, 228.

defendant did not cause the child's deplorable condition. . . . However, in breach of his obligation towards the mother to treat her, he failed to prevent by means of an abortion the birth of a child, the health of which was severely endangered and in whose person the danger materialized in a severe form'.[15] While in *Procanik* the court said', In the present case, the plaintiffs do not allege that the negligence of the defendant doctors caused the congenital rubella from which the infant plaintiff suffers. . . . The essence of the infant's claim is that the defendant doctors wrongfully deprived his mother of information that would have prevented his birth.'[16]

Moving next to more important matters, we notice that both systems also reach the same (negative) result concerning the most difficult claim in these actions, namely the child's claim for general damages for being born.[17] The American judgment, reviewing early case law, states simply that 'policy considerations have led this court in the past to decline to recognize any cause of action in an infant for his wrongful life'.[18] The German court takes the same view and states: 'this Division believes that in cases such as the present the limits within which claims can be adjudicated according to law have been reached altogether and even exceeded'.[19] A long line of subsequent cases has not budged on this point.[20]

Thirdly, both systems are at *idem* in so far as they make sure that the child's basic needs will be taken care of through damages given to the parents. Could this solution be running counter to the philosophical stance taken by those courts which have argued that life cannot be damage and cannot justify the award of damages? It is very tempting to give an affirmative answer to this question. But this would produce an

15 BGHZ 86, 240, 250. This elementary point was, apparently, misunderstood by the *Cour administrative d'appel* of *Lyon* and its decision was thus quashed by the *Conseil d'Etat* of 14 Feb. 1997, *Semaine Juridique*, 1997, 228 (with approving note by Prof. Moreau).

16 *Procanik v Cillo* 478 A 2d 755, 760 (1984).

17 The position of French law is, probably, the same despite the 2 recent important decisions of the *Cour de Cassation* which are discussed below.

18 *Procanik v Cillo* 478 A 2d 755 760 (1984).

19 BGHZ 86, 240, 254.

20 In *BGH*, (1994) NJW 788, an attempt to argue this point on appeal was abandoned, obviously because it was hopeless. Likewise, *BGH*, (1996) NJW 2432, which involved an attempted abortion of twins which succeeded in the case of one but left the other fertilized egg alive. The most recent case—*BGH* 4 Apr. 1997, (1997) NJW 1639, reached the same conclusion by stating, somewhat blandly, that the child was not included within the protective scope of the contract between mother and doctor. This continuing case law is also giving rise to interesting literature with the result that Germany is no longer following the American debate but, in one sense, leading it. Thus, see Cramer, 'Pränatale Diagnostik und Fetaltherapie. Auswirkungen auf die Rechtsprechung des Bundesgerichtshofes zur Zeugung oder Geburt eines genetisch geschädigten Kindes als Schadensfall ('wrongful-birth action')', (1992) MedR 1, 14; Deutsch 'Das Kind oder sein Unterhalt als Schaden—Eine methodische Grundfrage des geltenden Rechts', VersR 1995, 609.

overall result which would be too harsh for most. The decision of 16 November 1993 of the *Bundesgerichtshof*[21] ingeniously wriggles through the (puritanical) obstacles laid before it by the Constitutional court.[22] This section of the judgment of the *Bundesgerichtshof* thus concludes with the following peroration:

> This Division is rather of the opinion that, especially in cases such as this, granting compensation not only has no detrimental effect on this child [honestly, how could it!] but can rather be beneficial to it, since it improves its financial situation and possibly even its standing within the family. The shifting of the maintenance burden to the attending doctor appears especially satisfactory where, due to his faulty consultation, he is co-responsible for the economic burden which, if a severely handicapped child is in constant need of care, can even threaten the family's existence.[23] As this Division has previously stated . . . even in cases where the doctor is fully liable for all extra expenditure calculated by means of an economic comparison, the parties are still burdened with the total personal care of the child and also with a certain amount of financial losses and sacrifices which they cannot transfer to the person who created the damage. The Court fails to detect any constitutionally objectionable attack on the honour of the child from this partial economic alleviation of the parents' burden'.[24]

The teacher who uses material such as this in the classroom can, of course, digress here and refer to the cat and mouse jurisdictional game which the Constitutional and Federal Court play from time to time, as the latter shows signs of 'irritation' by the generalized fiats which the former sends down from its Olympian heights. Indeed, the discerning teacher or reader obtains a clear glimpse (from judgments such as that of the *Bundesgerichtshof* of 16 November 1993) of how the Federal Court handles these 'directives'; and can, thereby at his discretion, add further dimensions to his exposition of foreign law.

Differences between the Systems

The appreciation of the two systems comes more into relief when we look at the differences between the approaches of the two courts. They lie in three areas.

Firstly, style. As I have discussed this elsewhere,[25] little need be added here. Special note, however, must be taken of two features of the cases. The first is how each court uses its respective case law; and let it be noted

[21] BGHZ 124, 128; (1994) NJW 788; *BGH*, (1997) NJW 1639.
[22] BVerfGE 88, 203, s D.V.6. See n. 10 above.
[23] This point, as well, is made by the New Jersey decision: *Procanik v Cillo* 478 A 2d 755, 762 (1984).
[24] BGHZ 124 at 144.
[25] 'A Matter of Style' (1994) 110 LQR 607.

that, yet again, we are confronted with an area of the law which in almost all countries but England has found its answers through cases and not statutes. The second is the use of the comparative method in the German case (albeit here, unfortunately, displaying a mistaken appreciation of American law).

Secondly, methodological approach. For reasons which have, again, been explained elsewhere,[26] German law often resorts to contract to perform what we would regard as tort functions. Thus, here, too, the remedies of the various plaintiffs are seen as stemming from the main contract made by the mother of the affected child with the hospital. This part of the German reasoning makes little sense to a common lawyer so little more need be said on this point.[27]

The last area of difference can be found in the substantive answers given; and here we note two major differences.

First, in German law the mother is not allowed any damages for pain and suffering except for that which 'exceeds the inflictions which accompany a birth without complications'. If, for instance, she was forced because of the damage to the foetus, to have an *abortion*, a small sum would be claimable under this heading. More importantly, 'no pecuniary damages can be awarded . . . in respect of a violation of the right to plan a family as an emanation of the general right to one's personality'.[28] By contrast, the American case allows such claims; indeed, *Roe v Wade*[29] is the *fons et origo* of the developments in this part of the law.

Secondly, the cases differ in the way they deal with the affected child's claim for special damages. Unlike the New Jersey court in *Procanik*, the German court refuses the child's claims, (for what we would call general *and* special damages), and this irrespective of whether the claim is based on contract (the child being seen, as stated above, as a third-party beneficiary of the contract made by the mother and the hospital) or in tort. On the other hand, both parents are, as already noted, compensated to the tune of all living and medical expenses incurred for the handicapped child.[30]

Despite this last-mentioned similarity, the American decision remains

[26] See, e.g., *German Law of Torts*, n. 13 above, 46f.

[27] The recent double decision of the *Cour de Cassation* of 26 Mar. 1996 (*Bull. Civ.* 1996, 109) also chose to base liability on art. 1147 CC, i.e., a contractual rule; but this has puzzled some French commentators. See, e.g., Prof. Jourdain's observations in (1996) 623 Rev. trim dr. civ. 4.

[28] BGHZ 86, 240, 248. Point re-confirmed by *BGH*, (1994) NJW 788.

[29] 410 US 113, 93 S Ct 705.

[30] BGHZ 86, 240, 247.The Federal Ct recently stressed forcefully that the damages must include both normal and extra-ordinary expenses: *BGH*, (1993) NJW 788. See also *BHG*, (1997) NJW, 1639. In France, on the other hand, the lower courts are less generous since they limit damages to extra-ordinary expenses incurred on behalf of the 'abnormal' child. See cases cited by Le Tourneau in DS 1990, 287.

more generous than the German in that damages for 'medical and other expenses' are given to the parents *and* the child. Though the American court is quick to clarify that such damages are not 'doubled',[31] in the sense that the damages to the child become payable only when the parental obligation to maintain ceases, the difference is significant since it means that in New Jersey law (but not in German) law the child can go on receiving compensation in the event of surviving its parents. In one sense, however, the extent of this generosity may be exaggerated: statistics suggest that victims with serious injuries rarely live beyond their majority.

The Influence of Legal Background on the Outcome of These Cases

Professor Fleming made this the central theme of his excellent comparative analysis of the American legal system entitled *The American Tort Process*.[32] There he showed how the differences between American and English tort law lay not in the concepts or values adopted by the two systems but on the impact that backdrop factors such as the presence or absence of a written constitution, a Bill of Rights, juries, the welfare state, a differently trained and organized legal profession, and the like had on the final outcome of the cases. His pioneering study has not yet been replicated at a Continental European level; but it is submitted that his main ideas hold true also for the comparison of English, American, and German law. This further and significant dimension to the study of the law is well-illustrated by the two cases discussed in this paper.

Thus, first, we note how the German court categorically asserts that 'Human life . . . is a legally protected interest of the highest order deserving absolute protection. No third party may determine its value'.[33] The court goes on to hold that 'it is impossible to determine . . . whether a life affected by serious handicaps as an alternative to absence of existence can be regarded at all in law as damage'. Significantly, the court alludes to its not so distant past and states 'generally, having regard to the experience under the National Socialist regime of lawlessness, the practice of the courts in the Federal Republic does not permit, with good reason, any legally relevant judgment about the value of the lives of others'.[34] Considerations such as these have led the German courts, as we have already noted, to deny the child/plaintiff any legal redress.

31. *Procanik v Cillo* 478 A 2d 755, 762 (1984).
32. (1988).
33. BGHZ 86, 240, 252.
34. BGHZ 86, 240, 252.

But there is another, more contemporary and pragmatic argument for denying the child special damages; and it is one which, in Professor Fleming's terminology, is dictated by the different national background. A hint of this comes towards the end of the German judgment where the court states that its solution to grant the parents special damages may not be enough 'once the duty to maintain [the child] comes to an end, as for instance, when they die'.[35] Here, as stated, the American solution appears, if not preferable, certainly more generous to the child; that is until one notes the way the German court completes the above-mentioned thought. 'In all these cases', says the court 'a fateful development takes place, the interruption of which cannot be demanded by the child and the effects of which must be made good by the community within the bounds of the possible'.[36] An admission here, that the social security net (effectively absent in the USA) will thus take over, but also a very important explanation for the fact that American tort law is so often more generous than its European counterparts. That this will provide only a limited relief—'within the bounds of the possible'—and will be less generous than the tort or damages system of compensation, is an undoubted fact. But as Frederick the Great said over two centuries ago: *'Der Mantel des Königs ist Warm aber Kurz'*.[37] One could not better this summary of one of the advantages and drawbacks of the social security versus the tort method of compensation!

The way the American court deals with some of the philosophical points of the case is also instructive. With regard to the child's claim for special damages, the court said:

> We need not become preoccupied . . . with . . . metaphysical considerations. Our decision to allow the recovery of extraordinary medical expenses is not premised on the concept that non-life is preferable to an impaired life, but it is predicated on the needs of the living. We seek only to respond to the call of the living for help in bearing the burden of their affliction.[38]

[35] Note here that in German law the obligation of maintenance continues for life and does not, as in many American jurisdictions, come to an end upon the child attaining majority. This difference in the family law rules may thus explain the lesser generosity of the German tort rules. To put it differently: under English common law, tort law often makes up for the defects of the law of contract, family, and succession. Yet, in German law, at the end of the day a difference still remains at the expense of the child. For what happens to it when the parents die? The solution, as we explain in the text, is found in German social security law.

[36] BGHZ 86, 240. In BGH, (1997) NJW 1639, the Federal Ct refused the child's claim on the ground that the child was not included within the scope of the contract made by its mother and the doctor. Why this is so, is not explained, though a few lines further down the court alludes to the dangers of enlarging unnecessarily the extent of medical liability.

[37] 'The cloak of the King is warm but small'.

[38] *Procanik v Cillo* 478 A 2d 755, 763 (1984).

Without too much distortion one can read into these lines the idea that something must be done about these unfortunate victims of human errors; and, in the absence of any social security provisions in the United States, tort law must perform this function. This agenda was clearly in the minds of such eminent American scholars as Fleming James Jr. who advocated with such passion the expansion of American tort law in the fifties and sixties.

If true, this is an important new optic for looking at American tort awards, for it suggests that to the extent that they deal with future medical expenses they are rightly more generous than their European counterparts. Additionally, one must also bear in mind that a large slice of the damages awarded will, in America, go to counsel under the contingent fee system which, in one respect at least, is nothing more than a way of financing litigation, alternative to but just as defective as our Legal Aid system.

The judgment in the New Jersey court in *Procanik* becomes even more interesting when it comes to give its reasons for denying the child's claim for general damages. The relevant section deserves to be quoted in full not least because it provides an open admission of how the jury system has affected the operation of tort law in practice. It said:

> Underlying our conclusion is an evaluation of the capability of the judicial system, often proceeding in these cases through trial by jury, to appraise such a claim. Also at work is an appraisal of the role of tort law in compensating injured parties, involving as that role does, not only reason, but also fairness, predictability, and even deterrence of future wrongful acts. In brief, the ultimate decision is a policy choice summoning the most sensitive and careful judgment. From that perspective it is simply too speculative to permit an infant plaintiff to recover for emotional distress attendant on birth defects when the plaintiff claims that he would be better off if he had not been born. Such a claim would stir the passions of jurors about the nature and value of life, the fear of non-existence, and about abortion. That mix is more than the judicial system can digest.[39]

This is a pragmatic and admirable assessment of conditions in the jury room, especially in the context of contemporary American politics. Arguably, it is also a more convincing explanation for denying damages than resorting to philosophical or metaphysical statements which, even when proclaimed with great conviction, do not enjoy unanimous support.

[39] ibid at 763.

Inductive and Deductive Reasoning

In his perceptive lecture entitled 'Two Ways of Thinking'[40] Lord Macmillan suggested that the Scots and continental Europeans opt for a deductive way of reasoning while the Anglo-Saxons prefer the inductive approach. 'To proceed from principles to instances is the characteristic of the one school [continental European]; to proceed from instances to principles—or perhaps not to proceed beyond instances—is the characteristic of the other [common law]'. This central theme, however, failed to bring out the fact that the two worlds, though starting from different positions, tend to meet in the middle.[41] For our purposes, therefore it is interesting to note that one can find abundant German case law, which goes from its starting premise to its conclusion, without really using either other way of reasoning.

The 'wrongful birth' and 'wrongful life' cases we have been comparing offer such an illustration; and to the extent that they do not follow the reasoning pattern one expects of them, but proceed to the finishing point in a very similar fashion, they can help bridge the gap between the two major legal families of the world by showing that even their so-called cardinal difference—their different ways of thinking—is not as omnipresent as one has been led to believe. For one must stress the fact that there are large areas of German law where the same holds true. This tends to happen where the statutory material in the Code (*Bürgerliches Gesetzbuch* (*BGB*)) is slender; and the pegging of the result on a provision in the Code tends to be more a formality than a logical necessity.

Here only a few instances of this can be given; but in all of them one can attempt the kind of interpretation or analysis of the decisional law which we have tried in this piece.

From the German law of torts we thus note that the development of contractual ways of circumventing the tort rule of vicarious liability can be included in this group.[42] This tendency to move away from the strict reasoning of the Code can also be seen in the judicial development of the general right to one's personality. The deductive reasoning which one finds here derives its force from the hierarchically superior Constitution; and that is as far as deduction goes. Yet even here one is left with the impression that the courts are trying to do justice to a problem which has become more acute in our times than it was when the Code was drafted and less concerned to pursue the Code's merciless logic to its end. In that

40 Reproduced in his book *Law and Other Things* (1938), 84.

41 To be fair to the great jurist he does say that in Scotland 'the edges of distinction have been blurred by constant contacts' with England.

42 This 'peculiarity' of German law is extensively discussed in Markesinis, n. 13 above, 685 ff & 774 ff.

sense, therefore, one could apply to these cases the American dictum that 'Law is more than an exercise in logic, and logical analysis, although essential to a system of ordered justice, should not become an instrument of injustice'.[43]

The absence in any meaningful way of any deductive or inductive logic is even more obvious in important areas of contract law which have been transformed over the last century by the courts, the result being dictated by purely practical considerations or iniquities of the solutions based on the Code. This is progressively obvious in the slow enlargement of the notion found in the Code of the impossibility of performance which culminated in the ability of German courts to readjust *(Ausgleichsanspruch)* the contractual obligations of the parties. Here, a mere perusal of the judgments shows how a reference to the Code—§ 242 *BGB*—amounts to little more than paying lip service to the notion that the courts are applying statutory law and hardly disguises their creative powers, often prompted by little more than the desire to do justice during a period of drastic dislocation of the German economy. How creative this power can be, can be seen not only by the courts' ability to move away from the wording of the contract chosen by the parties but also in the extent of their power to re-draw the contract, the entire process finding but the slightest of justifications in the Code. A number of interesting illustrations of this are given in *The German Law of Contract and Restitution.*[44] Two can be mentioned here as illustrations of the point we are trying to make. In these decisions the scant reference to the Code's provisions, coupled with the insistence, commonly found in cases turning on § 242 *BGB* that they each turn on their facts, demonstrate that neither deductive nor inductive reasoning is dominant here. Instead, the result is dictated by the court's feeling of fairness, at times coupled with an economic analysis of the circumstances of the case before it.

In 1966 the *Bundesgerichtshof*[45] heard a case involving a city dweller who had decided to live in the country and was offered the possibility of a lease of land on which the defendant (a builder) was to erect for him a pre-fabricated house. When, to the surprise of both contracting parties, the local authority declined to give building permission for the works to proceed, the plaintiff sought to recover his down payment from the builder. In such a case and in accordance with the traditional application of the doctrine of impossibility, the defendant would have been excused his obligation and the plaintiff entitled to recover the pre-paid amount

[43] *Procanik v Cillo* 478 A 2d 755 (1984).

[44] B. S. Markesinis, W. Lorenz, & G. Dannemann (1997). This work forms the first part of the author's 2-vol work, *The German Law of Obligations.*

[45] *BGH* (1966) JZ 409.

by way of restitution.[46] Yet the court went down a completely different path. For the defendant builder argued that he could build a house on another piece of land, lying nearby and having the same characteristics as the first plot (view, clean air, etc.). This land belonged to a different landowner who, argued the builder, was willing to grant the plaintiff a similar lease of it as the one the plaintiff had originally obtained of the first piece of land. The *Bundesgerichtshof* was of the view that if these assertions could be proved—it was left to a lower court to verify them—the substitute performance should be allowed to go ahead. In our view, it is entirely unconvincing that this bold result flowed deductively from any provision in the Code even though it was, on the face of things, based on the mundanely-phrased provision about good faith of that enactment.

A more recent decision of the *Bundesgerichtshof*[47] shows the extent of praetorian powers which the German courts have arrogated to themselves when solving a case through the good faith provision of the Code (§ 242 BGB). Talk of deductive reasoning once again serves no meaningful purpose in such cases.

The litigation arose after the recent re-unification of Germany when the old 'West' swallowed up the bankrupt 'East'. The case involved a buyer (defendant) and a seller (plaintiff) of a machine originally acquired from Austria. Both parties operated within the state-controlled economy of communist (the former East) Germany. The two Germanys agreed to unite in 1989; and the currency of East Germany ceased to exist in July 1990. East German marks (EDM) were converted into West German marks (WDM) at a rate of 2:1. The purchase price of the sold object was 1.7 million EDM; and before the disappearance of the EDM, the plaintiff had paid 400,000 EDM. The *Bundesgerichtshof* took the view that the two parties should share the cost of the fiscal disruption to the transaction which the unexpected political and economic changes had wrought. Pegging this result on § 242 *BGB* was only the first step. The way the court thought the sharing of the costs should be undertaken is even more intriguing; and, again, it bears no connection to deductive or inductive reasoning.[48] Arguably, the result is thus not really based on

[46] Subsequent decisions have shown a greater reluctance to order substitute performance. See *OLG*, Karlsruhe, JZ 1972, 120.

[47] *BGH*, (1993) NJW 259. Some of the post reunification cases are discussed by W. F. Ebke, 'Legal Implications of Germany's Reunification' (1990) 24 Int. Lawyer 1130.

[48] The *BGH* calculation was as follows. 1.7 EDM (purchase price) minus 400,000 EDM (deposit already paid) left 1.3 EDM unpaid. Exchanged for WDM this meant 650,000 WDM, half of which (i.e. 325,000 WDM) should be paid by the defendant (buyer). This may sound very much less than the originally agreed purchase price of 1.7 EDM but, in fact, it may have been too generous to the plaintiff (seller). For the 1.7 EDM were based on the unrealistically inflated value of the EDM against the Austrian schilling (from where, it will

any kind of 'legal principle' but on the court's desire to make some kind of economic sense of a transaction which had been completely falsified by the unexpected political developments that shook Germany during the late 1980s.

Cases such as the above are not, of course, the norm. In *The German Law of Contract and Restitution* my German co-authors and I discuss the kind of case which involves the typical German deductive syllogism which will take the judge through a series of paragraph chains before coming up with the result desired by the Code.[49] But not all decisions display these characteristics; and to the extent that one uses as teaching tools decisions which do not depend on deductive or inductive reasoning one can take the comparisons of different systems even further. For in such cases the methodological differences between common and civil law are attenuated and thus the mental block which discourages consultation of each other's law should also, in theory, be correspondingly weakened.

Concepts: Verbal Devices which Formulate Judgments but do not Really Explain Them

The starting idea is, again, Professor Fleming's. To be sure, it was formulated in the context of the common law and posited that there was often considerable equivocation between such legal concepts as duty, remoteness, foreseeability, and the like.[50] In later years, another imaginative tort scholar repeated this idea in somewhat more colourful language by maintaining that 'it is a question of aesthetics as much as anything else whether one feels that the acceptable solution is better produced by emphasizing causation or duty or damage'.[51] But all this can also be applied with profit to the comparative study of foreign law.

be remembered, the sold object was originally acquired). If one used the WDM/schilling market exchange rate, the purchase price would have been 380,000 WDM. Now it will be recalled that the plaintiff was allowed to claim 325,000 WDM; and he was allowed to keep the deposit already received (which was 400,000 EDM or, at a 2:1 exchange rate, 200,000 WDM). This means that the plaintiff (seller) ended up with a total of 525,000 WDM for a machine which, realistically priced, was worth 380,000 WDM: that covers its cost; and leaves a profit of about 40%. That the court would have used its adjusting powers under § 242 *BGB* is understandable and, possibly, even fair; that it should been so generous to the plaintiff is, however, more open to doubt.

[49] Markesinis, Lorenz, & Dannemann, n. 44 above, ch 1.

[50] 'Remoteness and Duty: The Control Devices in Liability for Negligence', (1953) 31 *Can. Bar Rev.* 471.

[51] T. Weir in P. Catala & J. A. Weir, 'Delict and Torts: A Study in Parallel' (1964–5) 39 *Tulane L. Rev.* 701, 705. However, this is not always true. Thus, in *Rondel v Worsley* [1969] 1 AC 191, e.g. the expressed policy aim of the court could not have been achieved through the mediums of causation, carelessness, or damage.

If we return to our wrongful life and wrongful birth cases and look at them from a broader comparative perspective than we have done so far, namely by bringing in French material,[52] we shall see that the results remain broadly similar even though they are justified through the use of different concepts. The French judgments in particular thus seem to be almost pre-occupied with whether the notion of causation is satisfied in these cases. Whether this is a convincing way of handling their facts is not really the issue. But what these decisions do show, especially when compared with the American or German case law, is that (in Professor Fleming's words) the concepts are only 'the means of formulating conclusions but do not often dictate them'.[53] The comparisons of the four systems we have been looking at in this essay confirms this; for though the concepts differ the results are broadly speaking very similar. Nevertheless, it is worth while discussing French law briefly because this reveals a different set of difficulties when studying foreign law.

The first problem with French law is finding out precisely what the courts allow in such cases. Sir Frederick Pollock is said to have written that 'this [i.e. Britain] is the only country in Europe where quite a large portion of important affairs, from the Constitution downwards, are worked by just doing the thing you want and saying as little as possible about it even to yourself'.[54] This statement could apply with equal force to the decisions of the highest French courts.

Until March 1996 and February 1997, the French law was basically to be found in two decisions of the Conseil d' Etat[55] and one of the *Cour de Cassation*.[56] The following dense statement from the latter, denied any *damnum* to the mother 'given that the birth of a child conceived by her could not, *in itself*, amount to a juridically recognizable harm to her, even if the birth followed an unsuccessful attempt at abortion' (emphasis added). The italicized words supply the only visible clue that the legal position is not as simple as the key statement implies at first glance; and even when the reconstruction of the picture has progressed—with the aid of the *arrêtistes*, the *conclusions du Commissaire du Gouvernement*, and the published versions of the decisions of the lower courts[57]—it is not as complete as the one which we have obtained from the German and

[52] Italian law, not discussed in this essay because of reasons of space, confirms the validity of most of the above general statements.

[53] n. 50 above, 497–8.

[54] Cited by Lord Macmillan, 'Two Ways of Thinking', n. 40 above, 82.

[55] 2 July 1982, DS 1984, 425; 27 Sept. 1989 GP 1990, 421.

[56] 25 June 1991, DS 1991, 566.

[57] We are lucky that in the present cases we have all three. In most instances, however, one or more of these 'clues' will be missing, making the reconstruction of the case very difficult. This, e.g. is the case of the very latest decision of the *Conseil d'Etat*. I have only seen extracts of the revealing *conclusions* of the *Commissaire du Gouvernement* in *le Monde*, 17 Feb. 1997.

American judgments. As instruments of teaching the law, the value of the French judgments is thus very low indeed. So, that observation apart, what is the picture which emerges from this puzzle?

The first decision of the *Conseil d'Etat* and that of the *Cour de Cassation* of 1991 dealt with the mothers' claims. We have no clue whether any claims were advanced on behalf of the children, though given that in both cases the children born were healthy, the probable answer is that none was made.[58] The words 'in itself', alluded to above, have nevertheless allowed the *arrêtistes* to argue that the mother's position might be different if *she* could prove that she had suffered *'une souffrance morale spéciale'*, for instance because the child was conceived as a result of rape;[59] or because the child was born with grave deformities.[60] However, this last-mentioned decision of the *Conseil d'Etat* was not, really, a case of 'wrongful life' or 'wrongful birth', but concerned a claim for damages for injuries inflicted by a negligent doctor to a living foetus. Thus, despite some academic[61] and journalistic[62] dicta to the contrary, the better view would appear to be that it cannot be used as a 'precedent' in genuine 'wrongful life' cases in order to justify any claim by the affected child. The validity of this view was recently confirmed by the *Conseil d'Etat* which re-stated its opposition to allowing the child (in contrast to its parents) any damages whatsoever.[63]

Thus far, the reconstruction of the French law has brought it closer to the American and German judgments than its opaque judgments would suggest at first sight. Though we cannot say how substantial this approximation is, since we do not have a comparable, settled list of compensatable headings of damage,[64] the overall picture is quite similar,

[58] In German law the doctor's liability is, in such cases, limited to that of a natural father. It is fixed by means of tariffs and tends to be much less generous than when tort law methods of compensation are used.

[59] *Cour d'Appel*, Riom, DS 1990, 284. It is interesting that the decision of the CA stressed that the plaintiff's only complaint seemed to be that the birth of her (healthy) child would make it impossible for her to lead the ordinary life of a young girl! Incidentally, there is no clue as to why she had allowed herself to become pregnant; nor indeed that she had been contributorily negligent in failing, despite medical advice, to have timeously an echo test to verify the successful conclusion of the abortion. At First Instance, this claim had led a more sympathetic court to reduce her damages by half.

[60] As is shown by *Conseil d'Etat*, (1990) 2 GP 421. In this case the liability of the hospital, which was held responsible for the doctor's negligence, amounted to just over 1m fr, 400,000fr of which had to go the Social Security for medical expenses etc. and 600,000fr to the child for *'des souffrances physiques et du préjudice esthétique'* which he suffered *'ainsi que des troubles dans ses conditions d'existence'*.

[61] Le Tourneau, DS 1991, 567.

[62] Alluded to by Prof. Moreau in his note to *Conseil d'Etat*, 14 Feb. 1997, *Semaine Juridique* 1997, 195.

[63] *Conseil d'Etat*, 14 Feb. 1997, Semaine Juridique 1997, 228.

[64] The cost of a new abortion, to complete a first and unsuccessful attempt, has been consistently allowed. See, for instance, *Trib. grande inst.* Evreux, 21 Dec. 1979, D. 1981, 185. Extraordinary expenses seem allowable; but what amounts to *'circonstances particuliermen*t

especially since the most recent cases have made it quite clear that the parents' claims for their pain and suffering and the child's cost of maintenance are recoverable.[65] Finally, this picture of similarities is completed by the fact that (until recently) there was nothing in these judgements which could be taken to support the view that any sum could be given to the child for its having been born. Indeed, the repeated insistence that life, in itself, cannot be seen as damage made this difficult to accept in any form.[66]

Yet this picture of trans-border uniformity of the law may have been shattered by two recent (1996) decisions of the *Cour de Cassation* which seem incompatible with American, English, and German law and, indeed, irreconcilable with the even more recent (1997) decision of the *Conseil d'Etat* to which we have already referred.

The first of these decisions of the *Cour de Cassation* was the result of an action brought against a 'geneticist' who advised a couple who consulted him to go ahead and procreate assuring them that the symptoms of neurological disorder that concerned them were not likely to be transmitted to any child which the mother conceived.[67] The second case concerned the familiar rubella drama. In both instances, the claims of the impaired *children* succeeded—the argument that life, itself, could not be considered as *dommage réparable* being reformulated to allow a pro-plaintiff result.[68] Once again, however, there is no complete clarity as to who is suing (the judgments only deal with the claims of the children). Opaqueness also exists as to what is being compensated. All that we have here is the almost meaningless generality 'dès lors leur

inopportunes ou exceptionnelles' is left to the courts of First Instance and access to their decisions is not always easy.

65 In *Conseil d'Etat*, 14 Feb. 1997, Semaine Juridique 1997, 228, a proper case of 'wrongful birth' claim, the court denied the parents' claim for 2m fr for pain and suffering and gave them, instead, a paltry 200,000fr. Additionally, the parents were given 5,000fr p.a. for as long as the child lived to cover the child's annual expenses.

66 Indeed, pro-life authors such as Prof. Le Tourneau wax lyrical about this. In his most helpful comment on the decision of the CA of Riom he thus states (DS 1990, 288): 'La vie même penible, est un don, peut être une grace . . . Toute notre civilisation nous souffle cet axiom et nous pousse à la chanter.' This view was, again, re-asserted by the *Commissaire du Gouvernment* in the recent decision of the *Conseil d'Etat* of 14 Feb. 1997 where Mme Pécresse said: 'Nous ne pensons pas qu'un enfant puisse se plaindre d'être né tel qu'il a été conçu par ses parents, même s'il est atteint d'une maladie incurable ou d'un défaut génétique, dès lors que la science médicale n'offrait aucun traitment pour le guérir *in utero*. Affirmer l'inverse serait juger qu'il existe des vies qui ne valent pas la peine d'être vécues et imposer à la mère une sorte d'obligation de recourir, en cas de diagnostic alarmant, à une interruption de grossesse.' *Le Monde*, 17 Feb. 1997. It is noteworthy that the judgment itself makes no allusion whatsoever to this important policy reason.

67 (1996) Bull. Civ. 109—decision of 26 Mar. 1996.

68 '[L]e dommage ne consiste pas à naitre, mais à naitre atteint des séquelles graves et irréversible d'une maladie contractée avant la naissance.' Jourdain, (1996) 623 Rev. trim. dr. civ. 4.

décision [des juges du fond] condamant le médecin à réparer les conséquences dommageables définitives des troubles de l'enfant est légalement jusitfiée.'[69] Notwithstanding these uncertainties, to foreign eyes at least, these decisions can only herald a further liberalization of the law in the direction of more extensive compensation rights, in addition to being in serious conflict with the pronouncements of the *Conseil d'Etat*.

Before we close this brief survey of French law it should be repeated that beyond the general and conclusionary statements alluded to above, the French decisions also display a particular approach to the issue of the existence of a causative link between the doctor's negligence and the harmful event. This, of course, is inevitable for a system that has no device such as a 'duty of care' under which it can subsume all the wider policy issues raised by the case. The consequence is that the notion of causation is understood in an overtly normative manner to end up with a result which we would also adopt relying on a different conceptual methodology. This point is made very clearly in the second decision of the *Conseil d'Etat* where the trier of fact held that the obstetrician's negligence did not take place in the operating-room but consisted of failing to check after the operation was over whether the whole of the foetus had been extracted from the mother's womb. The *Commissaire du Gouvernement* thus continued: 'Ainsi, peut-être certains d'entre vous trouveront-ils que le préjudice n'est pas du tout en relation avec la faute reprochée, mais bien plutôt avec la façon dont l'opération a été conduite ou avec la décision d'y recourir, c'est à dire avec des circonstances qui ne peuvent être imputées à faute à l'hôpital.' The concluding statement is full of meaning when the *Commissaire* proceeded to say that 'nous hésitons à vous proposer d'adopter un raisonnement où le droit paraît s'écarter de la justice'.[70]

The Utility of Studying Foreign Law in a Comparative Way

For some authors the major advantage of studying foreign legal systems is a cultural one. Professor Jolowicz, for instance, when asked to contribute a paper to a conference held in Paris under the general heading 'Les professions juridiques et le droit comparé' responded that 'le droit comparé ne s'avère pas de grande utilité pratique du point du vue d'un membre d'une profession juridique'.[71] Like many French authors he attributes to comparative law (a misleading term encompassing in this country foreign law and comparative methodology) 'une valeur . . . essentiellement culturelle'. That such a function exists, and must be

[69] (1996) Bull. Civ, 109. [70] (1990) GP 422. [71] (1994) 3 Rev. Int. Dr. Comp. 747.

encouraged, especially now that Roman law seems—unfortunately—to be in terminal decline in this country,[72] cannot be doubted. But this writer at any rate has seen much more in his subject than the cultural icing to a 'black-letter' law cake; and the benefits gained from this subject, in these days of increased legal borowings or legal harmonizations, are ones which, he feels, should be stressed more loudly.

Yet this view has yet to gain full acceptance in England. Thus, one learned contemporary writer who, because of his provenance, should have shared this view of a closer co-existence of the common- and civil-law worlds has, nevertheless, expressed doubts as to whether comparative law can achieve its full potential in the real world of practice. That these predictions appear to be partly prompted by (his openly admitted) resentment that comparative law may nowadays be taking good minds away from his own subject (Roman law) is no reason to pay these doubts any less attention or leave them unanswered.

Lord Rodger of Earlsferry, the author of such pessimistic predictions,[73] makes them even more poignant by linking them to Lord Goff's judgment in *White v Jones*.[74] He thus states specifically:

> I still wonder whether comparative law will achieve the kinds of practical results which are claimed for it. Certainly it will not do so if it is used as a substitute for analysis. . . . [Q]uoting chunks of law from other jurisdictions . . . can be really useful only as an aid to the proper analysis of the question before the court . . . references to the general principles adopted by Civil Law systems will usually have only a limited impact, especially since the approaches of those systems may very often diverge from one another. For this reason even Lord Goff . . . seems to have been able to draw only rather limited and inconclusive assistance from looking at Civil Law material on the concurrence of actions in *Henderson v Merrett Syndicates Ltd*.[75] In *White v Jones*[76] Lord Goff invokes German, French and Dutch law—along with Commonwealth and American authority—as support for the view that negligent solicitors should be held liable to disappointed beneficiaries. But when it comes to the actual analysis of the legal basis for any such liability, despite a fairly detailed discussion of two German doctrines, Lord Goff eventually falls back on an extension of *Hedley Byrne* as the actual foundation for his decision.[77]

[72] In Germany it has been 'saved' because it has been combined with the study of German legal history (increasingly viewed within the wider context of European culture) and comparative law. Thus, see, Reinhard Zimmermann 'Roman and Comparative Law: The European Perspective (Some Remarks apropos a Recent Controversy)', (1995) 16 (1) *Legal History* 21, esp. 27. This approach was put into practice in that author's magisterial treatise, *The Law of Obligations: Roman Foundations of the Civilian Tradition* (1992).

[73] 'Savigny in the Strand', John Maurice Kelly Memorial Lecture of 1994 (Univ. Coll. Dublin, 1995) 24. Dr Jane Stapleton has also expressed similar doubts in her learned contribution, 'In Restraint of Tort', P. B. Birks (ed.) *The Frontiers of Liability, Volume 2* (1994), 83, 101.

[74] [1995] 2 WLR 187, 194–5. [75] [1995] 2 AC 145. [76] [1995] 2 WLR 187, 194ff.

[77] 'Savigny in the Strand', n. 73 above, at 25.

This writer, who was involved in the *White v Jones*[78] litigation as a very junior junior, finds part of this criticism convincing; but he also feels that it misrepresents the respondents' efforts in that litigation.

First, no one advocated (in this or comparable cases) the introduction of 'general principles' of the civil law. What my side (the successful respondents in the case) wished to indicate, through the use of the abundant foreign material which it assembled, were three things: first, we wished to stress the fact that liability was imposed on such facts in the vast majority of legal systems. A rule which enjoys such wide recognition cannot be as bad as the appellants made out. Secondly, we wished to indicate that the rule had not caused an insupportable insurance crisis.[79] Finally, we felt that this material, so presented, could properly be taken into account by their lordships when considering English law, more precisely the heading of what is 'fair and reasonable' in the duty of care phase of the enquiry.

Is any of the above so revolutionary? In the view of this writer, the answer is clearly negative. Nor, in the light of this particular case, is it convincing to argue that the use of comparative material would *inevitably* add to the cost and length of litigation since the material which we introduced in the *White v Jones* hearing took less than an hour to present to their lordships compared to double the time that it took Counsel for the appellants to read extracts of the judgment of the judge at first instance.

Secondly, Lord Goff may not, on one reading of his judgment, have made as full use of this material as my side, at least, had hoped;[80] but merely by citing it he surely made lawyers of all kinds more aware of what another eminent British judge has described as another 'world elsewhere'.[81] We may not be ready to profit fully from that other world out there *yet*; but, as a result of changes in our legal education, we soon will be; and the earlier we start familiarizing English lawyers with the potential significance of the foreign material, the better.

Thirdly, that this material was not used as a 'substitute for analysis' can be seen in Lord Mustill's judgment and the effect the material had

[78] [1995] 2 WLR 187.

[79] An important point, given that in this case counsel for the appellants produced a series of examples from cases which the Law Society was expecting to flood the courts if the plaintiffs won in this case. Though the discussion over these cases took the better part of a morning, on closer analysis most turned out not to possess the particular features of *White v Jones* and to be able to produce their own answers in different ways. I have argued elsewhere that this prolonged discussion offered a good example of wastage of judicial time.

[80] Though he did refute the appellants' contention that a pro-plaintiff ruling would lead to unbearable insurance consequences; [1995] 2 WLR 187 at 199.

[81] Sir Thomas Bingham MR, 'There is a World Elsewhere: The Changing Perspectives of English Law', (1992) 41 *Int. Comp. L. Q.*, 513.

upon it. To be sure, the learned judge's opinion did not adopt the German reasoning. Yet, it is submitted that, if carefully read, the opinion shows how influenced the learned judge was by the Germanic debates about the contract/tort divide and the consequences which this entails. This view is reinforced if one reads Lord Mustill's opinion in conjunction with his thought-provoking article 'Negligence in the World of Finance'.[82] The doctrinal setting may thus be different in Germany; but forcing an English lawyer to try to understand it may, at the very least, be forcing him to rethink his own law. It is thus at least arguable that because Lord Mustill refrained from openly citing the German material he admitted to using, many English lawyers may have been quick to underestimate the effect this had on his thinking process.

Two additional points must be made to conclude this counter-thesis to Lord Rodger's views.

First, in his aforementioned article Lord Rodger states that what is needed is the supply of more detailed knowledge of foreign law. In this short essay and elsewhere, this author has always argued along similar lines, condemning René David's approach in his *Les grandes systèmes du droit contemporain*.[83] My two-volume work, *The German Law of Obligations*,[84] goes as far as the book of any one author can go in supplying over 250 German decisions in translated form—almost as many extracts as any English law student is likely to read in his preferred English case-book on contract and tort—and accompanies them by over one thousand pages of commentary and annotations. More importantly, if one looks at the number of works, translations, articles, and monographs, published by other scholars in the last ten years, and compares this situation with the three books my generation had when I started as a law teacher,[85] one must admit to great progress having being made in this area of the law. We would not have had this 'New Wave' had my generation not made the crucial shift from (old) civil law (i.e. Roman Law) to modern civil law (i.e. continental European law); and the scholar honoured in this *Festschrift*, admitted as much in an oft-cited book review.[86]

[82] (1992) 5 The Supr. C. J, 1–41.

[83] The English version of this work is *Major Legal Systems in the World Today: an Introduction to the Comparative Study of Law*, 3rd edn (1985).

[84] See n. 44 above; vol 2 is entitled *The German Law of Torts* (1997).

[85] E. J. Cohen's *Manual of German Law*; M. S. Amos & F. P. Walton's, *French Law* and A. R. von Mehren's *Comparative Law*.

[86] 'Comparative Law of Torts', (1984) 4 *OJLS* 235 where, referring to the Roman material which had been included in a book co-authored with the late Prof. F. H. Lawson, he wrote, 'the whole retention of the Roman law relic surely owes more to nostalgia than to functional justification'. The book reviewed is entitled *Tortious Liability for Unintentional Harm in the Common Law and the Civil Law* (1982) and is a revamped edition of Prof. Lawson's classic *Negligence in the Civil Law* (1950).

A further point, related to the above argument, must also be stressed. The new (translated and annotated) material does not merely describe the foreign systems but facilitates more active use of their case law; and in this piece I have tried to suggest ways of 'milking' this material of its rich contents. Thus, I have tried to show how, starting from decisions, we can come to appreciate the common factual backgrounds and the remarkable similarity of solutions. I have also suggested that studying foreign law through cases also gives the teacher the chance to compare judicial styles, reflect on the sources of law and the use made of them by various courts, and also look at the relationship of the civil courts to the constitutional jurisdictions which are growing ever more powerful in most Continental countries. With slightly more effort on the part of the teacher, delays in litigation, levels of compensation, and the interrelationship of tort awards and social security awards can also be discovered through this material. A 'lecture' on one case and its parallels in two or three jurisdictions can thus easily be spun out over two or three hours; and if the same is done systematically over a forty- or sixty-hour course on, say, foreign tort law or contract law, my experience has shown that the teacher will have imparted a great deal of knowledge on foreign law to his autochthonous student. More importantly, that material will already be in a shape and form that will make it more user-friendly to others who may subsequently wish to refer to it. All this, I suggest is both interesting and useful; and, as I already said, methodologically it is very different in style to what was available some twenty-five years ago.

This brings me to my last point: the receptivity of the judges of the future. I regard this as a very important issue and, again, regret to sense a difference of views between such an eminent jurist as Lord Rodger and myself. I am, however, encouraged to take issue with the learned Lord not only because I find comfort in the fact that others, as eminent as Lord Rodger, have differed with him on this issue. Thus Professor Koopmans, Advocate-General of the Dutch Supreme Court and former (Dutch) Judge at the Court of the European Communities, recently confirmed that what I have been advocating for a very long time is, actually, already happening in foreign supreme courts.[87] And if to this statement my English readers retort 'yes, it may be happening abroad but it cannot happen here', let me explain why I think that such an assertion will be proved wrong.

First, some of Lord Goff's contemporaries and most of his successors are likely to have a university *legal* education behind them, something which was not true as recently as thirty years ago. It is logical, therefore,

[87] 'Comparative Law and the Courts' (1996) 45 *Int. Comp. L.Q.* 55.

to expect such judges, nourished on textbooks as never before, to share a greater receptiveness to academic doctrine than their predecessors did.

Secondly and more importantly, we must soon be approaching a new crop of judges who will have visited Europe, not as part of some grand tour during their youth, a tour of the kind that was fashionable in the eighteenth and ninteenth centuries, but as participants in some kind of short or more sophisticated Erasmus-type programme. Take, for instance, the four-year double degree which King's College London has been running for years with Paris One. It attracts students at least as good as the best Oxbridge recruits; and it supplies then with a truly first-class double training, accompanied by a technical linguistic proficiency in both languages. Will lack of languages be an obstacle to such a generation of judges? And if knowledge of the French and German languages is likely to become more widespread, will the same reluctance to look at foreign material continue? The truth of the matter is that there is out there a whole new generation of excellent legal minds waiting to come 'to power' without any of the hang-ups (cultural or political) of the older generation but, on the contrary, conscious of the respective strengths and weaknesses of a number of European legal cultures.

We are creating such a generation of European lawyers in Oxford; and to anyone who argues that it will be along time before they have the influence on our law that I am predicting, I say that I am prepared to wait. And, while waiting, I will go on trying to devise better ways of introducing these new recruits to the mysteries and fascination of foreign law and enticing them to visit the foreign countries and work in them. What adversity in life gave to John Fleming, we would like to supply in a more normal and congenial manner to the young Oxonians of today in the hope that this might give them a mind as agile and as open as his.

11

Quieta Movere

Interpretative Change in a Codified System

Reinhard Zimmermann and *Nils Jansen*

Introduction

The present essay has been prompted by the recent renunciation of the maxim *error iuris non excusat* in the law of restitution of a number of common-law jurisdictions and mixed legal systems.[1] Ever since Lord Ellenborough's ill-considered decision in *Bilbie v Lumley*[2] a plaintiff has been denied recovery of a transfer which he had made as a result of a mistake of law. Sustained criticism of this rule finally persuaded the Canadian Supreme Court,[3] the High Court of Australia,[4] the Appellate Division of the Supreme Court of South Africa,[5] and the Scottish Court of Session[6] to abandon it. Within a period of six years these four courts thus reversed the position which they had previously adopted and removed the bar on restitution for mistakes of law. The House of Lords is very likely to follow suit. This change of opinion has induced a prominent English author to raise fundamental questions of legal methodology.[7] If a mistake of law is no longer taken to constitute a bar to recovery, any transfer made in accordance with what is generally accepted to be the law may be reclaimed whenever the courts

[1] For a detailed discussion, see Reinhard Zimmermann & Phillip Hellwege, '"Error iuris non excusat" und das "law of restitution": Zur Karriere einer gemeinrechtlichen Maxime in der Welt des common law', in *Festschrift für Bernhard Großfeld* (1999) 1331ff.

[2] (1802) East 469; 102 ER 448.

[3] *Air Canada v British Columbia* (1989) 59 DLR (4th) 161.

[4] *David Securties Pty Ltd v Commonwealth Bank of Australia* (1992) 175 CLR 353.

[5] *Willis Faber Enthoven (Pty) Ltd v Receiver of Revenue* 1992 (4) SA 202 (A).

[6] *Morgan Guaranty Trust Co. of New York v Lothian Regional Council* (1995) SLT (Reports) 299.

[7] Peter Birks, 'Konkurrierende Strategien und Interessen: Das Irrtumserfordernis im Bereicherungsrecht des common law' (1993) 1 *Zeitschrift für Europäisches Privatrecht* 554.

subsequently decide to interpret the law differently. The security of receipts, so it is argued,[8] will be gravely jeopardized in view of the flood of unjustified enrichment claims that may be unleashed as a result of interpretative change. May this tide be stemmed by abandoning the 'declaratory' theory of legal change? In terms of that theory, the courts are merely providing a new, and better, restatement of the existing law, when they overrule an earlier decision.

If, on the other hand, the courts openly assert that they are laying down new law rather than correcting a mistaken view of what has always been the law, there is no room for plaintiffs who earlier took the other view to claim that they have acted under a mistake of law. They acted in accordance with what was then (but is now no longer) the law.[9] But would the courts, under these circumstances, not usurp the function of the legislature and relinquish their traditional role as interpreters of the law? Arguably, the courts have done that anyway and a new, corrective theory of legal change resulting from judicial development of the law would merely acknowledge this more honestly.[10] Essentially, therefore, this debate focuses on what the courts are actually doing when they apply the law, on how the reasonable expectations of the parties to past transactions may be protected, and on how, generally, the requirements of legal certainty and flexibility of interpretation may be balanced.

Do these questions only arise in jurisdictions based on common law or do they also confront lawyers in codified legal systems? This question should no longer be surprising in view of what J. P. Dawson has described as the 'case-law revolution' that has occurred, in the course of this century, in one of the major civilian jurisdictions governed by a code of private law.[11] Nevertheless, certain doubts are still persisting as to whether the legal methods employed in common-law and civil-law legal systems are indeed converging[12] or whether we are faced with an insurmountable epistemological divide.[13] It is therefore proposed to look at

[8] Birks, n. 7 above, 567 f.

[9] See Thomas Probst, *Die Änderung der Rechtsprechung: Eine rechtsvergleichende, methodologische Untersuchung zum Phänomen der höchstrichterlichen Rechtsprechungsänderung in der Schweiz (civil law) und den Vereinigten Staaten (common law)* (1993) 439ff.

[10] Professor Birks, in this context, draws attention to a remark by Lords Goff and Browne-Wilkinson in *Woolwich Building Society v IRC* (1993) AC 70 at 168 and 196 (one of the seminal cases of recent years reshaping the English law of restitution), according to which the decision creates new law rather than merely corrects a mistaken view of what has always been the law.

[11] John P. Dawson, *The Oracles of the Law* (1968) 432ff.

[12] See generally, e.g., B. S. Markesinis (ed.), *The Gradual Convergence: Foreign Ideas, Foreign Influences, and English Law on the Eve of the 21st Century*, 1994; and see the interesting observations by Lord Mackenzie-Stuart, in David L. Carey Miller & Reinhard Zimmermann (eds.), *The Civilian Tradition and Scots Law: Aberdeen Quincentenary Studies* (1997) 351ff.

[13] This has been argued by Pierre Legrand, 'European Legal Systems Are Not Converging', (1996) 45 *Int. & Comp. L. Q.* 52; idem, 'Legal Traditions in Western Europe: The

the phenomenon of legal change in Germany, as effected by decisions at the highest appellate level in the field of private law. The relevant legal problems arise in cases where the Federal Supreme Court (or the Federal Labour Court) unexpectedly adopts a new interpretation of a legal rule and, even more pertinently, where this involves the overruling of a precedent which had previously been established.[14]

Seven Case Studies

Case 1: Is an Architect 'Rendering Services'?

The German law of extinctive prescription is characterized by an extraordinary degree of differentiation among prescription periods for individual types of claims.[15] Thus, for instance, there are a great variety of 'everyday life' transactions which the draftsmen of the German Civil Code (*BGB*) exempted from the regular prescription period of thirty years. In § 196 *BGB* they listed, somewhat clumsily, all claims they wanted to be subject to a two-year period, among them the claims of those who make a business of rendering services for the remuneration due to them from their business ('die Ansprüche . . . derjenigen, welche . . . die Leistung von Diensten gewerbsmäßig betreiben, wegen der ihnen aus dem Gewerbebetriebe gebührenden Vergütungen').[16] In a decision handed down on 25 April 1966 this rule was held not to apply to the claim of architects for their professional fees.[17] The architects' contract constituting a contract for work (*Werkvertrag*) rather than a contract for services (*Dienstvertrag*),[18] the plaintiff's claim could not be

Limits of Commonality', in R. Jagtenberg, E. Örücü & A. J. de Roo (eds.), *Transfrontier Mobility of Law* (1995) 63; cf. also Geoffrey Samuel, *On Obligations and Legal Remedies* (1995) 417ff.

[14] The following standard abbreviations are used, concerning German law, in this essay: *BGB*: *Bürgerliches Gesetzbuch* (German Civil Code); *GG*: *Grundgesetz* (Basic Law); *ZPO*: *Zivilprozeßordnung* (Code on Civil Procedure); *AGBG*: *Gesetz zur Regelung des Rechts der Allgemeinen Geschäftsbedingungen* (Standard Contract Terms Act); *EGBGB*: *Einführungsgesetz zum Bürgerlichen Gesetzbuch* (Introductory Act to the German Civil Code); *BGH*: *Bundesgerichtshof* (Federal Supreme Court); *BAG*: *Bundesarbeitsgericht* (Federal Labour Court); *NJW*: *Neue Juristische Wochenschrift*. For more information, see Reinhard Zimmermann, 'An Introduction to German Legal Culture', in Werner F. Ebke & Matthew W. Finkin (eds.), *Introduction to German Law* (1996) 1 (with an appendix on German legal materials and on how to use them, 35ff.).

[15] For all details, see Reinhard Zimmermann, 'Extinctive Prescription in German Law', in Erik Jayme (ed.), *German National Reports in Civil Law Matters for the XIVth Congress of Comparative Law in Athens* (1994) 153.

[16] § 196 I, no. 7 *BGB*.

[17] BGHZ 45, 223 at 225ff.

[18] See, e.g., Hans Hermann Seiler, in *Erman, Handkommentar zum Bürgerlichen Gesetzbuch*, (9th ed., 1993) Vor § 631, nn. 10ff.; Frank Peters, in *Staudinger, Kommentar zum Bürgerlichen Gesetzbuch* (13th ed., 1994) Vorbem. zu §§ 631ff., nn. 112 ff. The distinction between

classified as resulting from the 'rendering of services'. The Federal Supreme Court thus interpreted the crucial term used in § 196 I, no. 7 *BGB* in a technical sense and also refused to countenance an application *per analogiam*. As a result, the general prescription period of thirty years (§ 195 *BGB*) was held to apply.

Only a few years later, on 6 July 1972, the Federal Supreme Court was confronted with the same question once again. An architect sued for his fees. He had sent out his invoice in December 1963. On 30 March 1965 he filed a lawsuit against his debtor, but since he delayed the advance payment of costs required by the court, the summons was only served on the defendant on 8 May 1968. Prescription of his claim would have been interrupted on 30 March 1965 if the summons had been served on the defendant 'shortly after' the filing of the lawsuit (*demnächst*: § 270 III *ZPO*). May 1968, however, was much more than 'shortly after' 30 March 1965, and consequently a period of more than four years had elapsed since the fees had become due (December 1963). This should not have mattered in view of the fact that the thirty-year period of § 195 *BGB* had been held to apply in BGHZ 45, 223.

But now the Federal Supreme Court reversed its opinion.[19] 'Rendering of services', in terms of § 196 I, no. 7 *BGB* was, after all, to be understood in a wide and untechnical sense so that it did not matter whether the fees had been earned under a contract for work or services. The Federal Supreme Court drew attention to § 631 II *BGB* according to which the object of a contract for work may be the 'production or alteration of a thing, or any other result to be brought about by labour or the rendering of services'. The Code itself thus appears to acknowledge that services may be rendered in terms of a contract for work. The new interpretation was also supported by policy considerations. Since it can be difficult to distinguish a contract for services from a contract for work, it would be awkward to subject the respective claims for remuneration to two radically different prescription periods. And the *ratio legis* underlying the short period of § 196 I, no. 7 *BGB*[20] also, of course, applies to claims based on contracts for work. Here, no less than under a contract for services, all claims should be settled within a reasonably short period of time. The Federal Supreme Court did not fail to appreciate

a contract for work and a contract for services reflects the Pandectist subdivision of *locatio conductio* into *locatio conductio operis* and *operarum*; for details, see Reinhard Zimmermann, *The Law of Obligations: Roman Foundations of the Civilian Tradition* (paperback ed. 1996) 338ff., 384ff., 393ff.

[19] BGHZ 59, 163 at 164ff.; cf. also *BGH*, (1983) *NJW* 870f.; Helmut Heinrichs, in *Palandt, Bürgerliches Gesetzbuch* (56th ed., 1997) § 196, nn. 12ff.

[20] Cf. Motive, in Benno Mugdan, *Die gesammten Materialien zum Bürgerlichen Gesetzbuch für das Deutsche Reich*, vol 1 (1899) 516ff.

that it had abandoned its own precedent of less than seven years before (plus a long line of earlier decisions).[21] It did not, however, appear to regard that as a problem. No word of consolation was offered to the architect whose claim was now worth nothing and who had lost a lawsuit lasting more than four years.

CASE 2: BLANKET DECLARATION OF SURETYSHIP

§ 766, 1 *BGB* requires that the surety's declaration of intention to conclude a contract of suretyship be in writing. Until 1996, a long line of decisions dating back to the Imperial Supreme Court had consistently held that formal requirement to be complied with should the surety subscribe a document subsequently completed by a third party under the oral authorization of the surety.[22] A so-called blanket declaration of suretyship could thus be converted into a valid document in terms of § 766, 1 *BGB*. This had been expressly confirmed by the Federal Supreme Court as late as 1984[23] and a decision from 1991 was clearly based on that assumption.[24] Most standard textbooks and commentaries endorsed that view without further ado.[25] The main argument advanced in favour of it was the wording of § 126 I *BGB* which is applicable to all cases where the Code requires writing (including § 766, 1 *BGB*): the document has to be signed by the person issuing the document in his own hand by signature of his name, or by his mark being notarially authenticated.

In a decision handed down on 26 February 1996, however, the Federal Supreme Court reversed its opinion.[26] Attention was now drawn to the purpose of the form requirement: it is designed to provide an opportunity for thoughtful consideration and thus to prevent rash and precipitate suretyship declarations. These objectives, the Court argued, can only be achieved if the document contains not only a declaration of intention to stand surety, but also specifies the creditor, the main debtor, and the debt which is to be secured. In order to comply with the formal requirement, 'the surety must not only sign a document in which his intention to assume responsibility for someone else's debt is clearly apparent. The document also has to specify the risk assumed and thus to make the surety aware of this risk at the moment of his declaration'.[27]

[21] BGHZ 59, 163 at 166, referring to a *jahrzehntelange Rechtsprechung*; see the references at 164.

[22] Cf. RGZ 57, 66 at 69; RGZ 76, 99 at 100; RGZ 78, 26 at 29; *BGH*, (1962) *Wertpapier-Mitteilungen* 575; *BGH*, (1968) *NJW* 1131.

[23] *BGH*, (1984) *NJW* 798.

[24] *BGH*, (1992) *NJW* 1448 at 1449.

[25] Karl Larenz & Claus-Wilhelm Canaris, *Lehrbuch des Schuldrechts*, vol II/2, (13th ed., 1994) 5 f.; Seiler, n. 18 above, § 766, n. 15.

[26] BGHZ 132, 119 at 122ff.

[27] Ibid at 123.

Attention was also drawn to the strict formalities laid down in the Consumer Credit Act, evidencing the quest for an increased protection of the weaker party.[28] In terms of §§ 6 I and 4 I of the Consumer Credit Act the signature on a blank document is generally recognized as being insufficient.

Again, the Federal Supreme Court was quite aware of the fact that it deviated from a long line of earlier decisions. This time, however, the problem of whether the new approach could immediately be implemented and be applied to the case at hand was discussed at some length.[29] § 242 *BGB*, the famous general clause focusing on the notion of good faith, was mentioned as a possible obstacle.[30] Apart from that, in the opinion of the Federal Supreme Court, a party only deserved to be protected if he had (i) reasonably relied on the continuation of the old approach and if (ii) application of the new approach to his case would constitute an unacceptable hardship, even in view of the reasonable interests of the other party. In this context the Court referred, once again, to § 242 *BGB* as well as to the views of the Federal Constitutional Court concerning retroactive legislation.[31]

Case 3: How Comprehensive is a Comprehensive Suretyship Clause?

If a contract of suretyship is concluded, there has to be certainty as to the main debt for which the surety assumes responsibility.[32] After all, the surety has to be able to evaluate the risk involved in the transaction. § 765 II *BGB*, however, specifically permits a contract for a future debt. The requirement of certainty of the main debt is met, in cases of this kind, if it is possible to determine, at the moment when the main debt comes into existence, whether the latter is covered by the contract of suretyship or not. Even a surety's promise to be responsible for all debts of a specific debtor to a specific creditor is therefore reconcilable with the certainty requirement, since it is quite clear which debts are to be covered by the suretyship.[33] Thus, until very recently, and in spite of vigorous criticism,[34] the Federal Supreme Court consistently regarded

[28] BGHZ 132, 119 at 126.

[29] Ibid at 129ff.

[30] Reference is made to a number of cases where the Federal Supreme Court has regarded it as conduct infringing the principles of good faith to invoke the invalidity of a contract for failing to comply with the required formalities. Cf. Heinrichs, n. 19 above, § 125, nn. 16 ff.; Othmar Jauernig, in *Jauernig, Bürgerliches Gesetzbuch* (7th ed., 1994) § 125, VII.

[31] BGHZ 132, 119 at 129f.

[32] Cf., e.g., Norbert Horn, 'Globalbürgschaft und Bestimmtheitsgrundsatz', in Walter Gerhard, Wolfram Henckel, Joachim Kilger & Gerhard Kreft (eds.), *Festschrift für Franz Merz* (1992) 217 at 221; Mathias Habersack, in *Münchener Kommentar zum Bürgerlichen Gesetzbuch*, vol 5 (3rd ed., 1997) § 765, n. 68.

[33] BGHZ 130, 19 at 21f.

[34] Horn, n. 32 above, 219ff.; Larenz & Canaris, n. 25 above, 6ff.

this kind of comprehensive suretyship (*Globalbürgschaft*) as permissible, provided that it was confined to debts arising from a specific business relationship between the main debtor and one of his creditors.[35] As a result, a type of suretyship contract very popular with banking institutions was regarded as acceptable (even if standard contract forms had been used!): the surety undertakes to be liable for all debts arising under the banking relationship between the bank and the main debtor.

This approach, favouring the interests of the banks, was abandoned in 1995 when the Federal Supreme Court decided to bring § 9 *AGBG* to bear upon standard contract forms containing comprehensive suretyship clauses.[36] § 9 *AGBG* is the equivalent of article 3 of the EC Directive on Unfair Contract Terms[37] and provides for open control of standard contract terms under the auspices of good faith. The Federal Supreme Court, in this context, pointed to the provision of § 767 I 3 *BGB*, according to which the surety's obligation is not extended by any legal transaction entered into by the main debtor after the conclusion of the contract of suretyship. This rule was taken to imply that nobody but the surety himself may determine the range of his liability: he must not be subject to any form of heteronomous disposition. This, in turn, means that the surety's liability must be limited. For, the Court argued, this rule

> is not only to be applied if a limitation has been specifically agreed upon. Apart from the fact that the main debt must be determined, the Code takes for granted, in the interest of the surety's due protection, a financial limitation of his liability. This is supposed to prevent the main debtor and the creditor from arbitrarily extending the range of the suretyship. An unlimited extension of the surety's obligation as a result of the arrangements by third parties is inconsistent with the elementary protection of the surety's private autonomy.[38]

May the new approach be applied to contracts concluded in the past? Once again, the Federal Supreme Court devoted a number of paragraphs to this question to which it gave, in principle, an affirmative answer.[39] An exception was to be recognized if the party detrimentally affected by the new approach could reasonably rely on the continuation of the old one and if the protection of such reliance deserved priority after it had been balanced against the opposing interests of the other party and against the interests of the community at large. Whoever uses standard contract terms does not, however, deserve to be protected: he carries the

[35] Cf. BGHZ 25, 318 at 321; *BGH*, (1990) *NJW* 1909 at 1910; *BGH*, (1992) *NJW* 896 at 897; BGHZ 125, 206 at 208.
[36] BGHZ 130, 19 at 23ff.
[37] Dir. 93/13 [1993] OJ L95/29; concerning its implementation in Germany, see Helmut Heinrichs, 'Das Gesetz zur Änderung des AGB-Gesetzes', (1996) *NJW* 2457.
[38] BGHZ 130, 19 at 26f., 32ff.
[39] BGHZ 132, 6 at 11f.

risk that the terms drafted by him are valid.[40] The Federal Supreme Court expressly left undecided the question of whether a different view might have to be taken in cases where the adoption of the new approach resulted from a general change in evaluation (*allgemeiner Beurteilungswandel*).[41]

Case 4. Changing the Standard Terms of Employment

The conditions of employment in a large enterprise are usually determined by a set of standard terms which become part and parcel of the individual employment contracts.[42] Occasionally, the employer subsequently wishes to change these standard terms to the detriment of his employees. This may happen, for instance, if the economic position of the enterprise becomes precarious. In a long line of decisions, the Federal Labour Court had consistently held that the employer could indeed effect such change, albeit only by means of a shop agreement[43] with the works council of his enterprise.[44] In 1982, there was a sudden reversal of opinion, first by the VIth Division of the Federal Labour Court.[45] It was endorsed by a decision of the Combined Divisions of that Court in 1986: the individual employment contract may not be changed by means of a shop agreement to the detriment of the employee, even if the point at issue was contained in the standard terms of employment, as incorporated into the individual contract.[46] Once again, the question arose whether the new approach was applicable even though the parties did not (and could not) know about the decision of the VIth Division, let alone the decision of the Combined Divisions of the Federal Labour Court, when they concluded their shop agreement. It was answered in the negative. Strict application of the new approach, so it was argued,[47] would effectively entail retroactivity which, in turn, would pay insufficient attention to the protection of reasonable reliance on the continuation of the old approach. The need for such protection of reliance has to be balanced against the interests of the employees in

[40] Once again, the Federal Supreme Court discussed the question of whether there were any obstacles, on the level of constitutional law, to giving what amounts to retrospective effect to the new approach, by applying it to the case at hand.

[41] BGHZ 132, 6 at 11. Generally on 'Recent Developments in German Suretyship Law', see Mathias Habersack & Reinhard Zimmermann, in John Cairns & Olivia Robinson (eds.), *Festschrift for Alan Watson* (in preparation).

[42] On *allgemeine Arbeitsbedingungen*, see generally Reinhard Richardi, in *Staudinger, Kommentar zum Bürgerlichen Gesetzbuch* (12th ed., 1993) Vorbem. zu §§ 611ff., nn. 223ff.

[43] *Betriebsvereinbarung*; for details, see Richardi, n. 42 above, Vorbem. zu §§ 611ff., nn. 1429ff.

[44] BAGE 27, 252; BAGE 23, 257; BAGE 27, 194; BAGE 29, 379; BAGE 32, 293; BAGE 34, 238; BAGE 41, 118.

[45] See *BAG*, (1991) *Der Betrieb* 914 at 916.

[46] *BAG*, (1991) *Der Betrieb* 914.

[47] Ibid at 916f.

having the new regime applied to their contracts and against the interests of the community at large in maintaining the rule of law. In the present case, the protection of reliance on the part of both employer and works council was held to prevail, with the result that the shop agreement in the present case (which had reduced the retirement benefits as promised in the standard terms of employment) had to be treated as effective.

Case 5: Invalidity of a Consultancy Agreement

In a decision handed down on 25 March 1991[48] the Federal Supreme Court had to deal with a consultancy agreement of a stock company with one of the members of its supervisory board. In terms of § 114 I of the Stock Company Act (*Aktiengesetz*) such agreements may only relate to matters outside the range of activities of the supervisory board. In the present case the contract contravened the provision of § 114 I of the Stock Company Act, but it had been concluded before the person concerned had become a member of the supervisory board. The Federal Supreme Court held the contract to have been valid originally but to have become invalid at the moment of acquisition of membership of the board. The Court was, however, prepared to grant protection to the consultant:

> [Invalidity of the contract] is a legal consequence which, in the past, could neither be gauged from the statute nor from the views propounded in legal literature. From the latter one can discern a general consensus that §§ 113, 114 of the Stock Company Act are not applicable to these types of contracts. That a diverging view might be taken by the Federal Supreme Court (which had not, hitherto, pronounced upon the matter) could not, therefore, readily be anticipated. Thus, it is justified, in principle, to treat a contract that had previously been concluded as valid even for the time of membership of the supervisory board.[49]

Mere reliance upon the continuation of the legal position as it presented itself before the decision of the Federal Supreme Court is not, however, sufficient to treat the contract as valid. The verdict of invalidity would also have to affect the consultant much more seriously than the Company in economic terms. This is the case, particularly, where his entire professional existence is based upon the consultancy agreement.[50] Ultimately, therefore, the decision depends upon a balancing of interests with the result that invocation of the invalidity of the contract on the part of the company may constitute an infringement of the precepts of good faith.

[48] BGHZ 114, 127. [49] Ibid at 136f. [50] Ibid at 137.

Case 6: Transparency in Standard Contract Terms

The Standard Terms Act of 1977 empowers German courts to strike down unfair contract terms. Over the years, a large body of case law has been developed on the basis of this Act, particularly of the general clause contained in § 9.[51] In terms of this core provision, any clause is invalid which one of the parties has introduced into the contract and by means of which the other party, contrary to the precepts of good faith, is placed at an unreasonable disadvantage. In a decision handed down on 24 November 1988[52] the Federal Supreme Court introduced a new and interesting criterion in order to determine whether a set of clauses contained in the standard contract terms imposed by a mortgage bank was in accordance with the precepts of good faith. According to one of those clauses, the borrower had to pay a certain sum of money in quarterly instalments. Each instalment contained the interest due at that moment and also a part repayment of the capital sum. As a result of this clause, the capital sum still due was thus reduced every three months. Somewhat surprisingly, in view of the repayment conditions, the standard contract terms contained another clause according to which the interest had to be calculated on the basis of the capital sum due at the end of the previous year. This way of calculating the interest is, of course, distinctly disadvantageous to the borrower, since he is required to pay interest on a capital sum part of which he has already repaid. Nevertheless, the Federal Supreme Court did not object to the clause as such: in the interests of commercial convenience, banks not infrequently calculate interest rates on the basis of fictitious capital sums.[53] But since the borrower could only gauge its disadvantageous effect from reading it in conjunction with another, seemingly unrelated, clause the Federal Supreme Court held it to be invalid for lack of transparency (*Transparenzgebot*).[54] Insufficiently transparent standard contract terms—this is the premise of the Court's argument—may be unfair in terms of § 9 of the Standard Terms Act. This reasoning was, at first, vigorously criticized but has, in the meantime, been endorsed by Art. 5 of the EC Directive on Unfair Contract Terms in Consumer Contracts, which provides the background for the interpretation of the German Standard Terms Act, as revised in 1996.[55]

Of course, this new criterion for policing unfair standard contract terms, came as a surprise to mortgage banks. But the Federal Supreme Court did not hesitate to apply it to the case at hand, since anybody

[51] See, e.g., Hein Kötz, in *Münchener Kommentar zum Bürgerlichen Gesetzbuch*, vol 1 (3rd ed., 1993) § 9 *AGBG*; Heinrichs, n. 19 above, § 9 *AGBG*.

[52] BGHZ 106, 42.

[53] Ibid at 47f.

[54] Ibid at 49.

[55] See, e.g., Heinrichs, n. 19 above, § 9 *AGBG*, n. 15.

using standard contract terms always has to carry the risk that some or other clause might be declared invalid, even if it was used for a considerable time without any objection being raised.[56] That the defendant (and possibly many other mortgage banks) were now faced with unjustified enrichment claims concerning the excess payment of interest did not trouble the Court. The defendant had actually already conceded the claim in case the relevant clause was declared invalid. Whether possibly the short prescription period of § 197 *BGB* (four years) applied was left open.[57]

CASE 7: THE RENAISSANCE OF *LAESIO ENORMIS* IN INSTALMENT CREDIT TRANSACTIONS

In devising the general law of contract, the draftsmen of the German Civil Code proceeded from the assumption that the result of fair negotiations is likely also to be substantially fair. Thus, the courts only have to be concerned with the fairness of the bargaining process. More particularly, the will of the contracting parties must not have suffered from a defect induced by fear, fraud, or mistake. Of course, the content of a contract may not be illegal or immoral. But apart from that, there should be no judicial interference.[58] Today, however, the courts are no longer prepared to accept the results of such far-reaching party autonomy and thus German law has witnessed a surprising renaissance of the notion of equality in exchange.[59] An important tool in this process of transformation was the provision of § 138 *BGB*, another one of its famous general clauses. § 138 I *BGB* declares contracts *contra bonos mores* to be void. Even a striking disproportion in value between performance and counter-performance may not, however, be regarded as infringing the *boni mores*. This is apparent from § 138 II *BGB* which requires, apart from such disproportion, exploitation of the distressed situation, inexperience, lack of judgmental ability, or grave weakness of will of the party that has been overcharged.

Yet, contrary to the intentions of the draftsmen of the *BGB*, the courts have begun to water down these additional, restrictive requirements contained in § 138 II *BGB* and even to sidestep them by falling back on § 138 I *BGB*. This has happened particularly prominently in a number of cases concerning loans repayable by instalments and granted by

[56] BGHZ 106, 42 at 52. [57] Ibid at 53.

[58] See, e.g., Ernst Kramer, in *Münchener Kommentar zum Bürgerlichen Gesetzbuch*, vol 1 (3rd ed., 1993) Vor § 145, nn. 2ff.

[59] See, e.g., the discussion by Theo Mayer-Maly, in *Münchener Kommentar zum Bürgerlichen Gesetzbuch*, vol 1 (3rd ed., 1993) § 138, nn. 98ff.; Zimmermann, n. 18 above, 268ff.

instalment credit institutions.[60] Such credit transactions may be *contra bonos mores*, it was held, if there is an obvious disproportion between the obligations of the bank and of the borrower, and if the bank displayed a reprehensible attitude, either by deliberately exploiting the weaker economic position of the other party, or by grossly negligently failing to realize that the latter entered into the contract only because of his precarious situation. This subjective component, however, is of an almost fictitious character, since the courts are prepared to draw inferences from the objective circumstances of the contract (especially the disproportion in values) without requiring specific evidence as to whether the conduct in question was wilful or grossly negligent. Of central importance, therefore, is the interest rate charged by the bank, and here the rule has been established that the effective rate of interest must not exceed the current interest rate by more than 100 per cent (relatively) or 12 to 13 per cent (absolutely).

The first of these decisions dated from the latter part of 1978, and consequently the instalment credit institutions were only able to adjust their terms to the new situation by about spring 1979. Nevertheless, the Federal Supreme Court applied the new regime to contracts in the past, even if all obligations arising under them had already been entirely carried out. The change in the relevant evaluations (*Wandel der maßgeblichen Wertvorstellungen*), it was held, had not been brought about by those decisions; it had taken place already by the time the contracts in question had been concluded and had merely been identified by the Court.[61] As a result, many instalment credit banks were faced with a considerable number of unjustified enrichment claims.[62] The courts accommodated the interests of the instalment banks in not having all their past transactions unravelled by applying the four-year prescription period of § 197 *BGB* rather than the general prescription rule of § 195 *BGB* (thirty years!).[63]

Case-law in a Codified System

These seven case studies, of course, are merely examples of a phenomenon that was once (but is no longer) regarded as highly exceptional and problematic in a legal system dominated by a code: the courts develop

[60] Cf. *BGH*, (1979) *NJW* 805; *BGH*, (1979) *NJW* 2089; BGHZ 80, 153 at 160. For a discussion see, e.g., Volker Emmerich, 'Rechtsfragen des Ratenkredits', (1988) *Juristische Schulung* 925.

[61] *BGH*, (1983) *NJW* 2692 at 2693. The approach adopted by the Federal Supreme Court was endorsed by the Federal Constitutional Court in (1984) *NJW* 2345.

[62] See Emmerich, n. 60 above, 931f.

[63] BGHZ 98, 174.

the law in countless respects, in manifold ways and by a great number of different means.[64] Sometimes they introduce entirely new legal rules. This can come as a surprise both to the parties concerned and to the legal community at large: a surprise that is particularly understandable where the courts themselves have previously espoused a different view. It should be noted that judge-made law does not only flourish under the auspices of general clauses such as §§ 138 I, 242, 826 *BGB* or § 9 of the Standard Terms Act.[65] There are a number of open-ended concepts and clauses (such as 'or any other right' in § 823 I *BGB*[66]) that have to be interpreted. But even where the Code contains supposedly specific terms like 'compensation for non-performance', 'unlawful (infringement)', or 'damage to property', the courts have introduced subtle distinctions which have given rise to new pockets of case law.[67] Sometimes, the courts have to apply the rules and concepts of the Civil Code to situations which its draftsmen failed to contemplate, sometimes they have to accommodate new and unforeseeable developments. They have introduced new legal rules and institutions on the basis of somewhat specious analogies to existing provisions in the Code or by using the device of 'supplementative interpretation' of a contract. Or they have 'essentially created an autonomous field of law with its own specific criteria'[68] by reversing the onus of proof in product liability cases.[69]

In our present sample of cases we have three which fall within the range of application of a general clause (cases 3, 6, and 7) and three (cases 1, 2, and 5) which turn around the interpretation either of a specific term ('rendering services') or the range of application of a specific rule. Case 4 is drawn from an area of private law where case law has played a more fundamental role than in any other: the law relating to labour relations.[70] A central point in all of them is whether protection

[64] See Dawson, n. 11 above, 432 ff.; Zimmermann, n. 14 above, 16ff.

[65] Cf. generally John Dawson, 'The General Clauses, viewed from a Distance', (1977) 41 *RabelsZ* 441.

[66] It has been used to introduce, *inter alia*, delictual protection of the personality (*allgemeines Persönlichkeitsrecht*) and of the established and operating business (*eingerichteter und ausgeübter Gewerbebetrieb*) into the *BGB*; see, e.g., Arndt Teichmann, in *Jauernig*, n. 30 above, § 823, VIII, A and C.

[67] Cf., as far as the three examples mentioned in the text are concerned, the intractable distinction between consequential loss closely related and not so closely related to a defective piece of work (§§ 635, 638 *BGB*; see Zimmermann, n. 18 above, 166ff.); the two different approaches to establishing the issue of unlawfulness, as predominantly recognized today (see Larenz & Canaris, n. 25 above, 364ff.); and the 'functionalization' of the concept of 'property' in terms of § 823 I BGB as evident, particularly, in BGHZ 55, 153; see Larenz & Canaris, n. 25 above, 388ff.

[68] Teichmann, n. 66 above, § 823 VIII E 1.

[69] The leading case is BGHZ 51, 91 ('fowl pest'); see Basil Markesinis, *The German Law of Torts* (3rd ed., 1994) 493ff.

[70] For an overview in English, see Abbo Junker, 'Labour Law', in: Ebke & Finkin, n. 14 above, 305. A standard reference is Richardi, n. 42 above, Vorbem. zu §§ 611ff., nn. 101ff.

has to be granted to the party who acted in accordance with the previous legal position and therefore lost his case, or whether the new approach may be implemented, without any equitable adjustment, to the case at hand. In two cases (4 and 5) such protection is granted, but more often it is not. In all seven decisions the Court was quite aware that it was changing the law, but in the earliest of them (case 1) the consequential problems were not discussed at all. All of the more recent cases do contain such discussion. Reference is made, *inter alia*, to § 242 *BGB*, to a balancing of interests, to whether the reliance has been reasonable, to the problem of the retroactive effect of legislation, and to decisions by the Federal Constitutional Court dealing with the latter issue. Whether the courts merely introduce a new legal rule or whether, by doing so, they overrule a precedent, or even a line of precedents, does not appear, in principle, to make a difference.

The Force of Precedents

It may be obvious by now that the kind of situation discussed in the present essay raises problems on three different levels: private law doctrine, constitutional law, and legal methodology. On the methodological level, an important preliminary issue is the status of precedents in German law.[71] It is obvious that, unlike in England, they do not have legally binding force. There is, in principle, no rule of *stare decisis*, either as far as previous decisions by the deciding court itself or as far as previous decisions by superior courts are concerned. On the other hand, it is equally obvious that precedents cannot be said to have no force at all. The courts themselves attribute considerable significance to precedents. Whenever they want to deviate from previous decisions, they openly refer to them and advance arguments which are designed to demonstrate that the earlier decisions were wrong and why the new approach is preferable. And if they follow a line of precedents, they usually refer to it without entering into a substantive discussion of the relevant legal problem. Clearly, the authority of the precedent relieves them from that burden.

In addition, it is noticeable that German law places considerable emphasis on uniformity of approach towards disputed legal issues.[72] German law obviously proceeds from the assumption that judicial pronouncements are not only addressed to the parties involved in the

[71] For a comprehensive recent analysis, see Robert Alexy & Ralf Dreier, 'Precedent in the Federal Republic of Germany', in D. Neil MacCormick & Robert S. Summers (eds.), *Interpreting Precedents: A Comparative Study* (1997) 17.

[72] See Alexy & Dreier, n. 71 above, 31f.

litigation at hand, but also to the legal community at large.[73] Thus, for instance, if one of the five Supreme Courts (Federal Supreme Court, Federal Labour Court, Federal Administrative Court, Federal Social [Security] Court, and Federal Tax Court) wishes to deviate from a decision of one of the others, it has to submit the matter to a Common Panel of the Federal Supreme Courts;[74] and if one of the Divisions of the Federal Supreme Court wishes to deviate from a decision of one of the other Divisions, the matter has to be submitted to the Joint Panel of all Divisions of the Court.[75] Moreover, a Regional Supreme Court (*Oberlandesgericht*) that does not want to follow a decision of the Federal Supreme Court has to grant leave to appeal on points of law in terms of § 546 I 2, no. 2 *ZPO*. Every student of German private law is made aware, again and again, of the importance of leading cases decided by the highest courts. *Herrenreiter*,[76] *Schwimmerschalter*,[77] *Jungbullen*,[78] or *Flugreise*[79] have become household names with which German lawyers have to be familiar. The contours of modern product liability law are discussed, in the most important comprehensive textbook on German private law,[80] in terms of the development from *Hühnerpest*[81] via *Apfelschorf*,[82] *Kupolofen*,[83] and *Honda*,[84] to *Mehrwegflasche*,[85] *Milupa*,[86] *Hochzeitsessen*,[87] and *Kondensator*.[88] A book containing the 100 most important decisions of the Federal Supreme Court and aimed at the student market has seen four editions within eight years.[89] It is not surprising, therefore, that the courts require practising lawyers to be familiar with the latest case law; they have to be acquainted not only with the decisions in the quasi-official series called *Entscheidungen des Bundesgerichtshofs in Zivilsachen* but also have to study the decisions published in general law reviews like *Neue Juristische Wochenschrift*.[90] Moreover, in taking care of the affairs of his clients, a lawyer has to be guided by the views taken by the Federal Supreme Court (and, of course, by its sister courts).[91]

[73] For details, see Christoph Louven, *Problematik und Grenzen rückwirkender Rechtsprechung des Bundesarbeitsgerichts* (1996) 170ff.

[74] See § 2 I *Gesetz zur Wahrung der Einheitlichkeit der Rechtsprechung der obersten Gerichtshöfe des Bundes*.

[75] Cf., e.g., § 132 *Gerichtsverfassungsgesetz*.

[76] BGHZ 26, 349ff.

[77] BGHZ 67, 359ff.

[78] BGHZ 55, 176ff.

[79] BGHZ 55, 128ff.; a more comprehensive report is to be found in (1971) *NJW* 609.

[80] Dieter Medicus, *Bürgerliches Recht* (17th ed., 1996) nn. 650ff.

[81] BGHZ 51, 91.

[82] BGHZ 80, 186 & 199.

[83] BGHZ 92, 143.

[84] BGHZ 99, 167.

[85] BGHZ 104, 323.

[86] BGHZ 116, 60.

[87] BGHZ 116, 104.

[88] BGHZ 117, 183.

[89] Haimo Schack & Hans-Peter Ackmann, *Höchstrichterliche Rechtsprechung zum Bürgerlichen Recht* (4th ed., 1997).

[90] For details, see Michael Martinek, in *Staudinger, Kommentar zum Bürgerlichen Gesetzbuch*, n. 18 above, § 675, C 15.

[91] *BGH*, (1983) *NJW* 1665; BGHZ 85, 64 at 66; BGHZ 87, 150 at 155 f.

The Retroactivity of New Rules of Judge-made Law

The Prohibition of Retroactive Legislation

If precedents are not formally binding, they still have considerable force, or authority. Does this preclude the courts from a retroactive change of opinion? This appears to be the central question within the present context. It affects one of the most elementary constitutional principles of German law: the principle of the *Rechtsstaat*.[92] One of its many emanations is the prohibition of retroactive legislation, as specified in a long line of cases by the Federal Constitutional Court.[93] A distinction has consistently been drawn, by that Court, between 'genuine' and 'non-genuine', or 'spurious', retroactivity.[94] A piece of legislation has genuinely retroactive effect if it attaches new legal consequences to past acts; it is only 'spuriously' retroactive if legal consequences are attached to an act which originated in the past but has not yet been completed. Genuinely retroactive legislation is unacceptable in principle.[95] Contrary to what the Federal Supreme Court appears to think,[96] the application of a new rule of judge-made law to the case at hand is often not merely 'spuriously' retroactive, for the courts are usually asked to pronounce upon a set of past facts.[97] Thus, for instance, the defendant in BGHZ 132,

[92] For an overview in English, see David P. Curry, *The Constitution of the Federal Republic of Germany* (1994) 18ff. and *passim*.

[93] Apart from the principle of *Rechtsstaat*, art. 14 *GG* (right to property) and art. 3 *GG* (equality) have been referred to as constitutional parameters which have to be taken into account in the present context. While it is well established that the constitutional guarantee of art. 14 I *GG* does not relate only to 'property' in the technical sense attributed to the term by the *BGB* (§ 903), but comprises all rights and assets protected by private law (BVerfGE 31, 229 at 239; 45, 142 at 179; 68, 193 at 222; 89, 1 at 6ff.), it does not follow that art. 14 I *GG*, as it were, supersedes the issue of retroactivity and renders consideration of the *Rechtsstaat*-issue obsolete (but see Bodo Pieroth, *Rückwirkung und Übergangsrecht* [1981] 192ff.). For even if it is problematic whether, and to what extent, a citizen may be deprived of a legal position (art. 14 I *GG*), it remains a separate, and usually much more pressing, question whether this can happen retroactively. Whether the principle of equality (art. 3 I *GG*) is relevant at all must be regarded as at least doubtful. Thus, with regard to legislation it does not pose a problem either. Even if, however, one regards art. 3 I *GG* as applicable (Rainer Riggert, *Die Selbstbindung der Rechtsprechung durch den allgemeinen Gleichheitssatz* [Art. 3 *GG*], 1992), the better reasons provided for the new decision can always justify the unequal treatment. This is all the more valid since it may be argued that art. 3 I *GG* does not require equality of unjust treatment (*Gleichbehandlung im Unrecht*; see Katja Langenbucher, *Die Entwicklung und Auslegung von Richterrecht* (1996) 109. See also Michael Reinhardt, *Konsistente Jurisdiktion* (1997) 450ff.

[94] For an overview, see Hans D. Jarass, in Hans D. Jarass & Bodo Pieroth, *Grundgesetz für die Bundesrepublik Deutschland* (3rd ed., 1995) art. 20, nn. 47ff.

[95] For details, see Jarass, n. 94 above, art. 20, n. 51; Klaus Stern, *Das Staatsrecht der Bundesrepublik Deutschland*, vol 2 (2nd ed., 1984) 833ff.; Hartmut Maurer, 'Kontinuitätsgewähr und Vertrauensschutz', in Josef Isensee & Paul Kirchhoff (eds.), *Handbuch des Staatsrechts*, vol 3 (1988) 222.

[96] See esp. BGHZ 132, 119 at 129ff.

[97] Along the same lines, see Eberhard Schmidt-Aßmann, in *Maunz/Dürig, Kommentar zum Grundgesetz*, art. 103 I, n. 240.

119 (case 2)[98] had signed the suretyship document, the validity of which was now disputed, in 1992. As far as both the creditor and the surety were concerned, the transaction had thus been completed. If that transaction is now subjected to legal consequences which differ from those prevailing in 1992, we are dealing with genuine retroactivity. If the rules concerning retroactive legislation were applicable to judge-made law, the new approach could therefore only be implemented *pro futuro*.

THE CONSTITUTIONAL STATUS OF JUDGE-MADE LAW

This brings us to the question whether judge-made law can be compared to legislation which, in turn, raises another, preliminary issue: to what extent is judicial law-making admissible in terms of German constitutional law? The Federal Constitutional Court does not apply the principle prohibiting retroactive legislation to new rules of judge-made law, even in areas of law which are nearly exclusively governed by pronouncements by the courts. The latter do not, according to the Federal Constitutional Court, bind in the same way as acts of legislation, for whether they are valid beyond the individual case at hand merely depends upon the persuasiveness of the arguments advanced and upon the authority of the court.[99] In the legal literature relating to constitutional law, judicial pronouncements are widely regarded as a legitimate source of law.[100] Inclusion of the term *Recht* in article 20 III *GG* suggests that the legal system does not only consist of statutes, codes, and the Constitution (*Gesetz*)[101] while the doctrine of the separation of powers[102] does not present an obstacle to judicial law-making, as long as

[98] See text at nn. 22–31 above.

[99] BVerfGE 84, 212 at 227.

[100] Cf., e.g., Reinhardt, n. 93 above, 84ff. and *passim*; Stern, n. 95 above, vol 1 (2nd ed., 1984) 43f., 800f.; idem, n. 95 above, 581ff.; Christian Stark, 'Die Bindung des Richters an Gesetz und Verfassung', (1976) 34 *Veröffentlichungen der Vereinigung deutscher Staatsrechtslehrer* 43 at 69ff.; Fritz Ossenbühl, 'Gesetz und Recht—die Rechtsquellen im demokratischen Rechtsstaat', in Isensee & Kirchhof (eds.), n. 95 above, 281 at 298ff.; Jörn Ipsen, *Richterrecht und Verfassung* (1975); Rolf Wank, *Grenzen richterlicher Rechtsfortbildung* (1978); cf. also Josef Esser, *Grundsatz und Norm in der richterlichen Fortbildung des Privatrechts* (4th ed. 1990); of fundamental importance is Martin Kriele, *Theorie der Rechtsgewinnung* (2nd ed., 1976) 60ff.

[101] 'Die Gesetzgebung ist an die verfassungsmäßige Ordnung, die vollziehende Gewalt und die Rechtsprechung sind an Gesetz und Recht gebunden' (Legislation shall be subject to the constitutional order; the executive and the judiciary shall be bound by statute and law). On the ambiguity of the terms *Gesetz und Recht*, in the present context, see Curry, n. 92 above, 18.

[102] As laid down in art. 20 II *GG*: 'Alle Staatsgewalt geht vom Volke aus. Sie wird vom Volke . . . durch besondere Organe der Gesetzgebung, der vollziehenden Gewalt und der Rechtsprechung ausgeübt' (All state authority emanates from the people. It shall be exercised by the people . . . through separate legislative, executive, and judicial bodies). For an overview in English, see Curry, n. 92 above, 102ff.

the *precedence* of legislation is not infringed.[103] Judge-made law is legitimate, and even necessary, in order to satisfy the demands of the principle of *Rechtsstaat*, as long as it remains *intra* or *praeter legem*. Judicial pronouncements *contra legem* have, at least in one case, been condoned even by the Federal Constitutional Court,[104] but they remain inadmissible in principle. Nevertheless, the textbooks and commentaries on the *Grundgesetz* generally do not even mention the problem of overruling, or judicial law-making in the field of private law, when they deal with retroactive legislation:[105] obviously they, too, regard judge-made law as a different species of law. According to Klaus Stern, for instance, it is based upon the gradual compression (*Verdichtung*) of individual precedents and always remains subject to the reservation that, one day, a better perception of the law may come to prevail.[106]

Do Judges merely Declare the Law?

Legal theory in Germany (just as in England) has long been dominated by a dispute between proponents of a declaratory concept of judicial development of the law and a number of approaches attributing a more creative role to the judge. According to the traditional view, propounded by Savigny,[107] taken over by Windscheid,[108] and still prevailing today (at

[103] See Ipsen, n. 100 above; Reinhard Zimmermann, *Richterliches Moderationsrecht oder Totalnichtigkeit?* (1979) 97 ff. with references; Otto Rudolf Kissel, 'Grenzen der rechtsprechenden Gewalt', (1982) *NJW* 1777; Stern, n. 95 above, 584; and see the references above at n. 100, particularly Kriele.

[104] BVerfGE 34, 269 (Soraya), condoning the judicial derogation of § 253 *BGB*; for background, see Zimmermann, n. 18 above, 1092 ff. But see BVerfGE 65, 182, reversing *BAG*, (1979) *NJW* 774 (relating to how claims based on social redundancy plans have to be treated if the employer falls insolvent).

[105] Cf. Stern, n. 100 above, 831 ff.; Friedrich E. Schnapp, in Ingo von Münch & Philip Kunig (eds.), *Grundgesetz-Kommentar* (4th ed., 1992) art. 20, nn. 26 f.; Christoph Degenhart, *Staatsrecht I* (11th ed., 1995) nn. 308ff.; there is also no discussion in the great standard commentary of *Maunz/Dürig*, n. 97 above. The problem is comprehensively debated, however, in the literature on criminal law. Here the discussion usually latches on to the special rule of art. 103 II *GG* ('An act may be punished only if it was defined by law as a criminal offence before the act was committed'). See Claus Roxin, *Strafrecht Allgemeiner Teil* (2nd ed. 1994) 116f.; Herbert Tröndle, *Strafgesetzbuch* (48th ed., 1997) § 1, nn. 11ff., with further references. Some authors used to regard the retroactive change of judicial interpretation as inadmissible in principle without differentiating between different areas of the law (Wilhelm Knittel, *Zum Problem der Rückwirkung bei einer Änderung der Rechtsprechung* [1965] 50ff.; Wolfgang Grunsky, *Grenzen der Rückwirkung bei einer Änderung der Rechtsprechung*, [1970]). Their writings are, however, regarded today as outdated; cf. Maurer, n. 95 above, 270ff. (who discusses the problem generally under the heading '*Vertrauensschutz*' [protection of reliance]).

[106] Stern, n. 95 above, 586.

[107] Friedrich Carl von Savigny, *System des heutigen römischen Rechts*, vol 1 (1840) 13ff., 45ff., 83ff.

[108] Bernhard Windscheid & Theodor Kipp, *Lehrbuch des Pandektenrechts* (9th ed., 1906) 72ff.; only statutes and customary law are recognized as sources of law.

least as far as German private law is concerned),[109] the formation of law must be distinguished from its perception by the lawyers required to apply the law. Judicial pronouncements, therefore, can only be regarded as binding so far as they correctly reflect 'the law'. They are to be followed *imperio rationis*: because of the persuasiveness of the arguments on which they are based. It is not *per se*, or inherently, right to follow a judicial precedent.[110] According to the other view, the courts do not merely find the law but actively and constructively develop it. In principle, therefore, precedents contribute to constituting the law. Thus, *pro tanto*,[111] they have to be followed. Unlike legislation, however, they are not strictly binding: they merely place a burden of argument on those intending to deviate from them, or postulate a presumption in favour of the correctness of the earlier decisions.[112]

Every declaratory theory of judicial adjudication necessarily proceeds from the assumption of the completeness of the law: there is one right answer for every legal problem.[113] Otherwise judicial pronouncements could not, in every case, be regarded as an attempt at 'finding' the law. But this assumption is implausible. Statutory rules never comprehensively cover the law or even a fairly specific area of the law. Nor can it be maintained that all 'gaps' in the law can be filled by means of customary law which, after all, is based on long and uniform practice (*longa consuetudo*) and on the general convictions of the community (*communis opinio*).[114] *Culpa in contrahendo* and positive breach of contract[115] may qualify as customary legal institutions supplementing the system of

[109] Eduard Picker, 'Richterrecht oder Rechtsdogmatik—Alternativen der Rechtsgewinnung?', (1988) *Juristenzeitung* 1, 62; Josef Esser, *Vorverständnis und Methodenwahl in der Rechtsfindung* (1970) 184ff.; Karl Larenz & Claus-Wilhelm Canaris, *Methodenlehre der Rechtswissenschaft* (1995) 252ff.

[110] Larenz & Canaris, n. 109 above, 255f.

[111] On the difference between *pro tanto* reasons (normative) and *prima facie* reasons (epistemic), see Susan Hurley, *Natural Reasons* (1989) 130f., 260f.: 'Reasons for action are pro tanto, not prima facie; they aren't bits of evidence about what should be done that yield to better, more comprehensive evidence'.

[112] See Robert Alexy, *A Theory of Legal Argumentation* (1989) 274ff.; Hans-Joachim Koch & Helmut Rüßmann, *Juristische Begründungslehre* (1982) 186ff.; cf. also Kriele, n. 100 above, 243ff.; Hans Martin Pawlowski, *Methodenlehre für Juristen* (2nd ed., 1991) 229ff.; Franz Bydlinski, *Juristische Methodenlehre und Rechtsbegriff* (2nd ed., 1991) 501ff.; and see the discussion by Alexy & Dreier, n. 71 above, at 43ff.; Peter Raisch, *Juristische Methoden* (1995) 190ff.

[113] See Ronald Dworkin, *Taking Rights Seriously* (1977) 81ff.; *idem*, 'No Right Answer?', (1978) 53 *N.Y. U. L. R.* 1 at 23; cf. also Jan Sieckmann, 'Zur Begründung von Abwägungsurteilen', (1995) 26 *Rechtstheorie* 45 at 68f., according to whom there is for legal decisons, at least, a subjective claim to the one correct answer. Thus, e.g., Picker set out to demonstrate that the *Betriebsrisikolehre* (cf. Zimmermann, n. 18 above, 195) is not based on evaluations going beyond those contained in the *BGB*: 'Richterrecht oder Rechtsdogmatik—Alternativen der Rechtsgewinnung?' (1988) *Juristenzeitung* 63ff.

[114] Cf. Larenz & Canaris, n. 109 above, 258.

[115] On which, see Zimmermann, n. 18 above, 11f., 244f., 812f., 1041.

remedies provided in the *BGB*,[116] but even the first decision establishing these institutions constituted 'law' in spite of the lack of long and uniform practice.[117] None of the decisions discussed above can be regarded as a manifestation of a rule of customary law. And while it is arguable that the application of the short prescription period of § 196 I, no. 7 *BGB* to architects' fees (case 1), or the invalidity of blanket declarations of suretyship (case 2), is supported by more convincing arguments than the opposite solution, and that it therefore represents, and has always represented, the correct solution to those legal problems, it can hardly be maintained that a legal rule according to which an interest rate of more than double the normal rate is unacceptable (case 7) represents a 'correct' concretization of the moral standards contained in § 138 I *BGB*. There is at least a discretional element involved in the judicial fixing of precise limits of this kind.[118]

None the less, the declaratory theory is today defended by the argument that judges always have to base their decisions on legally recognized reasons, such as arguments deduced from general legal principles.[119] But it does not follow from this proposition, either, that the legal system provides a right answer for each problem.[120] Even if it were correct in principle, it must be kept in mind that a decision always depends on the relative weight of its reasons. Legal reasons do not, however, have a predetermined and distinctive weight; weight must be assigned to them by way of reasoned argument. Criteria for this process of weighing-up can only be roughly gauged from the law.[121] Legal systems are therefore partly incomplete at least in so far as the relative weight of the arguments relevant for a decision are concerned. It follows that the courts, at least in part, create rather than merely find the law when they decide hard cases. A neat and clear-cut distinction as to when, and to what extent, the courts are declaring or creating the law is probably impossible to draw.

[116] Cf., e.g., Max Vollkommer in *Jauernig*, n. 30 above, § 276, V 1 d and VI 1 c.

[117] And in spite of the fact that the 'internal' legal arguments on which they were originally based are unconvincing. In the early *culpa in contrahendo* cases, the Imperial Supreme Court used the fictitious device of a pre-contractual contract; also an *argumentum per analogiam* was advanced on the basis of rules like §§ 122, 179, II, 307, 309 *BGB*. Positive breach of contract was originally read into § 276 *BGB*.

[118] Louven, n. 73 above, 190ff.

[119] Dworkin, n. 113 above, 105ff.; idem, *Law's Empire* (1986) 231ff.; cf. also, for Germany, Picker, n. 113 above, at 65. In actual practice, however, practical arguments like the potential consequences of a decision tend to play a significant role; cf. Ulfried Neumann, 'Rechtsphilosophie', in Dieter Simon (ed.), *Rechtswissenschaft in der Bonner Republik* (1994) 145 at 173f.; for England, see Rupert Cross, J. W. Harris, *Precedent in English Law* (4th ed., 1991) 219ff.

[120] Langenbucher, n. 93 above, 36ff.

[121] For a detailed discussion, see Nils Jansen, 'Die Abwägung von Grundrechten', (1997) 36 *Der Staat* 27 at 44ff.

Judicial Findings as a Source of Law but Different from Legislation

The mere fact that a declaratory theory of adjudication appears to be fallacious does not, of course, mean that judicial law-making has to be accepted. Substantive grounds must be advanced for recognizing judicial precedents as a source of law. By and large, German authors rely on the same grounds which have been put forward in England:[122] the principle that like cases must receive the same solution, the necessity of obtaining an authoritative clarification of disputed legal questions in order to deter further litigation (*interest rei publicae ut sit finis litium*) and the related requirements of legal certainty and protection of reasonable reliance. In Germany, these arguments are often derived from basic tenets of the Basic Law, such as the principles of equality and of *Rechtsstaat*.[123] Since they are today predominantly regarded as convincing, it has to be accepted that judicial pronouncements may constitute (in the sense of create) a legal rule and therefore develop or refine the legal system in some or other specific respect. The degree to which they are binding, however, depends on whether we are dealing with individual decisions or with a firmly established line of cases.[124]

Even if judge-made law is recognized as an independent source of law, the prohibition on retroactive legislation is not necessarily applicable. That prohibition is a special rule required to protect reasonable reliance in view of the fact that Parliament may—within the confines of the Basic Law—implement whatever legal rule it chooses: statutes do not have to be based on convincing arguments; nor do they have to pass a test of reasonableness.[125] Their validity is based on whether the body enacting them was competent to do so and on whether the procedural requirements for the enactment of statutes have been complied with. The prohibition on retroactive legislation corresponds to the substantive arbitrariness of statute law in a democracy. Judge-made law, on the other hand, is not in this, or any comparable, sense arbitrary. Judicial decisions have to be based on legal arguments.[126] Their validity rests, apart from the jurisdiction of the court, entirely on the quality of the reasoning processes employed. If courts were regularly to hand down indefensible

[122] See, e.g., Zenon Bankowski, D. Neil MacCormick & Geoffrey Marshall, 'Precedent in the United Kingdom', in: MacCormick & Summers (eds.), n. 71 above, 334f.

[123] Cf. Alexy & Dreier, n. 71 above, at 47. [124] Ibid at 50f.

[125] Arguably, of course, recognition of a statute as constituting valid 'law' depends on whether it conforms to elementary requirements of justice (see Gustav Radbruch, 'Gesetzliches Unrecht und übergesetzliches Recht', (1949) *Süddeutsche Juristenzeitung* 105 ff.; cf. generally Robert Alexy, *Begriff und Geltung des Rechts* (1992) 51ff.). This question is not, however, practically relevant as far as the Federal Republic of Germany is concerned since those elementary requirements of justice are enshrined in the *Grundgesetz*.

[126] This is no longer undisputed, but in Germany it still constitutes the prevailing (and in our view correct) opinion; cf. Langenbucher, n. 93 above, 22ff.

decisions, they would lose their authority, with the result that their judgements would lose their validity. Thus, with regard to validity and legitimacy, the procedural requirements for the enactment of legislation correspond to the reasoning process for the establishment of rules of judge-made law. Judge-made law, accordingly, does not have the definitive character of a statutory command but only a weaker, *pro tanto* nature:[127] it always stands to be corrected by better, countervailing arguments.

Even in the case of judge-made law the question may, of course, arise as to how the reliance of individual citizens may be protected. Such protection is essentially a constitutional requirement. For judicial rulings constitute an action of the state, the consistency and reliability of which remain indispensable elements of the *Rechtsstaat*-principle, even if statutory law and judge-made law cannot formally be equated.[128] But the prohibition of retroactivity can hardly be the appropriate means to implement such protection: it would either lead to the cementing of a line of precedents which is now regarded as wrong or it would require the courts consciously to lay down legal rules of general application—as, for instance, by means of prospective overruling.[129] This is not, however, reconcilable with the primary function of the judiciary to provide reasoned decisions for individual cases. It can also not be justified by pointing out that judicial pronouncements in fact may lead to judge-made law. For judge-made law always rests on the decisions of individual cases. The courts do not have any authority beyond deciding the case at hand; and, in particular, they may not establish general rules for deciding future cases. As a result, it may be stated that a prohibition of retroactivity is not required by considerations of constitutional law. On the contrary: judicial pronouncements with a merely prospective effect would appear to transgress the borderline between legislation and adjudication.[130] Retroactivity must therefore be the general rule when it

[127] Cf. n. 111 above.

[128] Reinhardt, n. 93 above, 474ff. Moreover, a change of judicial opinion must always be compatible with art. 14 I *GG* if it leads to the deprivation of a legal position which has been established by judge-made law and which enjoys the protection of the constitutional property guarantee (cf. n. 93 above).

[129] In favour of such an approach is *BAG*, (1982) *NJW* 788ff.; for criticism, see Larenz & Canaris, n. 109 above, 260.

[130] The contrary view is advocated by Probst, n. 9 above, 707f., 709 ff. But he fails to appreciate that statutory law and judge-made law cannot 'structurally' be equated (cf. above; but see Probst, 711). Judges may not take over the role of the legislature; judge-made law can therefore only be created through deciding individual cases. To grant to courts the power to overrule an earlier decision prospectively would mean to level out this structural difference. Paradoxically, it would only be such a power which would vest judge-made law with the definitive character of a statutory command which, in turn, would require the establishment of rules concerning the protection against retroactive change of law (such as 'prospective overruling'!).

comes to determine the effect of judge-made law. This means that the new view has to be applied to the case at hand—a result which would also seem to tie in with a simple rule implicit in the principle of *Rechtsstaat*: legal disputes have to be decided by applying what is perceived to be the correct, or at least the better, view of the law.

Protection of Reasonable Reliance on the Basis of Private Law

Situations in which no Need for Protecting Reliance Arises

Protection of reliance can therefore only be granted, in individual cases, on the level of private law doctrine.[131] For we are dealing here, in the first place, with a balancing of the conflicting interests of the parties concerned.[132] But it should be noted, first of all, that in a number of important situations[133] the need for granting such protection does not arise. Many legal consequences are dependent upon fault: the remedies for breach of contract or *culpa in contrahendo* provide notable examples. The relevant moment for assessing whether a party has been at fault is undoubtedly the time when the contractual or pre-contractual duty was infringed.[134] Such assessment will therefore have to be based on the legal position prevailing—or at least foreseeable—at that moment in the past. In other cases the particular contract has to be examined to see whether it is void for being *contra bonos mores* (§ 138 I *BGB*). But what is regarded as a violation of the *boni mores* may change over time.[135] Again, it is generally recognized that the standards prevailing at the time of conclusion of the contract are relevant.[136] Arguably, therefore, the Federal Supreme Court should not have held the credit transactions in case 7 to be invalid: they had been concluded in 1976 and it is questionable whether the relevant change in the evaluation of instalment credits, on which the Federal Supreme Court based its decision (in 1978) had already taken place at that stage.[137]

131 Cf. also, in particular, Dieter Medicus, 'Über die Rückwirkung von Rechtsprechung', (1995) *NJW* 2577; Langenbucher, n. 93 above, 134ff.

132 Thus, retroactivity in private law gives rise to much more complex problems than in public law. On the statutory level this is demonstrated by the transitional regime, contained in arts. 153–217 *EGBGB* and regulating the coming into force of the provisions of the *BGB*. For extensive discussion, see Hermann Habicht, *Die Einwirkung des Bürgerlichen Gesetzbuchs auf zuvor entstandene Rechtsverhältnisse: Eine Darstellung der Fragen des Übergangsrechts* (3rd ed., 1901).

133 See Medicus, n. 131 above, 2577ff.

134 Cf. Heinrichs, n. 19 above, § 276, nn. 70ff.

135 Zimmermann, n. 18 above, 714 f.; Mayer-Maly, n. 59 above, § 138, n. 17.

136 Cf., e.g., Heinrichs, n. 19 above, § 138, nn. 9f.; Jauernig, n. 30 above, § 138, 1 C.

137 For criticism, see Medicus, n. 131 above, 2579.

But in cases revolving around § 138 *BGB* another consideration frequently comes into play. § 138 *BGB* attempts to establish certain outermost limits on the parties' private autonomy: a contract has to be at variance with the sense of decency of all just and fair-thinking people, it has to scandalize the reasonable man, in order to be held invalid.[138] A party exploiting his freedom of contract so as to come close to such an extreme form of disapproval can hardly be said to have invested *reasonable* reliance in the continuation of a more liberal approach previously adopted by the courts.[139] Moreover, most of the relevant cases deal with the situation of one party unfairly placing the other at a disadvantage and the courts are, understandably, disinclined to grant protection to the former when they have just tightened up their approach in order to protect the latter. Very similar considerations apply to a particularly frequent situation (see cases 3 and 6): a clause in a standard form contract is held invalid in terms of § 9 *AGBG*. Standard contract terms are pre-formulated by one party and that party does not usually have the interests of his contractual partner at heart. Individual negotiation is replaced by virtual imposition of a uniform and often one-sided set of conditions. The corollary is obvious: whoever uses standard contract terms does so at his own risk. He does not deserve to be protected if it subsequently turns out that he has overstepped the borderlines of what is fair and reasonable.[140]

The Device of 'Supplementative Interpretation'

In order to restrict the retroactivity effected by a new rule of judge-made law, the courts of private law in Germany can avail themselves of two main tools: the interpretation of a contract in the light of the earlier case law (on the basis of § 157 *BGB*) and the general principle of good faith, as embodied in § 242 *BGB*.

Contractual regulations often contain gaps—they leave potential legal problems without regulation. In such cases recourse is had either to the rules of the *ius dispositivum* contained in the Civil Code, or to the device of 'supplementative interpretation' of the contract (*ergänzende*

[138] Zimmermann, n. 18 above, 706, with references.

[139] See also the discussion by Probst, n. 9 above, 543ff. concerning the protection only of reliance that is worthy of protection.

[140] Similar considerations have prompted courts and legal writers to argue that excessive clauses contained in standard contract forms may not be modified, i.e. reduced to an admissible level: cf. Heinrichs, n. 19 above, Vorbem. v. § 8 *AGBG*, n. 9; Teichmann, n. 66 above, § 6 *AGBG*, 2 b. For criticism, see Kötz, n. 51 above, § 6 *AGBG*, nn. 8ff.; cf. also, as regards the present situation concerning a change of judicial opinion, Medicus, n. 131 above, 2583 and BGHZ 130, 19 at 34ff.

Vertragsauslegung).[141] § 157 *BGB* provides that contracts have to be interpreted according to the precepts of good faith, giving consideration to common usage. There is unanimity that the so-called hypothetical will of the parties must be used as a yardstick. But it is also recognized that where the will of the parties cannot be determined, the court in fact makes its decision according to what it considers to be a fair solution of the problem.[142] As a result, § 157 *BGB* has become one of the most important foundations for judge-made law in the field of private law.[143] If there is reason for a change of judicial opinion in the field of *ius dispositivum,* or as far as judge-made law dealing with supplementative interpretation is concerned, it is always possible that the parties to the contract have based their incomplete regulation—consciously or unknowingly—on the judicial interpretation adopted in the past. They may have proceeded from the assumption that that interpretation conformed to the way in which they wanted to see their contract operate. If that is in fact the case, § 157 *BGB* requires the courts to base their decision on the earlier interpretation. The reason for this is not primarily the protection of reliance (as in the case of a change in statutory law) but the fact that the parties—within the framework of their private autonomy—have willed this regulation. At the same time, such a way of proceeding enables the courts to express doubts about their previous interpretation without having to resort to the device of prospective overruling.

Good Faith

The main tool in the hand of courts of private law enabling them openly to intervene on behalf of parties disadvantaged by the implementation of the new interpretation is the principle of good faith (§ 242 *BGB*).[144] They have to ask whether that principle would be disregarded if the party favoured by the new rule were to be allowed to invoke it against the other party.[145] This depends, in the first place, on whether the party

[141] On which see Jauernig, n. 30 above, § 157, 1; Mayer-Maly, n. 59 above, § 157, nn. 36ff.

[142] BGHZ 96, 313 at 320f.; cf. Mayer-Maly, n. 59 above, § 157, nn. 43ff.; Dieter Medicus, *Allgemeiner Teil des BGB* (6th ed., 1994) n. 343.

[143] Claus-Wilhelm Canaris, 'Die Problematik der Sicherheitenfreigabeklauseln in Hinblick auf § 9 AGBG und § 138 BGB', (1996) *Zeitschrift für Wirtschaftsrecht (ZIP)* 1109 at 1115f.

[144] This, essentially, represents prevailing court practice. For an early discussion along these lines, see Burkhard Rüberg, *Vertrauensschutz gegenüber rückwirkender Rechtsprechung* (1977), 206ff. For a general discussion of the background and the implications of § 242 *BGB* in German Law, see Simon Whittaker & Reinhard Zimmermann, 'Good Faith in European Contract Law—A Survey' in R. Zimmermann & Whittaker (eds.), *Good Faith in European Contract Law* (in preparation).

[145] This is not (as some writers think) a case of applying the principle of *venire contra factum proprium* (as recognized under § 242 *BGB*) in the relationship between the court

disadvantaged by the new rule had invested *reasonable* reliance in the old one. Here it must be taken into consideration, for instance, whether the old rule had been established by a few scattered precedents, had been supported by a consistent line of decisions, or had been subject to sustained criticism, etc. The age of the relevant case law must be taken into account as well as whether a general change in evaluation since the last decision has made the adoption of a new approach less surprising. But, as the Federal Supreme Court has repeatedly stated,[146] reasonable reliance as such is not sufficient to warrant an exception to the general principle of retroactivity. After all, the other party could easily point out that his own reliance on the 'correct' law being applied to his case deserves to receive (at least!) equal protection. Application of the new approach would have to constitute an unacceptable hardship, even in view of the reasonable interests of the other party. A process of balancing is thus required as a result of which the scales would have to be weighted heavily in favour of the party disadvantaged by the new rule. Factors to be taken into account include whether his entire economic existence would be jeopardized, whether both parties have carried out the transaction in the obvious belief that it was validly concluded, or whether implementation of the new rule would constitute an unwarranted windfall for the party favoured by it.[147]

If we turn our attention to the remaining four[148] of the seven cases at the beginning of this essay, we can see the courts engaged in this balancing process in all of the more recent ones. It is hardly conceivable that a plaintiff today would receive the kind of short shrift that makes the decision in BGHZ 59, 163 (case 1) so startling. It still smacks of the declaratory theory in its undiluted form: architects' fees are subject to a two-year prescription period and the plaintiff should have known this in spite of the fact that the Federal Supreme Court itself did not manage correctly to figure out the legal situation. In case 2 (blanket declaration of suretyship) the odds are evenly divided and no deviation from the principle of retroactivity was thus required. Protection of reliance in the old legal regime was granted in cases 4 and 5. This is hardly surprising in case 4, which deals with labour relations, a field of law which has very largely been established and regulated by case law and where precedents therefore enjoy an even greater force than in private law in

and one of the parties to the dispute (see Louven, n. 73 above, 158f.; Probst, n. 9 above, 531ff.). We are concerned rather with the balancing of the interests of the parties according to good faith.

[146] See, e.g., the decisions in cases 2 and 5 above.

[147] Statutory evaluations may possibly be gauged from arts. 168 ff. *EGBGB* (cf. n. 132 above). It must, however, be kept in mind, that these rules relate to a statutory change of regime.

[148] For cases 3, 6 and 7, see above.

general.[149] Moreover, the shop agreement had been properly concluded and both the employer and the members of the works council (that is, the workers' representative) had relied on its validity: the eventual invalidity could not therefore affect the reasonable expectations of the workers. In case 5 the consultant's economic existence possibly depended upon the contract which was now ruled to have been invalid for the time of his membership of the supervisory board (1978–84). Also, it has to be taken into account that during those six years he had fulfilled his contractual obligations and had duly received his payment, as agreed upon. It was only when he left the supervisory board and when, on the same day, his consultancy agreement was terminated by the stock company that the question of the validity of the contract for the previous six years somewhat unexpectedly and incidentally arose. A claim based upon unjustified enrichment against the consultant may therefore well be regarded as a windfall.

The Historical Dimension: England and Germany Compared

It will have become clear that precedents are of very considerable importance in German law. They constitute an independent source of law, albeit one of only 'outweighable force'.[150] In particular, they cannot be equated, as far as the degree to which they are binding is concerned, to legislation. Modern legal methodology is thus about to leave behind certain positivistic constrictions which have their origin in eighteenth and nineteenth century legal science. Under the older *ius commune* a much more open and flexible approach had prevailed. The *Corpus Juris Civilis*, it is true, had been ambivalent. *Non exemplis, sed legibus iudicandum est* was the famous exhortation contained in C. 7, 45, 13; but in D. 1, 3, 38 it was stated that where the law gives rise to ambiguity *consuetudinem aut rerum perpetuo similiter iudicatorum auctoritatem vim leges optinere debere*. By the eighteenth century, however, the *usus fori* was assigned considerable weight.[151] This was due to the authority which courts like the *Rota Romana*, the *Grandi Tribunali*, the *Hoge Raad* of Holland, or the *Reichskammergericht* enjoyed, as well as to the fact that

[149] For a comprehensive study of the problems and limitations of retroactivity with regard to decisions by the Supreme Labour Court, see Louven, n. 73 above.

[150] Cf. the terminology adopted in the questionnaire underlying the research project by MacCormick & Summers, n. 71 above, 555.

[151] See Helmut Coing, *Europäisches Privatrecht*, vol. 1 (1985) 125f.; Heinz Weller, *Die Bedeutung der Präjudizien im Verständnis der deutschen Rechtswissenschaft* (1979) 43ff.; Gero Dolezalek, *'Stare decisis': Persuasive Force of Precedent and Old Authority (12th–20th Century)* (1989) 13ff.

their precedents had become increasingly available in a large number of collections of decisions.[152]

Also, it has to be kept in mind that the *ius commune* during the period generally known as *usus modernus pandectarum* was, to a large extent, judicial law (*jurisprudentia forensis*) developing through lawyers' interpretation and judicial opinions, and that protagonists of this law in action were academically trained practitioners as well as professors who had usually spent part of their career as an advocate or judge.[153] Thus, Supreme Courts like the ones mentioned above were often staffed with internationally-renowned jurists. The *vis praejudiciorum* was widely recognized as vital for determining the law, the convenience of *conformitas in iudicando* was emphasized, and the typical case-law techniques were taught (*Si tamen casus decisus a casu decidendo, vel in minimo differat, allegatum praejudicium nil relevat*[154]). On the other hand, it was always recognized that the force of precedents was subject to a better, and more convincing, interpretation of the law being advanced. The weight of the argument was what ultimately counted.

In the course of time, however, the great number and complexity of legal sources gave rise to a widespread feeling both of legal uncertainty and inefficiency as far as the administration of justice was concerned. The rulers of the emerging modern territorial states were bound to find this situation unattractive. They had been raised in the spirit of enlightened absolutism and perceived it as their duty to centralize, to rationalize, and to clarify the law within the borders of their states.[155] Occasionally, strict rules of *stare decisis* were laid down: all courts within a specific territory were enjoined to follow the decisions of the highest tribunal as far as they were published in print.[156] In 1838 the King of Hanover even authorized the Supreme Court to publish important precedents in the government gazette.[157] Predominantly, however, these rulers turned to legislation as the most suitable means of providing their territories with a rational system of private law. Here, they could avail themselves of the theories of the new, secularized brand of natural law that had emerged in the course of the seventeenth century. A number of factors contributed towards a doctrine of legal sources that was inimical to judicial precedent: the desire of the absolutist monarch to be the

[152] Cf. Helmut Coing (ed.), *Handbuch der Quellen und Literatur der neueren europäischen Privatrechtsgeschichte*, vol II/2 (1976) 1113ff.

[153] See the remarks in (1992) 66 *Tulane L. Rev.* 1712f. (concerning Roman–Dutch law).

[154] Wolfgang Adam Lauterbach, *Collegium theoretico-practicum* (Tubingae, 1707) Lib. I, Tit. III, XLVIII.

[155] On the origins of the codification movement, see the remarks (and references) in (1995) 3 *Eur. Rev. Private L.* 95ff.

[156] Cf. Regina Ogorek, *Richterkönig oder Subsumtionsautomat?* (1986) 192 ff.; Weller, n. 151 above, 82ff.

[157] See Weller, n. 151 above, 85; Dawson, n. 11 above, 436f.

source of all law as much as the general quest for legal certainty, Montesquieu's doctrine of the separation of powers as much as the notion of the law as constituting an unchangeable and coherent system of rules and concepts from which legal conclusions could be drawn *more geometrico*, as espoused by the authors of the Law of Reason. The famous prohibitions to interpret, develop, and comment upon the codification in a specific territory (*Kommentier- und Auslegungsverbote*) enacted in the course of the eighteenth century,[158] remain the ultimate monuments to an ideology attempting completely to emasculate judges (as well as academic lawyers).

Nineteenth-century Pandectist legal science was not, on the whole, more favourably disposed towards judicial precedents as an independent source of law.[159] Like the Law of Reason it was based on the premise that the law constituted a closed system of rules and institutions on the basis of which the correct decision of individual cases could be reached by purely logical deductions. Each judgment was thus an act of scientific cognition, and each judge had the duty to find the one correct decision. A precedent *per se* was obviously of only epistemic, *prima facie*[160] value in this process of reasoning. The 'scholarly positivism', just like the statutory positivism by which it came to be replaced, aimed at protecting nineteenth-century civic society from arbitrary judicial interference, but it never correctly reflected legal practice. Nineteenth-century supreme courts played an active role in the development of the law[161] and the *Reichsgericht*—established in 1879, eight years after national unification had been achieved—also immediately 'equipped itself with the essential elements of a case-law technique'.[162] The obvious disjunction between legal theory and legal practice was, for a long time, 'obscured in the long-continued and cloudy debates over the continuing force of custom and the priority of "jurist's law" over "people's law"'.[163]

Developments in England display certain intriguing similarities. 'The duty of repeating errors' is a modern innovation:[164] it dates from the second half of the nineteenth century.[165] In previous times, English

[158] For details, see Hans-Jürgen Becker, 'Kommentier- und Auslegungsverbot', in *Handwörterbuch zur deutschen Rechtsgeschichte*, vol 2 (1978) cols. 963ff.; Heinz Hübner, *Kodifikation und Entscheidungsfreiheit des Richters in der Geschichte des Privatrechts* (1980) 29ff.

[159] Weller, n. 151 above, 98ff.; Franz Wieacker, *A History of Private Law in Europe* (trans. Tony Weir) (1995) 341ff.

[160] Cf. n. 111 above.

[161] Cf. Helmut Coing, *Europäisches Privatrecht*, vol. 2 (1989) 251f.; concerning the Imperial Supreme Court in Commercial Matters see the recent analysis by Herbert Kronke, 'Rechtsvergleichung und Rechtsvereinheitlichung in der Rechtsprechung des Reichsoberhandelsgerichts', (1997) 5 *Zeitschrift für Europäisches Privatrecht* 735ff.

[162] Dawson, n. 11 above, 449.

[163] Ibid at 442.

[164] J. H. Baker, *An Introduction to English Legal History* (3rd ed., 1990) 229.

[165] Cross & Harris, n. 119 above, 24ff.

courts displayed a surprisingly flexible attitude towards precedents.[166] 'You are not bound by any rule of law which you may lay down,' as Lord St Leonards stated as late as 1852,[167] 'if upon a subsequent occasion you should find reason to differ from that rule; that is, that this House, like every court of justice, possesses an inherent power to correct an error into which it may have fallen.' Again, a number of factors combined to produce the doctrine of *stare decisis* which had begun to emerge by that time:[168] the declaratory theory of adjudication which had been espoused by Sir Matthew Hale and Sir William Blackstone[169] and which reduced the role of judges to finding rather than establishing the law; the legal positivism culminating in, but by no means confined to, the writings of Jeremy Bentham[170] and John Austin;[171] the doctrine of separation of powers with its emphasis, in England, on the sovereignty of Parliament;[172] and the quest for legal certainty within a society dominated by vastly increasing trade and industrialization.[173] Thus, the same kind of legal formalism gained ascendency in England which had previously taken hold of German legal scholarship, except that in the one country it found its focal point in judicial precedent, whereas in the other it emphasized the role of legislation. Not accidentally, the same period also witnessed the rise of the literal approach to statutory interpretation in England.[174]

As a result of these developments, the general perception of the law and the approach towards its application and development drifted apart. Today, however, we see a *rapprochement* of thinking patterns, evidenced by the relaxation of the doctrine of *stare decisis*[175] (and the [re-]adoption of a purposive approach towards legislation!) in England and by the great and general sensitivity towards case law and its problems in Germany.[176]

[166] Just as they did with regard to legislation; cf. Baker, n. 164 above, 239ff. and the remarks and references in (1997) 56 *Camb. L. J.* 321ff.

[167] *Bright v Hutton*, 3 HLC 343 (388), quoted in Cross & Harris, n. 119 above, 25.

[168] See generally Jim Evans, 'Change in the Doctrine of Precedent during the Nineteenth Century', in Laurence Goldstein (ed.), *Precedent in Law* (1987) 35.

[169] See the references in Cross & Harris, n. 119 above, 27f.

[170] On the influence of Bentham's positivistic legal theory on the common law, particularly concerning the rule of *stare decisis*, see Gerald J. Postema, *Bentham and the Common Law Tradition* (1986) esp. at 192ff.

[171] John Austin, *The Province of Jurisprudence Determined* (4th ed., 1971) *passim*; cf. also the evaluation by H. L. A. Hart in the introduction to that volume.

[172] Cf. J. W. F. Allison, *A Continental Distinction in the Common Law* (1996) 72, with references.

[173] W. R. Cornish & G. de N. Clark, *Law and Society in England 1750–1950* (1989).

[174] This will be demonstrated in a forthcoming thesis by Stefan Vogenauer, *Die Auslegung von Gesetzen in England und auf dem Kontinent*.

[175] See Bankowski *et al.*, n. 122 above, 348ff.; Cross & Harris, n. 119 above, 6, 135ff.

[176] Cf. also the conclusions of Zenon Bankowski, D. Neil MacCormick, Lech Morawski & Alfonso Ruiz Miguel, 'Rationales for Precedent', in D. Neil MacCormick & Robert Summers (eds.), *Interpreting Statutes* (1997) 494, and those of D. Neil MacCormick & Robert Summers, 'Further General Reflections and Conclusions', ibid at 531.

Many differences, of course, remain.[177] Overruling, for instance, is a phenomenon occurring much more often in Germany than in England.[178] This does not mean that legal certainty is prized less highly in Germany for the Code, even if it does not fulfil the Utopian hopes of eighteenth-century legal theorists, does, of course, provide a general systematic framework which the common law appears to lack.[179] Thus, English law depends on the stability of case law to a greater extent than German private law (but not German labour law). On the other hand, it does not help to disguise the change of law that is always brought about when precedents are overruled by claiming that the courts have merely declared what anyone could have known anyway. Both in Germany and in England, the declaratory theory is increasingly being abandoned.[180] Removal of the maxim *error iuris non excusat* from the English common law does not, therefore, appear to open new floodgates of litigation: not, at least, as long as English law continues to allow recovery on the ground of mistake rather than transfer without legal ground. Whether it might not be preferable also to abandon that approach is an altoghether different question.[181]

[177] See, above all, the discussion by MacCormick & Summers, n. 176 above, 536ff.

[178] Between 1966 and 1990, there have only been 8 instances, in which the House of Lords has explicitly overruled a previous decision; see Cross & Harris, n. 119 above, 135f. Thomas Probst, who has compared the phenomenon of overruling in Switzerland and in the US has also come to the conclusion that overruling occurs much more often in the civil-law system: there are 731 pertinent decisions of the Swiss Federal Court within a period of 116 years as opposed to 208 decisions of the US Supr. C. within about 200 years: see n. 9 above, 199ff., 282ff.

[179] See also Veelken, (1997) 61 *RabelsZ* 154. The indifference to system and classification in modern English law has recently been highlighted by Peter Birks, 'More Logic and Less Experience: The Difference between Scots Law and English Law', in Carey Miller & Zimmermann n. 12 above, 167.

[180] For England, see Bankowski *et al.*, n. 122 above, at 332; for Germany see Stern, n. 100 above, 582ff.; Kriele, n. 100 above, 60ff.; particularly in labour law, Louven, n. 73 above, 197ff.

[181] For criticism from the point of view of comparative law, see the remarks in (1995) 15 *OJLS* 414ff.; for sustained and detailed 'internal' criticism, see Sonja Meier, *Irrtum und Zweckverfehlung* (forthcoming).

PRODUCT LIABILITY

12

Some Thoughts About International Product Liability

Werner Lorenz

The Fragmentation of Product Liability: Attempts at Harmonization

United States of America

If compared with the *embarras de richesses* of literature which product liability has thus far provoked both in the United States of America and in Europe during the second half of this century, there are relatively few cases and materials dealing with the private international law aspect of this subject. This is astonishing if one considers the enormous flow of goods across the borders of the major industrial countries. May we, therefore, surmise that conflict rules are rarely needed because the relevant substantive laws of these legal systems are basically identical? In the United States, section 402A of the *Restatement (Second) of Torts* (1965), dealing with the special liability of a seller of a product 'in a defective condition unreasonably dangerous to the user or consumer or to his property', initiated a nationwide development which its main proponent, Dean William Prosser, aptly described as 'the fall of the citadel' of privity.[1] Sellers' warranties, historically sounding in tort, served as a bridge from contract to strict liability in tort for personal injury and property damage caused by defective products. The impact of this innovation on 'the American Tort Process' has been brilliantly analysed by John Fleming in whose honour this essay is written.[2] He rightly draws attention to one of the major questions left open by the Restatement: when is a product defective? The answer is clear only as far as

[1] W. Prosser, 'The Fall of the Citadel (Strict Liability to the Consumer)' (1966) 50 Minn. L. Rev. 791.

[2] J. G. Fleming, *The American Tort Process* (1988), 56f.; idem, *The Law of Torts* (8th ed., 1992), 477. See also J. Stapleton, *Product Liability* (1994), 23.

concerns products which do not conform to the quality standard set by the manufacturer's own specifications (manufacturing defects or *Fabrikationsfehler*). But the situation is entirely different where the product, even though conforming to the manufacturer's design, is unsafe and liable to cause damage to the user of consumer (design defects or *Konstruktionsfehler*). In laying down strict liability the Restatement seems to have had in mind only manufacturing defects where the departure from the fault principle had already begun in actions for negligence with the aid of *res ipsa loquitur.* In actual practice, therefore, the next step to strict liability was not as big as might seem at first blush. The real difficulties came with design defects where strict liability, if taken seriously, would not permit a 'state-of-the-art defence'. A parallel problem is presented by products, the use of which is accompanied by a risk. Certainly, failure to warn against foreseeable risks not generally known to the public at large already entails liability under negligence principles, but it makes no sense to speak of a duty to warn (*Instruktionspflicht*) if, in the light of our scientific knowledge as it then was, the risk was undiscoverable. So it appears that liability for design defects and failure to warn has more affinity with negligence than with liability, irrespective of fault. However, the controversy about the New Jersey Supreme Court decision in the *Beshada* case may be taken as evidence that it is by no means clear whether or not this liability should be fault-based.[3]

Although section 402A of the Second Restatement is widely relied upon, or at least frequently cited, by the courts in the United States, it is fair to say that it has not brought about the desired harmony of legal decisions. Apart from the definition of 'defect', the defence of 'state of the art', and the role of fault, there are a number of other open questions which account for the fragmentation of product liability into nearly as many pieces as the number of states: there is no agreement on the measure of damages, especially in regard to non-economic and punitive damages, and there are differences in the lengths of limitation periods. Moreover, some states have enacted so-called 'statutes of repose' that cut off liability a number of years after the first sale of the product (commonly ranging from seven to twelve years). Neither the original proposal of the Interagency Task Force for a Federal Uniform Product Liability

[3] *Beshada v Johns-Manville Products Corp.* 90 NJ 191, 447 A 2d 539 (1982) applying the 'hindsight approach' to the liability of asbestos producers. But see also the subsequent decision of the same court in *Feldman v Lederle Laboratories*, 97 NJ 429, 479 A 2d 374, 385 (1984): 'The question in strict liability design-defect and warning cases is whether, assuming that the manufacturer knew of the defect in the product, he acted in a reasonably prudent manner in making the product or in providing the warning given. Thus, once the defendant's knowledge of the defect is imputed, strict liability analysis becomes *almost* identical to negligence analysis in its focus on the reasonableness of the defendant's conduct' (emphasis added).

Act (1977), nor the (Draft) Model Uniform Product Liability Act (1979), nor subsequent proposals were enacted.[4]

Europe

Turning now to Europe, the question is whether there is less diversity in the area of product liability. Has the EEC Directive adopted by the Council of Ministers in 1985 achieved the desired harmonization of the law?[5] One hesitates to answer in the affirmative. It is true that outstanding progress has been made with regard to liability for manufacturing defects to which article 1 applies without qualification: 'The producer shall be liable for damage caused by a defect in his product.' In this type of case, where the notion of 'defect' presents no problem of definition, it is unthinkable that a producer could successfully plead 'that the state of scientific and technical knowledge at the time when he put the product into circulation was not such as to enable the existence of the defect to be discovered' (article 7(e)). In a well-reasoned judgment, the *Bundesgerichtshof* has made it clear recently that this defence may be raised only in cases of design defects.[6] Thus liability for manufacturing defects really deserves the epithet 'strict'. However, taken as a whole, the Directive has achieved approximation of the law of product liability only to a very limited extent. This is already apparent if one looks at the three options granted to the Member States: they may exclude the development risk defence, they may include liability for game and unprocessed agricultural products, and they may provide that a producer's total liability caused by identical items with the same defect must not exceed a certain amount.

Moreover, a rather long list of important questions could be drawn up which the Directive has not touched upon and which have thus been left to the laws of the Member States. For present purposes, suffice it to mention that 'damage' does not include 'non-material damage' for pain and suffering or loss of amenities of life (article 9, paragraph 2). As far as property damage is concerned, the same article shows that the Directive merely protects the private consumer, whereas damage to commercially used items of property is left to the relevant national provisions. Finally, article 13 makes it clear that approximation of the different laws falls

[4] For more details, see P. E. Herzog, 'Recent Developments in Products Liability in the United States', (1990) 38 Am. J. Comp. L. 539 and P. J. Kozyris, 'Values and Methods in Choice of Law for Products Liability: A Comparative Comment on Statutory Solutions', (1990) 38 Am. J. Comp. L. 475.

[5] Council Directive (EC) 85/374 on liability for defective products OJL210, 29 (7 Aug. 1985).

[6] *Bundesgerichtshof*, 9 May 1995, BGHZ 129, 353: personal injury caused by an exploding bottle of mineral water.

short of unification, for the Directive does not affect any rights which the injured person may have according to either the national rules of contractual or non-contractual liability or a special liability system already in force. This applies, for instance, to the legislation enacted in Germany in 1976, imposing on the pharmaceutical industry strict liability with no development risk defence.

The Courts' Struggle for the Proper Law of Product Liability: diversity of approaches

United States of America

For some decades ranging from 1934, the year when the first Restatement of the Law of Conflicts of Laws was promulgated, to the sixties, the basic rule applied to torts containing a foreign element had been the law of the place of injury. In the words of the Restatement: 'The place of wrong is the State where the last event necessary to make an actor liable for an alleged tort takes place' (section 377). This conflicts rule was inspired and primarily prepared by Professor Beale, who was probably the last eminent advocate of the theory of territorialism.[7] For him it was only natural that an injured person should acquire an indefeasible right at the moment in which all elements of a tort are united and hence the cause of action arises. The leading product liability case of *Hunter v Derby Foods, Inc.*, decided in the Court of Appeals for the Second Circuit in New York in 1940, may serve as an example of this approach: an Ohio plaintiff recovered under Ohio law against a New York distributor of contaminated beef, because the plaintiff's deceased 'ate the food, took sick and died' in Ohio, and because the fact that the defendant had made the sale to an Ohio wholesaler in New York, who resold the merchandise to a retailer in Ohio, did 'not oust the law of Ohio'. Circuit Judge Patterson pointed out that the law of the place of wrong which governs the right of action for wrongful death is determined by the 'last event'.[8] In explanation of this rule he referred to the paradigmatic textbook case of shooting a firearm across the state line. Although no objection can be raised against the result of this decision, its reasoning has met with criticism from Professor Ehrenzweig, who puts the case of an Ohio citizen who, on a trip to New York, consumes, and falls ill from, contaminated food, produced and sold by an Ohio manufacturer in violation of an Ohio statute. Under the rule as applied in this decision,

[7] J. H. Beale, *Conflict of Laws* (3 vols) (1935)—a commentary on the Restatement.
[8] *Hunter v Derby Foods, Inc.* 110 F 2d 970, 972 (2d Cir. 1940).

recovery under the Ohio statute would be precluded because the harm occurred in New York.[9] This example shows that the place of wrong as defined in section 377 of the first Restatement is a fortuitous point of contact unless supported by other connecting factors.

Interestingly enough, the decision in the *Hunter* case, in spite of its insistence on the place of wrong, contains an important hint at a more modern solution, for the court stressed the fact that defendant had 'sent food into Ohio where the harm was done'. Indeed, the law of the country where the first sale to the ultimate consumer takes place has a much stronger claim than the place of injury, especially if such sales in a particular country are foreseeable. This is confirmed by a more recent case decided in 1964 in the Appellate Court of Illinois. A citizen of Iowa had bought a defective hair-spray manufactured by the defendant in Illinois, and sold to a local wholesaler who, with the knowledge and approval of the defendant, passed it on to retailers in other states. Although the plaintiff had suffered her injuries in Iowa, the court emphasized that the decisive point of contact was not the place of injury, but the ultimate sale in Iowa, no matter where the manufacturer directly or indirectly sold his product to the consumer.[10]

The growing dissatisfaction with the territorial approach and the idea of vested rights going along with it is evidenced by a number of parallel cases, even though they still pay lip-service to the first Restatement.[11] However, the decisive break with tradition came with the well-known traffic accident cases. It will suffice to mention *Babcock v Jackson*, decided in 1963 when Judge Fuld, writing for the majority of the New York Court of Appeals, questioned whether the law of the place of the tort should invariably govern the availability of relief for the tort or whether the applicable choice-of-law rule should also 'reflect a consideration of other factors which are relevant to the purposes served by the enforcement or

[9] A. A. Ehrenzweig, *A Treatise on the Conflict of Laws* (1962) 590; for a general critique of the place of wrong, idem, *Der Tatort im amerikanischen Kollisionsrecht der außervertraglichen Schadensersatzansprüche, Festschrift für Ernst Rabel*, Vol. 1 (1954) 655.

[10] *Hardman v Helene Curtis Industries, Inc.* 48 Ill App 2d 42, 198 NE 2d 681, 689 (1964). Drucker J, pointed out that the view that the law of the ultimate sale should govern 'comports with logic and common sense'. Since Iowa had been the place of injury and thus was the state with the most intimate contacts with the transaction, one must not attach too much weight to this statement.

[11] *Helene Curtis Industries, Inc. v. Pruitt* 385 F 2d 841, 848 (5th Cir. 1967) per Thornberry CJ: 'Although most courts in tort problems are moving away from the vested rights and territorial approach, Texas still follows the traditional *les loci delicti* rule.' See also *Getty Oil Company v Mills* 204 F Supp 179, 187 (WD Pennsylvania, 1962): although the damage caused by a leaking oil-pipe arose in an Arabian Gulf State, the place of wrong was deemed to have been Germany because 'the final step in perfecting plaintiff's loss or damage was the issuance, in Germany, of defendant's certificates of inspection. We therefore conclude that the German tort law governs.'

denial of the remedy'.[12] A few years later California finally abandoned the place-of-wrong rule in favour of an approach which weighs relevant government policies and interests. In the words of Chief Justice Traynor: 'The forum must search to find the proper law to apply based upon the interests of the litigants and the involved states.'[13]

Very soon this interest-weighing approach was also adopted in resolving product liability cases containing foreign elements. However, under the growing influence of the *Restatement (Second) of Conflict of Laws* (1971) it became modified by the 'most significant relationship test' which gives the courts some guidance along the lines of the traditional jurisdiction-selecting method (section 145), subject to the general principle stated in section 6, where consideration is given to the relevant policies of the forum and of other interested states as well as to such important matters as, for instance, the protection of justified expectations and certainty, predictability, and uniformity of result. This case-law development is reflected by several successive decisions turning on claims brought by the representatives of the estates of victims of air-crash disasters which happened in European countries, all of them involving aircraft designed and manufactured in the United States.[14] While the weighing of contacts as suggested by section 145 of the Second Restatement dominated the reasoning of the courts in the beginning, interest analysis became more important in subsequent decisions. In one of these cases the crash had happened in Germany, the victims having been mostly European passengers and some US servicemen. The defendant Boeing had urged the application of German law, but a Federal Court sitting in Pennsylvania and applying the conflicts rule of that state, combined the evaluation of contacts establishing significant relationship with a qualitative appraisal of the relevant states' policies in regard to the controversy. This 'mixed approach' takes into account both the grouping of contacts with the various jurisdictions concerned and the interests and policies that may be validly asserted by each of these jurisdictions. In the instant case Pennsylvania had been the place of design, manufacture, and assembly of the helicopter. Therefore the choice was between the place of the defendant's conduct and the *situs* of the crash and resulting death of the foreign decedents whose domiciles had been in Great Britain, France, and Germany. The result arrived at by the court's interest analysis was

[12] *Babcock v Jackson* 12 NY 2d 473, 477, 240 NYS 2d 743 746, 191 NE 2d 279, 280–1 (1963).

[13] *Reich v Purcell* 67 Cal 2d 551, 553, 63 Cal Rptr 31, 33, 432 P 2d 727, 729 (1967).

[14] *Melton v Borg-Warner Corp.* 467 F Supp 983 (WD Texas, San Antonio Div., 1979); *In re Paris Air Crash of March 3, 1974,* 399 F Supp 732 (CD Calif 1975); *Piper Aircraft Co. v Reyno* 454 US 235, 259–61 (1981), a case primarily concerned with the problem of jurisdiction (*forum non conveniens*), but with important obiter dicta regarding choice-of-law analysis; *In re Air Crash Disaster at Mannheim, Germany* 575 F Supp 521 (ED Pennsylvania, 1983).

that no legitimate interest would be furthered by applying German law, which would probably have meant protecting the defendants from excessive liability.[15]

Equally instructive is a more recent case concerning actions brought against the Japanese designer and manufacturer and the American distributor of an all-terrain-vehicle (ATV).[16] The accident had happened in Colorado where the plaintiff, a domiciliary and taxpayer of Rhode Island, was temporarily stationed at an army base. In the present case, Honda wanted Colorado and not Rhode Island law to apply to the measure of compensatory damages available to the plaintiff, but not to the substantive rules of liability governing the plaintiff's claims. The Court admitted that, in a tort case, different substantive issues may be resolved under the laws of different states under the doctrine of *dépeçage*, but this merely means that 'we must consider the states' interests regarding the distinct issue of compensatory damages, and not their interests generally'.[17] Since the number of contacts claimed by each state was deemed equivalent, the Court examined additional factors: predictability of results, maintenance of inter-state order, simplification of the judicial task, application of the better rule of law and, last but not least, advancement of the forum's governmental interests. It is, perhaps, not astonishing that the Court's reasoning turned almost exclusively on the last-mentioned factor. Would Colorado's policy be advanced by the application of its damage cap, or should preference by given to Rhode Island's policy, according to which a plaintiff should be fully compensated for his personal injuries, including pain and suffering? In the opinion of the Court the interests of the domiciliary state in the welfare of their plaintiffs tipped the scale in favour of applying Rhode Island law to the measure of compensatory damages.

Arguments of a similar kind may also be found in decisions where a court is confronted with different standards of product liability. Suppose a person domiciled in state X suffered injuries while working on a machine manufactured in state Y by a corporation incorporated there. Let us further assume that state X, where the accident occurred, does not recognize a theory of strict product liability for manufacturing defects, whereas state Y has introduced such liability. In a case like this, a plaintiff would probably prefer to sue the manufacturer at his principal place of business, hoping that a claim for damages based on the law of Y would have a better chance than an action for negligence under the law of X. A court rigidly adhering to the *lex loci delicti* would, of course,

15 *In re Air Crash Disaster at Mannheim, Germany* 575 F Supp 521 (ED Pennsylvania, 1983).
16 *La Planta v American Honda Motor Co., Inc.* 27 F 3d 731 (1st Cir., 1994).
17 *Ibid* at 741. Colorado law limits compensatory damages to $250,000, but Rhode Island did not impose any limit.

apply the substantive law of the place of injury. But what will happen in a state where the traditional rule has been abandoned in favour of the governmental interest approach? In dealing with such a case the Superior Court of New Jersey recognized two competing policies bearing on this issue: (1) those relating to the defect-free design and manufacture of a product, and (2) those that regulate the full and fair compensation of the injured party. In the opinion of the Court, the former would militate in favour of New Jersey law (= Y) and the latter for North Carolina's (= X). This conclusion is astonishing because North Carolina law was not as favourable to the plaintiff as New Jersey law, for North Carolina had not adopted the doctrine of strict liability in such cases. In reality, therefore, the second of the two noted policies did not control the outcome. On the contrary, the Court emphasized that New Jersey law had no interest in protecting the compensation rights of a non-domiciliary resident. Moreover, application of New Jersey law would have undesirable consequences in that state, such as deterring the conduct of manufacturing operations. There was also the fear of an unreasonable increase in litigation which might unduly burden the courts: any corporation conducting manufacturing activities in the state could then be sued successfully there.[18]

The interest of a state in deterring substandard conduct within its territory may be further diminished in a case where a defective product is manufactured abroad under licence of a local corporation which had designed and tested that line of products.[19] However, courts applying the governmental interest approach tend to a different conclusion if a citizen of the forum state sues a foreign manufacturer. If the foreign state recognizes strict liability of manufacturers, a more lenient *lex fori* is easily displaced.[20] In a situation like this, the line of argument may run as follows: the defendant cannot complain that application of the law of the place of manufacture is unfair. Moreover, this state must have an interest

[18] *Deemer v Silk City Textile Machinery Co.* 193 NJ Super, 643, 475 A 2d 648, 650–52 (1984).

[19] *Dorman v Emerson Elec. Co.* 23 F 3d 1354 (8th Cir. 1994): D, a Missouri corporation, had designed the product, a mitre saw, which had been acquired by P, a domiciliary of British Columbia, Canada, and had caused injury to him in that province. That particular mitre saw had been manufactured in Taiwan by a Taiwanese corporation, was then purchased by Emerson Electric Canada, Ltd., shipped directly from Taiwan to Vancouver where the saw was sold to a retailer from whom P had purchased it. Unlike Missouri law, Canada does not impose strict liability on manufacturers. Applying the Restatement Second (s 146), which is followed in Missouri, the forum state, the Court concluded that in this case the place of injury was not fortuitous. Therefore Canada's interests in and contacts with this case were regarded at least as substantial as Missouri's. Hence the presumption established in s 146 had not been overcome.

[20] *Magnant v. Medtronic, Inc.* 818 F supp 204 (WD Michigan, 1993). Diversity action before a court sitting in Michigan where strict liability was not recognized as a basis on which relief can be granted. It was different under Minnesota law where D had designed and manufactured the defective product.

in having its law apply to its corporations because this will provide them with certainty as to which law would apply. As for the forum state's interest in protecting citizens, nothing weighs in favour of the *lex fori* because the plaintiff would be better off under the law of the place of manufacture.[21]

Different periods of limitation of tort actions present no problem which is peculiar to product liability claims. The age-old problem of how statutes of limitation must be characterized for choice-of-law purposes can now probably be regarded as settled. The overwhelming majority of courts treats them as going to the substance of the claim. But the question remains whether the same can be said of statutes of repose which extinguish product liability actions a certain time after a product is purchased for use or consumption. Several more recent cases may give rise to some doubts. Thus it was held by the Supreme Court of Connecticut in 1994 that 'the fact that a statute of repose may bar a claim before the cause of action has accrued does not form a basis to distinguish it from a statute of limitation for choice-of-law purposes'.[22] Taken by itself, this statement is correct, but unfortunately in the case in question it meant that the statute of repose had to be treated as procedural by nature. The same characterization was deemed appropriate by the Supreme Court of Alabama when the majority refused to apply a North Carolina statute of repose, even though the law of that state was regarded as governing the substance of the plaintiff's claim. However, the dissenting judge rightly remarked that under North Carolina law the age of a product is a material and substantive element of a claim, and no cause of action arises after the period laid down in the statute has elapsed.[23] It appears that this view is gradually gaining ground with the courts. Indeed, both statutes of limitation and statutes of repose barring actions based on an alleged defect in 'old' products go to the substance of the claim. Therefore the 'functional approach' aimed at finding the most significant relationship of a set of facts with a certain legal system determines this choice-of-law issue as well.[24]

[21] *Ibid* at 207.

[22] *Baxter v Sturm, Ruger and Co., Inc.* 230 Conn 335, 644 A 2d 1297, 1301 (1994).

[23] *Etheredge v Genie Industries, Inc.* 632 So 2d 1324, 1327–8 (1994) per Houston, J. The majority of the court felt free to make its own characterization, even though the North Carolina Supr. Ct had previously characterized its statute of repose as being substantive. P was domiciled in Alabama, but the accident had happened in North Carolina while he had used a lifting device that had been rented by his Alabama employer from another Alabama citizen who had bought the product from D in Alabama. In spite of these contacts with Alabama the law of North Carolina was regarded as governing the substance of the claim because the injury occurred there.

[24] *Cosme v Whitin Machine Works, Inc.* 417 Mass 643, 632 NE 2d 832 (Mass. 1994); *New England Telephone & Telegraph Co. v Gourdeau* 419 Mass. 658, 637 NE 2d 42 (1995); *Rice*

England and Canada (Common Law Provinces)

Leaving aside for a moment Quebec, where a new Civil Code (adopted 18 December 1991 and in force since 1 January 1994) has laid down special conflict rules dealing with the liability of manufacturers (articles 3128 and 3129), the position taken by English and Canadian courts is not easily described in a few words. The main reason for this uncertainty is that the small number of reported cases on product liability containing foreign elements all turned on problems of jurisdiction. Therefore, one can only speculate on the choice-of-law issue. However, it may perhaps be taken for granted that the *lex fori* will be applied once an English or a Canadian court has decided that it can exercise jurisdiction over such a case. As far as Canada is concerned, this is confirmed by the recent Consumer Products Warranty and Liability Acts which are now in force in several Canadian provinces. Their common feature is that 'doing business within the Province' is a sufficient ground for exercising jurisdiction over a manufacturer who directly or indirectly markets consumer products in the province. This fact having been established, no problem of choice of law arises since the internal *lex fori* will then automatically be applied.[25]

The place where the tort was committed has been the decisive jurisdictional point of contact in England and the Commonwealth when plaintiffs sought to serve process outside the jurisdiction under Order 11 of the Rules of the Supreme Court (RSC).[26] However, this criterion was reformulated in 1983 so as to adapt it to the Brussels Convention of 1968 (article 5 number 3) and the construction put upon it by the European Court of Justice.[27] Under the new provision of RSC Order 11, rule 1(1)(f), English courts may exercise jurisdiction 'where the claim is founded on a tort and the damage was sustained, or resulted from an act committed, within the jurisdiction'. This may mean that the cases previously decided will be of no further significance.[28] As far as the choice-of-law process is concerned, it remains to be seen whether this new jurisdictional approach will promote the tendency to apply the *lex fori*. Leaving aside such speculations, English private international law, as it

v Dow Chemical Co. 124 Wash 2d 205, 875 P 2d 1213 (1994); see also *Farrell v Ford Motor Co.* 199 Mich App 81, 501 NW 2d 567 (1993) where the Michigan CA criticized *Mahne v Ford Motor Co.* 900 F 2d 83 (6th Cir., 1990) as an 'errant decision'.

[25] J.-G. Castel, *Canadian Conflict of Laws* (3rd ed., 1994), 656–8 referring to legislation in New Brunswick and Saskatchewan.

[26] RSC Ord 11, r 1(1)(h).

[27] *Bier v Mines de Potasse d'Alsace* [1976] ECR 1735. In construing article 5 no. 3 of the EEC Convention on Jurisdiction and Judgments in Civil and Commercial Matters, 1968, the ECJ held that the place of wrong was both in France where D acted and in Holland where the damage was suffered.

[28] This is the view held by J. G. Collier: see *Conflict of Laws* (2nd ed., 1994), 230.

stands now, is still committed to the 'substance of the tort' test as enunciated by Lord Pearson in the leading case of *Distillers Co. (Biochemicals) Ltd v Thompson*,[29] according to which the right approach consists in looking back over the series of events constituting the tort and asking the question, where in substance did the cause of action arise?[30] Thus, in a more recent case where a user of a machine manufactured in Germany was injured in England, the substantial wrongdoing was held to be putting on the English market a defective machine with no warning of its defects.[31] It is submitted that putting a defective product on the market should suffice as a point of contact, both in point of jurisdiction and for choice-of-law purposes, for it does not make much sense to re-interpret a manufacturing defect so as to give it the appearance of a failure to warn. A duty to warn may only be an independent cause of action where certain foreseeable risks are at issue.

It also remains to be seen whether the changes brought about by Part III of the Private International Law (Miscellaneous Provisions) Act 1995 will lead to results different from those thus far elaborated by English courts in the field of product liability. Although this Act has abolished the common-law rule requiring actionability both under the *lex fori* and under the *lex loci delicti*, it is not to be expected that the marked 'home-ward trend' will disappear. The new general rule adheres to the *lex loci delicti* which, in actions for personal injury, is the law of the country where the injury was sustained, and, in actions for damage to property, is the law of the *situs* of the property at the time of damage (section 11). However, this general rule is easily displaced if 'it appears, in all the circumstances, from a comparison of: (a) the significance of the factors which connect a tort or delict with the country whose law would be the applicable law under the general rule; and (b) the significance of any factors connecting the tort or delict with another country, that it is substantially more appropriate for the applicable law for determining

[29] [1971] AC 458 (PC), again a case turning on jurisdiction, i.e. whether P's cause of action against the manufacturers of the drug Distival, containing thalidomide, arose within the jurisdiction.

[30] See also *Multinational Gas and Petroleum Co. v Multinational Gas and Petrochemical Services Ltd* [1983] 2 All ER 563, 570 (CA) per Lawton LJ and *Metall und Rohstoff AG v Donaldson Lufkin & Jenrette Inc.* [1990] 1 QB 391, 436–47 (CA) per Slade LJ.

[31] *Castree v E. R. Squibb & Sons Ltd* [1980] 1 WLR 1248, 1252 (CA) per Ackner LJ, who pointed out that what gave, or gives, P her cause of complaint is not the mere manufacture of the defective machinery, which of course took place in Germany. In his opinion this was not even the beginning of the tort. The decisive act was putting the machine on the English market with no warning as to its defects. But see also *Monro (George) Ltd v American Cyanamid and Chemical Corp.* [1944] KB 432, 439 per Goddard LJ who subscribed to the theory of the place of acting rather than the place where the damage was suffered. This view may now be regarded as obsolete. See too, *Cheshire and North's Private International Law* (12th ed., 1992) at 554–5.

the issues arising in the case, or any of those issues, to be the law of the other country.' On such displacement the applicable law then becomes the law of that other country (section 12(1)). Section 12(2) gives some hints as to the factors to be taken into account: factors relating to the parties or any of the events which may constitute the tort in question or any of the circumstances or consequences of those events.

The few Canadian cases on our subject must be received with the same caution as the English authorities because they, too, arose in a jurisdictional context. But it is, perhaps, permissible to conclude that once a Canadian court assumes jurisdiction over a product liability case it will not hesitate to apply its *lex fori* to the substance of the claim. The leading case of *Moran v Pyle National (Canada) Ltd*,[32] decided by the Supreme Court in 1973, did away with the theory of the place of acting by emphasizing instead that the foreign manufacturer had put the defective product in the stream of commerce knowing that as a result of carelessness a user or consumer in another province might well be injured.[33]

Germany, Austria and Switzerland

For a long time it was taken for granted that German courts had little chance to deal with product liability cases confronting them with choice-of-law problems. However, recent research has revealed that, in spite of relevant cases, the courts only rarely took notice of private international law.[34] This is astonishing because under the Code of Civil Procedure (*Zivilprozessordnung* (*ZPO*)) foreign law is not treated as a fact which must be pleaded and proven by the parties. The court must take cognizance of it *ex officio* (§ 293 *ZPO*). It goes without saying that this holds good also for the preliminary question as to whether or not foreign law is applicable in a concrete case. It is an open question why the choice-of-law problem was ignored in a substantial number of cases. One

[32] [1973] 43 DLR (3d) 239, 250–1 per Dickson J (delivering the judgment of the court): 'Where a foreign defendant carelessly manufactures a product in a foreign jurisdiction which enters into the normal channels of trade and he knows or ought to know both that as a result of his carelessness a consumer may well be injured and it is reasonably foreseeable that the product would be used or consumed where the plaintiff used or consumed it, then the forum in which the plaintiff suffered damage is entitled to exercise judicial jurisdiction over that foreign defendant.'

[33] But see also the following decisions of the Ontario High Ct of Justice which give the impression that the place of harm as such, or even the place where the plaintiff was hospitalized, determines the exercise of jurisdiction and presumably also the choice of the applicable law: *Skyrotors Ltd v Carriere Technical Industries* (1980) 102 DLR (3d) 383 and *Vile v Von Wendt: Zürich Insurance Co.* (1980) 103 DLR (3d) 356.

[34] M. Wandt, *Internationale Produkthaftung* (1995), 164–7 lists 16 relevant cases, most of them having been decided by courts of first instance and courts of appeal, where German law was applied without any previous discussion of the choice-of-law issue.

hesitates to presume that these courts simply did not realize that foreign law might be involved in a pending case. The better and more probable explanation for this phenomenon seems to be that in these cases both parties based their claims, as well as the defence, upon German law. In a case like this, a court may treat these pleadings as a tacit choice of the German *lex fori*.

Leaving aside cases where the claimant is in direct contractual relationship with the person claimed to be liable, the starting-point will be the conflicts rule on extra-contractual liability. In German law this is still the *lex loci delicti*, which may either mean the place of acting or the place of harm.[35] Since the delict is located in two places simultaneously this has been given the name of 'the theory of ubiquity' (*Ubiquitätsstheorie*).[36] Under this theory the plaintiff may choose between these two legal systems. He will, of course, base his claim on the law which is more favourable. This theory obtains also in regard to jurisdiction: actions based on delict must be brought before the court of the district where the act was committed (§ 32 *ZPO*)[37] which includes the place of harm. Putting this construction upon the *locus delicti* has given German courts considerable freedom of action, both in regard to jurisdiction and in point of the applicable law. In practice, the court chooses the applicable law, at least in those cases where the parties cannot agree on the law to be applied. Again the cases provide evidence of the well-known 'homeward trend' in private international law leading to the *lex fori*, either as the law of the place of acting or, more often, as the law of the place of injury. Thus far in all of the German decisions which have faced the choice-of-law issue squarely, 'the theory of ubiquity' enabled the courts to apply the *lex fori* because Germany had been the place of harm.[38]

When Austria became a member of the European Union it had already enacted a special Product Liability Law (*Produktehaftungsgesetz*) which, for all practical purposes, was identical with the EEC Directive of 1985.[39]

[35] This is deemed to be implicit in art. 38 *EGBGB*, i.e. the Introductory Law to the Civil Code.

[36] This theory was first applied in cases involving negligent misstatements resulting in pure commercial loss; see *Reichsgericht*, 23 Sept. 1887 = RGZ 19, 382 (383) and *Reichsgericht*, 20 Nov. 1888 = RGZ 23, 305 (306).

[37] Although this provision has in mind only 'venue' (*örtliche Zuständigkeit*), it is also applied in a jurisdictional context (*internationale Zuständigkeit*). But see also n. 27 above concerning EEC Convention on Jurisdiction, art. 5 no. 3, which has priority over § 32 *ZPO*, in cases arising within the European Union.

[38] *Reichsgericht*, 21 Feb. 1899 = JW 1899, 222 no. 2; *OLG* Karlsruhe, 26 May 1977 = J. Schmidt-Salzer, *Entscheidungssammlung Produkthaftung*, vol 2 (1979), 57; *OLG* Düsseldorf, 28 Apr. 1978 = NJW 1980, 533 = *IPRspr.* 1978 no. 24; *OLG* Celle, 26 Oct. 1978 = IPRspr. 1978 no. 28; *Bundesgerichtshof*, 17 Mar. 1981 = BGHZ 80, 199 = IPRax 1982, 13–14; *OLG* Cologne, 11 Dec. 1991 = VersR 1993, 110.

[39] *Produkthaftungsgesetz*, in force since July 1 1988 (*ÖBGBL* 1988/89). For the EEC Directive, see above.

This piece of legislation has meanwhile been fully adapted to the Directive by the removal of certain technical discrepancies. Thus far it has had no impact on the system of private international law of Austria. In the opinion of the majority of Austrian scholars, the conflict rules developed under the regime of negligence would also be suitable for deciding cases concerning product liability under the Directive.[40] However, according to an isolated view propounded by Professor Schwind, an Austrian court would have to apply this new *Produktehaftungsgesetz* in any case because it should be classified as a *loi d'application immédiate*.[41]

The leading case of the Austrian *Oberster Gerichtshof* (*OGH*), decided in 1987, has led to some controversy among academic writers.[42] The reason is that in Austrian product liability law the line of demarcation between contract and tort is somewhat blurred because the last buyer of a product is protected by the contract concluded between the seller (retailer) and the wholesaler/importer or manufacturer.[43] This raises a problem of characterization: does a claim for damages brought by the last buyer against a remote party in the chain of distribution sound in contract or in tort? If the claim were regarded as purely contractual it would be governed by the proper law of the contract from which this protection is derived. However, the *OGH* classifies such claims as non-contractual and applies the conflicts rule on torts (§ 48 paragraph 1 *Bundesgesetz über das internationale Privatrecht* (*IPRG*)) which prefers the *lex loci delicti* unless both parties have a more real and common connection with the law of another state. This 'escape clause' has an important function in Austrian private international law, particularly in product liability cases, because the *locus delicti* is deemed to be the place where the defendant acted, or should have acted, in order to avoid the damage.[44] Therefore foreign manufacturers or sellers of defective goods could hardly be held liable under Austrian law if this were the only point of contact. This explains why the *OGH* had recourse to the 'escape clause'. In the instant case this meant that the closest contacts of both parties pointed to the (Austrian) market for which the goods in question were destined (*Recht des Marktes*). Again, the outside observer can but

[40] For this view, see P. Rummel & R. Schwimann, *Kommentar zum Allgemeinen bürgerlichen Gesetzbuch*, vol 2 (1992), § 48 n. 4a *IPRG* with further references.

[41] F. Schwind, *Internationales Privatrecht* (1990), 234: 'wirtschaftlich und sozial bedingte Eingriffsnorm'.

[42] *OGH*, 29 Oct. 1987 = IPRax 1988, 363 = VersR 1988, 1086.

[43] Contract with protective effect towards third parties', i.e. *Vertrag mit Schutzwirkung für Dritte*. In adopting this legal institution the *OGH* followed a suggestion made by F. Bydlinski, 'Vertragliche Sorgsfaltspflichten zugunsten Dritter', (1960) JB1. 359. It was 'invented' in German law some time ago, but it must be emphasized that German courts will not apply it to chains of distribution.

[44] See A. Duchek & F. Schwind, *Internationales Privatrecht* (1979), § 48 n 4 *IPRG*. Austria does not adhere to 'the theory of ubiquity'.

marvel at the ingenuity of the Court in finding the way home to the *lex fori*. A perusal of this decision reminds the reader of Dean Prosser's unforgettable pleasantry about 'the realm of the conflict of laws' which he described as 'a dismal swamp, filled with quaking quagmires, and inhabited by learned but eccentric professors who theorize about mysterious matters in a strange and incomprehensible jargon'.[45] The leading Austrian case shows that this 'jargon' is not confined to professors teaching private international law.

In Switzerland the *Produktehaftpflichtgesetz*, which has been in force since 1 January 1994, transposes the EEC Directive into national law. The new Swiss Federal Statute on Private International Law (*Bundesgesetz über das internationale Privatrecht* (*IPRG*)) had been passed several years before. It is one of the very few laws containing a special provision on product liability. Thus, article 135 *IPRG* gives the party who is injured by a defect in, or a defective description of, a product a choice between (a) the law of the state in which the tortfeasor has his place of business or, in the absence thereof, his habitual residence; or (b) the law of the state in which the product was acquired, unless the tortfeasor proves that the product had been marketed in that state without his consent. However, this provision also contains a proviso inspired by considerations of Swiss *ordre public*: when claims based on a defect or a defective description of a product are governed by foreign law, 'no damages other than those that would be awarded under Swiss law for such injury may be awarded in Switzerland; (article 135 paragraph 2 *IPRG*). Obviously, this provision has in mind the American practice of awarding punitive damages (treble damages) in cases of recklessness on the part of the person claimed to be liable.[46] Leaving aside this reservation clause as to the extent of damages, the Swiss legislature has tried to strike a balance between two conflicting interests: the injured person's position is strengthened by the option between two legal systems with which such facts are usually closely connected, but the tortfeasor is protected in so far as he may be held liable only under a foreseeable law for which adequate insurance coverage may be had. Whether this aim can be achieved will largely depend upon how the decisive point of contact, the place where the product was acquired (*Erwerbsort*), is construed. It would add to clarity if this were held to mean the country of the first sale to a consumer or user. But there remains, of course, the case of the bystander who is injured by a defective product. Doubts may also be raised in regard to persons acquiring possession as bailees. If these

[45] Citation taken from *Hughes v Hughes* 91 NM 339, 573 P 2d 1194, 1199 (Supr. Ct NM, 1978).

[46] See A. Meier-Hayoz (ed.), *Kommentar zum Schweizerischen Privatrecht—Internationales Privatrecht* (1996), art. 135 no. 17.

claimants are not covered by the special provision of article 135 *IPRG*, their cases would have to be dealt with under the general provision of article 133, paragraph 2, sentence 2, i.e., the law of the place of injury would apply, always provided, however, that this could be foreseen by the tortfeasor.[47] Since the Swiss Federal Tribunal has not yet been given an opportunity to decide a product liability case under the new *IPRG*, all these questions are still open.

More Recent Codifications: Louisiana and Quebec

The Swiss attempt at codifying international product liability law does not stand alone. Both Louisiana and Quebec have recently laid down special provisions for such cases. Article 3545 of the Louisiana Civil Code (1991), effective 1 January 1992, has created a one-sided conflicts rule in favour of the *lex fori* which applies (1) when the injury was sustained in the state by a person domiciled or residing in the state; or (2) when the product was manufactured, produced, or acquired in the state and caused injury either in the state or in another state to a person domiciled in the state. However, Louisiana law will not apply if the defendant can prove that 'neither the product that caused the injury nor any of the defendant's products of the same type were available in this state through ordinary commercial channels' (article 45). The incompleteness of this unilateral choice-of-law rule is underlined by its last paragraph which refers to other articles of the section on delictual and quasi-delictual obligations. Indeed, article 45 covers only those cases in which the application of the *lex fori* will be non-controversial. It does, however, not apply if only one of its four connecting factors points to Louisiana, for it always requires a combination of at least two of these factors. Therefore the controversial cases must be solved by applying the general conflict rules of this section (articles 42–4 and 46–8), most important among them being an 'escape clause' giving preference to the law of another state if the policies of that state 'would be more seriously impaired if its law were not applied to the particular issue. In such event the law of the other state shall apply' (article 47). In view of the flexibility of the general rule (article 42) the practical function of this 'escape clause' remains unclear, for the general rule already tries to strike a balance between the governmental interest approach and the jurisdiction-selecting method: the court must apply 'the law of the state whose policies would be most seriously impaired if its law were not

[47] For this view, see A. Heini, M. Keller, K. Siehr, & P. Volken (eds.) *IPRG Kommentar* (1993), art. 135 no. 35.

applied to that issue' (article 41 paragraph 1), but this state is determined on the strength and pertinence of the relevant policies of the involved states in the light of a number of traditional connecting factors as, for instance, place of conduct and injury, domicile, habitual residence, or place of business of the parties, and the state in which the relationship, if any, between the parties was centred (article 42 paragraph 2). Summing up, the impression remains that the new Louisiana conflict rules on delict are no 'counter-revolution' marking the end of a period of bewildering experimentation in this area of the law. Rather, it bears all the traces of a compromise surrounded by many uncertainties.[48]

The recent codification of private international law in Quebec (cited above), which is part of the new Civil Code of this province, has brought about radical changes of the conflict rules on civil liability. Thus the (former) English rule requiring double actionability (i.e. actionability under the *lex fori* and under the *lex loci delicit*) is replaced by the *lex loci delicit* as the basic principle. It may be noted that the Supreme Court of Canada has also abolished this 'double-barrelled' rule for the common-law provinces, replacing it with an unqualified rule in favour of the *lex loci delicti*.[49] Liability is governed by the law of the country 'where the injurious act occurred' (article 3126). In cases of damage occurring in a jurisdiction other than that in which the defendant acted, this means the (foreseeable) place of injury. Following a modern European tendency, the *lex loci* is set aside where the person committing the injurious act and the victim have their domiciles or residences in the same country. However, as far as manufacturer's liability is concerned, Quebec has laid down a more particular choice-of-law rule which is closely modelled after the Swiss rule (see above). Thus, article 3128 provides that the victim of damage caused by a defective product, including failure to warn of risks, may choose, as governing law, the law of the country of the manufacturer's place of business or, in the absence thereof, his residence or the law of the country where the product was acquired.[50] This differs from article 135 of the Swiss *IPRG* only in so far as the tortfeasor cannot

[48] See also S. C. Symeonides. 'Problems and Dilemmas in Codifying Choice of Law for Torts: The Louisiana Experience in Comparative Perspective', (1990) 38 Am. J. Comp. L. 431, 469, who rightly remarks that the Louisiana Project, as it then still was, 'makes its appearance on the national conflicts scene at the end of a not-so-glorious revolution and the beginning of a bitter counter-revolution, that is, at a period of transition, reorientation, and intense soul-searching in American conflicts law'.

[49] See *Jensen v Tolofson, Gagnon v Lucas* (1994) 120 DLR (4th) 289.

[50] But see also H. P. Glenn, 'Codification of Private International Law in Quebec', (1996) 60 Rabels Zeitschrift 231, 251 who maintains that the choice of the plaintiff may be even larger than that indicated by art. 3128. Thus, art. 3082, embodying the principle of proximity, might lead to the application of the *lex domicilii* of the victim if he or she has bought a manufactured product while away from home (cross-border shopping) and an obligation to recall or warn is not respected by the manufacturer.

escape liability under the 'law of the market' by proving that the product has been distributed in that state without his consent. The section on civil liability is concluded by a provision in the nature of a *loi d'application immédiate*: article 3129 dealing with claims brought in cases of damage suffered as a result of exposure to or the use of raw materials originating in Quebec.[51] This provision, which subjects such claims to the *lex fori*, is intended to protect the Quebec asbestos industry against strict liability under foreign law which is regarded as excessive.

The Hague Convention on the Law Applicable to Products Liability (1973)

This Convention, which has been in force since 1 October 1977, has thus far been ratified only by a relatively small number of states.[52] Its system is based upon a 'grouping of contacts'. The American revolution in the law of conflicts, which had not yet passed its peak when the Convention was drafted, remained without influence. Suffice it to recall the French delegate's classification of the American conflicts scene as *'impressionnisme juridique'*,[53] a view which prevailed among the members of the committee drafting the Convention. This does not, however, mean that the method adopted at The Hague has received much applause. On the contrary, the complicated system of combining several connecting factors has given rise to widespread criticism. But some of the critics do not seem to be sufficiently aware of the difficulties with which a diplomatic conference has to cope when drafting such a Convention on a subject bearing on the economic interests of states. This differs greatly from the work done in the ivory-tower of a scholar. The present author, who was himself a delegate to the conference, is of the view that nothing would have been achieved without the willingness to arrive at compromise solutions.[54]

[51] Art. 3129: 'Les règles du présent code s'appliquent de façon impérative à la responsabilité civile pour tout préjudice subi au Québec ou hors du Quebéc et résultant soit de l'exposition à une matière première provenant du Québec, soit de son utilsation, que cette matière première ait été traitée ou non.' The sceptical attitude towards strict product liability is fully borne out by H. P. Glenn, 'Judicial Authority and the Liability of the Manufacturer, of Jusqu'où Peut-on Aller Trop Loin?', (1990) 38 Am. J. Comp. L. 564–5.

[52] France, Yugoslavia, and Norway ratified first, but were joined by The Netherlands, Luxembourg, Spain, and Finland later.

[53] Y. Loussuarn, 'Cours général de droit international privé', (1973–II) 139 Recueil des Cours 270, 338 about 'l'essor de l'impressionnisme juridique'.

[54] See. W. Lorenz, 'Der Haager Konventionsentwurf über das auf die Produktenhaftpflicht anwendbare Recht', (1972) 37 Rabels Zeitschrift 317–56 and idem, 'Das ausservertragliche Haftungsrecht der Haager Konventionen', (1993) 57 Rabels Zeitschrift 175, 195–206.

One of the problem areas where a compromise had to be reached concerned the interaction of contract and tort which looms so large in cases of product liability. However, contractual liability is not within the scope of the Convention, which does not even apply to liability in tort if 'the property in, or the right to use, the product was transferred to the person suffering damage by the person claimed to be liable' (article 1 paragraph 2). Different notions prevailing in the various legal systems with respect to the transfer of property would have produced international disharmony in the application of the Convention, particularly in cases where the plaintiff acquired the product through an agent or a family member. This exclusion of contractual relations has given rise to the question whether it would not have been advisable to make provision against the application of different laws to concurring contractual and delictual remedies available in a substantial number of legal systems. The problem has recently become known as 'dependent choice of law' (*akzessorische Anknüpfung*), i.e. the contractual relationship existing between the parties is regarded as dominant for conflicts purposes. A parallel tort action would then have to be determined by the law governing the special legal relationship among the parties at the time of injury.[55] Unfortunately, this idea did not win the support of a majority of the countries represented at The Hague, the main reason being that this would amount to giving the parties freedom of choice in regard to the law applicable to liability in tort which, in some legal systems, is deemed to be a matter pertaining to the *ordre public interne*. But there is also another reason why, seen in the light of a legal system like that of France, this proposal did not recommend itself to a majority of delegates: in a country where concurring tort actions are not admitted if the plaintiff can sue in contract (*non-cumuldes responsabilités*), there is no room for such a 'dependent choice of law', the more so if such a legal system permits a direct contractual action even against a remote seller (so-called *action directe*).

In international product liability cases, there are essentially four connecting factors which may be regarded as important: the place of injury, the habitual residence of the person directly suffering damage, the place of business of the person claimed to be liable, and the place where the product was acquired by the person directly suffering damage. During

[55] The German delegation had made the following proposal: 'If the victim has acquired the product under a contract made with the defendant, liability in tort, if any, shall be governed by the law applicable to that contract.' See Document de travail No. 22: Actes et Documents de la Douzième session, 2 au 21 octobre 1972, III 151. It must, however, be admitted that this problem has meanwhile lost some of its significance since the coming into force of the Convention on International Sales Law (CISG) which does not contain provisions on product liability.

the preparatory work in a special committee of the conference the prevailing opinion had been that none of the possible connecting factors, taken by themselves, can be regarded as a proper localizing element. For this reason the idea of establishing a 'hierarchy of connecting factors', starting out with the victim's habitual residence, was finally abandoned. It was also thought that 'the proper law of the tort' would not have been a true solution because this is, in reality, nothing but a heuristic principle. But would the idea of an option between several potentially applicable laws not have been a way out of this dilemma? It will be remembered that in countries adhering to the 'theory of ubiquity' the plaintiff may already choose between the law of the place of injury and the law of the place where the defendant acted or should have acted. However, a general option between four legal systems would have gone much further and would no longer have been in keeping with the idea of liability under a foreseeable law under which adequate insurance coverage may be had.

The key provisions of the Convention (articles 4 and 5) provide that either 'the state of the place of injury' or 'the state of the habitual residence of the person directly suffering damage' will determine the applicable law if the case has one or two more designated contacts with that state. So, under article 4, 'the state of the place of injury' will be the state of the applicable law if, in addition, that state is also the place where the injured person had his habitual residence or acquired the product, or where the person claimed to be liable had his principal place of business. Under article 5, and 'notwithstanding the provisions of article 4', the state of the habitual residence of the person directly suffering damage will be the state of the applicable law if, in addition, that state is either the place where the person claimed to be liable had his principal place of business or where the product was acquired by the person directly suffering damage. Only in the relatively rare cases where no such combination of contacts as envisaged in articles 4 and 5 exists is the claimant given an option to base his action on the internal law of either the state of the place of injury or the state of the principal place of business of the person claimed to be liable (article 6). However, even this limited option is subject to the 'foreseeability test' of article 7: the law of the state where the claimant suffered injury may not be chosen if the defendant 'establishes that he could not reasonably have foreseen that the product or his own products of the same type would be made available in that state through commerical channels'. As a result, there will be rare situations where the plaintiff must base his claim on the internal law of the state of the defendant's principal place of business even though he, the plaintiff, has no connection whatsoever with that state. In other words, a manufacturer must always be prepared to face liability under the law of his own state.

As has already been mentioned, the system of 'contact grouping' chosen by the Convention has been much criticized, the main thrust of this criticism being that it is too complicated.[56] But the alternative proposals cover such a wide range of connecting factors that they again prove how difficult it is to find a satisfactory solution in an area of private international law dealing with sets of facts which usually have a variety of contacts with several legal systems. One may also challenge the proposition that a manufacturer should only be liable under a foreseeable law. This is to the disadvantage of the person suffering damage. Apart from that, it appears that insurers calculate their risks upon a different basis, for they are, first of all, interested in their clients' turnover and, secondly, they want to know the countries to which the products are exported. It goes without saying that this has some influence on the premiums if, for instance, a manufacturer puts his products on the US market.

As a matter of principle, rules of conduct and safety laid down by the law applicable under the Convention have to be observed by manufacturers exporting their products to other countries. Suppose, however, the product in question was introduced into the market of a country whose internal law is not applicable by reason of articles 4, 5 and 6. In a situation like that, it might be asked whether the pertinent rules of safety of the market should have any influence on the standard of conduct required of the person claimed to be liable. The Convention tries to answer this question in a rather vaguely formulated provision (article 9) which had given rise to disputes until the last (plenary) session of the Hague Conference. This article empowers, but does not require, a court to give consideration to the rules of safety prevailing in the state where the product was marketed as well as to similar rules of the state whose internal law is made applicable by the Convention. The effect of this provision is uncertain because it may, or it may not, be to the advantage or disadvantage of the one or the other part if these safety standards diverge.

Conclusions

The development of international case law, as well as the recent codifications in the field of international product liability, display at least five

[56] U. Drobnig, 'Produkthaftung', in E. von Caemmerer (ed.), *Vorschläge und Gutachten zur Reform des deutschen IPR der ausservertraglichen Schuldverhältnisse* (1983) at 311–13; H. Stoll, 'Anknüpfungsgrundsätze bei der Haftung für Strassenverkehrsunfälle und der Produkthaftung nach der neuren Entwicklung des internationeren Deliksrechts' in A. Lüdentz & J. Schroder (eds.), *Festschrift für Gerhard Kegel* (1977) at 127–34; F. Vischer, 'Das Deliktsrecht des IPR-Gesetzes unter besonderer Berücksichtigung der Produktehaftung', in I. Schwander (ed.), *Festschrift fur Rudolf Moser* (1987), 132.

possible points of contact for determining the applicable law: (1) domicile or habitual residence of the person suffering injury; (2) place of injury; (3) place of the first sale to, or acquisition of possession by, the consumer or user, and the place of marketing; (4) place of manufacture and/or design; (5) principal place of business of the defendant. Some of these connecting factors are liable to be construed differently in different jurisdictions. Thus 'domicile' as used in the present context is not necessarily identical with the concept as found in English law. It does not differ essentially from 'habitual residence', which has become a familiar contact figuring prominently in more recent Hague Conventions, denoting the home or place where a person lives permanently. More difficult is the definition of 'place of injury'. It will be remembered that under 'the theory of ubiquity' this may either be the place where the defendant's wrongful act had its first impact upon the person suffering damage or the place of the defendant's wrongful act, a theory which is also recognized by the European Court of Justice for jurisdictional purposes. Moreover, situations may occasionally arise where the damage does not manifest itself immediately upon impact as, for instance, in consequence of taking a medical drug. Leaving aside such isolated cases the modern tendency, at least for choice-of-law purposes, is to regard the 'place of the first impact' as the *locus delicti.*

The large variety of international situations of fact to be dealt with in this area of conflicts of law makes the choice of the appropriate connecting factor particularly difficult. The recent national codifications and the discussions in preparation of the Hague Convention are evidence of a common conviction that none of the possible connecting factors, taken by themselves, can be regarded as an appropriate localizing element. This explains the temptation to take refuge in 'the proper law of the tort' which empowers a court to determine the jurisdiction where a certain legal relationship has its 'centre of gravity'. Even more vague or objectionable than this particular method of selecting the jurisdiction is the attempt to find the applicable law by way of an 'analysis of governmental interests'. Experience has shown that this makes the choice-of-law process highly capricious because such interests are not openly pronounced by governments. In reality, therefore, it amounts to mere conjecture if a court asserts its belief in such specified interests as, for instance, New Jersey's interest in protecting the manufacturing operations of its industry so as to neglect the compensation rights of a North Carolina resident who had suffered injuries while working on a machine manufactured in New Jersey by a corporation incorporated there.[57] The

[57] See *Deemer v Silk City Textile Machinery Co.* 193 NJ Super 643, 475 A 2d 648 (Supr. Ct of New Jersey, 1984), discussed above.

example alluded to is one of the relatively rare cases where a court did not conclude its analysis by giving preference to the forum's own law. In general, however, a plaintiff may count on the courts' tendency to apply the *lex fori* which makes the choice of law dependent upon jurisdictional rules.

This leads to the question of whether it is a legitimate aim in private international law of product liability to select the applicable law with a view to the desired outcome of the case. Obviously, this goes far beyond the traditional influence of the *ordre public* of the forum enabling a court to correct an outrageous result which would follow from the legal system to be applied under the conflicts rule. Empowering the courts to look for 'the better rule of law' means something else, and the question immediately arising is, which of the two laws is 'better' if, for instance, liability under the law of state A is strict, but limited in amount, whereas in state B liability is based upon negligence, but without any such limit? One hesitates to answer this question. Should one, perhaps, carry the doctrine of *dépeçage* to the point of applying both laws, namely, law A to the basis of liability and law B to the extent of damages to be awarded? This would give the plaintiff the best of both worlds. Apart from that, who says that the choice to be made must necessarily produce a pro-plaintiff result?[58] All this shows how uncertain the choice-of-law process would be for the parties.

In this context it deserves special attention that Professor Cavers, not uninfluenced by the Hague Convention, has modified his earlier 'principles of preference' so as to adapt them to the special needs of product liability. He now recognizes that combining coinciding contacts diminishes the risk of arbitrary results that single-contact rules would create.[59] This is in basic agreement with the territorial approach of the Hague Convention. It is followed also in the recent Louisiana statute, by requiring at least two contacts to merge in one jurisdiction before that jurisdiction's law becomes applicable. Does this approach lead to an unjustified protection of the person claimed to be liable?[60] What about the legitimate expectations of the claimant as to the applicable law? It may be said with some confidence that the typical combination of the place of injury and the habitual residence of the plaintiff exactly meets these expectations.

The same holds good if the plaintiff acquired the product in the state

[58] It appears that, in actual practice, the 'application of the better rule of law' is by far the most important among the five choice-influencing considerations propounded by Robert A. Leflar, L. L. McDougal & L. Felix, *American Conflicts Law* (4th ed., 1986), 279 & 297.

[59] D. F. Cavers, 'The Proper Law of Producer's Liability', (1977) 26 Int. & Comp. L.Q. 703, 728–9.

[60] This is the view of E. F. Scoles & P. Hay, *Conflict of Laws* (2nd ed., 1992), 636.

of his habitual residence, no matter where the injury was sustained. It will be remembered that both these combinations are the hard core of the Hague Convention (articles 4 and 5). Doubts may only be raised in regard to the 'foreseeability test', for it does not seem to be too far-fetched to presume that a manufacturer exporting his goods will be in a position to obtain insurance coverage not merely for the countries for which his products are primarily destined, but also for other countries and the standards of liability prevailing there. It is to be welcomed that article 3128 of the Quebec Civil Code, which was drafted along the lines of article 135 of the Swiss *IPRG* has abstained from incorporating the foreseeability requirement to which the Swiss legislature still attaches importance. Under both statutes the plaintiff is given an option. In principle this is the solution which favours the plaintiff most. But this depends, of course, upon the number of laws among which such choice is permitted. The Swiss model of granting the injured party the liberty of choosing between the law of the state where the tortfeasor has his place of business or habitual residence and the law of the state in which the defective product was acquired restricts this freedom of choice to the minimum.

13

The Smoking War and the Role of Tort Law

Stephen D. Sugarman

Introduction

In the forty years between the first edition of *Fleming on Torts* and the completion of the ninth edition, products liability law has come of age. In country after country, the number of product liability cases has grown enormously. The quantity of academic writing about product liability has exploded. The law now provides compensation for injuries in ways that would have astounded torts scholars in the 1950s. Doctrinally, 'strict liability' for product injuries is said to have taken over centre stage, at least in the United States.

Yet, the world's most dangerous consumer product has so far remained essentially untouched. Cigarettes cause millions of deaths every year, including more than 400,000 in the United States. But the tobacco industry has yet to pay a single penny in tort damages to any individual smoker (or to a smoker's heirs) because of the inherently lethal nature of cigarettes. Why is this so? Is this about to change with the announcement in 1997 that tobacco companies in the United States are suddenly willing to put more than $350 billion on the table in order to put some of their litigation fears behind them? Would it be desirable for tort law to play a strong ongoing role with respect to cigarettes?

The Cigarette Stories

Think of the career of a smoker as having a series of stages. Visualize a path with forks along the way. At the beginning of the path lies the 'initiation' stage. Head down the path, and you become 'a smoker'. Everywhere along the path, there is the possibility of getting off. You do so by entering the 'cessation' stage. Some who leave the path rejoin it later. If you settle in along the path, you enter the 'possibility of harm' stage. At that stage you might harm yourself or others. This might pull you off the path. Otherwise, you eventually come to the end of the path at the end of your life.

For decades the tobacco industry has told a simple story about these stages: younger people see other people smoking—perhaps their friends, their siblings, their fellow workers, or their parents—and many of them give it a try. Some don't like it, but others do. The latter pass through the initiation stage and become smokers. Later, some decide they no longer enjoy it and quit. The rest remain life-long smokers. To be sure, some carelessly dispose of their lighted cigarettes and the matches or lighters they use. But with enough reminders, we can hope to keep the number of carelessly set fires to a minimum, thereby limiting the amount of harm incurred by both smokers and others.

For a long time now, hardly anyone outside the tobacco industry has believed this story. Yet, the public seemed of shrug it off: what could you expect the tobacco companies to say—that they were aggressively marketing the most lethal product in the world?

Some years ago, anti-smoking activists in the public-health field in both the United States and elsewhere began to engage in activities designed to demonize the cigarette companies, their chief executives, and others who act at their behest. These activists tell a very different story: the marketing arms of the tobacco industry prey on vulnerable children, seducing millions into taking up a vile habit. Before long, nearly every smoker wants to quit. But a majority just cannot. They try and try, but they are hooked. Some briefly stop smoking, only to be enticed back. Eventually, more than half of these addicts die of tobacco-related diseases. On top of that, each year they also kill tens of thousands of loved ones and strangers who are forced to inhale their smoke.

What is perhaps most remarkable about this story is that, at least among élites in the United States, it has very quickly become the culturally dominant narrative. The cigarette companies and their minions, all of a sudden, are decidedly the bad guys.

It is understandable, if not admirable, that the tobacco industry would stand by its story as long as it could. Not only is it psychologically difficult and a questionable business practice to go around admitting that your product kills when used as directed, but also there are the legal risks.

The Legal Landscape

Are Cigarettes Defective Products?

In the United States, it was in 1964 that the Surgeon General first issued his famous Report linking smoking to disease and death. This was the very time that US tort law embraced strict liability for defective products, as reflected in the publication of section 402A of the *Restatement (Second) of Torts*.

The first thing to try to understand is why cigarettes *per se* have not been viewed as defective products for tort law purposes even though they kill so many people. This result seems odd to some people, who wonder whether Berkeley's Law Dean, William Prosser, then Chief Reporter for the *Restatement (Second)*, wasn't mistakenly shortsighted when he included in his comments to section 402A the statement, 'Good tobacco is not unreasonably dangerous merely because the effects of smoking may be harmful'.[1] Yet, it isn't just this bald assertion that stands in the way.

It turns out that, in the products liability area generally, tort law judges across America have been unwilling to hold manufacturers liable on the ground that their product is simply too dangerous. It is true that American product liability law in most jurisdictions employs the so-called 'risk/benefit test' in deciding whether a product is defective or not.[2] And it is quite easy to see that, if asked, an American jury might well conclude that the risks of cigarettes outweigh their benefits, notwithstanding Prosser's assertion.

But, as the forthcoming *Restatement (Third)* makes clear, the risk/benefit doctrine, in the end, has been essentially restricted to cases involving design alternatives and has not been applied to products *per se*.[3] Only the New Jersey Supreme Court started seriously down this road—by allowing liability to be imposed on the manufacturer of a one-metre-deep, above-ground, backyard swimming pool solely on the basis that people were being hurt when diving headfirst into such pools.[4] Yet, not only did that Court go no further, but also its approach in the swimming pool case was later rejected by the New Jersey legislature.[5] California's Supreme Court once pointedly left open the question of whether a product might be found defective even when no alternative design is feasible because the product's 'norm is danger',[6] but it never embraced that outcome.

Why is that? The answer, I believe, is that our courts have decided that the judicial system is not the proper institution for second-guessing the market in these settings. If a product is legally made and sold, if people are aware of its dangers, and if they choose to buy it and use it anyway,

[1] *Restatement of the Law (Second) of Torts*, s 402A, comment i.

[2] See, e.g., *Barker v Lull Engineering Co. Inc.* 20 Cal 3d 413 (1978).

[3] *Restatement of the Law (Third) of Torts: Products Liability*, s 2(b).

[4] *O'Brien v Muskin* 94 NJ 169 (1983).

[5] For a discussion of the new statute and its impact in a cigarette context, see *Dewey v RJ Reynolds Tobacco Co.* 121 NJ 69 (1990).

[6] See *Barker v Lull*, n. 2 above at fn. 10.

then, if no safer alternative is available, it would be improper for the legal system to decide that this product's risks outweigh its benefits and that the product is therefore 'defective'. Put differently, since a finding of 'defect' means that the product should not have been sold, condemning products *per se* has seemed to smack too much of paternalism—at least, as with cigarettes, when the product's risks are aimed at the consumer or under the consumer's control.

TRUE STRICT LIABILITY FOR CIGARETTES?

Because American tort law imposes liability only on those products that it is willing to condemn, this, of course, means that it has been decidedly unwilling to go even further and embrace what I call true strict liability. True strict liability would not require a judgment that cigarettes are unreasonably dangerous because it would reject the 'defect' requirement. True strict liability would instead use tort law to force injury-causing products, including cigarettes, to internalize in their price the social costs they impose, including their costs to smokers. Would that have been a good idea?

I would like to suggest, first, that this is not a solution that smokers would want. It would mean, in effect, that all smokers would, in the price of the product, contribute to a fund from which those who have the misfortune of getting injured or killed by the product could claim. Suppose that would eventually be half of the long-term smokers. As a practical matter, as they buy cigarettes, smokers would be buying insurance against the risk they will fall into the unlucky 50 per cent. But from the smokers' viewpoint, this would be extremely expensive insurance, given the huge transaction costs associated with tort law generally, costs that would almost certainly be associated with the application of true strict liability in this setting. Moreover, most of these victims already have some health insurance, some life assurance, and so forth. So, for a great proportion of smokers, strict liability would force them to purchase insurance to duplicate compensation they would obtain in any event.

What about the idea of using true strict liability in order to confront buyers of cigarettes with the full cost of this product? There is something to this argument. Behind it lies the notion that, if smokers realized in this vivid way how costly smoking was, on average and in the long run, then many would decide to spend their money elsewhere. Yet, it bears emphasizing that this is something we simply do not do in other areas of tort law. For example, we don't confront drinkers with the full costs of drinking, or drivers with the full costs of driving. We don't confront buyers of prescription medications with the full cost of their unavoidable side effects and so on. In short, accident costs are not now fully internalized through tort law. So, it would be a truly radical transformation of the law to do this for cigarettes, and it would not be principled to limit it to cigarettes.

Some may respond that even if smokers may not want strict liability, society should insist on it on the ground that smokers are sponging off the rest of us by incurring such high health costs that the rest of us must pay for. But studies have shown this to be a simplistic analysis. In the bigger picture, it seems rather that smokers already more than pay their way for the health-care and other costs they impose on others through a combination of the current excise taxes on cigarettes they pay, plus all of the social security, public nursing home, and other such costs they save us by dying early.[7] Moreover, picking out smokers to pay extra for health care is an undesirable form of discrimination in my view. We do not, for example, pick out in this way those people who engage in other dangerous recreational activities. If we look at the Consumer Products Safety Commission's list of the products that cause the most hospital visits in the United States, things like bicycling, playing football, skiing, and so on stick out. But we don't ask those people to pay for the extra health-care costs they impose on us. I'm particularly troubled about singling out smokers for this especially disfavoured treatment now that they are viewed as social pariahs in many quarters.

One more argument for true strict liability is that this will force the companies to develop safer and less-addictive cigarettes. Theoretical economic models can be constructed that predict this result.[8] In practice, however, my sense of the historic record is that this argument has it backwards. Most importantly, there are already very strong market incentives to develop safer cigarettes, if that were possible. To be sure, the existing companies may not have incentives to develop addiction-free cigarettes, but if cigarettes posed no significant health risks, it is not so clear how much of a problem their addictive qualities would be. Smoking, after all, is not like using other drugs. You can smoke and still work, raise a family, engage in politics, and so on. Cigarettes don't make you engage in degenerate or violent behaviour. If anything, they help calm people down.

So why haven't safer cigarettes emerged? Maybe this is an impossible objective. But, in any event, I believe that the fear of tort liability may

[7] See, e.g., Willard G. Manning, Emmett B. Keeler, Joseph P. Newhouse, Elizabeth M. Sloss, & Jeffrey Wasserman, 'The Taxes of Sin: Do Smokers and Drinkers Pay Their Way?' *J. Am. Med. Assoc.* (1989) 261; and Robert E. McCormick, Robert Tollison, & Richard E. Wagner, 'Smoking, Insurance and Social Cost', (1997) Summer *Regulation* 33. For a contrary view, see Jon D. Hanson & Kyle D. Logue, 'The Costs of Cigarettes: The Economic Case for Ex Post Incentive-Based Regulation', (1988) Yale L.J. 107.

[8] See generally, Hanson & Logue, n. 7 above.

well have discouraged the existing companies from pursuing this goal. That is because the companies have good reason to fear that their very success in developing a safe cigarette would put them much more at risk of being held liable in the cases brought against them. Plaintiffs could then point to a design alternative. Of course, the dominant (although not exclusive) US rule now appears to be that products are judged as of the time of distribution, rather than at the time of trial.[9] Yet, once a safe cigarette were identified, plaintiffs would surely assert that the defendants knew, or should have known, about it earlier. Hence, it is arguable that, in this context, the development of a safer cigarette would have been furthered more by clear tort immunity than by existing tort law.

Certainly, true strict liability would force the companies to keep paying until they developed a safer cigarette, but even then one wonders what exactly this would achieve beyond the market incentives they already have. Perhaps the industry would devote any new resources to fighting claims (say, on causation grounds, where, for example, smokers who attempt to link cigarette use to heart disease face substantial difficulties because many of them would have suffered from coronary problems anyway). In any event, as with the idea of using true strict liability to force smokers to face the full costs of the product they buy, the use of true strict liability as a technology-forcing strategy is simply not a role that product liability law has turned out to play. So here, too, a principled solution would not be limited to tobacco products. For example, by parallel reasoning, automobile makers would be strictly liable for the consequences of all automobile accidents on the ground that this would force them to make safer cars. But when this very proposal was made by Professor Howard Latin about fifteen years ago, no one seemed to take it seriously.[10]

Liability for Failure to Warn?

Of the Diseases Caused By Smoking

If the tobacco industry was never really at risk of true strict liability for the costs of smoking, and if, as a practical matter, there has been no real prospect of liability for defective design defects, then what was the industry's worry?

Let's first go back to 1964 and the Surgeon General's Report. Simply put, since there were millions of smokers out there in 1964, if the

[9] *Restatement of the Law (Third) of Torts: Products Liability*, s 2, comment a.

[10] Howard Latin, 'Problem-Solving Behavior and Theories of Tort Liability', (1985) 73 Cali. L. Rev. 677.

manufacturers then admitted that smoking was very dangerous, how were they going to fend off the potential avalanche of lawsuits by those who would say 'Why didn't you tell us? Had you done so, we never would have started smoking, or at least we would have quit long ago.' These claims, essentially rooted in negligence, would immediately have ensnared the industry in a fight over who knew what and when. Although this is a fight which the tobacco companies might win, they must have realized, based upon what they knew they had in their files, that they risked a finding that they knew and should have warned earlier.[11] Without any industry admissions, plaintiff victims have found it daunting to prove in court both that smoking is dangerous and that the industry knew that that was so before the victim did.[12]

By 1998, however, admitting that smoking causes disease and death is much less of a problem for the industry (and we have seen in recent months that some US tobacco executives have finally, if perhaps grudgingly, accepted what just about everyone else has long believed). First, because governments have forced the companies to warn of some of the dangers of smoking for more than thirty years now, there are fewer and fewer smokers around who began before those warnings were placed on the packs and on advertisements. Second, in the United States at least, the Supreme Court decided in the *Cipollone* case that the Congressional statute requiring those warnings pre-empts tort claims based on a duty to warn.[13] Third, research shows that just about everyone in the United States (including children) knows that smoking is very dangerous, regardless of what the official position of the industry has been. This is probably true around the world. Indeed, there is reason to believe that Americans over-estimate the risk that smoking will give you lung cancer.[14]

In other words, admitting today that smoking is deadly might not be a legal disaster after all, so long as the industry could re-tell its story like this: everyone knows smoking is dangerous; but people choose to smoke because of the pleasure they get from it; they could stop, but they elect not to do so. If the only viable basis for a tort claim is the failure to warn of the diseases and death caused by smoking, cases brought today that rest on that theory would be very difficult to win.

[11] See generally, Stanton A. Glantz, John Slade, Lisa A. Bero. Peter Hanauer, & Deborah E. Barnes, *The Cigarette Papers* (1996) and Richard Kluger, *Ashes to Ashes* (1996).

[12] For discussions of the US cigarette litigation from the 1950s through to the start of the 1990s, see Robert L. Rabin, 'Institutional and Historical Perspectives on Tobacco Tort Liability' and Gary T. Schwartz, 'Tobacco Liability in the Courts', both in R. Rabin & S. Sugarman (eds.), *Smoking Policy: Law Politics & Culture* (1993).

[13] *Cipollone v Liggett Group Inc.* 505 US 504 (1992).

[14] See W. Kip Viscusi, *Smoking: Making the Risky Decision* (1992).

About Addiction

But that isn't the only warning that plaintiffs are claiming they were denied. More and more they are alleging that they should have been told that smoking is addictive. As we have seen from its story, the industry has long denied this. Unlike admitting that cigarettes can give you lung cancer, heart disease and the like, admitting that the nicotine in cigarettes makes smoking addictive still looks very risky from a legal viewpoint.

For one thing, smokers who began before the warnings went on the packets can argue that they learned of the danger of cigarettes only after they were hooked. But even more important, those starting after 1964 can claim that they assumed they could always quit, not realizing that, in many cases, starting to smoke would turn into an involuntary lifetime commitment. This argument could be especially troublesome when put together with the findings that once you quit and are 'clean' for several years, the health risks you face from having previously smoked decline sharply.

To be sure, even though there is no addiction warning on the packet, the industry could argue in court that, despite its official line to the contrary, most people know that you can get hooked on smoking. Moreover, in the court-room the tobacco companies can resist the addiction claim of an individual smoker with the argument that he or she could have quit—after all millions of others have. And, indeed, individual juries so far still don't seem inclined to embrace the addiction theory.[15] Yet, as more and more well-funded and experienced plaintiffs' lawyers get on board the anti-tobacco company litigation bandwagon, and as the cultural understanding of smoking in America increasingly becomes one in which the tobacco companies, rather than individual smokers, are primarily responsible for the harm smoking causes, the industry has good reason to be fearful.[16]

This is especially so once the reality begins to sink into the public consciousness that nearly all long-term smokers start smoking as children. Whatever they could be said to 'know', who could maintain with a straight face that young teenagers make a mature judgement to become lifetime smokers? Any characterization of youth smoking as 'voluntary' is now being put even more into question as the anti-smoking activists have been able to portray the tobacco companies as deliberately seducing children into becoming smokers with ads featuring the cartoon *Joe Camel* and other youth-oriented marketing measures.[17]

[15] See generally, Frank J. Vandall, 'Reallocating the Costs of Smoking: The Application of Absolute Liability to Cigarette Manufacturers', (1991) 52 Ohio St. L.J. 405.

[16] See generally, Philip J. Hilts, *Smokescreen: The Truth Behind the Tobacco Industry Cover-up* (1996).

[17] *Mangini v R. J. Reynolds* 7 Cal 4th 1057 (1994).

In short, even if the industry were to concede that cigarettes are somewhat addictive and then try to shift the debate from 'whether' to 'how much', there are some potentially very dangerous time bombs out there waiting to go off. But at the same time, to try to stonewall the addiction theory entirely is becoming less and less tenable.

Other Legal Assaults

Even if the cigarette-makers could fight off individual lawsuits, or at least most of them, they are now under fire in the United States on other fronts. For one thing, several smoker class-action cases have been brought against them. It now looks as though a single national class-action case won't get anywhere.[18] Yet, there is the possibility of a series of state class-action claims, each on behalf of hundreds of thousands of claimants (or more). Even if the judges were to dismiss these class actions as involving too many complications and too many individual problems of proof, there remains the possibility of the consolidation of thousands of claims. Perhaps the most serious threat in all of these group lawsuits is the possibility, however small, that a single case could trigger billions of dollars in damages, especially in punitive damages, if the tide of public opinion turns sufficiently against the industry. Armed with recently disclosed documents, plaintiffs increasingly appear to be alleging fraud and other misconduct, where earlier complaints alleged only negligence.

In addition, the tobacco companies are now being bombarded by lawsuits seeking to force them to reimburse others for the cost of health care provided to smokers. So far, the most aggressively fought of these cases are around forty claims filed by the attorney-generals of most of the states.[19] At their core, most of these lawsuits seek to win back the money the states have spent for the smoking-related, medical expenses of indigent smokers.

I have yet to see presented a coherent legal theory underlying these attorney-general cases that would justify this remedy.[20] If the theory is 'subrogation', then the state stands in the shoes of the smokers themselves, but the attorney-generals argue that they should not have to prove individual causation, individual lack of warning and the like.

[18] *Costano v American Tobacco Co.* 84 F 3d 734 (5th Cir. 1996).

[19] See generally, Karen E. Meade, 'Breaking Through the Tobacco Industry's Smoke Screen: State Lawsuits for Reimbursement of Medical Expenses', (1996) 17 J. Legal Medicine 113.

[20] For one effort, see Raymond E. Gangarosa, Frank J. Vandall, & Brian Willis, 'Suits By Public Hospitals to Recover Expenditures For the Treatment Of Disease, Injury and Disability Caused by Tobacco and Alcohol', (1994) 22 Fordham Urb. L. J. 81.

Some complaints allege 'unjust enrichment', but that legal theory, as conventionally understood, just doesn't fit the facts.[21] It might well be that the industry violated state laws on unfair business practices and consumer protection laws, perhaps even state antitrust laws. But it is hard to see why the repayment of millions or billions in indigent medical expenses is the right remedy. If nothing else, the state ought to have a remedy for those sorts of violations even if it never paid a penny for anyone's medical care. Yet, the attorney-generals like pointing to those medical expenses because the conventional remedies for violating things like the consumer protection laws are likely to involve far smaller financial penalties.

But the lack of a convincing legal theory may not matter. We are talking about a home-state prosecutor going before a home-state jury, and who knows what might happen. This perhaps explains why the industry has already settled these state claims in Mississippi, Florida, and Texas for large sums, and is trying to settle the Minnesota case during its trial, which is taking place as this is written.

Furthermore, having not long ago sworn to what now strike many people as preposterous statements in testimony before a Congressional Committee chaired by Congressman Waxman, individual tobacco company executives have grounds to worry about possible criminal prosecution. Newspapers lately report that several grand juries are actively looking into possibly bringing indictments.[22]

A Transition Strategy

In this state of affairs, it may well have dawned on the tobacco companies that they could very much use a transition strategy. They may have decided that they need to be able to make some admissions, but without getting clobbered into bankruptcy. They seem to be eager to put up a substantial amount of money if this can get the most serious of their legal problems behind them—especially if they can arrange to put that money up together, over time, and in a way that probably will permit them all to pass that financial obligation on in the price of cigarettes. And, most importantly, I believe, they need to try to gain public accep-

[21] See *Restatement of the Law of Restitution*, s 1, comments a, b, & c.

[22] For a discussion of potential criminal liability, see the remarks of Frank Tuerkheimer (Univ. of Wisconsin) in Proceedings of the Conference on the So-Called Global Tobacco Settlement: Its Implications for Public Health and Public Policy, University of Wisconsin–Madison Law School, October 15–17, 1997 (Institute for Legal Studies, Univ. of Wisconsin Law School 1997).

tance of a new story about the stages in a smoker's life that isn't the one being pushed by the anti-smoking groups.

Sure enough, as indicated earlier, during 1997 the tobacco industry in the United States said it would agree to a so-called 'global settlement'.[23] This is not a world-wide settlement by any means. 'Global' here refers to the idea that many legal issues would be resolved and new public policy set in a variety of areas. This settlement, which all the parties say requires legislation to be enacted by the US Congress, would foreclose future class actions and consolidated tort claims; it would resolve the state attorney-general cases; and it would put an end to punitive damages for past conduct. Individual tort claims could be brought as before, although they would be subject annually to an individual and aggregate ceiling. If awards in any one year were greater than either ceiling, the excess would be carried over to be paid out in future years. Although analysts have reached different estimates as to the precise amount of money involved, the parties to the deal talk in roughly terms of $350 billion. Perhaps this is better understood as something like $12–15 billion a year for twenty-five years. Money not paid out to successful individual tort claimants would go to a variety of public health programmes and to the states, in effect, to help pay for those tobacco-related indigent medical care costs, although there is no indication that the funds would have to be used in that way.

If this settlement were to go through, it is altogether unclear just how many individual tort claims would be successful in the future or how large a claim on the total fund they would be. Some predict that few, if any, individual tort judgments will be won. This view rests, in part, on speculation that lawyers will be less willing to take these cases once punitive damages are no longer available. And, in part, it is based on the assumption that in a one-by-one fight, the industry will continue to overwhelm its opponents, as it has in the past, forcing them to incur huge expenses, knowing that they might still lose at trial. The other prediction is that, what with all the recent revelations about what the anti-smoking advocates characterize as severe industry misconduct, claimants will start winning cases, the public will learn of these results, other juries will fall into line, a standard set of winning evidence and arguments will be generated, and the successful claims will quickly exceed the annual ceiling proposed in the settlement (and this has produced calls to double or triple the dollar amount of the settlement).

[23] For early accounts, see Barnaby J. Feder, 'No Clear Outlook From Tobacco Settlement', *New York Times*, 3 Aug. 1997, C3; Barry Meier, 'Tobacco Lawyers' Papers Are Made Public', *New York Times*, 7 Aug. 1997, A4; and Barry Meier, 'New Negotiations Reported On Tobacco Pact', *New York Times*, 10 Sept. 1997, A4.

As this is being written, it is very difficult to have confidence in either of these scenarios.

The proposed settlement would do a lot more than limit the tobacco industry's legal liability. It would, in addition, usher in a wide range of regulatory restrictions on tobacco products and their marketing—in many respects adopting the sorts of tobacco control measures that anti-smoking activists have favoured. The settlement, I believe, would also put the industry in a position in which it could try to sell a new story about smoking to the American public.

In the new story, smoking is not for children. To make that story credible, the companies will first have to stop all promotions either aimed at, or generally reaching, children. This means abandoning outdoor advertising (mainly on billboards), eliminating tobacco-product advertisements in magazines that a significant number of children read, discontinuing the sale or give-away of gear (clothes, backpacks and the like) with tobacco brands and logos on it, ending the sponsorship of sporting events that some youths admire (like motor racing), down-scaling in-store advertising, and so on. Second, the companies will have to embrace strict controls on the sale of cigarettes to minors. Third, they will have to co-operate with other measures designed to reduce youth smoking—such as the funding of anti-smoking counter-advertisements, the posting of warnings about the addictive nature of cigarettes, and so on. And, indeed, the proposed settlement contains all of these features.

There is, of course, a great danger to the tobacco companies in this approach. It is possible that, even if children didn't smoke, people would take up smoking in droves once they turned 18, with the result that smoking rates of people in their mid-20s would not be much lower than they are today. But this is an unlikely scenario. If, under the new regulations, you don't start smoking before you turn 18, and you are the sort of person who would already have taken up smoking in the past, you will probably have other risky habits already in place when you turn 18. Besides, since you are now an adult, you have less need to take up smoking in order to pretend to the world that you are. I'm not saying that no one would start to smoke after reaching age 18, but only that such a scenario would probably lead to a radically diminished number of lifetime smokers.

Instead, I imagine that the tobacco companies will figure that, even without their old marketing practices and even with all the youth access controls in place, lots of children will still smoke—perhaps not at current rates, but still lots. Just look at how many young teens drink, despite the tough legal controls on access that exist; or, if that isn't a good analogy because of all the beer, wine, and spirits advertising that children see, think about how many American teens regularly smoke marijuana.

But in a world of tough access controls and sharply restricted advertising, it is much more difficult to blame the cigarette companies for children's smoking. Of course, in the story that the anti-smoking activists tell, the tobacco companies are still to blame. Indeed, they will remain at fault so long as they make their product available for sale. Put differently, the logic underlying the anti-smoking story is that 'prohibition' is the most desirable public policy—if it could only be successful. After all, if many children still smoke and if nearly all adults regret that they ever started, then the real goal has to be to get rid of cigarettes altogether. The objections to the prohibition solution are not principled, but only practical: (1) how to deal with those millions smokers who are currently addicted, and (2) how to deal with the huge black market in cigarettes that almost surely would be created, just as we see with so-called 'illegal' drugs.

In the tobacco companies' story, however, prohibition is inappropriate in principle. Their new story, as I see it, would go like this: while there are some adults who are truly addicted and can't quit, most adults smoke because they enjoy it, and they probably could quit if they wanted to. So long as we are careful that other people aren't involuntarily assaulted by too much second-hand smoke, people who enjoy smoking should be allowed to do so. If a number of years might be cut off the end of their lives, this is a risk they should be allowed to take. It is regrettable that some children still smoke, but dealing further with that is the responsibility of parents, schools, and doctors. We've done what we can.

If this story is accepted and the proportion of adults in the United States who smoke settles down at, say, 15 or so per cent instead of around 25 per cent today, and if no new companies enter the cigarette market because advertising is so restricted, and if the tobacco companies save a lot of money because they all have to cut back so much on their advertising, then, even if a lot of money has to be paid out in a structured annual way as part of the global settlement, the tobacco companies can probably continue to keep the price of cigarettes within bounds and still make very substantial profits—which, I assume, remains their main objective.

Having conceded all those regulations aimed at youth smoking and having agreed to pay out what seems to most people a startlingly large sum of money, the tobacco industry has put the anti-smoking, public-health community in something of a quandary, a quandary that has caused division in the ranks. One side basically favours the settlement, pointing to the industry's acceptance of so many controls that it has previously successfully fought tooth and nail. To be sure, the supporters of the deal now generally concede that some of its details need tightening up a bit. But that isn't the crux of the problem, because it now appears that if any comprehensive measure is to get through Congress and not be vetoed by President Clinton, it will have to be made tougher in various ways.

But many in the anti-smoking movement are calling for a rejection of any sort of settlement. They argue that if the tobacco companies are for it, the public-health community must be against it. They can't stomach the idea of a deal that makes both sides better off. Sensing that the tide of public opinion is now on their side, they are unwilling to embrace a deal that would do anything for the tobacco companies. To bolster their resolve, many of the anti-smoking forces are taking the position that a non-negotiable principle is that none of the legal rights of smokers to sue may be sacrificed—a position that would clearly break the deal. They argue that, instead, the Congress should unilaterally impose tough regulatory controls on the tobacco industry and sharply raise the federal excise tax on cigarettes in hopes of financially discouraging teenagers from starting to smoke.

This might be the right strategy—if it succeeds and if it perpetuates the view that the 'bad guys' are the tobacco companies, while at the same time denying the industry the ability to sell its new story to the public. But it is also a dangerous strategy for the anti-smoking groups. For one thing, many of the very same lawyers, who have earned the praise of the anti-smoking activists for what they have done to bring secret industry documents to light, and who have been counted on to carry the litigation torch into the future, are now excoriated for getting into bed with the devil. Perhaps the public-health leaders believe there is an endless supply of plaintiff lawyers ready to step into key roles if those who negotiated the settlement are discredited. But this is not obvious to me.

In any event, a greater risk, I believe, is how the public-health hard line will finally play with the public as they think about its treatment of smokers. Remember that under the anti-smoking activist version of the smoking story, adult smokers are to be pitied. They were duped and they are stuck. Their right to sue must not be sacrificed. They are the people we are trying to prevent today's youths from becoming. All of those ideas fit together.

And, yet, look at the implications of the sharp increase in excise taxes that the anti-smoking groups are united behind. As an aside, I note that whereas some want to use the proceeds of this tax increase to pay for smoking-related medical expenses, President Clinton seems to want to use the money for new policy initiatives unrelated to smoking, like child care. His approach, of course, exposes the Government to the risk of winding up in the position currently faced by high taxing governments elsewhere. They need a high level of continued smoking in order to balance their budgets.

But regardless of how the excise tax is used, think about those addicted smokers. For a two-pack-a-day smoker, a $2-per-pack price increase (which is the minimum that many anti-smoking activists are calling for) comes to $120 a month. Even a $1-per-pack tax increase imposes genuine new costs on those who smoke even one pack a day. For the many moderate and low income smokers out there, where in their personal budget is this new money going to come from? Think about elderly smokers living on welfare or social security. Do they just eat less? Think about welfare mothers and minimum wage workers who smoke. Do they just feed their children less? A sharp price increase may cause some of them to quit smoking. But in the story told by the anti-smoking groups, it surely follows that the most addicted are least likely to do so.

Maybe some addicted smokers will be able to cope with a sharp price increase by switching to cheaper brands, or by cutting down a bit, or by smoking their cigarettes more carefully by inhaling more deeply and making sure they smoke down to the end of the cigarette. But more and more smokers have already made these adjustments. For them, a big new tax is a new agony—for the very people on whose behalf the anti-smokers say they are resisting the settlement.

Of course, many other Americans—unlike the anti-smoking activists—don't pretend to have much sympathy for smokers. More and more of them are vociferous about wanting the air wherever they go to be completely free from cigarette smoke. Indeed, as more adults from higher income classes don't smoke, they make up a potent block of voters who would be happy to have someone else pay the taxes that Government needs. They might be expected to be especially supportive of cigarette taxes that promised to help curtail youth smoking.

But even selfish non-smokers are likely to go only so far. We have perhaps seen a bit of this already in the early reaction in California to a new law that bans smoking in bars. I don't deny that such a ban can provide health benefits for employees in those bars. Moreover, the more we restrict where people can smoke, the more people are likely to figure out how to quit. Furthermore, many people would like there to be more 'no smoking' bars that they could go to. Nevertheless, not only are bar owners and smokers up in arms about this new smoking ban, but also I sense that, so far at least, they have public sentiment on their side. In other words, whereas there is strong support for smoking controls in workplaces and public places generally, I sense that most people feel that bars are places where smoking should be allowed (at least if this is the way the owner wants to run the business). In an extraordinary move reflecting that sentiment, the California Assembly voted to repeal this new law almost as soon as it went into effect and the negative public reaction was reported in the Press (although, as this is written, there is no indication that the California Senate will soon lend its needed support). Similar empathy for smokers is reflected in the laws of about half of the states that forbid employers from refusing to hire smokers.[24]

Of course, making smokers pay money is different from telling them that they can't smoke in bars and can't get a job. And certainly many other nations have had no qualms about imposing on smokers cigarette taxes that are much higher than the United States would have even with a $2-a-pack increase—although the culturally accepted cigarette story in many of those countries is that smoking is something the people do by choice. What I see lurking, then, is the danger that the anti-smoking forces will squander the great gains they have made in turning public opinion against the tobacco companies. That could open up the door to public acceptance of the industry's own new story that smoking is a voluntary adult activity.

Put generally, anti-smoking activists have to be very careful about how they tell their story. They may believe that, in the end, it is a fair trade-off to impose substantial new costs on addicted smokers in the hope that the higher cost of cigarettes will significantly reduce the number of smokers, especially among the young. Moreover, they may well believe that a high excise tax is the single most promising way to reduce youth smoking. Furthermore, they might argue that the proposed settlement is also expected to impose new costs on smokers—although, it should be noted, the cost of the settlement has been estimated to be less than a dollar a pack and this sum should be at least partly offset by sharply lowered industry marketing costs resulting from the settlement. Nevertheless, the risk here is that the public may find it hard to accept a story that portrays smokers as addicted victims whose right to sue must be maintained, and yet in the meantime tries to justify intentionally imposing a substantial new cost on them. Instead, a large excise tax may rather more easily be reconciled with the story that, I have argued, the industry will want to sell: smoking is not for children, but it is a valid choice for responsible adults.

In sum, in the United States we might now be at a critical moment in the smoking war. In this war, as in other wars, there comes a time when the best thing becomes, not to keep trying to bomb the other side into oblivion, but rather to declare victory and let the other side surrender and make peace. Maybe that time is not yet upon us. Perhaps the enemy

[24] See Sugarman, 'Disparate Treatment of Smokers in Employment and Insurance' in *Smoking Policy*, n. 12 above.

is not yet sufficiently weakened. Maybe the anti-smoking forces have not yet tasted enough victory, and it is psychologically necessary for them to do so.

But the US anti-smoking forces at least need to think more clearly about what a reasonable victory would be. How low can teen and adult smoking rates plausibly get? Does victory have to include keeping open all the theoretical tort rights of smokers? Must victory also include sharply higher cigarette prices? Otherwise, holding out for total victory may mean having to take responsibility for too many civilian casualties. As John Fleming would have counselled, moderation is usually a virtue.

Fleming would also have sought to draw on the lessons of other countries. On the tort side, there is little to learn. Until recently, there was essentially no litigation elsewhere, although now a few lawsuits have been filed that are modelled on the US cases.[25] But in terms of tobacco control policy generally, many other countries are more aggressive than is the United States. As I noted earlier, many other nations already have much higher cigarette tax rates. Youth access and advertising controls are also much tougher in many other countries. Yet, none has achieved, through those policies, anything like the low level of smoking to which US anti-smoking activists aspire. This is not to say that these measures count for nothing. But, rather, it is to emphasize that more is at work here.

What I find most striking in the international comparisons is the gender differences from place to place. In the United States now, men and women smoke at about the same rate. In some countries, for example, Japan, there is a huge gender imbalance. This tells me that culture is very powerful. We also know that within the United States, African–American teenage females smoke at extremely low rates as compared to white teens of either sex (even adjusting for family income). There has to be a cultural explanation for that, although no one seems yet to know precisely what it is.

So, if I were working on tobacco control, I would focus most on the cultural angle. Perhaps the best hope to marginalize youth smoking is to make it seem abnormal. Maybe if you go about on your daily rounds and you don't much see people smoking (except those who are miserably huddled around the doorways to buildings where they work), and you don't see billboards with people smoking, and you don't see cigarettes on display when you shop, and you don't see people smoking in films (if the industry could be enticed into voluntarily altering its

[25] See generally, the remarks of Eric LeGresley (Non-Smokers' Rights Assoc., Canada) and Geraint Howells (Univ. of Sheffield) in Proceedings of the Conference on the So-Called Global Tobacco Settlement, n. 22 above.

long-standing practice of having its stars smoke on screen), then you begin to see smoking as odd. To be sure, if you want to rebel against society, this may make smoking even more attractive. But for most youths, there will be much less of an adult world that you could sense you would fit into by smoking. Although this may be only wishful thinking, these changes just possibly could be more important than high taxes or tort rights in convincing children to avoid the initiation stage and never get on the smoking path.

After all, there has been a great reduction in smoking rates by adults in the United States in the past thirty years, and for those millions of former smokers who got off the smoking path, it has had nothing to do with tort rights and little or nothing to do with high taxes. For most middle-class and professional class adults in the United States, smoking has simply ceased to be 'cool'. This is partly, I believe, a result of scientific rationality a sensible response to the enormous risks of smoking by people who don't want to be thought of by their friends and work colleagues as stupid for doing such a dangerous thing. It is, as well, I believe, a result of a general cultural shift to an emphasis on fitness and health. It should not be surprising that in California, where healthy diets, working out, outdoor sports activities, and the like are very fashionable, smoking rates are decidedly lower than the US average.

This is all by way of saying that we in the field of tort law need to be modest about how much social change our special province—the common law—can be expected to achieve. If smoking rates are to come down to, say, 10 per cent of the adult population, it is unlikely that tort law will have played the primary role. As John Fleming taught me, the future for tort law, if anything, lies elsewhere.[26]

[26] See, e.g., John G. Fleming, 'Is There a Future for Tort?' (1984) 58 *Aust. Law J.* 131, also appearing as John G. Fleming, 'Is There a Future for Tort?' 44 La. L. Rev. 1193 (1984) (in honour of Prof. Wex Malone).

DELIVERING COMPENSATION

14

Traffic Accidents Compensation Under Tort Law and Under a Specific Law: The French Experience

*André Tunc**

In France, as in the United States and in many industrialized countries, innumerable proposals have been advanced since the beginning of this century for a specific statute dealing with compensation of traffic accident victims. Most of the proposals favoured a no-fault system of compensation of all victims. It would probably be pointless to study all these proposals. On the other hand, one text, the French 1985 statute on the matter, seems to deserve attention, because it is not a proposal, but a piece of positive law, and has been applied now for more than ten years.

To honour John Fleming, who did so much to modernize tort law, I would like to present the French experience by (1) briefly recalling what the law and practice was before 1985, (2) describing the 1985 law, and (3) trying to observe the results of that law.

Law and Practice Before 1985

Before 1985, the law applicable to a traffic accident was the law of the Civil Code—enacted 180 years before. It is true that the courts had been remarkably creative in the construction and application of the Code. That process, often described[1], can be briefly summarized here.

*The author apologizes for having on some points borrowed from a previous study, 'The "*Loi Badinter*": Ten years of experience', in (1996) The Maastricht Journal of European and Comparative Law 329–40. The statute and the circumstances surrounding its adoption are what they are; the author felt unable to change them for the sake of originality.

[1] See Arthur T. von Mehren & James R. Gordley, *The Civil Law System* (2nd ed., 1977), 590–702; Konrad Zweigert & Hein Kötz, *Introduction to Comparative Law* (trans. Tony Weir) (2nd ed., 1987), vol 2, 353–61.

The basis of the judicial construction has been article 1384, paragraph 1:

On est responsable non seulement du dommage que l'on cause par son propre fait, mais encore de celui qui est causé par le fait des personnes dont on doit répondre, ou des choses que l'on a sous sa garde.

This provision must be placed in its context. Articles 1382 and 1383 provide for liability for one's own fault. The following paragraphs of article 1384 provide for a certain number of cases of liability for another person, and articles 1385 and 1386 enunciate some cases of liability for damage caused by things. It clearly appears, therefore, that paragraph 1 was a mere transition, an *elégance de style* devoid from any autonomous meaning.

In 1896, however, the *Cour de Cassation*, in order to provide compensation to the family of a worker killed when the machine with which he was working exploded, due to a defect in construction, decided that article 1384, paragraph 1, was a sufficient basis of liability against the owner of the machine. The rule was thus established that a person (in this case, the owner of the machine) is liable for the damage caused by a thing which he has in his care. During the following years, this doctrine was confirmed, but two questions arose and were hotly disputed. Since the liability based on article 1384, paragraph 1, was probably not an absolute liability, the first question was what the '*gardien*' would have to prove in order to escape liability. The second was whether this new liability should apply to a traffic accident, since the damage done usually comes not from the car itself, but from a fault or error of one or more of the drivers. The two questions were settled, once and for all, by the famous *Jand'heur* case, decided by the *Cour de Cassation*, in plenary formation (*toutes chambres réunies*) on 13 February 1930[2]. The decision expressed two principles: first,

The presumption of liability established by article 1384, paragraph 1, of the Civil Code, against the person who has under his guard the inanimate thing which has caused damage to someone else, can be rebutted only by evidence of a fortuitous cause or *vis major* or an extraneous cause which cannot be imputed to him; it is not sufficient for him to establish that he has not committed any fault, nor that the cause of the prejudicial fact remains unknown.

And secondly,

The statute, for the application of the presumption that it creates, does not distinguish whether the thing that has caused the damage was or was not operated by the hand of a man: nor is it necessary that the thing has a vice inherent in its nature and capable of creating the damage.

[2] Ch. réunies, 13 Feb. 1930, *Veuve Jand'heur c. Les Galeries belfortaises*, D. 1930.1.57, rapp. Le Marc'hadour, concl. Matter, note Ripert, S. 1930.1.121, note Esmein.

The law was settled, at least in principle. All previous discussions could be forgotten. In particular, all traffic accidents were clearly put under the new regime. But the application of the first principle, on the causes of exemption from liability (or, more technically, on the causes of rebuttal of the presumption of liability) proved unmanageable. The Cour de Cassation itself wavered in its terminology: *présomption de responsabilité, responsabilité de plein droit, responsabilité de l'article 1384, al. 1, c. civ.*

Whatever the terminology, in the case of nearly every traffic accident, it was arguable that a cause of exemption had existed. The Cour de Cassation itself wavered on the question whether fortuitous cause or *vis major* had to be 'unforeseeable' or 'normally unforeseeable'. But, whichever was required, it was always difficult to decide whether it was in fact so in any concrete case. A number of decisions, for instance, relate to the case of someone killed or injured by a car which skidded because of ice on the road. Certainly, a traffic accident law should provide compensation to the victims of such accidents. But, under the law of torts, the question was whether, in the circumstances of time and climate, the formation of ice was unforeseeable or (normally?) foreseeable. The court had to make a decision on the basis of witness statements and, if available, the weather records of the previous years.

If the outline of the law was apparently clear, many secondary legal problems arose, which cannot even be summarized here. But, even within a clear legal framework, the application of the rules was often uncertain. The present writer, when he was promoting a reform, annotated a number of cases to show how contradictory they were. A dog crossing the road in front of the car was held an excuse for the driver,[3] but not a cat in front of a scooter.[4] In both cases, a decision of the court of first instance (three judges assisted by four lawyers) was reviewed by a court of appeal, with the same number of judges and lawyers, before going to the Cour de Cassation, with a larger number of judges. In another case, water on a road at a time of rain was held unforeseeable.[5]

By reason of the uncertainty inherent in nearly every case, the defendants, i.e. the insurance companies, were prompt to invoke the *fait de la victime* or *fait d'un tiers*, to refuse compensation or to offer a very reduced compensation in the negotiation stage. The result was, of course, permanent grave injustice and enormous litigation. In cases of personal injury, 36 per cent of the victims did not receive any compensation. 27 per cent

[3] Cass. 2e civ., 10 Apr. 1964, D. 1965.169, note Tunc.

[4] Cass. 2e civ., 24 Mar. 1965, D. 1965.405, note Tunc.

[5] Cass. 2e civ., 28 Oct. 1965, D. 1966.137, note Tunc. A certain number of the writer's Notes criticizing decisions of the Cour de Cassation in matter of traffic accidents are reproduced in Societe de Legislation Comparee, *Jalons. Dits et écrits d'André Tunc*, 1991, at 155–68.

of them tried their luck before a court: 250 on average, every day of the year. When compensation arrived, it was, on average, twenty-one months after the accident if the victim and the insurer reached a settlement, thirty-one months later if the case was decided by a judge.

The case for reform, and for automatic protection of all traffic accident victims, is a strong one. It has often been forcefully presented in the United States and will be only summarized here.

First, it is a fallacy to believe that the law of torts can and does settle liability for traffic accidents on the basis of fault. 'Fault' is commonly defined as behaviour departing from that of a good citizen, mindful of his duties towards his fellow citizens and towards himself. However, research, in the United States and elsewhere, has established that most traffic accidents occur as a result of errors, inadvertencies, blunders, and clumsiness. Such behaviour does not fit into the definition of 'fault'. It is statistically unavoidable, even on the part of the good citizen. It is the consequence of human nature: *errare humanum est*. Since most traffic accidents are the result of human nature exposed to traffic risks, it would seem fair to require those who create such risks—that is the motorists—to subscribe to an insurance which would cover all damages (at least all personal injury damages, since the owner of a car may insure it) resulting from traffic accidents.

It is true that some accidents result from fault in the precise sense of the word. When this is the case, one might wish that a victim who is at fault should not receive full compensation, and that conversely the insurer of a person who causes damage and is at fault should be given recourse against his client. But that does not seem practicable. The victim often suffers severe physical consequences—even death. A civil penalty does not appear desirable when the victim is wholly or partially at fault.

Another reason not to deal with traffic accident compensation on the basis of fault is the difficulty of knowing exactly how the accident happened and what judgement should be passed on the behaviour of each of the parties. It is important to underline that, if the victim's behaviour is allowed to reduce the compensation he will receive, this difficulty of judgment will bear heavily on the fate of all victims, even those who are finally judged not to be at fault. As mentioned above, in France, notwithstanding the *prima facie* liability of the driver, it was usual for insurance companies to accuse the victim of 'fault' and oblige him or her to engage in long discussions, and to accept an unfair settlement or to take the chance of a long and expensive litigation.

A last argument for no-fault compensation of all traffic accident victims may be even stronger. In France, automobile liability insurance has been compulsory since 1958. In traffic accidents, therefore, the application of the principle of liability for fault is only theoretical, or at least one-sided in its application. Liability never bears on the tortfeasor, but only on the victim. On the road or in the street, one may kill or injure one's neighbour with total civil impunity, provided he is at the wheel of a car. On the other hand, the victim's behaviour is sanctioned, often severely. The Cour de Cassation has approved a number of decisions refusing complete compensation to a pedestrian whose feet were on the pavement, but whose shoulders were over the street. In the same vein, the 'natural reaction' of a pedestrian has been held a 'fault'. Such a law cannot be defended. *C'est le monde à l'envers*. If the cost of damage caused by a driver who has committed an error or even a fault is legitimately spread to all drivers (through insurance), all drivers should also bear the cost of damage suffered, whatever the victim's behaviour.

La loi Badinter

In France, the law has been set in better order by a statute passed by the French Parliament on 5 July 1985, a statute 'tendant à l'amélioration de la situation des victimes d'accidents de la circulation et à l'accélération des procédures d'indemnisation'. As an acknowledgment of the work of the Minister of Justice, Robert Badinter, in the preparation of the statute, the latter was immediately called *la loi Badinter*. The vote in favour of the statute was unanimous, but it came at the conclusion of a long fight of a rare violence.

The idea of no-fault compensation for traffic accident victims was not a new one in France, any more than elsewhere. For a long time, however, no proposal was successful. The process which led to the *loi Badinter* started in 1963, when the Minister of Justice, Jean Foyer, convened an important commission, under his chairmanship, to prepare a project of automatic compensation for all traffic accident victims. The commission met a number of times under great internal tensions. After a few months, however, an insurer, a member of the commission who had great political experience and contacts, launched (anonymously) a powerful press and radio campaign against the project (with slogans as refined as 'On the road, every one will be allowed to do anything', 'The number of victims will greatly increase', 'The insurance premiums will be multiplied by four'). The great newspapers, *Le Monde* and, for a while, *Le Figaro*, carried articles explaining the reform. Eventually, Jean Foyer ceased to convene the commission: it was clear that the insurance industry, opposed to reform, was politically stronger than the Minister of Justice.

In 1981, however, elections brought a new government into office and, after a short while, Robert Badinter became Minister of Justice. He had two main projects in mind: abolition of the death penalty and no-fault compensation of all traffic victims. For this second purpose, he set up a small commission (three judges, two insurers, two practising lawyers, and a law professor) under the chairmanship of Pierre Bellet, a former *Premier président de la Cour de Cassation*. It was clear that the commission would be divided: the judges and the law professor would favour a radical reform; the practising lawyers would seek to preserve a system of law which was a source of much easy litigaton; the insurers might favour a reform (the industry was divided, but now on the whole rather favourable to a reform under certain conditions). In June 1982, Robert Badinter received the report of the commission. Probably because he was frequently attacked in the media (especially for his 'laxity toward crime'), he did not invite a public debate. Copies of the report were sent to the courts and the law faculties. With the help of his staff, Badinter conducted a discreet consultation with all parties concerned. This policy of consultation and conciliation did not protect him (and the proponents of reform) from persistent passionate attacks (including public insults and written defamation in *La Gazette du Palais*, a journal widely read by practising lawyers). These attacks, however, came only from members of the Bar, not from the insurance industry, as had been the case twenty years earlier. The climate, therefore, was very stormy. Thus, Badinter had to prepare a bill which, in order to have some chance of being passed by Parliament, had to be a compromise.

In the course of the consultation process, Robert Badinter was convinced by an insurer that it would not be possible to extend no-fault protection to drivers without a significant increase in the premiums. This was a crucial point: for economic and political reasons, any increase of premiums was ruled out by the Government. At the expense of the logic of the statute, Badinter felt obliged to restrict the automatic protection to 'victims except drivers'. Even after this severe amputation, Badinter was not sure that the bill would be passed by Parliament. However, his patience and diplomacy were rewarded when, on 5 July, 1985, the bill, after some amendments, all favourable to the victims, received unanimous approval from Parliament.

In the course of the long consultation process organized by Badinter, it appeared that the law could be improved on many points to the benefit, not only of traffic victims, but of other victims of personal injury. Thus, the statute ended up as a long and complex document, composed of three chapters. While the first exclusively deals with compensation of traffic victims, Chapter II aims at co-ordinating, to the benefit of every victim of a personal injury, insurance compensation and compensation from other sources (especially social security). Chapter III contains a number of procedural and substantive provisions which improve the law to the benefit of all victims of personal injury.[6]

We must concentrate here on Chapter I (*Indemnisation des victimes d'accidents de la circulation*) and, more specifically, on Section I (*Dispositions relatives au droit à indemnisation*) and Section III (*De l'offre d'indemnité*). Chapter I, section I contains the most fundamental and controversial set of provisions of the statute. The general philosophy of the law being compensation for all victims, article 2 abolishes a centuries-old tradition in eliminating the excuse of *vis major* and 'fact of a third party'. Thus, to refer to a case discussed above, if a car skids on the road by reason of the formation of ice, the pedestrian hit by the car shall be entitled to compensation even if the formation of ice was 'not reasonably foreseeable'.

Article 3 provides for quasi-no-fault compensation of traffic victims 'other than drivers'. This regrettable exclusion has already been explained. It is confirmed by article 4: a fault committed by a driver reduces or excludes compensation for the damage he has suffered.

Article 3 is a text of compromise on another score. While it starts in a very promising (if not elegant) fashion, 'Les victimes hormi les conducteurs . . . sont indemnisées des dommages résultant des atteintes à leur personne qu'elles ont subis, sans que puisse leur être opposée leur propre faute', the text goes on, 'à l'exception de leur faute inexcusable si elle a été la cause exclusive de l'accident'. This exception, which may cause surprise, was introduced at the last moment. Robert Badinter had asked the members of his staff to test on their friends the idea of no-fault compensation. The consultation produced negative reactions: the idea of no-fault compensation was not approved; it was considered as a denial of common sense and social values. Hence, as a compromise, the exception to the principle: no compensation for the victim of his or her own inexcusable fault, if it was 'the only cause of the accident'. In Parliament, Robert Badinter stressed that this exception should be invoked only in very exceptional circumstances. We shall observe its fate later.

Anyhow, the subsequent paragraph of the same article provides for an exception to the exception: the victim, whatever his or her behaviour,

[6] On the *loi Badinter*, see Geneviève Viney, *L'indemnisation des victimes d'accidents de la circulation* (1992); François Chabas, *Les accidents de la circulation* (1995); *Dixième anniversaire de la loi Badinter sur la protection des victimes d'accidents de la circulation: bilan et perspectives* (1996). See also the various works dealing with '*responsabilité civile*', the most recent being Philippe Le Tourneau & Loïc Cadier, *Droit de la responsabilité* (1996), 778–808; or with the law of insurance, the most recent one being Yvonne Lambert-Faivre, *Droit des assurances* (9th ed., 1995), 527–709. See also idem, *Le droit du dommage corporel. Systèmes d'indemnisation* (3rd ed. 1996), 565–629. All recent important decisions are commented on by Patrice Jourdain in each issue of the *Revue trimestrielle de droit civil* and by Hubert Groutel in the monthly *Responsabilité civile et assurance*.

shall always be entitled to full compensation if he or she is less than 16 years old or more than 70, or at least 80 per cent incapacitated.

Section III of Chapter I also contains important innovations. In the first part of this essay, I reported the high degree of litigation, with the unavoidable consequences of cost, delay, and frustration, and the danger of unfair settlements, which prevailed under the law of torts. If general compensation of traffic victims was the primary aim of the law, therefore, a secondary, but important, aim was the reducton of litigation and the fairness of agreed settlements.

Article 12 prescribes that the insurer who owes compensation must, within eight months of the accident (a long period, but necessary to permit the insurer to know what the victim receives from other sources and thus avoid double compensation), present an offer of compensation to the victim or, in case of death, to the spouse and the heirs. The offer may be provisional if the victim's condition has not stabilized; in that case, the final offer should be made within five months of the stabilization. The offer must contain an offer to forward the police documents; it should also remind the victim that he or she may require the assistance of a lawyer and of a physician. When two or more vehicles are involved in the accident, the insurers must agree between themselves which one is to act on behalf of all of them.

If the insurer fails to make an offer within the prescribed period, the amount of compensation which is finally decided bears interest at double the legal rate. If the parties do not reach an agreement and the case is settled by a court, the latter, if it finds that the offer was grossly unfair (*'manifestement insuffisante'*), will order the insurer to pay compensatory damages to the victim and a fine to the Guarantee Fund, which may amount to 15 per cent of the general compensation.

To give the victim a greater chance of a fair settlement, article 19 provides that the victim may cancel the agreement within fifteen days of it being signed by both parties, and must be notified of this right.

Payment of the amount agreed upon by the parties, or decided by the court, must be made within a month, after which interest at a substantial rate becomes payable.

In order to provide the parties with some guidance as to the reasonable amount of damages, article 26 prescribes that an official periodical publication shall report compensation payments agreed upon by parties to settlements or awarded by the courts. These reports are not compulsory schedules: they are only a means of guidance by offering comparisons.

The statute does not deal with property damage, especially damage to cars (article 5), where agreements between insurers provide for reasonably satisfactory solutions.

Under the *loi Badinter*

The *loi Badinter* was passed by a unanimous vote of Parliament. This was a great surprise, explained by the discreet lobbying by a member of Parliament who had previously lost two daughters in a traffic accident and was more sensitive to the fate of victims than to the income of lawyers. It might be expected that a unanimous vote would close the dispute. In fact, the dispute continued as passionately as before the vote. This strange phenomenon had a number of causes.

One was the feeling, current among lawyers as well as among laymen, that liability for fault is a cornerstone of our society. There is some truth in this feeling, as regards deliberate behaviour. But what is true of deliberate conduct may not be true of errors. Furthermore, if liability for fault is justified, it does not follow that compensation should never have some other source.

This attachment to liability for fault was reinforced by political reasons. After decades of centre-right government, the 1981 elections had brought the Left to power. This was a trauma for a significant part of French public opinion. A paper as influential as *Le Figaro* published daily editorials on the disasters threatening France. Out of all the members of the Government, Robert Badinter was the most frequent target of such attacks, especially since he had obtained the abolition of the death penalty. Abolition of the death penalty and no-fault compensation were considered as the utmost of *déresponsabilisation*—a process which it was feared, would lead to a society comparable to those of the Soviet Union or China. The reform was considered of 'leftist' inspiration, even though it had been launched by Jean Foyer, who prided himself on being strongly conservative.

Needless to say, the hostility towards the project and, later on, the statute, also had a financial basis: traffic accident litigation provided a significant part of many lawyers' incomes.

It may appear strange that many judges, probably most of them, shared the general hostility towards the new law. Of course, their feeling was not financially based. But most of them were, for moral reasons, attached to liability for fault and probably to a centre-right government. They were regular readers of *Le Figaro* and *La Gazette du Palais*, which had led the fight for partisan reasons. Finally, the choice made by Robert Badinter of a policy of consultation over a policy of confrontation was unfortunate in the respect that judges were bewildered by a philosophy which was not the one they had learned at law school and had applied for decades. The influence of *La Gazette du Palais* was particularly baneful: for a long period, it published with critical comments every decision applying the new law.

It is true that the task of the courts in applying the law was harder than has been expected. Many problems arose which had not been foreseen and which had to be solved in the framework of a new philosophy. It would be of no interest to give here a complete account of these difficulties.[7] Only the most important of them will be mentioned.

The most crucial problem was to know when the victim had committed a *faute inexcusable, cause exclusive de l'accident*. As explained above, this cause of refusal of compensation had been introduced at the last moment, and Robert Badinter had explained to Parliament that the notion had to be extremely narrowly understood, and applied only in most exceptional circumstances. The hostility of many judges, however, introduced great uncertainty. If a pedestrian inadvertently steps off the pavement and is hurt by a car, this is, in the philosophy of the new law, the type of error that any good citizen can commit and would not jusify a denial of compensation. But, in the traditional philosophy, to which a number of judges remained faithful, this behaviour was an inexcusable fault ('you should not have stepped from the pavement'), and it was obviously the only cause of the accident. Decisions of this vein were published in great number by *La Gazette du Palais*. At times, it appeared that the reform had been nullified by the courts.

The Cour de Cassation seemed to hesitate to intervene in the matter. A courageous decision in this field, some years before, while the statute was under preparation, had led to a revolt of many courts of appeal, which had refused to follow its doctrine—a situation without any precedent and of utmost gravity.[8] The Cour was certainly reluctant to take the risk of another revolt. The situation, however, was also highly regrettable—it was one of revolt against the statute.

Finally the Cour intervened—in the most spectacular fashion. In one afternoon on 20 July 1987, the Cour de Cassation examined eleven decisions in which the courts of appeal had refused compensation for *faute inexcusable, cause exclusive de l'accident* and it set aside ('*cassa*') ten of them,[9] leaving only one to stand to show its obedience to the statute. The Cour gave a narrow definition of *faute inexcusable*. The sociological impact of the afternoon was even more important: the Cour de Cassation had nullified the decisions made by a third of the French courts of appeal in cases where, under the previous law, it would have approved the denial of compensation. In order to suppress any attempt at rebellion, the Cour, on 10 November 1995, by a decision in plenary session, reiterated its *coup d'éclat*: it approved compensation in a case where all the

[7] See works referred to in n. 6 above.

[8] On the *Desmares* case, see Viney, n. 6 above, 8.

[9] Cass. 2e civ. 20 July 1987, *Bull. civ.* II, nr 160, p. 90. See Viney n. 6 above, nr 32.

circumstances were against the victim (the victim, drunk, wearing dark clothes, walking down the middle of a busy road by night, was trying to stop a driver to give him a lift home).[10] A final decision, of 6 November 1996,[11] deserves quotation:

> Pour retenir à la charge d'un piéton, victime d'un accident de la circulation, une faute inexcusable, cause exclusive de l'accident, l'arrêt attaqué retient qu'en complet état d'ivresse, chancelant et continuant à boire du pastis directement à la bouteille, le piéton s'est accroupi sur la chaussée d'un chemin départemental, hors agglomération, de nuit, par temps de brouillard réduisant la visibilité à 30 mètres, au milieu du couloir de marche du véhicule; en l'état de ces constatations qui ne caractérisent pas l'existence d'une faute inexcusable à la charge de la victime, la cour d'appel a violé le texte susvisé.

This is the type of decision which delights supporters of the *loi Badinter* and infuriates those faithful to tort liability. In any event, it shows that, practically speaking, all traffic accident victims other than drivers are now entitled to compensation.

Another concept in the statute which gave rise to great difficulties, probably because it had not been explained, is the concept of *implication*. From the traditional elements of civil liability the new law eliminates not only (to a large extent) the concept of fault, but also the concept of causation. In the hope of reducing litigation, insurers were called on to provide compensation as soon as the vehicle they covered was '*impliqué*' in an accident. That means that any kind of relation between the car and the accident is sufficient to create the insurer's duty. The difficult problem of causal connection was thus eliminated. Besides, with compensation flowing from a collective source, individual justice had become of secondary importance. In retrospect, the idea was certainly a wise one. However the courts, and even the *Cour de Cassation*, had great difficulties in freeing themselves from old conceptions. Fortunately, the matter now seems settled in a satisfactory manner.

Surprisingly, one of the most frequent problems facing the courts is that of deciding who is a driver (*conducteur*). When someone enters the car in order to drive it, is that person already a driver? If he stops the car on the side of the road, does he still remain a driver? When he stops and leaves the car, at which moment does he cease to be a driver? The problems are even more subtle for the user of a motor cycle. What is the legal status of someone who was driving a car or a motor cycle, but has been thrown out of his car or motor cycle and is then hit by another vehicle? On these problems and on similar ones, the courts have been

[10] Cass. ass. pl., 10 Nov. 1995, D. 1995.633, rapp. Chartier, JCP 1996 II 22562, concl. Jeol, note Viney. See also comm. Jourdain, (1996) Rev. tr. dr. civ. 187.

[11] Cass. 2e civ., 6 Nov. 1996, JCP 1996 IV 2547.

obliged to create a case law nearly as ridiculous and uncertain as the one which had developed under the previous law.

Fortunately, there is now a general consensus on the desirability of extending automatic protection to drivers. As soon as the law was passed by Parliament in 1985, some insurers offered to their clients, for an additional premium, full coverage (that is, for the amount which would be awarded by a court) of themselves and the members of their families in case of personal injury or death by traffic accident, even if the accident results from a fault or error of the driver or from a collision with a fixed obstacle, in which case civil liability would be of no avail.[12] The premium is quite reasonable[13] and the protection has been widely purchased. The insurance industry now favours drivers' automatic protection, either by voluntary coverage (which would be so attractive that it would be purchased by everyone) or by legislative reform.

The construction of the *loi Badinter* being now, on the whole, settled, and more than ten years having elapsed since its enactment, it is possible to establish a balance-sheet of its results. That was the purpose of a large conference organized in 1995 by the Editions du Juris-classeur with the co-operation of the Groupement des Entreprises Mutuelles d'Assurances. The proceedings of the Conference have been published by the Editions du Juris-classeur under the title: *Dixième anniversaire de la loi Badinter sur la protection des victimes d'accidents de la circulation: bilan et perspectives*. The reader of this document, who remembers the vehemence with which the project was opposed, will be struck by the change of climate. The law no longer has any enemies. On the contrary, there is a general consensus on the need to radicalize it and extend its compulsory protection to drivers. Its strengths and weaknesses have been objectively assessed.

From this document and certain others published by the quasi-official Fédération Française des Sociétés d'Assurances, a certain number of conclusions emerge. First, one of the main arguments against the law was that it would require a significant increase in insurance premiums. The argument proved groundless. Robert Badinter had obtained from the Treasury (which controls the insurance industry and, in particular, insurance premiums) a letter certifying that the reform would not entail any premium increase. As a matter of fact, a small increase occurred the year after its enactment, but entirely due to an increase in the cost of car repairs. Ten years later, it appears that, from 1985 to 1995, insurance premiums for automobile civil liability increased slightly less than the

[12] See Viney, n. 6 above, nr 87. Lambert-Faivre, *Le droit du dommage corporel*,(n. 6 above) nr 309–17, and *Droit des assurances* (n. 6 above) nr. 790–792.

[13] An important mutual company (to which I belong) offers this additional coverage for an annual premium of 280 fr. (£28).

cost of living. Obviously, automatic coverage of drivers would impose a certain increase, at least at the beginning. There is every reason to believe that it would be modest.[14] It might even be off-set by administrative savings, especially if the present system of compensation was replaced by a system of direct one-party insurance, which would then become possible.

It is obviously of paramount importance to know the proportion of victims who received compensation before and after the *loi Badinter* came into force. The increase is disappointing: the proportion went from 67 per cent to 72 per cent. The proportion was dragged down by the exclusion of the drivers from the automatic protection. For a better appreciation of the situation, however, two remarks should be made. First, the figures do not include the drivers covered by voluntary insurance, whose number has greatly increased as an indirect result of the *loi Badinter* (making it evident that the drivers have little legal protection). Secondly, under tort law, the compensation paid to a large proportion of pedestrians, cyclists, and even passengers, was reduced on the basis of contributory negligence, while all of them now receive full compensation. The progress, therefore, is more important than may appear at first sight. The situation, however, is not yet satisfactory. Drivers should be included in the automatic protection.

A drastic reduction of traffic accident litigation, with the reduction of delay, expense and frustration that it entails, is an unquestionable success of the *loi Badinter.* That reduction is not self-evident. It has often been denied by writers of good faith, misled by the fact that a greater proportion of decisions under the new law are published in the law reports. Still, the reduction is spectacular. According to documents produced by the insurance industry the proportion of cases going to court has dropped from 27 per cent to 10 per cent, 'perhaps less'.[15]

The delays of settlement have also been reduced. Before the *loi Badinter*, the delay for an agreed settlement averaged twenty-one months; it is now twenty months. These figures may not suggest much progress, but, as we have seen, they now relate to 90 per cent of cases instead of 73 per cent. In the case of judicial settlements, the delay, which was thirty-one months, is now forty months, and would be worse if the amount of litigation had not been significantly reduced.

The results of the new procedure obliging the insurer to present to the victim an offer of compensation are more questionable. On average, compensation payments resulting from settlements are lower than those

[14] See n. 13 above.

[15] According to Lambert-Faivre, *Le droit du dommage corporel*, n. 6 above, 629, the proportion of cases settled by judicial decisions would now be 7.6 per cent.

decided upon by judgment of the court. However, they save the victim the trouble, delay, expense, suffering, and frustration inherent to a law suit. Furthermore, the present writer considers that the courts are often over-generous as regards the compensation of non-pecuniary damage (which means that an agreed settlement may be less generous without being unfair). At the 1995 conference, the general feeling was that the victim was often at a disadvantage compared to the insurer, and that the system of publication provided by the statute should be amended to redress the balance. This does not mean that the principle of a compulsory offer does not represent a progress over the previous situation. Furthermore, it has probably contributed to maintaining insurance premiums at a reasonable level.

Conclusion

When comparing the fate of traffic accident victims before and after the *loi Badinter*, it seems objectively self-evident that considerable progress has been realized. Victims (apart from drivers) are now assured of total compensation without reference to their behaviour. Some difficulties of construction of the statute may remain; but they are rarer and rarer, and they are settled by judges who no longer bear any hostility towards the statute. A cultural revolution has occurred. The idea of no-fault compensation for personal injuries suffered by traffic accident victims is a *fait acquis*.

Consequently, the lack of automatic protection for drivers is considered the only failure of the new system, a failure which should be remedied as soon as possible. The following document is typical. It is the conclusion of the editorial of *Assurer*, the monthly letter of the Fédération française des sociétés d'assurance, in its issue of October 1996:

> L'évolution de la jurisprudence, puis l'intervention du législateur en 1985 (Loi Badinter) ont conduit à un système d'assurance de responsabilité civile obligatoire qui est sans conteste l'un des plus protecteurs des victimes en Europe. Les piétons, cyclistes et passagers, c'est-à-dire toute personne autre que le conducteur, sont entièrement dédommagés de leur préjudice corporel, sauf dans des cas tout-à-fait exceptionnels. En revanche, l'indemnisation du conducteur, dans près de la moitié des cas, ne relève pas de l'assurance automobile obligatoire et l'accident peut laisser la famille de la victime dans une situation financière dramatique. Or, la moitié seulement des conducteurs ont souscrit pour se protéger une assurance volontaire dite 'du conducteur responsable'. Il est du devoir des assurés envers leurs familles et des assureurs envers leurs clients d'aboutir, dans des délais rapides, à une totale généralisation de cette garantie.

15

The Collateral Source Rule Thirty Years On

*Harold Luntz**

Introduction

In 1966 John Fleming published 'The Collateral Source Rule and Loss Allocation in Tort'.[1] He later refined his analysis of the issue and extended the jurisdictions which he encompassed in a chapter of the *International Encyclopaedia of Comparative Law*.[2] One aspect, recovery from a tortfeasor which is insufficient to reimburse both the victim and the collateral source in full, was elaborated in a case note which he wrote in 1974.[3] The purpose of the present chapter is to update Fleming's treatment of the subject on a much more modest scale, with reference to only two jurisdictions, Australia and England.[4] No attempt will be made to canvass the law outside that affecting personal injuries.

* Thanks to Alan Clayton for research assistance and to Lizzie Barmes of the Law Commission for comments.

[1] (1966) 54 Cal. L. Rev. 1478. See also 'More Thoughts on Loss Distribution' (1966) 4 Osgoode Hall L.J. 161 at 167–73.

[2] 'Collateral Benefits' (completed 1 Jan. 1970) ch 11, vol XI (*Torts*).

[3] 'Insurance—Subrogation—Priority between Insurer and Insured' (1974) 52 Can. Bar Rev. 103. The case there noted, *Re Ledingham v Di Natale* [1973] 1 OR 291 (CA), revg [1972] 1 OR 785, was itself later reversed by the Supreme Court of Canada *sub nom Ledingham v Ontario Health Services Commission* [1975] 1 SCR 332; (1974) 46 DLR (3d) 699. Unfortunately, the Supreme Court did not respond to Fleming's call (at 112) 'for a policy analysis, not a capricious exercise in . . . statutory construction'.

[4] A 'brief, non-exhaustive review' of the current law on the topic in Scotland, Ireland, the United States, and Canada is to be found in the English Law Commission's recent consultation paper, *Damages for Personal Injury: Collateral Benefits* (Consultation Paper No. 147, 1997), Pt III. For full treatment of the law in Canada, see K. Cooper-Stephenson, *Personal Injury Damages in Canada* (2nd ed., 1995), ch 9; S. M. Waddams, *The Law of Damages* (3rd ed., 1997), paras 3.1490–3.1810.

Fleming's Analysis

When an injured party claims damages from a tortfeasor, the court almost invariably has only those two parties before it.[5] Where, as is frequently the case, the plaintiff is entitled to receive benefits in consequence of the injury from some other source, the options available to the court are usually only two: (1) to award the plaintiff damages without reference to the benefits available from the other source, so that the plaintiff, who is theoretically made whole by the award of damages, is better off by the amount of benefits retained; or (2) to reduce the damages by the amount of the benefits received and to be received, thereby relieving the tortfeasor of part of the liability which would otherwise have been incurred.[6] The insight provided by Fleming was to draw attention to the wider picture, which must acknowledge that there are three parties affected, not two, since the collateral source also has an interest in the way the funds are distributed. He was not the first to draw attention to this feature,[7] but the clarity of his analysis meant that it could not thereafter be ignored.

Fleming divided the possible solutions to the problem into four: (1) *election*, that is, requiring the injured party to elect between the benefits available from the collateral source and pursuing a remedy against a tortfeasor; (2) *cumulation* of benefits, that is, allowing the victim to retain the collateral benefits and to recover damages in full undiminished by the recovery from the collateral source; (3) *reimbursement*, that is, requiring the tortfeasor (or the victim) to reimburse the collateral source; (4) *relieving the tortfeasor* by reducing the damages which would have been payable if the collateral benefits had not been there.

[5] In some cases there may be multiple tortfeasors, but this does not affect the analysis.

[6] Occasionally, a court will claim power to order the plaintiff to pay over part of the damages to a collateral source or to require the plaintiff to hold part of the damages in trust for the collateral source. As we shall see, the House of Lords did this in *Hunt v Severs* [1994] 2 AC 350. This claim is denied in Australia: *Griffiths v Kerkemeyer* (1977) 139 CLR 161 at 177 per Stephen J; *Kars v Kars* (1996) 187 CLR 354.

[7] In his main article he referred extensively to Spencer L. Kimball and Don A. Davis, 'The Extension of Insurance Subrogation' (1962) 60 Mich. L. Rev. 841, whose main purpose, however, was to consider when subrogation is available against a tortfeasor under policies of insurance. He also drew attention to the 'categorical repudiation of the philosophy underlying the collateral source rule' by the Departmental Committee on Alternative Remedies ('the Monckton Committee'), *Final Report*, Cmd. 6860 (1946), which was set up following the Beveridge Report, Inter-Departmental Committee on Social Insurance and Allied Services, *Report*, Cmd. 6404 (1942): see 'Collateral Source Rule', n. 1 above at 1539–40. In the bibliography to the chapter in the *International Encyclopaedia* (n. 2 above), Fleming listed Fleming James Jr, 'Social Insurance and Tort Liability: The Problem of Alternative Remedies' (1952) 27 NYU Law Rev. 537, which presented a similar, though less comprehensive, analysis.

Election

Fleming found no need to dwell on election of remedies, which he said had gradually fallen into disfavour because of the immediate needs of the victim and the long delays before tort recovery.[8] He referred briefly to the unhappy experience with Anglo-American workers' compensation laws.[9] Indeed, in the current edition of his textbook, he omits it altogether at the point at which he deals with collateral benefits, referring only to three possible solutions to the general problem.[10] However, election has made a limited comeback in several Australian workers' compensation statutes, which now make explicit provision for non-pecuniary loss and sometimes require workers to make an election between common-law and statutory remedies of this type. Inevitably, problems have emerged in this context.[11]

Cumulation of Remedies

The usual United States solution found by Fleming was cumulation. Clearly he was not sympathetic to this. Although when he came to deal with reimbursement, he was much concerned with the overall costs and benefits, he displayed only the barest hints of the economic justification which would see the requirement that the tortfeasor bear the full cost of the harm as necessary to provide the appropriate incentive for an efficient allocation of resources.[12] He remained unpersuaded by the economic theories espoused by the Chicago school of legal analysis, applying them in the present context only with disdain.[13]

Reimbursement

The third solution, reimbursement of the collateral source, Fleming showed could be effected through various mechanisms. One is to give the collateral source direct recourse against the tortfeasor (a) by way of subrogation to the victim's rights, or (b) a common-law action such as for loss of *consortium*, or (c) a statutory right of indemnity (as under

8 *International Encyclopaedia*, n. 2 above, para 4.

9 The problem essentially arose from attempts by representatives of insurers to foist on workers some compensation at a time of need, so that thereafter they would be deprived of the common-law remedy.

10 J. G. Fleming, *The Law of Torts* (8th ed., 1992), 243; but see 522.

11 See, e.g., *Pye v Butterfield Cheese Factors Pty Ltd* (1996) 39 NSWLR 425 (CA) (election provision unable to operate where forum and *locus delicti* outside the state).

12 One such hint is to be seen in 'More Thoughts', n. 1 above at 172, where reference is made to G. Calabresi, 'Some Reflections on Risk Distribution' (1961) 70 Yale L.J. 499.

13 J. G. Fleming, 'The Pearson Report: Its "Strategy"' (1979) 42 MLR 249 at 256 ('"transaction costs" in economic jargon'; 'economists allergic to "externalities"').

workers' compensation legislation). Another mechanism for reimbursement of the collateral source is to require the victim to refund the benefactions; and, as he pointed out,[14] the same effect is achieved by termination of periodical payments once the need is met by tort damages. In the context of recourse against the tortfeasor he considered various types of benefit, such as private insurance, social security, workers' compensation, disability pay, and other contractual fringe benefits. He pointed to some special problems that arise when reimbursement applies. One is how one apportions the recovery when it is insufficient to satisfy in full both the victim's losses and the collateral payments, either because the damages have been reduced for contributory negligence, or the tortfeasor's liability is limited in some other way, or the tortfeasor is insolvent or has inadequate insurance cover.[15] Does the collateral source obtain reimbursement only *after* the victim's losses have been satisfied in full, does it take priority over the victim, or is there to be a pro rata sharing? A similar issue, dubbed by Fleming 'equivalence', is whether the collateral source is to be confined to recovery out of those heads of damages which can be said to be compensating for losses equivalent to the ones which the collateral source has met, or is it instead entitled to be reimbursed for its payments in full even if the equivalent heads of damages are insufficient for this purpose? He showed that different jurisdictions approach these issues in different ways; in some the solution varies between private and social insurance.

Workers' compensation systems generally favour reimbursement, frequently allowing the employer or fund that paid the benefits a direct action to recoup those payments even if the employee, say, by reason of having elected to take the workers' compensation, is precluded from pursuing an action for damages.[16] Social security systems, on the other hand, Fleming found, were divided on the issue because of the cost of recovery. Notably, the British social security system, which after Beveridge had absorbed workers' compensation, opted against reimbursement. Instead, this system had achieved an historic compromise between relieving the tortfeasor and allowing cumulation, legislation requiring the court to set off against damages half the value of certain social security benefits for up to five years.[17]

[14] See, e.g., 'Collateral Source Rule', n. 1 above at 1531.

[15] This was the subject of his case-note in (1974) 52 Can. Bar Rev. 103, n 3 above.

[16] Such action is predicated on liability on the part of the third party to the employee but for the particular bar; i.e. there must be someone who would be a tortfeasor vis-à-vis the employee if the employee had sued instead of accepting the benefits. In *Tickle Industries Pty Ltd v Hann* (1974) 130 CLR 321 a majority of the High Court held that the employer could recover an indemnity notwithstanding that the employee's dependants' action was barred by limitation of actions.

[17] Law Reform (Personal Injuries) Act 1948.

Relief of the Tortfeasor

Between Fleming writing 'Collateral Source Rule' and completing *International Encyclopaedia*, the House of Lords decided *Parry v Cleaver*.[18] He could thus state in the later work that the English position was 'not wholly dissimilar' to that in the United States, 'though somewhat more complex'.[19] As a result of that case, cumulation is allowed for charitable gifts and insurance purchased by the plaintiff, but otherwise the basic principle of compensation means that the tortfeasor is relieved.

To relieve the tortfeasor entirely requires not only that the damages be reduced in the victim's action, but also that the collateral source be denied subrogation or a direct action. As already noticed the social security system compromised between cumulation of benefits and relieving the tortfeasor. This was on the theory that in most cases both plaintiff and defendant would have contributed to the fund from which the social security benefits were paid. This theory would not have countenanced any subrogation rights in the social security payer. Workers' compensation had disappeared into the social security system, so there was no room for subrogation and indemnity, as continued to operate in Australia. In England employers were also denied a direct action for the recovery of, for instance, sick pay by *IRC v Hambrook*,[20] which had confined the action for loss of *servitium* to domestic servants, and *Metropolitan Police District Receiver v Croydon Corporation*,[21] which had held that no restitutionary claim was available.

Fleming, while recognizing the attractions of reimbursement, apparently favoured relieving the tortfeasor. By the time of the case note in the Canadian Bar Review, he openly numbered himself among the 'growing school of skeptics [*sic*] . . . concerning the value and efficiency of subrogation, in view of its high administrative cost and the fact that its supposedly disciplinary edge on tortfeasors is largely blunted by the interposition of liability insurance, so that in effect subrogation merely shifts the costs from one to another of two, usually equally well-placed, loss distributors'.[22]

[18] [1970] AC 1. [19] *International Encyclopaedia*, n. 2 above, para 11-37.
[20] [1956] 2 QB 641 (CA). [21] [1957] 2 QB 154 (CA).
[22] (1974) 52 Can. Bar Rev. 103 at 109. In the *International Encyclopaedia* he had documented 'mounting scepticism' as to the value of subrogation: see *International Encyclopaedia*, n. 2 above, para 11–66.

What has Happened Since

As between Plaintiff and Defendant

England

In *Hussain v New Taplow Paper Mills Ltd*[23] and *Hodgson v Trapp*[24] the House of Lords confirmed that the prima facie rule in England is relief of the tortfeasor and that the plaintiff is not to be allowed to cumulate the benefits, unless falling squarely within the exceptions of charity and insurance.[25] The former case involved payment of sick pay by means of an insurance policy paid for by the employer, who was also the defendant. The latter concerned social security benefits not dealt with in the legislative compromise, namely mobility and attendance allowance. All these collateral benefits were held deductible in the assessment of the plaintiff's damages. In *Hodgson* Lord Bridge gave expression to a view that accorded very much with Fleming's. He called for a recognition of the 'realities' of the situation, that the damages would not be paid by the defendant personally, but by insurers who would derive their funds from premiums contributed by employers, motorists, professional people, occupiers of property, and so on.[26] It seems that he did not perceive any difference between the two risk pools that provided the funds for respectively the collateral benefits and the damages payable to injured plaintiffs. These remarks are consistent with the view of the Royal Commission on Civil Liability and Compensation for Personal Injury under the chairmanship of Lord Pearson, which had concluded that '[s]ocial security should be recognised as the principal means of compensation. Double compensation should be avoided by offsetting social security benefits in the assessment of tort damages'.[27]

However, another decade later, an attempt to overturn, or at least distinguish, the actual result in *Parry v Cleaver*,[28] reached by a three-to-two majority — that disability pensions are more like insurance than sick pay and are not to be set off against wages lost — failed. In *Smoker v London Fire & Civil Defence Authority*[29] their Lordships not only unanimously refused to hold that *Parry* was wrongly decided, but also

[23] [1988] AC 514. [24] [1989] AC 807.

[25] In both Lord Bridge gave the only reasoned judgment on the relevant point, with which all the other members of the House of Lords who were sitting agreed.

[26] In *Hunt v Severs* [1994] 2 AC 350, where again the rest of the House agreed, Lord Bridge again emphasized that damages are to be confined to compensation of the plaintiff, but found too great the complexities of recognising that insurance would mean that the defendant did not actually pay twice. Contrast *Kars v Kars* (1996) 187 CLR 354, discussed below.

[27] *Report*, Cmnd 7054 (1978), vol 1, 'Summary of conclusions', 367.

[28] [1970] AC 1. [29] [1991] 2 AC 502.

declined to act on a dictum of Lord Pearce in that case that the situation might be different when the 'pension rights in question come from an insurance arrangement which [the employer defendant] has made with the plaintiff as his employee'.[30] According to their Lordships any trend towards disallowing cumulation of benefits was to be discerned only in relation to substitutes for wages, which they held such a disability pension was not. Significantly, in the interim Parliament had legislated for repayment of social security benefits,[31] which showed to their Lordships that it was capable of legislating in this field and there was therefore no need for the House of Lords in its judicial capacity to change the law which had stood for twenty years. Even more significant, perhaps, is the change in political philosophy which led to the enactment of this legislation, and which will be considered below. That change is probably also to be seen in one of the reasons why the trial judge, Auld J, had rejected arguments that *Parry v Cleaver* was to be distinguished. It was now possible for members of such pension schemes to opt out of them and make their own insurance arrangements. In these circumstances his Lordship thought that it would be illogical to deduct the benefits here and not in such cases.[32] Of course, consistency could have been achieved by deducting in both instances, but the insurance exception appears sacrosanct, Windeyer J having noted that it had 'stood too long and on too firm a foundation of policy and justice to be unsettled by demands for logical consistency'.[33]

In fact the inconsistency goes further. The law on collateral benefits has been comprehensively reviewed recently by the Law Commission[34] and there is no need to deal in detail here with the case law, except to note that the House of Lords has subsequently decided another case involving disability payments under a superannuation scheme by a defendant employer in which it recognized that by virtue of *Parry* and *Smoker* disability pensions fall outside the general rule that prima facie all receipts resulting from the injury have to be set off against losses so resulting.[35] The Law Commission's summary[36] of the position at the time of its report showed that charitable gifts (unless, possibly, if made

30 [1970] AC 1 at 37.

31 Social Security Act 1989, s 22 and Sch 4, discussed in its later manifestations below.

32 [1991] 2 AC 502 at 524.

33 *National Insurance Co. of NZ Ltd v Espagne* (1961) 105 CLR 569 at 588.

34 CP 147, n. 4 above. See also Law Commission, *Damages for Personal Injury: Medical, Nursing and Other Expenses: the Cost of Care* (Consultation Paper No. 144, 1996) and Law Commission, *Claims for Wrongful Death* (Consultation Paper No 148, 1997), paras 2.43–2.60. Particular treatment of death claims is outside the scope of this paper.

35 *Longden v British Coal Corporation* [1997] 3 WLR 1336 (holding that periodical payments of pension are not to be taken into account, but a lump sum had to be apportioned so as to deduct from claim for loss of retirement benefits that part which represented commutation of post-retirement pension).

36 CP 147, n. 4 above, para 2.92.

by the defendant), insurance payments (at least where paid for by the plaintiff), and disability and retirement pensions (except in so far as they relate to a claim for loss of retirement benefits) are all ignored in the assessment of damages. On the other hand, sick pay (at least if paid periodically) and redundancy payments due to the injury are deducted. Social security benefits are either recouped by the State,[37] taken into account to the extent allowed for in the historic compromise or, with the exception of State retirement pensions, are deducted in full.

Not only does this summary reflect the uncertainty in relation to what the court will do in particular cases, even within the established categories where there happens to be some unusual element in the nature of the collateral benefit,[38] but it shows some very basic inconsistencies between categories. The Law Commission in particular highlighted the striking inconsistency between the treatment of sick pay, which is deducted, and disability pensions, which are ignored.[39]

The Law Commission put forward six options as to what to do about this situation of uncertainty and inconsistency.[40] The first is to have a strong rule of deductibility, that is relief of the tortfeasor, including deduction of charitable and insurance payments, coupled with a requirement of equivalence and an exception if the collateral source has a right of recoupment. A possible modification of this to take into account insurance premiums paid by the plaintiff is mooted. The second option adds an exclusion for charitable payments to the basic rules of option one. The third option is to allow cumulation whenever the provider of the collateral benefit intends that it should be retained in addition to damages (this is the present theory in Australia). It asks whether uncertainty inherent in this option could be overcome by means of rebuttable presumptions. Option four involves only a very limited change to the present rules, by making disablement pensions deductible in the same way as sick pay. The fifth option is to allow cumulation of benefits in all

[37] The recoupment scheme is described below. At this point it should be noticed that Social Security (Recovery of Benefits) Act 1997, s 17, which provides for the recoupment by the Department of Social Security of benefits which are listed in the Act, reads: 'In assessing damages in respect of any accident, injury or disease, the amount of any listed benefits paid or likely to be paid is to be disregarded'. The listed benefits are those which correspond to three heads of damages: compensation, during the relevant period, for (1) earnings lost, (2) cost of care incurred, and (3) loss of mobility (Sch 2).

[38] See, e.g., *McCamley v Cammell Laird Shipbuilders Ltd* [1990] 1 WLR 963 (CA) (proceeds of ordinary accident insurance policy employers had taken out for different categories of workers prior to accident, of which plaintiff and union unaware, held not deductible, not because it came within exception based on insurance for which the plaintiff has paid, but because it came within principle of *ex gratia* gifts).

[39] See CP 147, n. 4 above, paras 2.104–2.109.

[40] See the summary, ibid, Pt VI, which contains references to the fuller discussion earlier in the paper.

cases. Subject to views which may be put forward on consultation, it expressly rejects this option. The sixth and last is to abandon the attempt to reform the law and to leave it to the courts to continue to deal with collateral benefits on a case-by-case basis. Although the Commission leaves this option open, it is difficult to accept in the light of the present uncertainty.

These options for reforming the law of collateral benefits as it affects the plaintiff and defendant must be viewed in the light of the Law Commission's further provisional views relating to the rights of the collateral source to recover its payments. If the rights of the collateral source are extended, then the deductibility of collateral benefits as between plaintiff and defendant does not have the effect of relieving the tortfeasor, but does prevent double compensation for the plaintiff. The question of the right of the collateral source to recover will be considered below. So far as rights between plaintiff and defendant are concerned, one should applaud the view that haphazard recovery of double benefits from the collateral source and as part of the damages should not be permitted merely because of the inadequacy of damages for other reasons. Therefore, it is hoped that the recommendations the Law Commission eventually makes will provide for maximum deductibility of equivalent benefits. The Commission notes that some people are sceptical that the consequence will be a reduction in insurance premiums, but supports the view that in theory competition should force this to happen.[41] One may be cynical that if this does occur it will release more funds for other disabled people in greater need, or even that it may provide funds for increased damages as a result of other aspects of the Law Commission's work.[42] Nevertheless, since insurance premiums are regressive in their impact, any reduction in premiums not bought at the cost of under-compensation would be welcome.

Australia

In *Parry v Cleaver*,[43] although four members of the House of Lords relied on statements of principle enunciated by Dixon CJ and Windeyer J in *National Insurance Co of NZ Ltd v Espagne*,[44] they differed on their application to the facts. An even more remarkable difference of opinion as to the application of these principles emerged in *Redding v Lee*,[45] where the High Court of Australia unanimously adopted those principles but divided into different majorities and minorities in the characterization

[41] Ibid, paras 4.27–4.28. [42] Ibid, paras 1.2, 4.25 and 4.29. [43] [1970] AC 1.

[44] (1961) 105 CLR 569. See at 573 per Dixon CJ; at 599–600 per Windeyer J, though both acknowledged the difficulty of generalizing for all types of benefit. Fullagar J agreed with both.

[45] (1983) 151 CLR 117.

of each of the two benefits under consideration.[46] Unanimity was, however, reached in *Manser v Spry*[47] and *Harris v Commercial Minerals Ltd.*[48] Both arose out of workers' compensation legislation, which, while allowing workers to proceed with common-law action notwithstanding receipt of workers' compensation, unusually did not provide for repayment of the benefits once damages were recovered.

In these cases the High Court reiterated that the fundamental principle is that damages for mere negligence are compensatory only. However, in *Manser* the Court noted that Windeyer J, who had stated this principle in *Skelton v Collins*,[49] observed in *Espagne* that the collateral source rule is not necessarily in conflict with the principle. It depends on whether the intention of the collateral source is that the plaintiff should enjoy the collateral benefit in addition to the damages. The High Court adverted to three possible indicia of the relevant intention. The first is the financial source of the payment, for example whether the scheme from which it comes is a contributory one.[50] If a legislative scheme provides for employees or for employers and employees to make contributions to fund benefits in respect of personal injury, there would be strong grounds for concluding that the legislation did intend that the benefits should be cumulated. The scheme would then be like a personal injury insurance policy, the proceeds of which are not ordinarily deductible. In both these cases the scheme was funded by employers[51] and no contribution was made by employees.[52] This indicium, therefore, did not

[46] Since both types of benefit, invalid pension (now known as disability support pension) and unemployment benefit (now known as newstart allowance or mature age allowance), are now subject to the regime of recoupment by the Social Security Department to be described below, the actual decisions of the High Court in the two cases are no longer directly relevant, though the reiteration of the *Espagne* principles remains authoritative.

[47] (1994) 181 CLR 428. [48] (1996) 186 CLR 1. [49] (1966) 115 CLR 94 at 128.

[50] The High Court saw this as the explanation of *Parry v Cleaver* [1970] AC 1 and *Smoker v London Fire & Civil Defence Authority* [1991] 2 AC 502. Although he was a party to both the joint judgments in *Manser v Spry* and *Harris v Commercial Minerals Ltd*, McHugh J appears to have overlooked the two cases in the House of Lords in a case which was decided between *Manser* and *Harris*. In *Medlin v State Government Insurance Commission* (1995) 182 CLR 1 at 23 he reached the preferable solution that the 'defendant is entitled to have credited against the loss of salary any benefit to the plaintiff arising from the accelerated payments of his pension and lump sum entitlements'.

[51] There might have been some contribution from Parliament in the *Harris* case.

[52] The High Court implicitly rejected the view that an employee can always be said to have 'bought' employment benefits by taking lower wages than would be the case in the absence of the benefits. This view had long ago been rejected in relation to sick pay in *Graham v Baker* (1961) 106 CLR 340 at 350. See also *Hussain v New Taplow Paper Mills Ltd* [1987] 1 All ER 417 (CA), affirmed [1988] AC 514 (HL); cf. *Dews v National Coal Board* [1988] AC 1 (HL) at 18 per Lord Mackay. In *Hussain's* case the Court of Appeal held that the trial judge was wrong to find that the plaintiff had in effect 'bought' the entitlement to sick pay by taking lower wages. Kerr LJ reserved his opinion on the result if it were established in a particular case that the plaintiff had accepted lower wages in return for a sick-pay scheme

indicate an intention of non-deductibility. The second indicium, that the benefits are repayable, was also absent in both.[53] The High Court therefore turned to the third relevant indicium, the nature of the benefit. This requires characterization of the benefit. Presumably, one is to understand by this Fleming's concept of equivalence, so that a benefit of a different nature from a head of damages is not to be deducted from the damages awarded under that head. In respect of the workers' compensation benefits in these two cases, the Court concluded that they were intended to replace the same losses as common-law damages, that in the circumstances the fundamental principle should prevail, and that they should therefore be taken into account in reduction of the damages.[54]

The second of the above indicia shows that where workers' compensation benefits are repayable to the employer or statutory fund from which they came, they must not be directly taken into account by way of reduction of the damages. Nevertheless, they do affect the assessment of damages in two ways. First, receipt of workers' compensation which is repayable must be taken into account for the purposes of calculating interest, since it means that the plaintiff has not been kept out of the money which is due for the full period. This rule applies to the appropriate head of damages whether the workers' compensation is a substitute for damages for loss of earning capacity[55] or for non-pecuniary loss.[56]

The second point relating to repayable workers' compensation benefits arises because in Australia, a lump sum award of damages is not taxed.[57] Periodical payments of workers' compensation, on the other hand, are taxed in Australia. Where the workers' compensation statute

(at 429). Cf. the Canadian cases of *Ratych v Bloomer* [1990] 1 SCR 940 and *Cunningham v Wheeler* [1994] 1 SCR 359, each decided by a narrow majority.

[53] See *Spry v Manser* (1993) 60 SASR 586 (FC) with regard to this in the first of the cases. There was no appeal on this point.

[54] *Harris* was followed by Cole JA in *CSR Ltd v D'Arcy* (1996) 40 NSWLR 721 (CA) in respect of medical benefits under the same legislation, even though the plaintiff had not applied for the benefits and had no intention of doing so (and accordingly there was no double compensation). The majority in this case reached the same result by holding that the plaintiff had failed to mitigate his damages. An application for leave to appeal to the High Court was lodged, but appears not to have been proceeded with.

[55] *Batchelor v Burke* (1981) 148 CLR 448 (deduction must be made whether the defendant is the employer or a stranger).

[56] *Haines v Bendall* (1991) 172 CLR 60.

[57] Income Tax Assessment Act 1936 (Cth), s 26(j), as interpreted in *Cullen v Trappell* (1980) 146 CLR 1. As Fleming recognized ('Collateral Source Rule', n. 1 above at 1542 n. 257), this non-taxation of damages designed to replace earnings which would have been taxed is also a collateral benefit. England and Australia have dealt with it by relieving the tortfeasor (*British Transport Commission v Gourley* [1956] AC 185 (HL); *Cullen v Trappell* (1980) 146 CLR 1); in Canada cumulation is allowed (*The Queen in right of Ontario v Jennings* [1966] SCR 532; reaffirmed in *Cunningham v Wheeler* [1994] 1 SCR 359). The Canadian position is criticized by Cooper-Stephenson, n. 4 above, 277–88, but defended by Waddams, n 4 above, paras 3.950–3.980.

provides for repayment of the benefits to the employer or statutory fund, the *gross* income replacement benefits paid have to be reimbursed, though the worker would have received only the *net* amounts after payment of income tax. Since the damages are calculated on net loss of earnings, workers would lose the amount of the tax.[58] In *Fox v Wood*[59] the High Court held that payment of tax on workers' compensation weekly benefits is such a natural and foreseeable consequence of injury that the amount of tax must be included in the damages as an additional item of loss.

The major advance that *National Insurance Co of NZ Ltd v Espagne*[60] made over earlier cases was that it rejected an approach to the collateral source rule based on causation, which involved distinguishing between the Latin tags *causa sine qua non* and *causa causans*. Some causal principles nevertheless remain relevant. If a person is forced to give up a job because of injury and chooses to retrain for a more remunerative profession, the higher earnings resulting from the new occupation are not to be seen as a benefit consequent on the injury and to come within the principle of deductibility.[61] The High Court had long ago concluded that a widow's earnings are not to be taken into account in reduction of her damages under Lord Campbell's Act because 'the wages which the plaintiff earned and received were no more and no less than the reward for her labour'.[62]

Fleming noted that 'the oldest and yet weakest form of social security' is support from relatives.[63] At one time, the fact that nursing and similar services were provided to the plaintiff gratuitously meant that it was not possible to claim their value as expenditure with which the plaintiff was entitled to be credited.[64] The rule was changed in England in *Donnelly v Joyce*[65] and in Australia in *Griffiths v Kerkemeyer*.[66] The courts in these two cases saw the loss as the plaintiff's because of the need for the services that had arisen, not as the loss of the carer. This enabled the loss to be included in the assessment of the plaintiff's damages. The source from which the need was met was disregarded, so that the provider's care was not treated as a subvention with which the defendant was entitled

[58] Unless they were able to recover the tax paid from the Commissioner of Taxation. J Dooley and A Cassimatis, 'Recovery of the "*Fox v Wood*" component in personal injury actions' (1997) 17 Queensland Lawyer 109, suggest that they could under Taxation Ruling IT2623 (13 Dec. 1990), though there are problems with time-limits.

[59] (1981) 148 CLR 438.

[60] (1961) 105 CLR 569.

[61] e.g., *Tucker v Westfield Design and Construction Pty Ltd* (1993) 46 FCR 20 (Fed Ct of A, FC) (injured carpenter obtained university degree and qualified as accountant).

[62] *Carroll v Purcell* (1961) 107 CLR 73 at 78 per Dixon CJ, Kitto, Taylor and Windeyer JJ.

[63] *International Encyclopaedia*, n. 2 above, para 11–70.

[64] e.g., *Groves v Lingston* [1965] WAR 186; *Haggar v De Placido* [1972] 2 All ER 1029.

[65] [1974] QB 454 (CA).

[66] (1977) 139 CLR 161.

to be credited.[67] The High Court reaffirmed the principle of recovery in *Nguyen v Nguyen*[68] and *Van Gervan v Fenton*.[69] There are sound policy reasons for allowing such recovery.[70] However, in *Hunt v Severs*[71] the House of Lords disapproved of the reasoning in *Donnelly v Joyce*. It held that the loss in these cases is the loss of the provider of the services and that, although the victim is the person entitled to recover the amount of the loss sustained by the provider, the plaintiff must hold the damages so awarded in trust for the provider. Since in *Hunt v Severs* the provider was also the tortfeasor, no damages could be awarded under this head. The High Court in *Kars v Kars*[72] promptly repudiated this view and reaffirmed that the loss is the plaintiff's, not the provider's. In a joint judgment strongly influenced by the fact that in practice such damages are nearly always paid by a compulsory insurer and that therefore there is no risk of the defendant personally having to 'pay twice', four members of the court held that for policy reasons the defendant should not be credited with the defendant's own subvention. Dawson J, in a separate judgment, found the reason for not debiting the plaintiff with the subvention in the more traditional explanation derived from *Espagne* of the probable intention on the part of the provider that the services should be enjoyed in addition to the damages. The Law Commission has provisionally determined that *Hunt v Severs* should be reversed by statute, though it too favours the view that the loss is the provider's and that there should be an enforceable obligation on the victim to account to the provider for the damages recovered.[73] This presents considerable problems in relation to the assessment at the trial of future loss, when the relationship between the plaintiff and the provider of the services is likely to change.[74]

[67] The distinction between expenditure with which the plaintiff seeks to be credited and subventions with which the defendant seeks to have the plaintiff debited was made by Fullagar J in *Blundell v Musgrave* (1956) 96 CLR 73 at 93. Cf. how Fleming himself put the distinction in his textbook, n. 10 above, in the context of 'wages and wage-alikes': 'they are treated not as gains which might or might not be set off against an actual loss, but as preventing a loss from ever arising'.

[68] (1990) 169 CLR 245 (a Lord Campbell's Act case in which a father himself provided services to his children that had previously been supplied by his wife who had been killed).

[69] (1992) 175 CLR 327 (where it was held that the value of the loss was ordinarily to be ascertained by reference to the commercial cost of providing the necessary services).

[70] These were best expressed in *Hodges v Frost* (1984) 53 ALR 373 (Fed Ct of A, FC) at 379–80. See also *Hunt v Severs* [1993] QB 815 (CA) at 831; and CP 144, n. 34 above, para 3.48.

[71] [1994] 2 AC 350. [72] (1996) 187 CLR 354.

[73] CP 144, n. 34 above, para 3.68. The Commission recognizes that there are problems with the trust concept espoused by the House of Lords and that the obligation to account to the provider should be a personal one. On the difficulties with such a trust, see P. Matthews and M. Lunney, 'A Tortfeasor's Lot is not a Happy One?' (1995) 58 MLR 395.

[74] As Regina Graycar notes, '[p]resumptions about the continued availability of the care by the volunteer care provider ignore the potentially disruptive effect of the injury on the

Reimbursement of the Collateral Source by the Tortfeasor

Australian Workers' Compensation

Workers' compensation statutes usually provide for the employer who pays workers' compensation to recover an indemnity from a third party tortfeasor. In *Tickle Industries Pty Ltd v Hann* Barwick CJ said that '[t]here is obvious and necessary justice in giving the employer, who has been involved in the payment of compensation by the wrongful act of another, a right of recovery against that other'.[75] The justice is less obvious when one recalls that 'the employer' is either a compulsory insurer or an organization large enough to be accorded the status of a self-insurer and that 'the other' will only be sued where it too falls into a similar category. The history of this right to recover an indemnity in Australia reinforces the scepticism Fleming expressed as to the worth of the shifting of the loss from one good loss distributor to another.[76] Several factors have contributed to an increase in the scope for recovery. Reported litigation, manifestly between two insurers or their equivalents,[77] is common.[78] The relevant factors accounting for the increase in litigation appear to be:

relationship': 'Love's Labour's Cost: The High Court Decision in *Van Gervan v Fenton*' (1993) 1 TLJ 122 at 129–30. See also Queensland Law Reform Commission, *The Assessment of Damages in Personal Injury and Wrongful Death Litigation: Griffiths v Kerkemeyer; Section 15C Common Law Practice Act 1867* (Report No. 45, 1993), 51–6.

[75] (1974) 130 CLR 321 at 327. [76] See n. 22 above.

[77] See, e.g., *Technical Products Pty Ltd v State Government Insurance Office (Queensland)* (1989) 167 CLR 45 at 50 per Dawson J ('It is apparent that the present argument is in effect between two insurers').

[78] At least 20 cases have been resolved only in the High Court, several of which will be referred to below. Canadian employers and their insurers appear to have been more sensible. The Ontario Law Reform Commission was 'advised that disability insurers and employers generally do not exercise their rights of subrogation. Most disability and accident insurers apparently regard the cost of establishing a system of subrogation to be unwarranted in light of the benefit that would be derived and, accordingly, prefer to absorb and spread the amounts paid to the insured through their own funding structure. Employers also regard the exercise of subrogation rights to be impractical and costly, particularly where recovery would be attempted months or years after providing the benefit. They often have no effective means of monitoring the progress of the injured person's claim, or of identifying what parts of a settlement represent lost wages. Furthermore, there is a reluctance on the part of employers to exercise such a right of recovery because of its possibly detrimental impact on employee relations': *Report on Compensation for Personal Injuries and Death* (1987), 189–90. The OntLRC went on to recommend that recovery by the injured person should be held in trust for the collateral source: ibid, 194. Cf. *Cunningham v Wheeler* [1994] 1 SCR 359 at 388 per McLachlin J, dissenting ('The rare exercise of the right of subrogation suggests that the best approach is a regime of deductibility of employment plan benefits, subject to the plaintiff's right to claim the benefits if it is established that they will be paid over to the subrogated third party').

- First, so long as contributory negligence was a complete defence to an action by the injured party, the employer could not recover an indemnity if the worker's own negligence had contributed to the injury. Apportionment statutes removed that impediment.[79]
- Secondly, the employer was denied a right of recovery if it was itself guilty of contributory negligence.[80] Given the broad scope of the employer's liability to provide a safe system of work, extending to a duty to ensure that care is taken even by independent contractors,[81] there would be few instances of on-site negligence by a third party that did not also constitute negligence on the part of the employer. In due course, the statutes were amended to allow the employer to recover at least a reduced indemnity in such circumstances.[82]
- Thirdly, in *Watson v Newcastle Corporation*[83] the High Court held that an employer was unable to recover an indemnity under section 64(b) of the Workmen's Compensation Act 1926 (NSW) as it then stood from a third party against whom the worker had already obtained a judgment for damages. The current statute provides a mechanism to ensure that the employer is not prevented in this way from enforcing its remedy before the judgment is satisfied.[84]
- Fourthly, and probably most significantly, Australian statutes deemed injuries sustained during certain protected journeys, in particular between home and work, to arise out of or in the course of the employment and so to carry an entitlement to workers' compensation.[85] As workers came to work in increasing numbers by motor vehicle, they had an increasing number of accidents that could plausibly be attributed to the fault of a third party, 'the other driver'. This might frequently lead to the absurdity of determining which of the two compulsory insurers should bear the cost of the worker's injuries by reference to which of the two drivers beat the red light immediately before the collision.

[79] e.g., Law Reform (Miscellaneous Provisions) Act 1965 (NSW), Pt III.

[80] *Public Transport Commission (NSW) v J Murray-More (NSW) Pty Ltd* (1975) 132 CLR 336, following *Cory & Son Ltd v France, Fenwick & Co Ltd* [1911] 1 KB 114.

[81] *Kondis v State Transport Authority* (1984) 154 CLR 672.

[82] See now, e.g. Accident Compensation Act 1985 (Vic), s 138.

[83] (1962) 106 CLR 426.

[84] Workers Compensation Act 1987 (NSW), s 151Z(1)(e1).

[85] Recently some jurisdictions have cut back on the coverage of journey injuries: e.g. Accidents Compensation Act 1985 (Vic), s 83, as amended in 1992. This reduces the scope for litigation of this nature, but it will still occur where the journey is in the actual course of the employment, as opposed to the deemed course of the employment. There is also scope for this type of liability whenever the worker works away from the employer's place of business, eg on a building site, and there is negligence of, say, the occupier of the premises which has contributed to the worker's injuries.

- Fifthly, no-fault motor accident compensation schemes in some jurisdictions[86] raised the possibility of shifting the loss to the statutory fund even when there was no fault on the part of another driver.[87]

Perhaps the extreme example of how long a dispute between the workers' compensation insurer and the compulsory third-party-motor vehicle insurer might take to resolve is *Bain v Frank G. O'Brien Ltd*,[88] where the motor accident out of which the claim arose occurred on 10 October 1958, the worker's incapacity was found to have ceased on 30 March 1962 (though he continued to receive workers' compensation for more than another five years) and judgment was given in the High Court on 21 June 1976, nearly eighteen years after the claim arose, holding that it was all recoverable from the motorist by the employer.

Similar wasteful litigation arises in circumstances where the employer is liable to the worker, either directly or vicariously, in connection with the use of a motor vehicle. Normally, two insurers who are both liable for the same risk, even under different types of policy, share the loss through contribution.[89] Frequently, however, the workers' compensation insurer attempts to shift the full loss for which it is initially responsible to the compulsory third-party motor-vehicle insurer.[90] After years of similar skirmishing between the statutory funds out of which workers' compensation and motor-accident compensation are paid in Victoria, the legislature eventually imposed what appears to be a sensible solution in the form of an agreement between the funds for a sharing of the aggregate payments.[91]

Australian Social Security

Income Maintenance Benefits

From their inception in 1944, sickness benefits payable by the Commonwealth in Australia were repayable on recovery of damages.[92] In 1987

[86] Motor Accidents Act 1973 (Vic) (replaced later by the Transport Accident Act 1986 (Vic)); Motor Accidents (Liabilities and Compensation) Act 1973 (Tas); Motor Accidents (Compensation) Act 1979 (NT).

[87] In the US strict product liability, coupled with relatively low workers' compensation benefits and the inability of workers to sue their own employers, has led to much litigation by employees against product manufacturers: see American Law Institute Reporter's Study, *Enterprise Responsibility for Personal Injury* (1991), vol II, 'Approaches to Legal and Institutional Change', 183–4.

[88] (1976) 135 CLR 158.

[89] *Albion Insurance Co Ltd v Government Insurance Office (NSW)* (1969) 121 CLR 342.

[90] See, e.g., the Queensland cases referred to in the dissenting judgment of Fitzgerald P in *A R Griffiths & Sons Pty Ltd* v *Richards* (1996) 24 MVR 296 (Qld CA) at 297.

[91] See Transport Accident Act 1986 (Vic), s 94A; Accident Compensation Act 1985 (Vic), s 137A; both as inserted in 1994.

[92] Unemployment and Sickness Benefits Act 1944 (Cth), s 23.

recovery was extended to a range of other income maintenance benefits.[93] Originally, recovery of sickness benefits was from the damages in the hands of the injured person. Presumably because this would often be ineffective, in 1948 the right of recovery was extended to allow recovery from the tortfeasor.[94] Since the principle of equivalence applied, it was necessary to amend the legislation frequently to overcome collusion aimed at denying the need to repay. Assume that a person had received $10,000 in sickness benefits which would have to be repaid on settlement of a common law damages action. The injured person might be willing to settle if allowed to retain, say, an additional $20,000. This would require the defendant's insurer to pay $30,000. If repayment of the sickness benefits could be avoided, a settlement anywhere in the range of $20,001 to $29,999 would benefit *both* parties. There was therefore a strong incentive for the parties to disguise the settlement as being entirely for pain and suffering or future loss, with little or no allowance for loss of earning capacity during the period when sickness benefits were received, and to settle at around $25,000.[95] It became necessary for the legislation to incorporate presumptions as to what proportion of the settlement was to be taken as being for loss of earning capacity and to specify methods for calculating a 'preclusion period' during which no benefits of this type were payable.[96] The fact that no benefits were payable as of right during the preclusion period meant that there was a 'termination' of the collateral benefits in Fleming's terms.[97]

The interpretation of the legislation for recovery of benefits and the calculation of the preclusion period has often led to appeals to the Administrative Appeals Tribunal[98] and to the Federal Court of Australia.[99] Provision has also had to be made for people who have exhausted their lump sums before expiry of the preclusion period; thus the legislation allows for part of the lump sum to be disregarded in 'special circumstances', so attenuating the preclusion period.[100] This too has led to numerous appeals to the Administrative Appeals Tribunal[101] and the

[93] The legislation at the time was the Social Security Act 1947 (Cth), as amended in 1986.

[94] Social Services Consolidation Act (No. 2) 1948 (Cth), s 19.

[95] This occurred perhaps even more frequently with the commutation of workers' compensation weekly benefits.

[96] Social Security Act 1947 (Cth), Pt XVII.

[97] See text at n. 14 above.

[98] e.g., *Re Secretary, Department Of Social Security and Williams* (1995) 37 ALD 753.

[99] *Secretary, Dept of Social Security v Banks* (1990) 23 FCR 416; *Secretary, Dept of Social Security v Sword* (1991) Aust Torts Reps 81–101 (Fed Ct of A); *Blunn v Cleaver* (1993) 47 FCR 111 (Fed Ct of A, FC), which contains a blistering attack on the 'plain English' drafting of the Social Security Act 1991 (Cth), Pt 3.14 (Compensation Recovery) at 127–8.

[100] The current section is s 1184 of the Social Security Act 1991 (Cth).

[101] A review of many of the decisions on the point and the factors which may be taken into account (such as financial hardship, legislative changes, incorrect legal advice, and ill health) is to be found in *Re Secretary, Dept of Social Security and Vys* (1995) 40 ALD 745.

Federal Court,[102] an exercise which must be costly for all concerned. Such costs are purely additional transaction costs which would not be incurred if the principle of relief of the tortfeasor, as opposed to reimbursement of the collateral source, were adopted. Furthermore, a system has been put in place whereby insurers and the Department of Social Security exchange notices so as to ensure that the damages are not paid to the injured person until the Department has been reimbursed.[103] This system too constitutes an extra expense which results from the shifting of the loss from the collateral source; the actual amount of the collateral benefits is not 'saved', but just differently distributed. In addition to the actual amount of those benefits, the community has to bear the cost of shifting them to the tortfeasor's insurer. Insurance premiums must rise not only by the amount of the collateral benefits paid, but also by the costs of loss shifting, which are duplicated on the side of both the government and the insurers. Unless the increased insurance premiums reduce the total number of accidents—a most unlikely possibility, whatever the economic theory—total welfare is diminished. Total government revenue may not necessarily be higher as a result of the recoupment when one takes into account the administrative costs of recovery; greater tax deductions from increased insurance premiums for many businesses; shortened preclusion periods because of 'special circumstances'; and the costs of determining, at initial decision-making level and on appeal, whether 'special circumstances' are present.

Even if total government revenue is higher as a result of the clawback of social security benefits, theoretically allowing the government to reduce taxes, or at least not increase them, this is likely in Australia to affect income tax, which, again theoretically, is a progressive tax. On the other hand, increased insurance premiums are either directly levied on the public, as with third-party motor-vehicle insurance, or passed on to the public in the form of a component of the cost of goods and services which they buy. Since there is no differentiation between higher and lower earners in this respect, the effect is regressive.[104]

At one time incorrect legal advice was thought to be irrelevant, the applicant theoretically having a remedy against the solicitor, but the Tribunal in this case expressed a preference for taking such advice into account and this was followed in *Re Secretary, Dept of Social Security and Hickman* (1996) 43 ALD 75.

[102] *Secretary, Dept of Social Security v Hulls* (1991) 13 AAR 414; 22 ALD 570 (Fed Ct of A); *Secretary, Dept of Social Security v Thompson* (1994) 53 FCR 580.

[103] Social Security Act 1991 (Cth), Pt 3.14. For an explanation of how the system of notices works, see *Re Secretary, Department of Social Security and Williams* (1995) 37 ALD 753.

[104] Cf., however, the fuller discussion in J. F. Keeler, 'Social Insurance, Disability, and Personal Injury: A Retrospective View' (1994) 44 Univ. of Toronto L.J. 275.

Health insurance benefits

Commonwealth hospital and medical insurance benefits have had a different history. Under amendments made to the National Health Act 1953 (Cth), sections 21 and 59, in 1962, Commonwealth hospital and medical insurance benefits were not supposed to be paid if there was an entitlement to damages; if paid provisionally, as they could be, they were supposed to be repaid when damages were recovered. When the first version of Medibank, the Australian universal health insurance scheme, was introduced on 1 July 1975,[105] it was intended that it would bear all the costs of accident compensation.[106] This lasted only until 1 October 1976. New provisions reinstated the rule of non-payment where compensation had been paid and provisional payment while eligibility for compensation was established.[107] Again the success rate of recovery by the Commonwealth was not high, mainly because of the need to identify in advance which payments were made in respect of injuries for which compensation would become payable.[108]

Eventually, the Commonwealth made a decision to accept responsibility for future medical insurance benefits, notwithstanding that a plaintiff had received a lump sum award or settlement of a damages claim, and not to seek to recover such future benefits. This means that it opted out of termination of the benefits and it is now for the courts to decide as between a plaintiff and a defendant whether cumulation or relief of the tortfeasor applies in respect of such future medical benefits. However, it decided to pursue more vigorously from insurers and their equivalents reimbursement of past medical insurance and nursing home benefits. A system of notices similar to that operating for income maintenance

[105] By the Health Insurance Act 1973 (Cth).

[106] See the *Report of the National Committee of Inquiry into Compensation and Rehabilitation in Australia* (Woodhouse Report, 1974), para 372(a). Such an arrangement was seen as 'efficient' by Murphy J in *Jaensch v Coffey* (1984) 155 CLR 549 at 556.

[107] See Health Insurance Act 1973 (Cth), ss 18 (medical benefits) and 35A (daily bed payments for hospital treatment) and National Health Act 1953 (Cth), s 59 (nursing home benefits), as inserted in 1976. S 35A was repealed by the Health Legislation Amendment Act 1986 (Cth) as part of the Commonwealth's 'deregulation' of private hospitals and the termination of daily bed payments for patients in such hospitals.

[108] See T. Brennan and J. Deeble, *Compensation and Commonwealth Health and Community Services Programs (A Discussion Paper)* (June 1993). Cf. the figures given by Cassidy, n. 109 below, at 474, which show that in the year ended 30 June 1995 Medicare recovered *more* than it paid out on provisional payments. Presumably, not only did the recoveries relate to many past years (which would not be relevant if the scheme had plateaued), but recoveries in some instances must have been of payments which were not provisional because Medicare did not know that the services were rendered as a result of a compensable event. In Canada, where the provincial health insurance funds are given a right of subrogation (eg the legislation interpreted in *Ledingham v Ontario Health Services Commission* [1975] 1 SCR 332, n. 3 above), such rights are apparently not vigorously pursued: R. Solomon & J. Payne, 'Alcohol Liability in Canada and Australia: Sell, Serve and be Sued' (1996) 4 Tort L. Rev. 188 at 207 n. 114.

payments was put into place to ensure recovery.[109] These notices have a further role to play in that they are necessary for identifying which of the insurance payments that the claimant has received were in respect of services that were in consequence of the injury (or disease) for which compensation is being claimed. It is noteworthy that the system exempts from the obligation to repay an individual defendant who is uninsured.[110] The legislation also makes provision for agreements between compensation payers, such as insurers, and the relevant government agency, the Health Insurance Commission (HIC), to recover payments in bulk and for a waiver of recovery in individual cases when such an agreement is in force.[111]

The new system for recovery of health benefits from the compensation payer, which commenced operation on 1 February 1996, rapidly ran into difficulty. Since the number of compensation cases had been vastly underestimated,[112] delays occurred in processing the notices. Until a certificate was received from the HIC, settlements (and judgments) could not be paid out. Often large sums had to be held back for trivial or, in the end, non-existent amounts thought to be owing to the HIC.[113] Conflicting decisions were given on applications by insurers for a stay on the accrual of post-judgment interest.[114] An amending Act[115] had to be rushed through to enable insurers, in cases where the compensation is $3000 or more, to pay 10 per cent (or such other percentage as may be prescribed) of the amount of the judgment or settlement to the HIC by way of an advance payment. The balance of the judgment or settlement may then be paid to the compensation recipient.

The objections to the recovery of income maintenance benefits on the grounds of increased transaction costs and a shift from progressive to regressive taxation apply also to the recovery of past medical insurance and nursing home benefits under the new legislation. The costs can at

[109] Health and Other Services (Compensation) Act 1995 (Cth), described by D. I. Cassidy QC, 'Health and Other Services (Compensation) Act 1995' (1996) 70 ALJ 473.

[110] S 4(2)(a) provides that 'compensation' (which, under s 4(1)(a), includes a payment of damages) does not include a payment by an individual who is not insured or otherwise indemnified for liability in respect of the injury in question, and who is not required by law to be so insured or indemnified.

[111] Health and Other Services (Compensation) Act 1995 (Cth), Pt 3 Div 3.

[112] In NSW the estimate of 25,000 cases in the first year was greatly exceeded when almost twice that number of notices was received in the first 3 months. The Government also had to abandon a proposed administration fee (Health and Other Services (Compensation) Administration Fee Bill 1994 (Cth)) after objections from insurers.

[113] See Hansard, *HR*, 22 Aug. 1996, p 3610.

[114] Contrast, e.g., *Carlyon v Mason* (NSW SC, Abadee J, 21 Feb. 1996) (BC9600251) with, e.g., *Wight v NSW Insurance Ministerial Corporation* (NSW SC, Dunford J, 23 Feb. 1996) (BC9600284). Cf. the arrangements made in the District Court of NSW as described by Cassidy, n. 109 above at 481.

[115] Health and Other Services (Compensation) Amendment Act 1996 (Cth).

least be reduced if the HIC enters into bulk agreements with compensation payers. Since this provision only came into operation eighteen months after the Act came into force, it is too early to know how much use will be made of it. Similarly, it is too early to tell whether the provision in the Health and Other Services (Compensation) Act 1995 (Cth), section 8, which seeks to ensure that equivalence operates when allowance for contributory negligence is made in a judgment or settlement by reducing the amounts payable to the HIC in proportion to the degree of negligence attributed to the injured person, will lead to collusive settlements. Perhaps as a result of its experience with the social security repayments, the Government was aware of this possibility and promised to monitor the legislation carefully, threatening the use by the HIC of broad fraud investigation powers if necessary.[116] The low level set for the minimum amount prescribed for repayment under section 38[117] reduces the opportunity to avoid repayments by collusive settlements below the minimum.

Hospital benefits today are treated differently again, though the principle is the same, namely that the tortfeasor (or its insurer) should pay. An agreement between the Commonwealth and the states provides for the delivery by the states of free hospital services to patients who choose to be Medicare patients.[118] The Commonwealth subsidizes the cost through block grants. However, patients who have claims for compensation may be charged by the states.[119] New South Wales has made special provision for recovery of these charges direct from motor-vehicle insurers who admit liability.[120]

United Kingdom Social Security

Benefits under the Social Security Act

Fleming noted that '[t]he most drastic and principled elimination of recoupment from the area of Social Security occurred in the UK in the course of the post-war reforms giving effect to the *Beveridge Report* (1942)'.[121] He observed that the Monckton Committee[122] had

[116] See the Minister's speech quoted by Cassidy, n. 109 above at 477.

[117] $150 (indexed according to the CPI): Health And Other Services (Compensation) Regulations 1995, reg 4.

[118] The agreement is made pursuant to the Health Insurance Act 1973 (Cth.), s 24 and is in force from 1 July 1993 to 30 June 1998 (a new agreement is in the course of negotiation).

[119] Cl 10 of the present agreement excludes 'a compensable patient' from those entitled to receive public hospital services without any charge. There is an exception for the NT, whose residents are not covered for hospital treatment under the no-fault motor-accident scheme, but under the Medicare scheme: T. Brennan and J. Deeble, n. 108 above, paras 3.11–3.12.

[120] See n. 159 below.

[121] *International Encyclopaedia*, n. 2 above, para 11-75.

[122] N. 7 above.

recommended the adoption of the principle of no recoupment by public authorities from tortfeasors on the ground that it was economically wasteful, if not also socially undesirable.[123] The Pearson Commission did not even consider any change to this position since its recommendations, which were designed to avoid cumulation of benefits and to ensure equivalence in relieving the tortfeasor,[124] would have resulted, in its own words, in tort becoming the 'junior partner' of social security.[125] These notions, however, could not survive the coming of Thatcherism. So-called economic rationalism, with its concerns for principles of 'user pays' and privatization of costs, so that they do not appear in government budgets, even if overall the cost to the community is greater, prevailed. Thus in the Report of the National Audit Office in 1986, it was said:

> Since the Report of the Royal Commission on Civil Liability and Compensation for Personal Injury in 1978, Governments have subscribed to the principles that those who are responsible for accidents should not expect the State to pay for their wrongdoing, whether in the form of treatment under the National Health Service or in cash benefits under the social security system, and that accident victims should not benefit twice, both from tort damages and social security benefits.[126]

Similarly, elsewhere in this Report it was said: 'The wrongdoer should not have the cost of his negligence met by public funds'.[127] This ignores the reality that those who cause accidents almost never pay for them and that it is the public in a different guise which actually does so. It overlooks the broader issues of social policy which motivated the Monckton Committee. But to give effect to the narrow perspective of the Government then in office, the Department of Health and Social Security in 1988 commissioned a report from management consultants to assess how much would be recoverable and what difficulties would face insurance companies.[128]

Despite the consultants having found opposition to the principle of the proposed scheme among all those they interviewed on the grounds of equity, legitimacy, and practicality,[129] Parliament enacted the Social Security Act 1989.[130] This provided for a clawback from tortfeasors

[123] *International Encyclopaedia*, n. 2 above, para 11-75.
[124] Cmnd. 7054 (1978), vol 1, ch 13. [125] Ibid, para 1732.
[126] 'Summary of National Audit Office Report on Recovery of Social Security Benefits when Damages in Tort are Awarded', App A to the Memorandum submitted by the Dep of Social Security, as set out in the Fourth Report of the House of Commons, Social Security Committee, *Compensation Recovery* (1995), 10.
[127] Quoted in the Report by Touche Management Consultants, *Recovery of Benefits in Tort Damages Awards*, Appendix 5 of the SSC Report, n. 126 above, 107.
[128] Ibid, App 5. [129] Ibid, pp viii, 104.
[130] Later consolidated in the Social Security Administration Act 1992, Pt IV, and recently re-stated with amendments in the Social Security (Recovery of Benefits) Act 1997.

and their insurers of social security payments that were made for up to five years and pending the outcome of litigation to enforce any common-law rights the injured victims might have. Certain benefits were exempt, particularly survivors' benefits and those not caused by injury (such as retirement pensions and child benefit) and invalid care allowance (which is intended for the carer, not the victim). For administrative reasons the clawback did not apply if the judgment or settlement did not exceed a relatively small amount, which, after negotiations with insurers,[131] was fixed by regulation at £2,500. The legislation, requiring an exchange of notices between insurers and the Government, and direct payment by the insurer of the amount to be recouped, preceded the similar system adopted in Australia.[132] The Government established a separate Compensation Recovery Unit (CRU), which in 1995 was staffed by 190 people.[133] Despite forebodings by insurers, the problems which accompanied the implementation of the Health and Other Services (Compensation) Act 1995 (Cth) seem to have been avoided.[134]

At first sight the amounts recovered and the relatively low cost to the Government are impressive.[135] Still, the amount recovered constitutes an insignificant proportion of the social security budget and the taxpayer could expect little relief in consequence.[136] On the other hand, insurers estimated that their claims costs went up by some 8 per cent on average in order to recover the amounts which they became required to pay to the CRU and to cover their own administrative costs.[137] These would have had to be passed on in increased premiums. Victims of injury were no better off and many would have had to pay increased premiums to insure their motor vehicles, etc.

The House of Commons Social Security Committee heard evidence in 1995 of many victims who were significantly worse off, mainly because the principle of equivalence did not apply, so that social security benefits were recouped out of damages which were intended as compensation

[131] See paras 3.1–3.6 of the Memorandum submitted by the Association of British Insurers as set out in the SSC Report, n. 126 above, 67.

[132] Social Security (Recoupment) Regulations 1990.

[133] See App C of the Memorandum submitted by the Dep of Social Security, as set out in the SSC Report, n. 126 above, 12.

[134] '[O]ur initial reaction was that this was cumbersome, our experience of working with the DSS was not desperately satisfactory and we thought there would be a lot of red tape. . . . I have to say that the DSS have operated this with some efficiency and it runs relatively smoothly; we do not have the problem we anticipated': Evidence of representatives of insurers to the House of Commons, Social Security Committee, 15 Feb. 1995 (SSC Report, n. 126 above, 70).

[135] Over £110m recovered in 1994–5 at a cost of about £4m: SSC Report, n. 126 above, p xi, para 21 & 1, para 6.

[136] General government receipts in 1996–7 were £286.3bn; social security contributions were £47.4bn: *Financial Statement and Budget Report* (House of Commons Paper No HC 85).

[137] SSC Report, n. 126 above, Minutes of Evidence, 15 Feb. 1995, 71–2.

for pain and suffering.[138] Similarly, the full amount of benefits was recouped though there was a high degree of contributory negligence or the damages were heavily discounted in the settlement because liability was doubtful.[139] Recovery sometimes defeated the purpose for which interim payments were made.[140] Numerous settlements were negotiated at or just below the minimum of £2,500, since this would give the victim that amount clear, whereas often the difference between the insurer's offer and the amount to be repaid to the CRU was less than this.[141] The victims were often resentful because they regarded themselves as taxpayers or at least insurance contributors and believed that the contributory principle under which the United Kingdom social security system had been established as a result of Beveridge was being undermined. The Committee expressed sympathy with this view.[142] But, it embraced the ideology underlying the legislation, believing 'that it was right for the Government to shift advantage of recovery to the taxpayer who lost out to the insurer under the old scheme'.[143] But, it considered that too great a burden had been passed to individual claimants, that some of the cases it had heard were 'revolting to the ordinary man's sense of justice', that the system operated in a way which was 'contrary to public policy',[144] and that it did not 'accept that the general taxpayer should be reimbursed out of damages awarded for an individual's pain and suffering'.[145] The Committee also found that some claims were not pursued because recoupment of benefits made it not worthwhile to do so. It thought that it 'is not in the interests of justice that this should be so'.[146] It believed that the problems it found with the scheme could be overcome by requiring solicitors to identify the separate heads of damages allowed in out-of-court settlements,[147] that an express amount be included in every claim for the amount of the social security benefits to be recouped and that recovery be allowed only from this head of damages.[148] In the light of the Australian experience, this belief appears naïve.[149] The Parliamentary Under-Secretary of State for Social Security, in his evidence before the Committee, seems to have had a much more realistic understanding of how settlements are arrived at,

[138] Ibid, *passim*. [139] Ibid, pp xxiv–xxv, paras 61–3.
[140] Ibid, pp xxv–xxvi, para 64.
[141] Ibid, pp xix–xxi, paras 46–51. Cf. *McCafferey v Datta* [1997] 1 WLR 870 (CA), where the full amount of the judgment obtained by the plaintiff went to the CRU and she would have been better off accepting the insurer's offer of £2,500. At least the CA reversed the trial judge's decision that she was not entitled to the costs of the action.
[142] SSC Report, p xvii, para 41.
[143] Ibid, p xxvi, para 65. See also pp xxviii–xxix, paras 75–7.
[144] Ibid, p xxvi, para 65. [145] Ibid, p xxviii, para 74. [146] Ibid, p xxvii, para 66.
[147] Ibid, p xix, para 45. [148] Ibid, p xxvii, para 75.
[149] Or might it be that UK solicitors are more ethical than their Australian counterparts?

taking into account issues of liability, contributory negligence, causation of particular aspects of the injury, and what is acceptable to the parties, all of which may make it impossible to dissect the final round figure into specific heads.[150] The Department specifically defended the scheme as it existed on the grounds of its workability, pointing out that if limited to loss of earnings it 'could be easily avoided by the artificial increase of other components and reduction (or abandonment) of any claim for loss of earnings or profit'.[151]

As a result of the Committee's recommendations a new Act was introduced, which came into force in October 1997. This lists benefits recoverable by the Department against corresponding heads of damages.[152] Only the corresponding heads are then reduced by the amount of the recoverable benefits; if the amount of the recoverable benefits attributable to a particular head exceeds the amount allowed under that head, that head is reduced to nil, but other heads are not affected.[153] The compensation payer remains liable to pay the full amount of the benefits to the Secretary of State.[154] The Act makes provision for appeals against decisions by the Department as to the amount of benefits payable, refunds of overpayments, and for other such matters as complex cases involving more than one compensation payment or more than one compensator, all of which would be unnecessary if the Government did not make the effort to shift the loss from itself to the premium-paying public.

National Health Service benefits

In its recent Consultation Paper, the Law Commission formed the provisional view that, on an analysis of legal principle, the National Health Service should have a claim to recover from tortfeasors the costs of NHS care resulting from a tort.[155] It recognized, however, that what it called the principled case might be outweighed by the cost and that the detail of any proposed arrangements for recoupment should be subject to a cost-benefit analysis.[156] It noted that in several European countries,

150 SSC Report, n. 126 above, Minutes of Evidence, 15 Mar. 1995, 81–8.

151 Ibid, Memorandum submitted by the Dep. of Social Security: Minutes of Evidence, 1 Feb. 1995, 7, para 38. The Dep. submitted that the scheme operating in the Netherlands meant that the taxpayer continued to subsidise the tortfeasor because it attempted to recover only 'like-for-like' and that the Pearson Commission had not worked out the practicalities of its proposal to match social security benefits with particular heads of damages: ibid, 22.

152 See n. 37 above.

153 S 8.

154 Ss 6 & 9(4). This is contrary to the position under Australian workers' compensation legislation, where the employer's right of recovery is usually limited to the extent of the tortfeasor's liability: e.g. *Xpolitos v Sutton Tools Pty Ltd* (1977) 136 CLR 418. Cf. *Neal v Bingle* [1998] 2 WLR 57 (CA), interpreting the previous UK legalisation.

155 CP 144, n. 34 above, paras 3.19–3.42.

156 Ibid, para 3.20.

particularly Scandinavia, subrogation of the State insurer has been abandoned because of transaction costs, or standard loss-sharing agreements have been entered into, or that internalization is achieved through taxation. While being of the provisional view that, if a recoupment scheme were introduced, it would be sensible to adopt administrative arrangements similar to those adopted in respect of social security benefits, it pointed to differences between NHS costs and social security benefits.[157] Without waiting for the outcome of the Law Commission's consultation, the new Labour Government announced its intention to 'act to recoup in full the cost of treating road traffic accidents from insurance companies'.[158] There are already rights for the NHS to recover limited costs from motorists,[159] but a newspaper report indicates that only about half the NHS trusts attempt to do so.[160] Commenting on the new proposal, a letter to *The Times* observed that, since '[n]early all motorists are taxpayers, and relatively few taxpayers are non-motorists', £100 million could be given to the NHS out of general taxation and be paid for by all taxpayers out of their taxed income, instead of effecting the transfer of a similar amount at a cost of about £200 million of untaxed income, 'paid not only by the guilty but by all of us'. 'The proposed scheme', the writer concluded, 'is an unbelievably inefficient way of funding the NHS, but a wonderful way of funding administrators and the legal profession'.[161]

[157] Ibid, para 3.39.

[158] Budget speech by the Chancellor of the Exchequer, Mr G. Brown, *Hansard*, 2 July 1997 (http://www.parliament.the-stationery-office.co.uk/pa/cm199798/cmhansrd/cm970702/debtext/70702–21.htm#70702–21_spmin1). See, later, J. Landale, 'NHS costs mean car insurance will rise', *The Times*, 5 Dec. 1997 (insurers to be 'forced' to pay hospitals directly).

[159] Road Traffic Act 1988, ss 157–8. Similar provisions, without the upper limits, exist in NSW for recovery of hospital and ambulance costs, etc., where any payment is made (whether or not with an admission of liability) by a licensed insurer or the Nominal Defendant: Motor Accidents Act 1988 (NSW), Pt 4A. That legislation makes provision for bulk billing: s 39B(4). Interpreting a predecessor of these provisions, a judge in NSW has said that '[a]ny reduction for contributory negligence will not . . . result in any diminution of the payment required to be made': *Wills v Black* (1990) 12 MVR 222 at 224. It is therefore surprising that it was apparently the plaintiffs in this case who were pressing for payment, since the effect of payment in full to the hospitals etc, gives priority to the collateral source over the victims themselves. As Fleming asked in the case note on the Canadian case (n. 3 above at 112), 'What justifies treating the fiscal self-interest of a social security fund as paramount or at least of equal importance, with the welfare interest of the beneficiary?'

[160] M. Curphey and I. Murray, '1997 Budget: Accident insurance: Cost of motor cover likely to increase', *The Times*, 3 July 1997.

[161] J. C. Banks, Letter to the Editor, *The Times*, 19 Dec. 1996. Legislative power to recover costs may also work to the detriment of health authorities: see *Avon County Council v Hooper* [1997] 1 WLR 1605 (CA) (local authority entitled to charge for care of severely brain-damaged child where child had cause of action against hospital in which he was born).

Other Types of Collateral Benefits

Employment Benefits other than Workers' Compensation[162]

Although the matter is not clear, at common law the employer's *actio per quod servitium amisit* might have enabled an employer who paid sick pay and other benefits to an employee to recover the benefits from a third party tortfeasor.[163] Although in England *IRC v Hambrook*[164] removed virtually all practical importance from the action until its eventual abolition,[165] in Australia *Commissioner for Railways (NSW) v Scott*[166] held that the action lay for injury to employees generally.[167] Nevertheless, it has been little used in practice, the employer's right of indemnity under workers' compensation legislation usually proving sufficient for the employer (or its insurer) to recover the bulk of its expenditure when the employee has been tortiously injured by a third party. Recently, both the Supreme Court of Canada[168] and the Court of Appeal in Victoria[169] have held that there is no independent action for negligence causing pure economic loss available to the employer against the third party.

The Law Commission, however, has formed the provisional view that a restitutionary remedy may be available.[170] It prefers the decision at first instance in *Metropolitan Police District Receiver v Croydon Corporation*[171] to that of the Court of Appeal, which denied such a remedy.[172] In any event, it takes the view that providers of collateral benefits have open to them the remedy of contracting with victims for repayment of the benefit if a successful tort action is brought by the victim or making the payment conditional on non-recovery of tort damages.[173] As a matter of policy, it notes the complexity of the arrangements that are entered into in European countries for reimbursement of collateral sources and

[162] Workers' compensation in Australia is dealt with above, text at nn. 75ff.

[163] e.g., *Sydney CC v Bosnich* [1968] 3 NSWR 725 (CA); *Marinovski v Zutti Pty Ltd* [1984] 2 NSWLR 571 (CA); *GIO Australia Ltd v Robson* (1997) 42 NSWLR 439 (CA). *Contra A-G v Wilson & Horton Ltd* [1973] 2 NZLR 238 (CA).

[164] [1956] 2 QB 641. See text at n. 20 above.

[165] Administration of Justice Act 1982, s 2(c).

[166] (1959) 102 CLR 392.

[167] Except soldiers or policemen, who are not 'servants' in the requisite sense: *Commonwealth v Quince* (1944) 68 CLR 227; *A-G (NSW) v Perpetual Trustee Co Ltd* (1952) 85 CLR 237 (HC), [1955] AC 457 (PC).

[168] *D'Amato v Badger* [1996] 2 SCR 1071.

[169] *Scott v Bowyer* [1998] 1 VR 207 (CA).

[170] CP 147, n. 4 above, paras 5.5–5.6.

[171] [1956] 1 WLR 1113.

[172] [1957] 2 QB 154.

[173] CP 147, n. 4 above, para 5.9. In Australia there is some doubt as to whether a conditional payment will allow recovery of the amount from the tortfeasor if its effect is to reduce the loss which would otherwise be recoverable. *Blundell v Musgrave* (1956) 96 CLR 73, esp. at 95 per Fullagar J; and *Treloar v Wickham* (1961) 105 CLR 102, esp. at 114 per Fullagar J, at 121–2 per Menzies J, suggest that conditional payments are excluded from the assessment of damages. If this view were followed the collateral source would not be able to recover its payment from the victim, who would not recover damages from the tortfeasor for the amount of the payment.

the increase that would result in the already high transaction costs of allocating tort liability, though these could be mitigated to some extent by agreements for bulk payments.[174] It also notes that a general recoupment right which was enforced undermines an argument for deduction of collateral benefits as between plaintiff and tortfeasor, namely the release of funds to make better provision for the ill and injured who are currently inadequately provided for.[175] It therefore doubts the need to create a statutory right of recoupment, but asks consultees for their opinion on this.

As Fleming wrote, to allow recovery to both the victim and the employer exposes the tortfeasor to double liability, which is 'untenable'.[176] Thus any proposal to allow recovery to the employer must be understood in the context of the adoption of one of the Law Commission's options which would provide for the deduction of all such benefits in the assessment of the victim's damages.[177] Although there may be particular cases of hardship caused to small employers and although one would not want to discourage employers from providing their employees with sick pay, pensions, and similar benefits, it is better to leave the loss to fall on employers than to encourage wasteful litigation to allow the employers to recoup the benefits from tortfeasors and their insurers by means of a second action.[178] The costs to employers are part of their cost of doing business and often can be passed on in the price of their goods and services. The Australian experience with workers' compensation described above,[179] where the litigation tends to be between two insurers and the outcome may turn on which of two non-parties was negligent, should discourage the creation of any new remedy for employers.

Insurers' Right of Subrogation

An insurer who paid benefits directly to the injured person by virtue of a contract of indemnity insurance would be subrogated to the rights of the victim to recover those benefits from the tortfeasor. As the Law

[174] CP 147, n. 4 above, para 5.19. [175] Ibid, para 5.20.

[176] 'Collateral Source Rule' n. 1 above, at 1495. [177] See above, text at n. 40.

[178] See the views of the Law Commission in its previous investigation of the subject, *Report on Personal Injury Litigation—Assessment of Damages* (Law Com No. 56), para 149. A contrary view was expressed by the English Law Reform Committee in its 11th Report on *Loss of Services, etc* (1963), but a minority (including Lord Diplock) dissented from this view on the grounds that it would make settlements difficult and that employers did not want such an action and would prefer not to be drawn into the victims' actions. As the Ontario Law Reform Commission observed, 'there are today other means of ensuring the provision of injury benefits to employees' than what amounts to a revival of the *actio per quod servitium amisit*: OntLRC, *Report on Compensation for Personal Injuries and Death* (1987), 69. See also P. S. Atiyah, 'Negligence and Economic Loss' (1967) 83 LQR 248 at 274–6.

[179] See text at nn. 75ff above.

Commission observes, such 'simple subrogation'[180] has the advantage that only one action would be available against the tortfeasor.[181] Under the present law, the insurance benefits are disregarded in the assessment of the victim's damages,[182] but if the insurer exercises its right of subrogation cumulation of benefits is avoided. Nevertheless, the Commission recognizes several arguments for abolishing the right of subrogation.[183] At the end of its Consultation Paper it raises the question of whether indemnity insurers' automatic subrogation rights should be abolished.[184] However, since subrogation rights are particularly important in relation to property insurance and more information is needed about the practice of insurers, it provisionally takes the view that abolition would be too radical a step in the context of a review of the law of damages for personal injury. It refers to the discussion of the issue in the report of the Australian Law Reform Commission (ALRC), *Insurance Contracts*.[185] The ALRC questioned the utility of subrogation in its discussion paper on the subject,[186] mainly on the ground of unwarranted additional expense, but in the end was persuaded by insurers not to recommend its abolition entirely.[187] However, it did recommend prohibiting the exercise of rights of subrogation against members of the insured's family, tortfeasors who were uninsured[188] and the insured's employees, unless in this last instance the conduct of the employee was serious and wilful.[189] Sections 65 and 66 of the Insurance Contracts Act 1984 (Cth), gave effect to these recommendations. However, since workers' compensation and motor-vehicle personal injury insurance were outside the terms of reference of the ALRC's inquiry and are excluded from the legislation,[190] most personal injury cases are not affected. Despite the Law Commission's reluctance to act, it must be doubtful that it is worth preserving the doctrine in the personal injury context and, at the least, its exercise should be prohibited so as to prevent actions against family members, employees, and uninsured tortfeasors.

180 The description is taken from C. Mitchell, *The Law of Subrogation* (1994), who contrasts it with 'reviving subrogation'.

181 CP 147, n. 4 above, para 5.28.

182 *Bradburn v Great Western Railway Co* (1874) LR 10 Exch 1.

183 CP 147, n. 4 above, para 5.29. The arguments acknowledged are the difficulty of distinguishing indemnity from non-indemnity insurance (no right of subrogation exists under the latter); over-compensation may result from non-exercise of the right; the insurer has the opportunity of providing contractually for repayment; deduction of insurance from damages with a separate right of recoupment may be preferable. For a full critique of the law of subrogation, see R. Hasson, 'Subrogation in Insurance Law—a Critical Evaluation' (1985) 5 OJLS 416.

184 CP 147, n. 4 above, para 5.27.

185 ALRC No. 20, 1982, 184–93.

186 See ibid, para 309.

187 Ibid, para 313.

188 Cf. the exclusion of the right of recovery of medical insurance benefits from uninsured tortfeasors under the Commonwealth legislation, n. 110 above.

189 ALRC No. 20, 1982, paras 305 & 306.

190 Insurance Contracts Act 1984 (Cth), s 9(1)(e).

Reimbursement of the Collateral Source by the Plaintiff

Subrogation not only allows an indemnity insurer to exercise rights which the victim has against third parties, but enables the insurer to recover the benefits it has paid from the insured victim if the latter receives them by way of cumulation in the victim's own damages action. If the first or second of the Law Commission's options[191] were adopted, there would be few benefits that the victim would be allowed to cumulate. The other options would permit more cumulation. The Commission raises the question whether, in so far as cumulation survives, there should be a general right of recoupment of the nature of the insurer's right of subrogation for collateral sources.[192] Its provisional view is that this should be left to the development of the common law. In the context of voluntary services rendered by relatives and friends it approves the development of such a personal obligation, though not the trust obligation recognized by the House of Lords in *Hunt v Severs*.[193] Given the tendency for the relationship between carer and victim to break down,[194] it probably is insufficient for it to be left, as the High Court would have it, to the moral obligation of the victim to account.[195] It is desirable that in this one area a legally enforceable obligation be created. Apart from limited social security carer's benefit,[196] there would be no other way that the carer could be assured of any compensation for the effort of caring for the victim. As a practical matter a requirement that the victim account to the care-provider can only apply to past services.[197] Once the damages are awarded to the plaintiff to provide for future care, the plaintiff must be left to make whatever arrangements he or she chooses with future carers; a court, and *a fortiori* a settling insurer, should not be able to bind a plaintiff to make use of the services of any particular person, especially when the services are of an intimately personal nature, as they usually are in this type of case.

[191] See above, text at n. 40. [192] CP 147, n. 4 above, para 5.22–6.

[193] [1994] 2 AC 350. See n. 73 above. [194] See n. 74 above.

[195] *Griffiths v Kerkemeyer* (1977) 139 CLR 161 at 176–7 per Stephen J, at 193–4 per Mason J (rejecting the trust concept); *Kars v Kars* (1996) 187 CLR 354 at 371–2.

[196] Social Security Act 1991 (Cth), Pt 2.5.

[197] See the Queensland Law Reform Commission's Report, n. 74 above. This Report falls short of recommending that the provider have a *right* to recover the damages awarded to the victim for voluntary services. It merely recommends that the court be required to consider whether or not the pre-trial component of such damages should be paid direct to the provider: at 52. This is not very satisfactory when only a small percentage of cases actually go to trial.

Conclusion

At the time when John Fleming was applying his matchless analytical skills to the collateral benefits problem, there was little consistency in the treatment of these benefits within either Australia or England, let alone the rest of the world. In *Browning v War Office*, Donovan LJ had said that 'in this field logic is conspicuous by its absence'.[198] Subsequent decisions have done little to clarify when plaintiffs will be allowed to cumulate damages and when, as between plaintiff and defendant, the defendant will be relieved of liability for a portion of the damages. It remains to be seen whether in England the Law Commission will succeed in achieving its object of ensuring that plaintiffs are unable to cumulate benefits so that more funds may be released for the benefit of those who currently receive nothing at all,[199] or even to provide more adequate damages to those who receive insufficient. If it does succeed in having a statute enacted that denies the plaintiff the benefit of cumulation in nearly all cases, it will still have to achieve politically the difficult task of having the funds which are released used for the benefit of other disabled people. In Australia even the first task is made almost impossible by the need to persuade more than six legislatures to act. The political difficulty is aggravated by the division of powers between the Commonwealth and the states and their respective taxing and spending abilities. For a long time yet, we shall have to live with the vague common-law principles of *National Insurance Co. of NZ Ltd v Espagne*.[200]

In looking at the bigger picture, Fleming regarded Britain as in the vanguard in being content to see some of the accident cost absorbed by the community at large in relief even of tortfeasors and the special risk community they happen to represent.[201] As he pointed out, this attitude affords major relief to tortfeasors without prejudicing their victims. It lends authority to the philosophy that the community at large may fairly be expected to share in bearing the eventual cost of repairing tort injuries. He thought that it was bound to lead to a review of the whole future of tort liability.[202] Perhaps these thoughts were prompted by the appearance, between the publication of his California Law Review paper and the completion of his chapter in the *International Encyclopaedia*, of the first

198 [1963] 1 QB 750 (CA) at 762.

199 Cf. the recommendation of the ALI Reporter's Study, n. 87 above, 182, for the almost complete reversal of the collateral source rule. The one exception proposed in this Study would be for life assurance. In respect of other private insurance, the Study proposes that the plaintiff be given credit equal to the amount of premiums paid for the previous 2 years. See ibid, 176–7. The Law Commission found the latter qualification 'difficult to justify in terms of principle or practicality': CP 147, n. 4 above, para 4.46.

200 (1961) 105 CLR 569.

201 'Collateral Source Rule' n. 1 above at 1542.

202 *International Encyclopaedia*, n. 2 above, para 75.

Woodhouse Report.[203] In 1979 he noted approvingly the vindication of the majority report of the Monckton Committee[204] by the Pearson Commission,[205] himself 'emphasising that, apart from Scandinavia, Britain stands alone in this advanced posture'.[206] A few years later, he predicted that 'the law of tort will yield more and more ground to accident compensation'.[207] Although a few Australian jurisdictions have moved some way towards the replacement of fault-based compensation schemes with specific no-fault schemes,[208] nowhere other than in New Zealand[209] has personal injury litigation been replaced completely with a no-fault accident insurance scheme. And in Britain, the climate changed. It was seen to be a 'serious' problem with the pre-1989 scheme that 'the negligent party or his insurer was receiving a subsidy at the expense of the taxpayer'.[210] Calls from bodies such as the National Audit Office and Public Accounts Committee for the Government to take action[211] resulted in the establishment of the CRU and the clawback of social security benefits.[212] In Australia the Commonwealth has followed suit. Mrs Thatcher and so-called economic rationalism have left their mark in the United Kingdom and Australia. Governments have not learnt from the wisdom of John Fleming.

[203] *Report of the Royal Commission of Inquiry on Compensation for Personal Injury in New Zealand* (1967).

[204] N. 7 above.

[205] Royal Commission on Civil Liability and Compensation for Personal Injury, *Report*, Cmnd. 7054 (1978).

[206] J. G. Fleming, 'The Pearson Report: Its "Strategy"', (1979) 42 MLR 249 at 255–6.

[207] 'Is There a Future for Tort', (1984) 58 ALJ 131 at 142.

[208] The NT and Victoria have gone furthest in abolishing common-law actions when workers' compensation or no-fault motor benefits are available: see Work Health Act 1986 (NT); Motor Accidents (Compensation) Act 1979 (NT); Accident Compensation Act 1985 (Vic); Transport Accident Act 1986 (Vic), s 93.

[209] Accident Rehabilitation and Compensation Insurance Act 1992 (NZ).

[210] SSC Report, p vi.

[211] Ibid, p vii. See also text at n. 126 above.

[212] Perhaps ironically, in the US, the home of the collateral source rule, recent statutory changes have been away from its application and the ALI Reporter's Study, n. 87 above, 182 recommended 'a bar to any subrogation or reimbursement rights exercised by loss insurers against the tort award'. Cf. the recommendation in respect of workers' compensation, 197–8.

A BIBLIOGRAPHY OF THE PUBLICATIONS OF JOHN GUNTHER FLEMING

John Gunther Fleming

A Bibliography of his Publications 1947–1998

Books and Pamphlets

1952 *Evasion of Law and Divorce Adjudication* [reprinted from (1952) 1 *The International and Comparative Law Quarterly* 381–90].
1957 *The Law of Torts* (Sydney, Law Book Company).
1961 *The Law of Torts* (2nd ed.) (Sydney, Law Book Company).
1964 *Sales under Division 2 of the California Commercial Code* (Berkeley, University Extension, University of California).
1965 *The Law of Torts* (3rd ed.) (Sydney, Law Book Company).
1967 *Introduction to the Law of Torts* (Oxford, Clarendon Press).
1971 *The Law of Torts* (4th ed.) (Sydney, Law Book Company).
1977 *The Law of Torts* (5th ed.) (Sydney, Law Book Company).
1983 *The Law of Torts* (6th ed.) (Sydney, Law Book Company).
1983 *Introduction to the Law of Torts* (2nd ed.) (Oxford, Clarendon Press).
1987 *The Law of Torts* (7th ed.) (Sydney, Law Book Company).
1988 *The American Tort Process* (Oxford, Clarendon Press; New York, Oxford University Press); Supplement (1989).
1992 *Introduction to the Law of Torts* (Chinese Translation, Hong Kong).
1992 *The Law of Torts* (8th ed.) (Sydney, Law Book Company).
1998 *The Law of Torts* (9th ed.) (Sydney, Law Book Company).

Articles, Essays, Notes

1947 'Conception of Marriage in English Law', (1947) 11 Conv. & Prop. Lawyer 201–11.

'Recovery of Money Mistakenly Paid by Personal Representative', (1947) 11 Conv. & Prop. Lawyer 275–8.

'Position of a beneficiary within the marriage consideration under an incompletely constituted trust', (1947) 12 Conv. & Prop. Lawyer 132–6.

'Secret Trusts', (1947) 12 Conv. & Prop. Lawyer 28–40.

1948 'Hybrid Powers,' (1948–9) 13 Conv. & Prop. Lawyer 20–30.

'Wills Cases', (1948–9) 13 Conv. & Prop. Lawyer 61–2, and 133–9.

'Choice of Law in Nullity Proceedings', (1948) 11 MLR 98–102.

1949 'Can a Trustee Sell to his Wife?', (1948–9) 13 Conv. & Prop. Lawyer 248–53.

'Domicil in nullity proceedings', (1949) 1 U. Western Australia Annual L. Rev. 193–210.

'The Oak and the Acorn', (1949) 13 Conv. & Prop. Lawyer 338–47.

'Choice of Law in Nullity Proceedings', (1949) 23 ALJ 458–64.

1950 'Reflections on Cannon v. Hartley', (1950) 24 ALJ 149–53.

'The Sanctity of Contracts in Eclipse?', (1950) 24 ALJ 306–11.

'The contractual and residence bases of nullity jurisdiction', (1950) 2 Int. Law Q. 9–27, 228–42.

'Recent Australian decisions on private international law', (1950) 3 Int. Law Q. 566–71.

'Substance and procedure: the Gaming Acts', (1950) 24 ALJ 487–9.

1951 'Misrepresentation and the Sale of Goods', (1951) 25 ALJ 443–8.

1952 'The Action Per Quod Servitium Amisit', (1952) 26 ALJ 122–9.

'Interstate Enforcement of Maintenance and Alimony Decrees', (1952) 26 ALJ 407–12.

'Common Mistake', (1952) 15 MLR 229–32.

'Legitimation', (1952) 1 Int. Comp. L.Q. 66–70.

'Evasion of law and divorce adjudication', (1952) 1 Int. Comp. L.Q. 381–90.

1953 'Remoteness and Duty: The Control Devices in Liability for Negligence', (1953) 31 Can. Bar Rev./Revue du Barreau Canadien 471–502.

'Recognition of foreign nullity decrees', (1953) 2 Int. C. L.Q. 453–9.

'Duty of Care and Standard of Care', (1953) 1 Sydney L. Rev. 69–77 (with W. L. Morison).

'Divorce and Domicile', (1953) 2 Int. Comp. L.Q. 303–8.

1956 'Accident law and social insurance', Inaugural lecture delivered at Canberra University College, 3 October 1956.

'Running down cases: conduct before action', (1956) 100 SJ 705–6.

1957 'Vicarious Liability for Breach of Statutory Duty', (1957) 20 MLR 655–58.

1958 'Liability for Suicide', (1958) 31 ALJ 587–589.

1959 'Tort Liability for Damage to Hire-Purchase Goods', (1959) 32 ALJ 267–75.

'Action for Loss of Services', (1959) 22 MLR 682–86.

'Developments in the English Law of Medical Liability', (1959) 12 Vanderbilt L. Rev. 633–48.

1961 'The Passing of Polemis', (1961) 39 Can. Bar Rev./Revue du Barreau Canadien 489–529.

1962 'The Lost Years: A Problem in the Computation and Distribution of Damages', (1962) 50 California L. Rev. 598–618.

1966 'The Collateral Source Rule and Loss Allocation in Tort Law', (1966) 54 California L. Rev. 1478–549.

'More Thoughts on Loss Distribution', (1966) 4 Osgoode Hall L.J. 161–73.

'Trespass and the Vagaries of Agency', (1966) 82 LQR 25–9.

1967 'The Role of Negligence in Modern Tort Law', 53 Va L. Rev. 815–46.

'Governmental and Charitable Immunities', Proceedings of 14th Conf. of Chief Justices.

'Defamation', *Encyclopedia Britannica.*

1969 'Damages: Capital or Rent?', (1969) 19 Univ. of Toronto L.J. 295–325.

1970 'Liability, Insurance and Risk Pooling in the Field of Injury Compensation' in *Legal Thought in the USA Under Contemporary Pressures* (US Report for VIIIth Congress of the International Academy of Comparative Law), Hazard, J. N. & Wagner, W. J. (eds.) (Brussels, Etablissements Emile Bruylant), 183–201.

'Collateral Benefits', ch 11, vol XI in *International Encyclopedia of Comparative Law.*

'Transnational Trends in Tort Law. Contemporary Roles of the Law of Torts: Introduction', (1970) 18 Am. J. Comp. L. 1–2.

1971 'Insurance for the Criminal', (1971) 34 MLR 176–81.

'Defamation', *Encyclopedia Britannica.*

1972 'Distant Shock in Germany (and Elsewhere)', (1972) 20 Am. J. Comp. L. 485–91.

'Die Haftung der Massenmedien, ins besondere der Presse, bei Eingriffen in persönliche oder gewerbliche Rechtspositionem: American Law (1972) 61 Arbeiten zur Rechtsvergleichung 45–61.

1973 'The Decline and Fall of the Law of Delict', (1973) 6 Comp. & Int. L.J. Southern Africa 259–71.

'Non-Material Injury', Special Lectures 1973, Law Society of Upper Canada.

1974 'The Patient or His Victim: The Therapist's Dilemma', (1974) 62 California L. Rev. 1025–68 (with Bruce Maximov).

'Insurance—Subrogation—Priority between the Insurer and Insured', (1974) 52 Can. Bar Rev./Revue du Barreau Canadien 103–12.

'Exculpatory Clauses' in *Law in the USA in Social and Technological Revolution* (US Report for IXth Congress of the International Academy of Comparative Law), Hazard, J. N. & Wagner, W. J. (eds.) (Brussels, Etablissements Emile Bruylant), 105–21.

'Teaching Compensation Systems: Some solutions for a common quandary: A symposium. Approaches Developed', (1974) 26 J. Legal Education 423–5.

1975 'Draft Convention on Products Liability (Council of Europe)', (1975) 23 Am. J. Comp. L. 729–41.

'Operating Defective Automobiles: The French Code and its North American Cousins', (1975) 23 Am. J. Comp. L. 513–20.

'Chapter 9: "Tort Liability for Work Injury"', ch 9, vol XV, in *International Encyclopedia of Comparative Law.*

1976 'Foreword: Comparative Negligence at Last—By Judicial Choice', (1976) 64 California L. Rev. 239–83.

1978 'Retraction and Reply: Alternative Remedies for Defamation', (1978) 12 U. British Columbia L. Rev. 15–31.

'The Impact of Inflation on Tort Compensation', (1978) 26 Am. J. Comp. L. 51–70.

'Changing Functions of Succession Laws', (1978) 26 Am. J. Comp. L. 233–8.

1979 'The Restatement and Codification', (1979) 2 Jewish Law Annual 108–125.

'Report to the Joint Committee of the California Legislature on Tort Liability on the Problems Associated with American Motorcycle Association v. Superior Court', (1979) 30 Hastings L.J. 1465–514.

'New Compensation Systems: Woodhouse and Pearson', (1979) Haftungsersetzung durch Versicherungsschutz 11–23.

'The Pearson Report: Its Strategy', (1979) 42 MLR 249–69.

1980 'International Incidents', (1980) 8 Student Lawyer 28–9.

1981 'Perspectives on Compensating Accident Victims' in *Compensating for Research Injuries* (President's Commission for the Study of Ethical Problems in Medicine), 175–203 (with S. Sugarman).

1982 'The Effect of Inflation on Civil Liability', (1982) 30 Am. J. Comp. L. (Supplement: Law in the US for the 1980s), 97–116.

'Drug Injury Compensation Plans', (1982) 30 Am. J. Comp. L. 297–323.

1983 'Is there a future for tort?' (rev. paper presented to the 22nd Australian Legal Convention, Brisbane 1983), (1983) 13 Queensland Law Soc. J. 235–246, (1984) 58 ALJ 131–42.

'The Collateral Source Rule and Contract Damages', (1983) 71 Californian L. Rev. 56–86.

'Drug Injury Compensation Plans', (1983) 32 U. New Brunswick L.J. 9–34.

1984 'Sistemi no fault e riforma nella disciplina dell' assicuriazione Obbligatoria', (1986) Rivista Giuridica della Circolazioni e dei Transporti 473.

'C'è un futuro per i torts?', (1984) 2 Rivista Critica del Diritto Privato 271–296.

'Comparative Law of Torts', (1984) 4 OJLS 235–43.

1986 'Torts Damages for Loss of Future Earnings', (1986) 34 Am. J. Comp. L. (Supplement: Law in the USA Faces Social and Scientific Change. Guest editors Hazard, J. H. & Wagner, W. J.), 141–56.

1988 'Negligence and Property Rights', (1988) 104 LQR 183–5.

'Contributory Negligence and Multiple Tortfeasors', (1988) 104 LQR 6–9.

1989 'Of Dangerous and Defective Products', (1989) 9 Tel Aviv Univ. Studies in Law 11–32.

'Mass Torts', (1988) Denning L.J. 37–50.

'Property Damage—Economic Loss: A Comparative View', (1989) 105 LQR 508–11.

'Must a Solicitor Tell?', (1989) 105 LQR 15–18.

'The Contingent Fee and its Effect on American Tort Law' in *The Butterworth Lectures* (London, 1989), 50–81.

1990 'The Insurance Crisis', (1990) 24 U. British Columbia L. Rev. 1–18.

'Probabilistic Causation', (1990) 68 Can. Bar Rev./Revue du Barreau Canadien 661–81.

'A Requiem for *Anns*', (1990) 106 LQR 525–30.

'The Negligent Auditor and Shareholders', (1990) 106 LQR 349–352.

'Is Wrongful Dismissal a Tort?', (1990) 106 LQR 8–11.

1991 'Probabilistic Causation in Tort Law: A Postscript', (1991) 70 Can. Bar Rev./ Revue du Barreau Canadien 136–41.

'Libel and Constitutional Free Speech' in Cane, Peter & Stapleton, Jane (eds.), *Essays for Patrick Atiyah* (Oxford, Clarendon Press), 333–49.

'Negligent Economic Loss in American Law', in *Negligence After Murphy v. Brentwood D.C.: Papers presented at a seminar held by the Legal Research Foundation at the University of Auckland, 7 March, 1991* (Auckland, Legal Research Foundation), 26–38.

'Damages, Reflections', paper presented at 27th Australian Legal Convention.

'*Donoghue v Stevenson* and the Modern Law of Negligence', in *Procs of the*

Paisley Conference on the Law of Negligence (Vancouver, Continuing Legal Education Society of British Columbia).

1992 'Torts' in Clark, David S. & Ansay, Tugrul (eds.), *Introduction to the Law of the United States* (Deventer, The Netherlands, Kluwer Law and Taxation Publishers), 181–98.

'Insurer's Breach of Good Faith—A New Tort?', (1992) 108 LQR 357–60.

'Damages Against the Helpful Tortfeasor', (1992) 66 ALJ 388–9.

'The Economic Factor in Negligence', (1992) 108 LQR 9–12.

'Once More—Economic Loss', (1992) 12 OJLS 558–63.

1993 'The Solicitor and the Disappointed Beneficiary', (1993) 109 LQR 344–9.

'Economic Loss in Canada', (1993) 1 Tort L. Rev. 68–74.

'Defamation: Political Speech', (1993) 109 LQR 12–16.

'Assumption of Risk—California Style', (1993) 1 Tort L. Rev. 93–98.

'Employee's Tort in a Contractual Matrix: New Approaches in Canada', (1993) 13 OJLS 430–9.

'The Old Pieties Must Give Way', (1993) 28 Aust. Lawyer 24–5.

'Tort in a Contractual Matrix' (paper presented at Australasian Law Teachers' Association Annual Conference, 1993). Reprinted in (1993) 5 Canterbury L. Rev. 269–79.

1994 'General Report to International Congress of Comparative Law: Mass Torts', (1994) 42 Am. J. Comp. L. 507–29.

'Injury Caused by Stolen Motor Vehicles', (1994) 110 LQR 187–191.

1995 'The Fall of the Crippled Giant', (1995) 3 Tort L. Rev., 56–62

'Torts in a Contractual Matrix', (1995) 3 Tort L. Rev., 12–25; (1995) 33 Osgoode Hall L.J. 661–78.

'Once More: Tort Liability for Structural Defects', (1995) 111 LQR 362–6.

1996 'Product Liability De-Constructed', (1996) 16 OJLS 185–90.

'Property Damage or Economic Loss?', (1996) 4 Tort L. Rev. 177–81.

Book Reviews

1947 Odgers, *Construction of Deeds and Statutes*, (1947) J. Soc. Public Teachers of Law 140–1.

1948 Cheshire, *Private International Law*, (1948) 64 LQR 556–8.

Lorenzen, *Selected Articles on the Conflict of Laws*, (1948) 64 LQR 558–61.

1949 Falconbridge, *Essays on the Conflict of Laws*, (1949) 65 LQR 99–102.

1953 del Vecchio, *Justice*; Pound, *Justice According to the Law*; and Hamburger, *Morals and Law*, (1953) 69 LQR 271–5.

Paton (ed.), *The Commonwealth of Australia—Development of its laws and Constitution*, (1953) 69 LQR 123–6.

Hamburger, *Morals and the Law*, (1953) 69 LQR 271–5.

1956 Morison, *Cases on Torts*, (1956) and Wright, *Cases on the Law of Torts*, (1956) 2 Sydney L. Rev. 212.

1958 Belli, *Ready for the Plaintiff*, (1958) 46 California L. Rev. 137–8.

1964 *Prosser on Torts*, (1964) 52 California L. Rev. 1068–70.

1967 Frhr. Marschall v. Bieberstein, *Reflexschäden und Regressrechte*, (1967) 15 Am. J. Comp. L. 579–80.

1971 Gitter, *Schadensausgleich im Arbeitsunfallrecht*, (1971) 19 Am. J. Comp. L. 805–7.

1972 Jayme, *Die Familie im Recht der Ünerlaubten Handlungen*, (1972) 20 Am. J. Comp. L. 364–7.

Weyers, *Unfallschäden*, (1972) 20 Am. J. Comp. L. 565–8.

1973 Linden, *Canadian Negligence Law*, (1973) 11 Osgoode Hall L.J. 349–51.

Lobedanz, *Schadenausgleich bei Straftaten in Spanien und Lateinamerika*, (1973) 21 Am. J. Comp. L. 614–16.

1974 Hellner, *Skadestandsrätt*, (1974) Rabels Zeitschrift 228–9.

1976 Wagner, *Obligations in Polish Law*, (1976) 24 Am. J. Comp. L. 358–62.

1977 Kötz, *Deliktsrecht*, (1977) 25 Am. J. Comp. L. 592–5.

1978 Hirschberg, *The Impact of Inflation and Devaluation on Private Legal Obligations*, (1978) 26 Am. J. Comp. L. 132.

von Marschall, *Die Produktenhaftpflicht in der Neueren Rechtsprechung der USA*, (1978) 26 Am. J. Comp. L. 133–4.

Stoljar (ed.), *Problems of Codification*, (1978) 26 Am. J. Comp. L. 369.

Stone, *Tort Doctrine (Louisian Civil Law Treatise*, vol XI), (1978) 26 Am. J. Comp. L. 673–7.

Zweigert & Kötz, *Introduction to Comparative Law*, (1978) 26 Am. J. Comp. L. 495.

1979 Weir, 'Complex liabilities' in *International Encyclopedia of Comparative Law, vol IX, ch 12*, (1979) 27 Am. J. Comp. L. 115–7.

1980 *Rapports Généraux au IXe Congrès International de Droit Comparé*, (1980) 28 Am. J. Comp. L. 147.

White, *Tort Law in America: An Intellectual History*, (1980) Am. Bar Foundation Res. J. 614–7.

Zepos & Christodoulou, 'Professional Liability' in (*International Encyclopedia of Comparative Law*, vol XI, ch 6) (1980) 28 Am. J. Comp. L. 339–44.

1981 Bernstein, Drobnig & Kötz (eds.), *Festschrift für Konrad Zweigert*, (1981) 29 Am. J. Comp. L. 747.

1982 McGregor, *McGregor on Damages*, (1982) 45 MLR 238–40.

Giesen, *Arzthaftungsrecht/Medical Malpractice Law*, (1982) 30 Am. J. Comp. L. 704–8.

Cooper-Stevenson & Saunders, *Personal Injury Damages in Canada*, (1983) 60 Can. Bar Rev./Revue du Barreau Canadien 778–81.

1983 Horn, Kötz & Leser, *German Private and Commercial Law: An Introduction*, (1983) 31 Am. J. Comp. L. 572.

von Hippel, *Der Schutz des Schwächeren*, (1983) 31 Am. J. Comp. L. 572.

1984 Lawson & Markensinis, *Tortious Liabilities for Unintentional Harm in the Common Law and Civil Law*, (1984) 4 OJLS 235–43.

1985 Smith, *Liability in Negligence*, (1985) 63 Can. Bar Rev./Revue du Barreau Canadien 254–8.

Will, *Quellen Erhöter Gefahr*, (1985) 33 Am. J. Comp. L. 127–32.

1988 Harper, James & Gray, *The Law of Torts*, (1988) 104 LQR 147–9.

Atiyah & Summers, *Form and Substance in Anglo-American Law*, (1988) 37 Int. Comp. L.Q. 445–7.

Cosgrove, *Our Lady the Common Law*, (1988) 37 Int. Comp. L.Q. 445–7.

1989 Giesen, *International Medical Malpractice Law*, (1989) 37 Am. J. Comp. L. 838–41.

1991 Clark (ed.), *Essays in Honor of John Henry Merryman on His Seventieth Birthday*, (1991) 39 Am. J. Comp. L. 444–6.

1992 Cane, *Tort Law and Economic Interests*, (1992) 12 OJLS 558–63.

1994 Mullany & Handford, *Tort Liability for Psychiatric Damage*, (1994) 2 Tort L. Rev. 202–4.

1996 Stapleton, *Product Liability*, (1996) 16 OJLS 185–90.

Editorial Positions

Special Editor, *Transnational Trends in Tort Law*, (1970) Vol. 18 No. 1, Am. J. Comp. L..

Editor-in-Chief, Am. J. Comp. L. 1971–1986

Letters

1953 'Duty of Care and Standard of Care', (1953) 1 Sydney Law Review 69–70, 74–77; letters to W. L. Morison.

Index

The manufacturer's authorised representative in the EU for product safety is Oxford University Press España S.A. of el Parque Empresarial San Fernando de Henares, Avenida de Castilla, 2 – 28830 Madrid (www.oup.es/en or product.safety@oup.com). OUP España S.A. also acts as importer into Spain of products made by the manufacturer.

www.ingramcontent.com/pod-product-compliance
Lightning Source LLC
LaVergne TN
LVHW101454200926
848483LV00001B/126

9780198264842